Discovering Leadership

SAGE PUBLISHING: OUR STORY

We believe in creating fresh, cutting-edge content that helps you prepare your students to make an impact in today's ever-changing business world. Founded in 1965 by 24-year-old entrepreneur Sara Miller McCune, SAGE continues its legacy of equipping instructors with the tools and resources necessary to develop the next generation of business leaders.

- We invest in the right **authors** who distill the best available research into practical applications.

- We offer intuitive **digital solutions** at student-friendly prices.

- We remain permanently independent and fiercely committed to **quality, innovation, and learning**.

Discovering Leadership

Designing Your Success

Anthony Middlebrooks

University of Delaware

Scott J. Allen

John Carroll University

Mindy S. McNutt

Wright State University

James L. Morrison

University of Delaware

Los Angeles | London | New Delhi
Singapore | Washington DC | Melbourne

FOR INFORMATION:

SAGE Publications, Inc.
2455 Teller Road
Thousand Oaks, California 91320
E-mail: order@sagepub.com

SAGE Publications Ltd.
1 Oliver's Yard
55 City Road
London EC1Y 1SP
United Kingdom

SAGE Publications India Pvt. Ltd.
B 1/I 1 Mohan Cooperative Industrial Area
Mathura Road, New Delhi 110 044
India

SAGE Publications Asia-Pacific Pte. Ltd.
18 Cross Street #10-10/11/12
China Square Central
Singapore 048423

Acquisitions Editor: Maggie Stanley
Editorial Assistant: Alissa Nance
Production Editor: Laureen Gleason
Copy Editor: Ashley Horne
Typesetter: C&M Digitals (P) Ltd.
Proofreader: Liann Lech
Indexer: Molly Hall
Cover Designer: Karine Hovsepian
Marketing Manager: Sarah Panella

Printed in the United States of America

Library of Congress Cataloging-in-Publication Data

Names: Middlebrooks, Anthony E., author.

Title: Discovering leadership : designing your success / Anthony Middlebrooks [and three others].

Description: Los Angeles : SAGE, [2020] | Includes bibliographical references and index.

Identifiers: LCCN 2018034158 | ISBN 9781506336824 (pbk. : alk. paper)

Subjects: LCSH: Leadership. | Organizational behavior.

Classification: LCC HM1261 .M525 2020 | DDC 303.3/4—dc23
LC record available at https://lccn.loc.gov/2018034158

This book is printed on acid-free paper.

19 20 21 22 23 10 9 8 7 6 5 4 3 2 1

• Brief Contents •

• Detailed Contents •

• Preface •

One way or another, we are all impacted by leaders and leadership. Individuals in leadership positions influence our life every day by the decisions they make, the behaviors they model and encourage, the way in which they influence others, the values and vision they hold, and the culture they foster. All of these leadership activities can be positive, supportive, life-affirming; negative, repressive, selfish; or anything in between. Within this incredibly complex, interconnected world, those leader behaviors directly and indirectly impact our life, our perspective, and even our aspirations. Leadership matters, and the behavior of a leader is both impactful and far-reaching.

Leadership matters. Leadership educators know this, and so do experienced leaders. Traditional leadership education has become considerably more interactive and experiential in and out of the classroom. Yet students often struggle to organize the many pieces of leadership knowledge, overlook key lessons from an experience, and default to prior patterns of behavior they rationalize as leadership. Out of the classroom, talented individuals are promoted to leadership positions where they are surprised to find that they are facing an entirely different set of challenges . . . and they too do not know where to begin learning about leadership.

Discovering Leadership: Designing Your Success provides a practical, engaging foundation and framework for individuals to purposefully *design* leadership. It is a core textbook for undergraduate or graduate students from any discipline seeking a framework and foundation upon which to build as their experience and future leadership learning continue. The textbook is also ideal for aspiring or new leaders outside the classroom—those who have found themselves with a real, immediate need to understand and apply leadership in their context.

What does one need to know, or be able to do, or be like to effectively engage in leadership? The answer to that question highlights the greatest challenge to leadership educators. Effective leadership is complex and situational—it depends on the specific person serving as the positional leader—his or her strengths, tendencies, style, perspective, values, and reputation, and how he or she is perceived by others. Effective leadership depends on the followers and their characteristics; on the specific organization and its vision, mission, and culture; on the specific challenges currently facing the organization; on the specific social and political culture within which the organization must operate; and on the norms, values, and tools of the current times.

Discovering Leadership: Designing Your Success uses a simple, powerful leadership definition as the backbone of the entire textbook—the process of influencing others toward a common vision. Each element of this definition drives the purposeful design of leadership. Many existing sources offer valuable insights relative to these many variables influencing leadership. A seemingly endless stream of leadership books, courses, consultants, coaches, workshops, blogs, and other sources provide a wide array of good advice. Without a foundation and framework, however, these valuable resources can be overwhelming. When people are overwhelmed, they default to established patterns, try to simplify, or walk away.

Our Vision: Designing Leadership, Building CORE™

Our vision in writing this book was to create a tool that could serve as *the one thing* that a new leader would need, and later, it could provide a foundational framework that students could continuously add to as they learn and experience more. Some students may currently be in a leadership position, others aspire to one, and many will one day find themselves in that position. All individuals, however, will experience the impact of leadership. We want students to understand that leadership matters, that it is much more complex than a position, and most importantly that they can do things now to prepare for the challenges ahead. Two unique themes are emphasized across all chapters of this book: the purposeful design of leadership and developing core capacities to face an unpredictable future.

Designing Leadership

Discovering Leadership: Designing Your Success applies a uniquely useful design framework and engages students in the purposeful design of their own leadership. Design is the process of originating and developing a plan. This design approach organizes leadership into five major design challenges, each of which comprises a distinct and separate module aligned with the core components of the leadership definition. This starts with the students' design of *themselves*. Each chapter begins with the framework shown below, highlighting the key question for that design challenge.

The design approach also offers new ways of seeing and engaging challenges. The tools and perspectives from the design field are used to help leaders see differently as they solve problems, make decisions, navigate and build relationships, and find innovative ways to address challenges. Specific chapters focus on design process and design thinking, which significantly enhance creative problem-solving and innovation. And the Leadership by Design feature throughout the book asks students to apply design principles to different aspects of leadership.

Module	Leadership Design Challenge (and Module Title)	Leadership Definition	Key Question
1	Design Leadership of Self	Leadership	How can I design myself as a leader?
2	Design Leadership Relationships	Is a process of influencing	As a leader, how can I design my relationships with others?
3	Design Others' Success	Others	As a leader, how can I design success for others?
4	Design Culture and Community	Toward a common	As a leader, how can I design the culture of my organization?
5	Design the Future	Vision	As a leader, how can I innovate?

Building CORE™

Many professionals try to predict the future so that they are adequately prepared and positioned for success. Unfortunately, the future is constantly surprising everyone. While leaders cannot predict the future, they can prepare for the future by building capacities that could be flexibly applied to a wide variety of challenges. Leaders cannot know what specific knowledge, skills, or experiences will be needed. This is particularly true for students. However, there are some core capabilities that will help leaders navigate any future challenge and effectively facilitate the process of influencing others toward a common vision, also known as leadership. Just as an athlete exercises to build the physical core that will improve performance, so too must leaders develop their psycho-social-emotional CORE™—an acronym for Confidence, Optimism, Resilience, and Engagement. With a strong CORE™, students are better prepared for the unpredictable future.

Discovering Leadership: Designing Your Success starts with the individual designing themselves. However, individual leadership development is a continuous, life-long process. The goals for any student of leadership are emphasized throughout the book, and include:

1. Find your leadership self and begin to identify as a leader and recognize your potential.

2. Change the way you look at leaders and leadership, developing a clear foundation from which to see the field more broadly and note the complexities.

3. Develop your leadership dispositions—the mental habits you use to see, think about, and respond to the world.

4. Build your leadership CORE™—confidence, optimism, resilience, and engagement—personal attributes that will enhance your leadership now and long into the future.

5. Acquire both a road map and a toolkit to effectively design your leadership into the future.

The information and insights within each chapter provide an important foundation for any individual seeking to make sense of this complicated field. The ideas and activities in this text have been used with college students, adult professionals aspiring to leadership positions, new leaders and managers in many fields and organizations, co-curricular college leadership programs and leaders of student organizations, and even with upper-level high school students.

Unique Approach

Conceived and designed by experienced, engaged leadership educators and generations of their students, *Discovering Leadership: Designing Your Success* provides a unique approach that will maximize student engagement and retention.

- Interactive and engaging—As leadership educators, we strive to bring information and ideas to life. Learning is a process of codesign, and this textbook is structured in that manner. The action-oriented design approach makes leadership learning a purposeful activity. The variety of special features appeal to new leaders, enhance the breadth and depth of the topic, and provide instructors with additional learning tools.

- Flexible—The full textbook is divided into five modules that each focus on a different aspect of designing your leadership, all within a larger, connected logic. This allows professors and other trainers the maximum amount of flexibility to fit chapters and modules into their existing courses and curriculum to best meet current needs of students and faculty expertise.

- Accessible—The language of professions can discourage newcomers. This text clearly and simply defines the terms students will need in a way that is understandable to those with limited to no experience in leadership or with leadership studies/terminology. Organized within an easily understood framework, the content connects to the limited experiences of the new or aspiring leader.

- Practical—The textbook starts with practical definitions and examples that highlight perceptions and misperceptions about leaders and leadership. Throughout the text, leadership theories and research are balanced with lessons from experienced leaders and applied tools. Content is filled with real-world activities, skill-building exercises, and effective practices in leadership and its related disciplines (i.e., collaboration, conflict resolution, team management, etc.).

- Distinctively focused on future success—While much leadership wisdom focuses on helping students meet current challenges, this text also focuses on helping students meet the unknown future. We focus on topics that help students build capacity such as change management, creativity, design thinking, innovation processes, culture design, entrepreneurship, systems and sustainability, and building personal CORE™.

- Inspiring and aspirational—As leadership educators, we want nothing more than for students to be inspired to learn more and then go make a difference in whatever world they choose. This text wants to inspire students to be the individual and leader whom others want to follow and be like and assure them that every leader had a first time.

- Sustainable—This is one of the few texts that students will want to keep for their college career and beyond, to refer to over and over again. With every reading they will find new aspects of themselves and their leadership to learn and explore further.

Unique Content

In addition to the design framework and emphasis on developing CORE™, *Discovering Leadership: Designing Your Success* offers an array of unique content amidst the important, more commonly found topics.

- Instructors are provided with **interactive and experiential learning activities** to use inside and outside the classroom, including specific activities to develop confidence, optimism, resilience, and engagement.

- A unique chapter on **design thinking and brain learning** helps students understand important mental attributes and habits that they can apply now and develop over time.

- Invaluable **innovation tools** throughout unique sections on creativity, idea generation, problem-solving, and leading innovation.

- Unique section on **designing the future**, with introductions to cutting-edge topics such as fostering a culture of innovation, entrepreneurial leadership, and seeing the long-term and big picture with sustainability and systems.

- Perceptions and **misconceptions of leaders and leadership**—in the words of new leaders, often overlooked in textbooks—including a Myth or Reality? feature using research to address common questions.

- Content **designed to maximize learning** by reinforcing and integrating concepts throughout multiple chapters, including an early section on what to expect when learning leadership.

Leadership is a very complex, multidisciplinary subject that is often field-specific. Many important leadership topics are not part of this textbook such as in-depth examination of leadership research and different leadership theories, the historical development of leadership, various philosophies of leadership, and leadership in specific contexts or with specific populations. This book positions students well to explore and learn more about this fascinating world. Your expertise and interests as a leadership educator enhance and continue that journey.

Features

Leadership That Makes a Difference at the start of each chapter profiles a leader, leaders, or leadership that had an impact. Many of the subjects are unexpected, as this feature is designed to broaden students' conception of who is a leader and what it means to make a difference. For example, Chapter 14 highlights three women who successfully created cultures of innovation within predominantly male fields.

Leadership by Design introduces students to different design principles—rules that designers use to enhance their product. These rules can often be applied to leaders and leadership to encourage exploration, discussion, and new ways of thinking. For example, the principles of balance and repetition are key to visual design. Applied to leadership, what are the many things that leaders need to balance? Where might repetition be important in leadership? Can you have both?

The **Myth or Reality?** feature examines commonly held beliefs through established research and practice. For example, the feature in Chapter 4, "Values," asserts, "I don't have a title, I can't make a difference." Experienced leaders know the answer, but new, young, or entry-level leaders wonder if this is true.

Experts Beyond the Text: Insightful Leaders Know About a lot of very interesting things. Invited experts provide a brief introduction to a topic that is beyond the scope of this introductory text, yet students should be aware that it is an important topic. For example, experts Rob Koonce and Marc Hurwitz tell students all about followership in this feature found in Chapter 3.

For every leader there are **Moments of Awareness**—critical decision-making, ethical challenges, or difficult truths. This feature shares short quotes and stories of the most challenging self-reflections with which aspiring leaders must grapple. For example, in the "Introductions and Foundations" chapter, one undergraduate student realizes that one of her most important jobs as a leader is to create opportunities for others to lead.

CORE™ Attribute Builders at the end of every chapter comprise engaging activities that emphasize one or more of confidence, optimism, resilience, and engagement. These activities ask students to actively work to develop their CORE™, while **Skill Builder Activities** at the end of each chapter are self-directed activities, tested for learning success in and out of real classrooms, in which students can develop important skills and gain richer understanding of specific concepts.

Reflection Questions throughout the features and the text prompt deeper thinking and discussion about the topics. And **Chapter Summaries** and **Key Terms** at the end of each chapter highlight important points, reinforce learning, and provide guidance for studying and instructor assessment.

Content and Organization

Discovering Leadership: Designing Your Success comprises 16 chapters within five modules. The "Introductions and Foundations" chapter provides a detailed overview of the logic and framework, and previews the many features found in each chapter. Each module begins with a three- to five-page introduction of the design focus of that module, and it includes some valuable topics and tools related to that focus. For example, Module 4 starts the Designing Culture and Community section, and introduces some of the tools of strategic planning as key to designing the shared values and vision that connect individuals to the community.

Introduction and Foundations

This important chapter includes some of the most important things instructors and students need to know, including the definition of leadership, overall logic and framework, and organization and features of the text, including some fun and interesting examples.

The two major themes of the text are elaborated in this chapter: designing your leadership and building your CORE™. Here the tools of design are distinguished between design process, design thinking, and the unique lens of design principles. Likewise, the elements of CORE™ are clarified along with suggested activities for further developing each.

Chapter 1: A Framework for Leadership Success: Design and Your CORE™

Module 1—Design Leadership Self

Module 1 begins where all leadership begins—with the individual, the leader. For students, there is a lot to know about themselves. And similar to all subjects, the more they know, the more effective they will be as leaders. Understanding as a leader starts with how one perceives leaders and leadership. All of us have had a variety of experiences with leaders—our parents, teachers, coaches, siblings, friends, bosses—and those experiences form our values, expectations, assumptions, and behaviors as leaders. Some of those personal characteristics are very effective for leadership, but unfortunately, many are not. The chapters in this section explore those personal attributes that characterize effective leaders and guide students through the process of designing their leadership self.

Chapter 2: Designing Your Perceptions of Leaders and Leadership

Chapter 3: Designing Your Leadership Capacity

Chapter 4: Your Values and Ethical Actions

Module 2—Design Leadership Relationships

Module 2 focuses on designing relationships with others. An amusing old leadership saying goes, "If you think you are leading, you might want to turn around and see if anyone is following." Without followers, there is no leadership. The nature of the relationships leaders design with followers and other stakeholders will greatly determine leadership success. The chapters in this section examine the foundations of powerful and influential leader-follower connections and guide students through the design of relationships.

Chapter 5: Design Thinking and Brain Leading

Chapter 6: Decision-Making

Chapter 7: Influence, Power, and Motivation

Module 3—Design Others' Success

Module 3 shifts focus to the success of others. If the first rule of leadership is *It's about you*, the second rule is *It's not about you*. We all want to feel successful. One's ability as a leader to facilitate learning and development in others is critical to the organization and achieving the vision. The chapters in this section examine what a leader needs to know to design others' success, beginning with expanding the capacity to creatively generate ways to do so.

Chapter 8: Creativity, Problem-Solving, and Idea-Generating

Chapter 9: Effective Practices for Leading Others to Success

Chapter 10: Utilizing Change Processes Effectively

Module 4—Design Culture and Community

Module 4 expands the leadership lens to focus on designing culture. Simply put, culture is the way we do things around here. All groups have a culture—teams, organizations, communities—a visible and invisible set of rules that defines the group. Culture happens, but a good leader designs the culture to influence others toward a common vision. The chapters in this section guide the design of culture, with special emphasis on leading effective teams and fostering an ethic of care.

Chapter 11: Culture

Chapter 12: Leading a Team

Chapter 13: Designing a Culture That Cares

Module 5—Design the Future

Module 5 applies students' growing leadership capacity to ensuring future success, focusing on perspectives and tools that develop the ability to see the big picture and long-term. The inevitability of change, unpredictable future, and interconnected nature of individuals and ideas require leaders who can innovate and maximize the value of their ideas. Leaders need to foster this capacity in others to sustain success. The chapters in this section guide efforts to design the future by introducing new ways of seeing, taking the initiative, and understanding the interconnected systems that comprise sustainable organizations, communities, and world.

Chapter 14: Creating a Culture of Innovation

Chapter 15: Entrepreneurial Leadership

Chapter 16: Systems and Sustainability

Starting Your Journey

As leadership educators, we have heard many experienced leaders and experts assert various qualifiers to those aspiring to lead: *You need to go through the crucible of experience! You need to study the leaders of the past. You must carefully study leadership theory. You are too young. You are not skilled enough.* All of this is good advice and certainly important to becoming an experienced and wise leader. But individuals—even you, perhaps—are assuming leadership positions right now, with or without the prerequisites the experts recommend. Understanding the influence, impact, and importance of leadership, as well as a bit of how-to knowledge, is just the start any student needs. We, the authors, want your students to be successful, to facilitate the success of others, and to make a difference. We have designed this textbook to that end.

Digital Resources

SAGE edge offers a robust online environment featuring an impressive array of tools and resources for review, study, and further exploration, keeping both instructors and students on the cutting edge of teaching and learning. SAGE edge content is open access and available on demand. Learning and teaching has never been easier! You can access your SAGE edge content at **edge.sagepub.com/middlebrooks**.

   SAGE edge for Students provides a personalized approach to help students accomplish their coursework goals in an easy-to-use learning environment.

- Mobile-friendly **flashcards** strengthen understanding of key terms and concepts

- Mobile-friendly **practice quizzes** allow for independent assessment by students of their mastery of course material

- **Chapter summaries** with **learning objectives** reinforce the most important material

- **Video and multimedia links** appeal to different learning styles

SAGE edge for Instructors supports teaching by making it easy to integrate quality content and create a rich learning environment for students.

- **Test banks** provide a diverse range of prewritten options as well as the opportunity to edit any question and/or insert personalized questions to assess students' progress and understanding. Questions are correlated to Bloom's taxonomy and the current AACSB standards.

- Editable, chapter-specific **PowerPoint® slides** offer complete flexibility for creating a multimedia presentation for the course

- The **instructor's manual** provides teaching tips and guidance for best utilizing the book's unique approach and feature set

- **Sample course syllabi** for semester and quarter courses provide suggested models for structuring one's course

- **Video and multimedia links** appeal to students with different learning styles

Tony Middlebrooks, PhD
On behalf of the author team

• Acknowledgments •

Leadership and the success of a project require that different individuals take initiative, but the reality of any accomplishment lies hidden under the vast array of interconnected influences, quiet contributions, and culture of support. This text is no different. I, Dr. Tony Middlebrooks, am grateful for the many individuals and teams that both purposefully and unknowingly influenced my development as a leadership educator, as well as to those contributing to the achievement of designing and crafting this textbook. Thank you to the generations of students, colleagues, family, friends, and mentors who have graciously shared both their triumphs and challenges as leaders, educators, and humans. This book is for all of us.

A very special thank you to those directly involved with this text: students who agreed to contribute their insights; guest experts who wrote features and chapters; Kelsey Edmond, who helped write the Leadership by Design features; colleagues and friends who reviewed various parts of the text; and of course my talented coauthors Jim, Mindy, and Scott, who made facilitating this process a pleasure—truly exemplars of collaborative, authentic leaders.

Great thanks to the supportive teams at SAGE for simultaneously guiding, educating, and supporting a bunch of professors through the professional publishing process. I would specifically like to thank Maggie Stanley, our acquisitions editor, for shepherding us through this multiyear process. Your kind, positive, professional, and insightful approach was critical to our success. How fortunate we are to work with you.

Finally, we are truly a product of those with whom we spend the most time. Lucky for me that means our children (quickly becoming adults) Jakob, Hannah, and Sydney. Thank you for your patience, support, and continuous reality check outside the academy. And the greatest thanks goes to my amazing wife, partner, collaborator, friend, and (when requested) critic, Dr. Jules Bruck. Thank you for your incredibly generous support, encouragement, and insights. I strive to meet the standards you model, and I am thankful every day to share my life with you.

Dr. Scott Allen would like to acknowledge his wife Jessica and three children, Will, Kate, and Emily, for their love, patience, and encouragement.

Dr. Mindy McNutt would like to thank her daughter Alexis and mother Penny for their support, patience, and encouragement.

Dr. James Morrison would like to thank Dr. Pamela Porter Morrison for her insight in editing and providing assistance in designing innovative strategies for generating a highly interactive writing style. Her expertise in the field of communication was most helpful in designing a unique writing style for having students be continually engaged as they read each chapter. Her continuous support was extremely appreciated.

SAGE would like to thank the following reviewers:

Kris L. Baack, University of Nebraska

Cheryl B. Baker, Plymouth State University

Tondalaya O. Carroll, Lincoln University

Robert Dibie, Indiana University Kokomo

Linette P. Fox, Johnson C. Smith University

Megan W. Gerhardt, Miami University

Michele Goins, Santa Clara University

Madinah F. Hamidullah, Rutgers University–Newark

Kimberly A. Hunley, Northern Arizona University

Chris Hutchison, Chapman University

Daniel M. Jenkins, University of Southern Maine

DeNisha McCollum, John Brown University

Patricia Mitchell, University of San Francisco

Don Mulvaney, Auburn University

Kerry Priest, Kansas State University

Kirk A. Randazzo, University of South Carolina

Julie K. Roosa, Des Moines Area Community College

Rian Satterwhite, University of Nevada, Las Vegas

John Silveria, Suffolk University

Nicole LP Stedman, University of Florida

Ramon Tejada, California State University Channel Islands

Joshua H. Truitt, University of Central Florida

Pamela R. Van Dyke, Southern Methodist University

Heather A. Vilhauer, California State University, East Bay

Ellen J. West, California University of Pennsylvania

Tara Widner-Edberg, Iowa State University

Michael A. Williams, Thomas Edison State University

Patricia Wilson, Otterbein University

• About the Authors •

Tony Middlebrooks, PhD, creates tools, explores, and teaches at the intersection of leadership, innovation, creativity, and design as Associate Professor and Director of the Siegfried Leadership Initiative for Horn Entrepreneurship at the University of Delaware. Dr. Middlebrooks has created and taught more than 35 different courses for all collegiate levels, as well as numerous experiential abroad programs. He presently teaches leadership theory and practice, decision-making, creativity and innovation, and social entrepreneurship. He received both the University of Delaware Excellence in Teaching and Excellence in Advising Awards, and regularly helps faculty develop their teaching.

Previously Dr. Middlebrooks codeveloped the Organizational and Community Leadership program at UD, as well as the doctoral program in leadership as a professor at Cardinal Stritch University, and spent ten years prior in nonprofit leadership positions.

Dr. Middlebrooks has published numerous articles and book chapters, and he has delivered hundreds of presentations. He is coauthor of *Public Sector Leadership*, and cocreator of the *Idea Fan Deck* and *Design Thinking Cards*, and he has served as Symposium Editor for the *Journal of Leadership Studies* since 2011.

A firm believer that leadership learning can benefit everyone and can make a difference, Dr. Middlebrooks consults and facilitates workshops for a wide variety of organizations and audiences. His current scholarly interests focus on methods of leadership education and the integration of leadership, creativity, and design thinking. Dr. Middlebrooks has a PhD in Educational Psychology from the University of Wisconsin–Madison. He resides in Wilmington, Delaware, with his wife and collaborator Dr. Jules Bruck.

Scott J. Allen, PhD, is the Standard Products–Dr. James S. Reid Chair in Management at John Carroll University. He is an associate professor and teaches courses in leadership, management skills, and executive communication. In 2008, he was voted the favorite teacher and in 2014, he was awarded the Wasmer Outstanding Teaching Award for his work in the classroom. Scott served as a Mulwick Scholar in the Boler School of Business, and his primary stream of research focuses on leadership development. Scott has published more than 50 book chapters and peer-reviewed journal articles. He is the coauthor of *The Little Book of Leadership Development: 50 Ways to Bring Out the Leader in Every Employee* and *A Charge Nurse's Guide: Navigating the Path of Leadership.* Scott is also a coauthor of *Emotionally Intelligent Leadership: A Guide for College Students.* In addition to writing and speaking, Scott consults, facilitates workshops, and leads retreats across industries. Scott is the chair and cofounder of the Collegiate Leadership Competition and has served on the board of the International Leadership Association, Association of Leadership Educators, and OBTS Teaching Society for Management Educators. He resides in Chagrin Falls, Ohio, with his wife, Jessica, and three children—Will, Kate, and Emily.

Mindy S. McNutt, PhD, is an Associate Professor of Leadership at Wright State University in Dayton, Ohio. She earned her BA in Communication Studies, MS in Personnel Counseling, and EdS in Educational Leadership from Wright State. She earned her PhD in Higher Education Administration from Bowling Green State University. Currently, she teaches in all three leadership programs at Wright State: the undergraduate program in Organizational Leadership, the master of science in Leadership Development, and the doctorate in Organizational Studies.

Dr. McNutt has engaged in leadership curriculum development for over 30 years for high school youth, and undergraduate curricular and extracurricular programs, and most recently she served with several faculty colleagues to write the proposal for the doctorate in Organizational Studies. At Wright State and at several area community colleges, she has held a variety of leadership positions including, among others, academic vice president, campus dean, and dean of student services and institutional advancement. Additionally, Dr. McNutt is or has been involved in a number of boards and committees at the local, state, and national levels.

Among her varied research interests are leadership education, transformational leadership, women in leadership, leader values, and a current project examining the relationship between values and organizational culture. She has been involved in several projects of significance: serving as an associate editor of the International Leadership Association Building Leadership Bridges book entitled *LEADERSHIP 2050: Contextualizing Global Leadership Processes for the Future* and collaborating with a nationwide team to create and serve as faculty for the international Leadership Education Academy.

James L. Morrison, PhD, is currently a Professor of Organizational and Community Leadership in the School of Urban Affairs and Public Policy at the University of Delaware in Newark, Delaware. His research interest focuses on issues surrounding senior leadership accountability. Currently, he is researching the effectiveness of CEOs in preparing for the possibility of a natural disaster. He has published two books and over 80 manuscripts in a variety of professional journals. In addition, Dr. Morrison has presented over 90 papers at regional, national, and international conferences. He is currently serving on three refereed editorial boards for academic journals and also is serving as the executive editor of the *Journal of Education for Business*. He has been the recipient of seven outstanding teaching awards in the College of Education and the College of Human Resources at the University of Delaware. Within the leadership major at the University of Delaware, his teaching focuses on preparing future leaders to initiate change within organizations by adopting a new set of principles and practices that have emerged in recent years.

• Introduction and Foundations •

The pure and simple truth is rarely pure and never simple.

—Oscar Wilde

Learning Objectives

0.1 State the definition of leadership and summarize why leadership matters

0.2 Understand the big picture of how to design your leadership (and how the textbook is organized)

0.3 Recognize special features of the textbook that will enhance your learning and leadership design

Detailed Chapter Outline

Leadership Matters

Organization of This Textbook:
  The Leadership by Design
  Framework

Content: Topics and Special
  Features
    Leadership by Design Model
    Leadership That Makes a
      Difference
    Leadership by Design

Myth or Reality?

Experts Beyond the Text:
  Insightful Leaders Know
  About _____

Moments of Awareness

CORE™ Attribute Builders

Skill Builder Activities

Chapter Summary

Key Terms

Leadership Matters

Learning Objective

0.1 State the definition of leadership and summarize why leadership matters

This is not your standard textbook because you do not want to be a standard leader. You want to be uniquely extraordinary—a leader who inspires others, a leader whom others remember and aspire to become, and a leader who seeks to make a positive difference. In whatever world you choose to work or operate, no matter the size or scope, you can be that effective leader who impacts others. You can *design* your leadership.

Leadership the process of influencing others toward a common vision

Leadership is the process of influencing others toward a common vision.[1]

There are many definitions and ways to explain leadership, and all offer some interesting and valuable insight into this complicated, dynamic activity.[2] But when you are trying to observe leadership, practice leadership, explain leadership, or further develop your leadership, you are going to want a simple, meaningful definition. So, right here in the introduction is your first and perhaps most important assignment. Memorize this simple definition—*Leadership is the process of influencing others toward a common vision.* You will see this definition many more times throughout this text, and Chapter 2 explains the full depth of each component. Do you have it memorized? Try again—say it out loud, say it to a friend, write it down—*Leadership is the process of influencing others toward a common vision.*

The importance, and consequences, of leadership are evident throughout the news. The world is full of complex challenges and wicked problems.[3] Yet addressing those global issues can begin at any level, even one relationship at a time. Along your leadership learning journey, you may hear experts telling you that the only path to leadership is years of experience and extensive knowledge. You will certainly hear that you are too _____ to make a difference. In reality, individuals are put into leader positions every day, all over the world . . . with no formal leadership training. Those persons are influential, for better or worse. You are influential.

Leadership feels most important when it is personal. For example, have you ever had a bad boss—someone in charge who was less than effective? Do you wish that person would have had some training in how to be a better leader? If you do not believe your own answer, ask a few others. While everyone has his or her own definition of *bad*, the reality is that everyone has *felt* the impact of leadership. When you are part of an organization, those feelings matter. Those relationships matter. Leadership matters. An effective leader can mean greater productivity, efficiency, innovation, satisfaction, retention, and a host of other personal, organizational, and cultural benefits.[4]

Leadership is an extraordinarily powerful tool that can be used to advance a variety of values and ends through many means. Wielding influence comes with great responsibility to carefully consider what you are doing, to whom, how, to what end, and so much more. And an ineffective leader, or worse, a bad leader, can destroy an organization, poison a culture, and negatively impact lives—with lasting effects long after the bad leader departs. There is a considerable and important difference, however, between an ineffective leader (i.e., someone who is just not good at influencing others toward a common goal) and a bad or toxic leader (i.e., someone who is unethical, immoral, or otherwise intent on harm). Many definitions of leadership include an ethical dimension, and there certainly is a good reason to advocate for that kind of *good* in leaders.

So, why doesn't the definition used in this text specify that leadership must be *good* in the moral sense? Because with a value-free definition, *you* must be thoughtful and consider all the distinctions and perspectives of how and to what end you practice leadership. Leadership is *always* a specific, value-laden activity because everyone brings their values, ethics, norms, and experiences to the group. An effective leader recognizes that the situation, persons, context, culture, time, and so forth, help define what kind of leadership is most ethical, most preferred, and most effective.

Fortunately, few individuals *try* to be either ineffective or bad leaders. Rather, most poor leadership results from lack of action, specifically the failure of individuals to think carefully and strategically about themselves as leaders, the individuals they are leading, and the culture required for success. In other words, you have a choice: You can consciously *design* your leadership, or you can just act (or react), see what happens, and hope for the best.

This introductory text to leadership engages you in the design of leadership over the course of five distinct modules, starting with your design of *you*.

Organization of This Textbook:
The Leadership by Design Framework

Learning Objective

0.2 Understand the big picture of how to design your leadership
(and how the textbook is organized)

Leadership is the process of influencing others toward a common vision. Within this definition lay the most important elements of leadership *and* the organizing structure of this text. Look at that definition in a slightly different way (**Leadership extended** definition):

> *Leadership comprises your perceptions, strengths, style, skills, and the way you make decisions and solve problems, including how you persuade, guide, teach, and build relationships with others. But leadership goes beyond you—it is also how you help others succeed and create a culture of success so that you, your followers, your organization, and your society can make a positive difference in the world.*

That definition sounds a bit more complicated. Here is how it aligns with the simple definition:

Leadership	Your leadership comprises your perceptions, strengths, style, skills, and . . .
is a process	the way you make decisions and solve problems, including . . .
of influencing	how you persuade, guide, teach, and . . .
others	build relationships with others. But leadership goes beyond you—how do you help others succeed . . .
toward a common	and create a culture of success so that you, your followers, your organization, and your society . . .
vision.	can make a positive difference in the world?

Design is the process of originating and developing a plan. This textbook guides you through the process of *designing* your leadership, focusing on practical skills and valuable attributes that will maximize your leadership success now and into the future. Two things to know about this text:

1. Organization—How this text is organized using the Leadership by Design framework.

2. Content——The topics and special features that will fill your leadership toolbox.

Each of the major components of the leadership definition can be *purposefully* planned and developed (i.e., designed). The framework for this textbook takes a design process approach to leadership, organizing that design process into five major design challenges: (1) design yourself as a leader, (2) design your relationships with others, (3) design others' success, (4) design your culture and community, and (5) design the future. This framework is outlined on the side of the pages throughout the textbook, highlighting the section you are reading.

Leadership (extended) Leadership comprises your perceptions, strengths, style, skills, and the way you make decisions and solve problems, including how you persuade, guide, teach, and build relationships with others. But leadership goes beyond you—it is also how you help others succeed and create a culture of success so that you, your followers, your organization, and your society can make a positive difference in the world.

Design (noun) a proposed plan, solution, or product; (verb) the process of originating and developing a plan, which comprises three phases: understand, imagine, and implement

Table 0.1 below lays out this framework.

TABLE 0.1 ● Leadership by Design Framework Modules			
Module	Leadership Design Challenge (and Module Title)	Leadership Definition	Definition Explained
1	Design Leadership Self	Leadership	Your leadership comprises your perceptions, strengths, style, skills, and . . .
2	Design Leadership Relationships	is a process	the way you make decisions and solve problems, including . . .
		of influencing	how you persuade, guide, teach, and . . .
3	Design Others' Success	others	build relationships with others. But leadership goes beyond you— how do you help others succeed . . .
4	Design Culture and Community	toward a common	and create a culture of success so that you, your followers, your organization, and your society . . .
5	Design the Future	vision.	can make a positive difference in the world?

Designing your leadership is different from learning *about* leadership or learning *to lead*. If you were to visit your local bookstore (virtual or real) and look at all the books on leadership, you might conclude that either (a) leadership is anything and everything or (b) learning leadership is simply too big of a task. The truth is that every one of those books is both correct and incorrect—filled with wisdom and insight, as well as with content that will never be relevant to you. You can, and will, learn a great deal about leadership from many sources. But then you must decide what is and is not relevant to you—what works for you and how—and what does not.

Leadership is such a personal, subjective, situational, and context-based endeavor that individuals often simply default to acting and reacting based on their prior experiences and then explaining it as leadership (often because they occupy a leadership position). Do not be that person. Instead, purposefully *design your leadership*. Read, observe, interview, discuss, interact, engage as much as you can with people, organizations, and leadership. Fill your toolbox of knowledge and skills and then draw from it to design who you will be as a leader and how you will execute the process of leadership.

Content: Topics and Special Features

Learning Objective

0.3 Recognize special features of the textbook that will enhance your learning and leadership design

What does it take to practice leadership? This should be an easy answer after having memorized the definition. Leadership requires engaging in and facilitating the process of influencing others and progressing toward achieving a vision you have crafted with followers. Sounds simple. But as many have noted, leadership would be simple if it were not for the people.

Central to every design project is the end user or client—the human element. Excellent design begins with a human problem, focuses on human feelings and perceptions, and ends with human assessment. Even for folks who design toasters or buildings or websites—the user is central. Designing your leadership is no different. The content of this text focuses on the heart of leadership—the individuals involved in leading and following—starting with you, the leader, and expanding outward. Chapters comprise topics and information that you can use now and long into the future as your leadership journey unfolds. Table 0.2 (shown below) reiterates the Leadership by Design framework, listing the chapter titles as they align with the definition.

As you work through this textbook, there are also many special features included to enhance your learning. The features are designed to highlight the focus of each chapter and expand your understanding, often by introducing alternative perspectives or stories from real students. Read the special features, think about them, and engage in any activity they prompt. Many of the features will also pose questions for reflection and discussion. While the special features are valuable in and of themselves, they also serve as a model for how you can pursue additional learning outside the classroom.

This section profiles each of the special features you will find within each chapter. Each special feature is explained, followed by an example of that feature illustrating the most common misconceptions about leadership—that leadership is all about the leader (hint: it is not).

TABLE 0.2 ● Leadership by Design Chapters

Module	Leadership Design Challenge (and Module Title)	Leadership Definition	Chapters
Intro	A Framework for Your Success		Chapter 1: A Framework for Leadership Success: Design and Your CORE™
1	Design Leadership Self	Leadership	Chapter 2: Designing Your Perceptions of Leaders and Leadership
			Chapter 3: Designing Your Leadership Capacity
			Chapter 4: Your Values and Ethical Actions
2	Design Leadership Relationships	is a process	Chapter 5: Design Thinking and Brain Leading
			Chapter 6: Decision-Making
		of influencing	Chapter 7: Influence, Power, and Motivation
3	Design Others' Success	others	Chapter 8: Creativity, Problem-Solving, and Idea-Generating
			Chapter 9: Effective Practices for Leading Others to Success
			Chapter 10: Utilizing Change Processes Effectively
4	Design Culture and Community	toward a common	Chapter 11: Culture
			Chapter 12: Leading a Team
			Chapter 13: Designing a Culture That Cares
5	Design the Future	vision.	Chapter 14: Creating a Culture of Innovation
			Chapter 15: Entrepreneurial Leadership
			Chapter 16: Systems and Sustainability

Leadership by Design Model

Each chapter begins with what you will learn (learning objectives), a detailed chapter outline, and the Leadership by Design Model highlighting the design focus (module) of the current chapter. The key question within each module should prompt and focus your thinking as you read the chapters of that module.

Design Self (Module 1)

How can I design myself as a leader?

Design Relationships (Module 2)

As a leader, how can I design my relationships with others?

Design Others' Success (Module 3)

As a leader, how can I design success for others?

Design Culture (Module 4)

As a leader, how can I design the culture of my organization?

Design Future (Module 5)

As a leader, how can I innovate?

Leadership That Makes a Difference

This special feature, found near the start of each chapter, highlights leaders and leadership that played a role in addressing social problems and improving social well-being. This feature will help you visualize the broader implications and applications of leadership activity, including those skills and characteristics used by successful social entrepreneurs and leaders. Across the entire textbook you will see the wide variety of forms effective leadership can take. Here is an example of a Leadership That Makes a Difference feature:

LEADERSHIP THAT MAKES A DIFFERENCE

There are a good many stories about leaders who make a positive difference addressing the big challenges of our world, and you will read about many of these individuals throughout this text. Did you ever ask yourself where that leader was *before* they made a big impact or became a story? The following story highlights one of the key attributes of leadership that makes a big difference . . . and it all starts with how you define *difference*.

When I was in high school, I participated in a charitable event. The president of our club put the entire event together and did a lot of hard work. At the event another girl was taking all the credit for the event in front of the retirement community for whom the event was organized. My friend and I were so confused and honestly, kind of upset for the president, who put it all together. We did not understand why someone else would think it was okay to take all of the credit when they did not do anything. I wanted to say

something and then asked the president about it. She said, "It doesn't bother me. The event was a success and all of the houses that needed work got done and look at how happy it made all of these people! That's all that matters." I was humbled by the president's positivity and realized how amazing a leader she was and how big her heart was. She did not care about any of the credit, just that the job got done. Real leaders want the best for their followers and whomever else they are helping or contributing toward; they do not care about their personal success or gains. Since that day, I have been inspired to help and lead others without expecting anything in return.

—Brooke Hoffman, Undergraduate

Making a positive difference on a large scale begins with doing so on a small scale, or even observing and learning from someone doing so. Effective leaders know that there is no small scale, only small attitudes.

REFLECTION QUESTIONS

Remember, *you* are designing *your* leadership. What difference would you like to make? What local actions can you take now that will prepare you?

Leadership by Design

Throughout the textbook you will find many examples of how you can apply lessons from other design worlds that will be very helpful to designing leadership. Here is an example: Designers follow rules, which they call principles. Following the right rules makes a design effective. This is true for leadership design as well. Within the overall model of this text, the Leadership by Design feature highlights these design rules and translates them into insights and applications for leaders. How can various design principles (rules) used in the design world be applied to effective leadership practice? Here is an example of a Leadership by Design feature:

LEADERSHIP BY DESIGN

Design Principle: Visibility

Definition: "The usability of a system is improved when its status and methods of use are clearly visible."[5]

In Other Words: Designs that tell you what is going on are more useful.

For Example: The battery icon on your cell phone that tells you how much charge you have left makes the phone much more useful. Without that little image, you would not know when the phone might shut off.

For Leaders: Leaders can use the design principle of visibility by considering what important systems, behaviors, or activities they could make more visible—not only as a matter of transparency but as a mechanism of feedback regarding the status of those things. If you are a more introverted leader who tends to process information in your head, visibility is a key design principle to consider. What would followers need to know about you at a given moment to make you more useful as a leader? Your mood? Your credibility? Your decision-making process? How could you design yourself to enhance visibility?

Myth or Reality?

Leadership is filled with myths and misconceptions, many of which will be addressed in Chapter 2 as you design your leadership self. The Myth or Reality? feature simply and directly addresses the common misconceptions about chapter topics. Here is an example of a Myth or Reality? feature:

MYTH OR REALITY?

THE LEADER IS THE ONE WHO TAKES CHARGE AND DOES MOST OF THE TALKING.

Myth . . . and Reality. Leaders come in all shapes and sizes (and volume levels). Some leaders influence others through charismatic speeches where all eyes are on them, much like depicted in the movies. But other leaders influence by quietly listening, building relationships, and creating room for others to shine and *take charge*.

REFLECTION QUESTION

Describe one of your initial misconceptions about leadership. How did you come to understand it differently?

Experts Beyond the Text: Insightful Leaders Know About _____

Understanding and effectively practicing leadership is a complex, life-long learning adventure. Insightful leaders understand that what they know about leadership today is only one part of this developing and dynamic field. This textbook facilitates you in the design of your leadership, yet there are many important topics that expert leadership researchers and practitioners continue to think about, explore, and test. This special feature briefly highlights an area of leadership study that you will find more extensively outside the textbook. As your leadership knowledge grows, you will encounter these topics in more depth. This feature will give you a brief familiarity now to prepare you for later learning.

Moments of Awareness

For every leader there are moments of critical decision-making, ethical challenges, and difficult truths. These short quotes and stories highlight some of the most challenging self-reflections with which aspiring leaders must grapple. This feature may also highlight ethical issues relevant to each chapter, as ethical issues permeate leadership practice. Here is an example of a Moment of Awareness feature:

MOMENT OF AWARENESS

Leaders create opportunities for others to lead.

When I thought of a leader, I thought of someone who was tough, hands on, loud, and assertive. Leadership style really depends on the followers and the overall situation, not necessarily the leader themselves. A leader I valued was my campus minister. She developed personal relationships with the young women at my school and inspired us to be confident, giving, respectful, and patient.

I volunteered to go to nursing homes, help with the retreat, and go to soup kitchens under her leadership. She set up so many opportunities for the students to better themselves and offered her genuine experiences to girls in need. She talked about coming into her own and growing into the person she is today. She led by example in terms of giving to those in need, being available, and being a leader for the good of the community. —Morgan Smith, Undergraduate

REFLECTION QUESTION

Describe a Moment of Awareness that you have had as a leader. What was the *big* lesson that you will not soon forget?

CORE™ Attribute Builders

When are you going to be serving as a leader? What challenges will you face? How can you know what you will need, when you do not even know the situation? The best thing you can do now is to develop the personal characteristics or attributes that will come in handy when facing that future leadership challenge—building your CORE™—Confidence, Optimism, Resilience, and Engagement.

Chapter 1 discusses the importance of these CORE™ attributes, and at the end of each chapter, you will find brief lessons and activities designed to develop those dispositions. With strong confidence, an optimistic mindset, significant resilience, and full engagement, you will be ready to effectively lead across multiple situations and challenges. Here is an example of a CORE™ Attribute Builder feature:

CORE™ Attribute Builders—Build Now for Future Leadership Challenges

Attribute: Engagement

Builder: Moment of Awareness

You will not learn unless you engage. Consider what happens when your mind is occupied with something other than what you are currently doing. You look up and wonder what happened, the events have little meaning, and you do not really remember much. If that happens while you are in a leadership position (or in class), you will miss valuable learning opportunities. To raise your level of engagement, take a Moment of Awareness. A Moment of Awareness, as you read about in the special feature example, raises your awareness of important aspects of a context or situation. The greater your awareness, the more likely you will not miss something and consequently make a great decision. Here are two cards that you can copy and cut out that you can reference to take a Moment of Awareness. Keep the cards with you—they will fit into your purse or wallet. One is for decision-making and the other for general leadership moments. Practicing both will build your engagement.

Moment of Awareness (MoA)—Decisions

1. What is happening *right now*?
   a. What am I doing?
   b. What am I feeling?
   c. What am I thinking?
2. What do I want right now?
3. What am I doing right now to prevent myself from getting what I want?
4. *Make a decision/choice*
5. And move on!

Senge, P. M. (1994). *The Fifth Discipline Fieldbook.*[6]

MoA: Critical Reflection for Leadership

1. What is happening? Describe it.
2. What is *important* about context, others?
3. What am I thinking and feeling?
4. **How might I be wrong?**
5. Have I experienced something similar?
6. **How do my strengths apply?**
7. What leadership theory/practices apply?
8. **What did I learn?**

©Middlebrooks, 2011[7] (tmiddleb@udel.edu)

Skill Builder Activities

Effective leaders know things, but they can also do certain things (i.e., have skills). At the end of each chapter, you will also find some self-directed activities, tested for learning success in and out of real classrooms, in which you can engage to develop important skills, gain richer understanding of specific concepts, and move your ideas forward. Make a promise to yourself that you will take at least one idea from the end of each chapter and apply it to your leadership practice. Here is an example of a Skill Builder Activity feature:

Skill Builder Activity

Get ready to design your leadership. Think about who through your life has served as a model of leadership for you. Identify one individual from your past or present. Consider each of the facets of the leadership by design framework:

> Design Self—What great strengths did they exhibit?

> Design Relationships—What made them easy to relate to?

> Design Others' Success—What did they do to help others be successful?

Design Culture—What kind of an impact did they have on the larger team or group?

Design Future—What positive difference did they seek to make?

You might consider e-mailing or calling them to find out more about how they lead.

When you have some answers, pick one of their skills that you would like to develop in yourself and try it out for a day.

Chapter Summary

Leadership is the process of influencing others toward a common vision. Leadership matters for individuals, teams, organizations, communities, and the world. Effective leaders consciously and purposefully design their leadership.

Design is the process of originating and developing a plan. The organization for this textbook aligns important elements of the leadership definition with the different aspects of designing your leadership: yourself, your relationships with followers, others' success, culture, and the future. And because your learning will come from

many different sources, the text provides lots of interesting special features that reinforce and extend the main ideas: Leadership That Makes a Difference, Leadership by Design, Myth or Reality?, CORE™ Attribute Builders, and Skill Builder Activities.

Leaders learn in a variety of ways—from the models they observe, their experiences, what they read, the conversations they have, and their own reflections. You will get the most out of each of these engagements if you are observant at the time, reflective after, and open to changing your own concepts.

Key Terms

Design 3   Leadership 2   Leadership (extended) 3

1

A Framework for Leadership Success: Design and Your CORE™

Education makes people easy to lead, but difficult to drive; easy to govern, but impossible to enslave.

—Henry Brougham

Learning Objectives

1.1 Summarize design as a process, principle, and way of thinking

1.2 Interpret leadership as an act of designing

1.3 Identify yourself as a mindful designer of your own leadership

1.4 Assemble a plan to design your CORE™ (confidence, optimism, resilience, engagement)

1.5 Enhance your self-awareness as a developing leader

1.6 Create your initial leadership development goals

Detailed Chapter Outline

Leadership by Design Model

Design Self

How can I design myself as a leader?

Design Relationships

As a leader, how can I design my relationships with others?

Design Others' Success

As a leader, how can I design success for others?

Design Culture

As a leader, how can I design the culture of my organization?

Design Future

As a leader, how can I innovate?

Leadership is the process of influencing others toward a common vision. Do you have a plan for your leadership? Have you created a design for yourself as a leader? A design (noun) can be defined as a proposed plan, solution, or product. You likely have many thoughts about who you are and what you are good at as a leader. That is a great start. Leadership, as the definition states, is a *process*. That means that your design *should be* a work in progress. Designing (verb) your leadership means *the process of originating and developing a plan*. This textbook aims to facilitate your design-centered activity—that is, to help you develop the characteristics of thinking and activities that improve or enhance your leadership.

Design is the process of originating and developing a plan.

Designing your leadership is about *mindfully engaging*. **Mindfulness** simply means being aware. What are you doing right now? Presumably, you are reading this textbook. What else are you doing or thinking about? What are you feeling right now? What are you

Mindfulness
the mental state of being in the present and in tune with all that is happening in your immediate environment; being aware of the full, present moment, individuals, context, and/or situation

thinking, and more importantly, *how* are you thinking? Mindfulness in the broadest sense has been described as awakening to experiences. When you are more aware, you see more, learn more, and are better able to make effective decisions about your learning and your leadership. There are many advantages to becoming more mindful. Utilizing the Moments of Awareness questions from the end of the previous chapter can enhance your general mindfulness. For now, remember that when you mindfully design your leadership, you are the leader of your own learning and behavior.

The aim of this textbook is to enable you to design your leadership in a mindfully engaging manner. This chapter introduces two elements that will frame your work throughout the text and likely long into the future: Design and CORE™. The design frame provides both the mindset (purposeful and present) and the organizing model explained in the previous chapter (and summed up in the Leadership by Design Model box at the start of each chapter). The design frame also contributes processes, principles, and unique ways of thinking that will greatly enhance your leadership. The other frame, CORE™, will help build your **leadership capacity**—your fundamental attributes that can be applied to any leadership challenge in the future. Recall that CORE™ stands for your Confidence, Optimism, Resilience, and Engagement. Strengthen your CORE™, improve your future performance.

Leadership capacity
your fundamental attributes that can be applied to any leadership challenge in the future

LEADERSHIP THAT MAKES A DIFFERENCE

Imagine for a moment that you can look back across the history of humankind and survey everyone who held a leadership position from the earliest tribal leaders to military generals to presidents, business executives, and community organizers. From your observations and discussions with those leaders, what matters most? What were each of those leaders ultimately striving for: fame, fortune, land, survival, happiness, legacy, self-fulfillment? And how did they assert and maintain their leadership? What were they like? Whose leadership made a big difference?

In 1978, a political science professor and historian named James MacGregor Burns wrote a book entitled *Leadership*, and with it, he officially started the field of leadership studies.[1] Of course, leadership as a practice existed long before that book. James MacGregor Burns drew upon that long history of leadership activity, including his own experiences as a combat historian in the Pacific Ocean theater during World War II, to frame his initial impressions. When individuals talk about leaders and leadership, they refer to those in a position of power and authority. How can others do what great leaders do? The answer had always been to look at what those great leaders knew, could do, or were like, such as their characteristics and their charisma. But James MacGregor Burns saw leadership in a broader sense, as an interconnected system of situations and relationships over time—a process. "Leadership is an aspect of power, but it is also a separate and vital process in itself," he wrote.[2]

Even more important, James MacGregor Burns recognized that *power over* is less effective than *power with*. As he explains,

The crucial variable is *purpose*. Some define leadership as leaders making followers do what *followers* would not otherwise do, or as leaders making followers do what the *leaders* want them to do; I define leadership as leaders inducing followers to act for certain goals that represent the values and the motivations—the wants and needs, the aspirations and expectations—of *both leaders and followers*. And the genius of leadership lies in the way leaders see and act on their own and their followers' values and motivations.[3]

For James MacGregor Burns, there was a difference between leadership as a transaction (you work for me, I pay you) and leadership as a transformation (together, you and I can do great things). Transforming leadership, he explains, "occurs when one or more persons *engage* with others in such a way that leaders and followers raise one another to higher levels of motivation and morality."[4]

That is a tall order. How can a leader have such an impact on others? For James MacGregor Burns, the answer lies in carefully understanding yourself, your followers and their motivations, the goals, and the obstacles to those goals. "Essentially the leader's task is consciousness-raising on a wide plane,"[5] but he advises,

(Continued)

(Continued)

"In real life the most practical advice for leaders is not to treat pawns like pawns, nor princes like princes, but all persons like *persons*."[6]

You took this class or picked up this book because you want to be a better leader, because you want to make a big difference. At the start of each chapter of this text, you will read about a leader who made a big difference. What will your big difference look like? Start your leadership journey with a charge from the individual who made leadership studies possible, James MacGregor Burns: "Decide on whether we are really trying to lead anyone but ourselves, and what part of ourselves, and where, and for what purposes."[7]

Designing and Leadership

Learning Objectives

1.1 Summarize design as a process, principle, and way of thinking

1.2 Interpret leadership as an act of designing

1.3 Identify yourself as a mindful designer of your own leadership

Design comprises a broad variety of fields, many of which we equate to products like chairs and buildings. Take a moment to look around the room. What in the room has been designed? As you look around you might immediately notice the wide range of products that have been designed: the furniture, carpet, light fixtures, your pen, computer, even this textbook. You might also notice the less obvious: haircuts, room layout, architecture of the building, heating and cooling system. Those things were also designed.

Design also includes things you cannot see; things you can only feel or experience. For example, the class or meeting you may be sitting in right now was *designed*. In the case of a class, the instructor considered the learning goals he or she wanted to meet, and then carefully created a plan to help the students learn. In other words, the instructor went through a process of planning your *experience*. This is a field called instructional design. Organizational design does the same thing but for employees—who does what, when, why, reporting to whom—designing the experience of working at an organization.

Design Process as a Creative Problem-Solving Process: Understand, Imagine, Implement, and Iterate

"It can be argued that the best CEOs are effectively designers—grappling with ambiguous challenges, probing for creative solutions—even though few would accept that moniker," notes a feature in *Fast Company* looking at the applicability of design to business success.[8] Designers are problem solvers, and they follow a problem-solving process. Design professionals write up a design brief outlining the problem and the parameters based on what the client wants, such as a more efficient toaster, a faster bike, a bee-friendly landscape, a more challenging golf course, or a more appealing website. At the university, the problem might be a more secure dorm or a healthier menu at the dining hall. Finding and identifying the problem is the start of the process, which designers then continue to originate and develop a plan to solve the problem. Many design-related processes have been created, varying in length, specificity, and emphasis. A quick web search under design process, problem-solving process, creative problem-solving process, or innovation process yields hundreds of processes ranging from well-established to homemade and from general use to organization specific.

Despite this broad and lengthy list of processes, *all* of them can be mapped onto a general **design process** consisting of three major phases: *understand, imagine, and implement*.

Design process
a general problem-solving process consisting of three major phases: understand, imagine, and implement; with iteration occurring throughout

Each phase defines a significant step in the design process. Understand—what do we know about the problem, context, stakeholders, history, and so on? Imagine—what are the most creative ideas we can generate for addressing the problem? Implement—what activities, resources, and timelines are necessary to bring the idea to reality?[9]

When you look around at all the things that were designed, it is not always clear what the original problem entailed. A pen that feels good in your hand may have been designed to solve the problem of cost effectiveness or reliable ink transfer. Nevertheless, the designer had to *understand* the problem and all its variables to move forward, otherwise the designer is solving the wrong problem. Now look at your phone. What kinds of problems was the design team trying to solve? What did they need to understand before they could solve each problem?

The pen in your hand may not have been the only idea to solve that problem. In the *imagine* phase the designer generates many, many ideas; this is the most creative part of the process. Problem solvers find a solution, but creative problem solvers do not stop with the first good idea, they keep coming up with ideas to find that *great* idea.

Returning to the pen example, once that solution was chosen, what did it take to get that pen from idea to production to retail store and into your hand? The designer, or likely others in a collaborative team, needed to address all the facets of *implementation*. Lastly, throughout the process the designer needed to **iterate**, meaning to try things out and improve the design based on feedback, until the final solution was ready. Iteration is an important activity that happens throughout all three phases. At any point in the process, how might our current progress make us rethink or redesign? Figure 1.1 illustrates the general steps in the design process.

Iterate
the act of trying things out and improving the design based on feedback

You are going to design something much more complicated than a pen. Designing your leadership comprises a wide menu of problems. The leadership by design framework helps organize those problems. Following a process will greatly enhance both your innovation and your success. For example, to design yourself as a leader, you must first understand many things about yourself. For instance, what are your strengths, values, assumptions, and goals? As you grow in that understanding, you need to imagine the possibilities for yourself. Who will you become? What characteristics and attributes should you acquire and develop? And then, you must implement—how will you learn and develop? What resources do you need to acquire? How will you make those lessons stay with you over time? Through this process you will assess yourself in a variety of ways and then change directions, alter your plans, scrap some solutions for others, and iterate.

Understand, Imagine, Implement, and Iterate: Attending to the full process will help you design your most effective and innovative leadership. But the design process is only part of the picture. How you think, see, and process information makes a big difference in how effectively you utilize each part of the process. That is called *design thinking*.

FIGURE 1.1 ●   Design Process

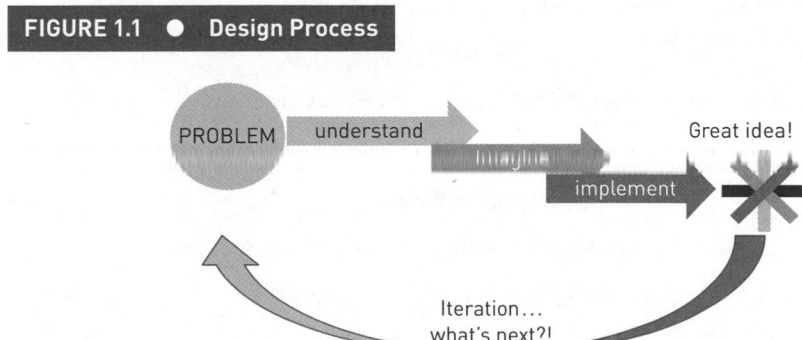

Design as a Mental Habit: Design Thinking

Design thinking
This is a cognitive approach to engaging problems that embodies a specific mindset that is **Explorative:** mindset that assumes purposeful ambiguity and curiosity; **User-centered:** mindset that focuses on the user and how they experience and feel; **Divergent:** mindset of generating many, many ideas for a single problem; **Multidisciplinary:** mindset that engages many minds and pursues multiple areas of expertise; **Integrative:** mindset of attending to and balancing multiple criteria, particularly viability, feasibility, and desirability; and **Iterative:** mindset of always seeing solutions in process—assessing and improving. Also, habits of mind (dispositions) that designers use to help enhance and guide their process.

Disposition
habits of mind often seen as tendencies or characteristics

Designers follow a process (Understand, Imagine, Implement, Iterate), *and* they have specific habitual ways of thinking that help them see the world, their process, and their design challenge in a unique way. This set of dispositions is called **design thinking**. A **disposition** is defined as habits of mind that are often seen as tendencies or characteristics. Tim Brown of the design firm IDEO describes design thinking as "an approach that uses the designer's sensibility and methods for problem solving to meet people's needs in a technologically feasible and commercially viable way. In other words, design thinking is human-centered innovation."[10]

Brown elaborates on what a design-thinking approach might entail, but the important part of design thinking is about your *thinking habits*. Bruck and Middlebrooks provide the following definition: Design thinking is a cognitive approach to engaging problems that embodies a specific mindset that is (a) user-centered, (b) explorative, (c) divergent, (d) multidisciplinary, (e) iterative, and (f) integrative—striving for feasibility, viability, desirability.[11] Engaging and developing these habits of mind enables you to more successfully and creatively work through ill-defined and dynamic problems, such as the kind you find in leadership, and certainly the type of problems you will face in designing your leadership. Table 1.1 aligns the design thinking dispositions within the understand, imagine, implement, iterate problem-solving process to better illustrate how design thinking helps each phase.

As you design your leadership, the important aspect of the process lies with the ability to think like a designer, adopting the mental habits that will maximize each phase of the process. For example, in your effort to understand your strengths as a leader, you might take many self-assessments. Considering the design-thinking disposition of user-centeredness, you might add interviews of your followers to your exploration, asking them about how it feels to be led by you; or perhaps, spend a day in their role to better understand their context. Developing your individual capacity to think like a designer ultimately helps you solve complex problems in more creative ways. Design thinking as a leadership tool is more extensively explained in Chapter 5: Design Thinking and Brain Leading.

TABLE 1.1 ● Design Thinking Dispositions by Creative Problem-Solving Phase
Design thinking is a cognitive approach to engaging problems that embodies a specific mindset that is:
Understand
User-centered: mindset that focuses on the user and how they experience and feel
Explorative: mindset that assumes purposeful ambiguity and curiosity
Imagine
Divergent: mindset of generating many, many ideas for a single problem
Multidisciplinary: mindset that engages many minds and pursues multiple areas of expertise
Implement and Iterate
Iterative: mindset of always seeing solutions in process—assessing and improving
Integrative: mindset of attending to and balancing multiple and contrasting variables and creatively resolving the tensions between them

REFLECTION QUESTION

If you were the leader of a group, how could you use each of the design-thinking habits to help you influence others toward a common vision? Here is an example for each disposition to get you started:

- User-centered: put yourself in the shoes of new students that your group wants to recruit; create fun new officer names and positions based on member strengths and interests

- Explorative: ask every member to generate a question about the history and practices of the group

- Divergent: challenge the group to generate 100 different ways you could raise funds

- Multidisciplinary: invite members from 10 very different groups to talk about how they would approach a problem your group is working on

- Iterative: try out a new activity with a few members and improve it before introducing it to the whole group

- Integrative: create numerous ways to assess the success of a new group activity, not just if people like it

Design Principles: Rules You Can Apply to Design Your Leadership

Designers follow rules, which they call **design principles**. Designers apply these rules to whatever they are designing to help the design better meet its goals. For example, the goal of a poster design might be to clearly communicate an event or to advocate for a cause. A product might strive for easy use or greater durability. The goal of a building design might be to encourage people to talk with one another or, by contrast, to focus on their individual work. Following the right rules helps a design more effectively meet its goals.

Design principle
rules that designers apply to help guide their process and enhance their product

There are hundreds of design principles, but they focus on typical, tangible design fields (i.e., fields that produce a product such as industrial design, architecture, graphic design) versus those fields that design things you cannot touch (i.e., experiences, services, systems). Over the course of this text you will see a feature called *Leadership by Design*. This feature highlights the insights leaders can draw from design. How might various design principles used in the design world be applied to effective leadership practice? On the next page you will find another example of what a *Leadership by Design* feature looks like using the most basic visual design principles: balance, focal point, contrast, repetition, proportion, and unity.

Could you draw a picture of your leadership? What if your leadership was a painting or photo? As you thought about the design of you as a leader, what would be most important? What rules might help you design? The main principles of visual design provide a very useful metaphor for guiding the design of your leadership self. The questions that emerge from these design principles are critical to your success, and because of that importance, you will see them again and again throughout this text.

LEADERSHIP BY DESIGN

Design Principles: Visual Design Principles: Balance, Focal Point, Contrast, Repetition, Proportion, Unity

Definitions: Explained from the artist perspective, "The elements and principles of design are the building blocks used to create a work of art. The elements of design can be thought of as the things that make up a painting, drawing, design, etc. The principles of design can be thought of as what we do to the elements of design. How we apply the principles of design determines how successful we are in creating a work of art."[12]

Balance—a sense of equilibrium

Focal Point—an area of emphasis that draws attention

Contrast—the notable or opposing difference between elements

Repetition—repeated elements that reinforce a theme

Proportion—a sense of order among elements

Unity—the relationship among elements that gives a sense of oneness

In Other Words: When the designer wants to convey a specific visual message, the above visual design principles can be applied to emphasize that message.

For Example: The first photo here illustrates *balance* and *repetition*, while the second photo shows an interesting *contrast* between the formal jacket and informal shorts, and clearly, those Bermuda socks are the *focal point*.

For Leaders: This segment of the feature is important for you as the designer of your leadership. This is the part that helps you apply the design principle to your leadership. The visual design principles hold many important implications and applications. Table 1.2 notes the fundamental application of each principle in the form of a prompting question for you to consider. Take a moment to note how each of these principles could be applied to your current context.

Courtesy of the authors

BALANCE AND REPETITION

Courtesy of the authors

BALANCE AND FOCAL POINT

TABLE 1.2 ● Reflection Questions	
You Might Apply This Design Principle	**By Asking Yourself This Key Question**
Balance	Am I seeing all perspectives? Is my approach balanced? What counterbalances what I am doing?
Focal Point	What needs to be highlighted? What needs to be the focus?
Contrast	What distinctions need to be drawn between things to highlight and clarify?
Repetition	What could be better learned, retained, or highlighted through consistency or repetition?
Proportion	What needs to be prioritized? Am I spending the right amount of time and energy on things relative to their importance?
Unity	Do all the things I am doing align with the vision?

Designing Your Leadership By Building Your Core™

Learning Objectives

1.4 Assemble a plan to design your CORE™ (confidence, optimism, resilience, engagement)

1.5 Enhance your self-awareness as a developing leader

"Who looks outside, dreams. Who looks inside, awakens." —Carl Jung

Life is challenging and leadership often more so. Humans become frightened, intimidated, tired, discouraged, distracted, saddened, overwhelmed, burned out, bitter, and disengaged. How can you prepare yourself for all the situations that you cannot see or even imagine now and stay positive and engaged as a leader through it all? Just as you can develop your core strength for physical activities, you can also develop your internal CORE™: confidence, optimism, resilience, and engagement. This section introduces these four elements and explains how you can develop each as a central part of designing your leadership.

Building your CORE™ is about developing the mental habits that will help you excel when things are going well and sustain you when things are most challenging. Your brain is a lean, mean, pattern-making machine; when you repeat patterns over and over they become habits. The foundation of CORE™ is rooted in positive psychology and the construct

PsyCap
an individual's positive psychological state of development characterized by confidence, optimism, hope, and resilience

Confidence
Latin root *con+fidere*, which means with intense trust—trust in yourself; the state of knowing you are capable and effective; as part of leadership CORE™ it is your ability to learn, adapt, and succeed

Optimism
the ability and tendency to see the positive, both now and into the future

Resilience
Latin root *resilire*, which means to spring back—your ability to withstand and recover from difficulties

known as psychological capital, or PsyCap. **PsyCap** has been defined as "an individual's positive psychological state of development and is characterized by: (a) having **confidence** (self-efficacy) to take on and put in the necessary effort to succeed at challenging tasks; (b) making a positive attribution (**optimism**) about succeeding now and in the future; (c) persevering toward goals, and when necessary, redirecting paths to goals (hope) in order to succeed; and (d) when beset by problems and adversity, sustaining and bouncing back and even beyond (**resilience**) to attain success."[13] Individuals with high levels of PsyCap display many positive constructive behaviors and abilities and fewer undesirable behaviors.[14]

Take a moment to assess your CORE™ by scoring yourself on the following statements on a scale from 1 (not at all) to 5 (a lot):

Confidence—self-efficacy and effort

1. When facing a new task, I know that I will succeed.	1	2	③	4	5
2. For nearly every task, I put in my best effort.	1	②	3	4	5
3. I do not let fear influence my efforts.	1	2	3	4	5

Optimism—positive about success

4. I will attain the goals I have set for myself.	1	2	3	4	5
5. When dealing with a difficult situation, I take a positive outlook.	1	2	3	4	5
6. My success is due to my effort and skill.	1	2	3	4	5

Resilience—perseverance and flexibility, using setbacks as set-forwards

7. When I encounter setbacks, I generally find ways around them.	1	2	3	4	⑤
8. When I fail to do something well, I want to try again and do it better.	1	2	3	4	⑤

Engagement—reflective and mindful

9. I integrate new experiences and ideas into what I already know.	1	2	3	4	⑤
10. I reflect and learn from what I experience.	1	2	3	4	⑤

In which of the CORE™ areas do you think you excel? Which need work? At the end of each chapter, the CORE™ Attribute Builders feature can help you build these valuable mental habits.

The CORE™ elements work together in a complementary and reinforcing way. When you are confident, you see the world and your success in more positive terms (optimism). When you are optimistic, you are more likely to bounce back from setbacks (resilience). When you are more resilient, every time you pick yourself up and try again, it builds your confidence. And driving the growth of all of this is positive engagement. The more you are engaged, the more you experience, the more you learn, and the more opportunities open up to you for further engagement. The model illustrating the interrelationship between the elements of confidence, optimism, resilience, and engagement is shown in Figure 1.2.

FIGURE 1.2 ● The CORE™ Model

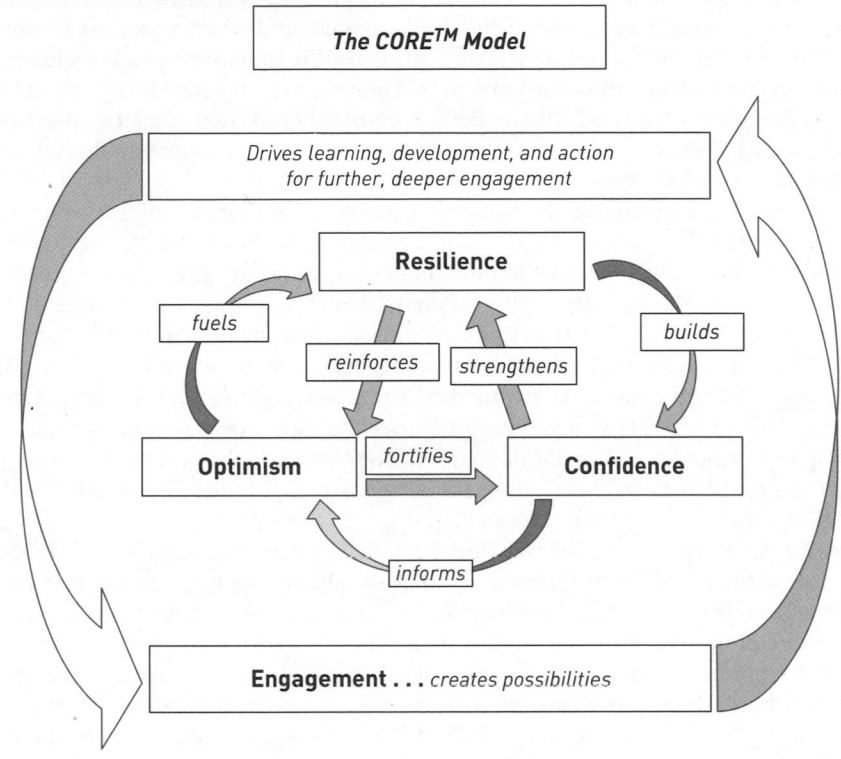

Confidence

Confidence as part of leadership CORE™ underpins your ability to learn, adapt, and succeed. You may have also heard the terms self-efficacy, self-confidence, assurance, self-esteem, or simply belief in yourself. But the key to confidence lies in its Latin root *con+fidere*, which means with intense trust. Trust in yourself. Consider what it means to intensely trust yourself. What would you do? How would you act? You would believe that your ideas are correct, be willing to take risks and make mistakes, be open to learning new things and hearing other perspectives, and likely feel very good about yourself. When you trust in yourself—who you are and what you think and do—you leave behind all the fear, doubt, self-consciousness, anxiety, and hesitation that limits your thinking and ultimately your success.

● REFLECTION QUESTIONS

When have you felt confident, and when have you not? Compare those situations. In what ways did you trust yourself? In situations in which you did not feel confident, what did you fear?

Your confidence as a leader has significant effects on you, your followers, and the organization. With great confidence, you can focus on others and the organization rather than yourself. For you as a leader, confidence results in greater influence with followers.[15] Followers are influenced by a leader they find credible, and when you trust in yourself, followers trust in you, too. Confident leaders also take the initiative to meet followers and build relationships, hear and discuss alternative perspectives, try new things regardless of who contributed the idea, and facilitate the success of others. When you are confident, you are not fearful that other perspectives will undermine your leadership; you do not need to take credit for new ideas nor be the sole font of information.

Confident leaders maximize the value that followers can offer, which in turn results in everyone's success. Building the confidence of your followers and fostering a culture of confidence has been described as the most important challenge for leaders.[16] Leadership guru Rosabeth Moss Kanter writes, "One difference between winners and losers is how they handle losing."[17] She explains that every organization, no matter how successful, faces setbacks and unexpected problems. But knowing that leadership is a process, she states, "Anything can look like failure in the middle." Confidence, along with the other elements of CORE™, can ensure that you successfully move through those failures. And that is the capacity your confidence will build in your followers and into the culture of the organization. In Chapter 11, you will learn more about the nature and nurture of culture and how to specifically utilize your CORE™ to shape it.

There are many ways that you can work on building your confidence, and all of them center around the sources of information you use to change your mindset and to increase your trust in yourself. Self-efficacy researchers note that there are four main sources that inform beliefs about self: enactive mastery experiences, vicarious experiences, social influences, and emotional states.[18] Enactive mastery experiences are activities in which you directly participate and are the most influential because they are the most authentic. When you engage and succeed, it builds confidence. When you engage and succeed over and over again, especially if you had to overcome setbacks, you develop a resilient confidence. And you develop an optimistic view of your success in future activities.

Again, note how the CORE™ elements work together (see Figure 1.3). Confidence strengthens resilience and informs optimism. Resilient activities build confidence, while optimism reinforces that confidence.

REFLECTION QUESTIONS

Consider an activity you feel confident about. Can you recall your early successes and small wins? How many times did you need to succeed before you felt generally confident?

Other ways to build confidence include observing what others do to succeed (vicarious experiences), receiving evaluative feedback that highlights your capabilities (social influences), and a wide variety of activities that impact physical wellness, including exercise, diet, and grooming. There is increasing evidence illustrating the connection between what you do physically and how you think about yourself and the world. This is obvious when you think about things like sleep and caffeine. You can even physically assume what social psychologist Amy Cuddy calls high and low power body positions that can change your brain chemistry and how others perceive you.[19] At the end of this chapter, you will find the CORE™ Adventure, which is a series of activities outside the classroom that will help you identify what aspects of your CORE™ need work and help jump start your development of these capacities.

MOMENT OF AWARENESS

One of the most influential factors in who I am as a leader, and the most overlooked, is my failures. Often in our society so much stress is placed on our successes, but little is put into our shortcomings. I feel that I have had enough of both to recognize that they both have played a lasting role in my leadership. I have been captain of sports teams and a leader in academic organizations . . . and I have been denied those positions. I have lived up to my potential in some regards, and I also have been a huge flop at times. I believe that being a good leader is not dependent on where you are at that certain point, but rather when you look back and consider the question: Did I make a positive difference? Would things be different if I wasn't there? Am I happy with what I provided?

—Benjamin Mergenthaler, Undergraduate

There are many assessments available online that you can utilize to assess your confidence and raise your awareness of the areas in which you are more and less confident.[20] However, as you plan for designing your leadership self and your confidence, there is a dark side that you must consider. Confidence is not arrogance. Trusting in yourself to the point of excluding other perspectives, and others generally, results in a dangerous level of overconfidence. Overconfidence has been described in three ways: "*overestimation*: thinking that you're better than you actually are . . . *overplacement*: thinking that you're better than others when you are not . . . (and) *overprecision*: being too sure you know the truth."[21] Overconfidence as a leader can result in poor decisions, failing to see deficiencies accurately, impractical goals, and disenchanted followers that soon become alienated.[22] In other words, you will make unnecessary mistakes that may irreparably harm your organization and your credibility.

Here are some suggestions for avoiding overconfidence: (a) question whether you are overlooking something, especially if performance feels too easy; (b) understand that there are many variables that account for outcomes and that you are only one of those variables; (c) seek out contrary and external perspectives, especially those that are the least noticed; and (d) back up your claims and your confidence with evidence. *Fake it until you make it* is a fine strategy for facing fears and building confidence, but it can quickly turn to outright falsehoods and deception, even deceiving yourself.

Within every experience lies the chance to build your CORE™ if you take the time to think about that experience and ask the right questions (remember the Moments of Awareness from the Introduction). At the end of this section, you will find another card called *CORE™: Assessing Leadership Challenges* (see Figure 1.3 on page 31). This card poses a few key questions that you can ask yourself during that moment of awareness, during or right after a leadership experience that you felt was probably impactful. Here are the questions related to building confidence:

- Did I put in my best effort?
- Did fear influence my effort?
- Did I take initiative?
- Did I focus and dedicate my attention to the effort?

Optimism

Optimism is the ability and tendency to see the positive, both now and into the future. You likely know people who you would describe as upbeat, positive, and always seeing the glass half full (and a host of other metaphors). But the key to optimism lies in its Latin root *optimus*, which means *the best*. What does it mean to see the best in yourself, others, and every situation? How would you act? You would likely work to try and bring out that best in yourself and others, which of course would feel great. As leadership gurus James Kouzes and Barry Posner note in their book *Encouraging the Heart*, people want to be in a relationship with someone who makes them feel good and brings out their best.[23] Optimism is your tool for building those great relationships. Of course, when you can see your best, you become more confident.

Optimism is both a learned mental habit and a characteristic you can inherit from your parents (lucky you). When people call someone an optimist, it sounds like part of who they are that cannot be changed. It has even been referred to as a core personality trait of managers.[24] You will read more about traits in the next chapter. But optimism can be learned, practiced, developed, and used by anyone. So, when you read *optimist*, it refers to someone with that ability and tendency to see the best, regardless of how they came to be an optimist.

A good deal of research has been done on the relationship between optimism and a variety of leadership variables. Optimists are perceived by supervisors as having leadership potential and being better able to cope with stressors.[25] Most importantly, focusing on the best things results in greater performance. One interesting study that has framed the power of optimism on performance involved two groups of bowlers. One group viewed videos of their mistakes and focused on not repeating those mistakes. The other group viewed videos of the things they did correctly and focused on repeating those behaviors. When comparing scores over time, the group that focused on their successes did far better than those focusing on their mistakes.[26] The previous section noted that confident leaders maximize the value that followers can offer. Leaders need to be able to *see* that positive value to capitalize on it.

REFLECTION QUESTIONS

How optimistic are those with whom you associate? Make a quick list of family and friends and order them according to how you perceive their ability and tendency to see the best. Compare and contrast the most and least optimistic. In what ways do you think their level of optimism has affected their life?

While optimism is a personal attribute, it is not necessarily an individual endeavor. If you have ever been part of a great team, you know how powerful and motivating a culture of optimism can feel. As each teammate communicates their positive perspective, the capacity of the entire team to see and strive for the best increases exponentially. Setbacks become opportunities for improvement. Problems become challenges. Achievements become affirmations of effort and capability. Even profitability and customer satisfaction increase based on the ratio of positive to negative comments among teammates.[27]

"I think I can, I think I can. I think I can. I know I can," wrote Watty Piper in *The Little Engine That Could*. Are you like the little engine, rooting your effort in a firm vision of your best? If not, you may want to very seriously consider developing your optimism. Optimism is a reinforcing cycle between what you highlight in the world and what you believe. The more opportunities you create to highlight the positive and the possible, the stronger you will make your mental habit of searching out those best elements in any situation. Try some of these ideas to build your optimism (or go online to find many more):

1. *Seek* positive perspectives, positive people, multiple perspectives, and upbeat words. Try responding to others' comments with "yes, and . . ." rather than "but . . ." even when you may disagree.

2. *Avoid* negative phrases, complaining, griping, and negative environments.

3. *Engage* in recognizing what is going well and what is going great; practice thinking about what could be; encourage open dialog and collaborate to build a compelling vision that inspires others.[28]

4. *Celebrate* to reinforce optimistic habits. When was the last time you celebrated a small win, learning something new, another person who did something well, or a moment of awareness of all that is going pretty well for you? Even small celebrations make a big impact.

Optimism is not about false confidence or pretending everything is happy and perfect. Nor do optimists avoid challenges and difficult people and situations. An optimistic approach is often rejected by those claiming that they are realists, and their perspective is more accurate. Do not be fooled or dissuaded. You can have a full understanding and acceptance of the real and still strive to see the positive and the potential. Within the CORE™ Model, optimism reinforces confidence and fuels resilience. If you can see the best and believe it is possible, then you will move forward without fear and keep moving forward even with setbacks.

Again, at the end of this section there is a card (*CORE™: Assessing Leadership Challenges*; see Figure 1.3) that poses key questions that you can ask yourself, this time related to building optimism:

- Did I feel I would succeed?

- Was my success due to my effort and skill?

- Did I need to redirect my efforts?

Resilience

Resilience is your ability to withstand and recover from difficulties. You may also have heard the terms hardiness, grit, stick-to-itiveness, and gutsiness. Once again, the Latin root captures the essence of the concept, in this case *resilire*, which means to *spring back*. Consider what it means to spring back. First, something must have pushed you over. A life without setbacks leaves no opportunity to display or build resilience. Second, there must be some initial resistance to the setback. A flower blown back by the wind started with enough resistance to stand upright in the first place. Third, there must be some energy to spring back, energy that exists before the setback, built in preparation for the challenge. Finally, there is a positive energy to springing back. You do not crawl, limp, hobble, or scrape your way back, you spring. As General George Patton stated, "I don't measure a man's success by how high he climbs, but how high he bounces when he hits the bottom."

REFLECTION QUESTIONS

Think about the last time you experienced a setback. How many times did you try again? What helped you to try again, and/or what kept you from doing so?

Once again, your mental habit-forming lean, mean, pattern-making machine of a brain can work with you or against you when it comes to resilience. The founder of positive psychology, Martin Seligman, and other researchers have summed up the mental habits you need. When something in your life goes wrong (or right), how do you explain it?[29]

1. Do you think problems happen for many reasons, or do problems happen because you are incapable, incompetent, and other bad things?

2. Do you see adversity as a challenge or chance to learn, or do you see it as a threat?

3. Do you see the problem as one specific thing or just another indication that your whole life is problematic?

4. Do you see difficulties as permanent situations or as something you can address or change?

5. Are *you* in control of the outcome, or is it out of your hands with nothing you can do about it?

For each of these questions, thinking and seeing as described in the first half of the question lead to very different outcomes than in the second. Resilient individuals, and leaders, work to develop psychologically positive mental habits.

Resilience in leadership goes beyond personal well-being, although it is critically important to the individual leader. A resilient leader not only springs back but also leaps forward, using the setback to advance the organization.[30] The cliché of seeing every challenge as an opportunity reflects the interplay of optimism and resilience and has been embraced by innovators and entrepreneurs as the power of failure.[31] Although no one wants to fail, those moments hold great value for individual learning and group modeling. Leaders who model resilience help create a resilient culture. Looking beyond the single moments of failure to the broader pattern of shortcomings brings even greater insights. In other words, sometimes many little failures are all hints at a more fundamental problem—a problem that you would not see otherwise, or worse, one that would build into a large problem.[32]

Great resilience does not come easily nor without considerable emotional consequence. Challenges and setbacks are exactly that; they are challenging and set you back. They are painful, disheartening, annoying, disorienting, and extraordinarily frustrating. The level, amount, and duration of these feelings varies; and what constitutes a challenge to one person may not be so to another. As a leader, you must understand the level of understanding for each follower. This means you must understand how others feel, which is part of a concept called emotional intelligence. **Emotional intelligence** is a person's ability to know and regulate their own feelings, perceive and understand the feelings of others, and effectively work between their own and others' feelings (see the *Experts Beyond the Text: Insightful Leaders Know About . . . Emotional Intelligence* feature at the end of this section).[33]

Resilience is not something one is born with, nor can you afford to purposefully engage in failure to build your resilience . . . or can you? The effort to develop resilience goes back to antiquity. Lucius Annaeus Seneca (4BC–AD65) was a Roman philosopher who, among his many wise letters, advised a friend on how to build resilience:

Set aside a certain number of days, during which you shall be content with the scantiest and cheapest fare, with coarse and rough dress, saying to yourself the while: 'Is this the condition that I feared?' It is precisely in times of immunity from care that the soul should toughen itself beforehand for occasions of greater stress . . . If you would not have a man flinch when the crisis comes, train him before it comes.

Emotional intelligence
a person's ability to know and regulate their own feelings, perceive and understand the feelings of others, and effectively work between their own and others' feelings

Not surprisingly, Seneca also noted that this activity for building resilience also provided insight that brought empathy (and emotional intelligence): "There is no reason, however, why you should think that you are doing anything great; for you will merely be doing what many thousands of slaves and many thousands of poor men are doing every day."[34]

REFLECTION QUESTIONS

Try holding your arms straight out away from your body for three minutes. As it starts to hurt, push through the pain. Keep them up. Were you able to keep your arms up for the full time? Why did you keep going (or why did you quit)? What did it feel like once you dropped your arms? What could you do without for a time that would build your resilience . . . and your appreciation?

Fortunately, there are many other ways to build resilience besides diving into failure. Developing your resilience as a leader depends upon engaging in experiences and mindfully learning from them. Here are a few suggestions based on attending to different kinds of health:[35]

1. Attend to your Physical Health: exercise, sleep, eat well, and destress

2. Attend to your Mental and Emotional Health: take time for yourself, develop your confidence, laugh

3. Attend to your Social Health: connect with others, foster relationships with family and friends, build your support system, ask advice

4. Attend to your Attitude Health: practice optimism, see problems as experiences you can learn from, put problems into perspective

5. Attend to your Aspirational Health: identify big and little goals for yourself, commit to them, act to move toward achieving them

Take a second look at the summary of resilience-building activities. If you are feeling good, have a great support system, see the bigger picture, and know leadership is a process, your capacity for resilience will grow. What one thing can you do today to start building your capacity to spring back?[36]

Again, at the end of this section there is a card (*CORE™: Assessing Leadership Challenges*; see Figure 1.3) that poses key questions that you can ask yourself, this time related to building resilience:

- Did I encounter setbacks or significant challenges?

- Did setbacks discourage my efforts?

- Did I confront problems directly?

- Did problems make me question my ability?

EXPERTS BEYOND THE TEXT

INSIGHTFUL LEADERS KNOW ABOUT . . . EMOTIONAL INTELLIGENCE

The Role of Emotional Intelligence in Leadership

By Scott Allen

The topic of emotions is central to leadership. After all, a central activity of leadership is engaging, inspiring, and motivating others to work above and beyond toward the goal or objective—all of which engages emotions. Likewise, because of the nature of leadership work, leaders must navigate any number of stressors, such as interpersonal conflicts, issue conflicts, rapid change, and organizational bureaucracy. The heightened levels of stress that come with leadership mean leaders must be acutely aware of their emotional state and that of others. In essence, leaders need to be *intelligent* about emotions and understand how emotions can influence themselves and others.

There are a number of different ways to make sense of emotional intelligence (EI). Some scholars feel that EI is a form of intelligence[37] and others believe it is simply a constellation of personality traits.[38] The most well-known model of EI explores the concept as a series of competencies.[39] Researcher Daniel Goleman provides a definition that nicely captures all three general approaches:

> *Emotional intelligence, at the most general level, refers to the abilities to recognize and regulate emotions in ourselves and in others.*[40]

As you look at the definition, note that having EI means that an individual *recognizes* their emotions and can *regulate* them as appropriate. This does not mean that they *stuff away* their feelings; it simply means that they are more aware of their emotional state in the face of a challenging situation. They can intentionally regulate their emotional state in an effort to move forward toward the end objective—aware of their emotions as they are *triggered* by the various stressors. Individuals who are more easily triggered will often react in ways that diminish trust and credibility. A second important highlight of the definition is the term *others*. The leader is responsible for awareness and regulation of both their own emotions and those of their colleagues. This means that leaders with EI can read the emotional state of the group and regulate that emotional state (e.g., pick them up during a difficult time).

Who in your life best maintains emotional intelligence when triggered by the various stressors that accompany their role? Who struggles to do so? What is the impact on the group?

Scholars have made positive associations that underscore the importance of leadership and EI. Here are several examples of what scholars from different paradigms have found based on their research.

- "The high EI individual, most centrally, can better perceive emotions, use them in thought, understand their meanings, and manage emotions better than others. . . . The person also tends to be somewhat higher in verbal, social and other intelligences, particularly if the individual scored higher in the understanding emotions portion of EI. The individual tends to be more open and agreeable than others. The high EI person is drawn to occupations involving social interactions such as teaching and counseling more so than to occupations involving clerical or administrative tasks."[41]

- "Both emotional and social competencies and personality traits are valuable predictors of job performance."[42]

- "Experienced partners in a multinational consulting firm were assessed on the EI competencies plus three others. Partners who scored above the median on 9 or more of the 20 competencies delivered $1.2 million more profit from their accounts than did other partners—a 139 percent incremental gain."[43]

- "In a national insurance company, insurance sales agents who were weak in emotional competencies such as self-confidence, initiative, and empathy sold policies with an average premium of $54,000. Those who were very strong in at least 5 of 8 key emotional competencies sold policies worth $114,000."[44]

While emotions can be a fuzzy or *soft* topic, research suggests that EI helps individuals succeed. Effective leaders understand emotional intelligence and strive to develop this key capacity.

Engagement

Have you ever been talking with someone and found yourself rushing to finish talking because it is clear they are not really listening but instead waiting for their *turn* to talk? Or worse, talking to someone while they look at their phone or around the room, mumbling an occasional "uh huh"? Engagement is key to connecting with others, as much as disengagement is off-putting. And, although rude and ineffective, the worst result of disengagement is the missed opportunities to learn, to connect, and to discover new ideas and possibilities. Engagement is one of the most powerful tools in your leadership toolbox. The origin of the word *engage* comes from the Old French *engagier*, meaning bind by promise or pledge. For example, engagement to a person means you pledge a binding promise to marry. Engaging the enemy binds you to the promise of conflict. For leaders, engagement promises the binding of your attention and involvement. **Engagement** is the degree of individual involvement, investment, and enthusiasm within and for a specific context or situation.

Engagement
the degree of individual involvement, investment, and enthusiasm within and for a specific context or situation

REFLECTIVE QUESTIONS

Are you involved? Invested? Do you notice the world around you? Do you actively listen to others and seek to discover more about them? How often would your friends say you are truly present?

Engagement drives the development of confidence, optimism, and resilience. If you are not paying attention to the things you are experiencing, or simply not involved enough to have a wide range of experiences, then you shortchange your chances for learning and growth. For effective leadership, engagement needs to add value, that is to say it needs to be *positive*. **Positive engagement** means that you initiate and participate in ways that add value in a reflective and mindful manner, critically and carefully integrating new information into your understanding. *Your most valuable internal asset is your positive engagement.* Engaged leaders are perceived as more charismatic, and they inspire performance and commitment.[45]

Positive engagement
your initiation and participation in ways that add value in a reflective and mindful manner, critically and carefully integrating new information into your understanding

Increasing your own engagement is a choice, but it is also a mental and behavioral habit. The best way to develop a habit is, of course, to repeat a behavior over and over again. Here are a few ideas for how you can increase your engagement:

- Take a leisurely walk and purposefully look up

- Eat with your eyes closed and focus on the flavors

- Unplug—set a time and time limit for dealing with social media

- Meet someone new and learn about their world

- Meet someone who you think is very different from you

- Meet someone you already know—interview them and get to know them better

- Learn to do something new in your leadership setting and beyond—learn to tie knots, learn a specific dance, cook a meal, identify trees

- Try sketching, even if you do not think you can—it forces you to really look at something

- Identify one activity that you would really like to do but never seem to have the time—commit to doing that activity every day for 30 days (and start by watching the Matt Cutts TED Talk for inspiration: http://www.ted.com/talks/ matt_cutts_try_something_new_for_30_days)

Similar to confidence, optimism, and resilience, engagement rubs off on others. Leaders model engaged behavior, and in turn, they become engaging. If you consistently positively engage—in any role, in any situation, in any context—you will ultimately find success. And, here at the end of this section is the card (Figure 1.3—*CORE™: Assessing Leadership Challenges*) that poses key questions that you can ask yourself. The questions related to building engagement are as follows:

- Did I reflect and learn from the experience?

- Did I integrate this new knowledge into prior?

One of the best ways to build your entire CORE™ is to raise your awareness of what is happening, what you are doing, how you are feeling, and what you could have done better. Use the prompting questions on the cards below to enhance your self-awareness as you engage in any leadership challenge.

"A well-designed product does not equal a well-designed business."[47] Likewise, a well-designed leader does not equal well-designed leadership . . . but it is a necessary start. This chapter focused on your perceptions and the task of designing your leadership self. Acquiring

---

FIGURE 1.3 ● CORE™ Card: Assessing Leadership Challenges

CORE™: Assessing Leadership Challenges

1. **Confidence**: self-efficacy and effort

   Did I put in my best effort?

   Did fear influence my effort?

   Did I take initiative?

   Did I focus and dedicate my attention to the effort?

2. **Optimism**: positive about success

   Did I feel I would succeed?

   Was my success due to my effort and skill?

   Did I need to redirect my efforts?

3. **Resilience**: perseverance and flexibility, using setbacks as set-forwards

   Did I encounter setbacks or significant challenges?

   Did setbacks discourage my efforts?

   Did I confront problems directly?

   Did problems make me question my ability?

4. **Engagement**: reflective and mindful

   Did I reflect and learn from the experience?

   Did I integrate this new knowledge into prior?

MYTH OR REALITY?

WITHOUT MOBILE PHONES AND SOCIAL MEDIA, INDIVIDUALS ARE MORE ENGAGED.

Myth . . . and Reality. A recent study asked a thousand students in ten different countries to go without all media for one full day. The resulting reactions, observations, and insights indicate that media use is more than a habit, but rather, it is "essential to the way they construct and manage their friendships and social lives," and it is critically useful for both practical performance and psychological and emotional security.[46] On the other hand, "Many students, from all continents, literally couldn't imagine how to fill up their empty hours without media," and limited their news and awareness to the brief and simplified media worlds in which they operate.

Could you go without media for 24 hours? Try it and note your observations.

---

a thorough and continually reviewed understanding of yourself will prove to be one of your most valuable assets as a leader. But as you know, leadership as a process extends far beyond your role, beliefs, values, and capabilities. Well-designed leadership must address the broader system and each of its component parts—and in the organizational structure of this text, well-designed leadership must address self, relationships, others' success, culture, and the future.

Designing Your Leadership—First Step: Your Goals

Learning Objectives

1.6 Create your initial leadership development goals

How rich are you? This is a more complicated question than you might initially think. Wealth in the form of money or valuable possessions is the typical measure of value. But consider what other forms of capital you can use to measure your wealth. For example, how positive and widely known is your reputation? How many friends do you have in the virtual world? How many friends do you have in the real world? How many very close friends do you have? How many connections do your friends have in their networks? All of these are measures of your social capital—the value created through common and stable individual relationships. A leader rich in social capital is likely to wield greater influence. This is one of many forms of value that you can build as a leader.

Learning leadership builds your human capital, and designing your leadership will require that you assess and build your human capital—not in the economic sense but rather in the personal sense—what knowledge, skills, and dispositions do you bring to any leadership position or challenge? Even though designing your leadership will be a collaborative endeavor, *you* must be the designer of your own growth. How rich do you want to be? You can start to address that question by setting your goals as a student of leadership.

One fun and effective way to better understand your capital is to explore where your assets came from in the history of you. You have identified many things about yourself: strengths, traits, skills, values, and more. All of these are you, but only some of them are *very* consequential and *very* foundational to you as a leader. Try this exercise:

1. Take a moment to gather or write out many of the words that describe you. Ask for input from friends or family if you like.

2. Now picture yourself in a leadership position. What are you doing? For whom or what are you responsible? How are you influencing others? What are others looking to you for?

3. Looking back at the list you wrote, circle the words about you that are *most* important for your leadership success.

4. Now choose *one word*—a value, a skill, an attitude, a strength—and *write the story* of where that personal attribute came from. How and when did you acquire it? From where or whom? What event or experience highlighted the importance of that attribute? And how will you continue to apply and develop the attribute?

5. Be prepared to share the story with others in a compelling manner (i.e., in a way that helps us understand the full importance of that attribute to you as a leader).

Purposeful, Present, Planning: 3 Ps for Your Leadership Journey

This chapter introduced the essential framework for your leadership success. Leadership is truly a life-long journey. That is not cliché or trite, but it is a fact to which every single experienced leader will attest. With such a long and winding journey, the best thing you can do to prepare for a lifetime of challenges and learning consists of three Ps: purposeful, present, planning.

Purposeful: As noted earlier, as a leader you can make conscious, mindful decisions about what you do, or simply be a nonparticipant and let things happen. *Present*: Mindful leaders are present and aware of the context, situation, individuals, relationships, and themselves. And if they are ill-informed, they get informed. *Planning*: Effective leaders design their leadership; they originate and develop a plan for themselves, their followers, their relationships, the culture, and the future of the venture.

Utilizing design process, design thinking, and design principles (3D) and focusing on building your confidence, optimism, resilience, and engagement (CORE™) will greatly enhance your abilities as a purposeful, present, and plan-oriented leader (3D + CORE™ = 3P for the math inclined). This textbook aims to help you achieve those goals and more. Some additional important leadership learning goals are listed below. Take a moment to consider how each of these goals fits into your understanding and your plan for developing. Then, *you* need to identify some personal goals for yourself.*

Goal 1. Find my leadership—begin to identify as a leader and recognize my potential.

Goal 2. Change the way I look at leaders and leadership, allowing me to see the field more broadly and note the complexities.

Goal 3. Develop my leadership dispositions—the mental habits I use to see, think about, and respond to the world.

Goal 4. Build my leadership CORE™—personal attributes that will enhance my leadership now and long into the future.

Goal 5. Provide both a road map and a toolkit to effectively design my leadership.

Additional Goals. As the designer of my own leadership, I will set additional goals by asking myself some of the following questions:

a. An immediate practical goal for me as leader is: _____.

b. One way I would like to become a more effective leader is: _____.

c. The *best* leader I ever saw or worked with did this: _____.

d. Other goals I have for designing myself as a leader are: _____.

*Reread all the goals and put a *large star* by the one that most appeals to you. Then, rewrite that goal here in your own words. This will help make it stick and help you stay focused on what is most important to you: _____.

The next chapter continues your design of leadership self, starting with how you learn leadership and clarifying important aspects of leadership that are often misconceived.

Chapter Summary

Leadership is the process of influencing others toward a common vision. Leadership matters for individuals, teams, organizations, communities, and the world. Effective leaders consciously design their leadership, and strive to be as mindful as possible.

The framework of this textbook emphasizes your purposeful design of your leadership and consistently working to build your CORE™—confidence, optimism, resilience, and engagement.

Design is the process of originating and developing a plan. Designers are problem solvers, and a complete design process will include understanding, imagining, and implementing.

The design process is enhanced by specific ways of thinking—design thinking—dispositions that include user-centered, explorative, divergent, multidisciplinary, iterative, and integrative. Developing design-thinking habits makes you a more effective problem solver and will result in a better design; in this case, that design is you and your leadership.

Leaders who develop deep, foundational capabilities are able to excel when faced with new challenges. Confidence, optimism, resilience, and engagement (CORE™) provide individuals with the capacity to lead now and into the future. The elements of CORE™ influence the development of each other, and there are very concrete activities that will build your CORE™.

Keep the goals of this text and your own personal goals in mind as you move forward and experience your own *aha* moments.

Key Terms

Confidence 20
Design Principle 17
Design Process 14
Design Thinking 16
Disposition 16

Emotional Intelligence 26
Engagement 29
Iterate 15
Leadership Capacity 13
Mindfulness 12

Optimism 20
Positive Engagement 29
PsyCap 20
Resilience 20

CORE™ Attribute Builders: Build Now for Future Leadership Challenges

Attribute: Confidence, Optimism, Resilience, and Engagement

Builder: CORE™ adventure

Complete the CORE™ development tasks noted below. For added fun, complete these as a group with each group member taking on *one* of the four CORE™ challenges: **Confidence, Optimism, Resilience, Engagement**.

Although each team member has a set of tasks, you must work as a team, observing the completion of each task and supporting each member.

Challenge Yourself

This adventure is designed to be a learning experience . . . but only if you really strive to make it so. Any of the tasks can be completed with minimal effort and zero learning; however, as aspiring leaders, you will want to fully engage the tasks, take some uncomfortable risks, question your assumptions, and reflect on the learning and development that each task has the potential to offer. Good luck and have fun!

Confidence

- Enter **two** establishments. Assuming your neutral face, ask the individual behind the counter to assess your confidence (circle their answer):

Not Confident   *Very* Confident

0	1	3	5	7	9	10
0	1	3	5	7	9	10

- Enter **two other** establishments, this time assuming a *big* smile, shoulders back, and with eye contact, clear voice, and power pose, ask the individual behind the counter to assess your confidence (circle their answer):

Not Confident   *Very* Confident

0	1	3	5	7	9	10
0	1	3	5	7	9	10

What did you observe?

_____

_____

_____

- Take a risk—try something new.

What did you try? _____

_____

_____

- Assume an attitude of gratitude—write a thank you note to someone who deserves your thanks.

To whom did you write?   For what did you thank them?

_____

_____

_____

- List out 10 great things about *you*.

1. _____
2. _____
3. _____
4. _____
5. _____
6. _____
7. _____
8. _____
9. _____
10. _____

- Ask each person in your group to add one.

1. _____
2. _____
3. _____
4. _____
5. _____
6. _____
7. _____
8. _____
9. _____
10. _____

Optimism ☺

- Name two establishments that you really do not like. ☹

  ○ _____,_____

  Reframe those by naming *five* things about *each* that are positive.

  ○ _____,_____
  ○ _____,_____
  ○ _____,_____
  ○ _____,_____
  ○ _____,_____

- Ask three individuals that you do not know to share a joke with you (and be sure to thank them).

  ○ What joke was your favorite?

  _____

  _____

  _____

  ○ What did you observe?

  _____

  _____

  _____

- Do *one* spontaneous thing.

  ○ What did you try?

  _____

  _____

  _____

- Encourage your team to complete their tasks.

  ○ Ask them to rate your optimism:

  Not Optimistic   *Very* Optimistic

  0   1   3   5   7   9   10

- Influence five separate groups of individuals to *smile*.

  ○ List out all of the things you did to make them smile:

  _____

  _____

  _____

Resilience

- For every decision your group makes, take a moment for *you* to *decide* what *you* want and assert *yes* or *no*.

  This does not mean you get to decide, nor that you will always get your way. Just make sure you get your *say*.

  - At the end of the adventure, have your group assess your assertiveness:

Not Assertive   *Very* Assertive

  0   1   3   5   7   9   10

  What did you observe?

  _____

  _____

  _____

- Make a request from someone where you will likely be rejected (nothing illegal or unethical).

- Make the request again from a different person.

- Make the request a third time from yet a different person and ask them to sign affirming that you did so:

  _____

  _____

  _____

  _____

  What did you feel?

  _____

  _____

  What did you observe?

  _____

  _____

  _____

- Apologize to someone to whom you owe an apology.

  What did you apologize for?

  _____

  _____

  _____

- And ask each person in your group to share one (or more) things they admire about you.

  Write them here:

  _____

  _____

  _____

  _____

  _____

Engagement

- Keep your team engaged and on task. Help them succeed.

  Ask them to rate your ability to encourage their engagement:

  Not Helpful   *Very* Helpful

  | 0 | 1 | 3 | 5 | 7 | 9 | 10 |

  What did you observe?

  _____
  _____
  _____

- Ask three individuals that you do not know to share a grand vision of excellence about themselves—who do they want to be, where do they want to go, and so forth (and be sure to thank them).

  What were some of those grand visions?

  _____
  _____
  _____
  _____
  _____

- Build a bridge—find two individuals that YOU know—connect them with someone in your group.

  How did you connect them?

  _____
  _____
  _____

  What did you observe?

  _____
  _____
  _____

- Recognize a great performance in EACH of your group members and reward it.

  What did they do?   And how did you reward them?

  _____   _____
  _____   _____
  _____   _____
  _____   _____
  _____   _____

Skill Builder Activity

Build Your Design Process: Explore Understand—Imagine—Implement

Design thinking involves building specific mental habits that enhance your process.

Design principles comprise rules that you apply that also enhance your process.

So, you need to have a process, and there are many from which to choose.

1. *Find a creative problem-solving process, innovation process, or design process* that tells you step-by-step how to go from zero to innovative idea or product. The process you find can be from a specific model, researcher, or company.

2. The process you find should be a *process* (first do this, then do that). And it should be a generalized process (i.e., follow these steps to solve a problem or generate an innovation in any context; not specific instructions on to how to do something). For example, Tesla's process is explained here: http://executive.mit.edu/blog/innovating-innovation-tesla#.WKXp7NgzWUk (you will have to put it into steps). And here is Hershey's process explained: http://insigniam.com/insigniam-innovation/primed-breakthroughs/.

3. Examine the steps of the process you found and note which steps fit within each of the three general phases: understand, imagine, and implement. Which phase(s) is (are) overlooked? Are there any steps that cross stages or help you move from one to the next?

4. Compare the process you found with those found by your classmates. What process steps seem particularly interesting and/or useful to creatively solve problems?

Note that every process provides useful tools to design your leadership. Explore processes, familiarize yourself with their tools, and utilize them to design your leadership. Most importantly, use a process.

Design Leadership Self

Module 1 begins where all leadership begins—with you, the leader. There is a lot to know about you. And like all subjects, the more you know, the more effective you will be. Understanding yourself as a leader starts with how you perceive leaders and leadership. Everyone has had a variety of experiences with leaders—parents, teachers, coaches, siblings, friends, bosses—and those experiences form your values, expectations, assumptions, and behaviors as leaders. Some of the personal characteristics modeled by your early leaders are very effective for leadership, but unfortunately, many are not.

The chapters in this section explore those personal attributes that characterize effective leaders, with a focus on understanding yourself—how you see leaders and leadership, your strengths and style, and the values and ethics that will shape your decisions. As you work your way through the three chapters of the Design Leadership Self section, keep the key question in mind: How can I design myself as a leader? Purposeful attention to *you* will be the most useful guide through the process of applying what you learn to your growing leadership capacity.

You: Student and Designer of Your Own Leadership

Leadership is a dynamic, personal, situation-specific, context-dependent, multidisciplinary process. With so many variables, learning leadership requires a rather different approach than a more static discipline (for example, the fundamentals of mathematics do not change based on the person applying them). As the designer of yourself, you will be the designer of your own learning. Before you continue your leadership journey, there are a few things you should know about your own learning.

Learning Leadership

What did you learn today? Most people would answer that question by recalling some new bit of information or new skill they acquired, but what they are really describing is new information that they were exposed to. *Exposure* to a new idea is only the starting point of learning, and that exposure quickly fades unless revisited and reinforced. The acquisition of new knowledge happens as you engage with information over and over again. Remember the leadership definition introduced a few pages back? You read, Leadership is the process of influencing others toward a common vision. And then you read it again and again. Every single time you interact with information, you reinforce your recall (and likely enhance your understanding) of that information. Designing your leadership learning means thinking about and *planning* all the various ways in which you can engage with the topic, every time reinforcing and refining your understanding.

Right now, you understand leadership and leaders. You also may have some experience serving in a leadership position. How did you learn to do that? Most likely, you learned by watching others who were in leadership positions or some position of power and authority. Think back on all those in leadership positions with whom you may have interacted— parents or guardians, grandparents, teachers, coaches, priests or pastors, club/organization leaders, managers or bosses, or perhaps a babysitter. Whether they had formal training or not, they did their best to fulfill the position, and in the meantime, they unknowingly served as a role model for you. That is how most individuals initially learn leadership—by interacting with and observing others.

REFLECTION QUESTIONS

Who were your leadership models? Does your approach to leadership look like any of theirs?

Crucible (of leadership)
a difficult challenge that has the potential to transform your values, assumptions, and future capabilities as a leader

The second way many learn leadership is through experience—by serving as formal or informal leader. Generally, without any notion of what leadership is or entails, individuals are tasked with a position that requires influencing others toward a goal such that the organization succeeds. If you have had a leadership position, you undoubtedly learned a lot. If you had some significant challenges that you had to work through while in that position, then you learned even more. Bennis and Thomas (2002) called this a **crucible** of leadership.[1] A crucible was a vessel used by medieval alchemists, who were scientists trying to transform metal to gold. For a leader, a crucible is a difficult challenge that has the potential to transform their values, assumptions, and future capabilities. As Bennis and Thomas (2002) explained, "The crucible experience was a trial and a test, a point of deep self-reflection that forced them to question who they were and what mattered to them."[2] As you focus on designing yourself as a leader, we will find out from Bennis and Thomas what leadership skills help you learn the most from a crucible experience.

REFLECTION QUESTIONS

Learning through experience is of great value but only if you reflect on the experience and are aware of the impacts and outcomes. What leadership experiences have you had? What were some of the greatest challenges? How did those experiences change your leadership and self-perception?

Of course, there are also many leadership courses, programs, and workshops—all purporting to impart the knowledge and skills that will make you the successful leader of tomorrow. Learning leadership is partly about knowledge and skills, but it is more so about developing dispositions—defined as habits of mind that are often seen as tendencies or characteristics, even a personality. As introduced in the previous chapter, both design thinking and CORE™ are great examples of dispositions. Optimism and pessimism are very clear examples of dispositions you see every day. Some of your peers habitually see situations as positive and possible, while others see the pitfalls and worst-case scenarios. For leaders, another useful disposition might be the tendency to empathize (i.e., to habitually consider the perspective of your followers). You will learn even more about dispositions in Chapter 5 on leadership and the brain.

Learning comes with every encounter you have with information. Sometimes that information comes in the form of a professor or a textbook, and more often information comes in the form of engaging with others—discussing ideas, internships, student organizations, asking questions, interviewing leaders, and working through problems together. Consider the full range of where your learning can come from and how you can access those sources. Information comes from exposure to role models, experiences, prior courses and readings, and social interactions with others, but that is just the start. *Insight* and consequent learning come from your reflection and taking the time to integrate that information into your current understanding. To that end, a word of encouragement and caution from economist John Kenneth Galbraith: "Faced with the choice between changing one's mind and proving that there is no need to do so, almost everyone gets busy on the proof."[3] As you learn more about leadership you will be asked to change—change your behavior, change your mindset, change your understanding. Change is at the heart of learning. In Chapter 10, you will learn more about change as you design others' success (facilitating the learning of your followers).

What to Expect as You Learn Leadership

As you learn leadership and discuss your learning with your peers, you will find that everyone has their own unique significant learning moments—events or situations when a big insight changes the way we see the world. While the moment is unique, there are some common themes and lessons that developing leaders tend to experience. Here are some insights you might encounter while learning leadership. Of course, they will not seem as consequential to you now just reading them, but seeing them will prime your brain to spot these lessons in action later. Here are six very important lessons, shared by leadership students in their own words, which you can expect to learn again and again:

1. Leaders develop real relationships with each individual.

   There was a specific point in my life when I took a step back and saw the person in everyone. I was home during vacation when my mom walked into the room. She started talking about why she was stressed and how it was affecting her, and for the first time, I looked at her and didn't see my mom. I saw who she was, and I responded how I would if a friend had come to me in a bad place . . . I don't know why it took so long for me to notice everyone individually and the importance of taking into account the personal thoughts, experiences, and feelings of every person . . . —Daniel Clark, Undergraduate

2. There are many ways to solve a problem.

   There are so many different ways of tackling an issue . . . think of ways that are different and something that you'd never expect to do. —Tyler Saltiel, Undergraduate

3. Leadership and the concepts and aspects of the process are deeper and broader than you think. You will find that some things that you do well, that you seem to do naturally, are actually explained by leadership theory and best practices. Learning more about leadership concepts will help you use those strengths more effectively.

   For a long time, I have led best by seeking to help those struggling around me and have found it to be incredibly rewarding. It was not until we learned about empathy's role in leadership, however, that I realized it was what I had been doing and found so rewarding. . . . Only after learning about it, did I realize that I could reflect on, and improve, my empathy for others. —Matthew Divis, Undergraduate

4. The leader and the followers are both important.

The greatest "aha" moment for me in learning about leadership was learning that the leader is no more important than his or her followers. When learning this, it really made me stop and think. People have been subconsciously trained to believe that the most important person in a situation is the leader. A leader wouldn't get anything done without loyal followers. If Abraham Lincoln didn't have any followers, he would not have won the presidency or gone on to be one of the greatest leaders of all time. Yes, Abraham Lincoln is the big name, but he is no more important than his followers. They are the ones that made his successes possible. —Marina Wells, Undergraduate

5. Anyone can be a leader.

My greatest "aha" moment in learning about leadership came from a seven-year-old at a day camp. This boy was one of my campers, and he wanted to win Color Wars (the day camp version of the Olympics) extremely badly because he didn't win the past two summers. Formally, his role was very small because there were more than 100 campers on our team ranging from three to twelve years old; however, he was a leader and motivator. Throughout the week, he was involved and got others who were sitting out of activities to participate. He would strategize activities, including who would go in the front during tug of war and who would be better in the back. He screamed his head off (spirit points were considered the highest point bracket) the whole week, and I was not surprised when he had no voice during the last week of camp. In Color Wars, he was a true leader. I realized that anyone can be a leader and at any age. He was passionate about the activities, and I could see how his passion rubbed off on my other campers. He led for a reason, and I realized that anyone (even a seven-year-old) could influence others toward a common vision. —Daniel Auerbach, Undergraduate

6. Even quiet people can lead. Leadership starts from within.

For me, the greatest "aha" moment was when I realized that you don't need to be loud or extroverted to be a leader. I am not a loud person whatsoever and used to be extremely small. This discouraged me, but when we talked about creativity and resilience, it made me realize that the power comes from within, not the physical presence. Leaders come in all shapes and sizes; it's the influence you hold from the traits and skills you obtain. —Maxwell Gold, Undergraduate

The examples are just a few of the more common themes that you can expect to encounter as you design your leadership. Earlier, you were introduced to the notion of mindfulness—the concept of being as fully aware of your present learning and moment as possible. Did you notice a common theme across the six lessons you just read? They all required that the developing leader pay attention to what was happening. These students needed to pay attention to their context, the situation, the interactions between individuals, and the personal characteristics of everyone. The most important thing they needed to be mindful of, however, was their own understanding of leaders and leadership. If you don't know what you know, how will you learn what you do not know? You should probably read that sentence again—it is a bit confusing, but it is very important.

Designing Your Perceptions of Leaders and Leadership

There are very few human beings who receive the truth, complete and staggering, by instant illumination. Most of them acquire it fragment by fragment, on a small scale, by successive developments, cellularly, like a laborious mosaic.

—Anais Nin

Learning Objectives

2.1 Explain how conceptions and perceptions guide leaders

2.2 Identify common misconceptions about leaders and leadership

2.3 Critique the characteristics of leaders based on research and your perceptions

2.4 Contrast leadership skills with management, expertise, and established competencies

2.5 Appraise your leadership credibility relative to follower expectations

Detailed Chapter Outline

Your Brain Is a Lean, Mean, Pattern-Making Machine: You Construct Your World

Misconceptions About Leaders and Leadership

Leadership Is . . . a Process
Misconception:
Leaders Are Born
Misconception: Leaders
Need to Have a
Specific Set of
Traits, Particularly
Extroversion
Leadership Is . . . a Process
of Influencing
Misconception:
Leaders Do the
Talking and Take
Charge
Misconception:
Leaders Do the
Influencing
Leadership Is . . . a Process
of Influencing Others
Misconception: There
Is Only One Specific
Way to Be an
Effective Leader
Misconception: A
Leader Cannot Be
Friends With Their
Followers
Leadership Is . . . a Process
of Influencing Others
Toward
Misconception:
Effective Leaders
Are Always
Collaborative

Leadership Is . . . a Process
of Influencing Others
Toward a Common
Misconception:
Confident Leaders
Who Celebrate
Their Success Are
Arrogant and Selfish
Misconception:
Explaining the
Vision More Clearly
Is the Best Way to
Acquire Follower
Support
Leadership Is . . . a Process
of Influencing Others
Toward a Common Vision
Misconception:
Leadership
Education Is Not
Applicable to the
Real World
Effective Leaders Are

_____:
Characteristics and Traits
Effective Leaders Can Do

_____:
Skills and Expertise
In Competency Terms
Management? Leadership?
Both
The Expert Leader
The Credible Leader
Chapter Summary
Key Terms

Leadership by Design Model

DESIGN SELF
HOW CAN I DESIGN MYSELF AS A LEADER?

Design Relationships
As a leader, how can I design my relationships with others?

Design Others' Success
As a leader, how can I design success for others?

Design Culture
As a leader, how can I design the culture of my organization?

Design Future
As a leader, how can I innovate?

This chapter, *Designing Your Perceptions of Leaders and Leadership*, introduces the notion of leader and leadership by exploring *your* ideas and experiences with leadership, and it examines what others have thought and found about the leader in leadership. As a leader, you have a choice: You can act as a leader in whatever way *feels* right and then try to explain why you did what you did later, or you can understand your options for action *before* you act, using your leadership knowledge to *design* your leadership activity.

LEADERSHIP THAT MAKES A DIFFERENCE

When you think of great leaders, those who make a *big* difference, the names that arise are usually famous politicians, military or business leaders, or maybe social entrepreneurs. This chapter is all about perceptions and misconceptions, and what counts as a *big* difference may not be very accurate. Yes, there are indeed many individual leaders who have famously influenced broadly. The missed conception, in this case, lies in the considerable (a.k.a. big) difference made by tens of thousands of leaders at the local level. Indeed, when we asked students to describe who has most influenced their idea of leadership, nearly all described parents, colleagues, teammates, coaches, or immediate supervisors. Why? Because leadership is the process of influencing others toward a common vision—not just *any* others—but others with whom you have built a relationship. Those individuals are the most influential in your life. So, cumulatively, the big difference in leadership is made by a sea of individualized relationships that impact who you are and how you see the world. The following student example could likely be anyone's story:

> The best leader I have ever had is my grandfather. He taught me virtues through his stories and showed me the compassion and empathy needed to be a good leader. My grandfather truly had a love for all of those around him and wanted to see and help others to succeed. My grandfather saw potential that I could not see myself, and he taught me that anything less than my best is simply cheating myself. As a man who worked his way out of poverty, served in World War II, and became a successful entrepreneur, he had more to teach me about resilience and work ethic than anyone else I have met. He taught me never to quit and to set my goals high. He has helped me to understand how to have a vision and follow it, and I would not be the person or leader that I am today without him. —Matthew Divis, Undergraduate

Take a moment to consider who you would identify as a leader who has made a big difference. What matters most about that difference—how broadly it influences others or how deeply it influences a few? Both matter, just in different ways.

Your Brain Is a Lean, Mean, Pattern-Making Machine: You Construct Your World

Learning Objective

2.1 Explain how conceptions and perceptions guide leaders

Autobiography in Five Short Chapters*

By Portia Nelson

I

I walk, down the street.

There is a deep hole in the sidewalk.

I fall in . . . I am lost . . . I am helpless.

It isn't my fault. It takes forever to find a way out.

II

I walk down the same street.

There is a deep hole in the sidewalk.

I pretend I don't see it. I fall in again.

I can't believe I am in the same place.

But, it isn't my fault.

It still takes a long time to get out.

III

I walk down the same street.

There is a deep hole in the sidewalk.

I see it there. I still fall in . . . it's a habit.

My eyes are open. I know where I am.

It is my fault. I get out immediately.

IV

I walk down the same street.

There is a deep hole in the sidewalk.

I walk around it.

V

I walk down another street.

Have you ever kept doing the same wrong thing over and over? How did you know when to make an adjustment in your thinking and behavior? In the introduction chapter, you learned about the concept of mindfulness—being aware of the full, present moment, and you learned about the importance of taking moments of awareness and being mindfully engaged. But the five chapters of this poem illustrate that there is more to mindfulness if you are going to design your leadership. Even when you see the hole in the sidewalk, you still fall in because "it's a habit." Peter Bregman, author of *Four Seconds*, notes, "It doesn't take long to change a habit, but it's hard. Really hard."[4] Bregman writes, "we have no hope of changing anything that we're not aware we're doing. A moment of awareness allows us to pause (that's the four second part of *Four Seconds*)." You will see this valuable technique employed again in Chapter 6 as it relates to decision-making and emotional intelligence.[5]

Your brain is a lean, mean, pattern-making machine.[6] Do you remember where you read that funny phrase earlier in the text? Repeat it a few more times: My brain is a lean, mean, pattern-making machine. Can you feel the pattern forming? Every interaction you have with the world influences the connections your brain has made about the world, culminating in your mental model. A **mental model** is your mental representation of things in the world—not just the picture in your head but how you understand things and even how you process information. Your mental model guides your behavior and your thinking. For example, everyone *knows* what a classroom looks like, right? But what if you attended a nature-based school where every class was held in the forest, or what if you were part of an indigenous tribe that educated their young through apprenticeships without formal schools, or perhaps your grandchildren will meet their

Mental model
your mental representation of things in the world—not just the picture in your head but how you understand things and even how you process information

classmates in a virtual space. These conceptions of classroom are formed by experiencing something over and over.[7]

Have you ever heard traditional Hawaiian folk music? Surely a rush of images just filled your head as your mental models about Hawaii were triggered. If you have never been to Hawaii, then your mental model is likely filled with clichés from media—palm trees, hula dancers with grass skirts, coconuts to hold your drink, beaches. This is the case for everyone who has limited experience and/or exposure to a phenomenon. But if you have lived in Hawaii, those mental models are far more detailed and accurate. More interesting, mental models built from first-hand experience go beyond information and visuals, and include multiple senses and emotions. For example, when you think about *home*—whatever that might mean to you—your mind fills with far more than just an image. That is the power and strength of mental models—a strength you must both recognize and utilize. The legendary Hawaiian folk singer Israel "Iz" Kaʻanoʻi Kamakawiwoʻole created a record entitled *Facing Future*. For the aspiring leader, facing the future means addressing the mental models built from the past—mental models in the deeper sense—models of feeling and reacting, habits of perceiving and processing others and the world, and the personal challenges interwoven with your sense of self.

Mental models are very useful—they help you remember details, categorize new information, and generally navigate the world effectively and efficiently. But that construction comes with two great cautionary warnings: (a) the illusion of validity (My ideas about the world are true.) and (b) the illusion of verification (What *I see* in the world is true.). Mental models are constructed from your experience, and that experience may or may not be accurate, complete, or even true. In many ways, they are like an illusion, *your* illusion of the world. The only way to know if your conception of the world is accurate is to first be aware of your conception, and then to question, test, and revise that model. The second caution is that mental models influence what *you see* in the world. If you conceive that all leaders are out to get you, then you will perceive leaders through that lens, interpreting a leader's behaviors as somehow negative and nefarious and emphasizing negative outcomes, while overlooking anything to the contrary. That is how your brain works—how you think about the world influences what you see in the world, which reinforces how you think about the world.[8] The model below (Figure 2.1) illustrates this reinforcing relationship and how it ultimately influences your conception.

For aspiring leaders, the key question is how to continue growing in your conception of the world, versus narrowing to a rigid, single-view perception of the world. The answer: Leaders must understand that their brain constructs and interprets the world, and then knowing this they must explore and verify their conceptions (and misconceptions). The next section explores the common misconceptions about leaders and leadership. As you work your way through the next section, keep your lean, mean, pattern-making machine of a brain in mind and be open to exploring new ways of thinking about leadership.

Misconceptions About Leaders and Leadership

Learning Objective

2.2 Identify common misconceptions about leaders and leadership

You already have a mental model of leadership, one that you have built from all your interactions with the world—leaders you have observed, worked with and for, heard about, seen on television and the Internet, and even your experience and feedback from being the leader. Perhaps the image below represents your idea of leadership—the conquering hero inducing fear and dominance, victorious on the backs of others' hard work. And of course,

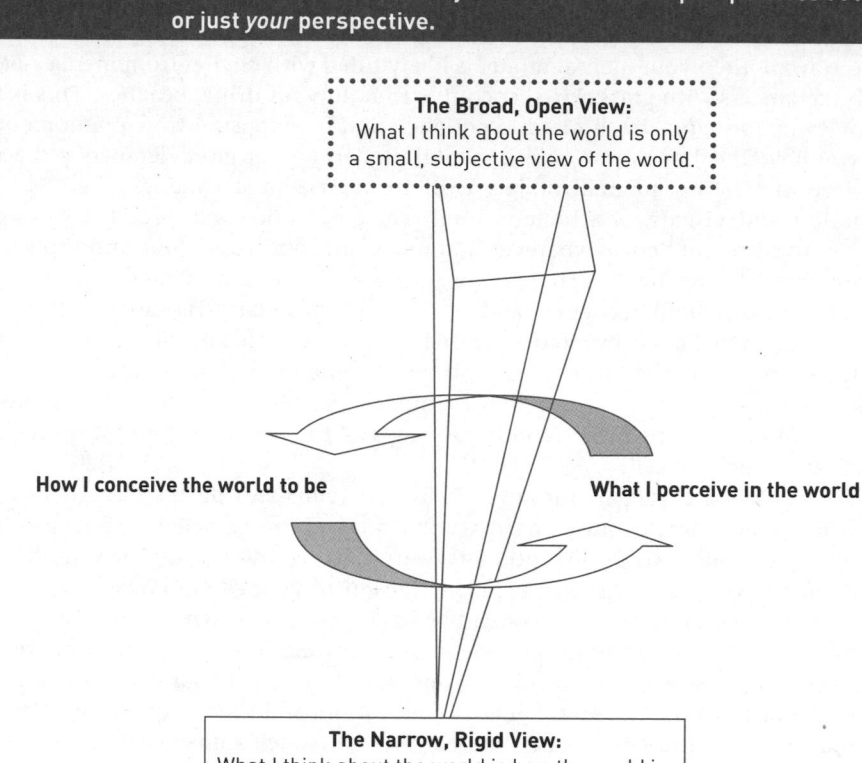

FIGURE 2.1 ● What you think about the world influences what you see in the world—that can ultimately be a broader set of perspectives . . . or just *your* perspective.

The Broad, Open View:
What I think about the world is only a small, subjective view of the world.

How I conceive the world to be

What I perceive in the world

The Narrow, Rigid View:
What I think about the world is how the world is.

there are always the random tourists for whom life continues, unaffected by the leader or leadership overhead.

Once again, recall the definition of leadership from the introduction chapter—the process of influencing others toward a common vision. It should sound more and more familiar, because you continue to repeat it, forming and reinforcing that connection. Using the definition of leadership, this section introduces important distinctions in leadership by exploring common misconceptions. As you make your way through this textbook, you will find that many of the most common leadership theories and approaches explain away these misconceptions. However, for now, the focus is on expanding the definition. As you learn more about leadership, the terms within that definition will take on greater meaning for you—that is you building a mental model about leadership.

REFLECTION QUESTIONS

What terms from the leadership definition can you identify in the image of the heroic leader statue? What could the leader do to more effectively influence each of the other individuals in this photo?

Leadership Is . . . a Process

The *leader* is a person. The person has characteristics that you can identify, which may or may not be effective in each situation and may change but only with time. *Leadership*, on the other hand, is a process. A process consists of a series of steps or activities over time. When you consider leadership as a process, many possibilities emerge. First, the positional leader becomes the facilitator of the process versus the person in charge. Thus, the task of moving the individuals and organization toward the goal is more accurately seen as a dynamic, situational, and context-dependent adventure. Second, leadership as a process means that mistakes can be made, and that is okay. Too often, leaders believe that any mistake is a setback. In fact, making minor mistakes helps the organization learn and better orient toward the goal relative to the ever-changing context. Third, the person in the leadership position does not always need to be (nor should be) the person taking the lead. Quite often there are others within the organization that are better suited, better skilled, or simply available to take the lead for a time or for a specific project.

Although leadership is a process, there are still individuals who hold the responsibility to facilitate that process. For those individual leaders, there are two simple rules:

Rule #1: It's about you.

Rule #2: It's not about you.

HEROIC LEADERSHIP AND THE MANY FACES OF FOLLOWERS

The first rule is clear to most aspiring leaders. *It's about you* means that you have the responsibility and accountability for the success of the organization and its followers. But it also refers to your designing your leadership self. Leaders must know about themselves, and the more they know, the more effectively they can respond to situations, facilitate the process, and further design their leadership.

The second rule is a little less obvious, particularly given the assumptions many have about leadership. *It's not about you* means exactly that; the activities of leadership should be focused on the success of the organization and the followers, they should not be focused on calming *your* fears, addressing *your* needs, or pumping up *your* ego. Making leadership not about you when you are in the leader position is more difficult than you might think. You might call this the paradox of confidence: Effective leaders must simultaneously be confident and humble. Yet, that pairing is not as contradictory as it may first appear. A most compelling illustration of the idea that true confidence results in humility is captured by the many stories of leadership guru Jim Collins.[9]

The pinnacle of leadership development found in Collins' research, which he calls **Level 5 leadership**, consists of high-level resolve coupled with compelling personal humility. In other words, leaders who are so confident in their abilities and sense of self are more interested in putting all their focus on the success of the organization and its people. You can be a highly capable individual (Level 1 in Collins' model) all the way up to an effective leader (Level 4), but to move from good to great (the title of his book), you need to get your own ego out of the way. Humility—making it not about you—is the true measure of confidence and can build confidence.

Level 5 leadership leadership consisting of high-level resolve coupled with compelling personal humility

If you are still doubtful about this connection, try the following: The next time you have to give a presentation, write yourself a large prompting sign and place it where you can see it often while you speak. The prompt should say, "Do they get it?" You will find that when you shift your focus from how *you* feel about your presentation (Did *I* say that right? Do *I* sound ok?) to how well the audience understands your message (Do *they* get it? What more do *they* need to know?), you not only feel more confident, you perform the task far better, which was to help the audience learn in the first place. Confidence with humility; it's about you, it's not about you.

These rules will be revisited throughout the text, just as you should revisit them throughout your leadership journey as they underpin numerous misconceptions about the individual leader. Throughout this section you can read the voices of students as they debunk these mistaken assumptions.

Misconception: Leaders Are Born

Well, technically everyone is born. And yes, there are obvious differences between persons. But the reality is that most of those differences were developed over time and can be altered if so desired.

> One of my biggest misconceptions about leadership is that people are born to be leaders. Ever since I was a little girl, I have always heard people say "so and so is a born leader," and to me that meant that I could only be a leader if I was born to do so. However, after growing up and taking a few leadership courses (I realized) that you do not have to be a born leader or that is even a real thing. Sure there are qualities that a leader possesses, but more often than not, these traits are acquired. I have learned that people can be successful leaders if they are good people and have the ability to understand what people want and need. —Aubrey Seeley, Undergraduate

> Early on in my life, one of my greatest misconceptions about leadership was that leadership wasn't something that could be learned. Throughout elementary and middle school there was this one kid who everyone listened to. Back then I thought that I could never be a "leader" like he was. Little did I know, I only considered him to be a leader because no one ever questioned his authority, and it made it seem like he was almighty. I always thought that in order to be a great leader, you must be born with the skills and qualities to be one. . . . I realized that is so far from the truth. Leadership can be learned and can be mastered . . . —Jamie Wolf, Undergraduate

Misconception: Leaders Need to Have a Specific Set of Traits, Particularly Extroversion

Some traits are pretty much always helpful to leaders, while other traits are helpful in some circumstances. But there is no specific set of traits. What is a trait anyway? You will learn more about traits later in the chapter, but for now, **traits** can be defined as well-habituated, stable, and consistent personal characteristics.

Traits
well-habituated, stable, and consistent personal characteristics

> I always thought leaders needed to be extroverts. However, learning about the trait theory, one of its weaknesses is that there is not a specific set of traits that qualifies someone to be a good leader. You need different types of leaders for the different types of situations. —Melissa Cabrero, Undergraduate

> One of the misconceptions I had about leadership was that when I thought of a leader, I thought of someone who was tough, hands on, loud, and assertive. I did not know that you could be a hands-off leader and still be considered an effective leader. Leadership style really depends on the followers and the overall situation, not necessarily the leader. —Morgan Smith, Undergraduate

Leadership Is . . . a Process of Influencing

Leaders influence others in a variety of ways. The most important thing to understand is *how* you most effectively influence others and *with whom* you are most influential, under what conditions or in what situations. Sometimes influence is grandly inspirational, and other times it is simple and subtle to the point of being nearly invisible. There are a great many techniques and tools that leaders can learn to influence others—build your influence toolbox. Consider a few more misconceptions:

Misconception: Leaders Do the Talking and Take Charge

Sometimes leaders influence by taking charge, and acting in a directive manner is necessary, but sometimes listening and observing are more effective. Your strengths and style, explored in Chapter 3, are adaptable enough to address a variety of needs.

> I always thought that the leader leads the discussion and comments on everything. A leader should be aware of everything around them and put the pieces together without saying a word. A leader who listens gains credibility and trust because they give a fair chance for everyone to share their thoughts and feel they are in a safe environment. —Brandon Bellina, Undergraduate

> A big misconception that I held about leadership was that to be an effective leader you only had to be able to "take charge" of a group. I viewed it as a very individualistic concept, but I now know that leadership goes far beyond having authority within a group or team setting. It requires a willingness to motivate/inspire followers to the point where you're not just making the plan, delegating tasks, and telling them what they have to do but instead working collaboratively to come to the best solution. —Jamie Fisher, Undergraduate

Misconception: Leaders Do the Influencing

Every human interaction results in reciprocal influence, and leaders are no exception. As a leader, you are constantly influenced by many things, particularly your followers. For example, consider a time you presented to a group. As you noticed the reaction of the audience to your talk, did you find yourself making slight changes in your delivery or explanation? You are in a constant process of interacting with your world, constructing and reconstructing your understanding, and reacting accordingly. Acknowledging the influences around you is both honest and accurate. So, while you are building your influence toolbox, note also what influences you and how.

> Growing up you are constantly surrounded by leadership figures such as your teachers, but you never hear about who helped them get there. For me, that realization came with maturing and realizing that everyone, even the leaders throughout your life, are just people. —Daniel Clark, Undergraduate

Leadership Is . . . a Process of Influencing Others

At the heart of all leadership lies the relationship between leader and follower. If there are no *others*, then you are not leading but simply acting alone. Considering the individual followers is critical to how effectively you are able to influence and move them and the organization toward the common vision.

Misconception: There Is Only One Specific Way to Be an Effective Leader

Your leadership approach may be consistent at this stage in your leadership design, but expert leaders can shift their style to complement and meet the needs of different followers.

A misconception about leadership is that there is one way to be a good leader. What I learned is that there are so many ways to be an effective leader. It all depends on who you are leading and what they react to positively. —Trevor Cox, Undergraduate

Misconception: A Leader Cannot Be Friends With Their Followers

This misconception might really surprise you. After all, how can you tell a friend what to do? How can you be their boss? (Are you seeing all the misconceptions in those questions already?) There has been a lot of research on the leader-follower relationship, called leader-member exchange (LMX), which will be explained more fully in Chapter 5 when we focus on designing your leadership relationships. The truth is that close relationships, even friendships, generally enhance the organization. Consider this . . . would you work harder and be more committed to the success of a friend or a stranger? While it might seem difficult to supervise a friend, especially if you must assess them or be critical, the benefits of building strong relationships far outweigh that possible momentary discomfort.

Leadership Is . . . a Process of Influencing Others Toward

Leaders move their organization toward success. They do not influence others to keep the status quo, do nothing special, stay the course, or just live with it. Leadership dynamically advances the organization.

Misconception: Effective Leaders Are Always Collaborative

After reading all the previous misconceptions, you are likely noticing a pattern: As a facilitator of the leadership process, leaders need to effectively navigate the ever-changing sea filled with unique waves, weather, sea creatures, and crew. In other words, the dynamic nature of leadership requires that leaders be equally flexible to meet needs as they arise, whether predictable or not. Sometimes the best approach is collaborative, and sometimes it is directive, and sometimes it will be entirely different. This student sums it up well:

> One of my greatest misconceptions about leadership was that leaders had to pick only one leadership style/concept to stick with to live and lead by. For example, while I was leading in my roles and facilitating meetings, I am naturally transformational, supportive, and understanding; however, there were some moments where it was necessary to be more firm and structured, and it was essential to assign due dates and specific assignments or roles. —Brooke Hofmann, Undergraduate

Whatever set of behaviors, skills, and actions moves your organization toward the vision is ultimately the right set of leadership tools for the job. As you design your leadership, you will find a number of tools that can do more than one job, such as confidence, optimism, resilience, and engagement—the CORE™ attributes. Remember to utilize the CORE™ Attribute Builder activities at the end of each chapter to build your most versatile tools.

Leadership Is . . . a Process of Influencing Others Toward a Common

Rule #2 states that leadership is not about you. The vision of your organization will be most successful if you craft a *common* vision. Not common in the sense of indistinguishable, but common in that everyone has a stake in and supports the vision.

Misconception: Confident Leaders Who Celebrate Their Success Are Arrogant and Selfish

Maybe, but probably not. Quite often we see leaders taking credit for the success of their organizations, but what we do not see are the relationships and interactions between the leader and followers—celebrating individual and organizational success, passing along acknowledgments and words of thanks, and continuing to inspire others around the common vision.

> I always thought leaders were cocky/over-confident. I have learned that as a leader you can acknowledge your success to a point without being greedy. It's important to be able to pat yourself on the back because you need to congratulate yourself at times—you earned it. I learned the difference between confidence and arrogance. It's vital to have confidence so that you believe in your abilities. I found this quote, "Confidence isn't walking into a room with your nose in the air and thinking you're better than everyone else. It's walking into a room and not having to compare yourself to anyone in the first place." —Erin Grady, Undergraduate

Yes, some may mistakenly see arrogance in your confidence, but that is not a reason to discount accomplishment or discontinue celebration for yourself and your followers.

Misconception: Explaining the Vision More Clearly Is the Best Way to Acquire Follower Support

The power of a common vision lies in the connections between leader and follower. While the elements of the leadership definition can be independently explained, those elements work together. For example, in this case, how you—as a leader—influence others will determine the extent to which followers feel part of the vision. Influencing others through intimidation, reasoned argument, or appeal to your position of authority is far less effective than connecting with followers' emotions, values, and their stake in the vision.

> A misconception I had about leadership is that the leaders are the boss and the system is a hierarchy. However, I learned that there are leaders who influence followers to accomplish more by being concerned with followers' emotions and values. The leader serves to help their followers grow. —Becca Estes, Undergraduate

A common vision entails more than general agreement on the vision; rather, it requires a sense of shared contribution and emotional connection. Leaders skilled in emotional intelligence, discussed in Chapter 6, excel at designing relationships.

Leadership Is . . . a Process of Influencing Others Toward a Common Vision

Extensive research on the nature and power of goals positions this element of the leadership definition as perhaps the most powerful. If you do not know where you are going, what are you facilitating? How can you influence others toward nothing? More than simply a goal, a **vision** is a picture of the future you seek to create.[10] The organizational vision serves many purposes and has great power. A vision can be inspirational, aspirational, a means by which individuals in the organization connect, a way of assessing progress, and a guiding light for leaders and followers to navigate the day-to-day challenges without getting sidetracked. A common vision provides meaning and purpose to the work of the organization, and ultimately, it reflects the values of those sharing the vision. Highly effective leaders utilize the power of the common vision.

vision
an aspirational image that provides short- and long-term direction for an organization and its members

Misconception: Leadership Education Is Not Really Applicable to the Real World

The benefits of learning leadership and designing your leadership are often difficult to measure and may in some cases be more long term than immediate. This often results in the final misconception of this section, namely the usefulness of leadership in the face of so many ineffective leaders. The real misconception in this case is that individuals in leadership positions believe that they are effective leaders simply by holding the position or title. Typically, individuals are promoted to leadership positions because they excel in the technical aspects of their job (e.g., you are an excellent accountant, so you are now promoted to manager). This is the equivalent of saying, "Hey, you're really good at fixing cars, so you are now promoted to quarterback for the football team." Huh? Exactly. Leadership is an entirely different field of expertise, requiring specific knowledge, skills, and abilities. And that is primarily why so many leaders are ineffective, if not downright detrimental to the organization.

> I think one of the greatest misconceptions about leadership is that people always wonder why it is a college major and how learning about leadership can help you later in life. I agree; when I first enrolled in a leadership class I wasn't really sure what to make of it, it made me think differently and how there was often no single right answer. Now to me this kind of sounded like a joke, but I was entirely wrong. Over the last two years, I have learned so much about leadership and that in the future when you have an "adult job" (is how I put it) being a leader and knowing how to influence others to reach a common goal is very beneficial. You are considered a trusted individual, and you understand the way people think and what they need to succeed. My respect for leadership as a study has changed dramatically, and I believe those lucky enough to learn about it will be better off in their futures. —Jessica Szymanski, Undergraduate

Table 2.1 provides a summary of the misconceptions discussed in this section but stated as a more accurate conception for your use in (re)designing your leadership self.

This chapter began with explaining how you construct ideas with your lean, mean, pattern-making machine brain. We then examined many of the most common misconceptions about leaders and leadership. At this point in the chapter, you should feel a little skeptical about what you thought you knew about leadership, and you should be ready to dig deeper into what makes an effective leader. Before you continue, revisit the definition of leadership as seen on the card in Figure 2.2. Make a copy of this card, cut it out, and put it in your purse or wallet so that you have a ready reference and reminder to access when you are facing a leadership challenge.

TABLE 2.1 ● Summary of Misconceptions	
Misconception	**Instead . . . Consider That**
Leaders are those who have the position or title of leader.	You are a leader when you influence others toward a common vision, which does not necessarily require a title or position.
Leaders are born.	You can learn the skills and habits of effective leadership.
Leaders need to have a specific set of traits, particularly extroversion.	Leadership is dynamic and situational—your characteristics may be effective in some cases and not in others.

Misconception	Instead . . . Consider That
Leaders do the talking and take charge.	Leaders need to sometimes talk and sometimes listen, sometimes take charge and sometimes observe or encourage others to take charge.
Leaders do the influencing.	Leaders are also influenced.
There is only one specific way to be an effective leader.	There are many different ways to influence others toward a common vision.
A leader cannot be friends with their followers.	A leader depends on close, authentic relationships, and that often defines friendship.
Effective leaders are always collaborative.	Effective leaders are sometimes collaborative, sometimes directive, and sometimes other behaviors are necessary.
Confident leaders who celebrate their success are arrogant and selfish.	Confidence is not arrogance, and celebrating success is key to effective leadership.
Explaining the vision more clearly is the best way to acquire follower support.	Followers, like all people, are driven more by their values and their emotions than a rational argument.
Leadership education is not really applicable to the real world.	Leadership is a distinct field of study, and applying it in the real world makes a big difference.

FIGURE 2.2 ● Leadership Definition Reference Card

Leadership is . . .

Process . . . beyond person, over time, dynamic

Influencing . . . explicit and implicit, ethical

Others . . . building and developing relationships

Toward . . . advancing and improving

Common . . . socially just, all voices heard

Vision . . . creative, clear, shared, sustainable

Rule #1: It's about you.

Rule #2: It's not about you.

Comparison
Design principle—to accurately understand and assess something, you must look at it next to things that relate.

LEADERSHIP BY DESIGN

Design Principle: Comparison

Definition: A method of illustrating relationships and patterns in system behaviors by representing two or more system variables *in a controlled way*.[11]

In Other Words: To accurately understand and assess something, you must look at it next to things that relate.

For Example: If you want to assess the quality of an apple, what you use for comparison must be related

(Continued)

(Continued)

to what you want to assess. An apple is great as a healthy food compared to a donut. An apple is not so great as a weapon compared to a spear.

For Leaders: To what do you compare aspects of your leadership? How can you use an appropriate comparison that makes it easier for others to understand? Think about ways to highlight different parts of your leadership compared to others. Leaders can use comparisons to illustrate relationships between values, between different people, or between themselves and others by presenting information in a controlled way. What do you want at this moment or for the organization . . . compared to what?

©iStock.com/xavierarnau

Who in the photo is the happiest? Are these individuals friends? Without being able to compare this moment to other times, you can only guess. What else would you want to know before you made any deductions?

Effective Leaders Are _____: Characteristics and Traits

Learning Objective

2.3 Critique the characteristics of leaders based on research and your perceptions

When you read the title of the section, what word did you want to put into the blank space? Early leadership researchers asked that same question, seeking those individuals in leadership positions whose organizations were successful or who appeared to emerge as leaders in groups. Effective leaders are tall, imaginative, and agreeable. Maybe some individuals fitting that description are indeed effective . . . in some contexts . . . in some situations. But so too are others with different characteristics.[12]

The trait approach to leadership asserts that a specific set of personal attributes (initially including physical characteristics) enable and explain effective leadership. Recall, traits can be defined as well-habituated, stable, and consistent personal characteristics. At first glance, this appears to make sense—everyone can describe leaders with whom they've worked, and there seem to be similarities between effective and ineffective leaders. Not only did researchers agree and pursue many studies trying to identify those specific traits, but other researchers studied those studies (this is called a meta-analysis, and it provides a big summary of many prior related studies). A scholar named Ralph Stogdill did a meta-analysis on leadership traits—twice.[13] His latest, in 1974, looked at 163 different trait studies. Table 2.2 displays the common traits he found, but after all that research, even Stogdill said there is no evidence for a single set of effective leader traits.

TABLE 2.2 ● Common traits and skills from Stogdill's meta-analysis—which ones do you have?	
Traits	**Skills**
• Adaptable to situations	• Clever (intelligent)
• Alert to social environment	• Conceptually skilled
• Ambitious and achievement orientated	• Creative
• Assertive	• Diplomatic and tactful
• Cooperative	• Fluent in speaking
• Decisive	• Knowledgeable about group task
• Dependable	• Organized (administrative ability)
• Dominant (desire to influence others)	• Persuasive
• Energetic (high activity level)	• Socially skilled
• Persistent	
• Self-confident	
• Tolerant of stress	
• Willing to assume responsibility	

REFLECTION QUESTIONS

The list of traits and skills noted by Stogdill in Table 2.2 are from the period 1949–1974. A lot has changed in the world since then—in how people communicate, structure organizations, and view leaders and leadership. What traits and skills from that list seem relevant today? Which ones feel outdated? What might you add?

Presently, five major traits have been highlighted as those most closely tied to effective leadership: intelligence, determination, sociability, self-confidence, and integrity.[14] You probably have a few questions right at this moment:

- *If I possess all five, will I be an effective leader?*

- *If I lack all five, does that mean I will never be an effective leader?*

- *I have lots of other great things about me—a good sense of humor, outgoing, creative, focused—do these not count for anything in leadership?*

Maybe, no, and yes, of course, are the answers to the three questions. Trait approaches provide valuable information about the range of attributes you can draw from, develop, and highlight as situations or context requires. The five traits noted also provide insight on what you should consistently work to develop in yourself and in your followers (because followers today will be the leaders tomorrow—it's your job to help them get there).

Leadership is a process, and traits, like all useful tools, must be used for the right project in the right setting. What traits do you possess? You likely could describe yourself pretty well, but you are far more complex than you realize. That complexity takes time and tools to understand. The Skill Builder Activity at the end of this chapter prompts you to discover more about your traits and attributes.

The traits you possess are like a set of tools. They are only as handy as your ability to use them. Sometimes you have tools buried in the toolbox that you discover later. Sometimes other people give you new tools by modeling their use or direct instruction. And sometimes you focus on a single tool just because you're good at using it. As the common saying goes, everything looks like a nail to the person holding a hammer. Here are some suggestions as you design your leadership:

1. Identify your traits and learn about them

2. Find out what others see as your traits

3. Consider what contexts and situations best fit your traits

4. Note traits you aspire to acquire and then create opportunities to do so

5. Know that traits are quite stable, so it takes time and effort to change them

Charisma
the personal quality that commands attention, respect, and attraction

One trait often associated with leaders is charisma. **Charisma** can be defined as the personal quality that commands attention, respect, and attraction. Charismatic leaders are described as inspiring, charming, and confident—powerfully alluring to their followers. Charisma would seem to be the ultimate trait to possess, yet an elusive treasure for most. And indeed, it is a powerful tool. However, the charisma tool can be misused if, for example, the leader inspires followers in the wrong direction or toward unethical ends.[15] The leader must also possess the competence to back up their charismatic approach—even though the lure of appearance is so strong.[16] The following story illustrates this phenomenon:

> Who is the leader? That was the question we asked the group. We had been together as a group for only a short time—three orientation meetings, each a couple hours long, and now three days into a month-long study abroad trip. There were 30 students on this trip, all focused on leadership and creativity but coming from a variety of majors. While all were highly engaged, some were clearly more outgoing and charismatic than others. But one stood above the rest—literally and in personality. Jake was tall, dark, and handsome with a constant, winning smile and nonstop energy to talk, explore, and meet people. He was the personification of charisma, and the students loved him. So, it was no surprise when we asked our question (write your answer in confidentially and anonymously) that Jake was deemed the leader. But an interesting thing happened over the course of a month together. At the end of the trip, we asked the group to again write down on a slip of paper who they thought of as the leader of the group. Jake's name was nowhere to be found among the votes. Instead, the group deemed another student the leader—a student who had a valued set of traits and skills and had used those tools to build relationships and facilitate others toward the common vision of the trip. For this leader, charisma was not part of their leadership toolbox but that just meant taking a bit more time. As for Jake, he didn't change a thing, and was still the happy, charismatic person throughout the trip; but he did realize the limits of charisma for leaders. —Tony Middlebrooks, Leadership Professor

Charisma used well and appropriately is a very useful trait to cultivate, although perhaps it needs to be reframed to focus on its great value as *initiating*—the very important person with the courage, tenacity, enthusiasm, willingness, and wherewithal to start something that others look to and follow. Sounds like leadership. But before you get carried away with the charismatic excitement, remember that leadership is a process. Jim Collins asks with what do we replace the charismatic leader because organizations are not sustainable long term when they are based on an individual. In other words, once you and your charisma and competence as a leader are gone, will the organization survive and thrive without you? Collins notes,

> Building mechanisms is one of the CEO's most powerful but least understood and most rarely employed tools. Along with figuring out what the company stands for and pushing it to understand what it's really good at, building mechanisms is the CEO's role—the leader as architect.[17]

The skill of building mechanisms and systems transitions the design of leadership self from what leaders *are* to what leaders *can do*—what skills do effective leaders wield to success?

REFLECTION QUESTIONS

Many would argue that organizations and history are shaped by a few extraordinary individuals. Do you agree or disagree that this was the case? Should it be the model in the future? What are the advantages and disadvantages of having a *hero* as leader?

Effective Leaders Can Do _____:
Skills and Expertise

Learning Objectives

2.4 Contrast leadership skills with management, expertise, and established competencies

2.5 Appraise your leadership credibility relative to follower expectations

Skills
what leaders can do—their competencies

The **skills** approach to leadership focuses on what leaders can do—their competencies. Unlike traits, skills can be more readily acquired and in turn seem to be more teachable. Similar to traits, the list of important, useful, and relevant skills is very long. One early attempt to simplify skills that has stood the test of time is Katz's three-level model of skills focus.[18] The three-level approach categorizes skills into technical skills, human skills, and conceptual skills. As individuals move up in an organization, the requisite skills needed shift accordingly. For example, imagine you are a skilled portrait artist recently hired by a company that does just that—produces high-quality portraits for customers. On the job, you are judged on your technical skills, in this case your ability to paint the portrait. There are likely some human skills needed as well—working with clients and colleagues—and at some point perhaps mentoring new artists. Over time, the boss notes what an excellent artist you are, and so you are promoted to division manager overseeing the portrait making of ten other artists. With this change in role comes a change in skills. Now, the big focus is on human skills—motivating, inspiring, solving conflicts, training, communicating, recruiting, and retaining. Your technical skills still come in handy for training others, but you simply don't have time to do portraits. At this level, you also start to consider the success of the overall organization but mostly as it intersects with your artists. Finally, after many successful years as division manager, you become the big boss, the CEO. Now, the success of the organization as a whole—big picture, long term—is your focus, and you need conceptual skills such as strategic planning, market forecasting, and fostering innovation. You clearly will need those human skills you have developed, but you are now far removed from needing to know how to paint a portrait.

Katz's model of shifting technical, human, and conceptual skills is an important moment for all individuals within an organization as it explains why certain roles focus on what they need to, as well as what specific skills need emphasis and development (and which can and should be ignored, which is no small thing given we can't focus on everything). More important, this model exemplifies that skills, while specific in practice, need to be considered categorically when applied to developing leaders. In other words, many specific skills represent human skills—you can acquire some and not others and still have human skills. This notion is of great importance as the field of leadership matures and is tempted to frame itself too constrictively with required competencies.

In Competency Terms

As you design your leadership, and others' success in future chapters, it is tempting to grab for a set of very concrete competencies. Easy to list out, easy to measure and assess, but not necessarily appropriate or mindful. In an analysis of leadership models and competency frameworks, the Center for Leadership Studies stated the following about competencies:

> The "leader" (as post holder) is thus promoted as the sole source of "leadership." . . . Fewer than half of the frameworks cited refer directly to the leaders' ability to respond and adapt their style to different circumstances. . . . This almost evangelistic notion of the leader as a multi-talented individual with diverse skills, personal qualities and a large social conscience, however, poses a number of difficulties. Firstly, it represents almost a return to the trait theory of leadership, just with a wider range of attributes. Secondly, when you attempt to combine attributes from across the range of frameworks, the result is an unwieldy, almost over-powering list of qualities. . . . Personal qualities of the leader are undoubtedly important but are unlikely to be sufficient in themselves for the emergence and exercise of leadership.[19]

Although dated, the ideas critical of competencies are timeless.

Developing your leadership with a checklist of competencies is contrary to mindful design. Nevertheless, any organized list of attributes can be useful as a menu from which to identify useful and necessary characteristics.

Management? Leadership? Both

You have no doubt heard leader and manager used synonymously, likewise leadership and management. The good news is that the person in the position must be both leader and manager, and consequently possess (or develop) some of the skills for both. The better news is that a skilled leader and manager will know how to discern and address leadership problems with leadership and management problems with management. The concepts are separate but complementary—like eating and drinking—same players, same ends; different means, different processes; and some overlap, which is what everyone argues about.

Management
the process of organizing, controlling, and coordinating resources to achieve organizational value

Leadership is the process of influencing others toward a common vision. Classic **management** activities include forecasting, planning, organizing, commanding, coordinating, and controlling.[20] Many leadership scholars have weighed in on the distinction between leadership and management, with Jon Kotter providing one of the most prevalent distinctions: Management produces order and consistency, while leadership produces change and movement.[21] You will find that there are many quick and quirky ways to differentiate the two concepts, generally making management and the manager appear to be the less appealing role (e.g., The manager is the classic good soldier; the leader is his or her own person.[22] Who would *not* want to be their own person?).

The practical reality is that there are a variety of activities, skills, and roles necessary for an organization to succeed. Some organizations are highly complex and require a great deal of organization and coordination, while others may be more dynamic and require adaptability and continual strategy readjustment. This situational and contextual nature means that sometimes you need leadership skills and activities, and sometimes you need management, and usually it is a combination of both. The flexible leadership model proposed by Yukl and Lepsinger outlines a number of critical activities where leadership behaviors and management programs and systems must work together.[23]

The Expert Leader

The ultimate end of any skill development effort is to achieve expert status. Expertise has been carefully studied much the way leadership has—find experts, observe them, interview them, identify what makes them experts (and others not). Experts—in chess, tennis, firefighting, and so forth—are characterized by how they think and what they perceive. Table 2.3 lists the characteristics of experts found by two researchers.

Based on the dynamic, situational, and context-based nature of leadership, the idea of an expert leader seems implausible.[26] How could you possibly know/be able to do/be like every known trait and skill related to effective leadership? Take another look at the characteristics of experts noted in the table. Positional leaders who have mindfully practiced their role for many years display these abilities. As a developing leader, you can benefit from knowing what you do not know as well as the *how to* of what you do not know. In a dynamic field like leadership, expertise may be rooted in one's ability to excel adaptably. For example:

- Recognizing other people's emotions and regulating your own?

- Connecting and working with a wide diversity of individuals?

- Seeing the big picture of how things interact and impact a situation?

- Learning new things and adjusting how you learn to meet new conditions?

- Generating unique ideas that are of value and facilitating others to do the same?

What other skills or capacities will enhance your leadership no matter what the context or situation?

TABLE 2.3 ● Characteristics of Expertise	
Bransford, J., National Research Council. (2000). *How people learn: Brain, mind, experience and school.*[24]	**Klein, G. (1998).** *Sources of power: How people make decisions.*[25]
• Notice features and meaningful patterns of information not noticed by novices	• Notice patterns that novices do not notice
• Have acquired a great deal of content knowledge that is organized in ways that reflect a deep understanding of their subject	• Notice anomalies—events that did *not* happen and other violations of expectancies
• Knowledge that reflects contexts of applicability, not just simple facts	• See the big picture—context and situation
• Ability to flexibly retrieve important aspects of their knowledge with little attentional effort	• Understand the way things work
• Possess varying levels of flexibility in their approach to new situations	• Notice opportunities and can improvise
	• See differences that are too small for novices to detect
	• Deeply understand their own limitations

As you design your leadership, the skills you choose to develop will often overlap and work in a complementary way. For example, skills as a systems thinker enable you to see underlying variables, which will enhance your ability to solve conflicts. Thinking creatively enhances your ability to make great decisions by helping you see more options, which would also help solve conflicts (more ideas for compromise).

REFLECTION QUESTIONS

If you could possess one extraordinary trait, what would it be and why? Have you ever met someone with a trait you thought could never be useful and then were surprised when that person proved you wrong?

The Credible Leader

The broad palette of traits and skills offer you many possible design options. Yet, underlying every effective leader is an effective person, regardless of what combination of skills and traits they possess. The effective person can be seen from two perspectives: internally and externally; it's about you, and it's not about you. Internally, effective individuals have developed a strong CORE™—confidence, optimism, resilience, and engagement—attributes that work in unison to maximize success in any situation. Externally, you are only as effective as others perceive you to be, also known as your credibility and reputation. *Your reputation as credible is your most valuable external asset.*

Credibility
the quality of being believed, and in practice, doing what you say you are going to do

Credibility is the quality of being believed, and in practice, doing what you say you are going to do. Kouzes and Posner consider credibility the first law of leadership: "If you don't believe in the messenger, you won't believe the message."[27] Without credibility, a leader has no positive relationship with followers, and without a positive relationship, there is no positive influence. "When people perceive their immediate manager to have high credibility, they're significantly more likely to feel proud about their organization, feel a high degree of team spirit, feel a strong sense of ownership and commitment to the organization, and be motivated by shared values and intrinsic factors," they note.[28]

Credibility comprises the foundational external attribute for a leader—external because it is based on the perceptions of followers. You cannot possess credibility without the approval of others. You cannot develop it within yourself. You can, however, learn ways to build your credibility—a task that must begin the very moment you meet a follower, if not before by reputation. Research has found that individuals judge you within microseconds. And knowing that people construct knowledge and form mental models, your first impression (no matter how professional, humble, relatable, and so forth) may run headfirst into followers' past negative mental model of leaders. So, step one of establishing your credibility is simple—talk to followers, find out what they know, want, need, aspire to, enjoy—and do so with genuine interest and enthusiasm.

Why should anyone be led by you? That is the question Goffee and Jones posed, highlighting four qualities effective leaders employ: showing their humanity, intuitively sensing timing and actions, managing with empathy, and capitalizing on their uniqueness as the leader.[29] The Graham Jones Credibility Pyramid indicates that 50% of a leader's credibility comes from the perception that they care (and another 25% based on their enthusiasm about the organization and its people).

Focus on small wins, because people pay attention to the little things, especially when it directly relates to them. The perception of leaders and leadership brings forth what you might call the gray matter. Not the stuff between your ears, although directly relevant, but rather the situation where ambiguity lies. Many things in leadership are rife with those "it depends" situations. This includes your credibility as a leader. When there is no clear black and white, when the answer is not readily apparent, then you are in gray territory. And when it comes to gray matters, the little things matter because followers are still trying to decide your credibility. "Respect is carried not in great, bold proclamations, but in small moments of surprising intimacy and empathy."[30]

Table 2.4 lists a number of other actions you can take to establish and build your credibility. Consider each one and the actions you might take to display these attributes.

> Leaders need to understand more about why people work, what matters to them, how they can support them more effectively and what might motivate them to perform better. Tomorrow's leaders in the public sector will . . . be coaches not kings.[31]

Just as important as knowing how to build your credibility, you must also be aware of what will tarnish, if not destroy, it. Not doing something you said you were going to do, without explanation or apology, will crush your credibility. Withholding information and not being transparent in your decisions and actions communicates to others that they don't matter, that they are unimportant, and that you don't care. When followers ask themselves whether they can trust you, the answer is a deafening no. Even if a leader is a brilliant expert and wildly successful, followers will know they are working *for* a leader, not *with*, and will invest themselves accordingly.

Other ways a leader can diminish or destroy their credibility include trying to fake any credibility-building activity, all of which then appears dishonest. Leaders who try to earn *likes* rather than respect, and demand respect because of their position (versus through building a relationship and demonstrating care and expertise) also risk loss of credibility. Lastly, many leaders continue to operate under a top-down, hierarchical mindset. When a problem occurs, the top blames the next level down, who blames the next level, and so

TABLE 2.4 ● Credibility Actions

How you treat people	With respect, honesty, and accountability
	Trust in follower capability and intentions
	Staying loyal to followers and backing their success
	Seeking to inspire
	With humility, gratitude, and confidence
	Celebrating and recognizing others' strengths and accomplishments
How you treat the job	Staying focused on goals and vision
	Fully engaging and leading by example
	Bringing current expertise to the table
	Admitting what you need to learn more about
How you treat yourself	Authentically—be true to your genuine self
	With respect and honesty
	Continuing to learn and grow
	Seeing mistakes as learning opportunities
	Being resilient in the face of critics and setbacks

Closure
Design principle—we tend to see complete figures even when part of the information is missing, which means what you do not show people, they will fill in the blanks on their own.

on to the bottom. Credible leaders accept personal responsibility and build that mindset into the organization. When a problem occurs, the first question at the top should be: How have I created the conditions such that this problem occurred? Did I not train someone effectively? Did I delegate too much, too quickly? Did I not provide sufficient resources? There certainly are times when a problem lies with a follower, but far more often, leaders inadvertently set others up for that problem. The credible leader admits mistakes, learns from them, and is willing to say, "I don't know."

How, then, can you become someone others desire to follow? Establishing your credibility in a specific leadership role or context is critical to your success, and it is something you will need to attend to every time, all the time. The next chapter continues your design of leadership self, looking at how your strengths and style align with the dynamic needs of tomorrow's organizations.

LEADERSHIP BY DESIGN

Design Principle: Closure

Definition: "The principle of closure applies when we tend to see complete figures even when part of the information is missing."[32]

In Other Words: What you do not show people, they will make up on their own.

For Example: *Skimming* a chapter that is due tomorrow (although not recommended) can be beneficial if you are already familiar with the material because you will automatically fill in missing information in order to understand something.

For Leaders: Use closure to think about how you can best design yourself as a leader and what might be missing. What is lacking from your personal leadership brand that your followers will have to fill in for themselves? Are you being clear with your goals, values, and expectations, or leaving room for interpretation? Are there facets about yourself that you *do not* want perceived as a single element and would rather them

stand alone? When conveying a vision, use closure to reduce complexity and increase interest—let groups fill in the gaps that lead up to the common goal.

The streams of water in this photo that you perceive as fluid are simply many tiny droplets, but you subconsciously use closure to make them seem like one cohesive element.

©iStock.com/Imgorthand

MANY OR ONE?

Chapter Summary

Your brain is a lean, mean, pattern-making machine that loves to construct mental models of the world as you interact with the world. Those interactions and experiences have helped form your conception of leaders and leadership . . . some of which might be mistaken. But the more you become aware of your own conceptions,

the more broadly you can perceive the world, including leadership.

Misconceptions about leaders and leadership can be more easily understood within the framework of the definition: Process of influencing others toward a common vision.

Rule #1 (It's about you.) and Rule #2 (It's not about you.) provide additional guidance.

Effective leaders possess specific traits—the challenge lies in identifying what specific traits fit a specific situation, context, challenge, and group of followers. Nonetheless, as you design your leadership it is important to know what traits you possess, where they are best utilized, and what traits you aspire to develop.

Likewise, effective leaders have a menu of skills that can be learned and developed as tools for a variety of leadership activities—influencing others, developing relationships, crafting vision, facilitating others' success, and so forth. Skills can be very specific or fall into general categories. One helpful way of organizing skills is by technical, human, and conceptual skills. Leaders need to shift their emphasis to different skills as they move to different roles and levels within an organization.

The list of what effective leaders could or should know, be able to do, or be like is quite vast. Some have tried to make sense of these by creating competencies, distinguishing between leadership and management, and envisioning what an expert leader might look like. Whatever combination of personal attributes you possess, developing your credibility and CORE™ provide you with transferable assets for effective leadership.

Key Terms

Charisma 60

Closure 66

Comparison 57

Credibility 64

Crucible (of leadership) 42

Level 5 Leadership 51

Management 62

Mental Model 48

Skills 61

Traits 52

Vision 54

CORE™ Attribute Builders: Build Now for Future Leadership Challenges

Attribute: Optimism

Builder: Send a thank you

Studies have shown that expressing gratitude increases happiness and optimism.[33] Take a moment right now to consider someone you could thank for something. The something could be big (thanks for helping me get into college) or small (thanks for showing me how to solve that math problem). Send that someone a thank you right now. You could simply email a thank you, but to get the maximum impact—for them and yourself—try writing and sending a note. Try doing this on a regular basis. Not only will you build your optimism, but you will further develop relationships that may someday be helpful.

CORE™ Attribute Builders: Build Now for Future Leadership Challenges

Attribute: Confidence

Builder: Reflected Best Self

This activity is based on the Reflected Best Self (RBS) exercise out of the Ross School of Business at the University of Michigan. Utilizing the idea that self-awareness and focusing on your strengths are two very important facets of your development as a leader, the RBS seeks to provide you with a more objective sense of what your *best* self entails. Here is your task:

1. Identify five to eight individuals who know you very well. Consider who will provide honest feedback for you, and who will take the time to provide a thoughtful answer.

2. Email those individuals and tell them you are taking a class that requires you to find out more about yourself and your potential as a leader. Ask them to provide three examples of when they have seen you at your best. Ask them to think carefully, provide you with a detailed answer, and then thank them.

3. Ask those individuals to complete the following:

   a. One thing you (the student) do very well, one of your most valuable attributes is:

      i. For example, the time you . . .

   b. One situation that really brings out the best in you is:

      ii. For example, the time you . . .

   c. One way that you add value/make an important contribution is:

      iii. For example, the time you . . .

4. Create a table with the following categories:

Best Attributes	Example Noted	My Interpretation
EXAMPLE 1. Honest	1. Found and returned that big pile-o-cash	I am very empathetic to how others feel, and my honesty follows from that perspective.

5. Using the data from the table, craft a single page (1-page) summary portrait of your Reflected Best Self—reflected from others, and reflected upon by you.

Skill Builder Activity

Leadership Either/Or

How do you perceive leaders and leadership?

Below you will find some contrasting choices. Pick the one with which you most agree. No, you cannot say *both*, even if that is what you think.

Then choose the other option and try to justify your (second) choice to a friend.

A leader:

1. Is inspirational   or   instructional

2. Is a model   or   a teammate

3. Is a friend   or   a boss

4. Is an expert   or   a good problem solver

5. Knows themselves   or   knows their followers

6. Is born   or   learns and develops

7. Has fun   or   assumes responsibility

8. Dresses to impress   or   dresses to fit in

9. Produces winners   or   wins

10. Makes it happen   or   facilitates a process

11. Challenges and critiques   or   maintains the current success

12. Decides based on their values   or   decides based on others' values

13. Achieves through their own initiative   or   achieves through creating conditions for others to succeed

14. Motivates others   or   removes barriers to allow others to pursue their motivation

15. Creates vision   or   allows vision to emerge

Skill Builder Activity

Who Are You?

Understanding yourself is key to leadership. There are many ways to describe oneself, some of which are very specific to an individual and others that describe general traits and tendencies shared by many. And many self-assessments have been created to help define you. None of them are the full picture, but *all* of them provide some interesting insight for you. Find a few new ways to describe yourself and how that personal insight relates to you as a leader. Here is the assignment:

1. Start a new folder or file that is all about you. Have you previously taken any personality or other assessments, such as Myers-Briggs or True Colors? Find those results and revisit them.

2. Find three other personal assessments online (or elsewhere) and assess yourself (take the test, etc.). You might start with a general search, but dig a little deeper and find some interesting aspects that you assess about yourself.

3. Using the results from #1 and #2, answer the following—in a personal journal or in a conversation with a friend:

   a. Describe your assessments—What did they measure? What are the different ways in which the assessments describe people? What are the different categories or types of people described by each assessment?

   b. Describe *your* results—What characteristics would you describe as defining you (based on these assessments)? What characteristics are definitely not you?

   c. Explain two things you need to know about yourself as a leader based on the results of these assessments.

3

Designing Your
Leadership Capacity

This may be the moment that changes the rest of your life.

—James Morrison

Learning Objectives

3.1   Describe important new challenges of leadership in a changing workplace

3.2   Identify cutting-edge skills for leaders now in demand

3.3   Design your leadership capacity to reflect your personal strengths

3.4   Formulate a preliminary leadership style and brand that connects your strengths and skills

3.5   Make a commitment to begin a new journey that will accelerate your career

Detailed Chapter Outline

Introduction
New Challenges . . . Need New
    Leadership . . . Need You
        Risk-Taking Replaces
            Status Quo
        Workspace Transforms the
            Workplace

Streamlined Organizational
    Structure Displaces the
    Hierarchy
Renewed Interest in
    Social and Corporate
    Responsibility
    Arises

Leadership by Design Model

DESIGN SELF

HOW CAN I DESIGN MYSELF AS A LEADER?

Design Relationships

As a leader, how can I design my relationships with others?

Design Others' Success

As a leader, how can I design success for others?

Design Culture

As a leader, how can I design the culture of my organization?

Design Future

As a leader, how can I innovate?

Introduction

Every individual has the capacity to positively impact someone else's life. You also have the ability to live a different kind of life from those who choose to follow someone else's lead. What kind of person do you need to be in order to take the lead? What personal strengths do you need to adopt to become a person of influence? How can *you* effectively facilitate the process of influencing others toward a common vision?

Designing your leadership self requires the identification of individual attributes that can be developed into effective leadership tools. This chapter focuses on designing your leadership capacity by taking an inventory of what you have, looking at what you will need, and crafting a plan for building and acquiring your leadership tools. Some leadership capacities are useful in all situations and contexts, such as the CORE™ (confidence, optimism, resilience, engagement) capacities; however, others are particularly effective in certain situations or contexts. The five learning objectives at the start of this chapter focus on those capacities that will best serve you in tomorrow's changing world and workplace.

LEADERSHIP THAT MAKES A DIFFERENCE

One never knows when a moment will arise that will change one's life forever. Your awareness of your capacity to lead may become evident when least expected. Put yourself in the position of a 15-year-old girl living in Pakistan. She is attending a public school in your home town. She gets on a bus to go home at the end of the day. On the way home, her bus is stopped by two young men who are specifically searching for her because she had previously spoken in public about how she wanted to be educated and become someone special. At that moment, she is shot in the head. This is a day that not only changed this 15-year-old's life but also that of a country and eventually the world. This individual endures several operations, suffers from a partial paralysis on one side of her face, and is without a country in which to reside. However, her confidence, resilience, and vision for change continues with her as she has a desire to take on leading a movement that is not expected of any 15-year-old. With the assistance of a global press, she gains the world's attention through her courageous attempts to spread the word of not only her own plight but those of millions of other children around the world. Remarkably at age 17, she stands before officials in the United Nations in New York City, thousands of miles from her home country, and addresses a global audience about the plight of over 60 million children who are deprived of an education, some deprived of equal opportunity with their male counterparts, and others deprived of any opportunity to engage in employment outside of the home. The story continues. In 2014, at 17 years old, she receives the Nobel Peace Prize for leading a movement to end the suppression of children's rights to receive an education. This is a remarkable accomplishment of a young person that began at age 11, when she took the initiative to influence others to allow girls to have an education; in just six years, she has demonstrated leadership in a movement to change the lives of millions of others. Now her vision for change has spread to every corner of the world. Who is this individual?

The moment to assume leadership often comes quickly and perhaps unexpectedly. In this instance, a 15-year-old faces that moment, and she rises to meet the challenge. In five short years, she had made a significant impact on world opinion, both in terms of how the world sees residents of Pakistan, as well as the challenge to eliminate extreme poverty, and to improve the future for over 60 million young people. Her name is Malala Yousafzai. This extraordinary young woman experienced the worst and best of humanity. One moment can change your whole life. Will you be ready for that moment when you have the opportunity to assume leadership that can make a difference?

New Challenges . . . Need New Leadership . . . Need You

Learning Objective

3.1 Describe important new challenges of leadership in a changing workplace

Leadership is for someone else, not me. The initial feeling that often arises when facing a difficult challenge or thinking about the complicated, messy problems of the world is one of skepticism. However, by stretching your perspective to broaden an awareness of your own capabilities, you can change both that feeling and mindset—and much can be accomplished. The question that underlies a hesitant leader is: *Do I have the capacity to lead others?* When presented with such a challenge, it is crucial to look within yourself to determine your strengths and engage in an important process of self-analysis. This also involves pushing your boundaries for evolving a mindset that envisions the excitement of a new challenge, the courage to take it on, and the willingness to collaborate and facilitate the process.

Examining and understanding yourself is not just a logical process, but involves your emotions. Reading the brief story of Malala Yousafzai, you can see how emotions are a key component in all aspects of her experience. The brief introduction to emotional intelligence in Chapter 2 noted the importance of self-awareness. Daniel Goleman's work connecting leadership and emotional intelligence regards self-awareness as a critical element when laying the groundwork for making better choices as to how to transition oneself into a leadership role, whether it is in a family, an organization, or a community.[1] Becoming aware of how the environment around us also changes to accommodate a new generation of leaders is your first step.

You are living in a world that is changing as you read this text. Not only is the structure of institutions and organizations changing but also the nature of leadership. There are numerous opportunities to assume leadership roles all around you—not just in the workplace. Leadership can be applied to most any situation whether at home, socially, or professionally. Remember the person profiled at the start of this textbook—James MacGregor Burns?[2] In his seminal book on leadership development, he introduced the notion that individuals initially must learn to lead themselves before they can lead others. This crucial step involves analyzing our existing personal strengths through a thoughtful self-awareness process.

Risk-Taking Replaces Status Quo

There is an extraordinary opportunity accessible to each of you. The need to remain competitive in a global economy has resulted in rethinking leadership roles in the private sector as well as in the nonprofit and public sectors.[3] Leadership is the process of influencing others toward a common vision. For the moment, consider what leadership looks like when that process is *inspiring others to want to achieve something special*. This outcome of effective leadership is exemplified by numerous individuals who in the past have taken a risk to produce a new product or service that had never existed before. The attributes demonstrated by these leaders are great examples of the way leaders emerge.

Risk-taking requires *imagination*. It was the imagination of Steven Jobs at Apple that drove his passion, which evolved into a new wave of creativity and produced the iPad and the iPhone. Risk-taking requires **perseverance**—the steady persistence in a course of action in spite of unexpected delays. It was the attribute of perseverance of Helen Clark, former prime minister of New Zealand, that enabled her to become the first female director of the United Nations Development Group in 2009. And risk-taking requires *passion*. It was the passion of Madeline Bell of Children's Hospital of the University of Pennsylvania that invigorated new approaches for treating childhood diseases through family-centered care programs. History has witnessed these individuals coming out of nowhere to lead a decade of progress. These individuals were like you in that they had a dream but also acted to see their dream become a reality. They are part of a new cadre of leaders that challenged themselves and at the same time conquered their fears. The word *can't* was not in their vocabulary.

Perseverance
a steady persistence in a course of action in spite of unexpected delays

Workspace Transforms the Workplace

Leadership is not about assembling individuals into a *workplace*, but rather creating a work*space* for others to thrive. Advanced technology has enabled individuals to achieve outcomes that were never considered a reality. Accordingly, working environments have become more virtual, dynamic, and digital.[4] Technology has enabled individuals to form innovative, collaborative work teams that are more capable of taking on the challenges of a global economy. For example, the emergence of freelance workers enables organizations to flatten their hierarchies by requiring smaller physical facilities for fewer managers and operatives. A more virtual workspace is not only more cost efficient to organizations, but it also allows for developing partnerships with those with specific skills required. Crowdsourcing is an example of how structures are changing to accommodate a dynamic working environment. This is the process of getting work performed or generating new ways of doing things, usually online, from a crowd of people. The idea is to enhance productivity by outsourcing it to a crowd of independent workers. It has had considerable impact on the way work is accomplished in retailing and food services. For example, companies such as Samsung, Lays Potato Chips, Starbucks, and Legos have taken advantage of crowdsourcing to bolster operations.[5]

The workspace is now often viewed as an environment where knowledge is valued as a critical component to creating an innovative culture. However, it takes an accumulation of new ideas to produce an innovative product or service. Creating something different from the past involves redesigning how people interact and communicate. Getting both yourself and others to change by establishing higher expectations for increasing your own productivity will require a new set of leadership skills.[6] For example, face-to-face interaction will continually change as the digital workspace is transformed from a physical space of cubicles to a virtual space with endless boundaries.[7] Therefore, instead of leading others in your physical presence, a different set of leadership skills will be required to motivate, monitor, and assess the actions and outcomes of followers and colleagues, whether in public institutions, private-sector organizations, or NGOs. Work will not be defined by physical space but rather by how you opt to perform your work.

Streamlined Organizational Structure Displaces the Hierarchy

The opportunity now exists for a new generation of leaders to take the successes of the past to a new level, one beyond the development of the Internet, a variety of social media, and digital networks. According to Colvin, every aspect of organizational structure is about to change.[8] The context for how we organize ourselves and inspire others to accomplish a shared vision is in transition. For example, traditionally, leadership has been based on one's position or title, such as president or CEO of an organization, in an environment of command and control over others from the top down. This organization reflects a hierarchy where individuals are closely supervised by someone above them. However, other organizational structures such as matrix, team, network, and virtual are being considered for what best fits the mission, values, and culture of a specific organization. Alternative organizational structures also change the way leaders communicate with and influence followers, make decisions, and facilitate success. For example, at the world-famous Longwood Gardens, Director Paul Redman uses strategic planning and a collaborative process to emphasize broad buy-in across all levels of the organization. By including as many stakeholders as possible in the vision-crafting process and then identifying and allowing experts to make that vision happen, Longwood is able to streamline activities and build an inclusive culture.[9]

Renewed Interest in Social and Corporate Responsibility Arises

There are issues in the workplace that seem to continue year after year, such as employee retention, engagement, development, and so forth. However, leaders across all sectors are recognizing the importance of the bigger picture and how their organizational success is intertwined with the success of their community, nation, and world. While public agencies attempt to address such issues as climate change, the wage gap, and workplace discrimination, these areas are starting to catch the interest of the private sector. For example, in terms of climate change, the National Aeronautics and Space Administration (NASA) and the National Oceanic and Atmospheric Administration (NOAA) data show that global temperature averages in 2016 were 1.78 degrees (F) warmer than the average of the mid-20th century, making 2016 the third year in a row with record-setting surface temperatures. This trend continued in 2017.[10] This development alone represents a considerable current and future challenge that will impact all sectors.

In terms of the wage gap between male and female employees, according to the National Committee of Pay Equity, since the Equal Pay Act was signed in 1963, the wage gap between male and female workers persists. In 1963, women who worked full-time made 59 cents on average for every dollar earned by men. In 2016, women still only earned 77 cents compared to every dollar for men.[11] These and many more issues of social responsibility can be addressed by leaders in the private, nonprofit, and public sectors, as well as those pursuing entrepreneurial opportunities.[12]

Humans Compete With Technology

Another intriguing aspect of the future is how humans will continue to add value to the workplace as technology intervenes in almost every aspect. Balancing the application of new technology for job creation with the effects of technology altering and eliminating jobs may be the defining economic concern of this era.[13] Advances in artificial intelligence, which have resulted in an explosion of new applications for technology in the workplace through big data analytics, social media, and robotics, may replace decision makers at various levels in the future. Although the fear of technological unemployment remains a concern, the good news is that humans will be needed to think through the consequences of our decisions, something that machines are unable to do effectively. Decisions about values, ethics, civil rights, and social welfare will require human assessment.

Leadership is always about people. The conflict between technology and human values often occurs in a subtle and emotional manner. For example, this conflict between technology and human values played out in a small town with a proposal by a university to build an extensive power plant to fuel electricity for both the town and a special new data center. The technology was deemed *safe*. The algorithm used to determine costs and benefits supported the decision that this was feasible. However, based on an analysis by the citizens of the town, the noise, pollution, and disruption to local quality of life was determined to be significantly detrimental to those residing near the site. After a significant debate, the project was rejected. The value of human input into the decision-making process proved to be the difference. Whereas technology suggested a cost-efficient project, the residents clearly delineated a human component that technology was incapable of processing.[14]

LEADERSHIP BY DESIGN

Design Principle: Form follows function

Definition: Beauty in design results when it is designed to function well. "A thing is defined by its essence. In order to design it so that it functions well—a receptacle, a chair, a house—its essence must first be explored; it should serve its purpose perfectly, that is, fulfill its function practically and be durable, inexpensive and 'beautiful.'"[15]

In Other Words: The shape of something is determined by what it needs to actually do.

For Example: Your resume is an example of form following its function—the point is to provide a brief summary of your skills, abilities, and accomplishments. The function of a resume is not to tell a life story, mystify with intrigue, lull others to sleep—if it were any of the latter, its form would be different.

The simpler and more succinct it is in form, the more usable it is perceived to be from an employer's perspective.

For Leaders: What form does your leadership need to take? That depends on what you need your leadership to actually do. Leadership can be applied to almost any situation, whether at home, socially, or professionally. Start with the functional question: What actually needs to be done here? Then form your leadership—your method of influence, your style, strengths you apply—to the required function. Do you lead differently depending on the environment? The constituency? Form follows function reminds designers to be as usable as possible in order to best serve a need—one way in which a leader can mimic that idea is to develop a repertoire of varying leadership styles and be familiar with when to use each one.

REFLECTION QUESTIONS

Can you think of at least three challenges that you as a future leader are likely to face? Have you faced similar challenges in your past work experience? How do you expect to face the challenge of technology possibly taking your career from you? List your perceived challenges here by degree of severity in terms of impacting your future.

1. _____ (Most Severe)

2. _____

3. _____ (Least Severe)

New Leadership Skills in Demand

Learning Objective

3.2 Identify cutting-edge skills for leaders now in demand

So far, this chapter has identified attributes of leaders who have succeeded in navigating a dynamic, changing world (imagination, perseverance, problem-solving); the changing nature of organizational structure (changing from workplace to workspace); and the importance of the human factor in the face of continuously increasing technological advances. In a very interesting article called "Humans Are Underrated," the author elaborates on the human factor, advocating skills that revolve around the value of human interaction, such as feeling empathy, exhibiting social intelligence, and respecting differences among individuals.[16] The essential CORE™ foundational attributes identified in Chapter 1 are critical components for becoming an effective leader. However, given the unique contexts in which you will someday lead, there are additional skills to fully designing your leadership: empathy, digital competence, organizational culture building, social intelligence, and perseverance. As you read about each of these skills, which one would you identify as the most critical leadership skill for the 21st century and beyond? Also, these skills cross many of the levels of design you will focus on in the rest of this textbook. In other words, skills required for 21st-century leadership will help you design yourself, your relationships, others' success, culture, and the future.

Exhibit Empathy

To Meg Bear, Vice President at Oracle[17], the new leadership skill for the 21st century is that of becoming more socially sensitive to the feelings of others in a more encroaching scientific workspace. You may be surprised that feeling empathy is a cutting-edge skill for our future leaders.[18] As an example, Pat Summit, former basketball coach for 38 seasons at the University of Tennessee with eight national titles, was demanding of her players. But she also showed a caring respect by ensuring that they all graduated from college while participating in the sport. Being demanding and caring at the same time may be unusual, but achieving excellence in what you do relies on setting high standards and fostering the success of each person.

What is empathy and how is it defined? Empathy is about caring about others. It is symbolic of your *heart*, which generally implies a sense of love or respect toward another. In this regard, **empathy** is defined as the ability to sense the feelings of others with the capacity to detect another's mindset. Empathy is one aspect of your emotional intelligence

Empathy
the ability to sense the feelings of others with the capacity to detect another's mindset

that you read about in Chapter 1 and is a very important tool you will need for design thinking in Chapter 5.

Why is empathy important to leadership? Empathy is considered the basis for forming a trustful relationship with others, and trust is the foundation of credibility. When you feel that someone truly understands your perspective, you feel heard and considered. Also, empathy is a key building block of morality since it places you in the shoes of another. It becomes a key component for building quality relationships.[19] Consequently, empathy also reduces prejudice, bullying, and inequality in the workplace.[20]

How well have you developed empathy? Most individuals already possess elements of empathy. Suppose you enrolled in a university course and volunteered to work on a team project with five others. One person in the group is from Italy and learned English as a second language. Your Italian team member has difficulty understanding the nuances of the English language and is often confused about what is happening at meetings. You had a similar experience when you took a course in China, when you had difficulty understanding the native language during class. You remember being confused about what was going on in class and when interacting with your classmates. If you had to select an action based in empathy, which of the following would you do to prepare your Italian classmate to participate in a team presentation? You can only select one action, so this may be challenging. What would an effective and empathetic leader do?

Choose One

___ 1. You would suggest they enroll in an English Language Institute immediately to help refine their English language skills.

___ 2. You would give them an easy part of the project to do so they can get it done.

___ 3. You would isolate them from the others and have someone help them after the meetings.

___ 4. You would match up with them during the project and concentrate on listening to them.

___ 5. You would match them with another foreign student on the team so they could support one another.

___ 6. You would choose a different course of action from the above options. Explain: _____

Each of the above alternatives is intriguing. Which one did you select and why? Are there other things (Option #6) you could do to show empathy? One important point is to separate having sympathy (feeling sorry for) and/or acting in a condescending manner from exhibiting empathy. Demonstrating empathy also helps when assisting others to gain confidence through active listening and equitable action. The other alternatives are more about having sympathy by removing yourself from the issue while having someone else assist. In this instance, Option #4 is perhaps most empathetic since you took the step to take on a personal relationship with your classmate from Italy and devoted time to listening to their suggestions, points of view, and concerns. You were attempting to identify with their feelings about the project.

What can you do to further develop empathy? Here are some specific practices you can implement to take your own empathy to a higher sense of awareness.[21]

• First, concentrate on becoming an active listener. By demonstrating to others that you are interested in what they are saying, an open dialogue can be generated that enables individuals to express their feelings as well as their ideas.

• Second, list what you have in common with your coworkers. Since you are likely to be working with someone who is very different from you—maybe with age, nationality, or gender difference—identifying what you have in common with others may reduce the stress of the unknown.

- Third, use your imagination to visualize what the other person may be experiencing at the time. This practice will likely get you to focus on the other person more than yourself.

These are just a few but important things you can do immediately to bring empathy totally into your life.

Engage Digitally

Another skill set growing in importance relates to a leader's ability to digitally engage employees and customers.[22] Digital tools, such as mobile technology and cloud computing, create a virtual workspace for getting things done.[23] Consider work life before computers, cell phones, e-mail, and the Internet. Think of how much has changed because of all those things. Technology always changes, and those changes impact how work happens and how leaders can and should lead.

What is digital competence and how is it defined? **Digital competence** is having a set of skills, attitudes, and abilities that enables an individual to use a variety of technical tools (the Internet, platforms, mobile tools, and computers, etc.) when seeking, gathering, and analyzing data, and communicating findings to others. Being digitally competent requires an individual to understand how information and communications technology (ICT) interact for creating a real-time office space where immediate access to information is expected by employees.

Why is digital competence important to leadership? Competence utilizing technology can enhance the efficient use of time in the workplace. Perceiving technology as a work tool, future leaders can enhance employee productivity considerably, manage time more efficiently, and improve worker capacity to become more creative and innovative.[24] Therefore, expectations have changed as technical tools become more prevalent. Future leaders are able to inspire employees to get outside their comfort zones for generating new products and services using less time and resources. In other words, a lot more time can be devoted to performing tasks that increase profits. In this regard, a productive workplace is a profitable one. New leadership roles will reflect digital engagement, collaboration, and accountability at a different level. You will likely be transcending physical boundaries to incorporate a blend of in-person, online, and other virtual forms of smart technology when leading others into action.

How well have you developed digital competence? You are working for the local community branch of the Alzheimer's Association designing a packet of materials seeking contributions from potential donors. You need to put together an effective letter to go with the package. Your covolunteers basically work out of their homes. You decide to use Google Docs for designing your letter and funding package collaboratively with five other volunteers. Now, you realize that you need to be adept in performing in a virtual workspace using digital technology. Accessing real-time databases, digital documents, images, and motion video to produce a shared outcome with individuals situated in different locations is part of the operational style of this organization. If you find yourself in a similar situation in the future, to what degree have you already developed this attribute?

What can you do to develop digital competence? Being on the cutting edge of technology is something that can benefit you as a leader. To maintain your capacity to perform in a leadership role as a more virtual workplace emerges, there are several practices you might adopt to create a more collegial workforce. Initially, integrate digital tools into both your work and personal life. Stay tuned in to the most recent advances in technology, especially those you think could impact how employees communicate and relate in the workplace. Encouraging others to bring their own technological solutions to work for accomplishing tasks will also likely make sure you are up-to-date with current technology. Second, build a personal digital network whereby individuals are readily available for discussing problems, gathering information, and gaining access to an outside expertise. To do this, think about adding at least one person outside of your current network each week. Finally, both initiate and participate in digital ventures for personal, economic, or social value. A suggestion would be to form a team of users at work and meet at least once a week to discuss how new forms of digital technology can transform a current workplace practice into a more dynamic operation. Think about how much you can learn by continually experimenting with digital technology by engaging yourself in learning how to enhance its use on an everyday basis.

Enhance a Collaborative Work Culture

A third important leadership skill, espoused by Ken Blanchard, suggests creating a new collaborative organizational culture that empowers individuals to make decisions for achieving a new triple bottom line: treating customers, employees, and community fairly.[25] Learning how to guide others to want engagement with coworkers and avoid a toxic workplace is an expectation of today's organizations.

What is collaborative work culture and how is it defined? **Organizational culture** is defined as shared values and assumptions by organizational members. These shared understandings—things that are learned and developed over time—become a way of life for a group of individuals. In an organization, culture is cultivated through learned beliefs, values, customs, and norms established over time by those in leadership roles. In this regard, individuals in the workplace are programmed with a mindset that distinguishes the organization from others. (You will explore the concept of designing culture more fully in Chapter 11.)

Organizational culture a way of life for a group of individuals that has been learned and developed over a period of time

Why is collaborative work culture important to leadership? An organizational culture that rewards change reflects a working environment where success and failure are treated as part of the process. The ability to generate teams of workers that can collaborate—that is, gather and share information with others, elaborate on ideas, coordinate the work of many, and create harmony among workers with different views—requires leaders who can rally others around a single cause.[26] Your capacity to encourage others to nurture unorthodox thinking that unleashes the talent of coworkers forms the foundation for generating a culture of innovation. Think about it. Would we have a company called Tesla that produces totally electric automobiles if a team of workers did not take a risk and present the idea? This openness is based on the fundamental belief that ideas for new products and services can come from anyone, anywhere, and at any time. Promoting risk-taking as a norm requires a collaborative culture.

How well have you developed the ability to foster a collaborative work culture? Imagine that you are employed in an organization where 20% of your time may be spent beyond performing normal routines to devising new ways to accomplish your job or to produce a new product or service. The expectation is that this discretionary time provided during a typical workweek will result in something special. The goal of leadership in this case is to create new markets rather than fighting competitors for existing market share.[27] In this instance, you and your employer realize that it will require a new work culture to take current products and services to a higher order of quality, usefulness, and cost-effectiveness. Ask yourself, to what degree have you developed a capacity to motivate others to use different work patterns, such as the one above, for producing results?

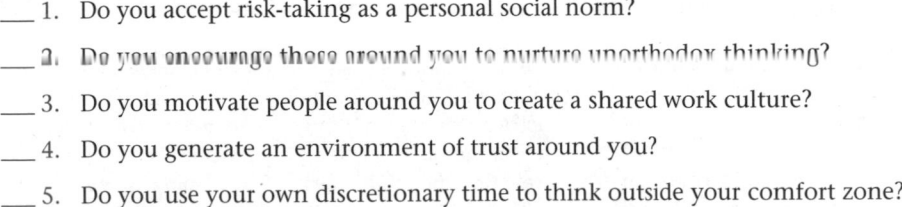

___ 1. Do you accept risk-taking as a personal social norm?

___ 2. Do you encourage those around you to nurture unorthodox thinking?

___ 3. Do you motivate people around you to create a shared work culture?

___ 4. Do you generate an environment of trust around you?

___ 5. Do you use your own discretionary time to think outside your comfort zone?

If you responded *yes* to at least three of the items above, you may already possess a great deal of organizational awareness.

What can you do to develop collaborative work culture? At first, one way to create a collaborative work culture is to have a clear vision of purpose. This vision will set the stage for how individuals set their own work goals and perceive your leadership. Second, establish clearly stated organizational values that blend with operational practices in that organization. Third, building an open organizational culture requires hiring individuals who will accept risk-taking as an organizational norm. Individuals generally stick with a culture they like, which brings some stability to the workforce. Finally, design an open architecture workspace where walls do not keep people apart. Placing individuals in spaces that encourage collaboration, communication, and camaraderie will go a long way toward establishing a culture of trust, respect, and collegiality.

Promote the narrative of the organization, the individuals, and its purpose. Most organizations have a heritage or tradition that illustrates past successes and milestones. This is a powerful way to carry on an organization's culture with a new generation of workers. Examples of organizations with a strong narrative are Coca-Cola with its World of Coke narrative, Apple with its fascination with small digital components, and Gore Industries with its legacy of people-centered operations. As you read further in this textbook, you will focus on designing various facets and types of culture, from organizational (Chapter 11) and team (Chapter 12) to designing a culture that cares (Chapter 13) and one that fosters innovation (Chapter 14).

EXPERTS BEYOND THE TEXT

INSIGHTFUL LEADERS KNOW ABOUT . . . FOLLOWERSHIP

By R. Koonce and M. Hurwitz

To obsess about superiors at the expense of subordinates is to distort

the dynamic between them. And it sends a message: to underestimate, or

to undervalue, the importance of those whom Shakespeare once referred

to as underlings is to disempower. So long as we fixate on leaders at the expense of followers, we will perpetuate the myth . . .

—Barbara Kellerman (p. xvii)[28]

The best people know when to lead and when to allow others to do the same.[29] When shared responsibility exists for accomplishing an established vision, no special emphasis should be given to a leader, or a follower; they equally cocreate.[30] Leaders and followers need to work as a partnership. Hollander writes, "Though the success of a team depends upon so-called 'teamwork,' it pivots around leader-follower relations."[31] Despite the perceived importance of the partnership between a leader and a follower, the partnership is still too often portrayed as a relationship between a parent and a child,[32] as a boss and an associate, or a superior and a subordinate.[33] If a partnership is to ever exist between

a leader and a follower, a follower must have a leader's interests at heart, as the leader correspondingly allows the follower to question or constructively challenge the leader's behavior or their policies.

In a paper presented in April and November 1927 conferences of the U.S. Bureau of Personnel Administration, management scholar Mary Parker Follett defined leadership as a problem of relating and the best leader as one who sought to arouse not "attitudes of obedience," but "attitudes of co-operation."[34] Her belief was that a leader who strived to organize the experience of a group in such a way that the specialized knowledge of its members could *actively*, rather than passively, contribute to the effectiveness of the group would inspire the group to work toward a common purpose.

Follett first used the term *followship*, pointing to the joint responsibility inherently described by the term leadership. She went on to suggest that if a follower should be expected to follow the common purpose of an organization (also referred to as the *invisible leader* in Follett's writings), so must the leader. While leadership for Follett represented a true partnership between leader and those being led, various historical accounts such as Thersites in Homer's Iliad, ronin in feudal Japan, and SS members in Nazi Germany also clearly demonstrate that "not all followers 'follow' in the same way."[35]

The next time you think about leadership, consider the role and influence of the follower.

Enact Social Intelligence

Another useful skill for those assuming leadership roles is that of exhibiting social intelligence when collaborating with others, especially in a workplace that is quite diverse.[36] Social intelligence reflects your pattern for working with others in an effort to achieve something special. The ability to collaborate with others intelligently and without excessive conflict and/or misunderstandings is a growing skill of importance.

What is social intelligence and how is it defined? **Social intelligence** is basically knowing how to engage others for establishing effective interactive networks. Specifically, it is defined here as the ability to get along well with others by getting them to collaborate and eventually partner with you for achieving a specific result. While the importance of social intelligence in leadership has been known for some time, its importance and practical application has grown stronger as work cultures have grown more collaborative.[37]

> **Social intelligence**
> the ability to get along well with others by getting them to collaborate and eventually partner with you for achieving a specific result

Why is social intelligence important to leadership? Socially intelligent leaders are more empathetic, more capable of influencing and inspiring others, and better able to bring out the best in a team.[38] In a leadership role, your social intelligence will help build quality relationships and ultimately enhance your credibility and effectiveness. Socially intelligent leaders are also better able to help others work through conflicts and challenges. This means leaders have the capacity to help people feel valued, respected, encouraged, and even competent.

How well have you developed social intelligence? Imagine you are working in the public sector in the mayor's office of your hometown. Your constituents are quite diverse but also vocal. A current issue concerning school budgeting has come forth. You need to read a situation as it unfolds, consider the appropriate ways to respond, and select an alternative that will yield the best result for all involved. The subset skills required for effective leadership are exhibiting active listening, utilizing a strong command of conversational language, differentiating cultural cues, reading subtle facial expressions, and negotiating. To what degree have you already developed this attribute yourself? This job is very political in nature, so think about how you would perform in this situation.

Yes/No?

_Y_ 1. When others disagree with you, do you manage conflict well?

_Y_ 2. Can you build partnerships (quality relationships) quickly?

_Y_ 3. Can you negotiate common ground from cultural differences?

_Y_ 4. Can you interpret cues (facial expressions) of others accurately?

_N_ 5. Do you know the impression you send of yourself to others?

If you responded *yes* to at least three of the items above, you may already possess a great deal of social intelligence.

What can you do to develop social intelligence? There are several practices that you can adopt that will enable you to intelligently create quality relationships with others. At the beginning, it is important to be perceived as acting with ethical motives that align with your personal values. In this regard, having authenticity is the foundation for creating collaborative work styles. Secondly, begin paying more attention to the social world around you. Work on becoming a conversationalist—not only with friends but with strangers also. For example, during social gatherings, being proactive by carrying on conversations with a variety of individuals will demonstrate your confidence in yourself. Greeting and being tactful with strangers reflects an individual comfortable with going outside his or her social comfort zone. Finally, become comfortable playing different social roles with individuals with different expectations. When there is a conflict among ideas, become an active listener by reflecting back on what you believe the speaker said. In other words, being capable of understanding what the other person is thinking or feeling is basic to reading the situation that you are in. People tend to make inferences about your competence based on the behavior they observe.

The demand for a new set of leadership skills, skills that will maximize the likelihood of your success in the workplace, requires that you become more sensitive to the value of human input during the process of creating a new array of products and services expected to emerge in the future. It will not only be *what* you know that will make a difference but *how* you perform in a leadership capacity. Blanchard depicts this emerging era as a movement toward *essence*.[39] To become an effective leader in the future, it is the essence behind the scenes that makes the difference. **Essence** reflects the process, the thought, the intent, and the motivation of the individual; that being, the actions of people who congregate for a common purpose. How clear are you regarding your essence? The four complementary skills identified here reflect this new essence.

Essence the process, the thought, the intent, and the motivation of the individual; that being, the actions of people who congregate for a common purpose

REFLECTION QUESTIONS

Can you recall the five Es that describe the complementary skills required for future cadres of leaders? List them below for your future reference. Circle the one skill that will challenge you the most and indicate why. What can you do to enhance your capacity to perform each of these skills?

1. E _____

2. E _____

3. E _____

4. E _____

5. Essence (yours): _____

Design Your Leadership Capacity: Highlighting Strengths

Learning Objective

3.3 Design your leadership capacity to reflect your personal strengths

Designing your leadership begins with you. In the first chapter of this text, you began to explore your perceptions and some of the CORE™ capacities required for effective leadership. In this chapter, you have also started to compare yourself to the new complementary skill set required for future leaders. This section illuminates three significant elements of designing your leadership self: Strengths, Skills, and Styles.

What if you simply ignored things you were not very good at? What if you focused on improving things you were already doing well? In fact, that is what most people generally do . . . except at work. Think about the things you like to do in your free time. Do you play a sport, have a hobby, dominate online games, or play a musical instrument? You are probably pretty good at the things you like to do. Would you take up a sport or hobby you are not so good at or even perform terribly? You probably would not. It would take significant interest (and resilience) to stick with it. So why in the work setting do leaders focus more on the things you must improve instead of those things at which you are already good? Development and growth do not need to mean fixing weakness, they can mean building on strengths. The main premise of **strengths-based leadership** is an emphasis on what you do well—your strengths.

Research conducted by a group of researchers at Gallup International identified 34 common strengths that individuals possessed to varying degrees.[40] Here are a few examples of strengths they identified:

Activator—the ability to make things happen, turning thoughts into action

Strategic—the ability to create alternative ways to proceed

Command—the ability to take control of a situation and make decisions

Individualization—the ability to identify the unique qualities of each person and help different individuals work well together

Maximizer—the ability to stimulate individual and group excellence—always seeking to transform something from great to super great.[41]

Do you see yourself possessing any of these strengths? Researchers subsequently developed a tool to identify an individual's top five strengths, enabling leaders and followers alike to strategically focus their performance on their already established strengths.

Leaders who focus on enhancing individual strengths find greater productivity than attempting to eliminate weaknesses of followers (such as through training programs). In their book *Strengths Based Leadership*, Tom Rath and Barry Conchie defend the position that there is no one strength that all successful leaders possess.[42] Most effective leaders are *not* well rounded, but instead they are acutely aware of their own talents and use them to their best advantage. Based on in-depth interviews with leaders around the world, they found that when leaders in an organization focus on the strengths of their employees, more effective work teams are formed, and productivity and employee engagement in decision-making increase substantially. Correspondingly, Rath and Conchie define strengths-based leaders as workers excelling in four specific domains, within which fit each of the 34 strengths: *executing, influencing, relationship building,* and *strategic thinking.* Individuals who apply these strengths in the workplace are likely to reap the benefit of having higher incomes, higher job satisfaction, and better health over time. A description of each domain is provided below. Take a close look at each of the four domains. Later in the chapter, you will be asked to consider your leadership relative to each leadership strength domain.

- **Executing**—working tirelessly to get something done by taking an idea and transforming it into reality

- **Influencing**—the process of promoting ideas and inspiring others to buy in

- **Relationship Building**—bringing people with diverse backgrounds and ideas together and maintaining a collective effort for getting things accomplished

- **Strategic Thinking**—absorbing information for making informed decisions while keeping coworkers focused on the future

Awareness of your strengths results in an increase in self-confidence, according to a 2008 study conducted by Charles Hurst and Tim Judge.[43] Based on a 25-year longitudinal study using a sample of 7,660 workers, they also found that people who had the opportunity to use their strengths early on (between the ages of 15 and 23) had significantly higher self-confidence but also greater job satisfaction and income levels 26 years later.

Strengths-based leadership
workers excelling in four specific domains: executing, influencing, relationship building, and strategic thinking

MYTH OR REALITY?

PEOPLE WHO USE THEIR STRENGTHS IN THE WORKPLACE ARE LIKELY TO HAVE BETTER HEALTH OVER THEIR CAREERS.

Reality. According to a Gallup Poll, employees who apply their strengths in the workplace tend to be much more engaged. Engaged employees lead healthier lives. And engaged employees will also likely reap two other benefits, which include higher income and higher job satisfaction. Relatedly, learning to use your strengths in the workplace in a leadership role requires you also to build trust, compassion, stability, and hope among your followers.[44] These four aspects of work generally create an environment that is conducive to generating a collegiality that reduces stress and conflict, leading ultimately to better health.

The bottom line is that people who are aware of their strengths are likely to reap a competitive advantage that continues to grow over a lifetime. These outcomes highlight the value of leaders knowing their own strengths and also reveal how important it is for leaders to help others uncover their strengths as early as possible.

REFLECTION QUESTIONS

Think about a time in the past when you assumed a leadership role, whether at work, for a charity, or for a community organization. How would you rate your performance in terms of influencing others, executing responsibilities, building relationships, and following through on strategic thinking? Which skill were you most efficient in carrying out? What specific strengths made the difference for your performance?

Design Your Personal Leadership Brand

Learning Objective

3.4 Formulate a preliminary leadership style and brand that connects your strengths and skills

Your personal leadership brand is your trademark; it reflects your journey of self-discovery. Your **leadership brand** involves identifying your assets—strengths, skills, and other desirable characteristics—and packaging them in a manner that enhances leadership efficacy and credibility. Ulrich and Smallwood, in their work, *Leadership Brand: Developing Customer-Focused Leaders to Drive Performance and Build Lasting Value*, state that your brand sets the stage for how others perceive you and thus how willing they are to engage you in collaborative working arrangements.[45] Your brand promotes a personal identity as relationships are built among colleagues, whether fellow employees, friends, or even family members. For those interested in developing leadership, you need to take charge and design your own personal brand—developing a total package to enable you to contribute to the success of work teams and organizations in general.

Leadership brand
identifying your assets—strengths, skills, and other desirable characteristics—and packaging them in a manner that enhances leadership efficacy and credibility

Designing your leadership requires a full-time commitment to a journey of defining oneself as a future leader. To start, here is a simple three-step process for creating and promoting a personal brand. Keep in mind that each of these steps, like you and your leadership brand, will evolve and change as you design and redesign your leadership self over a lifetime.

Step #1: How Would You Like to Be Perceived by Others?

The words we use to describe ourselves are critical to becoming aware of our capacity to lead. Words like innovative, curious, and insightful reflect a personal leadership brand as transformational or creativity oriented. On the other hand, words such as task-oriented, disciplined, and results oriented may reflect your personal leadership brand as transactional or task driven. How do others perceive you at this time? The self-analysis exercise below may assist in this endeavor.

Form a circle of at least five classmates, coworkers, or simply friends. Place your back to your classmates (facing away from others). Have the others talk about how they perceive your strengths and weaknesses. Initially, have the team focus on identifying your strengths, followed by comments related to your weaknesses. Then based on what you heard, turn around, face your classmates, and summarize your thoughts.

(1) **Five-Word Sum**—Attempt to classify the comments of others into five specific words that reflect your current brand.

(2) **Dis/satisfaction**—Is the conversation about you what you wanted it to be? If so, why? If not, why not?

(3) **Initial Improvements**—What can you do to enhance yourself for becoming an effective leader?

Step #2: How Can You Become the Person Others Desire to Follow?

Having self-awareness and a willingness to listen and learn from others will be helpful in keeping your personal leadership brand relevant to your actions. How can you become the person others choose to follow? The previous chapter (strongly) suggested you work on your credibility. Why not be incredible? That can only happen if you continue to learn and find out how *you* are most effective. Recall that your brain is a lean, mean, pattern-making machine—how you conceive the world is what you perceive in the world. Here are three things you can do to get followers to believe in you and desire to follow you: You are what you read, you are what you see, and you are what you do.

You Are What You Read

Followers admire those who know their trade. Take the initial step to become educated in the discipline of leadership. This is what you are doing right now. Establishing yourself as a continuous learner and knowing the principles of effective leadership provides the foundation for establishing a brand. For example, you should explore more about collaborative leadership from Bernard Bass[46] or about adaptive leadership from Ronald Heifetz.[47] Here is a little hint: All you need to do to find out more is follow those little numbers like the one after Heifetz. Then just Google it up. The more perspectives you read, the more options you have for executing leadership.

LEADERSHIP BY DESIGN

Design Principle: Affordance

Definition: The perceived and actual properties of a thing, particularly the properties that determine how something can be used.[48]

In Other Words: The things you can actually do with an object (throw it, eat it, write on it) are its affordances.

For Example: If you have ever pulled the door handle of a door that needed to be pushed (and wondered why someone put a pull handle on a push door), you have experienced a poor application of affordance.

For Leaders: What is your intended function as a leader? Then, what do you do that affords that function? For example, if your intention is to help followers recognize their strengths, you need to purposefully highlight their strengths, intentionally focus on strengths, strategically utilize strengths, and so forth. When the affordance of an object or environment (or leader) corresponds to its envisioned role, the design is more efficient and easy to learn. Followers' perception of you as a leader should match your personal intent and leadership style. Design things the way you want people to use them, and design your leadership the way you want others to see and utilize your capabilities.

You Are What You See

The second way to build your leadership credibility is to observe other people you admire. Identify those leaders who exemplify the behaviors and values that resonate with you and seem to be effective with followers. Whom do you admire for their ability to attract large numbers of followers? What is it about these leaders that can help you form your own leadership style? Consider a few individuals you may want to research to gain a perspective of why and how they inspire others to follow their lead.

You Are What You Do

The third and perhaps the most effective way to get followers to join you is by your actions—becoming a role model. This requires you to take the initiative to experiment when building relationships with others. Recall that leadership is about caring for others and making their lives successful (Rule #2: It's not about you). This aspect of learning requires you to take charge of your present and future.

There are basically two choices that you will be making at the end of this text. One choice is to sit by and do nothing and watch others accelerate their careers by applying what they have learned. The other choice is to be that individual who is accelerating in significance by putting into place a strategy for becoming an effective leader. However, you must first learn to lead (and manage) yourself before others will trust you to lead them. Do you manage your own time efficiently each day? Do you meet deadlines for your own work? When you commit to something with colleagues, do you follow through? If you responded with a *no* for any of these questions, this may be a wake-up call for you to reexamine your work style and adjust it if you truly want to assume a leadership function in the future.

REFLECTION QUESTIONS

If you are what you read, then what are you going to read first?

If you are what you see, then what leader are you interested in learning more about?

If you are what you do, then what could you do to impress others with your self-management?

Step #3: State Your Leadership Brand to Others

Your leadership brand is only as valuable as it is applied and communicated to others. Part of that task will be finding the right contexts for your leadership. But the other part is helping others find you, which starts with reflecting on the information above relating to what you would like to be known for. A personal brand also reflects your goals, beliefs, and expectations. Place your personal leadership brand into words that clarify exactly who you are. Most importantly, remember that actions speak louder than words. According to Ulrich and Smallwood, the most successful personal brand statements associated with leadership deliver what they promise.[49] Being capable of stating your brand to others in short but concise statements consistently will build trust. Use the Skill Builder Activity at the end of this chapter to assist you in both creating and promoting your personal leadership brand. For now, complete the questions below to begin crafting a leadership brand.

1. A follower would choose me because _____

2. I want to be known for being _____ so I can _____

Place Your Brand Into Action

Opportunity often comes when we least expect it to occur. Now is a time to invest in yourself by thinking about how you would like to lead others. As indicated earlier in this chapter, Blanchard considers two basic approaches to understanding leadership: through *outcomes* or *process*.[50] When your interest is primarily on achieving outcomes, then your framework reflects getting tasks done in an efficient and orderly fashion. If your interest is in generating processes whereby individuals can work collaboratively to achieve something new and special, then your framework reflects working in an environment where people and teamwork are valued. Look carefully at the table below and compare the focus between a task-oriented and people-oriented leadership framework.

Circle a total of six phrases from below that reflect your own mindset as a leader. In other words, what do you prefer doing each day when you assume a leadership role?

Outcomes-Oriented	Process-Oriented
Maintain the Status Quo	Be Change Oriented
Control Action of Others	Support Others
Complete Work Efficiently	Have Empathy and Sincerity
Meet Deadlines	Establish Group Harmony
Work Alone Primarily	Be a Team Player
Be Achievement Oriented	Be Creatively Oriented
Be Short-Term Oriented	Be Long-Term Oriented
Have Clear Role Expectations	Appreciate Role Ambiguity
Be a Power Seeker	Empower Others to Take Initiative
Promote Stability	Promote Risk Taking

Reflecting on the phrases that you circled, and exhibiting some personal creativity, come up with at least a five-letter acronym that visualizes your leadership framework. This word should reflect whether you lean toward an outcomes orientation, a process orientation, or perhaps a hybrid—a balance of each.

Commit to a Journey to Accelerate Your Career

Learning Objective

3.5 Make a commitment to begin a new journey that will accelerate your career

Convincing yourself that you can develop into an effective leader is essential to staying on track for accomplishing great things in your personal life. Now is the time to begin thinking about generating a personal commitment that results in a strategy for becoming an effective leader. In this regard, Jim Collins, author of the book *Good to Great*, points out that with rapid changes in work styles and expectations of the younger workforce entering the market, the need for different kinds of leaders is on the rise.[51] Moreover, volatile markets with an increasing demand by consumers for better products mean leaders now need to be more versatile by changing strategies quickly as new competitors also enter the marketplace.

Now that you have completed this chapter, you are ready to sign a letter of commitment. This acclamation on your part is the first step of your journey to become part of something new and exciting. Designing your leadership self means taking charge of your own destiny rather than letting someone else do it. Using the template provided in the exercise directly below, put together a commitment letter, sign it, and give it to your instructor.

Make a Commitment to Undertake the Leadership Journey

Directions: Fill in the blanks below to reflect your personal commitment to learning about leadership and submit your commitment letter to your instructor.

Dear _____:

Re: Commitment to Leadership

I am making a pledge to begin my journey for learning how to become an effective leader. My commitment shall entail learning how to use my present strengths to enhance my capacity to lead and make a positive difference.

My **three most significant current strengths** to be used in this endeavor are:

- _____
- _____
- _____

I also commit to learning additional skills that will support my future employability and meet my desire to grow as a productive leader. In this regard, I pledge to make considerable effort to **learn three new leadership skills** for the 21st century. They are:

- _____
- _____
- _____

Finally, I commit to invest in my future learning by completing a series of activities to **accomplish the following three outcomes** in my leadership development. They are:

- _____
- _____
- _____

My overall objective is to be a _____ leader who can be used in a(n) _____ organization.

Based on my strengths, my personal leadership brand is:

I want to be known for being _____ so that I can deliver _____.

I understand that this letter constitutes a voluntary commitment to my future.

Sincerely

(Your Signature)

Now you have an initial direction to designing your leadership self. But it is not enough to have a plan; you have to act on it. Your commitment letter is the vision you have designed for yourself. It reflects a promise to yourself and a reference point as your design develops. Keep this commitment letter nearby and refer to it as you proceed further.

REFLECTION QUESTIONS

Now that you have composed a commitment to leadership letter, what part separates you from all the other people you know—what makes you unique? Identify at least three aspects of your commitment that distinguish you. What will give you a competitive advantage as you prepare for taking an important step to enhance your career?

Leadership is about the heart, and it is often a process of caring about others as organizational goals are met. The heart is symbolic of what separates personal leadership from technology—computers cannot experience feelings. Technology generally disregards the impact on human psyche and life. Leaders who genuinely lead with their heart—not just their head—are more equipped to connect with the emotional needs of others. They understand that people need to be valued, respected, listened to, and involved. Carol Burnett, a television icon from the 1960s to the 1990s, had a highly successful career in show business and is a perfect example of a leader with heart.[52] She never criticized employees or appeared demanding. When she needed something done, she would simply ask for help with the task required. This leadership approach shows her respect for the abilities of subordinates. By acknowledging and honoring the human aspect of leadership, the heart-centered leader enhances the quality of work life for both themselves and for all those surrounding them. Do you know leaders like this? Do you want to be this kind of leader?

Five Es
This describes the skill set for future leaders: Exhibit empathy, Engage digitally, Enhance a collaborative work culture, Enact social intelligence, and identify your Essence.

Chapter Summary

The challenges you will face in the coming decades are only now providing hints at the skills and strengths future leaders will need. Changes in the nature of work, technology, and personal and organizational values are altering what works in leadership. Now, as ever, the process-oriented approach of effective leadership offers the dynamic flexibility to bring those newly required skills to bear. This new skill set can be summed with **five "Es"**:

- *Exhibit* empathy
- *Engage* digitally
- *Enhance* a collaborative work culture
- *Enact* social intelligence
- Identify your *essence*

The most applicable strengths and skills of a leader may change somewhat over time, but the need for human intervention remains critical. The changes demanded of each of you will reflect a more dynamic approach to learning leadership that is somewhat different from the past. The initial task for designing your leadership self is to identify your area of strengths (influencing, executing, relating, and strategic thinking) and to devise a strategy that will enable you to take advantage of these.

By designing a concise leadership brand statement through the process described in this chapter, you can develop an image for setting the stage for becoming a future leader. Finally, your commitment letter should be stored in a safe place and referred to as you proceed in this text.

Key Terms

Digital Competence 78

Empathy 76

Essence 82

Five Es 89

Leadership Brand 84

Organizational Culture 79

Perseverance 73

Social Intelligence 81

Strengths-Based Leadership 83

CORE™ Attribute Builders: Build Now for Future Leadership Challenges

Attribute: Engagement

Builder: Clearly delineate your leadership engagement style

Compare the dominant engagement style of leaders by decade as depicted in the three eras below. From each column, select one term that in your opinion *best* illustrates the emphasis behind the style of engagement of leaders in that era.

Past	Recently	Future
(1880–2000)	**(2001–2015)**	**(2016+)**
1. Control	Open	Virtual
2. Delegate	Volunteer	Initiate
3. Inform	Share	Discover

Past	Recently	Future
4. Powerful	Distributive	Empowerment
5. Efficient	Effective	Inspiring
6. Convergent Thinker	Divergent Thinker	Independent Thinker
7. Stability	Incremental Change	Extreme Change
8. Technical	Interactive	Team/ Collaborative

Which descriptive term do you prefer today that reflects *your* style of engagement as you assume a leadership role?

Skill Builder Activity

Design Your Own Personal Leadership Brand Statement

Think again about the workplace you would like to create along with the style of leadership that you prefer. Revisit that scenario by putting together a leadership statement that will guide you as you advance your career.

Design a Self-Portrait—What specific leadership strengths do you already possess?

Design a Leadership Style—What style of leadership do you prefer?

Design a Culture—What kind of working environment do you prefer to lead in?

Design a Future—What do you want to be the center of your leadership legacy?

Design a leadership brand using only two sentences. The initial sentence focuses on *who you are* and the second on *how you can serve others*. The more clear and consistent you are, the more influential your leadership brand. Your brand becomes what people recall when they think of you. Therefore, define it well and promote it enthusiastically as it is fundamental to gaining followers. A general template for designing a personal brand statement is provided here:

"I want to be known for being _____ so I can _____."

Here are two examples of personal brand statements. Which one do you prefer?

- I want to be known for being *passionate about finding the hidden potential in people* so I can *challenge others to accomplish tasks beyond their expectations.*

- I want to be known for being *innovative, respectful, and supportive* so I can *deliver results for my employer, colleagues, and work teams.*

Skill Builder Activity

Establish (or Revise) Your Social Profile on the Internet

Having a leadership brand is not sufficient. Gaining credibility as a leader requires you to make your brand known to others in your profession. Establishing a social profile using the Internet and other social media assists in gaining credibility among followers. Leadership is about connecting with others on a personal level. Followers generally want to know as much as they can about their leaders.

Design Your Profile—What key words describe who you are?

Design a Strategy—What social media are you comfortable with using?

Design a Support Team—Who can assist you in putting together an attractive profile? With whom do you want to associate on your profile?

Design a Charismatic Theme—What phrase or label can you use to quickly describe your style?

A profile where followers can readily access information about your leadership can help start relationships that result in productive collaborative arrangements. Examples of how leaders have used social media to reinforce their leadership brands are A. G. Lafley of Procter & Gamble with his *in touch* brand, Samuel Palmisano of IBM with his *integration of strengths* brand, and finally, Terry Kelly of W. L. Gore & Associates *encouraging feelings of self worth* brand.[53]

4

Your Values and Ethical Actions

It is only by tracing things to their origin that we can gain rightful ideas of them, and it is by gaining such ideas that we discover the boundary that divides right from wrong.

—Thomas Paine, Agrarian Justice, 1797

Learning Objectives

4.1 Examine ethical issues that directly impact the student experience

4.2 Define and identify key foundational ideas important to ethical leadership

4.3 Recognize the roots and leadership implications of moral development

4.4 Examine and assess the ethical challenges of leadership

4.5 Design your personal approach to ethical leadership

Detailed Chapter Outline

Introduction

Ethical Issues and the Student
  Experience

Ethics—The Key Concepts

Ethics/Code of Ethics

  Moral Principles

  Virtues

  Personal Values

Character

Integrity

Laws

The Roots of Moral
  Development

  Parents and Family

  K-12 Education

  College/University

Leadership by Design Model

DESIGN SELF

HOW CAN I DESIGN MYSELF AS A LEADER?

Design Relationships

As a leader, how can I design my relationships with others?

Design Others' Success

As a leader, how can I design success for others?

Design Culture

As a leader, how can I design the culture of my organization?

Design Future

As a leader, how can I innovate?

Introduction

At the heart of effective leadership is a strong sense of self and the values that guide the leader's work. Alignment between expressed values and actions is paramount when working with others. Individuals who align values and actions not only serve as role models for others, they build trust and credibility—some of the most important ingredients for leadership. This chapter helps you better understand the importance of ethical and moral leadership, highlights values-based challenges inherent in leading others, and provides tools to help you navigate ethical dilemmas in your own life and further design your leadership.

Leadership scholar and historian James MacGregor Burns wrote, "Leadership is morally purposeful."[1] How do you design your leadership to be ethical? Recall that leadership is the process of influencing others toward a common vision. Ethics is an area of study that is concerned with right or wrong behavior, and every word within the aforementioned definition contains ethical implications: the decisions you make and the behaviors you take. Ethical decision-making is about how one makes decisions as well as to what end, their course of action deemed right or wrong. When it comes to leadership, the end goal or *common vision* should leave others feeling like partners in designing a better future.

Leadership can be positional and non-positional. In other words, you can step in and out of leadership with a great deal of fluidity. As a group member, you may work to influence the group toward an ethical end without having any authority whatsoever. The key word is *influence*. You have an opportunity to engage in the process of influencing others toward a common vision multiple times every day, and the decisions you make come with the underlying decision about whether to follow your values and engage in ethical behavior . . . or not.

To *design* an ethical or moral approach to leadership (and followership), you first need to have a clear understanding of some key terminology. Once you have a baseline understanding of the core terms and ideas, it is important to ground yourself by having great clarity on your values, perspectives, and positions on important issues. Also, understanding the attributes of toxic or bad leadership helps further clarify what is, and is not, ethical. Each of you has faced ethical dilemmas as a student, and this will continue throughout your adult life. How will you work through those issues? In the end, each of you will have to decide your *true north*, which former Medtronic CEO Bill George describes as "the internal compass that guides you successfully through life."[2]

Ethical issues consist of many perspectives and are rarely simple, clear, or objective. The right decision often exists in the eye of the beholder. Fierce clarity about your view is critical to your leadership success. It is ultimately up to you to determine who you will be as a student, spouse, child, sibling, employee, and leader. If you are involved, engaged, and active in organizational life, your ethical decision-making will be tested on multiple occasions. You might consider these opportunities for practice and growth and having a solid base of self-awareness to work from will maximize your learning.

LEADERSHIP THAT MAKES A DIFFERENCE

In 1998, a 6-year-old Canadian named Ryan Hreljac learned that there are people in the world without clean water. What started as a goal to raise $70 for a school project turned into an organization that has helped more than 1 million people in 16 different countries around the world.[3] Because of Ryan's efforts, these people have access to clean drinking water—what many would consider a fundamental human right. Fifteen years after its founding, Ryan's Well Foundation has dug more than 1000 wells.[4] Ryan has designed his life and professional career in alignment with the moral values of commitment to something higher than himself, with respect and caring for others. In addition, his efforts serve as a model for the virtues of charity, diligence, patience, kindness, and humility. It is important to note that no one appointed Ryan *leader*—he found a way to make a difference in the lives of others and took action. In the process, he has influenced thousands to make a difference as well.

Ethical Issues and the Student Experience

Learning Objective

4.1 Examine ethical issues that directly impact the student experience

Some of you reading may not see how this topic applies to you. Moral and ethical issues seem like the stuff of classroom discussions, case studies, and corporate drama. What is fascinating is that much like corporate life, the collegiate context is filled with moral dilemmas. In fact, when you become more in tune with what is happening around you, you will begin to see multiple situations that require your attention every week. Here are a few hypothetical examples of ethical scenarios that you may have come across. Take a moment to consider your immediate answer to each. What should you do in each case? What would you do . . . especially if no one was looking or would find out? Then consider what other perspectives one might take on the matter. Choose one example that intrigues you. Discuss it with a friend, and note what values inform their perspective.

Rosario is a member of the hockey team. As a second-year member, this is his first time *on the other side*, part of the *in* group of veteran players. While he joined a successful team on every conceivable metric, the team has a culture of hazing, and he is feeling pressured to participate in activities that do not feel right. In fact, they are dangerous, and he feels uncomfortable even being involved. Rather than address his concerns with the team, he finds reasons to miss *newbie* activities and feels better that he does not actively participate. He wishes he knew how to convince his teammates that what was happening violated campus policy and was illegal, and the press would have a hay day if the activities were discovered. He does not want to be associated with such behavior but does not know what to do. How should he intervene?

MYTH OR REALITY?

I DON'T HAVE THE TITLE, I CAN'T MAKE A DIFFERENCE.

Myth . . . and Reality. Throughout this text, leadership is described as positional *and* non-positional. Every day, men and women without a title or formal position (e.g., the story of Ryan Hreljac at the beginning of this chapter) influence others toward a common vision and make great change in the world. Under normal circumstances, *you do not* have to have a title to make a difference. However, to say that this is an absolute would also be false. Of course, there are situations and contexts where a title or formal power can help greatly.

Jeff is a third-year undergraduate biology major. Getting into a top medical school has been a goal of his (and his parents) for as long as he can remember. But in recent months, he has been having second thoughts. The work is not exciting, and he finds himself working on anything but his coursework. He is behind and feeling desperate. He knows that his grades and test scores will have a major impact on his options. Likewise, he knows that if he does not bring home a 4.0 GPA, his parents will be disappointed and angry. Rather than put in the time to earn the grades, he has been focusing on how he can beat the system. In recent months, he has identified and used some unethical resources to circumvent the system (i.e., websites, technology, etc.) so he can keep up the façade. He knows what he is doing could get him kicked out of school, but he is so far behind at this point, he does not have many options. How does he unravel himself from the situation he created?

REFLECTION QUESTIONS

When was the last time you witnessed or engaged in cheating behavior? What action did you take—if any?

Marissa just witnessed one of her small group members cheat on multiple exams. Every part of her wants to bring this behavior to the attention of the professor, but she cannot bring herself to tell him. What if the cheater, Peter, finds out that it was her? Quite honestly, she does not want to deal with the potential drama of outing her classmate. However, she has become more and more agitated as he seems to move farther and farther ahead of her. People like Peter unfairly skew the curve, and the behavior has an impact on her grades. How should Marissa proceed?

Jamal is your best friend. The two of you went out to celebrate your birthday, and it has been a long night. Both of you have had more than your share of alcohol, and it is time to head home. Even though he is well above the legal limit, he is dead set on driving home. You have done all you can to persuade him not to drive, but he does not want to leave his car downtown overnight. You decide to take a hard stand and call a cab, and he has become more and more agitated. He starts calling you names and is making more and more of a scene. You know you could overpower him and take his keys, but he may become more and more physical. What do you do?

Juana is the recently elected president of the student government association (SGA) and one of your closest friends. In fact, you helped her get elected, and she was instrumental in helping you secure a Senate seat. In passing, you have noticed that she has been making some unilateral decisions that probably have not been discussed with others on her team. While it is likely no one will see, unilaterally allocating money to specific organizations and intentionally keeping others in the dark is becoming standard practice. In fact, she is highly skilled at not inviting key stakeholders that may stand in the way of her vision. When you bring it up, she becomes defensive and lashes out. What are your options moving forward?

If these examples are not enough to convince you that ethics should be a critical part of your leadership design, you might consider a real-world finding. When asked to choose the 15 most essential leadership competencies from a list of 74, leaders from across the world in over 30 different global organizations selected "has high ethical and moral standards" as one of the most important attributes—far more than most other competencies.[5] This finding, in conjunction with the other most important competencies listed, amounts to the importance of creating a safe and trusting environment. While morals and ethics seem to be an individual concern, the reality is that behavior shapes culture, which, in turn, influences both what followers expect and how they work with you.

Ethics—The Key Concepts

Learning Objective

4.2 Define and identify key foundational ideas important to ethical leadership

As you begin to think about how you would navigate some of the scenarios described in the previous section, understanding some key terminology is helpful. Like many other topics, ethics suffers from a lack of clarity around even the most common terms. While scholars may have clarity, most students do not; they end up using terms and concepts synonymously. As a result, the topic can be confusing and the application less effective.

Ethics/Code of Ethics

Ethics is an area of study that is concerned with codifying and defending right or wrong behavior in multiple contexts. Thus, a **code of ethics** is often a document that seeks to clarify right or wrong behavior in a profession or organization. For instance, there is a nursing code of ethics, a code of ethics for social workers, and even a code of ethics for librarians.

Ethics
an area of study that is concerned with codifying and defending right or wrong behavior in multiple contexts

Code of ethics
often a document that seeks to clarify right or wrong behavior in a profession or organization

REFLECTION QUESTIONS

Should there be a code of ethics for leaders? What would your leadership code of ethics say is right and wrong behavior?

Moral Principles

Each code of ethics will highlight several behaviors that have been deemed universal—these are **moral principles**. Moral principles are *truths* about behaviors that have been widely accepted and adopted by individuals, groups, and societies. It is important to note that moral principles held by one group of individuals may not be held in such high regard by others. For example, the Universal Declaration of Human Rights adopted by many countries in 1948 works to codify acceptable and universal norms of behavior such as, "All human beings are born free and equal in dignity and rights. They are endowed with reason and conscience and should act towards one another in a spirit of brotherhood."[6] Some countries who have not signed the document may not see this as a moral principle.

Another moral principle highlighted in the Code of Ethics of the American Medical Association states, "A physician shall be dedicated to providing competent medical care, with compassion and respect for human dignity and rights."[7] Other examples of moral principles may include "Do good, avoid evil; Do unto others as you would have them do unto you (The Golden Rule); The end does not justify the means; Follow what nature intends;"[8] as well as those such as committing to something greater than oneself and caring for other living things and the environment.[9] In essence, moral principles are the philosophies upon which everything else is built. For instance, if the United States is built on the moral principle that "all men are created equal," it must follow through on this expressed principle. The fact that the United States *was not* living this principle was a foundation of Martin Luther King, Jr.'s *I Have a Dream* speech.

> "I have a dream that one day this nation will rise up and live out the true meaning of its creed: 'We hold these truths to be self-evident: that all men are created equal.'"[10]

Virtues

Virtues are concerned with *living* the moral code. These are often referred to as morally good traits, behaviors, and/or habits that determine an individual's character. Virtues are practiced and are often a mean between two extremes (see Figure 4.1). Virtues are not about what is right or wrong, but what a person *should* be. If the United States has a moral principle that "all men are created equal" then a virtuous man or woman would *act* in alignment with this statement. He or she would potentially practice the virtues of respect and justice. It should be noted that there is overlap between principles and virtues.

Thus, the real-world way of living your moral principles is by outlining and practicing your identified virtues. For some of you reading this text, you may choose to follow the thinking of others, such as Plato's four cardinal virtues—wisdom, justice, temperance, courage.[11] For others, you may choose your religion as a source. For example, in Christianity, the seven heavenly virtues are wisdom, justice, temperance, courage, faith, hope, charity (love).[12] Regardless of how you choose the virtues to practice, the fact that you are intentionally working to develop your virtuous activity is a worthwhile endeavor.

Aristotle first developed the deficiency/excess spectrum.[13] The Virtue Continuum (Figure 4.1) communicates the concept of virtue on this spectrum (in this example through the lens of servant leadership; you will learn more about servant leadership in Chapter 13: Creating a Culture That Cares). The key point for Aristotle in highlighting this continuum is to assert that it takes practical wisdom (phronesis) to determine the *golden mean* (i.e., a desirable middle ground). For instance, sometimes selfishness can be helpful and is the right thing to do. For example, every airline instructs that in the event of cabin pressure loss, you should secure your oxygen mask first, and then help others. This seems pretty selfish at first, but if you pass out because you are trying to help others first, everyone loses. The key is thoughtful intentionality. Intentionality allows the individual to *choose* the correct place on the spectrum more consciously. As you design your leadership, do you carefully consider the *golden* balance?

Moral principles
principles deemed *correct* or *incorrect* by individuals, groups, and societies

Virtues
a continuum of traits, behaviors, and/or habits

FIGURE 4.1 ● The Virtue Continuum: Examples of the Deficiency to Excess Spectrum

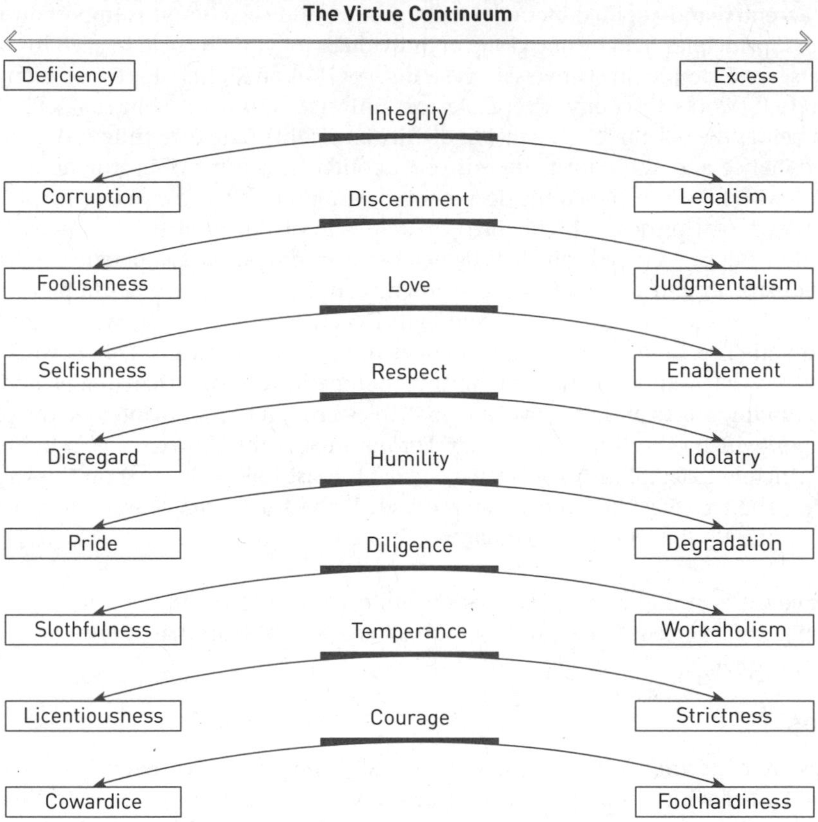

The Virtue Continuum

Deficiency		Excess

Integrity

| Corruption | Discernment | Legalism |

| Foolishness | Love | Judgmentalism |

| Selfishness | Respect | Enablement |

| Disregard | Humility | Idolatry |

| Pride | Diligence | Degradation |

| Slothfulness | Temperance | Workaholism |

| Licentiousness | Courage | Strictness |

| Cowardice | | Foolhardiness |

Source: Lanctot, J. D., & Irving, J. A. (2007). *Character and leadership: Situating servant leadership in a proposed virtues framework.* Retrieved from http://www.regent.edu/acad/global/publications/sl_proceedings/2007/lanctot-irving.pdf.

Practicing one's virtues helps an individual actively design their living moral principles or code. A common phrase is that "patience is a virtue." In other words, patience takes practice. For many of us, it takes intentional and deliberate work to master the virtue of patience. The American inventor and author Ben Franklin famously adopted 13 virtues[14] that he revisited on a *daily* basis. While his definitions of each virtue may not be academic sounding, they accurately describe his intentions. His areas of work for which, in the beginning, he struggled are listed below.

Franklin's 13 Virtues[15]

1. Temperance. Eat not to dullness; drink not to elevation.

2. Silence. Speak not but what may benefit others or yourself; avoid trifling conversation.

3. Order. Let all your things have their places; let each part of your business have its time.

4. Resolution. Resolve to perform what you ought; perform without fail what you resolve.

5. Frugality. Make no expense but to do good to others or yourself; i.e., waste nothing.

6. Industry. Lose no time; be always employ'd in something useful; cut off all unnecessary actions.

7. Sincerity. Use no hurtful deceit; think innocently and justly, and, if you speak, speak accordingly.

8. Justice. Wrong none by doing injuries or omitting the benefits that are your duty.

9. Moderation. Avoid extremes; forbear resenting injuries so much as you think they deserve.

10. Cleanliness. Tolerate no uncleanliness in body, clothes, or habitation.

11. Tranquility. Be not disturbed at trifles, or at accidents common or unavoidable.

12. Chastity. Rarely use venery but for health or offspring, never to dullness, weakness, or the injury of your own or another's peace or reputation.

13. Humility. Imitate Jesus and Socrates.

REFLECTION QUESTIONS

Which of Franklin's virtues do you find meaningful and important? Which are not very important? Why?

Personal Values

Personal values are what you find personally essential or of some *worth*. Even if you aren't aware of them or have not named them, values drive behavior. Many of your values are only visible through your behavior. You are conscious of some values, but others are not easily named or understood. Pay close attention to your behavior, and you will have a better understanding of your values—healthy and unhealthy. You could value your car, your social status, family, your wardrobe, or financial independence. Likewise, you could value "taking care of number one," but at an extreme, this may not be viewed as moral and/or virtuous. Visit https://corevalueslist.com for a list of 500 core values.

Personal values
beliefs or ideals that guide a person's behavior; what you find *personally* important or of some *worth*

Character

In essence, all of these concepts lead to an individual's **character**, which can indicate elements such as virtues, moral principles, and values. Hazing, cheating, stealing, lying, or treating another poorly could lead to being perceived as having weak moral character.

Character
the moral qualities of an individual

Integrity

The secondary definition of integrity describes something as having the condition of being whole, undivided, unified, and sound. When applied to a person, having **integrity** is often associated with having strong moral character and assumes alignment of one's word to deed. These may be promises we make to ourselves or others depending on the situation. When you as a leader are whole, the values on the inside show up as behaviors on the outside.

Integrity
having strong moral character; assumes alignment of word to deed

LEADERSHIP BY DESIGN

©iStock.com/Drazen_

STORYTELLING

Design Principle: Storytelling

Definition: A method of creating imagery, emotions, and understanding of events through an interaction between a storyteller and an audience. The elements of story typically consist of Setting, Characters, Plot, Theme, and Mood.

In Other Words: Once upon a time . . . somewhere . . . something really interesting happened . . . and they lived happily ever after.

For Example: Consider all the fun, interesting stories that also left you with a lesson: *The Little Engine That Could*, *The Three Little Pigs*, and so forth. Which stories immediately come to mind for you? Or consider more personal stories, such as how your grandparents started from nothing, the day you met that best friend, or that teacher who made a difference for you. All of those stories communicate values.

For Leaders: "Tell me a little about yourself" is one of the most common yet mystifying interview questions. Incorporating storytelling into your response illustrates a strong sense of self-design. Who are you? Use elements of storytelling to help highlight and demonstrate your values. Who are you, as a character in your story? What is your setting, and how do the aforementioned elements tie into the plot? Think to yourself, how can I as a leader better design myself so I can engage in the art of storytelling when necessary? How can I help other people read my personal road map?

Laws

Laws
rules developed by a social institution (e.g., state or nation) that govern correct behavior

Finally, **laws** are rules developed by a social institution (e.g., state or nation) that govern correct behavior. An act can be legal but not ethical, moral, or virtuous (e.g., cheating on your boyfriend or girlfriend). Conversely, you may break the law but still act within your values (for example, driving over the speed limit to get someone to the hospital). As a result, some values are legal, ethical, moral, and virtuous, while some are not—you can be immoral and still be following your values.

TABLE 4.1 ● Key Definitions and Questions			
	Definition	**Key Question**	**Key Question**
Moral Principles	Principles deemed correct or incorrect by individuals, groups, and societies	What moral principles underpin the major religions?	Can you identify moral principles that in hindsight were deemed immoral and/or illegal?
Virtues	A continuum of traits, behaviors, and/or habits	What are the opposite virtues associated with the seven deadly sins?	Which of Franklin's virtues intrigue you the most?

	Definition	Key Question	Key Question
Integrity	Of strong moral character	Can one lack moral character and have integrity?	Can you think of an organization that lacks integrity?
Character	The moral qualities of an individual	Are you perceived as an individual of strong character?	Which of your personal values may conflict with your objective of being known as an individual of strong character?
Personal Values	What you find *personally* important or of some *worth*	Can an individual value good looks?	Can personal values be immoral?
Laws	Rules developed by a social institution (e.g., state or nation) that govern correct behavior	Thinking globally, can you identify a law that is immoral?	Can an act be legal but immoral?

REFLECTION QUESTIONS

- What does your online persona say about your character? Look at the list of virtues in the Skill Builder Activity and see which words do and do not align.

- What are examples of personal values you hold that could be perceived by others as immoral or lacking virtue? How could these values damage your character? Look to your behavior(s) for clues.

- What are the triggers that cause you to act in an immoral manner? Alcohol? Greed? Pride? Pressure? Ego?

- What virtues and moral principles were modeled for you in your home growing up? How about your community and school? How did your environment impact who you are today?

- Realizing that everyone is a *work in progress*, what does version "You 2.0" look and act like when it comes to this topic? Who or what will help you live a more virtuous life?

The Roots of Moral Development

Learning Objective

4.3 Recognize the roots and leadership implications of moral development

Parents and Family

So where do your moral principles, virtues, and personal values come from? Few would deny that your parents/primary caregivers and immediate family have a significant influence on character development. Good character "consists of knowing the good, desiring the good, and doing the good."[16] In those critical early years, it is these people who model right and wrong. The literature in this realm of research is quite fascinating. As you read the following passage, reflect on your own experiences. Do they align with the research?

Parents who were responsive to children's signals and needs and had a warm, loving relationship with their children produced children of strong, multifaceted character. Families who used an open, democratic style of family discussion, decision-making, and problem-solving produced children who exhibited five characteristics (compliance, self-esteem, conscience, moral reasoning, and altruism—all but empathy, self-control, and social orientation). Parents who used *induction* (praising or disciplining with explanations that include a focus on the consequences of the child's behavior for others' feelings) produced children with relatively more mature empathy, conscience, altruism and moral reasoning. Parents who set high expectations (*demandingness*) that were attainable and supported, had children who were high in self-control, altruism, and self-esteem. Parents who *modeled* self-control and altruism had children high in self-control and altruism.[17]

K-12 Education

Along with your parents, early childhood and your school experience have an important impact on character development. In his article, *The Science of Character Education*, Berkowitz highlights several findings based on the character education literature. First, the quality of relationships in the child's life matters. Said relationships need to be "benevolent (nurturant, supportive), authentic (honest, open), respectful (inclusive, valuing the student's voice), and consistent (predictable, stable)."[18] Second, the child's environment is critical because they are learning about right and wrong based on what they observe. As a result, it is critical to pay attention to how people are treating one another in the child's presence. Clear, yet realistic and attainable, expectations is the third ingredient. By setting the bar realistically high, a child can build their efficacy and esteem. A fourth ingredient is communicating the importance of strong character. Students who engage in activities that allow them a chance to practice good character is the fifth ingredient. According to Berkowitz, students need "schools that promote student autonomy and influence. They need the opportunity to build skills such as perspective-taking, critical thinking, and conflict resolution, necessary for being a person of character."[19] One type of practice may be opportunities to debate, reflect, and view multiple perspectives on critical issues.

College/University

The ongoing design of your character is happening even now. In their research on character development and college students, Kuh and Umbach found that the collegiate experience can accentuate an individual's character development.[20] Another study found that students who engage in volunteerism in high school showed the most amount of significant growth in college.[21] Opportunities to expand one's horizons in and out of the classroom correlate strongly with character development (e.g., academically, socially, culturally).[22] Opportunities for students to engage with people unlike themselves (e.g., political views, religion, ethnicity) also had a positive impact on students. In fact, roughly 60% of respondents reported that the collegiate experience helped shape their ethical code.[23] Learning about and developing your moral and ethical self continue through life, but this happens only if you mindfully engage, recognize your value-driven behavior, and strive to be the leader you want to be.

The Ethical Challenges of Leadership

Learning Objective

4.4 Examine and assess the ethical challenges of leadership

Ethical Issues in Five Domains

In essence, your parents, your teachers, and your community have been training you on what is, and is not, moral behavior from the time you were a baby. And while you may think that ethical decision-making is an academic topic, relegated to political and organizational leaders, nothing could be further from the truth. In fact, as a student, each of you has more than likely encountered an ethical dilemma in the last couple days. Regardless of age, country of origin, or economic status, ethical issues for an average student occur in five primary domains.

1. The academic domain (e.g., the classroom, group projects)

2. The family domain (e.g., parents, children, siblings, extended family)

3. The work domain (e.g., jobs, internships, co-op)

4. The extracurricular domain (e.g., activities, athletics, community)

5. The friendship domain (e.g., classmates, peers)

In the classroom, the most common ethical issues involve academic dishonesty (e.g., cheating, plagiarism). In families, ethical issues often present themselves as keeping secrets, end-of-life decision-making for loved ones, or issues of fairness and equity. In the work domain, ethical problems usually have to do with individual and group decision-making around money (e.g., expense reports, spending), human resources (e.g., layoffs, hiring), and strategy (e.g., legal vs. moral, environmental impact, ensuring growth/profit). Ethical issues in the extracurricular domain are similar to others because they involve topics such as equity/fairness (e.g., who is or is not included), dishonest behavior (e.g., cheating to win), and day-to-day politics of organizational life (e.g., popularity, power, access to resources). The friendship domain can be particularly challenging to navigate because it involves close-knit social circles (e.g., groups of friends) with their norms of what is, and is not, appropriate behavior (e.g., drug use, drinking and driving, treatment of significant others).

You are also embedded in a broader context. Each community, state/province, and nation also faces ethical dilemmas and issues that are rarely simple. They often involve multiple competing commitments that do not always lead to a clear resolution. For instance, between 2015 and 2017, the United States and other countries around the world struggled with the question of allowing Syrian immigrants into their country. In essence, the country's leaders were struggling with the competing commitments of inclusion and security. How leaders at the community, state, national, and global levels address issues such as terrorism, individual privacy, climate change, and trade have significant ramifications for their citizens.

REFLECTION QUESTION

Which of the five domains prove the most challenging for you to navigate ethically?

LEADERSHIP BY DESIGN

Design Principle: Propositional Density

Definition: The relationship between the aspects of a design and their meaning. Designs with high propositional density are more interesting and memorable than designs with low propositional density. "If your propositional density is below one, you probably have superfluous, merely decorative elements in your design, which do not add to the deep reading."[24]

In Other Words: It is better to create something simple with deep meaning, rather than something with many superficial messages.

For Example: Symbolism in literature is a textual form of high propositional density; the author

is conveying multiple meanings in a single written component.

For Leaders: A leader can use the concept of propositional density to think about his or her values as elements and their actions as the meaning they convey. What is the relationship between what leaders do and what they *say* they will do? Successfully designing relationships means putting forth thought, energy, and effort to create the desired effect. A high propositional density makes relationships engaging and memorable. Increased engagement and meaningful values lead to stronger relationships. As a leader, how can you foster relationships that have the most impact?

Why Individuals Fail to Behave Ethically

Decision-action gap
That space between deciding what you *should* do and actually *doing it*, which exists when an individual or group knows what the correct course of action should be, but struggles to make the *right* or *best* decision.

It is a rare human being who has not fallen victim to the **Decision-Action Gap**[25]—that space between deciding what you should do and doing it. According to the Air Force Academy's research, there are two primary reasons for this phenomenon—the individual succumbs to the challenge (e.g., pressures, fears/doubts) and/or the individual lacks the necessary character strengths (e.g., courage, self-discipline, resilience).[26] Other reasons may be that the individual simply lacks awareness that they are involved in an ethical dilemma or lacks the skills to navigate the situation successfully.[27] Interestingly, characteristics of the issue at hand may also affect an individual's willingness to follow through on an ethical decision. For instance, there may be varied levels of perceived moral intensity (the degree to which the individual sees an issue as an ethical dilemma).[28] For example, one individual may not feel that drinking and driving is a significant offense, while others will perceive it as such. Another factor could be that the individual may be a victim of moral disengagement, which means that they lack ownership.[29] Moral disengagement "explains why otherwise normal people can engage in unethical behavior without apparent guilt or self-censure" (e.g., hazing).[30] A lack of moral ownership will also stall action.[31] If an individual does not feel ownership for acting (e.g., curing hunger in a developing nation), it is unlikely they will engage.

So why do student leaders fail to act ethically? According to Schwartz,[32] the literature points to six possible reasons (of course there are others). As you read each reason in Table 4.2, reflect on when and where you have experienced each over the course of your time in school.

REFLECTION QUESTION

When was the last time you fell victim to one of the reasons listed above?

TABLE 4.2 ● Schwartz's Six Reasons for Unethical Behavior	
Reason for Failing to Act Ethically	**Example**
Performance pressure (us vs. them; winning at all costs)	An individual who gets so caught up in *winning* that they sidestep the rules or lose sight of their values. For instance, a college athlete takes performance-enhancing drugs to gain an advantage.
Threats to self-efficacy (pressure to be successful)	Students who feel pressure to achieve a particular score or obtain a specific grade to be successful. For instance, a student cheats on a final exam because they need an *A* for their graduate school application.
Decision-making autonomy (nobody will find out)	The threat of being caught is low, and the perceived *gain* is enough to take the risk. For instance, a group of resident advisors violates the hall's policy on drugs because students have not yet moved in.
Interpersonal conflicts (who cares?)	An individual fails to do what is correct or *right* out of spite toward another. For instance, a faction of members does not attend the organization's philanthropy because they dislike the coordinator—they do not want her to succeed.
Bias (friends help friends)	An individual sidesteps the routine *process* because of a relationship with the decision maker. For instance, although many qualified individuals applied, a student supervisor only interviews his friends for a position on campus.
Managing important relationships (wink-wink)	An individual in authority overlooks a rule or requirement to avoid conflict or keep a relationship intact. For instance, a professor lets a favorite student slide on the attendance policy but not others.

Toxic and Bad Leaders and Leadership

Unfortunately, not all human beings are moral and virtuous—nor do they navigate the previously mentioned challenges in an effective manner. Whether it is a fraternity man hazing new members, an athlete accepting unapproved services and gifts, or a student leader intentionally keeping key players *out of the loop*, all are shades of what could be called toxic leadership. According to Jean Lipman-Blumen, toxic leaders are "individuals who, by virtue of their destructive behaviours and their dysfunctional personal qualities or characteristics, inflict serious and enduring harm on the individuals, groups, organizations, communities and even the nations that they lead."[33]

Men and women with power and authority have done unimaginable damage to the lives of others. Distinguishing between toxic/bad leaders and ineffective leaders is essential. We witness *ineffective* leadership each day. For instance, an athletic coach who does not achieve results on the field, an organization that does not meet its quarterly numbers, or a student leader who fails to lead his organization to success. While ineffective leadership is not desirable, it is also not surprising. Remember, leadership is a process, and sometimes that process includes setbacks that offer new opportunities to learn and reposition activities. High performance and effective leadership is usually the result of many adjustments, realignments, and lessons learned as an organization grows, pivots to meet new demands, or rebuilds after a difficult challenge. Ineffective leadership is also a part of any leader's growth and development. Failure is inherent in leadership.

So, what distinguishes toxic/bad leadership from ineffective leadership? Keywords and phrases, such as "dysfunctional personal qualities or characteristics" and "inflict serious and enduring harm," provide guidance. Under normal circumstances, a good individual with moderately poor results would not be deemed *toxic* by most. A team captain who is physically abusing freshmen team members or a student leader diminishing the financial health of a student organization for personal gain is another story. However, a challenge with this conversation is that one person's toxic leader may be another's heroic leader (e.g., the names Donald Trump and Barack Obama will likely yield strong reactions at the dinner table depending on your family's political persuasion).[34]

Recall again the definition of leadership—the process of influencing others toward a common vision. Embedded in the definition is the sense that followers have a choice and have a voice in what constitutes common vision. Choice and voice are two words that one must keep in mind when exploring the topic of toxic leadership. In the case of toxic leadership, it is often the case that one or both of these are missing, and the leader and/or a small group of individuals holds power—often left unchecked. The *others* in the definition (e.g., group, organization, team members, citizens, employees) lack voice and choice. Because of this reality, horrible atrocities are happening across the globe as you read this text.

Toxic leaders present themselves in many ways, and various types of toxic leaders have been identified (see the work of Barbara Kellerman or Jean Lipman-Blumen). While not to the extreme of some of the examples explored in this chapter, it is likely that you have and/or will encounter the various shades of toxic leadership at some point in your career. Toxic leadership has a lot to do with the leader's intent. While you may disagree with the policies of President Donald Trump or former President Barack Obama, as long as they are honest and allowing voice and choice, their perspectives can be viewed as well intentioned. However, each of us may have strong feelings around topics such as the war in Iraq, gun control, the Affordable Care Act, the Patriot Act, and Islamic State of Iraq and Syria (ISIS). These intense feelings often translate into perceiving a leader as toxic or bad. Likewise, if the leader's well-intended actions fail (e.g., had Abraham Lincoln lost the Civil War), you may perceive it as bad or toxic leadership. As a thoughtful leader, and follower, you must be able to mentally separate leadership behaviors that stifle voice or choice, or have harmful intentions, from those behaviors that merely differ from your values or ideas.

A starting point to determine if an individual is toxic is to view the individual and their actions through the filters of voice, choice, and intent. Some simple questions around each of these may include:

Voice—Did the leader actively work to eliminate the voice of the people (in particular, people who may have disagreed)? Did he or she do so by fear, intimidation, and force? Were dissenting voices actively suppressed?

Choice—Did the leader actively work to eliminate the choice of the people? In particular, were others stuck with this individual and forced to adhere? Did the leader act with the best interest of the followers in mind?

Intent—Did the leader have the best intentions of the people/followers in mind? Did the leader and his/her followers work in alignment with generally accepted moral and ethical behavior? Did the leader lie, deceive, or cheat? Was he or she trying to protect power, authority, or wealth?

Courageous Followers and Dissent

In the face of the challenges and difficulties mentioned in the previous section, followers are often on the receiving end of toxic leadership. Sometimes designing your leadership means first designing yourself as an active follower and having to confront or address the bad behavior. Everyone is a follower at one time or another. As introduced in Chapter 3 (see the *Experts Beyond the Text* feature), effective followership is every bit as important to your development and success as a leader. When considering followership, Chaleff notes a few key ideas:

- Follower is a role assumed at various times when working collaboratively.

- A follower shares responsibility for a common purpose with a leader, wants the activity to succeed, and works towards this end.

- In hierarchies, followers usually accept direction from formal leaders while influencing them to make choices that serve the common purpose better.

- Followers can dissent or can withdraw support from leadership actions they feel are not serving the common purpose well.[35]

Followers construct their role in different ways. Carsten, Uhl-Bien, West, Patera, and McGregor found that these roles often comprised three general categories: passive, active, and proactive. At one end of the followership schema, *passive* followers were more likely to do what the leader wanted, displaying deference to the leader. *Active* followers sought to play a larger part in decision-making but only when leaders included them. At the other end of the followership schema, *proactive* followers wanted ownership in the endeavor: "Active and proactive followers emphasized the importance of constructively challenging their leaders and voicing ideas or concerns. Moreover, proactive followers identified blind obedience as a behavior that was associated with ineffective followership."[36] Likewise, followers who romanticize the leader and view their role as subservient are more likely to follow through on unethical requests.[37]

Pioneering scholars on the topic, Robert Kelley[38] and Ira Challeff,[39] have identified several follower styles that can help you better understand the choice you have when determining which role you would like to play as a follower. Summarizing the work of Kelley and Challeff, followers often take on the following styles: Partner, Individualist, Implementer, and Resource/Sheep.

The ideal style of followers for achieving a shared vision is that of Partner. An expressed goal of every leader should be to develop a team of engaged followers who feel like partners in the process of moving toward the common vision.[40] Recall from Chapter 1 that engagement is the degree of individual involvement, investment, and enthusiasm. Creating an environment where people feel and act like partners is challenging work. The leader must give away some of his or her authority and open themselves up to the thoughts and perspectives of others. By doing so, followers will *feel* engaged and work far above and beyond what they may typically give.

Men and women who do not feel that they are engaged as partners, but rather are outsiders with a slightly different vision or perspective than the leader, play the role of Individualist. Individualists are often openly opposed to the direction of the leader/group, but at times, they may be silent about their opposition. Individualists can play an essential role on teams—they can keep the group in check and help the team avoid groupthink. By playing a *devil's advocate* role, the individualist helps a group explore multiple options before moving forward. However, taken to an extreme, an individual playing this role may damage group dynamics or marginalize themselves if they cannot separate their opinion from the desires of the group.

A third style that followers play is that of an implementer. Implementers consistently *fall in line* with the leader and support them in their endeavors—they are conformists or *yes* people. As with the other styles, context matters as to when this approach is, or is not, appropriate. In one sense, everyone needs to fall into this approach from time to time. If the stakes are low, and you authentically agree with the direction, you can comfortably fall in line to support the leader. However, blindly following a leader in all instances can be dangerous and destructive. History's toxic leaders (e.g., Joseph Stalin, Jim Jones, William Aramony) needed implementers to enact their visions.

A fourth follower style is Resource/Sheep. These individuals function as a *pair of hands* and will likely do whatever they are told. In many ways, they are indifferent. They are not partners, will not speak up, and will rarely take the initiative or implement anything. They merely follow instructions and do as they are told. At times, it may seem contextually appropriate for you to serve as a resource; however, the best followers are those who are mindful of what they are doing and why.

In summary, followership takes courage. It takes an exceptional amount of courage to intervene. In each case, followers logically know that something should be done, but the challenge lies in the decision-action gap—that space between deciding what you *should* do and actually *doing it.*[41]

REFLECTION QUESTION

What is the followership role that you most often assume?

Designing Your Ethical Leadership

Learning Objective

4.5 Design your personal approach to ethical leadership

Ethical Decision-Making

Are you ethically fit? Athletes, musicians, and other performers put in a great deal of training and practice before the big event. How often do you consider the ethical dimensions of decisions you make, much less practice? As noted, your family, faith, school, and culture have shaped who you are and the values you hold. Have you considered the different dimensions of those values and their importance? How often do you recognize that your behavior has been influenced by one of those values? What can you do to develop and maintain your ethical fitness?[42]

For leaders and followers alike, ethics is more than analyzing all the sides of a situation. Leaders make decisions (even the decision to *not make a decision* is a decision). Hence, the term ethical decision-making involves acting on what you believe to be right or wrong in a situation—do I take part in hazing? Cheat on the exam? Cheat on my girlfriend? Drive drunk? Buy alcohol for underage friends? Misreport the expense report? Withhold critical information from my supervisor? In fact, the examples just provided are relatively straightforward examples of what students on college campuses face. And it is reasonably clear what the right or correct course of action would be in each instance. However, even though you know turning in a peer for cheating would be the right course of action, it can be challenging to act—this is the decision-action gap introduced earlier. Clarity about your values and vision of self is tantamount to ethical decision-making. This work takes practice,[43] and ideally, it occurs before finding yourself in an awkward position.[44]

The decision-action gap in ethical decision-making is often substantial. Stop reading here and revisit the vignettes shared at the beginning of this chapter. Would you have acted or stood by? Would you have had the uncomfortable conversation? Would you have taken a stand or just acquiesced? Ethical decision-making involves logic *and* emotion. You may know what is right, but you feel afraid to *do* what is right. And that is why emotional intelligence is so valuable in the design of you as a leader and your leadership.

As you consider your ethical fitness, you may find that you have a great deal of knowledge about ethical decision-making models, ethical perspectives, toxic leadership, and courageous followership but lack the *skill* to navigate a complex moral dilemma.[45] It takes a great deal of intentional practice to become skilled at influencing others to behave in a way that may not serve them well in the short run (e.g., not cheating, ending the hazing). The following section is designed to provide a simple, yet robust, process to help develop an ethical and moral approach to leading others. The purpose was to integrate the thinking of many scholars into a single model that provides you with a framework for leading self and others.

The BASE Model

The BASE model provides a framework for building the skills of ethical leadership. BASE comprises four activities—each a fundamental ingredient to create a thoughtful starting point: (1) Begin With You; (2) Assess; (3) Seek Options; (4) Elect and Evaluate.

Begin With You

The first step in designing a moral approach to leading others is ensuring that you have done the appropriate inner work. For example, you know about the topic of moral leadership—you have clarity around your moral principles, virtues, and blind spots, and a vision for who you want to be (your character). What is your ethical code? Use that code as a guide as there may be instances when it is appropriate not to follow your code. Can you think of an example?

By designing your ethical code and the virtues for practice, you are actively and intentionally entering into a state of growth and development. This becomes your *true north* to help guide your thoughts and actions during difficult times. An English proverb asserts that "a smooth sea never made a skillful sailor." In the beginning, a sailor must practice and prepare for what they will inevitably encounter; the more you engage in these turbulent waters, the more skilled you will become. The metaphor holds true for leadership—you will be tested in large and small ways. Are you ready with a basic framework, and are you practicing each day so that you are prepared when you leave the harbor for the open sea?

Key questions in this phase:

- What are the moral principles driving my behavior as a leader?

- What are the virtues I need to practice to help me better model a life of integrity?

- When do I have the most difficulty living a life of integrity? What are the triggers?

- What would people say about my character?

- What values do I hold that may prevent me from being who I want to be?

Assess

The second step is to assess. Although it may sound odd, many people fail to recognize when they are facing a moral dilemma. This can occur because of sheer ignorance, a lack of experience, an educational gap, an inability to scenario plan, a lack of empathy, or wrongly justifying/rationalizing behavior that is unethical. Awareness is paramount.[46] For instance, recall the brief vignette at the beginning of the chapter about Rosario, a relatively new member of the hockey team. Unless he is indeed in touch with his commitment to the moral principle of "do unto others" and his deliberate practice of the virtue of kindness, he may not consciously process that he is involved in a moral dilemma. Also, note that paying attention to your emotional reaction to a situation can be a biological indicator that you are facing an ethical dilemma. Being attuned to your responses to a situation is valuable data that may trigger the next phase.

In the Assess phase, you better define the ethical dilemma and perhaps better understand the problem. This may require research or further dialogue with peers, parents, or trusted advisors and mentors who can provide guidance and counsel. By exploring your thoughts and ideas with others, you can gain a better understanding of your thoughts, perspectives, and fears. Another option would be for you to benchmark the situation with your ethical code. By doing so, you may gain additional clarity on your potential courses of action and identify blind spots or cognitive biases that hinder your ability to think through the problem clearly.

Key questions in this phase:

- What emotions am I experiencing because of the situation?

- What worries me about this situation? What is at stake?

- What is the ethical dilemma I am facing, and what are the competing values at play?

- What is an appropriate use of my power and access to resources in this situation?

- What loyalties are at risk?

- What authority do I have to act? Am I a leader with formal authority? If not, how should I influence those with authority? What followership style is most appropriate?

Seek Options

Scenario planning and empathizing with others are critical skills during this phase. For instance, can you identify ten options for how Marissa could respond in her vignette on cheating? At one extreme, she could do nothing; at the other, she could turn the student in for his behavior. However, there are multiple options in between the two options previously mentioned, each of which has a set of positive and negative consequences for her and the cheating student. What options provide her with a win-win? Your goal should be to identify at least five options for moving forward. Move past the obvious choices and explore more complex options to resolve the dilemma.

In his book *The Ethical Challenges of Leadership*,[47] author Craig Johnson highlights five **ethical perspectives** that can help an individual view an ethical challenge through multiple lenses. By intentionally exploring numerous perspectives and options, you will be better prepared to land on a decision with a higher level of intentionality. Be advised that perspectives overlap, and each has strengths and weaknesses depending on the context.

The first of the five ethical perspectives is **Utilitarianism**, which means that one should do the highest good for the most significant number of people. This approach requires that the decision maker(s) explore the cost/benefits of their decision and the consequences of their actions—which can be difficult to predict.

The second approach is **Kant's Categorical Imperative**, which posits that an individual must do what is right at all costs. While this is noble, and indeed a plan that has its place, it can be difficult to employ this perspective in all situations. At the extreme, the costs may be your life or the lives of others. On the other hand, this approach can be a good reminder that doing what is right at all costs helps you to take a close look at what those costs could entail in all situations.

Justice as fairness asserts that individuals in a free and democratic society should have equal access and opportunity to benefit from specific rights. This perspective contends that as a leader, you should consistently work toward the idea that all citizens should have access to fundamental rights—not just a few in power. Of course, this aligns with the founding tenets of the United States. For instance, to quote the *Pledge of Allegiance*: "I pledge allegiance to the flag of the United States of America, and to the republic for which it stands, one nation under God, indivisible, with liberty and justice for all."

Ethical perspectives
This describes five lenses through which to view ethical decisions including **Utilitarianism**, which means that one should do the highest good for the most significant number of people; **Kant's Categorical Imperative**, which posits that an individual must do what is right at all costs; **Justice as fairness**, which asserts that individuals in a free and democratic society should have equal access and opportunity to benefit from specific rights; **Altruism**, which means that you should *love thy neighbor* and make decisions from a place of benefitting others; and **Pragmatism**, which engages any of the ethical perspectives to address ethical issues, understanding that no one perspective can be correct all of the time.

Altruism means that you should "love thy neighbor," and make decisions from a place of benefitting others. Highlighted in several religious texts, the principle of altruism requires that you work from a place of concern for the well-being of others. Like the other perspectives, altruism is an ideal outcome of any moral dilemma. In other words, you work to keep the needs, wants, desires, and views of others in mind as you decide a course of action.

Pragmatism may engage any of the other ethical perspectives. Its strength draws from the notion that no one perspective can be correct all of the time. Back to the vignettes, it will likely benefit you always to follow the principle of not drinking and driving or getting in a car with someone who has been drinking. In this instance, having a clear line of what is, and is not, acceptable and beneficial will protect you and your loved ones. However, Kant's Categorical Imperative combined with altruism may cause you to help find a solution that creates a win-win (getting your friend's car home and not drinking and driving).

A hallmark of the Seek Options phase is asking questions of yourself and others (depending on the challenge). Several scholars have outlined critical questions that may help you determine a course of action (e.g., Nash's 12 Questions[48]). Some of these may also help you better understand the problem (assess) as well.

1. How will my decision impact others?

2. What is at stake if I do not act? What is at stake if I do?

3. Which ethical perspective is most appropriate for this situation?

4. Who will be negatively impacted by my decision? Am I willing to take this risk?

5. How do others perceive the problem? Can I empathize with their experience of the issue?

6. What is my ultimate objective? What is the best case scenario or ideal future state?

7. Whom will my decision injure (physically/psychologically)?

8. Is my potential solution a long-term solution, or will this problem remain in the long run?

9. What are the unintended consequences of each option?

Elect and Evaluate

In the end, you need to select an option and decide. Only the rarest of decisions ends up being perfect or ideal, or addresses every nuance of the issue. There will be unintended consequences, people will respond in unexpected ways, and various other contingencies will come into play. A useful way of thinking about your decision is that you are running your best-formulated experiment to see if it yields desired results. Expecting the unexpected is a useful mindset. If everything does work out, great, but that may not be the case. As new data present themselves, you may need to revisit the Assess and Seek Options phases.

Two critical points require emphasis. First, ensure that you have done your best to scenario plan the good and the bad of your decision. Second, ensure that you monitor and reflect upon and evaluate the results of your chosen course. Seeking the counsel of trusted advisors *after* the decision is just as critical in this phase as it is during the Assess phase.

Key questions in this phase:

- What were the unexpected consequences of my decision? Are they significant enough to warrant a reexamination?

- Are the results consistent with my future desired state or are adjustments needed?

- How do vital players feel about the decision? What are they seeing and thinking?

Your values and ethical actions strongly impact your credibility as a leader. The previous chapter posed the questions: How would you like to be perceived by others? And how can you become the person others desire to follow? Designing yourself as a leader must include developing an awareness of your values, attention to the decision-action gap, and deliberate efforts to enhance your ethical fitness. Failing to attend to these aspects of your leadership, and then subsequently failing your followers and organization, constitutes a moral failure in and of itself:

> The failure (or refusal) of a leader to foresee may be viewed as an ethical failure; because a serious ethical compromise today (when the usual judgment on ethical inadequacy is made) is sometimes the result of a failure to make an effort at an earlier date to foresee today's events and take the right actions when there was freedom for initiative to act.[49]

Chapter Summary

This chapter examined ethical issues that directly impact the student experience and highlighted some key terminology and ideas. These concepts included foundational ideas around ethics and your ethical code, moral principles, virtues and finding balance, integrity, values, and laws. Your moral development is the result of many influences, mainly family and education. Your growth continues even today.

All aspects of the leadership process comprise decisions, and as such, they are filled with ethical challenges. Those challenges, in leadership and life, can be categorized into five domains: academic, family, work, extracurricular, and friendship.

Perhaps most important, this chapter helps you design several dimensions of your approach to ethical leadership. Ethical leadership may feel like a set of extremes. On one

end, there is an ideal state for men and women—including qualities such as altruism, justice, and caring. At the other extreme, there are examples of toxic and bad leaders who have engaged in horrific acts that have done significant damage. While you may not experience this extreme, it takes a great deal of moral courage to lead *and* follow.[50]

You can become a more skilled ethical decision maker by working on your ethical fitness. This starts with finding clarity about yourself and your values. Assuming your goal is to be an individual of sound character, you must determine your *true north*—who you are and what you stand for. The BASE model provides a strategy for you to practice ethical decision-making actively, so you are prepared when you face a significant ethical dilemma.

Key Terms

Character 99
Code of Ethics 96
Decision-Action Gap 104
Ethical Perspectives 110

Ethics 96
Integrity 99
Laws 100

Moral Principles 97
Personal Values 99
Virtues 97

CORE™ Attribute Builders: Build Now for Future Leadership Challenges

Attribute: Confidence

Builder: *Breaking Bad, The Making of a Murderer,* and *House of Cards*

We know that you have internalized information at a deeper level when you begin to see the concepts mentioned in this chapter in some of the television shows you binge on your favorite network. The three popular shows mentioned above are examples of programming where the main characters struggle to live a virtuous life. As you watch these and other shows, can you see some of the concepts discussed in this chapter as they occur on the screen? If so, you are beginning to internalize the content. Questions to explore while watching may include:

- How does the primary character display attributes of toxic leadership?

- Discuss the character of the main character. What personal values guide his or her way?

- How do the main characters benefit from their followers?

Skill Builder Activity

Moral Principles, Virtues, and Ethical Decision-Making

Part 1: Exploring the moral principles that guide your approach to leadership is a critical activity for any leader. Recall that moral principles are *truths* about behaviors that have been widely accepted and adopted by individuals, groups, and/or societies. Below, you will notice a list of widely accepted moral principles that can serve as a foundation for your approach to leadership. Use your favorite search engine to explore the meaning of examples provided (and others as you see fit). Next, place a check mark (✓) next to your core four. The check mark indicates that you have explored its meaning, you could explain it to a friend, and it is of high value to you. The core four will serve as the foundation for your approach to leadership.

- ❏ Do good; avoid evil
- ❏ The Golden Rule
- ❏ Justice
- ❏ Rule of rescue
- ❏ Love thy neighbor
- ❏ Respect for persons
- ❏ Self-love
- ❏ Wisdom
- ❏ The end does not justify the means
- ❏ Follow what nature intends
- ❏ All men are created equal
- ❏ Do the greatest good for the greatest number of people
- ❏ Commitment to something greater than oneself
- ❏ Respect and caring for others

- ❏ Caring for other living things and the environment
- ❏ Faithfulness
- ❏ Mercy
- ❏ Love
- ❏ Sanctity of life
- ❏ First, do no harm
- ❏ Always do what is right, no matter the cost
- ❏ Equal consideration of interests

Part 2: Next, review the list of virtues provided and place a check mark (✓) next to your core four virtues that you believe, with practice, will help you best model your moral principles. The check mark indicates that you have explored its meaning, you could explain it to a friend, and it is of high value to you. Recall that virtues are concerned with living your moral principles. Virtues are widely accepted, morally good traits, behaviors, or habits that determine an individual's character. Virtues are practiced and are often a mean between two extremes. Virtues are not about what is right or wrong, but they are about what a person *should* be. Use your favorite search engine to explore the meaning of those we have included (and others as you see fit). Your core four will serve as opportunities for practice. Remember that Ben Franklin started his list because he *did not* have mastery of them. You *practice* the virtues. Regardless of how you choose the virtues to practice, the fact that you are intentionally working to develop them is a worthwhile endeavor. You may tell a friend that you are "practicing the virtue of . . ."

- ❏ Charity
- ❏ Chastity
- ❏ Cleanliness

❏ Compassion

❏ Courage

❏ Diligence

❏ Frugality

❏ Generosity

❏ Hospitality

❏ Humility

❏ Independence

❏ Industry

❏ Justice

❏ Kindness

❏ Moderation

❏ Openness

❏ Order

❏ Patience

❏ Prudence

❏ Resilience

❏ Resolution

❏ Respect

❏ Self-control

❏ Self-efficacy

❏ Silence

❏ Sincerity

❏ Temperance

❏ Thoughtfulness

❏ Tolerance

❏ Tranquility

❏ Truthfulness

❏ Wisdom

Part 3: While a general framework for ethical decision-making (BASE) is explored in this chapter, it is helpful to have *your process*—a process that you can recall with ease. A simple acronym can help you remember your process. It is important to remember that your core four identified in previous sections can help inform your decision-making process. While not every decision will align with the core four you have chosen, it is important to acknowledge them as you move through the decision-making process.

What is *your* four- to five-step process or a visual model for making an ethical decision? Using the space below this box, draw a diagram of your process or model. After doing so, benchmark it with the mini case studies shared at the beginning of the chapter to see if your process is realistic.

Design Leadership Relationships

To have a friend you have to be a friend.

—Elbert Hubbard

*Friendship is born at that moment when one person says to
another, "What? You too? I thought I was the only one."*

—C.S. Lewis

The quality of your life is the quality of your relationships.

—Anthony Robbins

Leadership is the process of influencing others toward a common vision. This section focuses on *others*, specifically your connection to others and how you design leadership relationships. Unless you try really hard to avoid it, most of life involves engaging with others. The three quotes at the start of this section offer advice about relating to others. What advice and guidance would *you* give someone who wanted to know the most effective way to build a relationship? You would likely ask what kind of relationship—casual, professional, friendly, romantic—because each kind of relationship looks and feels different. As a leader, what kind of relationship should you have with your followers? What kind of relationship do you want? Individuals spend a great deal of time talking and thinking about relationships, much of it reactive.

Like the prior section that focused on designing your leadership self, your approach to relationships can be mindfully designed . . . or you can just see what happens and hope for the best. Perhaps a ride down the rapids would better illustrate. Imagine you are invited to kayak down a very turbulent river by a couple of friends. Both friends are experienced, but neither is an expert. One friend has taken a close look at the river, mapped out the turns and rapids, and plotted a route through each stretch of rough water. This took time, effort, and thought. The other friend is going to just *go with the flow* (pun intended), which of course required no advance work. One approach may be safer than the other, one more fun and exciting, one more interesting or more appealing. But the relative advantages and disadvantages are not the point. The important thing is the *mindful decision* about how each friend wanted to experience the kayak trip (i.e., their proposed plan, solution, or product). In other words, each friend got the experience they designed.

As a leader, the nature of your relationships with others will determine what and how you influence, how you and others see yourselves and the work, and a host of other variables that all add up to how it feels to be led by you. In Chapter 11, the idea of *culture* is explored, and defined simply as *the way things are done around here*. That larger culture begins with the individual relationships—how we relate around here. You can design your relationships (carefully planned or purposefully going with the flow), or you can choose not to design them and just hope we all get along and work well.

The Leadership Challenge: Designing Leadership Relationships

People are complicated. That seemingly trite statement truly captures the greatest challenge you will face as a leader. Designing yourself takes time and effort; designing others' success requires insight and engagement, and designing culture means seeing the bigger picture. But *designing relationships* requires approaching all of the above along with extraordinary patience, forgiveness, and emotional intelligence. Continuing to build your CORE™ (confidence, optimism, resilience, and engagement) will also help you design relationships.

Another key set of tools comes from the research of Jim Kouzes and Barry Posner, who interviewed thousands of individuals about their best leadership.[1] Kouzes and Posner captured these answers in five broad *Practices of Exemplary Leadership*: (a) model the way, (b) inspire a shared vision, (c) challenge the process, (d) enable others to act, and (e) encourage the heart. The seminal book in which they elaborate on these five practices and offer many practical applied tips is aptly named *The Leadership Challenge*. Take a second look at the five practices. Can you identify the common factor that ties them all together? Yes, they all focus on designing and developing relationships with others. Kouzes and Posner provide an invaluable how-to/what-to-do list of leadership practices that will come in handy long into your future career. The exemplary practices also supply a framework by which you can begin to address the greatest leadership challenge—designing relationships (see Table M2.1).

Take another look at the five leadership practices asserted by Kouzes and Posner. This time, consider how each of the effective practices align with the definition of leadership and the design challenge focus that forms the structure of this textbook (see Table M2.2).

TABLE M2.1 ● Designing Relationships With Kouzes and Posner's Practices of Exemplary Leadership

When you . . .	You design relationships by . . .
Model the way	Providing a vision and route to achievement; building credibility and establishing parameters of the relationship and acceptable behavior
Inspire a shared vision	Sharing power and responsibility, which develops mutual respect
Challenge the process	Guiding others to their best while reinforcing the importance of making mistakes and improving; building resilience
Enable others to act	Building motivation and trust through autonomy, confidence through self-efficacy, and optimism through achievement
Encourage the heart	Understanding and connecting with emotions, which in turn becomes the greatest source of influence and inspiration

TABLE M2.2 ● Aligning Design Challenges, Definition Components, and Best Practices

Your leadership design challenge . . .	Aligns with defining leadership . . .		And how you best practice leadership.
Design Leadership Self	Leadership	Your leadership comprises your perceptions, strengths, style, skills, and . . .	Model the way
Design Leadership Relationships	is a process	the way you make decisions and solve problems, including . . .	Encourage the heart
	of influencing	how you persuade, guide, teach, and . . .	
Design Others' Success	others	build relationships with others. But leadership goes beyond you—how do you help others succeed . . .	Enable others to act
Design Culture and Community	toward a common	and create a culture of success so that you, your followers, your organization, and your society . . .	Inspire a shared vision
Design the Future	vision.	can make a great difference in the world?	Challenge the process

MYTH OR REALITY?

LEADERS CANNOT AND SHOULD NOT BE FRIENDS WITH THEIR FOLLOWERS.

Myth . . . and Reality. You already know this is a misconception from reading Chapter 2. But why is it both myth and reality? Consider a time when you were working on a group project or with a team and a new member joined the group. If the new member was someone you knew well and considered a friend, your interactions with them would be considerably different than if they were a stranger. You would place greater trust in them, have more meaningful conversations, discuss actions and decisions, and feel a mutual respect and equality even if you were the leader of the group. The rest of the group would likewise see this new person as part of the team based on your relationship with them. But now consider what it feels like to be the new person joining the group when you do not know the leader or the others in the group. You likely are welcomed, perhaps even with enthusiasm, but the leader does not know you nor do you know the leader. So, you assume the role of follower, listener, and learner; you are more cautious about taking action or making decisions, you follow the rules, and your conversations with the leader are more professional. You might even feel like an outsider for a time.

These situations highlight the importance of the dyadic (two-person) relationship between the follower and the leader. Researchers who focus on this dyadic relationship have developed a theory called Leader-Member Exchange Theory or LMX.[2] They have found many positive individual and organizational outcomes when there is a high-quality relationship between a leader and follower. For example, you may have witnessed a boss, teacher, or coach taking the time to talk with and get to know each individual follower. Sometimes those conversations are about the task at hand, soliciting ideas about the work, or guiding individual development. But all of the time, those individualized conversations are moments where the leader indirectly communicates how much they value the individual. Those individual moments can add up to a relationship of mutual understanding, credibility, and trust.

Focusing on each individual relationship and building these relationships from stranger to acquaintance to partner, as Leader-Member Exchange Theory explains, leaders are able to design a higher quality of interaction and performance from each member and the team as a whole.[3] In addition, once individual followers feel good about their relationship with their leader, they are freed up psychologically and emotionally to take the focus off of themselves and shift it to focus on the greater success of the group.

When should a leader not befriend a follower? Leader-Member Exchange Theory also focuses on what happens as these relationships form and what happens when some relationships with the leader are close and others are not. When a new person joins a group, all the other individuals in the group have been building a relationship with the leader—they are considered the *in-group*, while the new person feels like they are in the *out-group*. The leader is not trying to form in- and out-groups, they just naturally occur because the dyadic relationships vary. This perceived unfairness can be detrimental.[4] The best thing you can do as a leader is work hard to build relationships with new individuals, be aware of the perception of in-out groups and the appearance of possible favoritism, and find unique ways to connect new and veteran followers.

This module on designing leadership relationships comprises three chapters: Chapter 5: Design Thinking and Brain Learning; Chapter 6: Decision-Making; and Chapter 7: Influence, Motivation, and Power. Effectively designing relationships also requires that you understand how others think. Chapter 5 highlights six dimensions of the brain with direct applications for leadership, and then it introduces a broad set of mental tools called design thinking that will greatly enhance your ability to understand, build, and sustain the leader-follower relationship.

5

Design Thinking and Brain Leading

Your brain is a lean, mean, pattern-making machine.

—Michael Dickmann

Design thinking is a mindset, not a toolkit or a series of steps.

—Arne van Oosterom

Learning Objectives

5.1   Translate important information about the brain into designing leadership relationships and others' success

5.2   Understand the effective application of design thinking to designing leadership relationships

5.3   Assess successful leadership relationship-building practices

5.4   Plan and engage user-centered methods to better understand followers and design relationships

5.5   Apply divergent thinking to generating ideas for building relationships

5.6   Formulate an iterative, integrative plan to sustain your leader-follower relationships

Detailed Chapter Outline

Leadership by Design Model		
Design Self		
How can I design myself as a leader?		
DESIGN RELATIONSHIPS		
AS A LEADER, HOW CAN I DESIGN MY RELATIONSHIPS WITH OTHERS?		
Design Others' Success		
As a leader, how can I design success for others?		
Design Culture		
As a leader, how can I design the culture of my organization?		
Design Future		
As a leader, how can I innovate?		

Introduction: Designing Self to Designing Relationships

If Rule #1 is "It's about you," and Rule #2 is "It's not about you," this section examines the middle ground between the two: "It's about us." This chapter examines one of the *most* influential facets of leadership—the leader-follower relationship—through the lens of two powerful sets of tools—the dimensions of the brain and design thinking.

Leaders influence others and are likewise influenced by others. How you see and act regarding yourself, others, the world, and its influences all happens between your ears—in your brain. And yet, despite how much is known about the brain and thinking, leaders apply very little of this knowledge to designing and practicing leadership. How, for example, would you lead differently if you knew that the brain—everyone's brain—could only focus on work after a short rest and being flooded with oxygen? Perhaps you would incorporate more breaks into meetings or install a treadmill desk. Or maybe you would invest in an oxygen bar for the break room and a set of bunkbeds in the spare office. This *physiological* dimension of the brain is one of six that form a handy framework to help you apply these brainy lessons.

Your brain constructs how you see the world based on how you have experienced the world (remember the model from Chapter 2 that illustrated your choice between having a narrow, rigid view versus a broad, open view). Another thing you know about your brain is that it likes to form habits. What you construct can become habits in how you think— habits that are referred to as dispositions. Some thinking habits are helpful, and some are not. As you should recall from the introductory chapter, the mental habits comprising design thinking consist of a very useful set of dispositions, which you can apply to a wide variety of challenges. Individual behavior comes from individual brains. If you know how the brain works, you can influence behavior.

LEADERSHIP THAT MAKES A DIFFERENCE

What if you could start your Monday morning with an alarm clock that giggled?

What if you could treat chronic pain without drugs?

What if there was a way you could make sure you took the right medications at the right time?

What if you could grow your own food . . . in the middle of a city . . . with no soil?

These are just some of the amazing design challenges that president and CEO Tim Brown and his teams at the design firm IDEO have pursued. While many design firms would have been content with market-based projects like designing a new toaster or phone, IDEO has been striving to live up to their value proposition: *We create impact through design.*[5]

IDEO began through a merger of four design companies in 1991. One of those design companies was founded by David Kelley, who created one of the first prototypes for the computer mouse inspired by the roll-on mechanism of deodorant. Since then, IDEO has led the way in their unique and socially impactful solutions as well as the continued development of how individuals think about and apply design *processes*, *principles*, and thinking to different contexts and challenges.[6] The big difference that these leaders have made lies in how individuals and organizations *see* problems and challenges and the process they ultimately follow toward innovation. What started for IDEO as coming up with innovative solutions has transformed into developing new *methods* for

coming up with innovative solutions . . . and then ways of teaching those methods to others. Kelley calls their approach design thinking:

> In a meeting with IDEO's CEO, Tim Brown, in 2003, Kelley had an epiphany: They would stop calling IDEO's approach "design" and start calling it "design thinking." "I'm not a words person," Kelley says, "but in my life, it's the most powerful moment that words or labeling ever made. Because then it all made sense. Now I'm an expert at methodology rather than a guy who designs a new chair or car."[7]

And now that new way of seeing and operating lies in their mission:

- We identify new ways to serve and support people by uncovering latent needs, behaviors, and desires.

- We envision new companies and brands, and we design the products, services, spaces, and interactive experiences that bring them to life.

- We help organizations build creative culture and the internal systems required to sustain innovation and launch new ventures.[8]

Nearly all of IDEO's projects involve working with the clients and other stakeholders in unique partnerships and collaborations that highlight one of the most

(Continued)

(Continued)

fundamental aspects of their approach—understanding the user. So, the challenges that Tim Brown and the team at IDEO face in all of their design projects always come down to relationships—the relationships they have with one another to work collaboratively, the relationships they have with the user or client in order to fully understand the problem, and the relationships they have with countless others as they dream up, test, and implement their design solution. All of these relationships influence the effectiveness of their work. The activities they engage in to design these relationships are not random, nor are they unique to IDEO. These activities follow a design process, apply design principles, and utilize design thinking to create a proposed plan, solution, or product (aka *design*).

David Kelley and Tim Brown, in collaboration with countless others (as fitting with their approach), have contributed to helping define, redefine, and help others reconceptualize the "how to" behind innovation. These tools have been adopted across sectors and disciplines, from education and business to government and nonprofit organizations, and right back to their own field of design. Design processes and design thinking are making a BIG difference.

Design process, design principles, and design thinking were briefly explained in the introductory chapter. You should flip back and reread those sections . . . for a couple of reasons. First, this design framework is both highly unique and uniquely effective in helping you see differently, ultimately enhancing your innovation and efficacy as a leader. Design is a tool you will use again and again. Second, the more times you revisit information, the more you strengthen the connections in your lean, mean, pattern-making machine brain, and the better you will be at using that tool. Finally, revisiting what you previously learned will position you to more effectively learn the new stuff. Seriously, go back and reread—it will only take a few minutes. Then check out Table 5.1 (below) and add a reminder for yourself.

TABLE 5.1 ● Design in Brief and Why You Should Care		
Wait . . . What? . . .	You Need It Because . . .	How Will *You* Remember This Concept?
Design process—the process of originating and developing a plan, which comprises three phases: understand, imagine, and implement	*Following a process ensures you remember each important part.* Try doing something in random order that you normally have a process for doing. Get dressed in random order, brush your teeth, cook a meal—you will likely miss a few things and end up with a poor outcome.	
Design principle—the rules that designers apply to help guide their process and enhance their product	*Certain rules and reminders help enhance your outcome.* What *rules* do you normally follow that enhance your life? Say please and thank you, wear sunscreen, hydrate on hot days, call your mom—these rules make things better.	

Wait . . . What? . . .	You Need It Because . . .	How Will *You* Remember This Concept?
Design thinking—the habits of mind (dispositions) that designers use to help enhance and guide their process A cognitive approach to engaging problems that embodies a specific mindset that is (a) user-centered, (b) explorative, (c) divergent, (d) multidisciplinary, (e) iterative, and (f) integrative	*Certain ways of thinking and seeing enhance your process and outcome.* Your brain is a lean, mean, pattern-making machine that forms habits. You can form habitual ways of thinking that are detrimental ("people always disappoint") or form mental habits that are helpful ("mistakes help others learn to do better next time").	

Brain Leading in Six Dimensions[9]

Learning Objective

5.1 Translate important information about the brain into designing leadership relationships and others' success

Take another look at the title of this section. Can you imagine what the title means or what this section will talk about? Does it sound like a science fiction movie? Is the title so odd that you simply breezed over it and moved on? Whatever your interpretation and reaction, your brain was the star of the show. Think about all the things that your brain was able to do with this simple request: focus and refocus attention, interpret symbols into letters into words into a sentence, dig into memory for definitions and examples, compare and contrast memories with new ideas, judge the amount of time worth spending, assess the accuracy of your answer, and imagine new possibilities. And you did all this without anyone else, and you did it quite quickly. That is amazing.

Individual behavior comes from individual brains. If you know how the brain works, you can influence the behavior. Yet too often leaders seem to disregard the characteristics and needs of everyone's brain, instead focusing on themselves and the individual follower. Consider for a moment what you know about the brain. Better still, consult with a friend and consider what you know about your friend's brain.[10] You will probably start your list with some of the physical properties you know or have heard. But think hard about what your friend's brain can really *do*. For immediate example, your friend's brain can speculate about you and your brain—like he or she is doing right now.

There is a lot to know about the brain. One important thing that everyone knows about the brain, especially students, is that long, random lists of unrelated facts are very difficult to remember, much less use. Luckily your brain is a lean, mean, pattern-making machine, and it loves to categorize and organize information. Michael Dickmann and Nancy Stanford-Blair provide a framework that you can use to keep all this brain information organized so you can apply it to your leadership—the six dimensions: physiological, emotional, social, constructive, dispositional, and reflective.

The six **dimensions of the brain** imply significant applications for leaders. And as you learn more about the brain beyond this class, you can utilize this framework to translate that knowledge into leadership action. The key question is: *If I know x about the brain, then to be effective as a leader I should do y.* What will you do differently because you now know something about the brain?

The sections that follow include the story of Ralph, a typical employee who wants to be successful. The only thing getting in Ralph's way is his own brain. Read on to find out how

Dimensions of the brain This is an organizational scheme for understanding and applying information about the brain to leadership activity. The six dimensions are the **physiological dimension**, which recognizes that there is a fundamental connection between your brain and your body; the **emotional dimension**, which influences how individuals see and react to situations and others based on feelings; the **social dimension**, which focuses on the critical and inextricable role that others play in how you see and react to the world; the **reflective dimension**, which is the capacity to consider and modify information and understanding; the **constructive dimension**, which emphasizes your process of conceptualizing the world based on what you interact with in the world; and the **dispositional dimension**, which highlights habitual ways of processing information, also seen as mental habits that influence what individuals perceive and how they conceive information.

you as Ralph's leader can use each of the six dimensions of his brain to design your relationship and his success. You may want to read through these sections now and take a few notes. Then, reread the sections and discuss the reflection questions with a peer. Finally, read through the sections one more time (yes, a third time) and note what *you could do* to positively use each dimension.

REFLECTION QUESTIONS

How did you initially feel about being asked to read something three times? How and why is it useful to look at (or read) something multiple times focusing on different things? After you have read (and reread) these sections, what dimensions of the brain explain the benefits of rereading?

Physiological, Emotional, and Social Dimensions

Ralph arrives at work with a huge yawn, still sleepy from the night before when he decided to stay up for that movie marathon. Because he was in a rush, he did not get a chance to grab his usual morning coffee or even eat any breakfast. Now, Ralph sits at the staff meeting, tummy grumbling, eyes falling shut, and unprepared. Up for discussion is an item that involves Ralph having to shift projects. He considered the shift when the meeting agenda came out, and thought through the advantages to both himself and the company. But right now he is too tired to remember those reasons. When the item is brought up, Ralph finds himself feeling very angry, and he reacts with sarcastic comments and then stone silence. His colleagues, generally very collaborative and fun to work with, react to Ralph's behavior by cutting him out of the conversation and disregarding his perspective. Poor Ralph—and to think this all could have gone a different way had he just eaten a donut.

FIGURE 5.1 ● Rubik's Cube

Source: Image by Booyabazooka via Creative Commons BY-SA 3.0 https://creativecommons .org/licenses/by-sa/3.0/deed.en.

Physiological dimension
See Dimensions of the brain

This example highlights the three dimensions of the brain discussed in this section: physiological, emotional, and social. More importantly, the scene above illustrates the real-world nature of the brain in action. *The six dimensions work together, complementing and contradicting each other, and they cannot be separated in practice.* Thus, the six-dimension framework is simply an organizational and strategic tool for applying brain knowledge to leadership activity, also known as brain leading. One way to think about this interconnectivity is with the old-school puzzle called the Rubik's cube (see Figure 5.1). The Rubik's cube consisted of a 3 × 3 × 3 cube with each of the nine blocks on each side of the cube a single color. Each of the nine blocks could be moved by physically spinning rows and columns, with the goal to get the cube back to having each side a single color. If you consider each side one of the six dimensions of the brain, it becomes quite clear that the dimensions blend into one another pretty much all the time, and the single configuration of each dimension being clearly alone is a remote probability.[11]

So, back to poor Ralph—physiologically, he is a mess. Physiological refers to the functions and activities of your body. The **physiological dimension** of the brain recognizes that there is a fundamental connection between your brain and your body. This is not a surprise, but it does seem to be constantly overlooked in leadership. Ken Robinson, in his wildly popular TED talk, asserts that university professors "look upon their body as a form of transport for their heads. It's a way of getting their head to meetings."[12] Although slightly in jest, his assertion accurately sums the approach most leaders have to designing relationships with their followers: I, as leader, will interact with your head, overlooking the fact that your brain is comprised of water, chemicals, and electricity, all of which are connected to larger systems in your body. When we want optimal performance from a car, we do not limit our tinkering to the software that controls the systems and overlook the need for oil and other physical parts.

In addition to the very basic physical needs, the physiological dimension also recognizes that the brain is made of physical structures that grow (and recede) based on activity. The neural connections throughout your brain that make thinking happen continue to change, physically, as you engage the world—experiencing and learning. Experiences can be positive or detrimental, like the stress of some jobs or work cultures. If manageable, that stress can stimulate neural growth; if never-ending or traumatic, stress can damage the brain.[13]

REFLECTION QUESTIONS

What physical conditions might be contributing to Ralph's situation? What role is stress playing in this culture and context? What other friendly or unfriendly brain conditions can you identify?

The brain has an **emotional dimension** that influences how individuals see and react to situations and others based on feelings. Emotion is formally defined as a brief experience of pleasure or displeasure; however, that definition highlights one of the shortcomings most individuals have regarding their emotions—their very limited emotional vocabulary. Remember Ralph and his not-so-good morning at work? How would you describe the emotions he is feeling? You would likely use the most common emotions—angry, happy, sad—rather than more complex yet accurate descriptors like anxious, disaffected, or lethargic. How aware of his own emotions do you think Ralph is at this meeting, and how are those emotions influencing his thinking and behavior? Knowing the answers to these questions is partly a matter of emotional intelligence.

Emotional dimension
See Dimensions of the brain

You can be smart in many different ways. As you read in Chapter 1, one very important way of being smart for leaders regards emotion. Emotional intelligence (EI) was defined as a person's ability to know and regulate their own feelings, perceive and understand the feelings of others, and effectively work between their own and others' feelings. Being smart with feelings would mean that Ralph would also be able to read the emotions of others, understand how his behavior is influencing his colleagues, and manage his emotions more effectively, even if he is hungry and tired. The interrelated nature of the dimensions becomes even more apparent when you look at the central role of emotion. What physiological and social conditions elicit emotions? What emotions result in social and physical outcomes?

A great deal of work on EI urges leaders and followers to better understand and manage their emotions for better health, performance, and success.[14] Although research in EI is relatively recent, the notion of understanding and managing emotions dates back to early philosophers. The implications and applications to leadership are apparent in this quote by Aristotle: "Anyone can become angry—that is easy, but to be angry with the right person at the right time, and for the right purpose and in the right way—that is not within everyone's power and that is not easy."

As a leader, what can you do to attend to the emotional dimension of the brain? As Ralph sits through the meeting described, he is feeling defensive, unsupported, and generally uncomfortable. In any context, when you are more concerned with feeling accepted, safe, and comfortable, you are not going to be able to concentrate or focus on the higher-level thinking tasks. For example, if you are worried about the judgment of your colleagues, if you are sitting across the table from an angry ex-boyfriend, if someone in the meeting threatened you before the meeting—those emotions will overwhelm the agenda, making you far less effective for the task at hand. Effective leaders are aware of and proactive in designing the emotional climate and consequently influencing followers.

REFLECTION QUESTIONS

What emotions does Ralph's situation elicit? What are the levels of emotional intelligence of the individuals involved?

Social dimension
See Dimensions of the brain

The **social dimension** of the brain focuses on the critical and inextricable role that others play in how you see and react to the world. Much of your mental model was (and continues to be) constructed from interactions you have with others, even instances where you only interact with others by observing their behavior. Effective leaders utilize the social dimension of the brain, realizing the power that others have on the individual in problem-solving, seeing other perspectives, generating ideas, engaging complementary strengths, observing the environment, and modeling and upholding norms and culture. Surprisingly, many leaders overlook the power of the social dimension, instead falling back on out-dated notions of individualism and fears of losing control. The education world is a prime example of this shortsightedness, where only recently have some educators moved away from the rows of individual note-taking students listening passively to a lecture. One of the authors of this text begins each course with the assertion, "Just because I am not talking does not mean you are not learning." In other words, creating opportunities for individuals to learn from one another—directly, as models, or even as a process of working toward understanding—makes for a far richer emotional experience and learning outcome.

Kouzes and Posner's practices of exemplary leadership introduced earlier lie at the heart of the social dimension, primarily because each of those practices focuses on designing relationships. When you think about who in your life has made the greatest difference, the list is not filled with celebrities but rather with family or friends—those who have connected with you emotionally. When leaders model the way, inspire a shared vision, challenge the process, enable others to act, and encourage the heart, they tap into the social dimension of the brain.

REFLECTION QUESTIONS

How would Ralph's situation differ if he was alone versus in a meeting with peers? Looking again at Kouzes and Posner's effective leadership practices, what would you do as a leader to design relationships in the context of Ralph and the other staff? What have you experienced as benefits to sharing, discussing, or working with others?

Reflective, Constructive, and Dispositional

Ralph arrives at work with a huge yawn, still sleepy from the night before when he decided to stay up for that movie marathon. Here we go again, except this time we know the physiological, emotional, and social implications Ralph is facing. These challenges impact the three higher level dimensions of the brain: reflective, constructive, and dispositional. Ralph thinks about his situation throughout the meeting—tired, hungry, frustrated, defensive—and knows that this is a temporary state. His prior interactions with his colleagues and the leader have established his credibility, and he knows them well enough to know they have good intentions. Even though this has been a less than productive or positive interaction, Ralph is optimistic and a creative problem solver who persists at projects and learns from mistakes.

This example again highlights three dimensions of the brain, in this case the reflective, constructive, and dispositional. And again, note that the six dimensions continue to operate together, reiterating that the six-dimension framework is only a tool for brain leading. In the example above, it seems there is less to worry about with Ralph. He has a good deal of self-awareness, a positive mental model that goes beyond this instance, and some productive dispositions.

The brain has a **reflective dimension**, which is the capacity to consider and modify information and understanding. Your reflective capacity allows you to engage a variety of critical thinking capacities, such as the ability to critically question both a situation and your understanding or mental model. Reflection enables you to predict outcomes, envision futures, prioritize information, and revise both real outcome and conceptual models. The reflective dimension also allows you to translate information into implications and action.

Reflective dimension
See Dimensions of the brain

The power of the reflective dimension, however, is only as effective as you allow . . . or a leader facilitates. In other words, leaders must provide time, space, and in some cases, guidance for reflection. Unfortunately for Ralph, he will have to find that time himself after the meeting.

REFLECTION QUESTIONS

What opportunities do others have to reflect on the situation? What prompts are guiding and framing their reflection . . . and yours? How can you integrate project/work-focused reflection into team meetings?

The object and outcome of the brain's reflection is the mental model you construct. The notion of mental model was introduced in Chapter 1—your mental representation of things in the world—not just the picture in your head, but how you understand things and even how you process information. Mental models are key to the **constructive dimension** of the brain. The constructive dimension emphasizes your process of conceptualizing the world based on what you interact with in the world. This includes how you later reflect on that construction, feel about those constructions, test those constructions in interactions with others, and continue to modify your constructions.

Constructive dimension
See Dimensions of the brain

As noted many times in this text, your brain is a lean, mean, pattern-making machine. As a leader, you can use the constructive dimension to help followers understand and apply information by providing organizational frameworks (like the six dimensions of the brain as a way to organize what you know and how to use it). What knowledge matters most for your followers, and how do you need them to understand and prioritize that information? What mental models might be holding followers back from thinking more creatively or seeing alternative perspectives? As the famous economist John Kenneth Galbraith noted, "Faced with the choice between changing one's mind and proving that there is no need to do so, almost everyone gets busy on the proof."[15] The constructive dimension is a powerful tool for designers of leadership. A strong first impression or concept will withstand many contrary examples.

A leader who understands that the brain has a constructive dimension will address these questions. What is the follower's mental model of this situation? What is your mental model? What other constructions of the world (and the context) may be influencing others and your leadership?

LEADERSHIP BY DESIGN

Design Principle: Performance Load

Definition: The greater the effort to accomplish a task, the less likely the task will be accomplished successfully.[16]

In Other Words: Tasks that take too much physical or mental effort will simply not get done.

For Example: Having to decipher messy handwriting increases the performance load of a reader (see Figure 5.2).

For Leaders: What do followers need to accomplish or achieve that may have a significant load? How and where can I simplify? Where would the path of least resistance lead? A leader can help others be successful by reducing unnecessary steps, energy expended, and repetitive tasks. To decrease superfluous information from displays, chunk information, and provide memory aids. If at all possible, allow your followers to directly touch, manipulate, and interact with objects firsthand. It reduces the cognitive effort needed to perform a task while making it more emotionally satisfying.

FIGURE 5.2 ● Increasing the Performance Load of the Reader

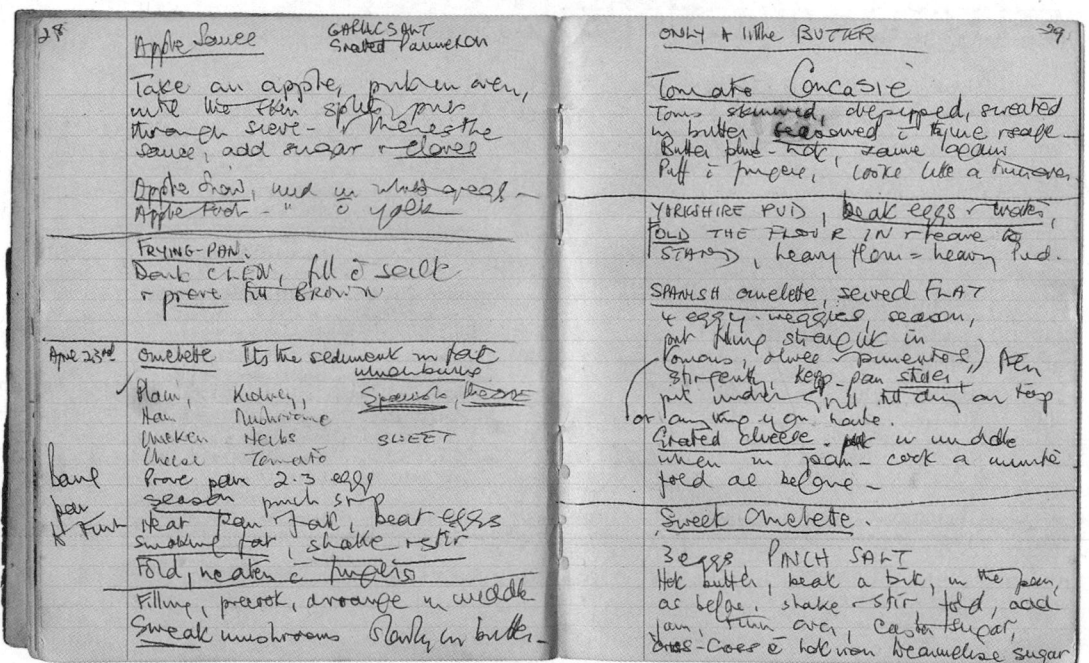

Source: ©iStock.com/whitemay.

The best news for Ralph and his situation is that he has strongly constructed some positive ways of thinking, so strongly that they have become habits. These habits of mind, as you might recall from the introductory chapter, are called dispositions—habits of mind often seen as tendencies or characteristics. The dispositional dimension of the brain asserts that everyone has formed habitual ways of processing information and that these mental habits influence what individuals perceive and how they conceive information. For Ralph, seeing the positive and the possible will carry him through this tough day, and ultimately, it will bring him success. His leader wishes all of Ralph's colleagues were as optimistic and persistent.

Dispositional dimension
See Dimensions of the brain

Dispositions are often thought of as personal characteristics because they appear to be so constant, but that is the nature of habits. Leaders who understand the dispositional dimension of the brain will seek to understand the different dispositions of their followers, as well as purposefully develop dispositions that will lead to success. Research has identified a number of dispositions related to effective thinking. These include a disposition (a) to be broad and adventurous, (b) toward learning, problem-finding, and investigation, (c) to build explanations, (d) to make plans and be strategic, (e) to be intellectually careful, (f) to seek and evaluate reasons, and (g) to be metacognitive.[17] Metacognition means thinking about your own thinking. In other words, if you have developed the mental habit of reflecting on how you thought about something—the approach or strategy you used, what you know and do not know, what you did well and did not do well in how you thought it through—then you have a metacognitive disposition, and that is part of good thinking.[18]

Metacognition thinking about your own thinking

Understanding different dispositions allows leaders to more effectively communicate and structure tasks to suit different strengths, which in turn help highlight the assets of what might appear otherwise. For example, what might appear as rebellious might be the perfect disposition for a team that tends to the status quo. Below is a list of troublesome characteristics, some of which could be dispositions, and how they might be alternatively seen as strengths. As a leader, how could you build a disposition that sees the strengths in others?

What Might Be Seen As:	Could Be This Strength:	What Do You Need to Do . . . 1. To see it that way? 2. To guide it to that?
Scattered	Creative	
Schedule-driven	Prompt	
Rigid	Organized	
Pushy	Assertive	
Loud	Outgoing	
Meek and deferential	Thoughtful and respectful	
Shy	Reflective or observant	
Very sensitive	Empathetic	
Unrealistic	Optimistic	
Pessimistic	Cautious and prepared	
Uncooperative and rebellious	Independent	

Effective Leadership: Creating Conditions Using Dimensions of the Brain

You are organizing a workshop for your regional managers. The regional managers are having a hard time with the site managers under their supervision, specifically, the regional managers are not happy with the leadership efficacy that they expect from their site managers. The regional and site managers know all sorts of information and practices of effective leadership; however, what they do not know is *how to create the conditions for effective leadership and success utilizing the dimensions of the brain.* What specific ideas and insight can your group offer the managers for how they might achieve the latter? Use the grid below to help guide crafting your recommendations.

Dimensions of the Brain	Key Questions for Leadership	What Should I Do as a Leader to Create Conditions for Effective Leadership, Design Relationships, and Achieve Follower Success?
Physiological	What physical conditions might be contributing to the situation? What role is stress playing in this culture and context? What other friendly or unfriendly brain conditions can you identify?	
Social	To what extent do individuals work and/or communicate with others? How do they do so advantageously and otherwise?	
Emotional	What emotions does this situation elicit? What are the levels of emotional intelligence of the individuals involved?	
Constructive	What are individuals' mental model of this situation? What is your mental model? What other constructions of the world (and the context) may be influencing others and your leadership?	
Reflective	What opportunities do others have to reflect on the situation? What prompts are guiding and framing their reflection . . . and yours?	
Dispositional	What dispositions (i.e., thinking habits) have individuals brought to this situation? What mental habits, in followers and yourself, would facilitate success?	

Developing Your Brain Leading

You can continue to develop your ability to connect what you know about the brain with your leadership activity. Here are two ways that you can purposefully build your brain leading:

1.   Continue analyzing situations through the lens of the six dimensions. Use a blank template and the prompting questions to list out what is going on across each dimension, and then compile some ideas for what a leader *could* do to address each of the oversights.

2.   Continue to add to your knowledge about the brain . . . and the implications of that knowledge. Using Table 5.2, continue to add ideas of specific things you might do as a leader in each dimension as you learn more.

3.   Get to know *your* brain. The more clearly you understand how *you* are influenced by your own brain, the more effectively you will be able to maximize your success and apply those lessons to leading others. The CORE™ Builder activity at the end of this chapter explains 11 different activities that you could have some fun with as you consider what dimensions are at work and how they are influencing you and others.

Dimension of the Brain	Applications for Leaders	What Specific Thing/s Can I Do as a Leader?
TABLE 5.2 ● Applications for Leaders From Connecting Leadership to the Brain[19]		
Physiological	-attend to physiological needs -stimulate neural growth -protect against stress	
Social	-create social opportunities -cultivate shared vision -invite diversity	
Emotional	-cultivate climate of trust and support -cultivate climate of challenge and passion -cultivate climate of emotional intelligence	
Constructive	-provide sites and structures for knowledge construction -construct knowledge that matters -challenge constructions of knowledge	
Reflective	-supply time, space, and structure for thinking -provoke thinking otherwise	
Dispositional	-proactively exercise multiple dimensions of intelligence -target productive thinking dispositions	

Design Thinking for Your Leadership Toolbox

Learning Objectives

5.2 Understand the effective application of design thinking to designing leadership relationships

5.3 Assess successful leadership relationship-building practices

5.4 Plan and engage user-centered methods to better understand followers and design relationships

5.5 Apply divergent thinking to generating ideas for building relationships

5.6 Formulate an iterative, integrative plan to sustain your leader-follower relationships

> *Excellence is an art won by training and habituation: we do not act rightly because we have virtue or excellence, but rather have these because we have acted rightly; these virtues are formed in man by doing his actions; we are what we repeatedly do. Excellence, then, is not an act but a habit.*
>
> —Will Durant, *The Story of Philosophy*[20]

Why would you want to think like a designer? Shouldn't you want to think like a leader? At this point in your textbook you should have a pretty good idea about what leadership is (and is not) and what effective leaders know, do, and are like. That was designing yourself as a leader. Designing beyond yourself, as the rest of the textbook examines, requires a more unique set of tools—tools that will facilitate your explorations, help you generate innovative ideas, and generally make you a more creative problem solver, better decision maker, and effective leader. The world of design has developed an extraordinarily useful tool in the form of **design thinking**.

The *way* people think determines the way people behave, as this text has often noted. If you have taken a philosophy course, you know that people have been trying to understand their own thinking for quite a long time, both generally and within fields of practice. Designers too have long discussed what a *designerly* way of thinking looks like.[21] Emanating from efforts to understand how designers give "form, organization, and order to physical things," designers have moved to apply this to human action, specifically to give form to "a desired state of affairs."[22] In other words, how does one design an experience that results in specific outcomes?

Design thinking provides a unique problem-solving methodology and mindset that is particularly well-suited to the wicked problems and ambiguous challenges of leadership, focusing on *what ought to be* (innovation) versus *what is* (analysis).[23] Picture yourself working on a group project with some classmates. You are all meeting about the project and trying to address the problem at hand. Can you envision the typical conversation? "Ok, what do we need to do?" "Anyone know anything about this problem?" "Anyone have any ideas?" "What if we do this?" And the conversation continues as it usually does—sometimes with innovative, excellent results, but most often, not so much.

But what if you were a design thinker? What if *you* were the person in the group who raised a question that was so unique that it guided the group in a more fruitful direction? That is what design thinking is and does. Take a moment to examine the key questions in Table 5.3. Imagine yourself raising each of these questions.

Design thinking is often used synonymously with design process, particularly as it has been applied to business settings.[24] You will read more about design process as creative problem-solving in Chapter 8 when you are designing others' success. However, although *doing* certain things when you solve a problem may influence your thinking, it does not entail a *thinking habit*. One of the best ways to distinguish design thinking from the activity of a design process lies in what and how a design thinker would think that is different from any other smart problem solver. Take another look at Table 5.3, this time focusing on the definitions of each of the dispositions. To what extent do you think like this, in each of these ways? Assess yourself on each of the design-thinking dispositions, and note which one/s are strengths for you and which one/s you need to further develop.

Design thinking can be applied to any problem, but it is uniquely suited to addressing complex, ambiguous, wicked problems. A **wicked problem** is a problem that is difficult or impossible to solve because of incomplete information, multiple perspectives, dynamic variables, and interconnections with other problems.[25] Because of this complexity, wicked problems resist solution, and solutions that are applied often result in additional problems. Social problems often comprise wicked problems—issues like poverty, homelessness, drug abuse, obesity, and . . . effective leadership. Wicked problems cannot be fixed or solved, but they can be incrementally and systematically improved. Design thinking, effective leadership, and you can help make that difference.

The next section of this chapter explores each of the six design-thinking dispositions, briefly (re)introducing each with definition and key question, followed by how that design-thinking disposition applies to designing your leadership relationships. More importantly, this section offers ideas and activities for developing each of the design-thinking dispositions (remember, these are mental habits). One helpful way to remember and apply the design-thinking dispositions is by embedding them into the design process: understand, imagine, and implement. When this process was introduced in Chapter 1, it was noted that you would be designing something much more complicated than a pen and that attending to the full process would be critical. Add design thinking to following a full design process to greatly enhance your design capability.

Design thinking This is a cognitive approach to engaging problems that embodies a specific mindset that is **Explorative:** mindset that assumes purposeful ambiguity and curiosity; **User-centered:** mindset that focuses on the user and how they experience and feel; **Divergent:** mindset of generating many, many ideas for a single problem; **Multidisciplinary:** mindset that engages many minds and pursues multiple areas of expertise; **Integrative:** mindset of attending to and balancing multiple criteria, particularly viability, feasibility, and desirability; and **Iterative:** mindset of always seeing solutions in process—assessing and improving. Also, habits of mind (dispositions) that designers use to help enhance and guide their process.

Wicked problem a problem that is difficult or impossible to solve because of incomplete information, multiple perspectives, dynamic variables, and interconnections with other problems

TABLE 5.3 ● Design Thinking Dispositions and Key Questions

Design Thinking . . . is a cognitive approach to engaging problems that embodies a specific mindset that is:	What If I Was the Person in the Room Who Asks . . .	How Likely Am I to Raise That Question? (0 = Not to 10 = Very)
Explorative Mindset that assumes purposeful ambiguity and curiosity	What if everything we know about this problem is wrong or untrue?	
User-centered Mindset that focuses on the user and how they experience and feel	How would the user view this problem? How would they feel? What user information do we need?	
Divergent Mindset of generating many, many ideas for a single problem	What processes can we use to generate many, many ideas?	
Multidisciplinary Mindset that engages many minds and pursues multiple areas of expertise	What other perspectives and expertise could inform? What less obvious fields might offer new perspectives? In what ways could we engage others in the process?	
Integrative Mindset of attending to and balancing multiple and contrasting variables, and creatively resolving the tensions between them	What are the various goals, issues, and stakeholders that we must consider? How could we increase solution viability, feasibility, and desirability?	
Iterative Mindset of always seeing solutions in process—assessing and improving	How can we assess and improve this solution? Can we build a prototype or pilot test?	

Explorative and User-Centered to Understand

One of the greatest challenges in working with others is not their misunderstanding but rather their conviction that their current misunderstanding is actually correct. They are unconsciously incompetent. This notion has been captured in a model of learning called the Four Stages for Learning Any New Skill.[26] In brief, when you learn something you go through four stages. First, you are unconsciously incompetent—you are so clueless that you do not even realize how clueless you are. Ouch. But it gets worse. The next stage is consciously incompetent, which means you now have a clue . . . but still limited skill. From there you slowly move into conscious competence—you know what you know and can do, and you can do it. Here is where things get a little strange. The final stage is unconscious competence. This is where you are so skilled and so experienced that you do not even have to think about what you are doing—you just do it and do it well. If you have a skill-based hobby, play a sport, or drive a car you might have a sense of this. You cannot really explain how to do it anymore because those details have become second nature—you just do them.

Knowing that your brain has a constructive and dispositional dimension, this model should be no surprise. However, this model helps you realize that there is more to learning than just the acquisition of skill or knowledge—that there are limitations to your awareness through the process. Possessing the metacognitive capacity to recognize this lack of awareness will give you a more accurate indication of where you are on your way to really understanding something. That is only half of the challenge. Ability is one thing, willingness yet another. As you grow in your confidence, experience, and expertise you will be increasingly looked to for answers. Your expectations of yourself as an expert who has answers will reinforce your desire to find the simple explanation. And you will be more likely to develop a deadly disorder: The God complex. Tim Harford describes the origins of this notion and describes the symptoms of the God complex: "No matter how complicated the problem, you have an absolutely overwhelming belief that you are infallibly right in your solution."[27] Recognizing, accepting, and acting on the idea that you might be mistaken—in the way you see a situation, your understanding of the problem or context, or in the solution you propose—is absolutely critical to designing leadership relationships and ultimately successful leadership. The explorative and user-centered design-thinking dispositions help you do just that.

Explorative

Explorative *See* Design thinking

The **explorative** mindset assumes purposeful ambiguity and curiosity, and it asks: What if everything we know about this problem is wrong or untrue?

Have you ever felt really stupid? Of course you have—we all have—and surprisingly we should strive to feel that more often. But why? The explorative disposition highlights the importance of being *productively stupid*. "I'm not talking about 'relative stupidity,' in which the other students in the class actually read the material, think about it, and ace the exam; whereas you don't. I'm also not talking about bright people who might be working in areas that don't match their talents," explains Martin Schwartz in *The Importance of Stupidity in Scientific Research*.[28] Productive stupidity means questioning and pushing your understanding and seeking out and allowing others to do so. "The more comfortable we become with being stupid, the deeper we will wade into the unknown and the more likely we are to make big discoveries."

REFLECTION QUESTION

What CORE™ (confidence, optimism, resilience, engagement) capacities are necessary for you to comfortably pursue productive stupidity?

Inquisitiveness
an inclination to ask questions, seek information, or otherwise inquire

The explorative disposition can best be described as a combination of curiosity and **inquisitiveness**, which is an inclination to ask questions, seek information, or otherwise inquire.[29] Curiosity piques your interest, but inquisitiveness puts that intrigue into explorative action. There are two facets to the explorative pursuit—one focused on a specific problem or a general, nonspecific approach. When focusing on a single problem the explorative disposition pushes you to find both the deep and the broad regarding that problem. The broad dimension of the problem includes understanding things like the context, history, other solutions that have been tried (and why and how they did and did not work), the range of stakeholders, and so forth. The deep dimension asks that you dig down to find the root of the issue or problem. Finding the more basic, underlying dynamics within a relationship will help you focus on the most impactful solution. The skill builder activity at the end of this chapter called Relationship Designer provides a checklist of activities covering the full design process and engaging all of the design-thinking dispositions.

In a group or work setting, the explorative disposition can be the most aggravating. Imagine having someone in your group who is persistent in questioning the group's understanding of things. However, this level of questioning, even when there is no *problem*, underpins innovation and continuous improvement.[30] As a leader, you can build a culture of inquisitiveness, curiosity, and questioning. One fun approach is by encouraging yourself and your followers to be *explorers of the world*, as author Keri Smith encourages. She offers some advice to help prompt your capacity to see things through new eyes like an explorer.

1. Always be looking. (Notice the ground beneath your feet.)

2. Everything is interesting. Look closer.

3. Alter your course often.

4. Observe for long durations (and short ones).

5. Notice the stories going on around you.

6. Notice patterns. Make connections.

7. Observe movement.

8. Trace things back to their origins.

9. Use all of the senses in your investigations.[31]

Exploratory activities can give you and your team a playful yet important start to observing more, seeing differently, and understanding more deeply.

User-Centered

The **user-centered** mindset focuses on the user and how they experience and feel, and it asks: How would the user view this problem? How would they feel? What user information do we need?

User-centered *See* Design thinking

What is it like to be you? What do you do all day? How do you feel? With whom do you interact and why and how? What spaces do you occupy during the day and night? What do you have in those spaces? User-centeredness has become an increasingly used design process because it seeks to deeply and authentically understand those individuals who will be affected by the design. More importantly, understanding the user will make it more likely the design will be accepted and used. For example, Christopher Charles was a Canadian student working in Cambodia to address anemia. He knew that anemia was caused by low levels of iron in the blood and that iron levels could be raised by simply putting a block of iron into the pots Cambodian families were using to cook food. After explaining this to families and distributing iron blocks, the families simply did not want to use the blocks because they were ugly and scratched up their pans. But in a stroke of user-centeredness, he researched his users and came upon the idea of combining the iron block with the Cambodian cultural reverence of fish. Shaping the iron into a fish made putting the lucky iron fish in cookpots very desirable. And consequently, anemia levels dropped substantially.[32]

Developing a user-centered disposition starts with respecting the perspectives of others and then seeking to discover what that perspective entails. But how do you find out what others think, feel, and see? Answering the question of how to get inside someone else's head is perhaps the most interesting and challenging facet of design thinking. How do you develop that level of empathy? Asking questions is a good start, maybe doing some observing, or perhaps a formal interview. Luckily, many additional methods have been developed to help discover and discern the user perspective. The design firm IDEO, highlighted at the beginning of this chapter, incorporates user-centeredness as a core phase in their process. In a particularly poignant user-centered example, the team at IDEO is asked to redesign the emergency room experience at a large hospital. They decide to capture the patient experience by putting one of their team through the emergency room while toting a large video camera to capture the experience. What they get back, to the surprise of the hospital leaders, is an extended video of ceiling tiles and lights. That is what it looks and feels like to be a patient in the hospital.

What does it feel like to be led by you? To work in your organization? To interact with you on a regular basis as a follower? These are the questions you need to answer as you design your leadership relationships. As noted, there are many tools for acquiring user-centered information, including two developed by IDEO: The Field Guide to Human-Centered Design and design Method Cards.[33] Each card in the method deck highlights a way of acquiring and interpreting others. Here are some excellent examples—try these with one of your friends and see what new things you learn about him or her:

- *Behavioral archaeology*—*look for the evidence of people's activities inherent in the placement, wear patterns, and organization of places and things—how do artifacts and environments figure in people's lives and highlight aspects of their lifestyle, habits, priorities, and values?*

- *Activity analysis*—*list or represent in detail all tasks, actions, objects, performers, and interactions involved in a process.*

- *Guided tours*—*accompany participants on a guided tour of the project-relevant spaces and activities they experience.*[34]

Right now, this generation of leaders—employers, managers, salespersons, teachers, clergy—is working hard to figure out how the next generation thinks. What do new employees value? How do they like to work? What will inspire them? In what settings and culture do they achieve? Currently, the buzz centers around millennials seeking jobs that offer a better quality of life rather than greater compensation.[35] What will be the driving force for your generation? More important, what will drive the generation after you—the individuals with whom you will be striving to design a relationship? A user-centered disposition will ensure that you pursue activities to really find out.

Empathy: User-Centeredness at the Deep End of the Pool[36]

Designing your leadership relationships must incorporate user-centeredness. Without this information and perspective, you are stuck at Rule #1 (It's about you). When followers perceive that your actions do not include them, they are unlikely to see their place in the organization and vision. "Humans react to emotional probes—solicited or not—that are often accompanied by emotional assurances rather than logic, reason, or dispassion. I call these 'emosurances.'"[37] What would you need to know from your leader in order to feel *emotionally* assured?

From the designing leadership relationships perspective, you are seeking much more than a deep and accurate understanding of your followers. Rather, you are seeking a level of trust and authenticity that only comes with a connection built with true empathy. Empathy is emotionally putting yourself in someone else's position—to share and understand their feelings, needs, concerns, and emotional state. Empathy only exists when you have experienced the same situation; and even then, you are not the same person who brings the same background, mental models, and dispositions to the situation. Nonetheless, the ability to emotionally and personally understand the needs of each follower fosters perceived leadership.[38]

What is the difference between your teacher and this textbook or the difference between you as a leader and an employee handbook that outlines all activities? That difference comprises the distinctly *human* part of leadership, and it matters. Consider some of the best relationships you have. They are generally based on a feeling that the other person really understands and can relate to you. Empathy builds trust, provides support and stability, communicates acceptance and authenticity, opens communication, and generally fosters a positive culture. "'You can't hate someone whose story you know.' You don't have to like the story, or even the person telling you their story. But listening creates a relationship."[39] Like all mental habits, engaging in the user-centered and empathic practices again and again will develop this disposition over time.

LEADERSHIP BY DESIGN

Design Principle: Mental Model

Definition: Your mental representation of things in the world—not just the picture in your head but how you understand things and even how you process information.[40]

In Other Words: How *you* see and understand anything and everything based on your experiences.

For Example: Your brain is a lean, mean, pattern-making machine (remember this from Chapter 2?). Picture a car. Now ask a friend to do the same and compare. There is often a common, generalized mental model shared by many, but your mental model will always be uniquely yours.

For Leaders: How would you describe your relationship with one of your friends? Would they describe it the same way? Effectively designing relationships means attending to your and their mental model of the relationship, how it functions, what it means. As you learned with LMX theory, the changing nature of a leader-follower relationship has many implications for how individuals successfully interact and work together. For design thinkers, understanding the mental models of others is critical to design success. User-centered methods help leaders understand and empathize with followers. Recognizing mental models also helps one break outside that model, which is a critical step for taking other perspectives into account, thinking divergently, and iterating your design.

Using This Design-Thinking Disposition:	Which I Could Further Develop With These Activities:	I Could Work to Design My Leadership Relationships by:
Explorative	Relook to find the more basic, underlying problem	What do I need to better understand others and my relationships with them?
	Engage preflection and reflection on your process	
	Choose an unrelated field and force a solution	
User-Centered and Human-Focused	Visualize the problem or solution from the user point of view	
	Spend a day in the life of the user (or an hour)	
	Interview, observe, interview, observe	
	Try to replace as many functions as possible with what a computer could do—what is left?	
	Visualize the problem or solution void of all technology	
	Research and engage in emotional intelligence and empathy building	

Divergent and Multidisciplinary to Imagine

In what ways might we . . . ? What would happen if . . . ? What are all the different ways we could . . . ? After working to understand your problem to the extent possible, it is time to shift to a period of imagining. Many leaders come up with a solution that seems workable and then head to implementation. This is called **satisficing**, which is a process of *satisficing* minimal criteria with a solution that will *suffice*. Design thinkers utilize two habits of mind that help maximize their idea-generating capability—divergent thinking and multidisciplinary thinking. While all the design-thinking dispositions help leaders to see differently, these two are particularly suited to the imagine phase, and in turn, they will help you generate many possible ideas for designing your leadership relationships.

Satisficing a process of *satisfying* minimal criteria with a solution that will *suffice*

Divergent

The divergent mindset generates many, many ideas for a single problem, and it asks: What processes can we use to generate many, many ideas?

Right now, can you set this textbook aside and write down 20 different uses for a pencil besides writing? Go ahead and try it. You probably came up with things such as something to poke someone with, a chopstick, a conductor's baton, a hair tie, a back scratcher, and maybe even something a bit odd like a crutch for a wounded squirrel. Now, imagine trying to generate 50 uses or 100—probably feels impossible, right? Wrong. This is what divergent thinkers do—and you can do it too. The immediate problem is that you have been trained in school for many years to be a convergent thinker. *Convergent* thinkers take lots of information and converge it into a single essay or test answer or model. By contrast, **divergent** thinking is the process of generating many ideas from a single problem, much like the multiple uses challenge, which is a classic creativity assessment.

Divergent *See* Design thinking

Divergent thinking underpins creativity, and it is key to generating ideas. But while generating ideas implies something of value, divergent thinking is really about quantity—coming up with as many answers as possible. Developing a divergent-thinking disposition requires confidence, comfort with ambiguity, a tolerance for intellectual risk-taking, and the mental habit of making distant connections, all without self-judging or self-editing. This challenging set of characteristics is why most individuals and groups satisfice, even when they say they are *brainstorming*. Brainstorming actually has strict rules that include going for quantity and no judgments, which are intended to facilitate divergent thinking. Chapter 8: "Creativity, Problem-Solving, and Idea-Generating" examines this concept and many other methods for generating ideas, in great detail.

Building your divergent-thinking disposition requires engaging in any activities where you need to generate many ideas from a single problem. Here are some fun examples:

- Choose an item from your pocket or purse or bag—list as many professions or roles that could use that item (and how).

- You are the dictator with great power. Think of as many ways as you can to control people.

- Alpha doodle—using a single letter, doodle as many different pictures as you can using that letter as the basis.

- Think of as many business ideas based on a childhood hobby or experience or toy. And then, think of all the worst business ideas . . . ever.

- Real-life superheroes—generate as many stories and scenarios for a given person/s you see in public. ("See that guy . . . he's a pirate . . . on his way to the big eye-patch sale.")

- You have a bag full of candy bars and a campus full of students. What fun things could you convince people to do with or for the candy (nothing illegal or unethical)?

Divergent thinking seems like all fun, and in fact, there is no reason why developing this disposition need not be fun. Unfortunately, the fun aspect often works against bringing divergent thinking into serious organizations because of two fears. The first of these fears lies in management believing that if followers are encouraged to think divergently and engage in this kind of go-for-quantity/no self-editing behavior that it will open up the gates of craziness and never end. This fear is easily remedied with a little management of the process, simply indicating when, where, and within what parameters the group will engage divergent thinking. And of course, making very clear when it will end and when the process will move forward to implementation.

The second fear is that the activity will be a waste of time, generating nothing but silly answers with no useful applications. This may be true . . . sort of. Any time invested in facilitating divergent thinking will be one step toward developing this disposition in others. So, at a minimum, the activity has that benefit. Realistically, however, the more ideas that are generated, the more likely that innovative idea will surface. There is no doubt the odds are in your favor when you generate 100 ideas for raising workplace happiness than if you generate five. Do not, however, expect those innovative ideas to be perfect and polished. Limited self-editing means you are looking for rough diamonds—the spark of an idea that will lead to the great innovation.

Multidisciplinary

The **multidisciplinary** mindset engages many minds and pursues multiple areas of expertise, and it asks: What other perspectives and expertise could inform? What less obvious fields might offer new perspectives?

Multidisciplinary *See* Design thinking

"It was six men of Indostan, to learning much inclined, who went to see the elephant, (though all of them were blind)."[41] Thus begins the poem by John Godfrey Saxe based on an ancient Chinese story about how each of six blind men touched a different part of the elephant and individually (and mistakenly) assumed what was in front of them. The man who touched the tail thought he had a rope, the one who touched the tusk thought he had a spear. In the end, the poem highlights their great dispute, rooted in their own conceptualization. How often have you worked with a group where everyone thought they had a grasp of the situation, yet each person had a different concept of the situation? And if you have ever worked with students majoring in fields different from yours, the differences are even greater. As the poem about the blind men and the elephant sums, "Though each was partly right, all were in the wrong."

> The fact is, encyclopedic knowledge is in the crowd, and specialized knowledge will rest with the individual. The leaders and experts of tomorrow have to be either polymaths (deep multidomain experts), curators (those who collect or collate different domains), polyglots (the overlay and meaning makers), or all three.[42]

A multidisciplinary disposition can also be described with the idea of the **T-shaped person**. This metaphor has been used since the early 1990s to describe a certain set of skills that were sought after in the design and technology fields.[43] The stem of the T represents an individual's depth of knowledge in their own field, while the cross of the T models an individual's capacity to collaborate and work with other disciplines. Researchers and practitioners continue to define the skills and experiences that enable one to effectively communicate their expertise to other fields and, in turn, hear and incorporate expertise from other fields. These include things you would expect such as oral and written communication, exposure to other fields, and emotional intelligence in working with those of different perspectives. None of these skills will matter, however, if you do not have the disposition to value, seek out, and work to interpret the connections across disciplines.

T-shaped person This is a metaphor for expertise within and across disciplines. The stem of the T represents an individual's depth of knowledge in their own field, while the cross of the T models an individual's capacity to collaborate and work with other disciplines

Developing a multidisciplinary disposition merely requires that you purposefully and frequently engage with very different perspectives. With whom can you engage this week to begin to develop your multidisciplinary design-thinking disposition? In addition to building a uniquely valuable network, this will significantly broaden your ability to lead and innovate. A common way to accomplish this in a more organized manner is to put together a personal board of directors. Just like organizations have a group of individuals providing guidance, each of whom brings a unique expertise, you too can thoughtfully put together a diverse group with whom you informally consult when wrestling with problems or simply thinking about future directions.

Similar to the dimensions of the brain, design-thinking dispositions also intertwine and work in a complementary manner. For example, the multidisciplinary mindset can function as a way to categorize user-centered information and further enhance divergent thinking. Taking a broader definition of discipline, you can construct a list of general person types or needs. If you were tasked to design a new park for your community, you might imagine a list of persons as follows:

- I need a place to reflect on big problems.
- My arthritic knees feel better when I can take a walk.
- I need to entertain my toddler safely.
- I need a place to meet with colleagues—a place where we can talk.
- I need a place to meet and impress important visitors.
- Healthy living and eating are important to me.
- I love to garden.
- I am training for a 10K run.
- I like to watch birds and identify new ones.
- I just want a place to eat my lunch in peace.
- I like to play Frisbee.
- I want to have a picnic with my family.
- I like to ride my bike to different places.
- I want a place to play with my kids.
- I need a place to run my environmental research studies.

If you put yourself in each of these roles, what do you envision yourself doing? In what kind of space do you envision yourself doing it? Adopting multiple perspectives is another idea-generating technique that will be further explored in Chapter 7 on creative problem-solving. The ability to consider these multiple and competing demands illustrates the next design-thinking disposition: integrative thinking.

Using This Design-Thinking Disposition:	Which I Could Further Develop With These Activities:	I Could Work to Design My Leadership Relationships by:
Divergent	Find 50 uses for an object; find 100 uses . . . Engage "What if" . . . current solutions were not possible Reverse the problem and brainstorm; then un-reverse solutions	In how many different ways can I build those relationships?
Multidisciplinary and Collaborative	Engage and interview experts in other fields Visualize your problem in another context Bring together diverse groups to discuss a problem Incorporate and build off the ideas of others Work in codesign and team-based projects Engage others to play devil's advocate and strive for consensus	

FIGURE 5.3

Source: By permission, John L. Hart FLP and Creators Syndicate, Inc.

Integrative and Iterative to Implement

The explorative and user-centered dispositions help you better understand others and your relationship with them. Divergent and multidisciplinary dispositions help you generate many ideas and approaches to building those relationships. The final two design-thinking dispositions help you sustain and grow your leadership relationships. Integrative thinking enables you to see multiple and competing facets of a relationship, to which you must attend, while iterative thinking prompts you to continuously assess and improve those relationships.

Integrative

The **integrative** mindset attends to and balances multiple criteria, particularly viability, feasibility, and desirability, and it asks: What are the various goals, issues, and stakeholders that we must consider? How could we increase solution viability, feasibility, and desirability?

Integrative *See* Design thinking

Have you ever tried to juggle? Juggling a single ball is easy. Your sole focus is on the one and only ball. Add a second ball and things get a bit more interesting but are still manageable. Add a third, fourth, fifth ball . . . and eat a sandwich . . . and text your friend, and your mind is racing to track and shift across many foci. At this point in life, you should know that multitasking is a myth; that in reality you are rapidly shifting your attention from task to task. Your brain is pretty nimble, and shifting focus is an early-acquired mental habit that has been well developed such that we seem to balance multiple thoughts in our head—a pretty handy skill for any complex endeavor such as driving a car, cooking a meal, or leading an organization.

The integrative disposition represents habitual ways of thinking that facilitate leadership performance. Roger Martin, dean of the Rotman School of Management at the University of Toronto, interviewed over 50 successful leaders. He

found that most of them share a somewhat unusual trait: They have the predisposition and the capacity to hold in their heads two opposing ideas at once. And then, without panicking or simply settling for one alternative or the other, they're able to creatively resolve the tension between those two ideas by generating a new one that contains elements of the others but is superior to both.[44]

Martin further explains integrative thinking in the context of decision-making, clarifying that the uniqueness of the integrative thinker lies in how he or she approaches and works through each step. Of course, that is a disposition by definition—a habitual way of thinking.

Interestingly, the disposition of an integrative thinker sounds similar to some of the characteristics of an expert as described in Chapter 1. Martin contrasts conventional decision-making with that of an integrative thinker by highlighting their tendency to seek, consider, and conceptualize more broadly and systemically. Likewise, experts are able to notice features and patterns that nonexperts miss, and experts conceptualize content in a more complex and integrated manner. This is important to note because you may need to acquire a level of expertise before or while you fully develop your integrative-thinking disposition.

There are still facets of integrative thinking that you can develop even if you are not an expert, and you can certainly put this thinking to use. Integrative thinkers recognize their own mental models and are both capable and comfortable considering information contrary to that model. Martin explains that "great integrative thinkers are fairly rare . . . because putting it to work makes us anxious. Most of us avoid complexity and ambiguity and seek out the comfort of simplicity and clarity."

The willingness to see complexity captures the great utility of integrative thinking. Applied to designing relationships, a leader with this disposition excels in identifying the broad range of variables and the systems that they comprise. Designing productive leader-follower relationships often depends on how well you can balance a variety of competing and contrasting aspects, as well as how you can creatively resolve those tensions. For example, an incompetent follower today will likely become competent over time. An employee you know to be skilled is having an *off* day. In one context, your follower shines, but not so much in another context. And a personal characteristic considered troublesome may have some uniquely positive applications in the eyes of an integrative-thinking leader.

Iterative

Iterative *See* Design thinking

The **iterative** mindset always sees solutions in process—assessing and improving, and it asks: How can we assess and improve this solution? Can we build a prototype or pilot test?

If you have ever watched an infant go from crawling to walking, you have seen them pull up, wobble, fall, and repeat. Each time may be only marginally better, but after what seems like thousands of falls, they become a toddler, then a walker, runner, and more. When *you* try something and fail, how many times do you typically try again? Two? Three? Although a toddler's degree of resilience is admirable, the fascinating aspect is that humans seem to be hardwired with the *try-fail-improve-try again* cycle. In other words, you are a natural at iteration. So, why is iteration so often left out of the problem-solving process?

Purposeful iteration is the process of revising based on feedback. As a disposition of design thinking, iteration requires both practice and the development of numerous supporting personal characteristics. Examine the list below. Which of the following do you find easy and which rather difficult?

- Willingness to change your idea and openness to being uncertain or wrong

- Critical-thinking ability to see shortcomings

- Creative-thinking ability to see potential

- Comfort with trying imperfect ideas

- Confidence enough to fail and see it as informative

- Resilient enough to try again

- Optimistic enough to know there's a better idea out there

- Purposeful trial and error, allowing you to make mistakes in the right direction and continuously improve

The iterative disposition is of great importance to every aspect of designing your leadership. An iterative leader constantly assesses and improves themselves, their performance, and their organization. Even though this activity may seem obvious, it is too often one of the last considerations in leadership. As a regular activity, iteration results in keeping up with current changes in market, users, and context; innovative ideas and possible new directions; and an accurate understanding of organizational quality. As a disposition applied to leadership relationships, iterative thinking communicates accountability, care, and reciprocal credibility. In other words, your attention and follow through as a leader build your credibility, and your work with followers to understand their performance and facilitate their improvement builds their credibility in your eyes.

Using This Design-Thinking Disposition:	Which I Could Further Develop With These Activities:	I Could Work to Design My Leadership Relationships by:
Integrative	Assess your solution for viability, feasibility, and desirability . . . improve each	What can I do to sustain and grow my relationships?
	Consider two competing interests . . . generate creative solutions to resolve . . . repeat	
	Again, identify a conflict . . . find an alternative perspective . . . find another	
Iterative	Force yourself to revise a solution . . . five times . . . ten times . . .	
	Assess anything and then generate ideas to make it better	
	Discard your current solution and start anew	

Assess Your Design Thinking, Then Design Leadership Relationships

Applying the design-thinking dispositions to designing leadership relationships can begin immediately. These ways of thinking can be used as conscious tools now. The more you actively use them, the sooner they will become habits. And the more practice you get with each disposition, the more specific uses you will uncover. You can revisit the summary tables at the end of each prior section and commit to engaging in different activities to build your design-thinking habits. The Design Thinking Assessment in Table 5.4 can better guide which dispositions you already tend to use and which could be further developed.

TABLE 5.4 ● Design Thinking Assessment

Instructions: Below are statements that describe how you may think during and about your own problem-solving. For each statement, please check one of the following: Always, Almost always, More often than not, Sometimes, Not very often, Never.

SCORE	6	5	4	3	2	1
Statement about your problem-solving	Always	Almost always	More often than not	Sometimes	Not very often	Never
1 When solving problems, I set aside time to imagine *crazy* ideas						
2 I research the history of the problem						
3 I think about how making my idea more affordable might make it less effective						
4 I establish written criteria for my solution						
5 I solicit ideas or feedback from others outside my field of practice/study						
6 I avoid viewing the problem through the eyes of those directly affected by it						
7 Setting aside the problem criteria for a time, I will generate at least 20 ideas for solving a problem before choosing one						
8 I make sure I am aware of nearly all the previous solution ideas to a problem						
9 I strive for excellence in meeting one goal (versus balance in meeting multiple goals)						
10 I am willing to start over on a problem						
11 I take time to explore how other fields have addressed my problem						
12 I note how individuals interact with the problem						
13 I utilize specific techniques (besides *brainstorming*) to come up with ideas						
14 In my problem-solving process, I purposefully set aside my initial ideas						
15 I note the competing needs of a problem						
16 I build and test prototypes of my solution						
17 I purposefully avoid *crazy* perspectives						
18 I take time to collect information about the user of the solution						
19 I will move forward with a good idea as soon as I find it						
20 Throughout your problem-solving process, from start to finish, estimate the percentage of time you spend on each of the phases listed below:						

Researching and focusing the problem	Researching the users	Generating ideas	Assessing and prototyping solution	Revising solution	Implementing solution

Scoring Key

Questions 1–19 are organized as follows:

Design Thinking Disposition	Questions	Notes	Score Total
Divergent—generating many, many ideas for a single problem	1, 7, 13, 19	Q19 is reverse scored	(out of 24)
Explorative—assuming purposeful ambiguity and curiosity	2, 8, 14		(out of 18)
Integrative—attending to and balancing multiple criteria, particularly viability, feasibility, and desirability	3, 9, 15		(out of 18)
Iterative—always seeing solutions in process—assessing and improving	4, 10, 16		(out of 18)
Multidisciplinary—engaging many minds and pursuing multiple areas of expertise	5, 11, 17	Q17 is reverse scored	(out of 18)
User-Centered—focused on the user and how they experience and feel	6, 12, 18	Q6 is reverse scored	(out of 18)

Reflections and Insights

Chapter Summary

Designing your relationships with followers comprises one of the greatest leadership challenges. Kouzes and Posner provide five general practices of exemplary leaders that offer tips on how to design relationships. Effective leaders design relationships with each individual follower and note the nature of that relationship as it develops. Leader-Member Exchange theory focuses on that dyadic relationship and cautions leaders to maintain awareness of the development of in- and out-groups as each one-to-one relationship develops.

Relating to others, and influencing them, requires understanding how people think and how their brain operates. There are many brain features and processes that all individuals share. If a leader understands these processes, they can more effectively relate to and lead others. While the brain consists of many, many detailed elements, your lean, mean, pattern-making machine brain loves when things are simplified and organized. Thus, one helpful way to understand the brain is by using six dimensions: physiological, emotional, social, constructive, reflective, and dispositional. The six dimensions can be examined separately for their impacts and influences on overall performance, even though the dimensions all overlap and influence one another.

The dispositional dimension of the brain describes how your brain constructs processes that are revisited so often that they become mental habits, which results in habitual ways in which you think about and see the world. Some of the most useful tools for you as a leader are dispositions that help you see more broadly and solve problems more creatively. Collectively, these dispositions are called design thinking, and they include: explorative, user-centered, divergent, multidisciplinary, integrative, and iterative. Each of these mindsets provides unique and valuable tools as you design your leadership.

Key Terms

Constructive Dimension 127
Design Thinking 132
Dimensions of the Brain 123

Dispositional Dimension 129
Divergent 138
Emotional Dimension 125

Explorative 134
Inquisitiveness 134
Integrative 141

CORE™ Attribute Builders: Build Now for Future Leadership Challenges

Attribute: Confidence, Optimism, Resilience, and Engagement

Builder: Getting to Know Your Brain activities.

Engage in the activity described below. Then think carefully about how leaders are influenced (and how they influence others) and what this means about what leaders know, do, or are like. As you do so, you will find many opportunities to build your confidence, practice your optimism, test your resilience, and engage. Write your insights in a 1-page paper.

Assignment #1: Eye Contact

Monitor your eye contact with others. For at least one day, try looking directly into the eyes of others. What are your thoughts and reactions? What reactions do you notice in others? Do you notice a reaction from others in days after?

Assignment #2: Dominant Hand

Consider things you do with your dominant hand— eating, brushing your teeth, steering your car, turning the pages of a book, and so forth. Choose 2–3 of these activities and complete them with your nondominant hand for a couple of days. Reflect on the experience.

Assignment #3: Emotional Quotient x3

Choose three individuals you interact with every day. Assess their emotional intelligence by observing their reactions to situations. Choose a day in which you are purposely contrary with these individuals and another in which you are consistently agreeable. Add this to your assessment.

Assignment #4: Big Smile

On your commute to school and/or work each day for a couple of consecutive days, smile continuously for the five minutes just prior to your arrival at work. Assess your mood and emotions each day and at the end of the week.

Assignment #5: Emotional Quotient Machine

Identify a machine that is used frequently (you decide the context). Inconspicuously place an 'Out of Order' sign on the machine and observe the comments and emotions you observe for 1 hour. Note how many individuals try the machine despite the sign. For added fun, step up and use the machine as dejected parties step away. Caution: Make sure you choose a machine that is not life or career threatening—to you or others.

Assignment #6: Routines

Consider a routine you have. It might be a morning routine before you start your day, when you first arrive at work, or a routine before going to sleep at night. Choose one routine and alter it so that you do something different or in a different order every day for a few days. At the end of that time consider how the experience felt and what you thought.

Assignment #7: Decision-Making Perspectives

Consider a decision you are about to make. On what are you basing your decision? Find three individuals very different from yourself: one of a different gender, one of a different generation/age, and one of a different ethnicity/culture. Find out their perspective on the decision (the one you are about to make). What would they decide, and on what would their decision be based? Write a letter to a friend explaining the decision, what you decided, how you decided and why, and what you learned from consulting with those different than yourself.

Assignment #8: Reflection

Choose a time during your day to sit alone in a quiet space for 15 minutes and listen to your own breathing— no television or phone, no colleagues, no Internet, no reading material, no lunch—nothing. Do this every day for a few days. After spending the time doing this, reflect on any changes in your reactions and interactions with others, as well as the overall experience.

Assignment #9: Something New

Resolve to find and experience something completely new (really, really new) to you every day for a few days. It may be eating a new food, listening to music you are unfamiliar with, going into a store you have never been in, visiting a town you have never been to, or talking to someone you do not know. At the end of this time, consider how you felt and what you thought during and after the experience. Did this change your view of things you were familiar with and the idea of exploring new things?

Assignment #10: Worn Out

Wear something out of character for you—not something ridiculous so that others assume you are being silly but rather something that clearly gets attention, has others questioning, but would not necessarily be considered a joke. Note how others react and interact with you. If you are really feeling daring, try wearing something that crosses gender or other cultural assumptions a bit, like men wearing a sparkly decorative pin or a college student pulling a little red wagon—if that is out of character for you, of course.

Skill Builder Activity

Relationship Designer—Follow and complete the different activities to facilitate your relationship design. Note how the different design-thinking capacities enhance the design process.

	Assignment/Prompt	Design-Thinking Disposition	Design Process Phase
1	Consider relationships of interest to you—which ones do you want to know more about and make a difference regarding?	Explorative	Understand
2	Write a brief history of specific relationships—both a professional history and your personal history.	Explorative	Understand
3	Create a visual model to better understand different aspects of the relationship—for example, a mental map or a systems diagram.	Explorative	Understand
4	Write the *story* of solutions as it regards these relationships and highlight *best practices*—when was the relationship at its best?	Explorative	Understand
5	Engage user-centered methods to collect information, identifying the stakeholders. Consider what kind of relationship you want with each individual.	User-centered	Understand
6	Envision the ideal solutions and/or outcomes—what would/could it look like, and how?	Divergent	Understand Imagine
7	Generate many, many, many ideas for *solving* your issue or achieving your ideal.	Divergent	Imagine
8	Examine multiple views and perspectives on both your specific relationships as well as those of other leaders.	Multidisciplinary	Imagine
9	Research and establish criteria by which you will judge the success of your solution. Create metrics as applicable.	Iterative	Implement

	Assignment/Prompt	Design-Thinking Disposition	Design Process Phase
10	Craft a strategic implementation plan to develop your relationships. What different demands do you need to balance?	Integrative	Implement
11	Consider and plan possible collaborations. Who could help you advance your relationships?	Collaborative	Implement
12	Consider unintended consequences, worst cases, and ethical issues arising from your envisioned plan.	Iterative	Implement

6

Decision-Making

Do nothing, and nothing happens. Life is about decisions. You either make them or they're made for you, but you can't avoid them.

—Mhairi McFarlane

In any moment of decision, the best thing you can do is the right thing, the next best thing is the wrong thing, and the worst thing you can do is nothing.

—Theodore Roosevelt

Learning Objectives

6.1   Interpret the role of decision-making in leadership

6.2   Describe two types of decisions and key terminology

6.3   Demonstrate decision-making at the individual level

6.4   Understand decision-making at the group/team level

6.5   Apply and practice the SOLVE model of decision-making

6.6   Assess several barriers to effective decision-making

Detailed Chapter Outline

Introduction
Decisions, Decisions, Decisions
   in Leadership

Technical or Adaptive?
   Types of Problems
   Leaders Face

Leadership by Design Model

Design Self

How can I design myself as a leader?

DESIGN RELATIONSHIPS

AS A LEADER, HOW CAN I DESIGN MY RELATIONSHIPS WITH OTHERS?

Design Others' Success

As a leader, how can I design success for others?

Design Culture

As a leader, how can I design the culture of my organization?

Design Future

As a leader, how can I innovate?

Decision-making and problem-solving are at the core of a leader's work. Navigating challenges in a creative and ethical manner helps a leader stand out, and best serves the organizations they work to advance. This chapter helps readers better understand the role of decision-making in leadership, acquire one very useful decision-making model, and think more intentionally about some of the inherent barriers that individuals and groups face when making decisions. The chapter also highlights decision-making styles and other tips for helping leaders navigate the process of reaching the best course of action.

Introduction

Learning Objective

6.1 Interpret the role of decision-making in leadership

When Steve Jobs returned to Apple as chief executive officer in 1997, he decided to focus the company's efforts on a few great products. Over the next decade, he created one of the world's most valuable companies and revolutionized film, music, phones, and computing in the process.[1] In recent years, IBM has continued to move away from the hardware/laptop business and placed its bet on artificial intelligence, cloud computing, and big data/analytics.[2] In 2016, Patagonia decided to donate 100% of its $10 million in sales from Black Friday to charities that support planet Earth.[3] Leaders make decisions—decisions about what to do, how to do it, when, why, with whom, for how long, assuming what, and resulting in what end. Decisions can be mindful and purposeful, or they can be random, avoided, uninformed, and misguided. For anyone interested in leading, decision-making is a core activity of leadership.[4] Sometimes your decisions result in positive outcomes and sometimes not. Decisions are made alone, at times with others, but always relative to others. Followers, too, make decisions, which at times makes them the leader. Regardless of one's actions, a decision is always made, even if the decision is not to decide. The best leaders make decisions based on priorities aligned with their values and accept and work within the consequences of those decisions.

If decision-making is so critical to leadership, what do you need to know about decision-making? The answer is a lot. Over the years, scholars, consulting firms, and leaders have each developed simple and complex models of decision-making to help leaders more skillfully navigate the many complex challenges they face. Consider the definition of leadership as a process of influencing others toward a common vision. Baked into the definition is the need to determine a course of action—to decide on an idea to pursue. Consider former President Barack Obama as a case study. Throughout his presidency, the decisions he (and any president for that matter) made were complex problems that rarely had a clear solution. No expert or authority figure could be called to make a decision that would *fix* challenges such as The Islamic State (ISIS), the shrinking middle class, reduction of the deficit, gang violence, gun control, approaches to solving immigration challenges, and the list goes on. Some have lauded President Obama for his decisions, while others fundamentally disagreed with his stance on the issues listed above. At the core of any president's work is making decisions that advance the nation from its current state to a better future state. In essence, decision-makers are often running their best experiment. While this language may sound odd, it is true, and this chapter will explore the notion of experimentation and decision-making further.

Many of the problems collegiate leaders face are complex and challenging as well. For instance, many fraternity presidents and captains of athletic teams have worked diligently to stop hazing in their organizations. Other complex challenges on college campuses include freedom of association, alcohol/drug abuse, Title IX, sexual violence/assault, student cheating and misconduct, and issues of inclusion, race, and diversity. Again, there are many possible decision routes for each of these issues. No authority figure or expert can fix these problems, but leaders can make a difference by learning more about how to make the best decisions possible.

If those of you reading this textbook have *entered the fray* and worked to reduce or eliminate the challenges mentioned above, you know leadership is challenging work. Factions emerge. Ideologies clash. Conflict ensues. And you, and perhaps a group of colleagues, find yourself at the center of a proverbial storm. Leading others is not all tulips, warm-fuzzies, and chocolate bars. At times, the work of leadership is messy, high risk, difficult, challenging, and scary.

Decision-making is a core activity of leaders as they move groups from Point A to Point B. Even individuals who have chosen not to take on specific issues have decided to stay safe and maintain harmony. Sometimes a nondecision is the correct intervention—other times, this choice is damaging and dangerous.

As you move through this chapter and consider how to make more effective decisions, you may want to revisit Chapter 4 on ethics. In the final analysis, many of your decisions (and nondecisions) will either fall in line or not fall in line with your true north. Being intentional and deliberate in how your decisions align with your values is critical—it determines your character and ultimately impacts your relationship with others.

LEADERSHIP THAT MAKE A DIFFERENCE

Students across the globe are making a difference and tackling some real-world challenges that even the best scientists have yet to solve. Based on their expertise, they are making decisions about new and innovative ways to address our most difficult challenges. The following are three unique examples of how students, such as yourself, are using the techniques discussed in this chapter to change the world.

- At Rutgers, biomedical engineering student Katherine Lau led a team that created a prosthetic hand for a young girl. Through the use of a 3D printer, Lau and her team fashioned a device to improve the life of another. In fact, Lau said of the experience, "Getting that opportunity was a great experience. . . . The reason I want to be a biomedical engineer is to improve the lives of others. This summer, I got to see what my work can do for people."[5] Her decision to use 3-D printing as a tool to tackle this issue is unique, innovative, and potentially ground-breaking.

- At Texas A&M, Elon Musk, founder and CEO of SpaceX, sponsored a competition for high schoolers and collegians from all over the world. The purpose was to bring Musk's vision for a "fifth mode of transportation," the Hyperloop,

closer to reality. Participants were challenged to focus specifically on the Pod that people will travel in. The undergraduate team from Massachusetts Institute of Technology (MIT) took home first place.[6] The many creative and innovative decisions the team from MIT made stood out and helped them secure the win.

- The iGEM Foundation is "dedicated to education and competition, advancement of synthetic biology, and the development of open community and collaboration."[7] Students from around the world were challenged to answer the following question—"How do you kill cancer cells without killing healthy ones at the same time?"[8] Teams decided upon a number of creative and innovative approaches to help scientists detect, treat, and prevent cancer. In fact, a team from Israel worked on ways to pinpoint cancer cells. "Using an innovative combination of molecular biology and engineering, the team devised a system they called 'Boomerang,' which detects cancer cells by identifying two cancer-specific promoters in cells, and only targeting those cells for treatment. The team's work earned them five awards at the competition, including First Runner Up and Best Health and Medicine Project."[9]

Decisions, Decisions, Decisions in Leadership

Learning Objectives

6.2 Describe two types of decisions and key terminology

6.3 Demonstrate decision-making at the individual level

Technical or Adaptive? Types of Problems Leaders Face

Often, leaders and groups are deciding because they are working toward a better future state—an ideal end that will leave others in a better place. Having a clear understanding of the type of problem you are working is critical if you hope to make progress. Sometimes a decision is relatively simple and straightforward; you could ask, "What would you tell your best friend to do?"[10] However, sometimes the decisions are much more complicated. Many terms are used, and they can mean similar things. Regardless, you must define what kind of problem you are working to solve.

Technical or Tame Problems—You know you are working with a technical problem when there is a known solution to the issue. For instance, fixing a flat tire or cleaning out an individual's arteries. You can call an authority figure or expert, go to your favorite search engine, or even take a course on how to fix technical problems. Technical problems are relatively straightforward.

Adaptive Challenges/Wicked Problems/Ill-Defined Problems—Adaptive challenges do not benefit from a technical solution. In essence, a solution does not yet exist. In fact, you and the team are going to have to run some experiments, learn quickly, and build a bridge to a better future.[11] And while you may not solve the adaptive challenge, ideally you have moved the needle and now exist in a better place. For example, smoking has not been eliminated, but in the United States, the number of smokers has decreased drastically. Another example would be obesity. While fast food has mostly dropped in popularity, fast-casual chains (e.g., Chipotle, Panera Bread) are growing at a more rapid rate than some of the traditional fast-food chains.[12] However, the fact remains that obesity is a significant challenge in the United States. There is no expert or authority figure one can call with the answer to the solution for the problem of the obesity epidemic. Challenges such as obesity, the war on terror, and immigration are adaptive challenges. It takes experimentation and engaging in continuous learning to best understand how to tackle adaptive challenges—the students involved in some of the issues mentioned at the beginning of this chapter (e.g., hazing) are working on adaptive challenges.

Defining Decision-Making

Decision-making generally feels very difficult. People believe they prefer many options. But in reality, more choices can feel overwhelming and actually stifle making a decision. The word **decide** is defined as the process of making a choice or determining a course of action. However, the origin of the word decide comes from the Latin *de+caedere*, meaning *to cut off*. When you make a decision, you essentially cut off other options in order to pursue the decided option. No one wants to cut off options—they *might* work out. You *may* have missed an opportunity. This choice *may* never happen again. Yes, all those maybe outcomes will disappear—that is why decision-making is so difficult. But unless you make a decision and follow one option, you essentially follow none, and that is a problem in both leadership and life.

Decide the process of making a choice or determining a course of action

Decision-making is a specific process of choosing the best option, and it is often part of a more extensive process of problem-solving (see Chapter 8). The more you know about decision-making, the more comfortable you will be cutting off options, making decisions, and facilitating the decision-making of others.

Decision-making a specific process of choosing the best option

There must also be a clear understanding of **decision criteria** (also known as decision rules[13]), which are factors deemed essential to consider in the process of choosing a course of action. For instance, when selecting a major, a student may use the following decision criteria for making the decision: prospects for getting a job, time, amount of passion for the topic, rigor/time commitment, quality of professors, and so forth. Some models suggest that weight is assigned to each criterion as well. For instance, an individual may place a higher weight on the passion for the topic than the time of day the class meets.

Decision criteria factors deemed important to consider in the process of choosing a course of action

Decision-making occurs at multiple levels. The first is the individual level. **Individual-level decision-making** consists of those decisions you make by yourself, most of which are rarely conscious (e.g., what to wear, when to eat, your route to work, the pace of your walk, the amount of time you keep shampoo in your hair). While there is no concrete number of how many decisions an individual makes in a day, some research suggests that humans make more than 200 decisions a day about food alone.[14]

Individual-level decision-making decisions made by an individual

Group/Team-level decision-making is a more complicated process. A **group** is made up of individuals who are coordinating their work for some reason or another (e.g., shared gym time, where to eat, a place to study). However, there may not be a mutually shared end goal the individuals are collectively working toward. A **team** is a group of individuals with a collective target (e.g., win the championship). In a general sense, group decision-making has less emotional energy than team decision-making. For this chapter, the term group is used, but be aware that there is an essential distinction between a group and a team. The following chart summarizes the advantages and disadvantages to group decision-making.[15]

Advantages to Group Decision-Making	Disadvantages of Group Decision-Making
can accumulate more knowledge	often works more slowly than individuals
broader perspective, more ideas	may involve considerable compromise, which may lead to less-than-optimal decisions
participation increases individual satisfaction, support, involvement, and buy-in	often dominated by one individual or small clique
serves important communication functions	overreliance on group can inhibit management's ability to act quickly and decisively when necessary

At times, groups can be part of the problem (or the main problem). For instance, a decision-action gap exists when an individual or group knows what they should do but struggle to make the right or best decision for various reasons.[16] Another example is that the group may be unaware of what is not being discussed. Specific topics are taken off the table (consciously or unconsciously) by decision makers—these are called **nondecisions**, which

are the covert issues about which a decision has effectively been taken that they will not be decided. They are controversial topics which go against the interests of the powerful stakeholders: they do not engender support, they do not fit with the prevailing culture, they are not considered acceptable for discussion, so they are quietly sidestepped or surpassed or dropped. A knowledge of what these issues are is likely to be as revealing, or more so, as knowledge of what is overtly being discussed. They are what is really going on, not just on the surface, but underneath it. The decisions which are being discussed in the board room, in meetings, by executives and management represent the tip of iceberg.[17]

When individuals and groups do make a decision, it can be rational or intuitive.[18] In a general sense, **rational decision-making** models follow a set process such as the PrO-ACT model.[19] Rational decision-making models follow an established process, and potential strengths include that it provides a standardized/predictable method and compares multiple options based on similar criteria. A downside can be the speed of decision-making, and the approach may not work when working through adaptive challenges. Likewise, the method does not take into consideration the role of relationships in the decision-making process. Decision-making at the group level involves others, and how the leader manages the social dimension is of critical importance. It is rare that humans are purely rational as economists and social psychologists have discussed.[20] In fact, while it would seem logical that decision makers would work to determine the ideal solution (maximizing), they often satisfice (put up with a good enough answer).[21]

Intuitive decision-making relies more heavily on an individual's gut feeling, a hunch, or intuitions, which are "affectively charged judgments that arise through rapid, nonconscious, and holistic associations."[22] When asked if they should conduct focus groups to see what the consumer wanted, former CEO of Apple, Steve Jobs, suggested, "A lot of times, people don't know what they want until you show it to them."[23] He was famous for asserting that Apple designers and engineers just built products for themselves. Strengths of the intuitive decision-making approach may include speed, and it gives the decision maker an opportunity to experiment and better define the problem. Sometimes doing first will help the leader better understand the problem.[24] Downsides may be that the decision maker may be subject to any number of cognitive biases, and the approach may be wrought with difficulties if, for example, the decision maker lacks expertise, emotional intelligence, self-awareness, and clarity of values (which all humans do at one time or another). At an extreme, this approach to decision-making can feel haphazard, random, and unpredictable. Thus, the importance of the leader's relationships is critical. A leader with healthy, long-term relationships will more intuitively read their team when making a decision.

Regardless of approach, leaders need to be skilled in both approaches to decision-making. There will be situations with a definite end state and need for a logical process, and there will be complex adaptive challenges that may not warrant a rational decision-making process. This requires intentionality in approach. The leader and group must first understand the type of problem and then intentionally choose a rational or intuitive approach.

REFLECTION QUESTIONS

- When was the last time you experienced the decision-action gap in a significant way? You knew what *should* be done, but you (or the group) failed to act for one reason or another.

- Which style of decision-making do you often default to—rational or intuitive? When has this default hurt you? When has it served you well?

In Leadership, Decision-Making Is a Team Sport (Much of the Time)

Learning Objectives

6.4 Understand decision-making at the group/team level

6.5 Apply and practice the SOLVE model of decision-making

As soon as you take on a formal or informal leadership role, you will be making decisions in groups. Discussing the role of the team in the process and how to establish an environment that will yield success is a critical task. You will need to focus on (at least) two dimensions—process/task and relationship. The first is the process of decision-making, or how the group arrives at the best way forward. The second dimension is your relationship with others in the group. Designing how you approach the relationships in the group is critical and cannot be underestimated.

Designing (and Deciding) How the Team Will Work

There are some critical ingredients to any competent team. First, there has to be a clear mission, problem statement, opportunity, or objective. Absolute clarity in this domain will help everyone better understand the ideal end state.

Second, develop a structure that will effectively capture and facilitate the work getting accomplished. Create a shared document and let the document drive all the work. Write down each individual's name, their role, and their specific/measurable/time-bound deliverables, and develop a set of group norms—the behaviors each team member commits to (e.g., submitting work on time, attending all meetings). On this document, include everyone's contact information, the team norms, and the agenda for each meeting. Be sure to take the time in your first meeting to establish a regular meeting time and include these dates/times on the shared document as well. Note, though, that at times, perfect can be the enemy of good. You may not get everyone to every meeting—you still need to meet. See if the missing person can call in, video conference in, or at the very least, update their section of the shared document, so everyone knows where they are.

Third, each meeting should begin with a discussion of the team norms, and then each member should report on their deliverables. As the leader, you may want to send out a reminder in advance of the meeting to remind people to update the shared document with their latest information. Be ready for one or two people to not follow through and/or complete their work. Plan for these conversations in advance, and as a group, identify a consequence for those who are not prepared. By setting up the team correctly (structurally and socially), you have a better chance at creating an environment where you can capitalize on the unique talents and perspectives of your team members. This is not common practice.

Fourth, once some tasks are identified, it will be essential to delegate said tasks in an effective manner. You will want to ensure absolute clarity of mission with the individual you are entrusting. Ensure that they are clear on the task, the deliverable, and the timetable, and be sure to answer any questions before they move forward. It will be necessary to check in (e.g., "How can I help?" or "Any unforeseen issues?") with each at a midway point. By doing so, you are reminding the individual, acting in a supportive manner, and providing them with an opportunity to check in. Maybe send another note to the group a couple of days before the next meeting and remind them to update the shared document, which will serve as the agenda for the next meeting.

REFLECTION QUESTIONS

In your experience, which of the ingredients listed are the most difficult for groups to achieve? Do you see some themes based on your experience?

LEADERSHIP BY DESIGN

Design Principle: Hick's Law

Definition: The time it takes to make a decision increases as the number and complexity of alternatives increases.[25]

In Other Words: One choice = quick decision; two choices = sort-of-quick decision; hundreds of choices = long and slow decision.

For Example: Drawing on their expertise, Secret Service agents can scan a crowd in seconds to recognize risk and take action. They combat Hick's Law by knowing what and who to disregard, knowing what they are specifically looking for, and training their eyes to limit options.

For Leaders: Leaders can enhance follower decision-making by applying Hick's Law in both directions. When and in what context are quick decisions necessary? On the other hand, when would you want to *slow down* decision-making? One thing to keep in mind: Hick's Law is not applicable as complexity of the decision increases. In other words, a complicated decision will (and should) take some time.

Designing Your Decision-Making Style

Once you have decided how to design the work of the team, how you approach the decision-making process is a meaningful discussion and intentionality is critical. As the leader, you must be intentional in your approach and how it will impact the relationships in the group. Theorist Victor Vroom and his colleagues developed five basic options a leader has (shown in Table 6.1 below): decide, consult individually, consult group, facilitate, and delegate.[26]

TABLE 6.1 ● Five Basic Options for Leaders	
Decide Alone	The leader makes the decision him- or herself and does not consult others.
Consult Individually	The leader speaks with one or two individuals to gain their perspective on the issues and then decides.
Consult Group	The leader speaks with the group or team to discuss the issue, solicit feedback, and then makes a decision.
Facilitate	The leader facilitates the decision-making process but does not share and/or promote his or her perspective.
Delegate	The leader delegates the decision to another individual or the group.

REFLECTION QUESTIONS

Can you think of instances where peers have used the wrong style for the situation? How did this impact their ability to lead the decision-making process?

Designing Your Approach to Decision-Making: The SOLVE Model of Decision-Making

There are several models of decision-making with varied levels of complexity.[27] Some models outline a series of steps to take in a process-oriented manner such as the three highlighted below.

- PrOACT: work on the right decision **Pr**oblem, specify your **O**bjectives, create imaginative **A**lternatives, understand the **C**onsequences, and grapple with **T**radeoffs.[28]

- GOFER: focus on **G**oal clarification, **O**ption generation, **F**act finding, consideration of **E**ffects, and **R**eview & implement.[29]

- DECIDE: **D**efine the problem, **E**stablish the criteria, **C**onsider all alternatives, **I**dentify the best alternative, **D**evelop and implement a plan of action, **E**valuate and monitor the solution and feedback when necessary.[30]

Other decision-making models, such as Multi-attribute Utility Theory (MAUT)[31] and Analytic Hierarchy Process (AHP),[32] involve a more complicated mathematical approach to help individuals, teams, and organizations make the best decision. In fact, there are sophisticated multiple-criteria software that support some methods and approaches.

Table 6.2 compares four decision-making models across general decision-making activities. Where do you see advantages to each of the models? What is missing (and why do you think that model does not include it)?

This chapter highlights the SOLVE model because it focuses on group decision-making and the role of leadership. What the SOLVE model leaves out—idea-generating and implementing—other chapters in this text cover more extensively. Of course, as the issues become more complex, so does a leader's approach to problem-solving. For most issues you will be working through in your student organizations, the SOLVE model will be a good starting place. However, while the model is presented as a process, steps can be skipped and/or prioritized out of order depending on the problem. For instance, if your group has an expert with *the* answer, it may be that you just begin by veering toward consensus versus taking the time to go through each step. Another important note about the SOLVE model is that people can have the impression that it needs to take a lot of time. When you step back and think about it, athletes move through this process in seconds. Coaches do the same from the sidelines. So, while in a general sense, it is important to go through all steps, it does not necessarily need to take a *long* time. For each phase of SOLVE, a brief description is provided along with common pitfalls. If you are genuinely tuned into what is happening in the meetings you attend, you will notice many of these pitfalls. Recognizing them in real time will not only help you keep the group on track, but it will also help your team progress through the decision-making process.

Set Roles

On any athletic team, players must have clear roles. When a player moves away from their position and takes over another player's role, it can cause confusion, frustration, and chaos. Team-based decision-making is no different. People need to know their role, and they need

TABLE 6.2 ● Decision-Making Models

Decision-Making Activity	SOLVE	PrOACT	GOFER	DECIDE
Preparing the decision makers	**S**et roles			
Understanding	**O**utline problem and decision criteria	Work on the right decision **P**roblem Specify your **O**bjectives	Focus on **G**oal clarification	**D**efine the problem, **E**stablish the criteria
Strategizing—what is the best approach?	**L**ist multiple strategies			
Imagining and option/idea-generating		Create imaginative **A**lternatives	**O**ption generation	**C**onsider all the alternatives
Making a decision	**V**eer toward consensus	Understand the **C**onsequences Grapple with **T**radeoffs	**F**act finding Consideration of **E**ffects	**I**dentify the best alternative
Implementing			**R**eview & implement	**D**evelop and implement a plan of action
Evaluating	**E**valuate decision and process			**E**valuate and monitor the solution and feedback

to be clear from the onset. Who is the timekeeper? Who is the note taker, or who is recording action items? Who is leading the discussion/process? Who is building the agenda? Who is following up to ensure completion of tasks? Who is leading the meeting? At times these roles are understood by the group, other times not. *Just be sure there is clarity.*

Common pitfalls at this stage

- *People forget their role.* The leader forgets she is leading a process, gets immersed in the conversation, and forgets she is responsible for meeting management. This can result in wandering conversations, a couple of people taking over, and rushed decisions.

- *People take on the role of others.* A team member begins leading the meeting, and the leader no longer has control of the tone, pace, and topics being covered.

- *Roles are not defined.* This is the most common pitfall when working with young adults. Roles are not assigned, and the group wanders. At times, a couple of roles may be appointed, but others—such as timekeeper or note taker—are not.

- *One individual takes on multiple roles.* At times, the leader may take on numerous roles. The leader is so busy trying to take notes, keep time, stay on task, and facilitate the conversation that it becomes unmanageable.

Outline the Problem and Decision Criteria

Challenges, problems, and opportunities come in many different forms (e.g., technical and adaptive). While the players in the National Football League (NFL) are changing, at least the rules and other variables remain relatively constant. With leadership, the context is shifting—media, political forces, cultural norms, technology, and so forth. Taking the time to outline the problem and your decision criteria are perhaps the most critical steps in the entire process. Until the group has a clear understanding of the parameters and an ideal end state, little can be accomplished. While this first phase may seem simple, you have to go a couple of levels down to get to the heart of the matter. For instance, think of a university band that hazes. A simple problem statement such as "we want to eliminate hazing" has many other problems bundled underneath the statement that need to be defined, discussed, and considered. For instance, with the example of the band's hazing, *problems underneath the problem* may include:

- Student leaders avoid conflict and do not want to make a faction mad.

- A faction of band members views hazing as fun and energizing.

- A faction of band members sees hazing as an integral way of bonding men and women.

- The group is unsure of what could replace the hazing activities.

- Some of the student leaders enjoy the hazing themselves and do not want to change. The risk of getting caught is worth the enjoyment.

- A faction of members enjoys the tradition of hazing. The experience is a rite of passage.

- Authority figures who know about the hazing do not want to spend the political capital on this issue.

To adequately address the issue, the leader will need to examine their appetite for disruption, identify the problems underneath the problem, clarify decision criteria (items to be compared to help determine the best option), define an ideal end state, and begin working with the broader membership to address the issues, especially if an external authority figure (e.g., the university, the band director) does not impose a decision on the group. What seemed like a simple problem actually has multiple components that need to be addressed, clarified, and understood.

Common pitfalls at this stage

- *The problem is not accurately/completely defined.* While difficult to be sure you have correctly identified all components of an adaptive challenge, give the time needed to ensure that the group has a good sense of the problem or opportunity.

- *Inaccurate assumptions are made about the problem.* While defining the problem, pay close attention to statements that may limit or truncate understanding of the issues. Words such as never, cannot, always, and every are indicators that you and the group may be making false assumptions.

- *Not enough time is given to this phase.* The group blows past outlining the problem and moves straight to brainstorming. A hallmark of this phase is the number of clarifying questions asked as the group works to define the ideal end state and identify the problems beneath the problem.

- *There is a lack of clarity around decision criteria.* The group has differing levels of agreement and/or understanding of the rules upon which they will be evaluating different options.

- *The leader does not notice some people are trying to outline the problem/decision criteria and others are brainstorming.* The leader will need to keep the group in the space of problem definition until the problem statement, decision criteria, and the ideal end state are articulated. Until these elements are clarified, it will be premature to move on to brainstorming. The leader has to skillfully keep those members who instinctually move ahead in the correct phase.

- *The problem statement is oversimplified.* In the example of the band, merely stopping at "we want to eliminate hazing" is an oversimplification of what the group is working to solve. This statement is like saying the U.S. government wants to "eliminate the deficit." The reality of what is underneath that statement has stalled lawmakers for years.

List Multiple Strategies

Once the group has consensus around the problem statement and decision criteria, it will want to move forward with brainstorming. The group will want to divide up the problems beneath the problem and address them one at a time or in small groups. Regardless, the group intends to brainstorm as many options as possible. Each of the above issues may have 10–15 ideas—do not worry about how silly or far-fetched the ideas are. Ideally, a group member is recording the thoughts in a place where everyone can see, and as discussed in previous sections, viewing the decision-making process as intentionally running a series of experiments is a useful way of thinking about how to move forward. While unlikely that the group will identify the perfect solution to please all parties, perhaps it will identify the best experiments to run. Asking the group, "What are the best experiments we should run?" will keep the group in a place of thinking in possibilities.

Common pitfalls at this stage

- *Perfect becomes the enemy of good.* The group searches for the one best answer and spends a great deal of time on one or two potential solutions. As a result, the group does not have many ideas to build upon and must rely on only a few options.

- *The group moves too slowly through the process.* A variation of the pitfall mentioned above, the group and its leader forget that the purpose of this phase is identifying as many potential solutions as possible.

- *Once an approach has been decided, the group stops thinking about other options.* Once the group is engaged in implementing a chosen solution, it can identify better solutions. However, the leader and members need to continue brainstorming, even in the midst of implementing a solution.

- *The group spends time discussing the merits of each idea while brainstorming.* The group stops to consider the value of each idea versus merely identifying as many options as possible. As a result, the group stalls on only one or two ideas or goes deep into one or two possibilities.

- *The group stays in a place of only seeing the barriers.* The group spends a large percentage of the time stewing on the obstacles ahead of them versus naming the barriers and then moving to brainstorming.

- *The leader is too democratic and loses control of the group.* The leader loses control of the process and is so concerned with everyone's voice being heard that she ineffectively manages the process.

Veer Toward Consensus

Once the group has identified a good number of ideas, the leader wants to help the group veer toward an agreement. While consensus is ideal, it may come down to a vote as well—so be prepared. The group works to identify its best guess about the correct experiment(s) to run—rarely will one individual have the answer. So keeping the group in a mindset of experimentation will be important. With an eye on the time, the leader may want to ask individuals to clarify ideas, seek out viable combinations, or even seek new ideas based on what has been identified thus far. However, the goal is to veer toward consensus, and one way to do so is to say the following—"I am hearing a general preference for XYZ approach. Does anyone have a major problem with us trying this first?"

Common pitfalls at this stage

- *The leader becomes overly concerned with finding the "right" answer.* There needs to be a balance. The goal is to outline the best guess but ensure that the group has given enough attention to the issue to be certain that it has a good number of ideas.

- *The leader is afraid to put the decision to a vote.* The leader becomes so fixated on gaining consensus that the process stalls or critical time is lost.

- *The leader does not spend enough time hearing the opinions of others.* Balance is key. Leaders who force their ideas through with little attention for general buy-in will struggle to gain widespread support. Conversely, leaders who are easily pulled in multiple directions may lose perspective on how to move forward.

- *The leader forgets to tap the quiet members of the group.* Just because individuals or factions are silent does not mean they have given consent or support. As a leader, you may want to quickly acknowledge individuals who have not spoken up to better understand the level of support.

LEADERSHIP BY DESIGN

Design Principle: Cost-benefit

Definition: Decisions and behaviors will only be taken if the benefits are equal to or greater than the costs.

In Other Words: People are constantly assessing the return on investment for every action. "Whenever people decide whether the advantages of a particular action are likely to outweigh its drawbacks, they engage in a form of benefit-cost analysis . . ."[33]

For Example: Have you ever grabbed a snack at the cafeteria and gotten in a long line and suddenly realized—you are not really *that* hungry? What is more likely happening is that you have mentally assigned the act of waiting in line a certain cost and subconsciously deemed the benefit of the food not worth it. The value you have placed on the time spent waiting is greater than the expected value incurred.

For Leaders: Cost-benefit is a common decision-making technique. But as a design principle, the costs and benefits are designed as a *perceived* factor. In other words, much of what drives decisions lies in what you *think* the costs and benefits are, versus some concrete measure. As you design your relationships with followers, consider these questions: What do followers see as the costs and benefits to working with you? How might you verify follower perceptions of costs and benefits?

Identify your costs and benefits. Then highlight what you need to for followers (while remaining authentic, transparent, and true). There are many forms of value beyond financial. Benefits might include a purposeful mission, a difference-making project, personal creativity, great autonomy, being part of something big, a fun and engaging culture, and great colleagues. Also consider benefits that might be indirect or deferred.

Evaluate Decision and Process

The group needs to circle back and evaluate its process. In the military, this phase is called an after-action review. This is a time to circle back, make sense of what occurred, and plan for next time. Groups that do not take time to evaluate may miss essential learning and could subject themselves to similar mistakes in the future. Similar to other phases, this does not need to take a great deal of time—just be intentional with the time being used.

Common pitfalls at this stage

- *The group does not complete this phase of the process.* The group is so caught up in the results (good or bad) that they forget, or do not prioritize, this phase of the process.

- *The group blames or externalizes others for results versus looking within.* While external forces may have hindered the group's ability to succeed, failing to recognize what the group could have done better may be a missed opportunity for learning. The group fails to own its part in the failure.

- *The group avoids the awkward conversation.* As a result, the group fails to discuss the real issues. Or the group works around the shortcoming of individuals or factions.

- *The group and/or the leader does not keep the discussion in a constructive space.* Tempers flare, frustrations boil over, and the group struggles to keep the dialogue constructive and civilized.

MYTH OR REALITY?

THE SOLVE MODEL TAKES A LONG TIME.

Myth. A leader can move the group through this process at a pretty good pace, and the model is merely a framework. A leader (and the group) may intentionally decide that one or two steps are·not needed depending on the problem being solved. The key is intentionality. A leader who unknowingly skips or forgets steps is limited in his ability to work any problem. The leader must balance speed of work with the quality of work, which is, at once, an exciting and challenging prospect.

REFLECTION QUESTION

Which phase of SOLVE do you need to focus on the most as you develop and practice?

How Did We Get Here? This Was Not the Plan: Barriers to Decision-Making

Learning Objectives

6.6 Assess several barriers to effective decision-making

Cognitive Biases That Hinder Decision-Making

All humans (individually and collectively) battle cognitive biases that hinder their ability to make good decisions. An understanding and an awareness of these biases will help you and the group be more mindful when working through the SOLVE process. In this section, some of the more common cognitive biases are highlighted. As you read, pay close attention to where you see each on campus, in your family, online/in the media, and in the workplace.

Confirmation Bias—Humans tend to pay closer attention to data that confirm their bias.[34] Their interest is peaked when a stimulus aligns with their perspective or worldview. For instance, in the United States, Republicans flock toward one television network, and Democrats tend to view another in more significant numbers. While fine, if the individual is unaware of the bias or sees no bias, then it can be difficult for the individual to understand both sides of an issue, and as a result, they may be heavily rooted in one side with little space for dialogue.

One-Right-Answer Thinking—Many of the challenges (e.g., hazing) discussed earlier in the chapter are adaptive challenges. In other words, no authority figure can fix the issue with their expertise. As a result, individuals who suffer from one right answer thinking are sure that they have found the silver bullet that will alleviate the issue at hand. While possible in theory, it is important to explore several options rather than just sticking with the one right answer[35] or the first correct answer. Research on problem-solving suggests that the first solution is rarely the most effective or efficient path forward.

Groupthink—Groupthink has three classic symptoms, which are "the belief in the correctness of one's own group, negative stereotypes of the out-group, and rationalizations concerning the issues."[36] Other precursors of groupthink may include crisis, external threat, group insulation, a culture of compliance, and recent group failure.[37] This is why the promotion of diversity of thought, culture, ethnicity, personality, and so forth is critical to effective decision-making. Without said diversity (and a culture that values essential debate), a group of human beings can come to some pretty poor decisions (e.g., hazing activities) that did not take into account other values, perspectives, worldviews, needs, and so forth.

Framing Effect—coming to different conclusions based on how an issue or topic is framed. A simple example of this cognitive bias is an individual's mindset—"Is the glass half empty or half full?" Another example, in the United States, is that a Republican-leaning television network and a Democrat-leaning television network will frame a single issue such as gun control or immigration in a different way.[38] Without awareness and understanding of how an issue is framed, people are susceptible to decisions that do not take into account other perspectives and points of view. The *Leadership by Design* feature in this chapter highlights this type of cognitive bias.

Overconfidence Effect—placing an unusually high value on the conclusion the individual or group has achieved.[39] Because of this cognitive bias, individuals and groups can lose sight of the limitations of their approach or strategy. Athletic teams and coaches can suffer from this quite easily. While the formula may have worked last year, the addition of new players, changes in other teams, and other contextual factors will likely impact the team in ways that make the formula obsolete in the coming year.

Law of Triviality—Individuals spend a significant amount of time avoiding tough, adaptive challenges and spend the majority of their time on less important, easily solved issues[40]—for example, Congress investigating steroids in baseball[41] versus fixing Social Security, immigration, education, and so forth. Student groups can suffer from this as well. More time is spent discussing t-shirt colors and food options than major issues facing the group or association. Is the group addressing the real, tough, critical problems, or is it focused on other, more trivial content?

Illusion of Control—This cognitive bias is defined as "an expectancy of a personal success probability inappropriately higher than the objective probability would warrant."[42] In essence, illusion of control is an overestimation of influence an individual had on an outcome or result. For example, an individual may view a successful sales call as a result of their skill versus luck or chance.[43]

REFLECTION QUESTIONS

Which cognitive biases can be seen in conservative or liberal media outlets? Why is it more difficult to see them when viewing the outlet that *you* align with politically?

Ways *You* Could Be the Barrier to Effective Decision-Making

As you become more and more deliberate in your leadership of the team, you will begin to notice themes and patterns of behaviors in yourself and others. It can be easy to identify the dysfunctional behaviors of others, but seeing them in yourself is another level of sophistication. As you become more and more experienced in facilitating the decision-making process, you will gain confidence, and ultimately, you will drive toward successful outcomes more intentionally and thoughtfully. However, along the way, you will make some common mistakes that may stall progress. The following behaviors may diminish the

LEADERSHIP BY DESIGN

Design Principle: Framing[44]

Definition: A technique that influences decision-making, risk tolerance, and judgment by manipulating the way information is presented or described.

In Other Words: What is emphasized is what you see *and* what you think.

For Example: Are you pro-bicycle or anti-car? The frame focuses your attention and influences your behaviors. How often are you lured to articles with click-bait titles: *You won't believe what happened next*!

For Leaders: Most people fail to bring the full or correct information into their conscious awareness at the right time. That is not a fault, it is a reality. Learning to expand the limits of your awareness before you make an important decision helps you avoid basing decisions solely on how the information is presented. How would you react to this photo if it were titled *Relaxing sunset yoga*? How would you react if the title were *Migrants beg for protection*?

RELAXING SUNSET YOGA, OR MIGRANTS BEG FOR PROTECTION?

Framing is a powerful design principle that you as leader must be wary of and utilize for good. Positive frames tend to influence toward proactive and risk-taking behavior, while negative frames bring out reactive and risk-averse actions. In what ways can you frame your organization or mission? How can you frame yourself to better design your relationships with followers?

quality of team decisions and your relationship (e.g., trust, credibility) with the group or team. When have you fallen victim to one or more of these behaviors?

- *Forgetful*—You forget that you are leading the meeting. You get sucked into the conversation, lose focus, and wander along with the group. You may even lose track of the purpose of the meeting. This may lead to additional meetings or rushed/poor solutions that are made at the last minute.

- *Unprepared*—You set the meeting but do not prepare an agenda, outline a clear purpose for the meeting, or determine how the group will spend its time. As a result, the group wanders in multiple directions with little aim or direction and is experienced as a waste of time by others.

- *My Way*—You take over, and/or talk over, and then wonder why others have not *bought in* and are not excited and energetic about the course of action.

- *Impatience*—You move to brainstorming before a clear problem statement has been identified. Group members have different levels of understanding about the end state and begin brainstorming before they fully understand the problem/opportunity.

- *Low Energy*—You are negative or struggle to keep the energy of the group in a curious and positive place. You fail to set a positive emotional tone or actively decrease energy levels.

- *Wet Fish*—You cannot keep the meeting on track when other, more dominant group members take over. And you watch and allow it to happen.

- *Overly Emotional*—You get really worked up, and yell, cry, and/or make others feel uncomfortable. Your lack of emotional intelligence impedes your ability to connect with the group.

- *Poor Delegation*—You ensured that people were delegated tasks but did not write anything down, failed to follow the tenets of effective delegation, and ultimately did not check in until the next meeting.

- *Non-Leadership*—You occupy a title, but no one really knows what you do beyond that. You are too busy, distracted, and/or overextended. You are leading nothing.

As previously mentioned, all humans fall victim to some of these dysfunctional behaviors at one time or another. Be mindful and reflective, and have trusted advisors who will provide you with unfiltered and honest feedback. Leading the process of decision-making is challenging work. In a general sense, you know you have arrived at a better place if you begin to see some of the following indicators of high-functioning teams:

- There is a general sense of enthusiasm for the decision.

- Within reason, people are laughing and joking during meetings.

- Individuals volunteer without you having to beg them to do so.

- Work is consistently done early or on time.

- There is a high level of trust among team members.

- Team members know their role and enjoy their position.

- The team is securing results and collecting small wins.

- The team has a deep bench of talent.

- People feel they can voice their concerns, thoughts, and observations. There is trust that their voice will be heard.

- It is understood that not everyone will get their way all of the time.

REFLECTION QUESTIONS

- When was the last time you fell victim to one or more of the behaviors mentioned in this section? How did it impact the group and your objectives?

Ways *Others* Could Be the Barrier to Effective Decision-Making

Decision-making is an emotional activity.[45] Depending on the issue, an individual or group will be asked to give something up or alter their behavior in some form or fashion. Decision-making involves change—an emotional process because "habits, values, and attitudes, even dysfunctional ones, are part of one's identity. To change the way people see and do things is to challenge how they define themselves."[46] Because decision-making often occurs in a team (especially in the collegiate context), the role of emotional intelligence is critical. At its most basic level, emotional intelligence is about awareness and regulation of emotions in self and others.[47] Throughout the decision-making process, the leader can be triggered in any number of ways, and maintaining emotional intelligence takes skill. Emotions run high around issues such as politics, religion, immigration, gender equality, gun control, the war on terror, free trade, quality, and so forth.

Leading a group of peers when you do not have formal power to hire or fire takes skill. Leading without authority is all about influence, and you may recall the proposed definition of leadership, which is "a process of influencing others toward a common vision." To do so takes a great deal of patience, wisdom, expertise, and awareness. And many leaders suffer from a cognitive bias called an empathy gap, which means that they tend to underestimate "how much emotional situations influence their attitudes, preferences, and behaviors."[48] After all, some of your team members can be pretty entertaining characters. Some will be responsible and level-headed, and display a strong work ethic. However, you will come across some other characters as well. The authors asked former students to make up some fictitious characters that represent real people they have worked with during group projects (we added a couple ourselves). The results were insightful, and as you read through them, you will notice some familiar characters.

- *Distracted Dhruv*: Dhruv is famous for not paying attention to the group at all. He is elsewhere—mentally and physically.

- *Noncontributing Neema*: The only thing Neema contributed was the text every week asking you what the homework was and if you could save her . . . again.

- *Finish Line Fred*: Fred's nowhere to be found for the whole project, but he shows up right at the end—just in time to get the big win when you turn in your *A*-level work.

- *Micromanaging Marisa*: Marisa obsessively insists on being the group leader, and she's micromanaging to ensure you do the work her way.

- *Reliable Ryota*: Ryota is dependable, level-headed, and consistent in getting her work done. She can always be counted on as the backbone of any group project.

- *Distant Dante*: Dante is always on his phone or texting during class or in group meetings.

- *Bossy Betty*: Betty can be very close-minded about other people's thoughts and prefers to tell people what they should do. Betty believes her way is the best way, which creates little space for the thoughts and ideas of others.

- *Ghosting Giotto*: Giotto disappears for days and weeks at a time. He will reappear but may disappear just as quickly again.

- *Silent Sofia*: Sofia says 3–4 words throughout the entire group project. Those words often occur during the final presentation.

- *Off-Task Olivia*: Olivia is more interested in spending the group's time talking about last night's party than focusing on the task at hand. She has excessive side conversations as well.

- *Forgetful Francesca*: Whether it was intentional or not, no one knows. What we do know is that Fran did not complete her work, the project is stalled, and the meeting is a waste of time.

- *Donneta the Downer*: Donneta's mood is frequently negative, and she works hard to help others see the downside of the group, the project, the class, the professor, and so forth.

- *Talkative Tiana*: Tiana takes up a lot of airtime, so much so that others in the group are visibly frustrated and put off by her lack of awareness.

What behaviors have you experienced working with others in a group? What character would you add to the list? Which group members do you act like sometimes? Maintaining emotional self-control when working with any number of these individuals can feel like a Herculean effort. You will encounter these same behaviors for the rest of your life. In the end, you need to walk into any group project understanding how these behaviors might trigger you emotionally and result in you not being your best self. It will happen. Giotto will ghost, Olivia will get off task, and Betty will boss. How you navigate these realities will make all the difference. In fact, now that you know what you are looking for, you may view this as an opportunity to practice working with individuals who display unique and different behavioral tendencies, achievement orientations, capabilities, and desires to succeed.

Other Factors That Impede Effective Decision-Making

Throughout history, poor decisions have been made—and at a significant cost in some instances. It may seem like the pitfalls to decision-making are endless, which is why skilled decision-making requires practice, awareness of all of the dangers, awareness of your habits as a decision maker, and then even more practice. Some problems are more common than others, particularly for developing leaders and groups. You can read about them in Table 6.3 (below). Which impediments have you observed in recent weeks? Consider choosing one to work on for 30 days and then choose another. Mindful engagement in decision-making will further develop your CORE™.

TABLE 6.3 ● Potential Decision-Making Impediments	
Time	The leader/group does not spend the time needed to successfully define and solve the problem they are working.
Emotions	The leader/group is emotionally tied to how things are, one course of action, and has unconsciously or consciously taken some options off the table.
Analysis Paralysis	The group is caught up in the process of analyzing all of the possible options and gets bogged down in the details and specifics.
Lack of Clarity	There is a low level of clarity around the ideal end state or even the problem being solved.
Conceptual Blocks	The leader/group has created fictitious rules or boundaries that hinder the ability to accurately define and/or solve the problem.
Politics	The leader/group lets internal and external politics hinder its ability to identify the *best* solution.[49]
Apathy	The leader/group does not have the energy and/or desire to work the problem.
Groupthink	The leader/group becomes *of one mind* and alternative ideas, perspectives, and opinions are pushed to the side.
Fear	The leader/group is afraid to fail or afraid to take an unpopular stance on an issue. As a result, viable options are taken off the table (consciously or unconsciously).
Power	Power dynamics in the group hinder the group's ability to have honest dialogue about the issues. As a result, individuals and groups do not bring their voice to the table.
Knowledge	At times a leader/group may not have enough knowledge to adequately solve the problem.

Chapter Summary

Leaders make decisions—decisions about what to do, how to do it, when, why, with whom, for how long, assuming what, and resulting in what end. Effective leaders make mindful and purposeful decisions as they design different aspects of leadership. Many can see the problems facing an organization, but very few are skilled at helping the organization make and execute the decisions to address and move *past* problems.

Deciding means cutting off options and making a choice that determines a course of action. Decision-making can address problems that are technical or adaptive, can involve processes that are individual- or group/team-oriented, and can be intuitive or rational. All of these conditions require careful consideration of the situation, context, and persons.

Your decision-making can be greatly enhanced by determining your style and by learning a model of decision-making similar to SOLVE: Set roles, Outline problem and criteria, List multiple strategies, Veer toward consensus, and Evaluate the decision and process. Recognizing and eliminating barriers such as cognitive biases and ineffective personal habits can also enhance your decision-making.

Decision-making is critical to designing relationships. Much of the decision-making work on teams and within organizations impacts and is influenced by how you relate to others and build relationships (e.g., consensus, coalition-building). Leaders balance two competing priorities—task and relationships. As you gain experience and wisdom in this work, you will become more and more valuable to any organization. Organizations need men and women who do both well.

Key Terms

Decide 153
Decision Criteria 153
Decision-Making 153
Group 154

Group/Team-Level Decision-Making 154
Individual-Level Decision-Making 153

Intuitive Decision-Making 154
Nondecisions 154
Rational Decision-Making 154
Team 154

CORE™ Attribute Builders

Attribute: Engagement

Builder: The iPhone 20

At the time of this book's printing, the Apple iPhone may be in its 11th iteration. A fun question to ask a group of friends is the following: "Can you imagine the hardware and software features of the iPhone 20?" This would be a device introduced around 2028. As you listen to the answers, pay close attention to what happens next. Some participants will forget that you asked about hardware and software. Their minds will only focus on one or the other, and they will immediately move to brainstorming one or the other. Rarely will they remember both, and many conceptual blocks will hinder their ability to think creatively. For instance, some will continue to think of the device in its current form—a phone as it looks today. Because of this, their ability to creatively brainstorm future iterations will be limited to a device as it seems today. Finally, pay close attention to the quality of their ideas. Are they limited to ideas that are just outside of current reach (e.g., longer battery life, waterproof) or are they genuinely transformational?

Additional questions to explore while watching may include:

- Could you see how your friends were limited in their abilities to understand your question and brainstorm truly innovative options?

- Do you think you could intervene skillfully and engage them in identifying creative opportunities that are more in line with a device on the cutting edge of technology in 2028?

- What conceptual blocks hinder your ability to help the work of the group move forward?

Skill Builder Activity

That Was the Best Group Project Ever

Group projects (as an undergrad and beyond) are rarely incredible experiences. The authors hear from students that they are a consistent source of frustration. Do you have the skills to lead a group project and at the end have people say to you—"That was the best group project I have ever worked on!" If you do, then you are a powerful individual. This is a challenging task, but you can do it. They key is to intentionally practice much of what has been discussed in this chapter.

Below are 10 key questions to consider as you think through how you will arrive at an *A* and a positive group experience.

1. How could your personality, mindset, outlook, and style hinder progress? Do you tend to micromanage or take over? Do you struggle to remain organized and on task?

2. How will you help the group clarify the desired end state? Note that this is more than just *securing an A*. In part, the task is about this being the best group project. What will that take? What are the expectations and norms of group members?

3. How will you organize your work? Would you use a platform like Google Drive?

4. What leadership style will best suit the group? A combination of democratic, affiliative, and coaching? Some other combination?

5. How will you divide the roles of group members and hold one another accountable?

6. How might Hick's Law apply to the work of the group?

7. What questions will you need to ask your professor as you outline the problem? Identify at least 10.

8. How will you hold one another accountable?

9. How will you celebrate some of the small wins and milestones along the way?

10. How will you make the experience enjoyable and fun?

While each of the questions is relatively simplistic, think through how you will navigate the project. Moreover, it will be important to revisit your answers to the questions so the group can gauge progress. When the project is complete, close the loop by going to lunch and discussing how the group did as a whole. Did you achieve your dual objective? Was it the best group project ever?

Influence, Power, and Motivation

No man is good enough to govern another man without that other's consent.

—Abraham Lincoln

Leadership is the ability to guide others without force into a direction or decision that leaves them still feeling empowered and accomplished.

—Lisa Cash Hanson

Learning Objectives

7.1 Describe the role of influence in leadership

7.2 Describe the difference between influence, manipulation, and authority

7.3 Identify 11 key approaches to influencing others

7.4 Analyze how people use power

7.5 Understand 10 sources of power

7.6 Analyze the difference between intrinsic and extrinsic motivation

Detailed Chapter Outline

Introduction
  The Path to the Goal
Forms of Influence
  The Difference Between
    Influence and Authority

The Difference Between
  Influence and
  Manipulation
Moving Individuals and Team
  From A to Z

Leadership by Design Model

Design Self

How can I design myself as a leader?

DESIGN RELATIONSHIPS

AS A LEADER, HOW CAN I DESIGN MY RELATIONSHIPS WITH OTHERS?

Design Others' Success

As a leader, how can I design success for others?

Design Culture

As a leader, how can I design the culture of my organization?

Design Future

As a leader, how can I innovate?

Introduction

Influencing others to be involved and engaged is a necessary skill for any leader. Understanding *how* you best influence others can make all the difference for the success of the followers, organization, and leader. This chapter explores the role of influence in leadership and how an individual's sources of power can impact his or her ability to lead others. The chapter concludes with a discussion on how to build a culture that motivates and empowers others.

This is the last chapter in the Design Relationships module, and intentionally considering how you will relate to and influence others is critical to leadership. Your actions impact relationships, and in many ways, determine your ability to succeed or falter. As you read this chapter, try to connect with the concepts on a relational level. In other words, consider what influence, power, and motivation look like *between* you and others and how these affect your ability and others' ability to succeed in the classroom, on the athletic field, or on the job. Whether you are inspiring a group of people to change behavior (Chapter 10), building a healthy organizational culture (Chapter 11), or encouraging others to behave in an ethical manner (Chapter 4), influence is at the heart of your work as a leader.

Most definitions of leadership include some mention of leadership being a process of influence. In the real world of leadership, influence feels like figuring out how to get followers to do something—how to get employees to work hard, get students to study, get constituents to vote. Note the language in those statements. Getting someone to do something is all about you and your motives, which means you are overlooking your most powerful tool as a leader, namely, the motivation of your followers. Why are your followers—each one of them, individually—doing what they do? What are their goals? What are their motives?

If you do not know, you should ask. If *they* do not know, ask them to think about it. And then talk about it relative to the goals of whatever organization or entity you are leading. Assuming the individual motives of others, or outright ignoring them and presuming that your goals as a leader will take precedence, will only result in frustration for everyone.

Similarly, the design framework of this textbook may lead you to think that purposefully designing the different aspects of your leadership is a solitary endeavor, similar to a "craftsman in a shed with lumber and nails, hammers and a saw, and a blueprint for a chair."[1] There will certainly be times where you will need to work alone, but the model of successful design is participative, collaborative, and a mutually influential codesign.[2] Fortunately, many of the concepts and tools in this textbook, such as empathy and design thinking, will reinforce the codesign notion.

Before you dig into the *how* of influence, power, and motivation, every leader must frame that influence in the context of their values and intentions. Why and to what end are you trying to influence others? Is that influence just and equitable? Are you fully considering the inequalities built into your context and community—even the ones you cannot readily see? How does the system perpetuate who does and who does not have power? Embedded within all influence are issues of privilege, class, protection of unjust systems, inequality, bias, and the potential to wield that influence in ways that can harm others and/or perpetuate unjust beliefs and systems. Only those who are vigilant about the dynamics of power and powerlessness—either leader or follower—will truly foster effective leadership.

As you read about the influence tactics and sources of power described in this chapter, reflect on the range of their application—when they have been used to achieve good, and when they have been abused and caused great destruction. Many individuals see the word influence (and design in some cases) as manipulation. In reality, you influence others all the time, and in turn, others influence you. The keys are (a) be aware of that influence, (b) be aware of how that influence fosters justice and equity within the larger context, and (c) mindfully and justly decide what and how you will influence others. If you want to be the leader who makes a just, equitable, and sustainable difference, then you must continue to develop your awareness of the full range of influence: visible and invisible; leader to follower; across and within genders, ethnic distinctions, and socioeconomic differences; and from the individual level through the cultures and systems that influence assumptions. You can further explore this topic within the leadership field in John Dugan's *Leadership Theory: Cultivating Critical Perspectives*.[3]

The Path to the Goal

Leadership is the process of influencing others toward a common vision. Let's pretend for a moment that the goal is not so common, or more likely, that the purpose (for the organization) is broad enough such that many other goals fit within it. Excellent organizational missions and visions are specific enough to guide the organization yet broad enough to allow many individuals to find the piece that motivates them. Each follower has unique, individualized goals for themselves relative to the organization. This reality is even more prevalent in creative and professional fields where great autonomy, innovation, and self-direction are necessary.

What happens on their path to that goal is where you, the leader, have significant influence. Path-goal leadership theory[4] highlights the variables that affect a follower's motivation to travel the path from the present to their goal. In simple terms, here is what you can do as leader:

1. Help define the goal(s)

2. Help clarify the most effective path

3. Remove obstacles (even if that obstacle is you)

4. Provide support in a variety of ways (that do not unintentionally become obstacles)

Leadership style This is how a leader goes about addressing the four elements of defining the goal, clarifying the path, removing obstacles, and providing support. Styles include **Directive:** The leader provides guidance and psychological structure; **Supportive:** The leader provides nurturance; **Participative:** The leader provides involvement; and **Achievement oriented:** The leader challenges others to work to the next level.

The key to maximizing follower motivation lies in how the leader goes about addressing these four elements, often called a **leadership style**. What does each of these elements look like from your perspective as a leader? How would you go about accomplishing these for each follower?

A leader's *style* represents the beginning of you understanding your tendencies but only as a springboard from which to shift and alter your behaviors to maximize follower and organizational success. Many leaders will justify their ineffective behavior by saying (and thinking), "Well, that is my leadership style; my followers will just have to get used to it." Maybe . . . or maybe they (your followers) will disengage, sabotage the mission, or just find another organization.

The great news: With work, you can change your default leadership style, and doing so is as easy as refocusing on what each follower needs, their goals, the path to those goals, and what the task/s requires. The fit between these variables, as shown by leadership scholar Peter Northouse,[5] is shown in Table 7.1 below.

TABLE 7.1 ● Fitting Leadership Behavior With Follower and Task		
Leadership Behavior (aka, your style)	**Follower Characteristics**	**Task Characteristics**
Directive Provides guidance and psychological structure	Dogmatic, authoritarian	Ambiguous, unclear rules, complex
Supportive Provides nurturance	Unsatisfied, need affiliation, need human touch	Repetitive, unchallenging, mundane
Participative Provides involvement	Autonomous, need for control, need for clarity	Ambiguous, unclear, unstructured
Achievement oriented Provides challenge	High expectations, need to excel	Ambiguous, challenging, complex

Effective leaders discern what style will work best given the situation, to what degree, at what point, and with whom.[6] If you are working with high-achieving individuals who are very self-directed, using a directive style will not only be ineffective but also be perceived as condescending and an obstacle in the path. We will explore this notion in greater detail later in the chapter.

There are many leadership styles—including more to this particular theory. However, the essential message remains: *To be effective, leaders need to facilitate followers by providing those things that will help their progress and by removing obstacles from that progress.*

LEADERSHIP THAT MAKES A DIFFERENCE

A challenge that has plagued college campuses for decades is hazing. For instance, in a study of more than 325,000 NCAA athletes, more than 80% reported having been exposed to "questionable to unacceptable activities."[7] Hazing most often occurs in Greek societies, athletic teams, and the band. And while one would like to think the problem has gotten better, there have been a number of high-profile cases in recent years that have brought shame and disgrace to individuals and their institutions.

The roots of hazing likely stem back to the military and other *rites-of-passage* ceremonies that new or younger members have endured. From a power and influence perspective, it is a fascinating topic because on a college campus the desire for inclusion can be overwhelming, and seemingly *good* people engage in activities that are dangerous, abusive, and demeaning. It would seem that the individuals engaged in the hazing have a great deal of influence and power over the individuals being hazed. According to Chaney, the practice of hazing continues in many organizations on college campuses, even though illegal in 44 states and highly discouraged by college administrations.[8]

Unfortunately, the leadership that makes a difference in this instance is the *toxic* leadership. While not all bands, teams, or fraternities haze, in this instance, the *common vision* is warped, lacks morality, and is illegal in many places. Perhaps even more disturbing is the number of bystanders who may not actively engage but do not have the fortitude and courage to stand up to the ringleaders. Why? What influence tactics are used? How is power being used or abused? What motivates someone to haze or be hazed?

At the heart of effective leadership is a strong sense of self and the values that guide the leader's work. Alignment between expressed values and actions is paramount when working with others. Individuals who align values and activities not only serve as role models for others, they build trust—a key ingredient for leadership and relationships.

Forms of Influence

Learning Objectives

7.1 Describe the role of influence in leadership

7.2 Describe the difference between influence, manipulation, and authority

Just like many other topics, there is an entire literature base on the topic of influence.[9] It is a complex subject and requires self-awareness, awareness and empathy for others, and a sound grounding in your values. **Influence** is the process of moving individuals or groups to the desired mindset, position, behavior, or place. Leaders need to consider an even more fundamental idea of influence, namely, that while they are influencing others, they too are subject to being influenced. Once this reality is understood, leaders can more fully understand their motivations. The leader can consider five dichotomous elements. For instance, what would be more effective? Direct influence, like an appeal to why this task is important, or an indirect influence, like appealing to a follower's colleagues who then influence the follower? Should the influence be overt such that they know you are trying to influence them in a specific manner, or covert such that the influence is masked?

Influence The process of moving individuals or groups to a desired mindset, position, behavior, or place

There are also physical, psychological, and contextual dimensions to influence, as shown in Table 7.2 on page 176. For instance, are you using some kind of psychological/cognitive means of influence (e.g., appeal to relationship, guilt inducement, etc.); a physical means (i.e., something more tangible like bonus pay); or contextual, where you alter the environment as part of influencing (e.g., play soothing music, take away the chairs so folks have to stand and talk)?

REFLECTION QUESTION

Which of the forms of influence listed above have you used in the last couple days with your peers, at your job, or in your student organization?

TABLE 7.2 ● Forms of Influence

Form of Influence	Form of Influence
Direct—Leader focuses influence efforts on the specific subject of influence.	Indirect—Leader seeks to influence the subject by way of other individuals.
Overt—Leader's efforts to influence are clearly seen.	Covert—Leader's efforts to influence are hidden.
Conscious—Leader wants subject to be aware of efforts to influence.	Unconscious—Leader wants subject to be unaware they are being influenced.
Active—Leader is currently purposefully trying to influence others.	Passive—Leader is influencing others even without purposefully trying.
Individual—Influence is focused on a single person.	Group—Influence is focused on a group and utilizes group dynamics.

LEADERSHIP BY DESIGN

Design Principle: Signal-to-Noise Ratio

Definition: The ratio of relevant to irrelevant information.

In Other Words: How much junk is in the way of important stuff?

For Example: How does a mascot clearly express themselves or tell a story without using any words? They have a strong signal-to-noise ratio since their actions are not muddled by speech. Likewise, PowerPoint presentations with too much information on each slide are filled with noise that distracts from key points.

©iStock.com/sshepard

For Leaders: What is your signal-to-noise ratio when it comes to your followers? How much of what you communicate is relevant (to them) versus not relevant? Leaders influence others through the many ways they communicate, but those messages need to be clear, focused, and relevant. Be mindful of the signal-to-noise ratio that you put forth in all the ways you and your organization communicate. Confirm shared meaning. Edward Tufte said, "There's no such thing as information overload, only bad design." What *noise* is getting in the way of your designing leadership relationships?

Authority figure an individual whose role provides them with formal power to determine the fate of individuals or groups

The Difference Between Influence and Authority

In addition to forms of influence, leaders should understand the difference between influence and authority or what is called legitimate or formal power. An **authority figure** is an individual whose role provides them with formal power to determine the fate of individuals or groups. **Formal power** is legitimate power bestowed upon an individual who holds a position or role (e.g., judge, police officer). For instance, a police officer has the formal power to give you a ticket, a judge can put you in jail, and your professor has the authority to issue you a grade. And while you may not agree with their decisions, they have the authority afforded to them by a larger body because of their role. Leadership scholar Ron Heifetz has a unique and interesting perspective on this concept.

> Our language fails us, too, when we discuss, analyze and practice leadership. We commonly talk about "leaders" in organizations or politics when we actually mean people in positions of managerial or political authority. Although we have confounded leadership with authority in nearly every journalistic and scholarly article written on "leadership" during the last one hundred years, we know intuitively that these two phenomena are distinct when we complain all too frequently in politics and business that "the leadership isn't exercising any leadership," by which we actually mean to say that "people in authority aren't exercising any leadership."[10]

It is important to remember that leadership is not about the use of formal power and authority. In many ways, it is about using **informal power**, which is derived from an individual characteristic such as charisma, expertise, experience, wisdom, and so forth. Leadership is about influencing others toward a shared vision. They are partners in the process and want to engage and commit to a better future.

Formal power legitimate power bestowed upon an individual who holds a position or role (e.g., judge, police officer)

Informal power power derived from an individual characteristic such as charisma, expertise, experience, wisdom, and so forth

The Difference Between Influence and Manipulation

There is also a very important difference between influencing someone and manipulation. **Manipulation** is similar to influence but often with more of a hidden or inauthentic intent. Manipulation usually involves an ulterior or hidden motive.[11] There is a level of deceit in manipulation. A general objective would be that leaders are transparent and upfront about their motives as they work to move individuals or groups to a desired mindset, position, behavior, or place.

Manipulation similar to influence but often with more of a hidden or inauthentic intent

Moving Individuals and Team From A to Z

Learning Objective

7.3 Identify 11 key approaches to influencing others

Influencing up, down, across—the process of influencing others is multidirectional, and it is likely you have been influencing others your entire life. Whether it is your peers when making plans on a Friday evening or influencing your parents to let you stay out just a little later in high school—you were practicing influence. Organizational life is very similar. Throughout your career, you will be influencing your peers, your subordinates, and your supervisor. An adage goes that "we all answer to someone." If you view your student organizations, your internships, and your job as practice fields, you will be ahead of the game. Likewise, if you pay close attention to how others in the organization are successfully influencing up, across, and down, you will glean important data as you progress through the organization.

According to authors Ricky Griffin and Jean Phillips, "all influential people have power, but not all powerful people have influence." As discussed, influence is a central activity when leading others, and as a result, it is an important skill whether you have formal authority or not. In other words, even when you are not *in charge*, you still have an opportunity to influence others. A number of the concepts discussed in this chapter are relevant regardless of your title or formal role.

People with real or perceived power can wield a great deal of influence.[12] An individual who brings a great deal of experience or expertise to a situation will often have influence over the group. People will place trust and confidence in their opinion. But this quality of being believed (i.e., credibility) is a powerful force that must be used with care. Individuals can overestimate their abilities, or they may underestimate the complexity of the context, which can mean proposed solutions are really not as straightforward and simple as suggested.[13] Likewise, group members need to think critically about the suggestions from people who have a great deal of expertise or experience. Blindly trusting can be a recipe for disaster.

REFLECTION QUESTIONS

Can you think of a time when you blindly placed too much confidence in an individual who had a great deal of experience or expertise? What was the context? What were the positive or negative results on you or the group?

Influence Tactics for Leaders

Influence tactics These are actions designed to move others to a desired mindset. Examples include (a) **Rational persuasion:** Sharing facts and using logic to persuade others; (b) **Lead a coalition:** Convening a group of like-minded people to convince decision makers; (c) **Win-win:** Helping others see how they will benefit from your idea or solution; (d) **Inspirational appeal:** Aligning your proposed direction with the values, mission, and vision of the group or organization; and (e) **Ingratiation:** Increasing the level of positive feelings among the key decision makers.

The following section comprises a list of influence tactics that is by no means exhaustive but provides a strong foundation for anyone hoping to lead others. Influence tactics are actions designed to move others to a desired mindset. Three words need to be top of mind as you influence others—*experimentation*, *authenticity*, and *intentionality*. First, no single resource will tell you exactly how to influence—not your mom, the team, your peers, or your supervisor—but they all will provide clues. In essence, you are running a well-planned *experiment*. Similar to the sciences, some experiments work, and others do not. The second word, *authenticity*, means that you are open and honest about your intentions. People do not want to feel manipulated or duped because of your ulterior motives. Likewise, tactics such as manipulation and deceit diminish trust—the foundation of stable relationships. The third word is *intentionality*. Purposefully plan and prepare for how you will influence others. An *off-the-cuff* influence attempt likely will not yield the results that a planned intervention will. As a result, you need to be intentional about how you intervene. It is not merely a default reaction or a last-minute, knee-jerk response.

Involve Others/Consulting—By involving others, you are providing them with a voice to help set the course and determine their role in the group's or organization's success.[14] Also, you are helping them acclimate to the new direction, provide input, and gain enthusiasm based on the energy of the group. By involving others, there is a shared sense of mission and shared vision which can unleash the energy needed to accomplish great things. Where have you seen this approach work in the last week?[15]

LEADERSHIP BY DESIGN

Design Principle: Horror Vacui

Definition: A fear of emptiness that results in a tendency to favor filling that emptiness with objects, sound, or meaning.[16]

In Other Words: People fear empty space and are compelled to fill it.

For Example: Essay questions on exams should be answered concisely, but if there is still room left over to write more, students may feel compelled to fill in the blank space with redundant information. Likewise, if you post a question with a blank space, people will be compelled to _____.

For Leaders: Leaders who can overcome the *horror* of empty space add considerably to their influence toolkit. When you leave open space for your followers, they will fill it—with activity, with meaning, with innovative ideas—all of which communicates that you value and trust their contributions. The simplicity of unfilled spaces can more clearly highlight and focus on what is in the space—like the mission or a particular project. Try sitting in silence with someone—they are inevitably compelled to speak—to fill the space with words. When you are comfortable with the empty space of silence, it communicates confidence, gives you time to think, and provides an opportunity for others. What empty spaces are you compelled to fill? When you purposefully leave an empty space, others will be compelled to fill it, often with their own meaning. Be cautious with *horror vacui* though. Who or what are you silencing when you choose to fill an empty space versus encouraging others to do so? Taylor Swift even sings about *horror vacui*—she has a blank space, so she wants to write your name.[17]

Facts/Logic/Rational Persuasion—While it is well established that humans do not always make decisions based on what makes logical sense,[18] helping others understand the logic behind your thinking is important because it will resonate with a faction of the individuals you are working to influence.[19] The key is to align your logic with the values and needs of the group you are working to influence. For instance, if you are influencing a group of sales managers, you would want to provide concrete information on how your solution could improve sales and increase their return on investment. When have you used this with a professor?

Relationships—Relationships and influence are closely interconnected.[20] As a result, it is vital that you do your best to build strong, lasting relationships when possible. While this is easy in concept, building relationships takes time and energy, which at times, individuals do not feel they have. However, strong relationships are an investment and a critical influence strategy. More often than not, people are influenced by others that they trust and like. Do you have a relationship with the last person you asked to write you a letter of recommendation?

Lead a Coalition—The adage of *strength in numbers* is an important concept when it comes to the topic of influence.[21] A lone voice has much less power than a group of individuals with a shared mission or vision for a better future. However, just because you have a coalition of motivated individuals does not mean everything is set. It will be wise to weave in elements such as logic, relationships, win-win, and empathy as well. When was the last time you were part of a collation of friends who wanted to get your way?

Emphasize Win-Win—When influencing others, it is important to emphasize the win-win. In other words, you are helping others see how they will benefit from the approach or strategy you are suggesting.[22] Framing an option as a win-win allows all parties

Rational persuasion *See* Influence tactics

Lead a coalition *See* Influence tactics

Win-win *See* Influence tactics

to benefit from the proposed solution. This approach requires empathy which means that you can place yourself *in the shoes* of the other individual. You can see the issue from their perspective and identify approaches that will help them accomplish their goals. When have you used this on your parents?

Create Positive Energy—If you have enthusiasm and energy for your proposed solution, it is likely that others will too.[23] Create positive and authentic energy around your recommended course of action. While not a silver bullet, positive energy is a necessary ingredient. When combined with other influence tactics in this section, positivity and optimism have enormous power to influence. One caveat: It is vital that your optimism and enthusiasm are authentic, measured, and appropriate. Who among your peers does this best?

Inspirational appeal *See* Influence tactics

Inspirational Appeal—Similar to creating positive energy, inspirational appeal is more focused on aligning your proposed direction with the values, mission, and vision of the group or organization.[24] You are appealing to the core of what the group was intended to be. A famous example of this would be Martin Luther King, Jr.'s *I Have a Dream* speech in which he aligned his words and hopes with the founding tenets of the United States of America. With an inspirational appeal, it is all about bringing your argument back to the mission and living into the purpose of the organization or institution. Can you think of the last cause you gave to? How did the concept of inspirational appeal influence your decision?

Negotiation/Bargaining/Exchange—Humans have been influencing one another via bargaining and exchange since the beginning of their existence. Also known as *reciprocity*, it means an exchange of *this* for *that*.[25] It is likely you have been using this influence strategy your entire life with peers, parents, siblings, and supervisors. It is an important tool because if both parties can feel like they are gaining something, it is more likely that an agreement can be made. The key is empathy. What do they need, and how will your exchange help them achieve *their* goals? How is this similar to but different from win/win?

Personal Appeal—A personal appeal relies heavily on the relationship between two individuals.[26] In a sense, it is using the connection as a primary reason for compliance. While it is true that relationships are critical to the influence process, it is important to observe when you are being asked to make decisions that go against what is ethically appropriate; fair; or, at an extreme, illegal. Personal appeal is a powerful force. Most people want to see their friends and inner circle succeed and progress. Have you used personal appeal in the last couple of days?

Pressure/Coercion—An individual using this influence strategy is often using their formal power or authority to dictate behavior.[27] There are many shades of this influence strategy, from offhand comments, such as "you better start studying because you cannot afford to fail this exam," to outright threats and violence. While pressure and coercion can seem extreme, they are valuable tools that most people in leadership have to use at one time or another. For instance, a chronically underperforming employee or an individual working outside of the rules and expectations may need to be pressured to act in line with organizational expectations and norms.

Ingratiation *See* Influence tactics

Ingratiation—An individual using this influence tactic is concerned with increasing the level of positive feelings among the key decision makers.[28] Making oneself more likeable to followers in order to influence them can be direct, or through association. A statement such as, "Under Xiaoting's leadership we have come so far, and this strategy is a way for us to continue his legacy," purposefully appeals to the positive feelings Xiaoting elicited as a leader. A leader using this appeal wants to influence followers to adopt the proposed strategy in the statement because followers liked Xiaoting and his actions. Similar to many other influence strategies, this approach combined with logic, win-win, inspirational appeal, and so forth can be a powerful combination. Can you think of a time you could have used this tactic?

TABLE 7.3 ● Influence Tactics for Leaders	
Influence Tactic	**Definition**
Involve others/consulting	Involving others in the decision-making process
Facts/logic/rational persuasion	Sharing facts and using logic to persuade others
Relationships	Using personal relationships to sway opinions
Lead a coalition	Convening a group of like-minded people to convince decision makers
Emphasize win-win	Helping others see how they will benefit from your idea or solution
Create positive energy	Building enthusiasm and energy for your proposed solution
Inspirational appeal	Aligning your proposed direction with the values, mission, and vision of the group or organization
Negotiation/bargaining/ exchange	Exchanging *this* for *that* or engaging in dialogue to establish a path forward
Personal appeal	Appealing to personal relationships as a way to sway opinions
Pressure/coercion	Using formal power or authority to dictate behavior
Ingratiation	Increasing the level of positive feelings among the key decision makers

Gaining Power in Groups and Organizations

Learning Objectives

7.4 Analyze how people use power

7.5 Understand 10 sources of power

At times, the word *power* can be perceived as a negative thing. In truth, power is neither good nor bad. Humans make it so. In other words, what people do with their power will make all the difference. As we explored in Chapter 4, some have used their power for destructive purposes or show up as "bosses from hell" as scholar Ron Riggio[29] suggests. These individuals are using personalized power, which is about using power for personal gain.[30] Another type of power is called socialized power, which is used to benefit the masses. For instance, for years Kiwanis has had a mission of "serving the children of the world." Through their Eliminate Project,

> Kiwanis' current global campaign for children, The Eliminate Project: Kiwanis eliminating maternal/neonatal tetanus, aims to raise US$110 million and save the lives of 129 million mothers and their future babies. In partnership with UNICEF, Kiwanis is committing by 2015 to eliminating maternal/neonatal tetanus, a disease that kills one baby every nine minutes.[31]

This story is an example of an organization using its power and ability to mobilize hundreds of thousands of men and women toward one cause and make a difference in the world. Leaders should consistently reflect upon how they are using their power. Likewise, a strong ethical foundation (see Chapter 4) and awareness can help leaders ensure that they are clear on what they stand for and are living their values.

Sources of Power: Personal and Positional Power

A relevant and interesting conversation for you reading this text is how an individual gains power and formal authority in an organization. What is the source of that influence? Sources of power comprise the specific origin of your capacity to influence others. After all, many of you reading this text hope to take on positions of leadership on campus, in your community, and perhaps across the globe. As you read this section, note that you have already achieved power and authority in multiple domains throughout childhood. For instance, as you review the sources of power in the following section, think about your peer groups, athletic teams, internships, student organizations, and so forth. It is likely you have three or more sources of power in many of these domains. The key to gaining power in an organizational context is intentionality. Are you purposefully working toward multiple sources of power? Are you consistently working to develop your knowledge, skills, and abilities in various domains? If so, you are likely on the right path.

Reward Power—Often associated with a formal position of power, reward power means that you can formally reward an individual for their efforts.[32] This recognition could be a monetary reward or some other perk that you have the authority to grant (e.g., vacation time, free meal). It could also mean that you can reward an individual with a promotion or opportunity to advance their career in some form or fashion. In many respects, your parents had this form of power and could reward you with benefits such as special privileges (e.g., staying out later), money, or gifts (e.g., a car). Here are some questions to help you determine your level of reward power.

- Do you hold a position on campus or in the community that allows you to reward others with special perks or money?

- Do you have the ability to reward an individual in your organization? Something that would exchange their hard work or effort with something they would value?

Personal Charisma/Referent Power—Some people have that *it* factor that others find attractive. Perhaps it is their optimism or enthusiasm[33] or perhaps their charisma that you read about back in Chapter 2. Not necessarily in a physical sense, but their humor, their zest for adventure, perspective on life, positive energy, view of a better future, endearing quirks, and ability to *connect* set them apart from the rest. Think of the person in your circle of friends who attracts others to be a part of the club, organization, or festivities. Those with referent power have strong interpersonal skills. Here are some questions to help you determine your level of charisma/referent power.

- Are you an individual who is a *hub* for the action? Do you have a wide variety of friends in many contexts? Are you a connector?

- Do your energy and enthusiasm attract others?

- Do people tell you that you are charismatic and an *attractor* when it comes to people?

Outmatched Effort—Individuals who consistently display superior effort. The term *outmatched effort* is contextual.[34] For instance, in an accounting firm during the busy season, it is not uncommon to work 12- to 14-hour days. In a similar vein, it is not uncommon for young medical residents to work very long hours—it is a part of the culture. In other contexts, an individual who worked these hours is an individual who puts in an extraordinary amount of time and energy. Here are some questions to help you determine your level of effort.

Sources of power This is the specific origin of your capacity to influence others. Examples include (a) **Referent power:** You attract others through your enthusiasm, energy, humor, and optimism; (b) **Outmatched effort:** You consistently display superior effort; (c) **Legitimate power:** You have actual authority over an individual or group.

Referent power *See* Sources of power

Outmatched effort *See* Sources of power

- Do your professors know you and your work? Would they say it is above and beyond the work of others or middle of the pack?

- Would your internship supervisor advocate for you? Did he or she see you work above and beyond the other interns, or are you in the bottom 50% when it comes to effort?

- Are you a *go to* person because people in your organization know you will get the task done?

Wealth/Resource—At first blush, you may be thinking about wealth as money, which of course is a source of power. However, wealth can be thought of as a *span of control*. Obviously, the president of a sorority has more wealth or span of control than a new member in the organization—the president is in charge of a $500,000 budget, the actions of 100+ women, and so forth. In corporate life, an individual running a multimillion-dollar division has more wealth than a director with a team of six (unless it is an exceptional group of six). Here are some questions to help you determine your wealth:

- Do you have a significant level of responsibility in your organization? Are you the captain of the team? President of the club? Senior resident hall advisor? Student body president?

- In the position(s) you hold, do you have control over how money is spent and allocated? Do you set the budget? Distribute the funds? Collect the dues?

- Do people see you as critical to the success of the organization?

Expertise—Individuals who display this source of power have a superior command of domain-specific knowledge. They have continually pushed well past the threshold of competence and are focused on developing their knowledge.[35] However, like other domains, expertise is relative. For instance, a senior resident advisor naturally has more expertise than junior advisors; however, one senior advisor likely knows policy much better than others. In a similar vein, some football players have spent more time studying the playbook than others—they have a strong command of the content. In organizational life (e.g., corporate, nonprofit), the individual with the most expertise has a great deal of power. Here are some questions to help you determine your level of expertise.

- Do colleagues or peers comment on your knowledge or command of the content?

- Have your peers, professors, or faculty advisors commented on your expertise?

- Do you enjoy the process of learning and building expertise in and out of the classroom?

Relevance—Relevance as a source of power means that you have responsibility for mission-critical work in your organization.[36] In health care, nurses and physicians are highly relevant to the task. At a college or university, the president is relevant to advancing the mission and vision of the institution. Individuals with highly relevant roles have power and authority. For instance, in a fraternity, the recruitment chairman may have a more relevant role than the chorister or secretary. High-quality meeting minutes mean nothing if you do not have members. Here are some questions to help you determine your level of relevance

- Are you a hub for activity? Do people need to work through you to complete their work?

- Is success in your role mission critical to the success of the organization?

- Is your role highly regarded as an honor?

Visibility—Visibility means that key decision makers or influential figures see you in action.[37] They see your skills or expertise in action, and this can open doors—quickly. Think of a coach watching a new player on the field display her talent—that visibility is a source of power because the individual moves forward from the pack in the eyes of the decision maker. Of course, this applies in the workplace as well, so how are you aligning yourself with committees, philanthropic endeavors, or projects that are critical to organizational success? If you don't, you may reside in the *cube farm* for longer than you would like. Here are some questions to help you determine your level of visibility.

- Your CEO, division leader, or department head knows your name and has seen your work, and they were impressed . . .

- On campus, you have an extensive network in and outside of your various organizations. Because of your involvement in the community, influential people in the community have seen your work and were impressed by your efforts.

- Strangers know who you are—and for good reasons.

Network—An individual's network is another source of power. The saying "it is not what you know, but who you know" can ring true. Individuals with a broad and vast network merely have access to resources that others may not.[38] So it is wise to invest in your network on campus, in your organization, and in the community. Investing in your network can pay off in many ways. First, your network can open doors that would otherwise be difficult to enter. Also, your network can provide guidance and mentoring in times of transition or change. Third, your network can serve as a peer group and social outlet. Investing in your network is a long-term process. It is a way of being. Here are some questions to help you think about your network.

- Do people make comments about the number of people you know on and off campus?

- Do you have coffee, lunch, or a drink with at least one or two people outside of your immediate peer group each week?

- Do you think of your family (e.g., aunts and uncles), family friends, and your friends' parents as part of your network? Have you connected with people in these realms to learn more about their path?

Legitimacy—Legitimacy means that you align with the written and unwritten norms, values, and goals of the group.[39] On an athletic team, an individual with this source of power may be a team player, behave well off the field, excel in competition, know the sport well, practice with great determination, embody the values of the team, and so forth. If the list mentioned above is what the team values, we could likely judge each team member on those dimensions and determine the person who most closely aligns with the list. Likewise, there would be some individuals with two or three but who are missing one or two important attributes (behave well off the field and practice with great determination). It is important to note that every group and organization has unwritten rules as well. It is important to observe these at play and understand how you do and do not align with them. For instance, it could be an unwritten rule that your boss promotes the people who work the longest hours. It is never said, per se, but her value for long hours is something you need to pick up on to be successful in that context. Here are some questions to help you think about your legitimacy.

- Do people say, "if we just had more of you we would be in a better position"?

- What did legitimacy mean at your last internship or job? What were the written and unwritten rules for success?

- What does a student with legitimacy look like in the classroom? Think of your courses and explore this concept.

Legitimate Power—Different from *legitimacy*, legitimate power means that you have actual authority over an individual or group.[40] For instance, a professor may have legitimate power over you as a student—they hold your grade in their hands. Or, you may have the authority to hire or fire an individual at your job. These are forms of legitimate power—a power granted to you by function of your role. Before using legitimate power to change behavior (e.g., putting someone on a 90-day plan or firing them), you should use influence to encourage a change in behavior. Here are some questions to help you think about legitimate power.

Legitimate power *See* Sources of power

- Have you served in a role where you had specific authority over others? Examples may be approving expenditures, setting someone's schedule, approval of requests, the power to hire someone, and so forth.

- When have you witnessed someone (coach, boss) using legitimate power to ensure compliance of a group? How did their use of this source of power impact the group's motivation or morale?

- Do your parents have legitimate power? If yes, how so? If no, why?

One final note on power. Reflect upon what happens if an individual lacks specific sources of power. In other words, you could have five to six of the sources of power listed in Table 7.4, but lack *expertise*, and you will be limited in your ability to connect at the highest levels. Likewise, it is likely you have a few of these sources of power in one domain (e.g., your athletic team) but not in others (e.g., the club you just joined). Depending on the context, it can take years to gain a position of formal authority or prestige. For instance, in your internship, it is unlikely you gainfully obtain many of the sources of power listed below in three to six months. All of this takes time, perseverance, resilience, patience, and a little luck.

TABLE 7.4 ● Sources of Power

Source of Power	Definition
Reward power	You can formally reward an individual for their efforts.
Personal charisma/ referent power	You attract others through your enthusiasm, energy, humor, and optimism.
Outmatched effort	You consistently display superior effort.
Wealth/resource	You have financial wealth or, in an organizational context, a wide *span of control* under your purview.
Expertise	You have a superior command of domain-specific knowledge.
Relevance	You have responsibility for mission-critical work in your organization.
Visibility	Key decision makers or influential figures see you in action.
Network	You have a wide and vast network.
Legitimacy	You align with the written and unwritten norms, values, and goals of the group.
Legitimate power	You have actual authority over an individual or group.

Motivation

Learning Objective

7.6 Analyze the difference between intrinsic and extrinsic motivation

Motivation the internal desire for a person to act

Motivation is the internal desire for a person to act. Everyone—believe it or not—is motivated. The trouble lies in *what* they are motivated to do, and in some cases *how* they are motivated. According to scholars, "To be motivated means to be moved to do something. A person who feels no impetus or inspiration to act is thus characterized as unmotivated, whereas someone who is energized or activated toward an end is considered motivated."[41] In this section, you will explore ways to create a culture that is energizing by capitalizing on intrinsic motivation and one that activates others toward a desired (by both the individual and the leader) goal or vision.

Intrinsic and Extrinsic Motivation

Intrinsic motivation engaging in an activity for the inherent joy of the task

Extrinsic motivation engaging in an activity because of external rewards for doing so

In 1971, Deci asserted that some activities have inherent benefits and do not need external rewards. These came to be known as intrinsic motivators.[42] **Intrinsic motivation** is about engaging in an activity for the inherent joy of the task, while **extrinsic motivation** is about participating in an activity because of external rewards for doing so. Interestingly, many scholars found that intrinsic motivation diminished with the presence of external rewards.[43] Other scholars have found that both intrinsic and extrinsic motivators jointly predict performance.[44]

LEADERSHIP BY DESIGN

Design Principle: Entry Point

Definition: A place where one enters, physically or in their attention focus, into a deeper space of your place, product, context, or concept.

In Other Words: Where and how do you enter or begin?

For Example: Common entry points you know: Judging a book by its cover; a class by its course title; a person by their look or handshake; or a store by its front space and door. An airport is an important entry point to a city that can influence the rest of the trip.

For Leaders: A first impression is the entry point of a person; it influences perceptions and attitudes that affect future interactions. Physical entry points have progressive lures to attract and pull people into the space, such as footsteps painted on the floor entering the door or sidewalk tent signs. How do you progressively lure followers to enter your organization, the mission, or the team? Good entry points also have minimal barriers and clear paths. What might be or

©iStock.com/4001tmax

WHAT DOES THIS ENTRY POINT TELL YOU?

appear too complicated or difficult for followers that keeps them from entering a project or the culture of your organization? Consider the entry point as a highly influential aspect of any design, including the design of your leadership relationships.

Sources of Intrinsic and Extrinsic Motivation

Sources of power represent your capacity to influence. **Sources of motivation** comprise the conditions that you design to alter someone's internal desire to act. The following section is a list of strategies that leaders and managers must have in mind when exploring the concept of motivation. By doing so, you can create a system that fits the needs and desires of your team members and your organization. And like other concepts explored in this text, you need to experiment. It is likely your first attempt will not yield perfect results. Also, it is important to pay close to attention to your employees. Are they behaving in a way that a motivated team member should?

Financial Compensation—Financial compensation is a motivating factor for some but not all.[45] Is your organization below the average income in your industry? At the top? Somewhere in the middle? What is your strategy? Starbucks has a history of compensating (pay and benefits) its employees in a very different manner from the industry standard.[46] In fact, it was an essential element of their strategy to make Starbucks your *third place* (first being home, second being work). By compensating their employees fairly, they bet on the fact that they would retain good people who had relationships with their customer base. Is money everything? No, but it is an important consideration.

Alignment With Values—Research has found that an individual will feel more motivated to perform when the mission and values of the organization align with their value system.[47] For instance, an individual who values service to their community will resonate with an organization that prioritizes *giving back* to the community as a core priority. Does your organization promote and live its values? Do your team members make connections between their values and the organization's?

Meaning—People who find significant meaning in their work are more motivated to perform at the highest levels.[48] For instance, an individual who sees purpose by helping people in the writing center will be more energized to produce *above and beyond* in their role. Of course, the key is to find work that is intrinsically meaningful to you. This takes exploration and a great deal of self-awareness. When you become a supervisor, it is important to coach and mentor others through this process as well.

Showing Appreciation—It sounds so simple, but think about all the people in your life who struggle to show appreciation[49] with a simple *thank you*. In addition to verbal appreciation, managers can praise via text, e-mail, or a handwritten note. Develop a habit of mind when it comes to appreciating others. Do you notice and acknowledge the *good* that your parents, peers, teachers, coaches, supervisors, and mentors do? People are motivated to work above and beyond when they feel appreciated for their efforts. If someone has given you their time, they deserve your appreciation.

Reward and Recognize—A more formal and sometimes more public way of showing appreciation, reward and recognition are other sources of motivation.[50] Often, reward and recognition involve structured systems of recognition (e.g., an employee of the month or employee of the year) or a bonus structure for meeting goals and objectives. While not a silver bullet, a reward and recognition program is an excellent addition to many of the other motivational techniques explored in this section.

Empowerment—The term empowerment has multiple meanings. In general, empowerment means that individuals feel a sense of ownership/control and competence in their work or projects.[51] From a situational leadership perspective, it may take some time until the leader can genuinely *turn over the reins* to a team member or employee. However, the most competent and committed followers are those individuals who are autonomous and who can be trusted to produce high-quality work with little or no direction. Autonomy and self-determination are significant sources of motivation. But in most cases, it is unrealistic to think that someone can achieve this level of trust and autonomy from the beginning. The road to empowerment is complicated and is a process that involves organizational analysis, coaching, and experience.[52]

Sources of motivation These are the conditions that you design to alter someone's internal desire to act. Examples include (a) **Empowerment:** You feel a sense of ownership/control and competence in your work; (b) **Autonomy:** You feel ownership in how tasks are accomplished; (c) **Career pathing:** You have a clear sense for how you can progress and move forward in the organization; and (d) **Psychological safety:** You have trust in the organization, your supervisor, and your peers.

Empowerment *See* Sources of motivation

MYTH OR REALITY?

ONLY ABOUT ONE-THIRD OF EMPLOYEES IN THE UNITED STATES ARE ENGAGED IN THEIR JOBS.

Reality. In 2014, about 31.5% reported being engaged, and in 2015, the number remained relatively stable at 32%. According to Gallup,

> research shows that employee engagement is strongly connected to business outcomes essential to an organization's financial success, such as productivity, profitability and customer engagement. Engaged employees support

the innovation, growth and revenue that their companies need.[53]

According to the article, disengaged employees simply show up and pass the time and really do not work above and beyond for the betterment of the organization. Gallup also found that disengaged workers cost the U.S. economy more than half a trillion dollars annually.[54]

Belonging—Feeling a sense of belonging and comradery with the group is another source of motivation which is founded in relationships.[55] As a result, it is important to focus on creating a sense of team so that all members understand their role and contribution to the team. In part, leaders have an opportunity to ensure that they have worked to create a sense of belonging. And while it is unrealistic to think that every team member will always mesh or fit in with the larger group, it is an important task and goal for anyone leading a team.

Achievement/Success/Competence—When people feel like they are successful in their endeavors, it is a source of motivation.[56] So a feeling of competence and achievement can drive motivation. As a leader, you have an opportunity to ensure that team members are provided with the correct coaching and feedback to develop as members of your team. The challenge can be to not overwhelm and to provide adequate tasks and activities that fit the individual's ability level.

Fairness—A lack of perceived fairness can diminish trust, which, in turn, can reduce an individual's motivation.[57] So, as a leader, ensure that (a) you are fair in your interactions with people and (b) you do everything possible to ensure that fairness is a norm in the organizational environment. At times, *in-group*[58] members (people with close relationships to decision makers) can be given (consciously or unconsciously) preferential treatment, which can lead to lawsuits, mistrust, decreased levels of motivation, and lower productivity.

Autonomy *See* Sources of motivation

Autonomy—People with a sense of independence feel ownership in the decision-making process.[59] Autonomy is a significant source of motivation for individuals who appreciate and enjoy the freedom to decide how their work is completed. However, like the other sources of motivation, this is not a panacea. Too much autonomy too soon can be disastrous for both the individual and the organization.

Feedback/Coaching—Feedback and coaching help the development and growth of team members.[60] As a formal or informal leader in your organization, coaching from one's immediate supervisor is vital. Without effective coaching and feedback, team members will struggle to work to their full potential and may struggle to meet expectations. At times, supervisors can feel uncomfortable when taking on a coaching role because it may involve conflict and accountability. When a supervisor avoids these opportunities, teaching moments are missed.

Flexibility the number of different answer categories comprising ideas as a measure of creativity

Flexibility/Freedom—Some individuals are motivated by flexible working hours, flextime, and remote working options.[61] Perhaps they can work from a home office or in a city removed from the home office. Another form of flexibility/freedom is that the role has clear benchmarks for success but does not require a set number of hours in one specific location. In other words, "we do not care when or where you work, we just care that you produce results."

Career Pathing—Team members want clarity about how their career will progress in the organization.[62] Providing team members with clear objectives, goals, and deliverables will help them better understand what they need to do to progress in the organization. Career pathing can be a challenge for some organizations that may not have this information clearly outlined or described. Again, the key is clear baseline expectations with consistent follow through for reward once expectations are met.

Psychological Safety—Trust is a fundamental ingredient for any human relationship. People want to have trust in the organization, their supervisor, and peers. When trust is missing, it is difficult for employees and team members to bring their *full selves* to the work.[63] In addition, when trust is lacking, individuals begin to focus more and more energy on their safety or well-being versus the task at hand. Note that as a leader, there will be times where you are actively holding people accountable or having difficult conversations with people. They may have reason to mistrust you, or they may feel unsafe . . . because they are. They are not living up to expectations. So, you need to think about trust and safety in a general sense—do your high-performing, well-adjusted, functioning employees feel like you have their best interest at heart? Do they trust that you want them to succeed? Do they know that if they meet baseline expectations, they will be *safe* and know where they stand?

Career pathing *See* Sources of motivation

Psychological safety *See* Sources of motivation

TABLE 7.5 ● Sources of Motivation

Source of Motivation	Definition
Financial compensation	You are fairly compensated for your work.
Alignment with values	The mission and values of the organization are aligned with your value system.
Meaning	You experience great meaning in your work.
Showing appreciation	Your superiors and peers show appreciation for your efforts.
Reward and recognition	You are formally rewarded and recognized for your results.
Empowerment	You feel a sense of ownership/control and competence in your work.
Belonging	You feel a sense of belonging and comradery with your team or group.
Achievement/success/competence	You feel competent in your work and enjoy a sense of achievement.
Fairness	You feel that your supervisor is fair and consistent.
Autonomy	You feel ownership in how tasks are accomplished.
Feedback/coaching	You receive consistent feedback and coaching on your performance.
Flexibility/freedom	You have flexible working hours, flextime, and/or remote working options.
Career pathing	You have a clear sense for how you can progress and move forward in the organization.
Psychological safety	You have trust in the organization, your supervisor, and your peers.

An important point to remember about this topic is that there is no *silver bullet* for motivating human beings. However, some concepts have emerged that, as a leader, you need to know. Your awareness of each of these concepts will allow you to more intentionally build a culture where both intrinsic and extrinsic motivators work in concert to drive individuals and the group to the desired end. Likewise, you will be in a better position to diagnose or understand why some individuals are not motivated or working to their full potential. For instance, *person/job fit* is an umbrella term for many of the elements explored in this section. In a general sense, individuals are more motivated when the job or role is a good fit.

Chapter Summary

Designing relationships involves the mindful application of influence, power, and motivation. These three constructs comprise a reality of leadership activity that requires careful consideration to ensure just, equitable, sustainable, and ethical application. At a minimum, leaders can capitalize on the natural motivation of followers by defining the goal, clarifying an effective path, removing obstacles, and providing support. Awareness of the appropriate behavioral style is also key.

Influence can come in many forms, and there are key differences between influence, authority, and manipulation. There are also many influence tactics leaders can use to

design relationships and effectively mobilize others to action. The roles and sources of power can drive influence tactics and often dictate the initial form of a relationship. Effective and ethical leaders should recognize these sources and their appropriate use.

Finally, leaders can design a culture that fosters motivation through a number of conditions and behaviors. Some of those characteristics enhance intrinsic motivation, while others rely on extrinsic motivators. This chapter provides many tools of influence, all of which can be employed to design relationships and ultimately influence others toward a common goal.

Key Terms

Achievement Oriented 174
Authority Figure 176
Autonomy 188
Career Pathing 189
Directive 174
Empowerment 187
Extrinsic Motivation 186
Flexibility 188
Formal Power 177
Influence 175

Influence Tactics 178
Informal Power 177
Ingratiation 180
Inspirational Appeal 180
Intrinsic Motivation 186
Lead a Coalition 179
Leadership Style 174
Legitimate Power 185
Manipulation 177
Motivation 186

Outmatched Effort 182
Participative 174
Psychological Safety 189
Rational Persuasion 179
Referent Power 182
Sources of Motivation 187
Sources of Power 182
Supportive 174
Win-Win 179

CORE™ Attribute Builders: Build Now for Future Leadership Challenges

Attribute: Engagement

Builder: Influencing others

It is likely that you see opportunities for improvement in your internship, family, student organization (fraternity, residence hall), or athletic team. For instance, recall the hazing statistics shared at the beginning of this chapter. Can you influence others to act upon the opportunity you see? Can you build a coalition of like minds in an effort to help the organization better live its values, achieve results, improve culture, and so forth? First, determine the opportunity and get clear on your thinking. How will your solution help? Next, read the influence strategies listed in this chapter and circle four or five that you think could work—perhaps it is inspirational appeal, building a coalition, and emphasizing win-win. As you plan, think through *how* others will respond, and be clear about the factions that will and will not support you. You could even run your thoughts by a few peers or a mentor as well to get some preliminary feedback. Finally, determine how you would like to communicate your plan and see who you can engage and *win over* to your perspective or thoughts.

Be sure to focus on listening, and be aware that you may need to compromise or collaborate with others. It is unlikely—especially if the issue has some heat around it—that your plan will move forward without some adjustment and tweaks.

After the meeting or discussion some critical questions may include:

- What happened that was unexpected? How did this impact results?

- In hindsight, what other influence techniques may have helped you make your case?

- Did you change the minds of individuals from other factions or subgroups? If not, why?

- How did your mindset and delivery help or hinder your ability to sell your ideas?

Skill Builder Activity

Motivating Leadership Presentation (Part I)— Conditions for Intrinsic Motivation

Your (large) group has been invited to present an introduction to leadership theory and practice to a group of high school students. Your presentation must be informative, accurate, entertaining, engaging, and memorable.

Your presentation must last between 5 and 8 minutes.

Every person in the group must be involved in a visible manner.

Your (small) leadership team has 4 weeks to prepare for this event (and all those events following):

How would you, as the leader, motivate your group—individually and as a group?

1. To what extent could you, the leader, incorporate the following conditions.
    a. Autonomy? How so?
    b. Individual achievement/success/ competence? How so?
    c. Responsibility and/or sense of meaning? How so?

Motivating Leadership Presentation (Part II)— Influence, Power, and Motivation

Your (large) group has been invited to present an introduction to influence, power, and motivation to a group of high school students. Your presentation must be informative, accurate, entertaining, engaging, and memorable.

Your presentation must last between 5 and 8 minutes.

Every person in the group must be involved in a visible manner.

Your (small) leadership team has 4 weeks to prepare for this event (and all those events following):

How would you, as the leader, motivate your group—individually and as a group?

2. How could you more effectively . . .
    a. define the goals of the task?
    b. clarify the path to achieve the goals?
    c. identify and remove obstacles to achievement?
    d. seek out needs and provide support?

Design Others' Success

"It made a difference for that one."

—Loren Eiseley

Forget about this notion of leadership for a moment. You find yourself with a group of individuals in a narrow canyon that is quickly filling with a raging river. With the temperature dropping and daylight fading, your group needs to find a way out or a way to contact help. You try to climb the canyon wall, but it is too steep. You try to hug the wall and work your way back upriver to where you started, but the current is too strong. You could ride the river to the end of the canyon, but hidden roots and rocks are a constant drowning hazard, threatening to pin you under the rapids. The situation is not good, and success is now reduced to survival.

Now bring yourself back to leadership, specifically as the leader of this canyon hike one week prior to the trip. What could you do to design a successful trip? What could you do to design each participant's success? Your list might include things like check the weather, know the route, anticipate problems, and secure necessary equipment and supplies. You might also make certain that participants understand the goal and the planned route, and that they generally know what to expect. You would try to think about and do everything possible to maximize your chances of success—right?

A week before disaster strikes your organization, what can you do as a leader to design others' success? This section flips the typical organizational chart upside down, putting those individuals who interface directly with the product or customer or service as most important, and placing those with lead titles in the support position—creating conditions for others to succeed—designing others' success. When a problem occurs in the typical organizational hierarchy, everyone looks down from the top to place blame—because, after all, that is where the problem happened. But when you are a leader who designs others' success, *blame-finding* becomes problem-solving. And the first question for you as a leader is, Did I create the conditions for this problem to occur, or did I create conditions for success? Did the problem occur because the person was not the right fit for the position or task? Was the person properly trained? Did they have the necessary resources to succeed?

Figure M3.1 illustrates this notion in the university setting. Take a moment to think about what you need to succeed as a student in the classroom. What conditions has the professor created to facilitate your success? Now think about what others have done behind the scenes to make sure your professor has what they need to succeed. If you do not know, ask them about it.

Your success as a leader happens only when you succeed in leader*ship* (i.e., you facilitating the process of influencing others toward a common vision). In the previous chapter, you read about what motivates others and how important it is to consider the path and goal of each person. This is where Rule #1 (It's about you) meets Rule #2 (It's not about you). Focusing on the success of others requires that you focus on your actions, attitude, and

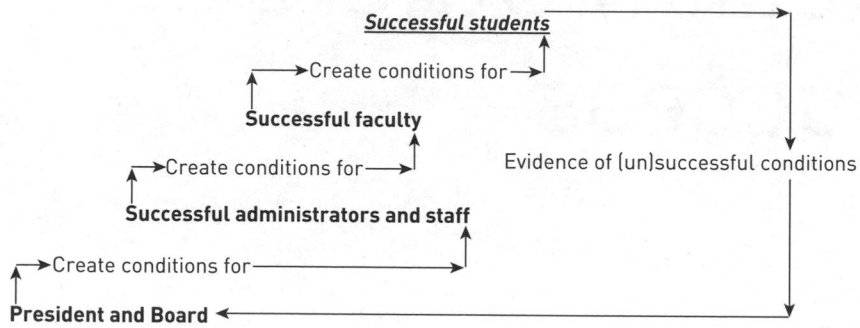

FIGURE M3.1 ● **Designing Others' Success Idea #1—The Bottom Is the Top**

Leaders create the conditions for others to succeed.

approach as collaborator in the common vision of the organization. This does *not* mean that every problem was the leader's fault for not preparing or facilitating success. Unanticipated problems, difficult circumstances, challenging individuals, and a host of other variables may be the root cause of a problem. For leaders, the important thing is shifting the mindset from individual blame to designing organizational and systemic excellence.

As you read the introduction to this section, were you able to visualize the canyon incident? You likely imagined all the terrible things that could have happened, and you probably wondered why the leader did not take the time to visualize how the day could unfold and the worst cases for which the group should prepare. Mindful, effective leaders do their best to proactively anticipate and prepare before a problem happens. **Proactive** means anticipating and preparing for a possible outcome, which is closely related to the notion of design (recall the definition of design as the process of originating and developing a plan). Reacting to a problem once the problem occurs leaves leaders and followers with too little time and limited options, which will likely end badly.

Proactive anticipating and preparing for a possible outcome

REFLECTION QUESTIONS

What if your goal as a leader was to develop and prepare your own replacement? How would you approach your followers differently if you saw them as aspiring leaders?

Individuals seldom *want* to fail. But leadership is a process and failure happens. Shifting your mindset from *who did it* to *why did it happen* reframes the situation and approach from fault to vault. In other words, how can you as a leader use the moment of failure to vault your organization and/or followers to the next level of development? As this chapter further explores, great innovations often begin with an annoyance or failure. Leaders need not wait for a failure to happen, but they can instead seek out shortcomings and areas for improvement. This complex activity will be further explained in the final chapter of this text, but the simple version can be explained by a simple formula: try it—assess it—improve it . . . or let it go (Figure M3.2). Like the design-thinking concept of iteration from Chapter 5, embracing limitations as opportunities for improvement should be a key part of your leadership.

FIGURE M3.2 ● Designing Others' Success Idea #2—Try It—Assess It—Improve It (or Let It Go)

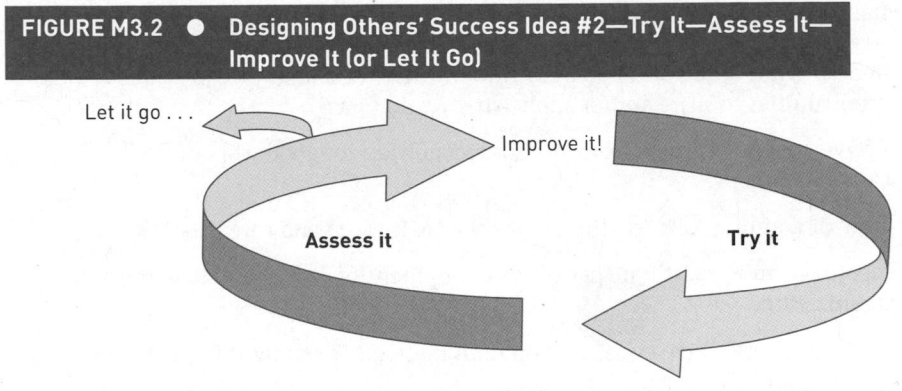

Let it go . . .

Improve it!

Assess it

Try it

Designing Others' Success: The Other Engagement

Throughout this textbook you have learned about building *your* CORE™—confidence, optimism, resilience, and engagement. Designing others' success means that you are also helping your followers build their CORE™: creating conditions that build confidence and optimism, ensuring that challenges are manageable but difficult enough to build resilience, and encouraging engagement.

The idea of engagement has become a popular topic as it relates to employees.[1] Chapter 1 defined engagement as the degree of individual involvement, investment, and enthusiasm within and for a specific context or situation. There are considerable individual and organizational benefits to having engaged followers, and many leaders focus on how they can increase their employee engagement in addition to their own.[2] The Gallup organization measures employee engagement and has created an assessment called the Q12—12 questions that best predict who will and will not be engaged and consequently perform and succeed. Gallup notes three categories of employees: engaged employees who work with passion and feel connected to their company; not-engaged employees who put in the time but without energy or passion; and actively disengaged employees who are both unhappy and busy undermining the organization.[3]

Gallup's extensive research highlights both the importance of engagement as well as the key role that leaders play in fostering that engagement. For example, if you have ever worked for a bad leader, it will not surprise you to learn that 50% of employees leave their job to get away from a manager. Further, 70% of the variance in employee engagement scores are tied to the manager.[4] Note that in the business setting, Gallup refers to leaders as managers and limits their definition of leader by those holding a supervisory position.

At the heart of engagement is follower satisfaction, if not downright enthusiasm. Satisfied, enthused individuals become cheerleaders for the organization, long-term invested members of the organization, and high performers. The consulting firm Aon Hewitt calls this the Say, Stay, and Strive model.[5] How will you engage individuals such that they will say great things, stay part of the group, and strive for greatness? The simple yet challenging answer lies in the human side of leadership. As a leader you must do more than design others' success, you must serve others' success. In short, supporting others, attending to social and emotional needs, and emphasizing the meaningfulness of the work bring forth the positive culture that leads to engagement.[6]

The Gallup Q12 measure illuminates what you might do to increase engagement. Following are a few questions based on the Q12 and reframed as prompts for generating ideas, specifically ideas for ways that you might increase engagement.

In what ways might I . . .

- identify what others and I do best? And in what ways might we provide opportunities to share and/or apply what we do best?

- receive and show others praise and/or recognition for good work or accomplishment?

- show or communicate to others that they are noticed and cared about?

- encourage and/or facilitate personal development of each individual in my organization?

- create a culture where everyone's opinion matters? How might I solicit those opinions and recognize/acknowledge them?

- consistently achieve really high-quality work? How might I ensure every activity greatly impresses others?

- build deeper relationships with others?

- regularly reflect on and discuss goals, activities to reach those goals, my role in those activities, and how I am progressing?

- create more opportunities to learn and grow both personally and professionally?

LEADERSHIP BY DESIGN

Design Principle: Biophilia Effect

Definition: Environments rich in nature views and imagery reduce stress and enhance focus and concentration.

In Other Words: Go outside and get some fresh air or at least look at a picture of nature!

For Example: Hospitals incorporate large murals of natural settings for their restorative effects. Pushing your desk up against the window can help you emotionally, cognitively, and physically do better in school.

For Leaders: As a leader, think about what conditions have the greatest impact on your team. Incorporating nature or natural images into daily work will prove beneficial to your team in a variety of ways. No matter how trivial they may seem at first, every element of engagement can provide a greater return on invested time or effort. What areas and/or activities in your organization require a context of healing, stress reduction, greater concentration, or enhanced learning? Apply nature.

The poet Loren Eiseley's quote at the start of this module refers to an often-told story about a boy picking up starfish off the beach and throwing them back into the ocean so that they did not die in the sun.[7] A passing man told the boy that there were miles of beach and endless starfish and that the boy could not possibly make a difference. The boy picked up another starfish and threw it back into the sea, stating, "It made a difference for that one." Likewise, leaders often view their role in designing others' success as too overwhelming—endless individuals and their needs and challenges. But as the story illustrates, your actions as a leader to facilitate individual success will make a difference to each and every person with whom you work, and ultimately, they will make you a more credible and effective leader.

Throughout this text, your approach to facilitating others can be mindfully designed, or you can just *see what happens* and hope for the best. This next module on designing others' success provides a wealth of tools that you will need to serve others on their journey. Three chapters comprise this module: Chapter 8—Creativity, Problem-Solving, and Idea-Generating; Chapter 9—Effective Practices for Leading Others to Success; and Chapter 10—Utilizing Change Processes Effectively. The first of these chapters introduces the value and role of creativity in leadership. Leaders solve problems—big and little, proactively and reactively, all day, every day, even in their sleep (more on that later in this chapter). The range of problems leaders face requires both creative problem-solving processes and a big toolbox full of idea-generating techniques to prompt innovation.

8

Creativity, Problem-Solving, and Idea-Generating

If you want something new, you have to stop doing something old.

People who don't take risks generally make about two big mistakes a year.
People who do take risks generally make about two big mistakes a year.

—Peter Drucker

Learning Objectives

8.1   Understand the value and role of creativity in leadership

8.2   Distinguish between different types of problems

8.3   Explore creativity within a general creative problem-solving framework

8.4   Construct your creative problem-solving toolbox with a variety of idea-generating techniques

8.5   Develop individual creative identity and activity

Detailed Chapter Outline

Yes, You Really Are Creative
  Myths, Fears, and Creative
    Thinkering
Yes, You Have Problems
  Reactive Problems to
    Proactive Opportunities

Algorithm, Heuristic,
  and the Important
    Thing
Yes, Creativity Will Help (a Lot)
  Product: Unique and
    Valuable

Leadership by Design Model

Design Self

How can I design myself as a leader?

Design Relationships

As a leader, how can I design my relationships with others?

DESIGN OTHERS' SUCCESS

AS A LEADER, HOW CAN I DESIGN SUCCESS FOR OTHERS?

Design Culture

As a leader, how can I design the culture of my organization?

Design Future

As a leader, how can I innovate?

Yes, You Really Are Creative

Learning Objective

8.1 Understand the value and role of creativity in leadership

Creativity. The concept shrouded in mystery—filled with the awe of amazing innovations and special individuals whose gifts are both enviable and unexplainable. Creativity stands as a prized and highly sought-after attribute, generally credited for the success of innovative organizations and on the grand scale hope for the future (i.e., if only we could find an innovative solution to [your problem inserted here]).

Creativity is perhaps the most valuable yet misunderstood attribute to personal and organizational success, as well as the most talked about yet least purposefully developed. Organizations, schools, policymakers, and leaders generally proclaim their affinity for creativity and how dedicated they are to the pursuit of innovation. Every leader wants to be innovative, and they value and seek creativity in their followers.[8] **Innovation** can be defined as new things or methods that deliver value, and it is the *new things* part of

Innovation new things or methods that deliver value; the collaborative process of translating creative ideas into something of value

innovation where creativity lives. Both innovation and creativity conjure images of magic, genius, and solutions that make all your dreams come true. And then . . . they wait and hope for a flash of inspiration and that breakthrough idea.

There is indeed great promise in creativity, and endorsing the concept can begin and sustain creative activity. Unfortunately, if you inquire as to how a leader is going to bring their love for creativity into practical reality, you will find considerable hesitation, misinformation, generalizations, and wishful thinking. After you read this chapter, you will not be that leader.

LEADERSHIP THAT MAKES A DIFFERENCE

Leaders and experts in every field struggle to concisely explain the complexity of their world, especially to those outside that world. How could one effectively popularize complex topics in a simple and fascinating manner? Have you seen a TED talk recently?

One of the most important things a leader can do to have an impact on both knowledge and practice is to alter and expand the way others see the world and its possibilities. Innovation is about opportunity—seeing potential challenges. Richard Saul Wurman—author, architect, urban and graphic designer, cartographer, teacher, and most notably the creator of TED, the entity that has brought innovative ideas from a broad variety of fields to millions—has been helping others see differently since his first books were published in 1962. As noted on his bio, "The acknowledged father of Information Architecture, Wurman has written, designed and published 83 books on a range of topics, while creating conferences and new mapping projects. All contribute to a greater understanding of complex information. They spring from his particular brand of innovation: *doing the opposite of what is rote or expected.*"[9]

The now-ubiquitous intellectual events themed TED were born in 1984 out of Richard Saul Wurman's observation of a powerful convergence among three fields: technology, entertainment, and design. The first TED included a demo of the compact disc, the e-book, and cutting-edge 3-D graphics from Lucasfilm. Designer Stefan Sagmeister states about Wurman, "He created and chaired TED Conferences, which might have become the single most important communication platform for our own field and many others, and thereby connecting design effectively to science, technology, education, politics and entertainment."[10]

As the TED history notes, "The roster of presenters broadened to include scientists, philosophers, musicians, business and religious leaders, philanthropists and many others. For many attendees, TED became one of the intellectual and emotional highlights of the year."[11] While others have grown TED into a multifaceted success, it was Wurman's initiative that provided the foundation. As TED notes, "In the fall of 2012, TED Talks celebrated its one billionth video view."[12]

Amusingly, Richard Saul Wurman's latest book "chronicles the adventures and musings of the eccentric main character, the Commissioner of Curiosity and Imagination."[13] If every organization, community, and culture had such a position, everyone would have the chance to see the world differently and further inspire creativity.

Myths, Fears, and Creative Thinkering

Creativity. The bolt of lightning from the gods that makes that light bulb appear above the head of the lone genius—eureka! Here is the real flash of genius for you: Yes, *you* can develop creativity. When students are asked if they are creative, most will initially say they are not. But asking why generally elicits answers like, "I am not artistic," or "I do not wear crazy clothes or do wacky things." The myths and misconceptions surrounding creativity rival those of leadership. Many of these false ideas stifle any chance for individuals or organizations to develop and utilize creativity. As a leader, you will need to know, confront, and debunk these myths in order to design others' success. Take some time to talk with others about their concept of creativity. The Creativity Myth Bingo card that follows can help guide your conversations.

The answers from those who identify as creative generally reveal more accurate answers about creativity. Why are you creative? "Because I think of lots of options and ideas before I make a decision." And "I consider many perspectives and try to see things in different ways." Those answers make creativity sound like it is more about *how* you think than something you produce. **Creativity** is defined as the personal capacities and process of generating a unique product that has value. The next section examines a more comprehensive definition of creativity, highlighting the components in this concise definition: person, process, product (and more).

> **Creativity** the personal capacities and process of generating a unique product that has value

Creativity Myth Bingo!

Eureka Myth	Breed Myth	Originality Myth	Expert Myth
New ideas are a flash of insight!	Creative ability is a trait inherent in one's heritage or genes.	New ideas are thought up by one person.	Only an expert or group of experts can generate creative ideas.
But . . . research shows that such insights are actually the culminating result of prior hard work on a problem.	But . . . evidence supports just the opposite. People who have confidence and work the hardest are the ones most likely to come up with a creative solution.	But . . . history and research show more that new ideas are actually combinations of older ideas and that sharing those helps generate more innovation.	But . . . research suggests that particularly tough problems often require the perspective of an outsider.
Incentive Myth	**Free Space!**	**Most Common Myth**	**Cohesive Myth**
Bigger incentives, monetary or otherwise, will increase motivation and hence increase innovation.	Yes . . . just like in real Bingo, you get a free space—it is true!	What have you heard the most that seems like it probably is not true?	If everyone gets along and plays, there will be creativity.
But . . . incentives often do more harm than good, as people learn to game the system.			But . . . creative companies are not *zany*, instead they find ways to structure dissent and conflict into their process to better push creative limits.
Constraints Myth	**Lone Creator Myth**	**Brainstorming Myth**	**Mousetrap Myth**
Constraints hinder creativity and the most innovative results come from people who have *unlimited* resources.	One person's hard work is how creativity happens.	Throwing ideas around, no matter how far out, will yield creative insights.	Once you have the creative idea, the work is done.
But . . . research shows that creativity loves constraints as it helps prompt creative potential.	But . . . creative work requires supportive work, collaborative preliminary efforts, and a great team.	But . . . without a focused problem, identifiable goal, and managed idea-generating techniques, there is no evidence that just *throwing ideas around* consistently produces innovative breakthroughs.	But . . . great ideas are only valuable if we communicate them, market them, and find the right customers. We all know of at least one *better mousetrap* that is still hidden.

Source: Based on Burkus, D. (2014). *The myths of creativity. The truth about how innovative companies and people generate great ideas.* San Francisco, CA: Jossey-Bass.

Even with an accurate understanding, individuals tend to limit or even avoid creativity. How can you design others' success when those others do not want to engage? The answer lies back in the introduction to this module on what facilitates engagement. Engaging in creativity is like any other task. Followers must feel competent, included, appreciated, and that their creative work is meaningful. Translating the engagement questions into facilitating creativity results in a leader asking questions such as

- How can I provide opportunities to create and co-create with others?

- How can I recognize creative behavior and production?

- How can I encourage and/or facilitate the personal creative development of each individual in my organization?

- How might I create a culture that encourages creative activity?

Try this thought exercise. Starting right now, you have five minutes to come up with a creative idea for any context you like, addressing any problem—as long as it is really unique and will work. Even with encouragement, this exercise is pretty stressful—not because of the time or expectations but because of the uncertainty:[14] Will I get a good idea? Will it be unique? Will others like it? Will it work? Everyone asks these questions *while they are thinking* about possible ideas, in effect scaring themselves and simultaneously stifling their creativity.[15] Self-editing or self-censoring kills creative ideas—what Matthew May calls *ideacide*.[16] Unique ideas are exactly that—unique. They are different—which makes you different. Recall that your brain is a lean, mean, pattern-making machine, and it loves the concept of the world you have constructed. Creative ideas, by definition, challenge the usual perspectives and are met with suspicion, skepticism, and sometimes even envious rejection.[17] Creativity requires courage; facilitating the creative capacity of yourself and your followers requires purposeful design.

LEADERSHIP BY DESIGN

Design Principle: Desire Line

Definition: Indications of common and frequent use that indicate preferred methods of interaction and activity.

In Other Words: You can see how people like to use things by looking at how that object or environment wears out.

For Example: A pumpkin patch may have premade rows that afford easy walking, but that is not where you will find the pumpkins. New paths are worn where people desire to walk.

For Leaders: Have you ever been in a creative session where ideas seem to have dried up, yet you just know there are many more ideas locked inside the group? When problem-solving, it is typical to follow the methods of thinking that have previously been laid out in front of you. Treat pumpkins in a pumpkin patch as solutions to your problem—you will not find the perfect one by taking the same path everyone else did. Thinking within the constraints of a certain situation is a barrier to creative problem-solving. You will only find that new idea if, as leader, you foster group

DESIRE LINE

©iStock.com/jeffbergen

brainstorming sessions in a way that encourages *mental off-roading*, which forces people to venture off the beaten track. When you allow desire lines to form, you get a more candid perspective that challenges what has already been done before and highlights its inefficiencies. Be attentive to desire lines to gain an unbiased understanding of how people interact with something.

Your concept of creativity has been shaped by many years of education and social norms. Those rules dictate that creativity is acceptable once in a while and only if there is a good idea attached. Beyond that, creativity as a focus or pursuit is fruitless, distracting, uncertain, and probably downright frivolous. And by the way, you are not that creative. Ouch. That thinking is not helpful, nor even accurate. In fact, that perspective is so bad you can almost smell it—hold your nose and exclaim, "That idea is thinky!" Even if puns are not your thing, how many different ways could you modify the word *think* to create new meanings? You would likely surprise yourself. In *Creative Thinkering*, expert Michael Michalko highlights a number of important realities about creativity that nicely frame the mindset that you will need moving forward—12 ideas:[18]

1. You are creative.

2. Creative thinking is work.

3. You must go through the motions of being creative.

4. Your brain is not a computer (and that is a good thing).

5. There is no one right answer.

6. Never stop with your first good idea.

7. Expect the experts to be negative.

8. Trust your instincts.

9. There is no such thing as failure.

10. You do not see things as they are; you see them as you are.

11. Always approach a problem on its own terms.

12. Learn to think unconventionally.

Creativity takes work, and our brains do not like to work if they do not have to. Research on brain activity shows that it takes less cognitive effort to choose a sure gain than a risky gain, and engaging in creativity is a risk (in many ways) with the potential gain of innovation.[19]

Yes, You Have Problems

Learning Objective

8.2 Distinguish between different types of problems

Reactive Problems to Proactive Opportunities

Do you have problems? Oh yes, you do. And if you do not have problems, that is, oddly, a problem. **Problem** can be defined as a challenge or difficult matter of uncertain outcome, and your ability to spot problems is key to effective leadership. After all, you cannot address much less solve a problem that you do not even realize exists. Most often problems are considered troublesome and troubling—something that pops up and gets in the way—a dissatisfaction with the current state. Addressing problems of this kind in this manner happens all the time in both leadership and life. This is the *reactive* problem-solving noted in the module introduction. By contrast, **proactive** problem-solving involves anticipating and addressing problems before they occur. The ability to see potential problems is even more powerful. But even the proactive approach is limited as it depends on the current state.

Problem a challenge or difficult matter of uncertain outcome

Proactive anticipating and preparing for a possible outcome

What if you created problems by visualizing a more ideal outcome than the present? In other words, what if you visualize making *something better*? The idealized design approach used in organizational design emphasizes defining the ideal end state and then addressing the current state as a problem to be solved.[20]

Proactively exploring problems is key to innovative leadership. Right now, it probably seems a bit strange to go looking for problems. But when organizations (and individuals) redefine problems as *opportunities*, finding new problems can lead to great success. Try addressing some of these questions as a way to seek out problems:

- Over the course of one day, what annoys me? Make a list. What annoyance, if solved, could be a great new product, process, or service?

- By contrast, what is working really well in my life that I use a lot? How could it be just a bit better?

- Who could I talk to in order to discover new problems? What could I find if all my friends and family kept track of what annoys them over a week?

Once you see the problem—reactively, proactively, or idealized—leaders set about solving the problem by engaging in a process. Your default, constructed process may or may not be effective for all problems, and it may or may not fully utilize the three general phases of problem-solving explained in Chapter 1: Understand, Imagine, and Implement.

Understanding the problem includes much more than simply knowing it annoys you. Consider the many questions that could prompt your understanding of the problem. What are the costs and consequences—current and long term? What has been done to solve the problem in the past, and what worked and did not work, and why? Who are the key stakeholders, and how are they affected? What are the different variables within the problem, and how are they connected? What is the history and context around this problem? What are the little problems within the larger problem? What would the ideal solution look like, and what consequences might that solution produce?

Unless you understand the problem, you may be working to solve the wrong thing. Experienced leaders appear to solve problems much more quickly than the time needed to answer all those questions because their experience has answered those questions already. The good news, as you may recall, about your pattern-making machine of a brain is that your experiences help make problem-solving more efficient. However, experienced leaders also know to take a slightly different approach to the Understand phase, namely, making sure they understand their own assumptions, biases, and limitations to how they see the problem. Knowing what might be influencing your perspective, or at least that your perspective is only one of many possible, positions you well for learning from experience.

Algorithm, Heuristic, and the Important Thing

Expert problem solvers recognize the different forms of problem, and then apply the most effective tools and approach for that specific problem. **Algorithmic problems** are those with a well-defined set of rules or instructions for solving, such as a mathematical equation. There are not very many algorithmic problems in leadership. Most leadership problems are open-ended, which means they have many parts that are often ill-defined and changing. These kinds of problems are referred to as heuristic. A **heuristic problem** is an open-ended problem with no specific formula for solution and thus needs a general set of guidelines to address. A heuristic approach is flexible enough to allow for variations in persons, situations, and context. For example, there are some general steps to things like building a team, strategic planning, crafting a vision, and conflict resolution. You can imagine how very different these heuristics look with differing players and situations. And that does not even include the other great variable—*you*. If you had to explain to someone how you generally solved problems, you would likely discover that you have already created a

Algorithmic problem a problem with a well-defined set of rules or instructions for solving

Heuristic problem an open-ended problem with no specific formula for solution and thus needs a general set of guidelines to address

habitual pattern—your informal problem-solving heuristic. Effective leaders design their problem-solving with a clear awareness of their tendencies, and have a range of heuristics to draw upon.

Problems are complicated, and every problem is comprised of many pieces—variables that lead to the problem, others that influence the problem, and still others that may be part of the problem some of the time. Heuristic problems include wicked problems (that were introduced in Chapter 5)—those generally social problems that are difficult to solve due to their incomplete, interconnected, and dynamic variables. How can you address such confusing and complex problems as a leader? You might start with *the important thing*. The children's book author Margaret Wise Brown (who also wrote *Goodnight Moon*) wrote *The Important Book* in which she illustrates a very important point about life (and leadership and problems):

> The important thing about a shoe is that you put your foot in it. You walk in it, and you take it off at night. And it's warm when you take it off. But the important thing about a shoe is that you put your foot in it.[21]

There are many characteristics about a given thing, but out of all those there is a fundamental characteristic—the important thing. The same is true of problems. Understanding the problem space helps you identify the important thing, which in turn focuses and specifies your problem. Trying to solve a problem that is too general leads to frustration and wasted effort because the solution is likely not targeted at the important thing. As management guru Peter Drucker notes, "There is nothing quite so useless as doing with great efficiency something that should not be done at all."[22]

When there is so much to understand about a given problem, and limited time to learn and explore, how does a leader make a decision and move forward? Decision-making research tells you that when faced with seemingly endless variables and an unclear path to the goal, the best thing to do is utilize the information you have, make a decision, and move forward. At first thought this approach is frightening. "What did I miss?" is the usual worry. Fear not. Effective problem-solving is *iterative*, which is to say, if you missed something important, you will notice it as you go through the process. Iteration happens automatically when you have developed the design-thinking capacity of iterative thinking—the mindset of always seeing solutions in process—assessing and improving (Chapter 5). As you read on into the Imagine phase of idea-generating, keep in mind that you may start to see the problem differently simply by generating possible solutions, which may then lead you to reframe the problem. That is not wasted time, it is effective problem-solving.

Yes, Creativity Will Help (a Lot)

Learning Objective

8.3 Explore creativity within a general creative problem-solving framework

Leaders solve problems—big and small, near and far, individual and organizational, algorithmic and heuristic, reactively and proactively, and in some cases creatively. Moving from a good problem-solving leader to a creative one consists of understanding the broad range of what facilitates and inhibits creativity, both in yourself and others. One effective way of organizing this understanding is around the classic **4Ps** that are often used to define creativity: Product, Person, Press, and Process. **Product**: The qualities and criteria that distinguish a solution as creative, namely, that it is unique and of value. **Person**: The knowledge, skills, and dispositions that support individual creative activity. **Press**: The contextual variables that foster or inhibit creative thinking and behavior. **Process**: The steps of thinking and doing that maximize creative possibilities. Each of these Ps can prompt activities that will encourage creativity.

4Ps This defines creativity: product, person, press, and process. **Product:** the qualities and criteria that distinguish a solution as creative; **Person:** the knowledge, skills, and dispositions that support individual creative activity; **Press:** the contextual variables that foster or inhibit creative thinking and behavior; **Process:** the steps of thinking and doing that maximize creative possibilities

Product (creative): *See* 4Ps

Person (creative): *See* 4Ps

Press (creative): *See* 4Ps

Process (creative). *See* 4Ps

Product: Unique and Valuable

Often when you come upon something that is very unique, you consider it creative. Indeed, uniqueness is one of the key criteria for a creative product. Note that the term product implies all forms of solution, which might be a design, a service, a strategy, or any other solution. What if you were to draw a messy scribble on a piece of paper right now and offer to sell it to your classmate? Would they buy it? You can claim it is unique—no others like it in the world. Try it and see what happens. From the conversation with your colleague, it quickly becomes clear that the quality of unique is both relative (ranging from unique to you, all the way through unique to the world) and varied (ranging from pretty much anyone can produce this, all the way through very few to perhaps only one person can produce this).

Did your classmate like your scribble? What if you clarified that this was done by someone famous, or that it was done at the top of Mount Everest? In addition to *unique*, a creative product must have value. The notion of value, however, may differ greatly in terms of both persons and forms of value. Usually the creative product is valued based on the degree to which it *solves* a problem. Your scribble may also be valued for its uniqueness, and therefore translate into monetary value. But it may have sentimental value, spiritual value, referential value, and a host of other forms of value as defined by individuals assessing it.

Both uniqueness and value are relative criteria for a creative product. That does not mean that anything you deem creative is so. In fact, what *you think* is creative is probably not. What matters more are numerous other measures, including how well the product solves the problem, how different the product is relative to a broad audience, and how and in what ways users value the product. This relativity also implies leaders must carefully research and consider both target population and value throughout the process.

Person: Divergent Thinking, Open-Mindedness, and Creative Confidence

Defining creativity as a product (i.e., this solution is creative . . . or not) helps leaders understand the nature of the solution, but it does not speak to the route to that end (process) or the tools to get there (person, press). The creative person comprises the knowledge, skills,

TABLE 8.1 ● Characteristics of Creative Individuals or Effective Leaders?			
Adventurous	Expressive	Open	Self-confident
Aggressive	Flexible	Open-minded	Self-sufficient
Ambitious	Humorous	Original	Sensation seeking
Assertive	Imaginative	Perceptive	Sensitive/perceptive
Autonomous	Impulsive	Persevering	Thorough
Complex	Independent	Playful	Tolerant of ambiguity
Courageous	Individualistic	Prefer complexity	Tolerant of disorder
Curious	Industrious	Questioning	Tolerant of incongruity
Dissatisfied	Inner-directed	Radical	Unconcerned with impressing others
Dominant	Internally controlled	Recognition seeking	
Emotional	Introspective	Reflective	Unconventional
Energetic	Intuitive	Resourceful	Uninhibited
Excitable	Liberal	Risk taking	Varied interests
Experimenting	Non-conforming	Self-aware	Versatile

and dispositions that support creativity. You are unique and of value, and you are the tool of creative production. Utilizing, emphasizing, and developing some key characteristics will best encourage creative outcomes.

Research into the creative person started much like effective leader research—identify individuals producing creative things, observe, and label their characteristics.[23] Over time, the list of characteristics became so long that it described lots of individuals, and it became too unfocused to identify what one should develop for greater creativity. Interestingly, many of these characteristics would be of great value to effective leaders. Look at Table 8.1. Can you tell if it is describing creative individuals or effective leaders?

REFLECTION QUESTION

How many of the above characteristics can you recognize in yourself? Put a check by those that describe you. Circle the five that you think are most valuable to your effectiveness as a *leader*. Now ask a friend to look at your choices and see if they agree that these are your most effective characteristics for *creativity*.

Many characteristics that you now possess can be leveraged to facilitate creativity. Three personal characteristics that are both skills and dispositions (mental habits) can be further developed to bring out your most creative self: divergent thinking, open-mindedness, and creative confidence. These three characteristics work together to enable you to see differently and generate new ideas from those new perspectives. Divergent thinking, introduced earlier as one of the key dispositions in design thinking, is defined as the mindset of generating many, many ideas for a single problem. This capacity underpins idea generation, and it pushes your thinking *outside the box* where unique solutions can be found.

Back in Chapter 5, you were challenged to come up with 100 different uses for a pencil—to think divergently. In a typical group of 50, with each person generating 100 ideas, you would be surprised to learn that out of that pile of 5,000 ideas there might be 10 that are original to *just that group*. You are more alike than you think, which is why it takes extra effort to be unique. Researchers have expanded the notion of divergent thinking to better assess creativity. The total number of ideas you are able to generate to a specific problem is called **fluency**, while the total number of unique ideas is termed **originality**. Guilford's alternate uses test[24] measures how many different uses you can generate for a common object—such as a pencil or a lollipop—and it measures how many different categories those uses comprise. This is called **flexibility**. Generating ideas that cut across many categories indicates that you are not stuck in one perspective. For example, a lollipop might be used for a variety of things in the category of *golf course* (e.g., a tee, a way to mark your ball on the green, a way to clean off your golf cleats), the category of *hospital* (e.g., a mini splint, test your reflexes hammer, cover one eye for an eye test), or the category of *landscape* (decorate your yard, aerate the lawn, create a squirrel lure). Finally, very few answers show **elaboration**, another measure of creativity based on the degree of detail in the answer. Saying you can use a pencil as a coffee stirrer is less elaborate than a temperature-sensitive coffee stirrer only found at literary cafes upon which famous phrases emerge with different temperatures to prompt writers.

Fluency the total number of ideas generated as a measure of creativity

Originality the total number of unique ideas as a measure of creativity

Flexibility the number of different answer categories comprising ideas as a measure of creativity

Elaboration the degree of detail in a given idea as a measure of creativity

MYTH OR REALITY?

THE PHRASE *THINKING OUTSIDE THE BOX* JUST MEANS TO THINK CREATIVELY.

Myth . . . and Reality. The phrase *outside the box* originally refers to a psychology experiment by Karl Dunker in 1945 where he asked individuals to solve a problem where they had to affix a candle to the wall using only a few items, one of which was a box of tacks. The key to solution was to overcome what he called *functional fixedness*, which is your lean, mean, pattern-making machine at work. Individuals were stuck seeing the box as a holder for the tacks rather than seeing it as an item available for use in solving the problem. When you take the tacks out of the box, you can tack the box to the wall to hold the candle. Thus, thinking (with the tacks) outside the box.

The phrase was popularized by management consultants in the 1960s and 1970s in reference to a classic puzzle from 1914[25] where you are challenged to connect nine dots (three rows of three . . . forming a box) with four lines.[26] The solution is to extend the lines out of the box formed by the dots. Try the puzzle and really *think out of the box*.

The metaphorical box you must now escape from is your own perspective and way of thinking. So, in reality, it does refer to thinking creatively.

Open-minded the mindset of being receptive to new ideas and perspectives

Open-minded can be defined as the mindset of being receptive to new ideas and perspectives. You cannot see new perspectives and possibilities if you are not receptive to doing so. Many individuals will claim that they are open-minded, but their behavior says otherwise. Open-mindedness requires both an awareness and a level of humility. In Chapter 5 (and earlier), you learned that your brain constructs information. When you encounter new ideas, your brain struggles to fit them into the way you see the world. And if you cannot, those perspectives are rejected. However, when you know that your perspective is only one of an endless parade, you open yourself up to looking more closely at new ideas. Admitting you have much to learn becomes more difficult as you become more experienced and expert, which is why open-mindedness requires humility. Can you admit the fallibility of your beliefs and perspective, or can you at least put them aside long enough to really consider something different?

Creative confidence trust in yourself as a creative individual or a "natural ability to come up with new ideas and the courage to try them out"

Supporting your open-mindedness and divergent thinking is a concept more recently popularized by David Kelley and his brother Tom from IDEO called creative confidence.[27] If the root of confidence is trust in yourself, **creative confidence** is trust in yourself as a creative individual, or as Kelley describes it (individuals), a "natural ability to come up with new ideas and the courage to try them out."[28] A strong creative confidence, like a strong CORE™, opens the door to many related creativity attributes such as comfort with ambiguity, the willingness to play and try things, willingness to take risks and to see failure as a learning opportunity. The Kelleys note a number of things you can do to build your creative confidence, all of which entail your active creative engagement and exploring new perspectives. Here are some specific suggestions:

- Choose creativity—at some point you need to simply make the decision that you are going to be creative and then go practice and engage.

- Build a creative support network—it is hard to be creative when everyone around you wants to stay in the box . . . and keep you in as well.

- Think like a traveler—seeing the world, even the one you live in every day, with wonder (as in, "I wonder why . . .") helps you practice seeing differently.

Press: Context and Culture

The creative press comprises those things in the environment that press on your creativity, either inhibiting or encouraging. Consider two scenarios as a practical way to understand press. In both situations, your team has been tasked with putting together some new, creative ideas for holiday gifts for your clients. In one scenario, the team meets in a windowless room, seated in rows facing the leader, given only a notepad and pen, and they are frequently reminded that the deadline is looming. In the other scenario, the team is sent off to visit other stores to explore and observe. They return to a wide-open, sunny space filled with arts and crafts materials and walls to write upon. They are encouraged to share their explorations and ideas, and they are told that even though there is a deadline, they should set the project aside for a few days and revisit it later.

Both scenarios really happen. Which one sounds more appealing? Which one would you choose if you had to focus on studying for a big test? And which one would more likely foster creativity? There is a great deal of research on what fosters and inhibits creativity in the immediate context and environment, in the local and larger culture, in the design of the space, timing of the activities, and style of interactions between individuals. Leaders can develop the creative capacity of their followers, and they can strategically engage elements of the creative press to influence creative behavior. Chapter 14 focuses exclusively on how to create a culture of innovation and will greatly inform how you design your leadership future.

Process: Understand, Imagine, Implement, and Iterate Revisited

Problem-solving is a process, and many models and approaches have been tried, recorded, and developed. Humans have been solving problems for a long time and learn processes from one another through experience and modeling. Everyone, including you, has a default problem-solving process that you learned through experience. Effective leaders have a range of processes that they can draw from depending on the needs of the problem and situation. By now, you should be familiar with the three phases of problem-solving: Understand, Imagine, and Implement. This general framework can be used to help you sort and organize other models you come across, taking the important steps and stages from each as you find useful.

Two of the earliest models of creative problem-solving were laid out by Graham Wallas (an economist) in 1926 and by James Webb Young (an advertising executive) in 1939. Wallas asserts four stages of the creative process: Preparation, Incubation, Illumination, and Verification.[29] Preparation clearly relates to understanding the problem, illumination is that mythical *aha* of imagine, and verification seems to fit implementation. But what is incubation? **Incubation** is a purposeful stepping away from consciously focusing on the problem to allow unconscious processing and connections. Wallas called it *mental relaxation*, and its importance to creativity has become increasingly recognized. Similarly, Young terms his model a technique, and it includes five steps:[30]

Incubation a purposeful stepping away from consciously focusing on the problem to allow unconscious processing and connections

1. Gathering raw material
2. Digesting the material
3. Unconscious processing
4. The Aha moment
5. Idea meets reality

Again, it is easy to see which steps comprise understanding the problem, imagining, and implementing. Many of the myths that have since been debunked are also evident because these models were based on experience and observations, rather than research. When you look at Wallas's and Young's models, how do you think their professions influenced them?

Perhaps the most famous and highly used process model has been the Osborn-Parnes Creative Problem Solving Model. Another advertising executive, Alex Osborn, took a

TABLE 8.2 ● Osborn-Parnes Creative Problem Solving Model—Stages and Activities	
Stage	**Activities**
Explore the challenge	Objective finding
	Fact finding
	Problem finding
Generate ideas	Idea finding
Prepare for action	Solution finding
	Acceptance finding

reflective approach to his work, partnering with Professor Syd Parnes to develop tools and techniques to enhance creativity.[31] The original model outlined seven steps in the creative problem-solving process,[32] but the power of this model has been its flexibility. Over the years, it has undergone many revisions, each striving to be a more useful tool. One of the recent iterations of this model identifies six steps within three stages (not surprisingly, they mirror Understand, Imagine, and Implement).

While not evident in Table 8.2, this model emphasizes two dynamic elements of the creative problem-solving process. First, the process is cyclical and iterative. In other words, reaching the end of the process is seen as additional insight to start again seeking further innovation. This dynamic mirrors the notion of continuous improvement and proactively seeking opportunities of effective leadership. The second dynamic is the complementary relationship between divergent and convergent thinking *at each stage* of the process. Divergent thinking is often characterized as the idea-generating mental habit, but in reality, you will need to think of many, many ideas throughout the creative problem-solving process. For example, during Fact Finding, you may have to generate many ideas for what to research and where to get that information, and then you have to converge those ideas into the best information and sources. Or for Acceptance Finding you could generate a list of the many individuals you may need to influence to bring an idea to practice, and again you need to converge on the most impactful individuals with whom you will work.

All of these models and processes can be a bit confusing. One very different and insightful approach is offered by creativity guru Roger von Oech, highlighted in his books *A Whack on the Side of the Head* and *A Kick in the Seat of the Pants* (sounds promising already).[33] Von Oech asserts that rather than go step by step, stage by stage, you should instead assume four different roles as you progress through the process: Explorer, Artist, Judge, and Warrior. An explorer seeks out new things but also talks with people, takes careful notes, and does considerable background work so they know where to look in the first place. Explorers probably feel excited, focused, eager, curious, and perhaps a little anxious. The explorer must be thoughtful, strategic, observant, courageous, and engaged. Take a moment to consider what each of these roles does, what they feel like, and what kind of personal characteristics are needed.

Role	What Do They Do?	What Does It Feel Like?	What Should They Be Like?
Explorer			
Artist			
Judge			
Warrior			

FIGURE 8.1 ● Von Oech Roles in Action

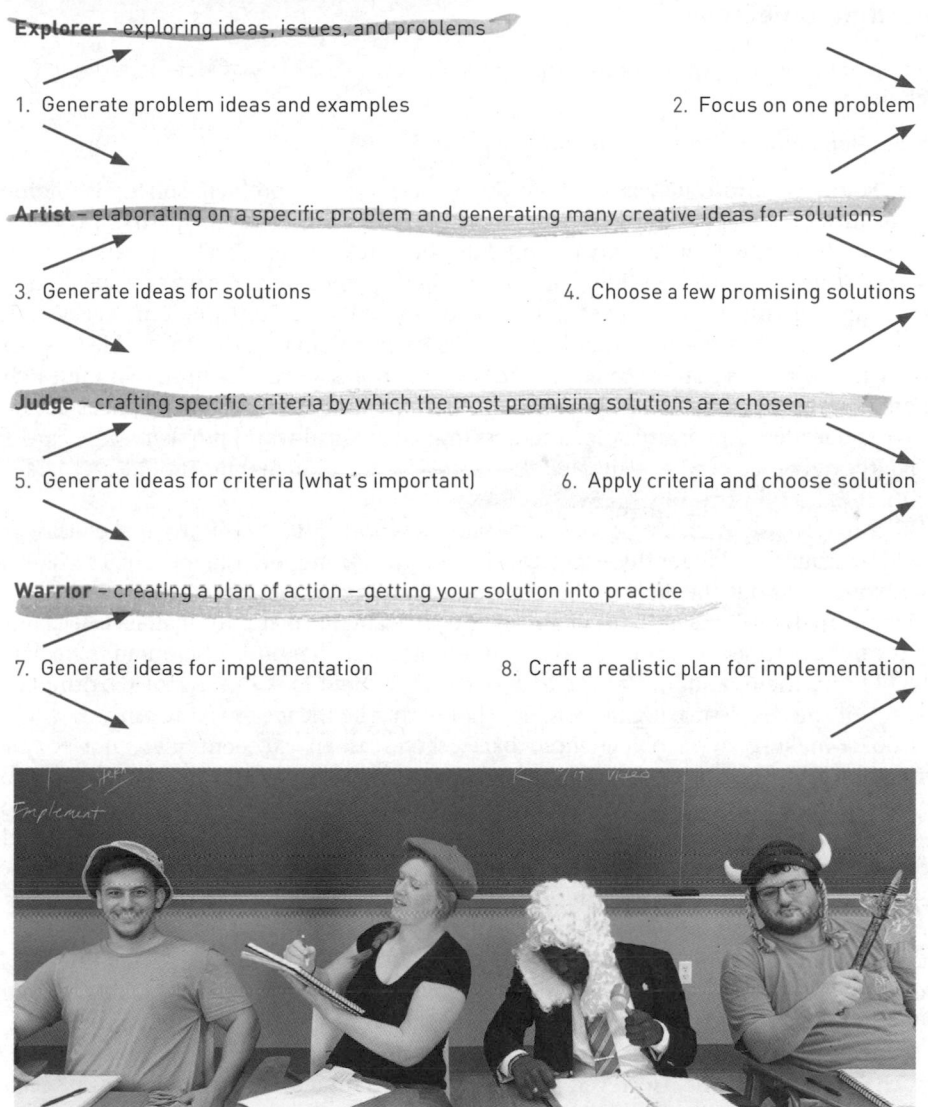

Explorer – exploring ideas, issues, and problems

1. Generate problem ideas and examples   2. Focus on one problem

Artist – elaborating on a specific problem and generating many creative ideas for solutions

3. Generate ideas for solutions   4. Choose a few promising solutions

Judge – crafting specific criteria by which the most promising solutions are chosen

5. Generate ideas for criteria (what's important)   6. Apply criteria and choose solution

Warrior – creating a plan of action – getting your solution into practice

7. Generate ideas for implementation   8. Craft a realistic plan for implementation

Von Oech notes, "When you're searching for new information, be an Explorer. When you're turning your resources into new ideas, be an Artist. When you're evaluating the merits of an idea, be a Judge. When you're carrying your idea into action, be a Warrior."[34] These roles can be translated into action by considering what divergent and convergent activities comprise each role. Figure 8.1 outlines these activities by role.

Creative problem-solving processes are easy to find and easy to follow, but they are challenging to fit to the appropriate problem and context. Your best approach as a leader is to know the general Understand—Imagine—Implement model and then continue to explore and add specific steps from other models to your problem-solving toolbox. The next section shifts exclusively to the Imagine phase, specifically looking at the many techniques for generating ideas. Get ready to put your divergent thinking to work.

Yes, You Can Generate Many, Many Ideas

Learning Objectives

8.4 Construct your creative problem-solving toolbox with a variety of idea-generating techniques

8.5 Develop individual creative identity and activity

Ideas. Solutions. Innovative answers. At the heart of creative problem-solving is finding a unique idea of value. But using the word *finding* takes leaders down the path of innovation as a treasure hunt without a map, playing into the Eureka myth. Great innovations are the result of many other ideas building off one another, crossing disciplinary silos, being tested and improved, and evolving over time and context. "We like to think our breakthrough ideas . . . are state-of-the-art technology, but more often than not, they're cobbled together from whatever parts happen to be around nearby," notes Steven Johnson, who researches where ideas come from.[35] That systemic and often random process, however, does not help individual leaders and organizations address immediate, real-world problems. Ideas are not *found*, they are produced or generated. This section introduces a number of idea-generating techniques useful in creative problem-solving.

If you went about making cookies the same way individuals typically make ideas, you would sit around looking at the empty cookie sheet for a while and wait for cookies to appear. Then you might put the sheet in the oven, again hoping cookies would form on the sheet. The more analytical or ambitious might buy a cookie and break it into small pieces, examining it carefully to see how it came to be. Others may grab handfuls of random ingredients, possibly mix them, and then shape them into what could look like a cookie. Fortunately, that is not the cookie-making process, nor should that be the idea-making process.

Cookie-making by an experienced baker serves as an excellent metaphor for idea generation. As a novice, you follow a recipe with ingredients and instructions on how to put them together, and end with how to transform them. The process is almost algorithmic—follow the formula, get the cookies. As you become more experienced, the recipe becomes more of a general guide for your experimentation and improvisation. You might add a bit more flour, substitute M&Ms for chocolate chips, or bake them at a higher temperature for less time. Finally, as an expert, you know and understand the ingredients and process at a more intuitive level (recall the characteristics of an expert from Chapter 1). This expertise allows for greater flexibility in your approach and process. Asking someone to find an idea is like asking a baker to find a cookie—both inaccurate and improbable.

Generating ideas may start as formulaic, using the algorithm of the techniques found in this chapter and beyond. However, idea-generating techniques are really heuristic because they prompt and guide your thinking in different directions. At the heart of all idea-generating techniques is a push to *see differently*. Think about all the ways that you could see something differently. You could look at the details or zoom out to see the larger context, you could see the opposite or reverse, or you could see through someone else's eyes. As you explore each of the idea-generating techniques, consider how each prompts you to see differently.

Divergent Thinking Techniques

Some problems are best solved by generating many, many ideas and then finding the best ones and developing them into something great. Divergent thinking, introduced in Chapter 5 as one of the dispositions of design thinking, consists of the mindset of generating many, many ideas from a single problem. While all the idea-generating techniques utilize divergent thinking, there are some for which that activity is central.

How often have you been asked to *brainstorm* for ideas? Generally, individuals use the term brainstorming when they really mean "let's just talk and shoot out some ideas." But brainstorming is a specific technique developed by advertising executive Alex Osborn back in the 1940s. Brainstorming has rules that facilitate the generation of many ideas:[36]

1. Go for quantity.

2. Withhold criticism and judgment—negative and positive.

3. Encourage wild ideas.

4. Combine and improve ideas by building off each other's ideas.

It may seem strange to apply rules to enhance creativity. Rules, however, provide guidance and context that foster idea generation. For example, each of the brainstorming rules prompts very specific thinking behaviors that would otherwise not emerge. This reasoning is noted in Table 8.3 below.

Brainstorming has many variations that suit different problems and contexts. Try this example: Take out a blank piece of paper and draw a line down the middle of the page from top to bottom. Writing only on the left side, generate as many ideas as you can for how to create the worst classroom space ever. Follow the brainstorming rules—go for quantity, go wild, with no judgment, and have some fun with others. Once you have filled up the left side, reverse your answers and build upon the reversals. Because the problem is really, How can we create the best classroom space ever? *Reverse brainstorming* allows you to see aspects of the problem and ideas that you would not have considered had you simply addressed the problem directly. For example, you might have said the worst classroom would have a really bad odor. Reverse that—a good space would not have the bad odor—and build off it. What if we added some pleasant scent to the classroom or perhaps a series of fun and pleasant scents? Take a few more minutes to work down your list and develop some ideas.

Sometimes as a leader you need to address a sensitive problem, one that others are hesitant to discuss. Likewise, you may have followers who are more quiet or private and

TABLE 8.3 ● Brainstorming Tips

Brainstorming Rule	Why It Is Important
Go for quantity	When solving problems, people tend to satisfice—settling on the first idea that will satisfy our needs—rather than generating more to find the best.
Withhold criticism and judgment—negative and positive	Asserting an idea is a bit of a risk and takes courage. The judgment of others is a very powerful influence. Individuals will withhold ideas to avoid negative judgments. On the other hand, positive judgments set a standard for idea quality that, if not met in your mind, will also stifle idea generation.
Encourage wild ideas	Individuals need encouragement and permission to escape their own self-editing and self-judgment. You can often see others dismissing their own ideas in their mind for fear that the idea is not feasible, viable, desirable, or unique enough. But without those *wild* ideas as seeds, there are no ideas to develop and build upon.
Combine and improve ideas by building off each other's ideas	The great power of brainstorming lies in the interactions between individual ideas. Without the constraints of judgment and quantity, the room fills with many *spare parts* that comprise an inventory of new possibilities.

simply not ready for the wild, no-judgment discussion in brainstorming. A technique called *Pass the Note* is an effective technique for generating ideas when discussion is limited. Write the specific problem on the top of the page and explain that you are looking for any and all ideas. Then, pass the note from person to person—either at a meeting or around an organization—allowing each person to write down their ideas after reading those that were written before (this allows some building off other ideas). The note can be sent around as many times as you like, but eventually, you end up with a big list of ideas for further development.

Problem Analysis Techniques

Another category of useful idea-generating techniques involves seeing the problem differently by analyzing it in different ways. Imagine you work for a local restaurant and the manager asked you to come up with a new sandwich for every day . . . for the next five years. That would be 1,826 different sandwiches (assuming one leap year). That is a lot of ideas to generate. You try brainstorming with a few groups but seem to stall out around 50 new sandwiches. So instead, you take a closer look at what generally makes up a sandwich: some kind of protein, some kind of garnishment like a cheese or vegetable, and then some way to hold it all together (i.e., the bread). Now instead of thinking divergently about the whole sandwich, you generate a list of different kinds of proteins (ham, tofu, turkey, etc.), different additions (Swiss cheese, cheddar, sweet peppers, etc.), and different wraps (wheat bread, lettuce wrap, pita, etc.). If you generate a mere 13 ideas for each of these three and then cross them in a 13 × 13 × 13 matrix, you will end up with 2,197 sandwich combinations—more than you needed. If you add another category such as sauces (ketchup, mayo, jelly), a list of 13 sauces would then bring the total combinations to 28,561. That is an incredible number of ideas, and it would take you nearly eight hours to list out if you could write one every second. This technique is called *morphological synthesis*, and the multiple effect of categories is made possible by the act of seeing the problem in parts rather than the whole.

Thinking about the *parts* as *attributes* helps to better identify the essential features of a problem. For example, the attributes of a sandwich include the generalized ingredients but also might include things such as (a) holdability—you can hold it in one hand and do other stuff; (b) preservation—you can pack it in your bag without cooling, and it will not spoil by lunch; (c) nutritional completeness—it includes all the necessary nutrients; (d) 10-bite timing—it does not take long to eat—about 10 bites. Of course, these terms are made up, but the idea behind them is not. Remember *The Important Book* noted earlier in the chapter? *You* need to determine the important attributes of the problem. And once you do so, those attributes can be modified.

The *SCAMPER* technique further prompts how you might modify attributes to generate new ideas. SCAMPER stands for Substitute, Combine, Adapt, Modify, Put to another use, Eliminate, and/or Reverse each attribute.[37] Each of these prompts represents numerous questions that could elicit new ideas. For example, for Substitute you might ask, Can we substitute one part for another? Could we change the name? The shape? The color? Can we use this in a different place or for a different purpose? Could we substitute different materials, processes, individuals involved, rules, and/or terms used? Attribute modification offers a seemingly endless supply of new ideas, each of which could be the seeds to your next great innovation.

At this point, you are probably thinking, yes, this is all good and perhaps fun, but how do techniques like this apply to something abstract like leadership? Many leadership problems can be reversed and brainstormed or broken into attributes that can be modified (again, problems include proactive opportunities, not just reactions when things go wrong). Quite often followers lose track of the vision, and leaders need to somehow help others remember and align their work with the mission. At the next meeting you might ask, What are all the ways in which we can stray from our mission? You will be surprised at the number of creative answers. Following that question to the group, of course, reverse the answers to see the unique possibilities.

Relatedly, what attributes comprise the *work* of individuals? For each of these attributes, note all the ways you might make the mission more evident or connected? Perhaps your organization is trying to come up with ideas for how to increase membership. You could come up with attributes of membership recruitment activities, such as forums, themes, activities, and follow-up.[38] Brainstorming a short list for each attribute, you could then apply morphological synthesis (remember the sandwich types example) to come up with a variety of events for recruitment. Try it out by adding to Table 8.4 below (the columns need not be even). From the examples below you have $5 \times 5 \times 5 \times 4 = 500$ event ideas. Who could resist a "Take a Selfie With an Ice-Skating Monkey Party," especially when the following week you get a singing e-mail reminder for the next meeting?

Visualization Techniques

Everyone is familiar with automobiles and their safety features. Many of those features were designed in response to an accident. But many were designed by visualizing what *could* go wrong. Your capacity to play out scenarios in your mind—even, if not especially, fictitious ones—represents a fundamental building block of creativity. The term ideation is often used to describe the entire creative process; however, it really means to form ideas in your mind. This capacity can be directed and used to generate new ideas.

The *Worst Case* technique asks you to visualize all the things that could go wrong and then address each of these *worst cases* by generating solutions, which may end up being new ideas. Worst cases need not actually be the worst, but rather they are all the things that might or could happen contrary to intent, use, or success. Try using this technique regarding your next organization meeting:

- What worst-case uses, interactions, or interpretations have you observed in the past?

- What could be misused or abused?

- What might your biggest critic say?

- What might wear out?

- How might I minimize the consequences if one of these bad things happens?

Visualization techniques more often focus on the ideal and fantastical. A common set of techniques (e.g., What would happen if ... magic wand, wish list) essentially entails asking the group to imagine ideal outcomes without the constraints of rules, budgets, personalities, procedures, or any of the other pesky implementation barriers. While the ideas generated are not practical, they do provide a different way of seeing the problem and

TABLE 8.4 ● Brainstorming by Attributes Example			
Forums (the when and where)	**Themes**	**Activities**	**Follow-up**
Classroom	Circus	Playing board games	Hand-written card
Local park	Cheese	Taking stuff apart	Picture of person
Main street	Monkeys	Eating	Singing e-mail
Swimming pool	Presidents	Taking pictures	Singing telegram
Ice rink	80s music	Balancing on things	

possible solutions. What if we could fly like a bird? What if all that power in a river could be captured? What would happen if we had light during all hours of the night? If you had a magic wand, what would your organization be doing right now? If you were granted three wishes for your followers, what would you wish for them? Each of these questions prompts new ways of seeing and ultimately new ideas.

The way that problems are framed and the level at which you view a problem can also change the way you see. *Framing* cars as a way to get from point to point is quite different from seeing cars as a status symbol or a sports implement. The designs would be (and are) significantly different depending on the frame. Likewise, designing a car from different perspectives results in very different innovations. Try the activity in Table 8.5 below. How would you innovate a car from each perspective? For example, at the micro level, you might consider new materials that would wick water off the windshield glass or conform the seat to your body, or perhaps you might infuse a pleasant scent to the exhaust. Those ideas are very different from those at the parking lot planning level, where the innovation might be wheels that turn to a full right angle to allow you to slide into a parking spot or a retractable bumper that makes the car two feet shorter.

Play and Build Techniques

Idea-generating in the Imagine phase is all about seeing differently . . . and playing. Many of the examples given are simply wacky and would not work for many reasons. But you are not judging those ideas at this point, only generating them. And again, quite often the bits of crazy ideas end up inspiring insights that lead to viable, feasible, and desirable innovation. Play and build techniques emphasize this iterative and cumulative notion in idea generation. Leaders need an open mind and trusting culture to engage their followers in play, which is discussed further at the end of this chapter (and a major focus of Chapter 14 on Creating a Culture of Innovation).

Many organizations promote the notion of play in their culture, but play in idea-generating is the specific, focused application of play to purposefully see differently. Tim Brown from IDEO, highlighted in Chapter 5, talks about three kinds of play that IDEO uses to generate insights about users and the problem in an effort to generate ideas: exploratory play, role play, and building play.[39] Exploration and inspiration for idea-generating will be discussed in the next section of this chapter. Role play and building play provide rich mediums for iteration and for alternative perspectives.

TABLE 8.5 ● Framing, Perspectives, and Ideas		
	Perspective	**Your Ideas for Car Redesign?**
1	Car from a distance—in action	
2	In the showroom	
3	Interior from driver's perspective	
4	Interior from passenger's perspective	
5	Engine level	
6	Micro level	
7	Urban setting—street level	
8	Parking lot planning level	
9	Urban core and evacuation route level	

No doubt you have dressed up for Halloween at some point, and perhaps you have even taken on the role of your character to some extent. Likely some of you have also performed in plays or other dramatic productions in which you had to take on a role. What was it like to see through that role? Everything looks like a chew toy to a baby; serious athletes structure their days and months around preparing for peak performance. Experienced professionals see the world in a manner that highlights their expertise. So too, as you learn more about leadership, you will begin to see more and more examples of good and bad leadership in your day-to-day life.

One of the origins of the word creativity is from the Latin *creare*, which means *to make*. For as long as humans have built things, they have used their hands as a tool to think and to generate ideas. Sometimes *making* ideas means you have to actually make stuff outside your mind so that you can see different dimensions of the problem and solution. Every design field incorporates sketching and prototyping into their process—not because they are *artsy*, but because each sketch is a step toward a more refined solution. Each prototype is a tool to help the designer see and try a solution.

In an introductory leadership course focused on creativity, students are challenged to create an innovation that makes dorm life easier and to build a cardboard prototype of their idea. Inevitably the cardboard models look terrible, but that helps emphasize the point. Making the model is not about how pretty it looks but about how well it illustrates and communicates the solution. Even more important, the process of making the model highlights alterations, improvements, and impossibilities that the students were unable to see without the physical model.

Senses and Emotions

Problems and solutions spend lots of time in your head. The power of play and build techniques brings that activity into the concrete world where there is more room to process. Have you ever worked on a paper or project where you had to spread different resources all over a table or an entire room? Why? Because you could not juggle all of those different elements in your head. Similarly, there are facets of problems that are often overlooked because they live in your brain. Applying role play, you are trying to conceptualize the world through someone else's mind. That effort can be significantly enhanced by adding two elements: senses and emotions.

Go on a sensory scavenger hunt, and focus on *all* of your senses. Most of our attention relies on the visual, but inputs to the other senses can make a huge difference. Think about how sound (a soothing voice versus a screech), touch (the firm handshake versus the limp), or smell (well . . . you can imagine this one yourself . . .) impacts the relationship you design with your followers. Considering a sensory component adds to your idea-generating as well. Attuning yourself to multiple senses promotes attending to this valuable perspective. Try this sensory hunt.

Sensory Scavenger Hunt

Sight: Find a defined space that is not the classroom.

What is your immediate focus? What is in the background? What is on the floor? What is over your head?

Sound: Close your eyes and listen carefully for a period of time. Note nine things you hear.

Now plug your ears—what/how do you hear (besides your own breathing/chewing)?

Smell: Find 10 different smells . . . describe them . . . rate them.

Item	Description of Smell	1 (Hated) to 5 (Loved) the Smell
1		
2		
3		
4		
5		
6		
7		
8		
9		
10		

Taste: Find five items to taste—pick some usual and some unusual. Close your eyes, take your time. Try small bites and big. Move the food around in your mouth, and focus on the primary flavor and then the more subtle flavors.

Item	Description of Flavors	1 (Hated) to 5 (Loved) the Taste
1		
2		
3		
4		
5		

Touch: Find five items to touch—again, pick some usual and some unusual. Close your eyes, take your time. Use your whole hand and then your fingers; touch without moving your fingers, then moving. Then try feeling touch with your body as a whole—close your eyes and feel the weather, wind, clothes on your body.

Item	Description of Touch
1	
2	
3	
4	
5	

Taking time to consider the emotional aspects of a problem can also contribute to idea generation. *Solving* a problem looks different when the outcome is to induce a specific emotion. For example, hotels gather extensive user-centered data to give people what they need and want. But what kind of room would you have if the hotel were designed to make you *feel* a certain way—like calm, or nostalgic, or energized? As you recall from the section on emotional intelligence, expanding your emotional vocabulary helps you better discern and work with your and others' emotions. In the most applied sense, consider what it feels like to be led by you? How do you want it to feel? Design your relationships with emotions in mind.

Incubation Techniques

The Eureka myth seems most applicable when you are least engaged with the problem. Although you may feel this as a flash of inspiration, that *moment* is really a culmination of many pieces of information swirling around over time. As that early Wallas model asserted, incubation in idea generation consists of any number of activities where you intentionally shift your attention away from the problem, with the intention of revisiting it later.

Suggestions such as "Why don't you sleep on it?" or "You should set it aside for a while," are suggestive of your brain's continuous processing. Attention and focus narrow your thinking and may further add stress, neither of which allow for new and random connections. Engaging in routine activities frees up one's cognitive load to process, even if unconsciously. In a world of increasing efficiency, multitasking, and on-demand, instant expectations, incubation is looked at with skepticism if not contempt. A boss might ask, "Why should I pay you to sit around and process?" Nevertheless, shower notepads were invented for a reason—to capture that brilliant idea that only seems to hit you when you do not have a pen. Contrary to the importance of engagement and the great value of engaging the problem, its components, other perspectives, and play, when generating ideas you sometimes need to engage in disengagement. Meditate, take a walk, play a game, or simply set a project aside for a few days. You will be pleasantly surprised by the creative results.

Alternative Perspective Techniques

Perhaps the most straightforward way to see differently is to see with someone else's eyes. Alternative perspective techniques take your idea-generating efforts outside the problem space, asking you to explore the problem from the outside in, through the eyes of another. Deep empathy becomes a vehicle to see differently and generate ideas. Two design-thinking capacities contribute to generating ideas in this manner: user-centeredness and multidisciplinary. Utilizing user-centered data collection methods (recall Chapter 5) directs your attention to see through the user's eyes and feel what they feel. And multidisciplinary thinking encourages you to invite other fields of practice and experience to the process. Together these design-thinking practices assist you in working as the T-shaped person described in Chapter 5, where working in the margins of your discipline helps you see ideas in the spaces where disciplines meet and overlap.

Alternative perspectives extend beyond other individuals and their disciplines. How else might you parse and pursue differences? Maybe a child would see the problem differently, or a veteran, or a small business owner, or a coin collector, or someone who has lived through a hurricane. There are endless ways to identify difference, each holding a unique and valuable perspective for contributing ideas. Yet another way of altering perspective lies in how people think: conservative, liberal, progressive; optimistic, pessimistic, nihilistic; and so forth to include any number of values and beliefs that would contribute a unique perspective.

REFLECTION QUESTIONS

Consider a problem on which you are currently working. Who would see this problem differently? Who has nothing to do with this problem or even the context? Whose opinion could you ask?

Hopefully it is now clear that ideas are generated, not found. What is found, however, is inspiration—ideas from sources outside the problem. Ideas build on other ideas and contexts, and the more you explore and experience the world, the greater your storehouse of concepts that can be applied, combined, and adapted into a new context and a new idea. If, as Steven Johnson noted earlier in this chapter, ideas are usually cobbled together from spare parts that happen to be around, where do you find the parts? You could work on your explorative design-thinking capacity and be more of an explorer of the world (review Chapter 5). But seriously, how much stuff can you have, and how many experiences can you keep track of before you are overwhelmed?

Inspiration and Exploration Techniques

Many individuals who work in a stereotypical creative field (remember, all fields should be creative) often surround themselves with a literal museum of interesting objects and images and regularly explore for new sources of inspiration. This approach can be fun and effective, but it is not always possible. Rather than random exploration, look to contexts that may parallel the problem you are addressing. The concept of **biomimicry** looks to see how nature has solved a similar problem and then tries to mimic that solution.[40] For example, no one likes to go to the doctor and get a shot. It hurts. How could scientists develop a pain-free needle? Turns out that there is an expert in the natural world at pricking others without getting caught or squished—the mosquito.

Biomimicry: a problem-solving technique that looks to see how nature has solved a similar problem and then tries to mimic that solution

Materials researchers and engineers at Kansai University in Japan saw amazing potential in the structure of the mosquito's mouth. They used sophisticated engineering techniques that can carve out structures on the nanometer scale. The result of this blend of materials science and biology was a needle that penetrates like a mosquito, using pressure to stabilize and painlessly glide into skin.[41]

What could leaders learn from how nature influences others or how to best work as a team?

LEADERSHIP BY DESIGN

Design Principle: Mimicry

Definition: The act of copying or imitating properties of something familiar. In design, looking to other objects, organisms, or environments for ideas and solutions.

In Other Words: Observe, copy, and paste.

For Example: Examples of mimicry are all around you. The famous Spanish architect Antonio Guadi mimicked patterns in nature for many of his very unique building features, such as the roof in this photo.

For Leaders: Creativity does not always suggest that an idea is brand new. Many great innovations take concepts and inner workings already found elsewhere and simply apply them to a new framework. Mimicry is actually

©iStock.com/sneska

MIMICRY

one of the oldest and most efficient methods for achieving major advances in designs. Leaders should use mimicry to further develop effective systems that have been previously designed—in their field and in others. Benchmarking identifies the goals of mimicry and helps quickly discern what ideas or practices would work in your organization without having to reinvent the wheel.

Even from a self-design standpoint, leaders can develop desirable skills the fastest by mimicking role models. Who is already doing a great job? Who can you mimic? When should an idea be entirely your own? How can you also use mimicry to model desired relationships after already established connections? A new idea can be created from two old ones.

If looking to nature to mimic how problems are solved is a good idea, why not look all over the place and find comparable ideas? *Metaphorical thinking* is an idea-generating technique wherein you compare two different things that share similar characteristics and then draw ideas for your context from the new context. For example, say your group has been challenged to find ways to improve the new student orientation at your college. Using metaphorical thinking, you would take a moment to generate ideas about what being a new college student is like—not the real experience, everyone has thought of that already. Instead, you think about metaphors.

Being a new student at college is like . . . stepping onto a school bus full of strangers . . . tasting a new food . . . visiting a country where no one speaks your language . . . walking through a haunted house where people jump out at you. You can probably already see the connections, but the next step is to make them explicit and then translate them back into your context as ideas. Table 8.6 provides an example. Note, the ideas generated are not necessarily good ideas . . . yet. But they are the result of seeing differently, and they may lead to innovation.

Many creativity experts assert that great ideas come from connecting with other ideas and making connections that others have not seen. *Forced connections* comprise a wide variety of techniques that direct you to examine and play with how one idea might fit with,

TABLE 8.6 ● Metaphorical Thinking			
Being a New Student in College Is Like . . .	**Because . . .**	**Which Means . . .**	**So, Here Are Some Possible Ideas . . .**
Entering a strange forest at dusk	You cannot see very far down the path.	It would be helpful to be able to see what is next and where the path leads.	Create a visual journey through the major, showing what comes next. Connect students across grades to discuss their experiences.
	Every little sound is new, strange and distracting.	Keeping new information and distractions limited to only those necessary for success.	Put together an easily accessible quick directory rather than separate flyers. Limit involvement in certain things to more experienced students.
	It feels fully immersive, like there is no way out.	Understanding where there are breaks (exits) and that there are guides in and out of the forest.	Have each new student return to their high school and share their experience. Build in *take a break* days into the semester where students share things about their home.

enhance, combine with, or otherwise alter another idea to create something unique. Say, for example, that you loved pizza and really wanted to create an innovation in pizza. This could include a unique new product, delivery system, restaurant, product packaging—any facet of the total pizza realm. The fun part is to find rich sources of inspiration with which to connect. See if you can force connections using the following sources (a few examples are noted—you should add to them):

Draw From This Source . . .	. . . to Create These Ideas for Pizza Innovation!
Random objects on your person (yes, make a list of them)	Rolled Pizza—like you would roll up your sleeves Pizza Passport—get stamped for each type of pizza until you have traveled the pizza world
Small businesses on Main Street (any Main St.—again, make a list)	Pizza Train—like the sushi train where you sit and the conveyor belt goes by with different small pieces of pizza, and you take what you want Pizza ATM—put in your card, get a slice out of the machine
Toys and board games	Pin the Pepperoni on the Pizza—a fun game for families at the restaurant
Random words—open a book at random, point to a word	
Tools and other things you would find in a hardware store	
A walk through the park	

Sources for ideas and inspiration are everywhere. Techniques like metaphorical thinking and forced connections are advanced techniques that involve some of the other idea-generating techniques (such as role play, attention to senses and emotions, attribute modification, visualization, play, and of course divergent thinking); however, the success of these techniques depends on your effort and ability to explore. Remember Roger von Oech's roles for guiding you through the creative problem-solving process (Explorer, Artist, Judge, and Warrior)? The Explorer role, while meant for finding and understanding the problem, offers considerable guidance for finding rich idea-generating sources.

Retype these, blow them up, and post them in front of your desk:

1. Ask questions and be curious

2. Start your explorations with a goal in mind

3. Be present and see what is around and in front of you

Retype these, cut them into strips, put them in a hat, and pick one to do each time:

4. Look at other disciplines, fields, practices, and industries

5. Allow yourself to wander and be led astray

6. Break up your routine

7. Look at different levels—up close to big picture

8. Visit places very different from your usual

And, tattoo this one on your hand:

9. Remember to take notes

MOMENT OF AWARENESS

Sources of inspiration are everywhere.

There are always new ways to take your ideas to the next level. Never again can I say, "I don't have any ideas." There are idea-generation techniques where you can just take a random image and start brainstorming ideas from there. There is no longer any barrier to entry to having an idea and no excuse for being unable to create something new! We drew inspiration from cartoons, skateboarders and our environment. We made connections between random words to form wild ideas. The number one problem I hear from people who say that they're "not creative" is that they don't have any ideas. After learning and experiencing all the techniques from this class, I'm confident that I could help people believe in their own creativity.

—Zachary Jones, Undergraduate

All the idea-generating techniques introduced in this chapter bring you to the heart of creativity—the ability to see differently. Table 8.7 (shown below) summarizes the different categories of idea-generating techniques with numerous examples. As you solve problems as a leader, know that there are many tools to help you and your organization imagine, generate innovative ideas, and develop your creativity.

TABLE 8.7 ● Categories and Techniques for Generating Ideas

When You Want to:	Use These Idea-Generating Techniques

Maximize ideas: Techniques that maximize quantity	Divergent thinking techniques:
	    Brainstorming
	    Reverse brainstorming
	    Pass the note

Examine problem and Modify parts: Techniques that analyze and deconstruct the problem and then alter some part or attribute of the problem	Problem analysis techniques:
	    SCAMPER
	    Morphological synthesis

Visualize outcomes: Techniques that involve mental simulation of various outcomes or scenarios	Visualization techniques:
	    What would happen if . . .
	    Worst case
	    Reframing problem
	    Wish list
	    Magic wand

Play and build: Techniques that emphasize idea emergence through random and/or playful manipulation of the problem and related facets	Play and build techniques:
	    Prototyping
	    Role play
	    Sketching

(Continued)

TABLE 8.7 ● (Continued)	
When You Want to:	**Use These Idea-Generating Techniques**

Sense and feel: Techniques that bring attention to the human facets of the problem such as emotions and multiple senses	Sense and emotion techniques:
	  Emotional prompts
	  Sensory focusing

Incubate: Techniques that purposefully relax and disengage the mind away from the problem	Incubation techniques:
	  Meditation
	  Exercise

See through other eyes: Techniques that apply a framework that is outside the problem	Alternative perspective techniques:
	  Cross-disciplinary
	  Empathy

Get ideas from elsewhere and purposefully explore: Techniques that acquire ideas from sources and contexts outside the problem	Exploration techniques:
	  Metaphor
	  Biomimicry
	  Forced connections
	  Be an explorer

No, You Are Not "Done": Iteration, Convergence, and Assurance

Generating ideas consists of many iterative reassessments and refinements. In classic brainstorming, the rule is to build off each other's ideas. In problem analysis, different attributes spark new modifications. In play and prototyping, there is a rapid cycle of try, assess, alter, try again. No matter how hard you try to withhold judgment (another brainstorming rule), you cannot help but make micro-judgments about each idea, which in turn spurs on more ideas. This iteration is crucial to idea-generating, and it can be purposefully built into the process.

As a leader trying to facilitate this process, you need two important actions: convergence and assurance. Convergent thinking as a complement to divergent thinking was explained earlier as happening at every stage of the problem-solving process. The convergent-divergent complementary process is a very important activity that is generally overlooked, primarily because in practice divergent thinking is relegated to the Imagine phase. Convergent thinking drives those little micro-judgments during idea generation. This is the Judge role presented by von Oech. You can put the Judge to work before the final solution decision. In reality, judges only render a decision after they spend a lot of time weighing arguments and evidence. In other words, the Judge helps refine the problem, which in turn generates more ideas. Here are some prompting questions by the Judge role that ultimately help generate ideas:

- What is the idea trying to do?

- What assumptions are you making, are they still valid, and are there assumptions you are not even aware of (ask someone)?

- What's interesting and worth building on?

- What are the idea's drawbacks?[42]

- Have I made things overly complicated?

- Are we playing by rules? What if we did not?

Like idea-generating techniques, there are many convergent thinking tools that facilitate your analysis and decision-making as you converge on the best ideas from the divergently generated list.

LEADERSHIP BY DESIGN

Design Principle: Iteration

Definition: A process of incrementally developing and refining a design based on feedback until a specific result is achieved.[43]

In Other Words: Go back to the drawing board. Again. On purpose.

For Example: Your educational curriculum is likely different now than it was when the program was first created; fields of study are often iterated to keep up with new knowledge and an increasingly complex, competitive society.

For Leaders: Iteration is arguably the most important component to a successful solution. It allows intricate ideas to build naturally on simpler ones, which brings order to complexity. Often leaders shy away from iteration because they fear failure; however, a failing design provides just as much, if not more, valuable information as a successful idea. People have an unlimited capacity for creativity—there is no reason to halt the process after the first idea. How can a leader involve as many constituents as possible to test concepts and solicit feedback? Why is that important? When should the iteration of a design actually stop, if at all?

Creativity takes practice. Creativity is (sometimes) hard work. These two assertions by Michael Michalko from the start of this chapter sum up the only thing between you and innovation. You have set aside your fears and recognize the myths of creativity. You understand creative problem-solving processes and idea-generating techniques. How, then, do you further develop your creative capacity? Frequent, purposeful engagement in creative challenges, along with the following suggestions, will help you maximize your creative potential.

1. Develop your CORE™—Creative activity involves risk. Taking creative risks is easier when you are confident, optimistic, and resilient.

2. Believe in yourself as a creative individual—This belief will grow as you engage.

3. Recognize and eliminate blocks—Creativity **blocks** are the many things that stifle your creative thinking. When someone says, "That is a terrible idea!"—that is a creative block. Blocks can also be psychological (fear), cultural (norms), social (others' judgment), conceptual (how you see things), and literal (deadlines, distractions, environment).

   Blocks the many things that stifle your creative thinking

4. Play and have fun—Positive emotions and humor enhance creativity and motivation to engage.[44]

5. Give yourself a kick—the idea doctor said, "It's a picture of the shoe I used to give you a kick in the seat of the pants. When you look at it, I want it to trigger these questions in your mind: Am I getting lazy? Am I too busy? Am I becoming arrogant? Am I getting timid?"[45] Developing your creativity takes work, time, humility, and courage. Some of these are internal and some external, but all are in your control.

Chapter Summary

Yes, you really are creative, and the first step toward developing your leadership is to understand the many myths that surround the concept. Perhaps the greatest obstacle to your creativity is you—your fear of being different, your self-editing and self-censoring, and the mental habits formed over the years.

But as a leader, you will have problems. Even if you do not have problems, you want to proactively seek out problems because those kinds of problems are heuristic opportunities to innovate. Creative leaders see more possibilities.

Creativity can be defined with the 4Ps. Creative products are unique and of value, and that uniqueness and value need to be clearly defined. Creative persons think divergently, able to generate many, many ideas from a single problem. They are also open-minded and have creative confidence. The creative press are the things in the environment that impact creativity. And, there are many creative processes, all of which offer some interesting divergent-convergent steps and stages, and all of which fall into the general organization of Understand—Imagine—Implement with iteration. But the important thing (remember to identify the important thing) is to follow a process.

Yes, you can generate many ideas. Wow, can you generate ideas. So many idea-generating techniques to add to your creative problem-solving toolbox. Fortunately, your toolbox is organized by category of technique: divergent-thinking techniques, problem-analysis techniques, visualization techniques, play-and-build techniques, human-centered techniques, incubation techniques, alternative-perspective techniques, and inspiration and exploration techniques.

Key Terms

Algorithmic Problem 204
Biomimicry 220
Blocks 225
Creative Confidence 208
Creativity 201
Elaboration 207
Flexibility 207

Fluency 207
4Ps 205
Heuristic Problem 204
Incubation 209
Innovation 199
Open-Minded 208
Originality 207

Person 205
Press 205
Proactive 194
Problem 202
Process 205
Product 205

CORE™ Attribute Builders: Build Now for Future Leadership Challenges

Attribute: Confidence (Creative)

Builder: Creating creativity workshop

Teach some idea-generating techniques to your friends. Better still, work with friends to put together a brief workshop (15 minutes) that engages your organization in divergent thinking activities or idea-generating techniques. Take the techniques and challenges right from this chapter or make up your own. The important thing is to continue to practice and involve yourself in creative activities.

Skill Builder Activity

Imagine Imagine Imagine what if . . .

Invite three friends out to coffee and discuss the questions below. Any time an interesting idea comes up, one that you think is really fun and has potential, write it down. Really push yourself and the group to have fun and be wacky.

- What would happen if animals became self-conscious?

- What would happen if men had babies?
- What would happen if college courses were only taught after 10 p.m.?
- What would happen if students wore uniforms?
- What would happen if all students used a wheelchair?
- What would happen if there was a 3 to 6 p.m. siesta?

Skill Builder Activity

Practice the creative process: Mission Positive Idea Challenge

Yay for happy!

Your challenge: Design an inexpensive, reproducible, product and/or experience that induces positive emotions in others. The broader the appeal (that is, the more people you impact), the better. If your idea can create positive emotions in the same person over and over again . . . well, that is really cool.

- Remember to *understand* the problem, context, solutions, etc.

- Remember to think *divergently* and generate many, many, many, many, many, many, many, many, many ideas . . .
- Remember to *iterate* and test and improve and test and improve and test and improve . . .
- And keep those other design-thinking habits of mind in mind: Explorative, User-centered, Multidisciplinary, and Integrative.

Skill Builder Activity

Activate multiple senses to generate ideas

Here are three challenges that ask you to activate as many of the senses as possible:

1. With a partner—Design a *date* focusing on each of the five senses (taste, touch, smell, sight, sound) and a sixth sense—a feeling of beauty, expectations exceeded, deep comfort, or an alternative you choose relative to positive emotion.

2. Create a campus map that is based on something other than geography (e.g., smells, mood, colors, etc.). Incorporate as many of the senses into the map itself or what it represents.

3. Design a greeting card for someone who needs a thank you. Again, think about a card that includes and activates as many of the senses as possible.

9

Effective Practices for Leading Others to Success

Helping others succeed may be your best success story.

—Joshua Becker

Leadership by Design Model

Design Self

How can I design myself as a leader?

Design Relationships

As a leader, how can I design my relationships with others?

DESIGN OTHERS' SUCCESS

AS A LEADER, HOW CAN I DESIGN SUCCESS FOR OTHERS?

Design Culture

As a leader, how can I design the culture of my organization?

Design Future

As a leader, how can I innovate?

Introduction

Leading is ultimately about influencing others. It is also about who you are as a person. In a leadership role, you will have an opportunity for setting direction for an organization, but that can only happen if everyone succeeds, including you. Inspiring others to follow your lead is a challenge. This chapter begins with a discussion of the context behind changing the mindset and expectations of today's workers that is requiring future leaders to modify how they practice leadership. What specific leadership and complementary managerial practices enable others to perform up to their capacity? More importantly, what leadership and management practices will you adapt to design your success? The chapter concludes with an overview of how situational leadership theory can assist you in designing the right approach for inspiring others to follow your lead.

LEADERSHIP THAT MAKES A DIFFERENCE

Life can take intriguing and unexpected turns. When things do not appear to be working out, opportunity may come along and change your current path . . . or it may not. You need not wait for opportunity. Building and utilizing your CORE™ leadership attributes from Chapter 1 can create your opportunity. This is what happened to a young man who seemingly had nothing going for himself. Put yourself into the shoes of a teenager who perceives that they have no future. What advice would you give to a young person trying to find their way to success?

Identify what you are good at and *engage*. You know you are good at working on projects with your hands. You enjoy fixing things by designing creative solutions. When you engage your strengths, you are putting your best self and effort forward. The resulting successes, even the small ones, build *confidence*. Your small successes may lead to a series of part-time jobs where your best self gets you noticed and builds your reputation. You finally land a full-time job, perhaps as a pipe fitter. Your *optimism* about your future continues to grow since you appear to be achieving a significant goal in your life, a job where you can excel. Optimism and confidence inspire your engagement when you meet and enter into partnership with an entrepreneur who runs a small plumbing business. As you organize and plan to expand your business, you run into stiff competition. Your leadership skills are tested as you lead a workforce that requires significant training. You work tirelessly as you overcome a series of setbacks, growing the company from a few employees to over 700. The many successes have increased your confidence so much that you are *resilient* in the face of unexpected challenges. And now, as an established leader, you begin to facilitate others' success. You help your employees identify their strengths and engage, build their confidence in themselves and their team, inspire their optimism in their future with the company, and ultimately help them become resilient experts who can help the organization succeed. Perhaps you then expand these efforts to help the greater community, such as creating an innovative nonprofit organization that installs free new furnaces in the homes of needy families. But that is a story for another day. Now, you look back and reflect on how your leadership journey unfolded, and you consider how you can help others design their journey. You realize that not only have you achieved great success yourself, you have also helped others around you become successful leaders themselves.[1]

The reality is that everyone faces an unclear future. But that cannot leave you paralyzed, and it certainly does not leave you powerless. Everyone matters, and effective leaders create conditions for others to succeed. Why bother designing success for others? Sometimes, that person could wind up creating lots of jobs and pump millions of dollars into the local economy. By the way, that teenager in the story above is Mark Aitkin. The company that Mark and his partner grew is Horizon Services, a multimillion-dollar heating, cooling, and plumbing company headquartered in Wilmington, Delaware. Mark's leadership journey continues by actively designing others' success, but it started with his CORE™.

Design for Followers' Needs and Motivation

Learning Objective

9.1 Describe the context behind adopting a new set of leadership practices

Designing success for others begins with how you *see* others. You are likely someone who wants to make an impact—an individual who wants to be seen by colleagues as a valuable contributor who makes a difference. Leaders need to see the same in their followers. Everyone wants to feel like they matter, whether the organizational objective is maximizing shareholder value in a for-profit corporation, better meeting an important social need through a nonprofit, or building sustainability, citizenship, or perhaps spiritual well-being through a public or religious organization. Leading others to success is actually pretty easy—it is already where they want to go. Facilitating that journey to success, and designing the conditions and actions to do so, is the tricky part for you as a leader. That facilitation begins with understanding what followers need and changing your mindset from *what can you (follower) do for me* to *how can I (leader) bring out your best.*

Know What Followers Need to Succeed

Your greatest achievements at work will ultimately be related to helping others around you succeed at their jobs. Organizations function as complex, interconnected systems where the actions of some impact the success (or not) of others. Knowing what those around you need to become successful requires constant vigilance and consistent planning. As you create conditions for others to succeed, their growing confidence will perpetuate those conditions for others.

Followers Need the Freedom to Raise Issues

You cannot help someone develop into a productive, confident employee if you do not know what concerns them. People generally know when you are truly interested in them. Asking thoughtful questions and providing serious consideration of answers to problems results in creating an atmosphere where success becomes a team effort. This is the objective of Appreciative Inquiry Theory, whereby you build unity among subordinates by focusing on what they are talking about, such as their achievements, stories, and dreams.[2] You will learn more about Appreciative Inquiry in Chapter 11. Applying this approach creates an open dialogue by permitting and encouraging those around you to ask questions unconditionally. This will likely result in a working environment where innovation and dream-making become a reality.

Followers Need to Be Believed In

People generally want others to believe in them regardless of how successful they might be. By showing support in the form of encouragement, it may be possible to get an individual to believe in themselves for accomplishing great things.[3] Recognizing the contributions of others on a daily basis shows respect and interest in their accomplishments. Giving credit to others for their successes will result in generating more confidence since the energy and enthusiasm at work become commonplace. When others see themselves as being respected and trusted, they are less likely to become negative and critical of others.

Followers Need to Possess Cutting-Edge Job Skills

Having the latest technology available, as well as up-to-date policies for using that technology, will help coworkers more readily gain access to information, connect with and network with others, and remain on the cutting edge of their work. While building relationships with coworkers requires a high degree of face-to-face interaction on your part, networking digitally around the world is also part of bonding with a wider audience. Competence in the use of various forms of social media, cloud computing, and connectivity enables coworkers to become more efficient in getting tasks done and more effective in designing their relationships. Network-enabled devices being *cloudy*, *social*, and *mobile* also allows individuals to complete many job routines remotely but in real time.[4]

Followers Need Time to Think Creatively

The ultimate confidence builder is coming up with a new idea that becomes a reality for an organization. Accordingly, you as a future leader must promote a framework that provides coworkers sufficient time to get away from job routines to think about innovative ways for getting things done. Setting time aside on a consistent basis, perhaps one day a month, allows individuals to think, plan, and organize their thoughts to advance the best interests of the organization. With organizations needing to stay on the cutting edge, having many employees at all levels of an organization spending time thinking outside the box and comfort zone increases the likelihood that new ideas will come forth.

Followers Need to Capitalize on Their Strengths

Double-bind
the phenomenon wherein even when women use the same leadership behaviors as men, they are judged more harshly than their male counterparts

Instead of focusing on rectifying employee weaknesses, as a leader you should identify their unique abilities and then help them use those skills to excel in their own way. Matching employees with a partner who has complementary skills can form a bond where individuals can focus on what they are good at in the workplace. During this match-up, reconfiguring work neutralizes weaknesses among coworkers and can lead to unconventional work designs that help individuals overcome obstacles. Offering incentives such as time off for planning creative approaches for getting things done can result in bringing out employee ingenuity.

EXPERTS BEYOND THE TEXT

INSIGHTFUL LEADERS KNOW ABOUT . . . WOMEN AND LEADERSHIP

Women and Leadership: Why It Matters

By Lisa DeFrank-Cole and Sherylle Tan

Women make up half the population in the United States. Since the 1980s more women than men have earned baccalaureate degrees.[5] Women participate in the workforce as managers at about equal numbers as men.[6] While women possess all the qualities required for impactful leadership in the 21st century, men continue to outnumber women in senior leadership positions in nearly every sector.[7]

This underrepresentation of women in senior leadership does not appear to be an issue of qualification or ability to lead. In fact, women are as capable of being effective leaders and exhibit the traits and skills necessary to advance contemporary organizations and society.[8] A meta-analysis found that women's leadership styles tend to be more transformational, and women tend to engage in more contingent reward behaviors than men—styles that are both associated with effective leadership.[9]

Despite research that shows that women are equally effective leaders as their male counterparts,[10] women face what is known as the "**double-bind**." Even when women use the same leadership behaviors as men, women are judged more harshly than their male counterparts. They are routinely categorized as either competent or likeable—but not both.[11] Women must work harder to prove their worth as a leader.

Prejudice, discrimination, implicit bias, and negative stereotypes continue to be pervasive and hold women back from ascending into leadership positions.[12] People have preconceived ideas of what a leader should look like, and these conceptions are often different from pervasive gender norms. This incongruence results in less favorable perceptions, attitudes, and evaluations of women leaders.[13] The bias persists in politics and in the workplace, creating obstacles for women to become leaders and achieve success in their positions.[14]

In addition to factors in the workplace and in society, women face additional responsibilities with home and family. While men have become more involved in domestic chores, women continue to bear the majority of those responsibilities even when they work outside the home.[15] This *domestic gap* contributes to the leadership gap in all segments of the workforce.[16]

Why does it matter? One significant reason to advocate for women in leadership is that heterogeneous groups outperform homogenous groups.[17] Acknowledging that one role of a leader is to solve problems, it makes sense to have the most diverse and creative thinkers working on solutions. The more diverse perspectives in senior leadership teams, the more beneficial and innovative outcomes will be found.

If women continue to be underrepresented in decision-making, then the expertise and skills of a significant part of the workforce are being underutilized. While great strides have been made and many "glass ceilings" shattered, there continue to be challenges and barriers in women's advancement to leadership. For parity in leadership to be realized, we need to see shifts in accepted gender roles and stereotypes. This needs to take place in the home with true equality in the division of labor as well as in all areas of work and society.

How can society (including men and women) advance women to leadership positions, and thus provide more diverse and creative teams? What can you do?

Motivate Followers to Have Impact

Highly engaged employees who contribute more of themselves at work are more likely to produce innovations that change the world.[18] Motivating employees to open their imaginations through creative expression will likely result in products and services that enhance the lives of customers. In this regard, how employees organize and collaborate does matter. You can generate a highly motivational work ethic among your followers by applying Kanter's Three Ms Theory that consists of three components: mastery, membership, and meaning. In her book *Confidence*, Kanter suggests that high-performance work teams generally are highly engaged and focused on impact rather than personal advancement.[19] Directly below is a brief description of this strategy for motivating your followers toward achieving success. Compare your own capacity for motivating others with each of the following factors.

Mastery of problem-solving skills. When individuals are competent in identifying and resolving especially difficult problems themselves, they possess the fundamentals for getting things done in a smarter way. Therefore, when coworkers possess the feeling that they can literally shape the future by being an active player at work, the pace of accomplishment increases.

Membership through community solidarity. Working in teams effectively is a strategy for developing community solidarity. **Community solidarity** is defined as unity (as in a group) which produces collegial interests, objectives, and points of view. It refers to the ties in a society that bind people together as one. By encouraging coworkers to network with others across an organization, you will enhance overall engagement and the opportunity for new ideas to be generated. Thinking laterally across organizational functions (marketing, human resources, accounting, research, design, etc.) results in an awareness of how the existing organizational system works. To build community solidarity among employees, clearly communicate unity whereby ideas, points of view, and feelings may be shared without fear of recrimination.

Community solidarity unity (as in a group) which produces collegial interests, objectives, and points of view; refers to the ties in a society that bind people together

Meaning by focusing upon the big picture. Having a view of the big picture takes a mental shift from the mundane to that of curiosity. Rather than continuously focusing on job routines and getting specific tasks done as part of an operational system, sitting back and looking at the overall purpose and impact of the work expands your perception of personal importance and that of others. Clarity about how organizational products or services improve the lives of others also results in guideposts for making future decisions. Changing the daily conversation about how to create new products energizes others to think beyond the typical.

REFLECTION QUESTIONS

When you have worked with others in the past, did you trust them enough to open your mind to their ideas? How did you help them feel comfortable enough to share concerns or new ideas? Do you think they felt like you believed in their capabilities? If you had to convince someone right now that you thought they could be successful, what would you say or do?

As a leader you work to build your CORE™. To design success for others, the bottom line is that you need to help others gain confidence, see optimistically, build up their resilience, and more fully engage. Another way to accomplish this is to consistently and authentically let others know that they are doing something important for the organization. People want others to believe in them. By showing support in the form of encouragement, you help others succeed at becoming innovative by tending to their needs rather than focusing solely on your own.

LEADERSHIP BY DESIGN

Design Principle: Garbage in—Garbage out

Definition: The quality of system output is dependent on the quality of system input.

In Other Words: Bad inputs results in bad outputs. You may also have heard this as *you get out what you put in*, or *you reap what you sow*.

For Example: The time and effort you put into studying for an exam is usually directly proportional to the grade you receive. Here is another example: If you make an apple pie with rotten apples, you will get a lousy pie. If you make a pie with good apples but add salt instead of sugar, again you get a lousy pie. The fault does not lie with the apples. Ponder, and read on.

For Leaders: This design principle captures the essence of designing for others' success. When follower performance fails, leaders often focus on that individual. But the real answer to why things went wrong lies long before the problem actually occurred. Assume for a moment that the source of the *garbage* is not the person—where could the garbage have been added? Did you advertise for the wrong positional skills? Was your hiring process flawed? Was the orientation lacking? Were the necessary resources not provided? Did the individual get any prior feedback or training?

Investing time and resources into the input processes (screening, interviewing, orienting, training, etc.) will ensure that you minimize the amount of garbage-in so you can maximize the quality of output. Can you trace the process of recurring issues back to the inputs and redesign it for follower success?

Move From Rigidity to Flexibility

The moment has arisen for a change in the line of authority, work practices, and accountability in today's organizations.[20] In the past, a traditional **vertical operational model** or hierarchy depicts a rigid structure that relies upon the leadership practices of senior executives to direct others for getting tasks done efficiently. In this model, followers simply do what they are told to do whether they agree or disagree. Leaders with authority and power at the top of an organization, whether the CEO or president or other senior executives, generally control every aspect of the daily operation.

Another, more contemporary operational model consists of moving from a hierarchy to a flatter or **lateral organizational model**, defined as a structure that enables individuals to come together in varying arrangements based on personal preferences for getting things done. Under this structure, there are fewer levels of management and more networking among employees having different functions. Collaborative work practices, where decision-making is expanded to include more personnel, allow for some flexibility in the way work gets done. In this model, job entrants have freedom to perform tasks based on personal preferences, whether digitally or face-to-face, and so forth. Examples of innovative companies that have adopted a lateral or flatter operational model with reduced layers of management that you want to look into are (1) game maker—Value Corp; (2) web hosting—Github; (3) marketing agency—Ciplex; and (4) maker of Gore-tex—W. L. Gore Associates.[21] Leadership in these organizations can come from anyone at any rank (or job title), thus giving everyone more presence in the decision-making process.

As a new employee seeking to eventually assume a leadership role, which operational model do you prefer? The following exercise may help you decide.

Vertical operational model a rigid structure that relies upon the leadership practices of senior executives to direct others for getting tasks done efficiently

Lateral organizational model a structure that enables individuals to come together in varying arrangements based on personal preferences for getting things done

Work Preference?		
Do you prefer to work:	Yes	No
(1) in a situation where senior executives control how work gets done with little opportunity for personal choice on your part?	___	___
(2) alone rather than with others in a team?	___	___
(3) where most decisions are made by a few key leaders?	___	___
(4) on the same tasks day after day rather than expand beyond routines?	___	___
(5) where you are held accountable by executives with no input from peers?	___	___

If you responded with a majority of *no* answers, then you prefer to work in an organization that does not rely on those in senior leadership roles to command and control all actions of their subordinates. You would probably prefer to be more personally involved by having more choices available to you regarding how you make decisions, conduct work, and are held accountable for your performance. Your context for performing in leadership roles reflects a preference for working collaboratively rather than independently. If you responded with a majority of *yes* responses, then perhaps you prefer a more traditional style of leadership whereby direction comes only from the top of the organization with little opportunity for input from those at lower levels of work responsibilities. Although this may seem restricting, it can also feel comfortable for a new employee who needs that level of direction. Your context for performing leadership is to be totally in charge by exhibiting your authority and power provided to you by your title (being CEO, president, etc.).

Change the Playbook

You are in the midst of the beginning of the third industrial revolution.[22] As a result, a new set of worker expectations is emerging. The **third industrial revolution** is defined as

Third industrial revolution the integration of science, technology, and personal choice for creating collaborative work strategies for getting people focused on the future

integrating science, technology, and a personal choice for creating collaborative work strategies for getting people focused on the future. This operational model calls for an enhanced interdependency among workers who need leaders who mobilize others to expand the boundaries of organizational outreach. This change in leadership approach recognizes a social revolution in which the sharing of knowledge, ideas, and your expertise becomes commonplace. The success of others depends on how they can be drawn into a system whereby both personal and organizational needs can be met simultaneously. Coworkers themselves desire to determine what technology to use, what programs to access, and who to contact. You may call this a **B**ring **Y**our **O**wn (BYO) work strategy for getting things done. To enable others to succeed, mold a strategy that connects individuals with one another, whether locally or globally.

Today's information technology enables individuals to collaborate with others easily. Correspondingly, the current generation now entering the workforce expects to connect to others instantly, advance in their careers quickly, and be successful at what they do—but somewhat on their own terms.[23] The power of social media has broken down authoritarian rule in many organizations. Workers at all levels of an organization are now actively engaged in making decisions that also builds confidence for action. By empowering subordinates to design their own work patterns and self-lead within the parameters of an existing operational system, you become a trailblazer for changing the playbook at work.

REFLECTION QUESTIONS

Think of a time when you worked with an individual who lacked confidence. What did you do to help that individual turn around and perform with confidence? What did you learn from that experience that may assist you in getting things done efficiently in the future? Do you prefer to work in an environment where you empower subordinates to design their own work pattern for building confidence or one where you control work practices? Justify your approach to leading others to succeed.

Augment Leadership and Management Functions: When Multitasking Really Matters

Learning Objective

9.2 Explain how leadership and management functions are different but complementary

There has been some dissension over the last several decades as to how leading and managing relate. The idea that leading and managing are both important is not new, but how the two roles interrelate continues as a topic of debate. Are leadership and management basically the same function, or are they entirely different activities? Revisit the definitions: Leadership is the process of influencing others toward a common vision. Management is the process of organizing, controlling, and coordinating resources to achieve organizational value. The function of leadership is to mobilize individuals—human resources—in an effort to move toward accomplishing something significant. The function of management is to coordinate the efforts of people to get those tasks done that achieve specific objectives.

Lead and manage, mobilize and organize. As noted in Chapter 2, these two functions require different but complementary skill sets. A leader in a relatively small organization generally takes on both functions simultaneously since limited resources invite a leader to be multifunctional. However, as organizations get larger and the complexity of operations becomes apparent, the need for taking on both functions becomes less apparent. In large organizations with many levels of responsibilities involving possibly thousands of individuals, it is practically impossible for those in leadership roles to manage coworkers on a daily basis. However, effective leaders are fully aware of leadership and management systems and activities as both impact success at many levels.

Visualize yourself down at the beach observing the ocean current. As you enter the ocean, you make waves. Similarly, in an organization there are existing currents—the flow of activity emanating from others, systems, and the overall culture. What waves do you introduce into the overall current, and how might your waves be most influential? How can you use the currents that already exist to your advantage? Creating waves requires the initiative of leadership. Directing your waves and those that already exist requires management. Only by designing others' success can you maximize the combined impact of both. Visualize how leadership and management are complementary functions.

Management Versus Leadership

Management Linking Leadership		
(Riding Waves)	Functions	(Making Waves)
Ask how to do it?	Planning	Ask why being done?
Match talent to task	Organizing	Hire the right people
Delegate tasks	Implementing challenge the process	Volunteer to engage
Micro-manage/monitor activities	Controlling	Empower others to act
Use top-down benchmarks	Assessing rely upon peer/personal	Accountability

As implied in the above illustration, management has the responsibility of maintaining order and discipline by ensuring that the right people are in place to perform required tasks. On the other hand, leadership is about obtaining and mobilizing resources to enable others to take on challenges to get things done. Now, in the next segment, you will look at several critical practices that individuals in leadership roles may undertake in order to make things happen in their organizations. But for now, reflect on your own past experience in regard to working as a subordinate to a leader and what you learned from that process.

● REFLECTIVE QUESTIONS

Consider a project you led. How did things actually get done? What practices of leadership and management did you exhibit? Why (do you think) you were successful or not? How could you have maximized the success of others to enhance the project outcome?

IGNITE as a Leader

Learning Objective

9.3 Engage in leadership practices to inspire those around you

MYTH OR REALITY?

THERE IS NO NEED TO LEARN A NEW SET OF LEADERSHIP PRACTICES. WHAT HAS WORKED FOR ME IN THE PAST WILL WORK FOR ME IN THE FUTURE.

Myth. To George Graen and Mary Uhl Bien, this perception is a myth. They point out that leaders in a hierarchy who rely on practicing leadership primarily based on their authority and power will likely find their leadership met with resistance among new recruits in the workplace.[24] Instead of practicing leadership from a position of power *over* subordinates, empowering others to act based on personal preferences is more amenable to the expectations of the new job entrant. Building on the success of others requires a new set of practices quite different from the command and control hierarchy of the past and the model many associate with the leader.

Practice: an activity used typically to maintain or improve one's performance

A **practice** is an activity used typically to maintain or improve one's performance. Recall the five leadership practices identified by James Kouzes and Barry Posner[25] as strongly correlated with successfully changing the behavior of those around you: (a) model the way, (b) inspire a shared vision, (c) challenge the process, (d) enable others to act, and (e) encourage the heart. Kouzes and Posner suggest that assessing your own capacity to put these practices into operation is an excellent way to begin your journey for learning how to grow into an effective leader.

How ready are your leadership practices? Using the five-point rating scale provided, assess yourself in terms of your confidence in performing each practice. Then have two other individuals also rate you and compare scores. Think about leaders you admire and how your current practices might measure compared to theirs. Testing yourself against these five practices of leadership should help you to determine who you are and what you have to do to emerge into this new role.

Assess Your Confidence for Effective Practices

1. Inspire others to act by appealing to common values 1 2 3 4 5

2. Be a role model by setting an example 1 2 3 4 5

3. Foster collaboration by strengthening others 1 2 3 4 5

4. Be a caring person by recognizing accomplishments of others 1 2 3 4 5

5. Challenge the process by searching for opportunities 1 2 3 4 5

   Average personal rating for all five categories_____

   Average rating by first reviewer_____

   Average rating by second reviewer_____

If you and your two observers recorded a personal average rating for all five categories of four or above, you are already doing things that leaders of the past have typically been remiss about doing. However, while the five practices identified above can provide you with a foundation to lead effectively, moving beyond the basics requires exploring outside your comfort zone.

In the leadership role, you act as a facilitator who brings people together in a united effort to accomplish something special. A new set of expanded operational practices (beyond that identified by Kouzes and Posner above) will make others look at you in amazement. To get followers to think for themselves, engage others, and overcome obstacles, you need to IGNITE their passion that will lead to action on their part. Here are six leadership practices that will enhance your capacity to IGNITE as a leader: I = Instill, G = Grow, N = Notice, I = Invest, T = Target, and E = Ensure.

Instill a Culture That Despises Complacency

As a human being, you have a tendency to become complacent. You often settle for doing things that are comfortable and routine. Complacency does not require much effort. To counter an organizational culture where complacency becomes the norm, your leadership should reflect an open work climate where all ideas for change are welcome. Organizations need to grow and change faster than the competition. You as a leader spur that change by designing new ways to address that reality. Jack Welch, former CEO of General Electric, said, "If the rate of change on the outside exceeds the rate of change on the inside, the end is near."[26] In other words, change what you are doing before you are forced to actually have to change due to competitive forces. We have witnessed a number of companies that at one time were among the top in their industries in 2010 but then failed to change and lost their prominence a few years later, such as Toys R Us, Lands End, Radio Shack, and Payless Shoes. To counteract failure, creating a work culture where *there is no place for complacency* reflects a new reality.

Grow the Use of Social Media

Leadership is about networking and expanding one's sphere of influence. Integrate a variety of social media such as blogs, apps, the Internet, Twitter, and so forth to create a bond with customers, suppliers, and employees at every level of the organization. To build respect and trust, capture the power of social media for generating a collaborative work culture where followers can thrive. As an example, it takes a team to win a competitive event whether in football, baseball, soccer, or hockey. In such events, it takes coaches, suppliers of equipment, trainers, and community support to make a winner. Similarly, in other organizations in the private, public, or nonprofit sector, it takes a similar team of players to come together to get products and services to customers. Social media enables you to initiate new ways for creating quality relationships.[27]

REFLECTION QUESTIONS

How do you currently use social media to stay connected with your friends? What is your favorite form of social media and why? Can you identify a time in your life when your ideas were substantially different from all of your friends? How did you feel about being outside the norm? How did your friends react to you?

Note and Study Your Competitors

Staying alert as to what competitors are doing enables you to remain on the cutting edge of your profession. As we all know, coming in second is not the benchmark for determining success.[28] Being first in any endeavor, especially your career, is your priority. Being aggressive about winning is a way to make certain that competitors do not suddenly overtake your product line or service.[29] Therefore, in the private sector, leadership is about scanning the marketplace and competitors to get new ideas. In the public sector, leadership provides high-quality services and an infrastructure to enhance the quality of life of residents. In the nonprofit sector, the objective is to provide clients with the best assistance to resolve illnesses, tend to the needy, and address sudden tragedies such as a hurricane or earthquake, among others. Knowing what competitors and other public service agencies are doing is an opportunity to reinforce what is currently being done or a source for new ideas. An example of being competitive-savvy is the leadership in Amazon.com, Costco, and PayPal, where each of these three organizations attempts to maintain a number one position in the marketplace. Similarly, in the nonprofit and public sectors, you need to be on the top of your game every day.

Invest in Real-Time Decision-Making

Leadership is about making the right decision at the right time. In order to achieve greatness, gathering information provides a framework for making decisions. Pulling together the latest technology along with an effective data analytics team produces the information required to become an informed decision maker. In addition, distributing decision-making among coworkers by connecting data to people results in more effective outcomes. Your expertise for diagnosing issues, identifying alternative solutions, and making decisions propels your capacity to make others believe in you. Working in an environment of ambiguity, uncertainty, and change adds urgency for useful data.

Think Differently From the Norm

A central idea in this textbook is that leaders must constantly be working on big ideas. Relying on incremental changes shortchanges long-term potential. It is through big changes that an organization builds success.[30] Effective leaders continually search for big, innovative ideas. As technology advances, new opportunities come into play. Building quality relationships along with technology generates a creative workforce that is willing to put its reputation on the line. But thinking of big ideas takes time. For example, a company called Intuit, the developer of TurboTax and QuickBooks, values the human aspect of their operation as witnessed by their policy to permit their employees to spend 10 percent of their working time on projects and ideas of their own.[31] This unstructured time has resulted in the creation of some of the company's best products.

REFLECTION QUESTIONS

Can you think of a time when you were complacent? How did you deal with complacency and ignite yourself into action?

Ensure a Clear Vision to Make It Happen

Effective leaders communicate their vision using clear, vivid messages that both motivate and provide direction. This involves identifying key constituencies that need to support your initiatives, enrolling them, and getting into place the support system that would give your efforts staying power.[32] Your vision as a leader promotes your leadership brand. It establishes the expectations behind the work culture in that organization. In this regard, Simon Senik's Golden Circle for Communication[33] depicts an intriguing strategy for connecting your vision to a successful effort. For example, leaders traditionally communicate their vision to coworkers by first focusing on *what* product or service is being produced, then explaining *how* to produce the end result efficiently, and finally emphasizing *why* the product will generate a profit. To Senik, successful organizations take a different approach. You inspire others to buy into your vision by first convincing followers on *why* there is a need for the product or service, then stipulating *how* to build the product or service creatively, and finally identifying *what* lifestyle need of consumers you are serving.

The IGNITE leadership practices delineated above should become part of your repertoire when helping others succeed, especially in a workspace where personal preference for getting things done becomes more prevalent. IGNITE those surrounding you by adopting these practices for becoming an exemplary leader.

REFLECTION QUESTIONS

Can you recall at least three leadership practices depicted above that will likely help you make waves and influence others to follow your lead? List them below in order of preference. Circle the one that you perceive yourself as being particularly adept in implementing right now. Put a square around the one that you need more confidence to use. What have you learned to ignite in yourself as a result of this reflection?

1. _____

2. _____

3. _____

DELIVER as a Manager

Learning Objective

9.4 Apply managerial practices to implement a strategic plan

A leader's vision is only as good as the delivery of resources toward that vision. In other words, things need to actually get done. In a leadership role, having knowledge of those practices in management that will result in moving followers and the organization along a path of success will be helpful. The collaborative nature of work today reinforces the notion that gaining knowledge is not a solitary act but a community affair.[34] An intriguing challenge for you as a leader is dealing with a growing number of **freelance workers**, defined as individuals who desire to work for more than one employer on a part-time basis rather than full-time for only one organization. Researchers predict that 50 percent of the workforce in the year 2020 may not be receiving a paycheck from just one employer.[35] With this new mobile worker emerging, you will be testing your capacity to prioritize tasks, motivate others for getting tasks accomplished, and hold individuals accountable for their results.

Freelance workers
an individual who desires to work for more than one employer on a part-time basis rather than full-time for only one organization

The acronym DELIVER reflects a set of practices that can focus you on managing to get things done. Placing this term in your own memory bank is a great way to expand your leadership presence because DELIVER should help remind you how to make your vision become reality: D = Designate, E = Empower, L = List, I = Initiate, V = Verify, E = Encourage, and R = Realign.

Designate One Individual Who Will Have Responsibility Over the Implementation Process

Selecting the right person for this responsibility is crucial. For credibility, this individual must have the capacity for communicating widely across all levels and functions (marketing, accounting, research/design, etc.) of an organization. Holding one person accountable allows for a quick assessment of the change process being undertaken. Getting continuous feedback as to how things are proceeding increases the pace of change.

Empower Followers to Make Thoughtful Decisions by Delineating Clear Lines for the Scope of Their Authority

As a leader, establish the framework for letting subordinates know what kind of decisions they are able to make without seeking approval from another. This practice provides clarity for determining when those surrounding you must seek permission before acting. Without such clarity, there will be a tendency for chaos or confusion. Pushing decision-making to lower levels in an organization enables followers to gain confidence. Giving individuals authority to perform is part of developing a learning organization whereby the work culture reflects an expectation to perform responsibly.[36]

List What Is Unique About Each Person, Then Capitalize on It

Turn talent into performance by challenging each employee to excel in his or her own way. Setting goals based on uniqueness is part of this process. Involve people in setting their own implementation goals, instead of dictating them. In a leadership role, you desire an individual's commitment, not just compliance. When people believe they can influence and shape their own goals, they are more likely to be motivated to achieve them.

Initiate a Risk Response Team to Assist Those Being Subjected to Significant Obstacles and Possible Failure

Having a tolerance for failure is important. During the implementation process, mistakes will likely occur. If followers are encouraged to learn from their mistakes, implementation efforts will proceed with less chaos and frustration. During this process, releasing resources to support risk-taking efforts (some of which fail) reassures followers that they are not left alone when difficult times occur. And making mistakes may also become a learning opportunity for followers, especially if they are encouraged to get together and discuss what is working and what is not. Creating a risk response team reduces the fear and frustration associated with setbacks.

LEADERSHIP BY DESIGN

Design Principle: Factor of Safety

Definition: The use of more elements than is thought necessary to offset the effects of unknown variables and prevent system failure.

In Other Words: Anticipating and addressing possible issues and trouble in your design.

For Example: Being asked a security question in order to verify your identity when logging into an online bank account. That verification step is designed to save you and the bank from fraudulent activity.

For Leaders: Think about all the many ways your followers might be *unsuccessful* at a given task. What can you add now to their knowledge, attitude, mindset, context, and so forth that can insure against possible future failure? One possible way to design around failure is to embrace small failure by encouraging controlled risk taking, using mistakes as an integral part of follower development. Consider how you can better design others' success by using factors of safety.

A note about designing your leadership self: Do you remember the most catastrophic error in leadership? Tarnishing your reputation and losing your credibility. What factors of safety can you design into your leadership to avoid this error?

<u>V</u>erify Progress by Establishing Checkpoints for Accomplishments

Convening coworkers on a periodic basis to evaluate work progress keeps everyone on track. Meeting, talking, and thinking together often brings the best out from each coworker. Creating momentum leads to systematic progress. Often, momentum itself will take on a life of its own for creating a winning climate. By having verification meetings, you learn about what actually works as you move forward—and you don't have to wait until the end to find out what worked and what did not. As individuals experience success, they will get better at implementation. They learn how to manage their own expectations, make better decisions, allocate scarce resources appropriately, and understand what actually works.

<u>E</u>xhibit Calm When Under Fire

Dealing with ambiguity, uncertainty, turbulence, and chaos that arise suddenly requires a steady hand and the ability to rally those around you to stay on track. An example of exhibiting calm came during an attack by aircraft by terrorists on September 11, 2001, when a large number of employees at different levels of operational responsibilities assumed leadership roles at the World Trade Center in New York City. In this instance, self-appointed leaders assessed that something was wrong and acted quickly to save lives. They reacted rationally during this tragedy by remaining calm when diagnosing the severity of the situation, then making decisions as to how to proceed, and finally executing those decisions quickly and effectively.

<u>R</u>edesign Work Patterns and Assignments So They Are Cross-Functional

Getting things done by yourself is very difficult. It generally takes a variety of individuals with complementary skills to get things done effectively. For example, by redesigning work assignments across functions, those in marketing can learn about product design by engaging in joint projects with those associated with manufacturing. Using the diversity of a workforce to your advantage leads to very impressive results. By redesigning work patterns, you energize workers to accomplish more than they think they can. Creating a learning organization propels managers to a vital role since they are the coaches in an organization.

REFLECTION QUESTIONS

Who have you met that is great at energizing workers to accomplish more than what those employees think they are capable of? What managerial practices did this leader implement to get followers to critically think about achieving important organizational goals? During your own previous work on a project where you were designated as the leader, what management practices did you adopt for generating results? What checkpoints did you put into place to ensure that your teammates were working efficiently? What did you learn from this experience that will help you as a future leader?

The acronym DELIVER should be helpful in remembering that management practices complement leadership practices to implement vision. Managers are the organizers and the doers; they get things done. Adopting practices that inspire others into action reflects the goal of leadership. However, change and innovation can also bring chaos and turbulence. Those in leadership positions must be capable of leading others during times when things are going well and managing when things get chaotic and unpredictable. The managing functions of producing, promoting, and pricing products and services require guidance for ensuring that work designs and output are compatible. Getting the best from followers is the goal of leadership.

REFLECTION QUESTION

Form a small group of at least three individuals. Put together a list of at least five managerial practices that a leader should be knowledgeable of for getting others to complete those tasks necessary for implementing a vision. List them below in order of preference. Place a circle around that one practice in which you feel you already excel. Put a square around that practice in which you need some work in order to be confident in performing. What did you learn about yourself as a result of this reflection?

1. _____

2. _____

3. _____

4. _____

5. _____

Design Others' Success With a Situational Leadership Approach

Learning Objective

9.5 Use a situational leadership strategy to design others' success

Applying both leadership and management practices will help enhance your effectiveness as a leader. How these practices are implemented depends on the situation in which you find yourself. As indicated earlier in this chapter, individuals born after 2000 are quite different as to how they think, work, and use technology. The present generation has high expectations in regard to balancing work responsibilities with personal lifestyle choices. They desire to grow on the job, share their strengths with others, and be part of an organization that produces goods and services that make a positive difference in people's lives. Working with different generations, within different fields, and across different levels of experience and expertise all comprise aspects of the *situation* within which you as leader must operate. For example, a study by Deloitte revealed that two-thirds of new entrants into the workplace now believe it is the leader's job to provide them with accelerated career development opportunities.[37]

In reality, leadership effectiveness is affected by situational factors often not under control of the leader. For example, in companies such as Google, Time Warner, and Samsung, in the private sector, goal attainment may be influenced by the actions of competitors, new legislation, and new technologies. Thus, situations shape how leaders must behave. Correspondingly, the kinds of followers you engage will likely vary in both readiness and willingness to perform. When assuming a leadership role, engaging employees with different motivations, goals, ambitions, and skills demands your attention.

Situational Leadership®: Adapt to the Capacity of Followers to Perform

Designed in the 1960s by Paul Hersey and Ken Blanchard, the Situational Leadership® Model promotes the idea that leaders generally must deal with a wide range of readiness levels of followers.[38] **Situational Leadership®** is defined as the behaviors used by leaders of an organization adjusting to fit the development level of the followers they are trying to influence.[39] With Situational Leadership®, you as a leader change your style based on specific parameters of your followers. There is no single best behavior to utilize at all times. Situational Leadership® Theory is arguably one of the most powerful tools used by leaders for designing a strategy to engage others.

As noted in Figure 9.1, the Situational Leadership® Model is based on the relationship between leaders and followers in terms of the amount of guidance provided (task behavior–horizontal axis); the amount of emotional support (relationship behavior–vertical axis); and the Performance Readiness® level of followers (the *R* level at the bottom). The outcomes of the interaction between getting tasks done and receiving emotional support are

Situational leadership behaviors utilized by leaders of an organization adjusting to fit the development level of the followers they are trying to influence

---

FIGURE 9.1 ●   Situational Leadership® Model

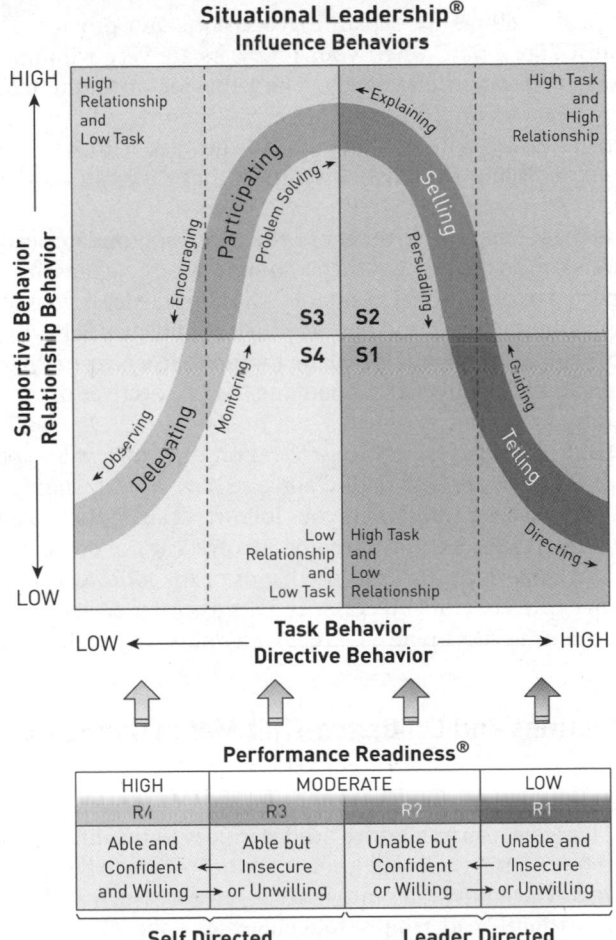

reflective in four leadership behaviors (telling, selling, participating, and delegating) that can be adopted for the different situations you may experience.

The process for applying the Situational Leadership® Model starts with your initial identification of the most important tasks to be accomplished. Second, you must consider the readiness and willingness of your followers (the R level at the bottom). Following the arrow of the R level up into the grid will identify the leadership behaviors most likely to facilitate that individual for that specific task. The leadership strategy you adopt, whether it be more supportive or directive, will depend on careful analysis of your followers' readiness level. The four universal leadership behaviors depicted in the model should prepare you for any situation you may find yourself in no matter the size or purpose of the organization.

As you read more about the application and significance behind the different leadership behaviors in Situational Leadership®, refer back to the model to keep you on track. Try applying this model to a current task you are working with others on. Do those individuals need your direction, coaching, support, or delegation?

S1—Telling: Telling others exactly what to do is an appropriate leadership behavior when your followers cannot actually do the job and are afraid to try. In such a situation, such behaviors as prescribing actual tasks to be performed and then directly supervising followers closely are in order. With insecure followers, you as a leader must recognize that being totally in charge of the work process is necessary if actions of followers are to be meaningful.

S2—Selling: Selling others by explaining decisions and providing opportunity for clarification is most appropriate when your followers are very willing to work but lack the skills necessary to perform effectively. The behavior of selling closely aligns with coaching whereby you work on a one-on-one basis—listening, advising, and helping your followers to gain necessary skills in order to do the task without assistance the next time. The outcome of Selling is convincing others that they can do the task with your guidance.

S3—Participating: Supporting others is the most appropriate leadership behavior when your followers can do the job, but they also show a lack of commitment or just refuse to perform to expected organizational standards. The key practice is your identifying incentives for both motivating followers and building their confidence. Behaviors such as getting others to participate in open dialogue by asking for input, listening to their comments, and empowering others to act are directed at changing the perspectives of those followers who are currently refusing to commit.

S4—Delegating: Entrusting others to perform on their own is an appropriate leadership practice when followers are very skillful and also have a great willingness to get things done. You should rely on delegating when your followers can do the job and are also motivated to succeed. You as a leader must become involved in the decision-making process, but the execution of those decisions is in the hands of the followers. The strategy of putting the follower in control of work processes enables a greater degree of creativity on their part. You as their leader are less involved in daily planning, organizing, and controlling of actual work.

Provide Instructions and Guidance That Match Capability

A very important part of Situational Leadership® is recognizing the readiness level of coworkers, which is the degree of ability and willingness of those around you to get work done effectively. Therefore, you as a leader need clarity as to the difficulty of the tasks others are being asked to perform, their skill levels, and their desire to be successful. These data can be useful in classifying individuals into a needs category (such as the S1, S2, S3, and S4 quadrants in the Situational Leadership® Model illustrated above).

Situational Leadership® is a good reminder that treating each coworker differently based on existing job skills is critical. Having knowledge of appropriate leadership and managerial practices and implementing them randomly will not likely result in being effective as a leader. Streamlining practices to the needs of each coworker depends on the situation at hand. It is during these personal moments between leaders and followers when opportunities for helping others develop new job skills arise. Building confidence is what success is all about, and your objective is to accelerate the development of followers through individual attention as they design innovative products and services.

LEADERSHIP BY DESIGN

Design Principle: Control

Definition: The level of control provided by a system should be related to the proficiency and experience levels of the people using the system.

In Other Words: Provide instructions and tasks that match understanding and capability.

For Example: Rock walls are designed to provide multiple courses to get to the top that vary based on a climber's ability.

For Leaders: As a leader, you should know the capabilities of your followers so you can provide an appropriate range of delegation. Are they beginners who need structure—or experts who need autonomy? Control as a design principle could mean a limit to follower authority when the task is above their experience. Accommodate varying abilities by offering

CONTROL

multiple ways to perform a task. Can you identify tasks that are not so easy that they bore followers, but not so difficult that they frustrate and overwhelm? What can be built into the system to allow your followers to succeed at each level of their development?

©iStock.com/SolStock

The Situational Leadership® Model is about demonstrating flexible leadership by adapting both leadership and management practices that address specific situations associated with followers. Situational Leadership® provides the flexibility to match a multiplicity of practices with appropriate behaviors to motivate others to perform above their own perceived expectations. Having a common purpose means that you and your coworkers are in this together. By respecting and dealing with differences, you as a leader have an added obligation to enhance the success of others by building quality relationships based on trust. Your behavior (whether telling, selling, delegating, or participating) is the ingredient that forms the foundation for putting your leadership practices into play. The innovation process requires utilizing and motivating individuals with the capacity to move a project forward at a reasonable pace. Getting workers with different levels of readiness for participating in a team effort is a challenge that you will likely address as you assume a leadership role in the future.

Respect the Culture of Engagement

An organization's culture depicts how things get done. **Culture** is defined as shared values and assumptions by organizational (or group) members; it is the way we do things

Culture shared values and assumptions by organizational (or group) members; the way we do things around here

around here. Culture is a major factor in selecting leadership practices that produce results, and it is a major theme of Chapter 11, entitled Culture. The leadership and management practices depicted earlier in this chapter reflect a new era whereby a different set of behaviors is required for getting others to buy in to your vision. They also reflect the emergence of a different kind of engaged workforce that relies on advanced technology to perform. Today new recruits do almost everything on a smart phone or tablet. Mobile usage through the use of apps on their cell phones has taken over the primary means of accessing the Internet.[40] It is easy to forget that organizations are comprised of people whereby organizational culture impacts upon the degree that job performance, positivity, and possibilities flourish.[41] Accordingly, 95 percent of job candidates currently believe that a culture of engagement at work is more important than compensation.[42] Achieving a common purpose requires an expanded outlook as to how people connect, interact, and support one another in an environment where face-to-face communication may be less of a reality.

REFLECTION QUESTION

Think of a time when you had a situation where you needed to assume a leadership role for getting others to complete tasks crucial to having a successful effort. Using the Situational Leadership® Model illustrated earlier in this chapter, what would you have done differently to meet the challenges of the situation you were in at that time? Give at least three examples.

1. _____

2. _____

3. _____

Chapter Summary

Leaders need a new set of practices to inspire a different kind of follower—one who now desires to succeed but also somewhat on his or her own terms.

IGNITE as a leader; DELIVER as a manager. IGNITE followers by **i**nstilling expectations for change, **g**rowing the use of social media, **n**oticing what competitors are doing, **i**nvesting in real-time information systems, **t**hinking differently, and **e**nsuring a clear vision. DELIVER results by **d**esignating responsibility, **e**mpowering followers to act, **l**isting employee strengths, **i**nitiating risk taking, **v**erifying progress, **e**xhibiting calm while under fire, and **r**edesigning work patterns. Your practices as a leader matter. Having command of both

leadership and managerial practices enables you to set the direction for an organization and design a working environment that produces results.

Design others' success by accommodating the situation. Situational leadership considers followers' competence and commitment as a basis for the kind of action that will best facilitate an employee. By leading with flexibility, you will likely be more capable of moving successfully into the third industrial revolution where personal expectations of followers will reflect their commitment and capacity to meet the challenges ahead.

Key Terms

Community Solidarity 233
Culture 245
Double-Bind 232

Freelance Workers 241
Lateral Organizational Model 235
Practice 238

Situational Leadership 245
Third Industrial Revolution 235
Vertical Operational Model 235

CORE™ Attribute Builders—IGNITE Your Leadership

Attribute: Confidence Building

Builder: Build your leadership rhythm

There is a rhythm to building your confidence as a leader. Just like a popular song, all parts of your strategy have to be in sync to be effective. This is similar to putting together a song where lyrics and score match perfectly. Have some fun by gaining some insight as to your personal rhythm and how confident you are in presenting yourself in a creative style.

Take those practices that will help you IGNITE your leadership and match each to a popular song. Using the lyrics, illustrate how that practice will help you become an effective leader for inspiring others around you to also become innovative.

Practice Song Title Matching Significance

(Example)

Be A Caring Person: *Stand by Me* (Ben E. King) Lesson: *Stand up for another person when an innovative effort stalls.*

Use the following from the chapter:

Instill Change _____

Grow Social Media _____

Notice Competitors _____

Invest in Data _____

Think Differently _____

Ensure a Clear Vision _____

Skill Builder Activity—DELIVER as a Manager

Working on your knowledge and abilities of management practices for getting things done is an important aspect to moving an innovative idea, whether a product or service, to actual production. Interview a leader of a nonprofit organization (United Way, American Cancer Society, American Diabetes Association) and one in the public sector (mayor, governor, county executive). Using the DELIVER acronym in the chapter, have each leader describe a situation, preferably regarding an innovative effort related to delivering a service

when that management practice was used. Compare the views of each leader in terms of strategy behind that practice for getting buy-in toward the innovative effort.

Questions for Interview:

1. How was each practice applied?

2. What were the similarities/differences in application among these two leaders?

[Guide for Your Notes]		
Management Practices for Interview	Nonprofit	Public
Designate responsible person	_____ :	_____
Empower followers to make decisions	_____ :	_____

(Guide for Your Notes)		
Management Practices for Interview	Nonprofit	Public
List unique aspect of each worker	_____ :	_____
Initiate a risk response team	_____ :	_____
Verify progress by meeting checkpoints	_____ :	_____
Exhibit calm under fire	_____ :	_____
Redesign work patterns	_____ :	_____

10

Utilizing Change Processes Effectively

Thinking about change is good; making change happen is better.

—Bradley Whitford

All meaningful and lasting change starts first in your imagination and then works its way out.

—Albert Einstein

Learning Objectives

10.1 Identify three levels of change typically initiated by those in leadership roles

10.2 Determine how individuals experience change

10.3 Examine key aspects of change that impact your leadership

10.4 Identify common barriers to change

10.5 Design a change strategy for implementation

Detailed Chapter Outline

Introduction: Change Happens—
    Lead It or Not
Identify Levels of Change

Refine Your Capacity to
    Change Yourself
(Level 1)

Leadership by Design Model

Design Self

How can I design myself as a leader?

Design Relationships

As a leader, how can I design my relationships with others?

DESIGN OTHERS' SUCCESS

AS A LEADER, HOW CAN I DESIGN SUCCESS FOR OTHERS?

Design Culture

As a leader, how can I design the culture of my organization?

Design Future

As a leader, how can I innovate?

Introduction: Change Happens—Lead It or Not

The idea of change filters through nearly everything. People are changing. Times are changing. You should make this change. Be open to change. At each level of leadership design within this textbook, change plays a significant role. Designing leadership self, relationships, others' success, culture, and especially designing the future—all talk about some facet of making things different (and hopefully better). Even embedded within the definition of leadership—the process of influencing others *toward* a common vision—speaks of movement from one state to another. Generally, people are not so good at change, and they dislike it. The current way of doing things is easy and efficient, and you really do not even need to think much about it. The new way, the changed way, requires learning and practice. Sometimes you feel frustrated and uncomfortable, and even if you know the change is for the better, you resist.

Change happens because the world and all those within it are dynamic. Even time changes. Every interaction you have with your world reinforces or changes your view of the world (remember your lean, mean, pattern-making machine brain?). Some of those changes are subtle, such as when you do not notice the paint fading on the fence in your backyard or how your sibling grows up a little every day. Those changes are easy to deal with—little changes require little change. But many changes, particularly in leadership, are a bit more significant and sometimes sudden. Those kinds of changes can overwhelm you since what you believed in the past may no longer be true.

This chapter helps you understand and lead change. In keeping with the general approach of this textbook, the important premise is that you proactively design how changes will be addressed rather than simply react to changes. And by facilitating change for yourself, others, and your organization, you help design others' success.

Change is intriguing in that it happens because someone cares to do something different and hopefully useful. People are making changes all the time. If you fail to pay attention or wait too long, especially in your job, organization, or industry, it may be difficult to maintain relevance. Designing others' success includes helping others change before they actually have to in order to remain a key player in adding value to the organization. What kinds of opportunities will you have to do something truly different from the past? Below is an example of an individual holding a PhD from Stanford University who decides to build a nonprofit organization to assist children suffering from diseases that are likely to end in death if untreated. As you read this story, note how one individual changes the process for delivering health care to families around the world who cannot get treatment due to its high cost, and consider how that one change resulted in myriad changes for many others.

LEADERSHIP THAT MAKES A DIFFERENCE

Imagine you are age 22 and receive a bachelor's degree in engineering. You graduate from a university with the world of opportunity at your fingertips. Soon after graduation, you notice that there are thousands of children dying from jaundice and other childhood diseases. Fifteen years later, you decide to change careers and create a nonprofit organization that brings medical devices to families around the world that earn generally less than $4 per day. The aim is to design first-rate medical equipment targeting children's health needs in developing countries and then license it to for-profit distributors for dissemination. Your desire is to change the way organizations can partner to produce and distribute products to those who cannot afford to purchase health care at all. You institute a change process based on a simple premise; that is, to design world-class products that perform better than the best product currently on the market. You become obsessed with a user-centric framework in that the end users of your medical devices, the patients, are key contributors in the design of your medical device. However, you change the process somewhat by making certain everyone who touches the product, whether the manufacturer or the repair person, also participates in its design and purpose. You realize that to build a better world, you need to *change the process* that includes building new relationships between the private and nonprofit sectors. And this, you believe, will best help change how medical devices are developed and how the medical society goes about delivering health care to those in desperate need.[1]

This is a real person and real story. In 2009, Krista Donaldson created a nonprofit organization known as D-Rev (short for Design Revolution). Since then, she has led the design and scaling in emerging markets of Brilliance, an affordable treatment for babies with jaundice, and the ReMotion prosthetic knee, which is worn by over 5,500 amputees. She has been recognized by *Fast Company* as one of the 50 designers shaping the future and by the World Economic Forum as a Technology Pioneer. The bottom line is that this could be you. Changing the way things have been done in the past provides opportunity to innovate and ultimately enhance the quality of life of others. You have the ability to innovate, but it takes action on your part to take an idea and make it happen.

Identify Levels of Change

Learning Objective

10.1 Identify three levels of change typically initiated by those in leadership roles

Change is the process of becoming different yourself or fostering difference in other persons or things, which is exactly the order for facilitating change. To successfully innovate within an organization, you need to be willing to change yourself first. If you cannot change yourself, it is difficult to inspire others around you to change. As a change agent, you are a role model. People look to you for setting the tone in the organization, and in the case of this chapter, how you deal with change. Do you model openness to change or resistance? Do your actions communicate a purposeful, goal-oriented focus, or one that is disorganized, hesitant, and lacking a vision? Back in Chapter 2, you established a personal brand for getting others to trust you. As a role model, you put your brand into action. One helpful model for leading change comprises three levels of change action.[2] As you read about each of the three levels, think about those things you would like to change and perhaps some that need to change. Ultimately, it is you who will change—into an effective change agent leader who designs others' success.

> **Change** the process of becoming different yourself or fostering difference in other persons or things

Refine Your Capacity to Change Yourself (Level 1)

How do *you* deal with change? What can you do differently to enhance your capacity to drive that change? **Refining personal change capacity** refers to making modest changes in your own behavior that people notice and at the same time convince them to follow your lead. As a role model, even minor things help refine your capacity to lead. Setting an example by getting to work a little earlier each day, engaging subordinates in opportunities to innovate, or becoming more complimentary by recognizing innovative efforts among coworkers are all symbolic of convincing others that you are the real thing. Can you identify at least three changes you made in yourself over the past 12 months that have enhanced your capacity to drive change? Consider one thing you could do over the next month and do it.

> **Refining personal change capacity** modest changes in your own behavior that people notice and at the same time convince them to follow your lead during the change process

Initiate Incremental Change That Enhances Interpersonal Effectiveness (Level 2)

The term **incremental change** refers to that extra effort needed in order to build effective working relationships for gaining the confidence of those with whom your future success depends. The importance of designing relationships with others was highlighted in the previous module. Trusting relationships with your followers makes you more influential, and that influence will be necessary to persuade others that a specific change is worth the effort. Incremental changes provide others the opportunity to test change and assure a supportive relationship. What incremental changes can you introduce to prepare followers for greater change? How can you highlight the importance and value of these small changes? For example, having special recognition days in which individuals are acknowledged for

> **Incremental change** that extra effort needed in order to build effective working relationships for gaining the confidence of those with whom your future success depends

their innovative efforts creates an appreciation of change. Setting aside time for individuals to reflect upon their past change accomplishments elevates the value of the change to coworkers. Can you identify at least three things you could do to encourage small change and assure supportive relationships?

Advance Large-Scale Change in Organizational Structure, Culture, or Systems (Level 3)

Leading innovative efforts throughout an organization and putting together a network of new thinking throughout an organization comprises a large-scale change. **Large-scale change** is a more complex process that requires integrating a strategic vision into change initiatives that redirect attention to entirely new processes, systems, or structures. Large-scale change requires a more extensive level of innovation than those indicated in the above two levels. For example, reducing the levels of hierarchy in an organization, designing an entirely new product line, or initiating a work-sharing practice reflects innovative processes at Level 3. What large-scale change would you recommend that benefits an organization with which you work? If you had a magic wand, what would that change process look like?

Effecting change relies on leadership to make it happen. It has been often said that what gets done in an organization is what leaders attend to. If you can design a framework where innovation occurs systematically, your credibility will become apparent to others. As opportunities emerge, you must be vigilant to change yourself routinely, then at the next level to lead innovative efforts by building productive relationships, and finally at the highest level to redesign operational systems to streamline functions. The key role leaders play in the change process is what this chapter is all about. The next section will focus on how change not only impacts you but also how it affects people around you.

> **Large-scale change**
> a more complex change process that requires integrating a strategic vision into change initiatives that redirect attention to entirely new processes, systems, or structures

Change Yourself Before You Can Change Others

Learning Objectives

10.2 Determine how individuals experience change

10.3 Examine key aspects of change that impact your leadership

How you view change influences how you communicate, make decisions, and solve problems. Ultimately, your view of change determines how quickly you will adjust to it. Change often comes suddenly, and it can be overwhelming if you are not prepared. Fortunately, there are many things you can do to anticipate change. If you view change as an opportunity to move on in a different role, then seeking alternatives becomes part of your plan. Entering into a dialogue about the change with others is also important as this is an opportunity for you to see new directions for yourself. However, if you view change with anxiety, frustration, and fear, you will likely struggle in attempting to find meaning as to what has happened to you.

Individual Change in Stages

Change affects how people interact with you and each other as innovative practices, policies, and expectations come into existence. For example, such innovations as Amazon.com with online retailing, Costco with membership consumption, and Walmart with warehouse direct shopping have resulted in structural changes in daily operations. Such innovations have led to employees being retrained to acquire new skills, transferred to another facility, and promoted with new responsibilities. These changes may also feel like loss, resulting in followers going through the classic stages of grief: shock, anger, depression, and possibly leaving the organization. You as a leader need to be sensitive to the five stages that you personally, as well as colleagues and followers, will likely go through as you attempt to move from denial to acceptance of change (see Figure 10.1).[3]

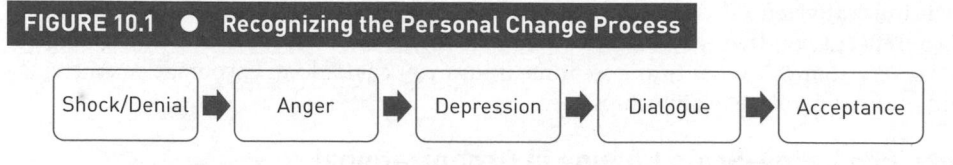

FIGURE 10.1 ● Recognizing the Personal Change Process

Shock/Denial ➡ Anger ➡ Depression ➡ Dialogue ➡ Acceptance

The first stage of *shock* or *denial* reflects an individual who is extremely confused and may blame others for what is happening. Following shock and denial is *anger*, whereby the individual has great anxiety, frustration, and embarrassment. The next stage is *depression*, which is characterized by being overwhelmed and helpless. This is where leadership is most needed and most influential. Moving from depression to dialogue, an individual begins to become more open to alternatives. As they continue *dialogue* with friends, cohorts, and others, the individual is ready to move on by *accepting* the need to explore options and place a new game plan into action.[4] As a leader, you may have witnessed those with whom you work not necessarily liking the change being undertaken. Individuals affected by radical change, such as losing a job, are likely to require your assistance for developing a new game plan.

The CORE™ attributes you are building are of great value to you in facing and working through change. Likewise, facilitating others to draw upon their confidence, optimism, resilience, and engagement will help them work through change. You may want to revisit some of the ways you can build these capacities (back in Chapter 1). One way to enhance resilience through a change is to commit to the change and craft a plan. Recall that the four CORE™ elements interact with and reinforce one another. Resilience can be strengthened by striving to remain optimistic, reinforcing your confidence, and fully engaging in the activities leading up to and through the change. You will need to be positive, focused, organized, and proactive rather than fight or run away from the change.

Understanding that change unfolds, and it results in somewhat predictable changes in individuals, empowers you to anticipate and prepare. How ready you are to convert these stages into personal action depends on how willing you are to change aspects of yourself by initiating a significant change in your own behavior. An intriguing and proactive model of personal behavior change is Prochaska's Model for Change.[5] This model, based on research in changing health behaviors, provides a practical guide for what individuals think and feel through the change process. Note that the actual change—the action—is only one of the five stages of the model, and that three stages come *before* any changing activity. The first stage, Pre-contemplation, is often overlooked in leadership. Individuals do not want to change because they do not even recognize that a change is merited, needed, or even possible. Thus, the earliest activities of a leader facilitating change should include pointing out all the possibilities for change—helping followers see differently (recall Chapter 8 on creativity)—what could be better, refined, reconsidered, or even simply noted.

The other stage of Prochaska's change process that is often overlooked is the final stage: Maintenance. People try to eat better, and then they do not; they try to quit smoking and pick it up again; they strive for work-life balance and slip back into working weekends. Change is challenging, and changing habits is even harder. But once the change has been made (especially after contemplation and preparation), individuals need a strategy, plan, and context to reinforce that change on a regular basis. When a change is dependent on individual willpower alone, it likely will not last. Leaders need to fully design change from before the need for change is even noticed to long after the change has occurred.

The prompting worksheet in the following exercise uses Prochaska's model to prompt you through a change, as well as assess where you are in the change process and consider your capacity to change. Think about a behavior that you would like to change about yourself—perhaps an unhealthy behavior such as arguing too much or engaging in conflict or being too negative—and follow the change process shown. See how things work out and what insights you find about changing yourself.

Exercise:
Prompting Change With Prochaska's Model
Note a change that you would like to make in your life: _____
Follow a Path to Personal Change

1. *Pre-contemplation* (Not Ready for Change): Generally, the first aspect which you are likely to feel is that of not being ready to change your behavior. This is what Prochaska depicts as "I won't" or "I can't." This is the time that you need someone who can work with you closely to understand your feelings. During this phase, you need to reflect on your own feelings without fear.

   Ask Self: Who has spoken to you about changing your behavior?

   List: Who can motivate me to change?

   Act: Talk to someone you trust about possibly changing your behavior.

2. *Contemplation* (Thinking About Change): This is the "I may" change, but I am not sure. At this stage, you are beginning to think about changing an unhealthy behavior. You need to gather some information to gain an understanding of the dimensions to such a change.

   Ask Self: What does my behavior look like to others?

   List: What are my reasons for wanting to change?

   Act: Talk to someone who has struggled and succeeded in making a change similar to one you are considering.

3. *Preparation* (Preparing for Action): This is the "I will" change. At this point, you begin to experiment with possible solutions. You realize you need a plan.

   Ask Self: What steps do I need to follow to change my behavior?

   List: Who will help keep me going when things get difficult?

   Act: Write out your plan and share it with a friend.

4. *Action* (Make Change Happen): This is the "I am" committed to implementing a change. You know what you have to do, so you begin to monitor your progress.

   Ask Self: What do I not have to give up when changing my behavior?

   List: What are those things that make me give up?

   Act: Avoid those things that make you want to give up.

5. *Maintenance* (Maintaining Your Changed Behavior): This is "I still am" committed to change. This phase begins when the new behavior change has become a habit and is done automatically. You are now confident that you can maintain the new behavior. In this stage, your own self-efficacy is both high and self-reinforcing.

   Ask Self: How can I continue with this behavior with ease?

   List: What are those things that will help keep me on track?

   Act: Ask someone you trust to keep track of your changed behavior.

Prochaska's Model of Change emphasizes your capacity for accessing information about effects of a proposed change, being moved emotionally to act, and reflecting how others are going to perceive you in the future. Therefore, making a commitment, being sensitive to cues around you to guide you in the right direction, and recruiting trusted friends to help you are all part of changing yourself. The storyline here is that you need to be able to first change yourself before you are likely to convince others to change aspects of themselves. Using your own example above, were you successful in changing aspects of your own behavior as a result of applying Prochaska's change model to your own situation?

Change Directly Affects Your Capacity to Lead Effectively

During a change process, you will learn a lot about yourself. Take a brief look at some situations where you may find yourself as change is implemented in the workplace. How would you personally react to each of these kinds of changes described below?

Be Reactive or Proactive

Remember how you felt and the stress upon you when you personally moved to a new school or neighborhood. As you just read, during the early stages of experiencing radical change, people generally feel fear, anxiety, and loss of control. A changing environment is like a problem to be solved. As you read in Chapter 8, problems can be approached in many ways, including reactive and proactive. A reactive approach, where you let an issue emerge before you act, frames change as a loss or threat. The opposite approach is being proactive whereby you plan for change before it occurs. A proactive approach frames change as a problem to be solved or even an opportunity to strategize a successful outcome. When you were subjected to a significant change in your life, how did you react? Were you a reactive victim of change, or a proactive strategic leader of change?

Gain or Lose Control Over Work Life

Change can evoke some intriguing reactions for those who appear to be losing control over their work life. One reaction is to continue to do those tasks the way they have always been done and to undercut the change process. This individual will likely resist change and make coworkers uncomfortable about accepting any change. Others, however, may desire to accelerate change by setting new goals and work routines to adjust to new conditions in the workplace. The challenge with change is that job routines remain to be done as a new system is designed and put into place. With two systems operating simultaneously, confusion and despair can become game changers. Discarding old ways of doing things is stressful. As a future leader, you need to be observant to the degree that coworkers deal with change. Here are four typical reactions by you and perhaps your coworkers as changes in how tasks are done are made:

- You embrace change in doing tasks to become better.

- You accept the need to do tasks differently although reluctantly.

- You resist changing at all and need some time to adjust.

- You are skeptical about doing tasks differently and undermine the change process.[6]

Adjust or Reject a Set of New Organizational Core Values

Changes in an organization's core values such as those arising from a merger or acquisition will directly impact upon your willingness to change. Depending on the size and impact of the innovation being proposed, typically employee engagement often declines initially when a change is actually proposed. However, as the process proceeds, employee engagement is likely to improve somewhat as the inevitable becomes apparent. In this regard, you—in a leadership role—are among the top drivers of employee engagement. In terms of organizational culture, the impact that you as a leader have on an organization's culture can be immense. This is the moment that the CORE™ attribute of *engagement* comes into play as individuals having conflicting personal and organizational values may need some interaction with their leaders. When designing others' success, the leader needs to be assured that coworkers are united in purpose for attaining the goals of the organization.

Transform How Careers Evolve

Typically, in the past, you entered an organization with the expectation of competing against your counterparts who are also attempting to move up the ladder of success. Particularly in a hierarchy, the path to success has been to work your way up the different levels of leadership (e.g. from supervisor to manager to director to senior leadership). As the career path emerges, the individual adjusts the career plan as new job openings become available. However, a change in the structure of an organization motivated by a merger, acquisition, or downsizing puts you at the mercy of external factors over which you have no control. As indicated earlier in the text, there appears to be some interest among new job entrants to stay in control of their careers by becoming freelance workers. In this regard, careers being multimodal, you will likely find yourself in a leadership role where employees may choose to work for more than one employer and thus receive more than one paycheck. The prevalence of a fluid workforce will challenge you when mobilizing resources for undertaking an innovative effort.

REFLECTION QUESTIONS

1. Think about some examples of how you have responded to change. Were you proactive or reactive? What could you have done differently to improve the process?

2. How do you feel about working in an organization where your core values are inconsistent with that of proposed changes in the way you operate? Can you give an example of when this has happened to you? How did you react and why?

3. How do you feel about becoming a freelance employee who works for more than one employer? How do you feel that will impact on your capacity to assume a leadership role?

Barriers to Change

Learning Objective

10.4 Identify common barriers to change

Organizations do not change unless the individuals within them change. Resistance to change at both the individual and organizational level is a normal response, so you need to plan for it, expect it, and accept it as part of the change process. People only change when they are Aware of the need for change and the alternatives, Desire the change, Know how to go about changing, are Able to implement the change on a day-to-day basis, and Reinforce the change so that it stays in place. This is called the **ADKAR model of change**, and many of the activities for successful individual and organizational change essentially follow these criteria.[7]

ADKAR model of change
This is a model of change starting with Awareness of a needed change, Desire to make the change, Knowledge about how to make the change, Ability to do so, and Reinforcement of the change once in place.

MYTH OR REALITY?

IMPLEMENTING CHANGE IS BASED ON USING ANALYTICAL TOOLS AND ALGORITHMS TO JUSTIFY MOVING IN A NEW DIRECTION.

Myth. Matthew Lieberman, a founding father of the field of social neuroscience, says this is a myth. In his book *Social: Why Our Brains Are Wired to Connect*, he points out that another driver of equal importance, if not greater, is the need to be socially involved in the change process by connecting to the values and expectations of others. A leader who knows what his or her staff really cares about will be able to succeed at change more effectively than one who is simply focused on the elements of a project.[8]

Thinking Rationally About Change May Not Work

Change from one thing to another is effectively a decision, and decisions are best if rationally calculated . . . right? As you may recall from Chapter 6 on decision-making, rational calculation is just one aspect of how decisions are made. Interestingly, it is not a lack of analytical skills but rather a lack of social skills among organizational leaders behind some of the biggest failures in organizations. If you are not good at understanding the needs of followers and their confidence levels, you are likely to develop a change strategy in a vacuum and thus fail. In fact, just 30 percent of change initiatives succeed, according to 15 years of data from McKinsey & Co.[9] Limiting your thinking to a rational analysis rather than social (or emotional) inhibits getting buy-in from followers who need to perceive how they fit into proposed changes.

If you adopt a mindset that discounts social cues, you are going to miss a lot of important information around you. A notable example of organizational failure is video game giant Atari, an early entrant in the video gaming industry in 1975. Rationally, the leaders in this company had the best technology at the time and thus gave little attention to social cues from both employees and customers by ignoring the increasing popularity of home computers for accessing such games. Other examples of notable failures are Blockbuster video, Kodak cameras, and Borders bookstores. Their leaders had rational plans for dominating their markets but again ignored the social aspects of their operations (employee input and customer feedback). Correspondingly, they failed to recognize that changing consumer preferences for online convenient access to video and reading materials would lead to their demise.

Not All Opportunities for Change Are Worth Taking

Change is about taking risks. The moment you stop looking for new opportunities, your organization is likely to become complacent. However, taking risks without thinking about consequences may be foolhardy. On the other hand, not taking risks may also be foolish since leadership is all about weighing the pros and cons of change for achieving something different. Therefore, a calculated risk is in order. **Calculated risk-taking** is making a decision that involves careful consideration of the possible outcomes. A calculated risk-taker has the following qualities:[10]

Calculated risk-taking making a decision that involves careful consideration of the possible outcomes

- Decisive, having good judgment as to whether information that is incomplete is sufficient for action;

- Analytical, being insightful when comparing the costs and benefits to a proposal;

- Predictive, using information to calculate the probability that actions will be successful.

Are you someone who can assess opportunities for change with a critical eye? Are you primarily driven by emotion, fear, or frustration? Or do you have confidence when taking on a challenge? Having a network of advisors in place to provide you with some objectivity is quite helpful. Realize that it is not feasible to pursue all proposals for change as you will likely be presented with numerous ideas for new approaches on how to operate. Moreover, once you initiate a change process, you may have to adjust your strategy as you may lose key personnel or the market may change. For example, it may be in your best interest to stop a current change proposal due to the emergence of a new technology that revolutionizes your industry.

Someone Will Resist the Change

As a change agent, you can expect to run into resistance from unexpected sources. For example, individuals who initially support your innovative idea may become active resistors over time. In addition, most significant change involves dealing with the power structure within an organization. Some people will gain influence while others will lose some. In addition, there is no guarantee that the change process you follow will work. Change is not only chaotic at times, it is quite unpredictable; all the planning in the world may not prevent failure from occurring. Therefore, the side effects to change are difficult to predict, maneuver, and manage. For example, change fatigue may set in over time. **Change fatigue** is a general state of disengagement from the change process due to natural cognitive, emotional, and social demands. When coworkers refrain from sharing or commenting on data generated during the change process or when progress reviews are not well attended, change agents should be on notice that an issue has arisen.[11] In this regard, you must be prepared to react to resistance, chaos, change fatigue, and other surprises that arise at times spontaneously. Table 10.1 notes some additional barriers to change. What could you do as a leader to overcome these barriers?

Change fatigue a general state of disengagement from the change process due to natural cognitive, emotional, and social demands

Leading Change

Learning Objective

10.5 Design a change strategy for implementation

You can unlock the keys to effective change. One fundamental key lies in rethinking the way in which you as a leader see yourself relative to your followers—focusing efforts on doing change *with* people rather than doing change to them. Based on interviews of leaders from 33 organizations, findings indicated that leader-centric behaviors, those shaping and

TABLE 10.1 ● Barriers to Change
1. Failing to be specific about the change
2. Failing to show why a change is important or necessary
3. Failing to allow those affected by the change to contribute to the planning
4. Using personal appeal to gain acceptance of change
5. Disregarding a work group's habit patterns
6. Failing to keep stakeholders informed about change
7. Failing to allay stakeholders' worries about possible failure
8. Creating excessive pressure/stress during change
9. Failing to deal with emotions and anxiety over individual issues during a change

controlling the actions of others, have an adverse impact on change implementation. In contrast, the behavior of leaders who are more facilitating and engaging is positively related to change success. The negative impact on change success of leader-centric behaviors (such as conflict, confusion, and resentment) was noted from data derived from their interviews, whereas more enabling behaviors (engaging and facilitating others) appear to promote a greater degree of successful change implementation.[12]

Transformational Versus Transactional Leadership

Your approach to your followers, and the way you fundamentally view your role in their life, represents one of the most consequential and influential aspects of leadership. Some leaders view their interaction with followers as a transaction: You (follower) work for me, and I (leader) pay you—a simple transaction that does not include anything beyond the terms of the agreement. In contrast, some leaders strive to maximize the success of followers—not just their success at work or for the organization, but their overall success as an individual—their personal fulfillment.

Transactional leadership
a process whereby those in leadership roles directly supervise change by setting clear objectives and goals for followers as well as by using either punishments or rewards in order to encourage compliance with these goals

Transformational leadership a change process in which leaders and followers help each other advance to a higher level of morale and motivation

Transactional leadership is defined as a process whereby those in leadership roles directly supervise change by the setting of clear objectives for their followers as well as the use of either punishments or rewards in order to encourage compliance with these goals.[13] In this regard, transactional change leaders also prefer to utilize rewards and punishment in traditional ways according to organizational expectations. Transactional leaders appeal to the self-interest of employees who seek out rewards for themselves, in contrast to transformational leaders, who appeal to group interests and notions of organizational success.

Transformational leaders strive to "*engage* with others in such a way that leaders and followers raise one another to higher levels of motivation and morality." According to James MacGregor Burns (you read about him way back in Chapter 1), **transformational leadership** is defined as a change process in which leaders and followers help each other advance to a higher level of morale and motivation.[14] The transformational approach creates significant change in the perceptions, values, expectations, and aspirations of employees. These include connecting the followers' sense of identity and self to the mission and the collective identity of the organization.

Transformational leaders focus on the higher order motivational needs of followers (i.e., helping followers and the organization reach full potential).[15] At the individual relationship level, transformational leaders appeal to followers' intrinsic motivation through what Bass and Avolio identified as four specific leadership actions:[16]

- *Individualized Consideration:* The leader respects each employee and pays attention to their individual needs. How would you as leader make every individual feel special, noticed, and/or relevant?

- *Intellectual Stimulation:* The leader provides tasks of considerable but possible challenge, encourages addressing problems in new ways, inspires critical thinking, and shares new ideas. How would you as leader keep every individual interested, intrigued, and positively challenged?

- *Inspirational Motivation:* The leader articulates an energizing vision that connects with each follower and provides a meaning for tasks at hand. How would you as leader infuse each individual with energy for the task, position, and organization?

- *Idealized Influence and Charisma:* The leader acts a role model for the employees, communicates and demonstrates a clear set of values, and builds trust and credibility. How are you as leader explicitly modeling the energy, engagement, and behavior you want in your followers or employees?

In practice, an effective leader influences others by modeling excellence, motivates others by emotionally connecting with them and steering their attention to the higher purpose, provides them with challenging and interesting work that is within their reach, and communicates the message that each individual is important, noticed, and considered by the leader. If what intrinsically motivates individuals is feeling competent (mastery) and feeling like they are doing something important (purpose), then having a transformational leader should significantly enhance the engagement of followers.

The transactional and transformational approaches can be applied to how you as a leader approach change. Table 10.2 discerns your preferred approach between the two. Use this to raise your awareness of the possible different approaches that could work best with followers.

Designing others' success relies on you to create a proactive work culture that instills pride, promotes involvement, and generates new ideas for change that becomes ingrained in an organization. The design process is a collaborative effort that results in mutual support and respect, meaningful work, and continual learning through timely feedback. In this regard, you will need to design a process that matches organizational and individual needs, moves innovative ideas forward by asking the right questions, and executes outcomes so all participants can see their contributions as part of a new reality.

Based on the premise that those leaders who act more as facilitators are generally more successful at change, four more keys to enhancing your effectiveness are also offered by Higgs and Rowland.[17] First, effective leaders are very self-aware of the importance of their physical presence to the change process. A second key is for you to learn everything there is to know about your organization, which involves mastering the politics of the workforce and in particular identifying those who will likely distort your ideas such as agitators, distractors, or combatants. Third, those effective at innovation are able to work in the moment, staying attentive to what is happening around them. A change that dramatically

---

TABLE 10.2 ● Your Current Leadership Framework for Designing Others' Success

Determine your current approach to leading change. Using an experience at work, in a community organization, or even on a class project where you have assumed a leadership role in the past, consider which of the two options you prefer. Place one check for each grouping.

1___ Be in control of the change process

2___ Empower others to take control of the change process

1___ Be reactive/responsive to solving problems as they arise

2___ Be proactive by addressing issues before they actually have to be resolved

1___ Prefer to work within the established organizational culture

2___ Prefer to work to change the existing organizational culture

1___ Administer rewards and/or punishments to get workers to achieve objectives

2___ Inspire others to achieve team objectives through pride and collegiality

1___ Motivate followers by appealing to their own self-interest

2___ Motivate followers by encouraging them to put group interests first

1___ Rather maintain the status quo and move cautiously to change

2___ Rather promote creative ideas to change continuously

Directions: Now add up your checks and place them in the scoring sheet below.

Number of #1 Responses _____

Number of #2 Responses _____

Note: If you had all your responses in #1, you have a transactional change approach.

If you had all your responses in #2, you have a transformational change approach.

If you had your responses split, you are basically a hybrid but likely leaning one way or the other.

increases organizational discomfort is doomed. Plan ahead by involving employees in planning changes. This will ameliorate some of the effects of change before you proceed. Fourth, effective change agents remain in tune with the bigger picture to ensure that the change process remains clearly connected to the wider audience. Resistance to change is likely at some point, but the above keys and a transformational approach should help tremendously.[18]

REFLECTION QUESTIONS

Having an insight that helps you grow in a leadership role can provide you with confidence that will help you endure through the bad times. Anybody can lead during good times. However, when things go bad, this is where your knowledge about effective leadership becomes critical. How can you distinguish yourself as a leader prepared for anything?

1. Identify at least three other companies or organizations that were well-known and are no longer in existence. Why did they fail? What can you learn from each that will help you in the future to not fail?

2. What is the most important thing that a leader has to know about confronting resistance during change process? Can you identify a time when you had considerable resistance to your change idea? How did you react?

Preparing to Execute Change

Change models used by those in leadership roles are important in that they set the stage for how individuals will go about achieving something new and different. Change by definition requires a new system and then institutionalizing the new approaches for getting things done.[19] While effective change depends on your mindset and approach as a leader, there are numerous models and strategies from which you can select to help you plan change execution.

As you prepare to implement any level of change whether personal, interpersonal, or organizational, you need (1) to operate within the work climate already in existence, (2) to adapt to the capacity or skill levels of your workforce, and (3) to identify the kind of support you will require for change to occur. One very helpful model is the Initiation, Implementation, Institutionalization (I3) model noted in Table 10.3 with prompting questions. This model can be used in advance to plan out the important elements and variables, or it can be revisited during a change process to reconsider the approach and improve the process.

TABLE 10.3   ●   The I3 Change Process With Prompting Questions[20]
Initiation
What is the need?
What is the vision of the end state?
What is the vision or model of how the process will unfold?
Who are your advocates?
What steps need to be prepared?
Implementation
Who communicates what to whom, when, and how?
Who should/could be part of the decision-making (i.e., *control*)?

Who/What will be supportive? And who/what opposed?
What technical assistance will be needed?
What intrinsic and/or extrinsic rewards could be engaged?

Institutionalization

How can the association between need and change be reinforced?
What assessment methods can inform further development?
How can the change be widened to include others/other areas?
What competing priorities/activities exist?
What policies need to be changed to make the change part of *doing business*?
Who are strong advocates that can offer continuing assistance/reinforcement?

When people are truly invested in change, it is 30 percent more likely they will be successful.[21] Leaders today need to make decisions quickly in a fast-paced environment where having competitive advantage comes to those who can set new priorities and implement change more quickly than their rivals. Perceiving yourself as being prepared at the start will bring along followers who are dedicated, strong, decisive, and organized.

LEADERSHIP BY DESIGN

Design Principle: Stickiness

Definition: The degree to which an idea, expression, product, or service is dramatically recognized, recalled, and/or shared with others.[22]

In Other Words: Designs that stick are remembered.

For Example: How can you make sure people remember your store? Try using an address that looks like someone dove into the wall and got stuck! Closer to home, college admissions tour guides work hard to ensure that your campus experience *sticks*. They use attention-grabbing elements of surprise, emotion, and storytelling to create a memorable experience.

For Leaders: Leaders designing success for others, particularly through a change process, need new ideas to stick. Anything that can be seen, heard, or touched can have an element of stickiness. To increase the memorability of a change, keep messaging succinct, yet thoughtful.

Consider what exactly you need to stick. Use the elements of SUCCESS: Simplicity, Unexpectedness, Concreteness, Credibility, Emotions, Stories, and Sincerity to increase the stickiness.[23] You may know what you want your audience to recall, but it is equally as

Courtesy of the author

STICKINESS AND SUCCESS

important to think about what you *do not* want them to remember, and make sure those items are not sticky.

Executing Change for Others' Success

Like any good design process, a good change process is iterative. In other words, as you execute the change you are constantly assessing, improving, and altering activities. A great change process strives to ensure others' success as much as achieving the change, since practically they are one and the same. Suppose you have been at a university for four years and have never met any administrator over that period. You could not recognize the president, provost, or even the dean of the college in which your major exists. You would like to create an innovative mechanism that would enable students to connect directly with such administrators face-to-face throughout a semester. You recognize this as a Level 3 change effort in which you are attempting to modify organizational culture in the way students and administrators connect. You could execute that change using an excellent model, such as John Kotter's foundational eight-step change model.[24] Detailed explanations of Kotter's model provide a very powerful tool for executing change. Adding a design frame enhances that process by focusing on the success of others through that change process (see Figure 10.2).

Justify an Opportunity to Act by Creating an Urgency for Change

The initial step in any change process is to justify that an opportunity exists. This involves gathering data from as many sources as possible to conceptually understand the need for change. As a design thinker, this is the opportunity to accurately define the challenge you are taking on by making sense of all the information you have gathered. In order to craft a clear definition of the issue at hand, you require data. Alternatives for gathering data digitally are conducting online interviews with current administrators, generating a Facebook discussion group, or placing a survey online for students, administrators, and faculty to participate, among others. You decide to create an online forum where you can interact with administrators and students directly for getting ideas about how to proceed.

Collaborate With Those Affected by Forming a Coalition

Now you realize you need to identify individuals who are likely to be affected by your innovative strategy. You must convince them that change is necessary on your campus.

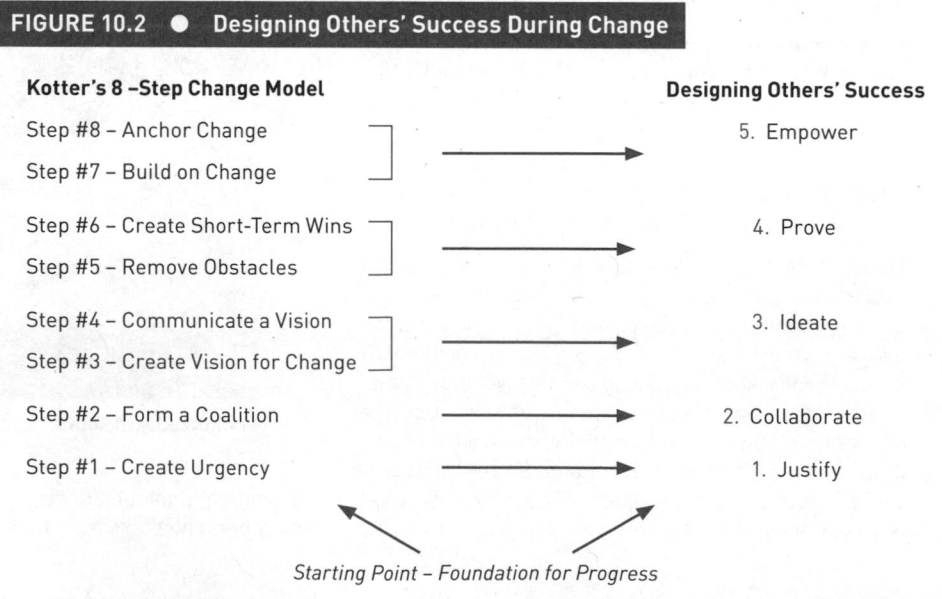

FIGURE 10.2 ● Designing Others' Success During Change

Kotter's 8–Step Change Model	Designing Others' Success
Step #8 – Anchor Change ⎤ Step #7 – Build on Change ⎦	5. Empower
Step #6 – Create Short-Term Wins ⎤ Step #5 – Remove Obstacles ⎦	4. Prove
Step #4 – Communicate a Vision ⎤ Step #3 – Create Vision for Change ⎦	3. Ideate
Step #2 – Form a Coalition	2. Collaborate
Step #1 – Create Urgency	1. Justify

Starting Point – Foundation for Progress

These individuals also will be those to whom you send out survey forms and connect with digitally, and so forth, as indicated in the first step. You decide to put together a leadership coalition of key administrators, faculty members, and students for designing actual questions for gathering data. You realize you need to understand the people with whom you will be working as well as those who will be impacted once the change is implemented. Having a change project leadership team in place will enable you to identify pockets of resistance as well as those who will support you.

Ideate and Communicate Possibilities Through a Clear Vision for Change

Using the divergent-thinking process, individuals working in teams build on each other's ideas for arriving at an innovative change idea. This step is about using your imagination to generate a wide range of ideas for solving an issue—and not simply determine the one most apparent. Based on the data obtained from your digital forums, online surveys, and interviews, three alternative solutions are proposed by your leadership team. One is to have a daily administrator-on-call online (similar to a physician's office). A second alternative is to schedule online meetings with a variety of students each month. Finally, a third possibility is to have special ask-the-administrator online chat sessions on the university website. This part of the change process encourages **lateral thinking**, defined here as having individuals step beyond the obvious solutions.[25] Getting back to the change project, in addition to the alternatives indicated above, another atypical solution could be using e-mail or posting notes to a Facebook discussion group for enhancing communication. Having the capacity for students to directly connect to administrators more frequently on their own time schedule is reflective of extending the conversation beyond the obvious.

Lateral thinking attempting to look at a situation from a unique or unexpected point of view; having individuals step beyond the obvious solutions

REFLECTION QUESTIONS

The capabilities of new technologies allow leaders and followers to communicate more quickly, more broadly, and more personally. In what ways might you utilize technology to provide just-in-time feedback? Build empathy, community, and shared purpose? Demonstrate progress?[26] Enhance any of the specific steps of the change process?

Prove the Change Is Acceptable

Ensuring that the changes proposed are realistic and compatible with existing organizational values, norms, and goals is critical if they are going to be ingrained into a new work culture. Pretesting the effects of alternatives allows for flexibility for possibly changing direction without committing excessive time, energy, and resources. Eliciting feedback from colleagues is a great way to get everyone involved. This is also an excellent time to gain an understanding of people you are designing the change for. This is similar to pilot testing the solution with a small group of individuals for gaining insight as to whether you are on the right track or not. After analyzing all of your findings, after collecting data by means of your surveys and interviews, you decide to experiment with the innovative idea of having a *provost-on-call* for an online discussion for one hour per week per month.

Empower Others to Implement and Build

After pilot testing a solution, you and your leadership group decide that having an online administrator forum once a month at the provost's level is feasible. However,

Project management
the application of knowledge, skills, tools, and techniques to a broad range of activities in order to meet the requirements of a particular project

you know that nothing will happen unless the necessary work is done to implement the proposed change. You put together a project management team to get the innovative strategy to actually happen. **Project management** is defined as the application of knowledge, skills, tools, and techniques to a broad range of activities in order to meet the requirements of a particular project.[27] Managing a project includes (a) putting together a team charter outlining the tasks to be completed, the budget required, and the deadlines for delivering important outcomes, and delegating authority to make decisions; (b) launching the implementation plan by identifying expectations of everyone in the change process and alerting stakeholders as to what is coming; (c) verifying that deadlines are being met according to actual implementation plans adopted; and (d) assessing the effects of the change process completed and the outcomes achieved. You also anchor the new practice of engaging an administrator by assigning a staff member to monitor the practice each day.[28]

While each step is critical, the task of getting others as advocates for the change process will make or break your effort. A large aspect of design thinking focuses on the human factor, that is, getting others engaged in the process of thinking about change. Therefore, Step #2 relating to understanding the needs and desires of those around you forms the backdrop for effective action. Without the support of your subordinates or coworkers, change at best will only be temporary.

LEADERSHIP BY DESIGN

Design Principle: Progressive Disclosure

Definition: A strategy for managing information complexity in which only necessary, requested, or user-understandable information is displayed at any given time.[29]

In Other Words: People get overwhelmed when they see too much information at once.

For Example: Having multiple small quizzes leading up to a final exam is not a form of punishment from your professor; it is a way to introduce students to the concepts a little bit at a time. Progressively disclosing prevents information overload.

For Leaders: When it comes to eliciting change, leaders and followers undergo many different phases: awareness of the need to change, desire to participate and support change, knowledge of how to change, what that change looks like, implementing the change, and then reinforcing it to keep the change in place. To facilitate this complex series of steps, use progressive disclosure with your followers to ensure only the necessary information is provided at any given stage. This does not mean keep secrets. Share the big picture and

©iStock.com/Steve Debenport

PROGRESSIVE DISCLOSURE

be transparent; but do not expect deep, focused understanding of everything at once.

Break tasks and information into small, understandable and achievable chunks. How can you, for example, teach unskilled people how to accomplish something as big as building a house? Hide options that are not essential at the moment and teach people as they go. Progressively disclosing big changes will help leaders design others' success.

Sustain Momentum and Resilience After Change Is Implemented

Perhaps the most challenging and frustrating aspect of change is how quickly and easily things can change back. How does one sustain the change? Maintaining a change once implemented also requires planning, persistence, and collaboration. Establishing an inclusive, positive working environment to involve as many individuals as possible for designing others' success is important to ensure a strong finish and an institutionalization of the change.[30] Most change plans fail to adequately anticipate internal resistance and other unforeseen factors that cause change to derail over time. Most resistance to change remains underground as managers and employees decide whether to support change, wait it out, or undermine it through inaction and sarcasm. Passive resistance is not lethal in small doses, but over time, it leads to a crippling of the change results. As a change agent, you need to create an organizational culture that reflects a rhythm for change, similar to how lyrics and a musical score, when put together properly, endure endlessly. Initially, having a work culture that performs in a rhythmic pattern sets the stage for accepting change.

Having change as an everyday expectation makes it easier to sustain it. Second, identifying and nourishing those individuals who both accept and initiate change themselves provides inspiration for others to follow along the same path. Creating an organizational culture that embraces change and nurturing change agents go hand in hand. To sustain change in an organization requires establishing an organizational DNA whereby change becomes a constant in the everyday flow of activities. You can reinforce sustaining change by holding a series of post-change meetings to keep on top of how things are progressing. In this regard, you must make certain that the infrastructure (e.g., performance management and reward systems) supports the continuation of the change and makes returning to the previous state less attractive. Having special recognition for those who excel in demonstrating the positive effects of the changes implemented will model an appreciation for follow through and outstanding productivity. Finally, you can celebrate successes along the way, not just final outcomes. People who see the connection between behaviors and outcomes are much more willing to embrace the desired change and sustain it over time. This keeps the focus on the achievement of the desired behavior in the short term as well as in the long term.[31]

Chapter Summary

Designing others' success is rooted in change as your charge as a leader involves facilitating others, and the organization, to become something better than before. Change is fundamentally a people process. Organizations do not change unless the individuals within them change. To achieve and sustain change, those in leadership roles need to look for new approaches for inspiring others to follow their lead. Change can be considered at three levels: personal, incremental, and large-scale.

Individual change happens in stages, which includes how people think about things (cognitive), how they feel (emotional), and how they interact with the leader and one another (social). Most people are uncomfortable with change and can initially react in very negative ways. The Prochaska model can help prompt individual change

from initial awareness of a need for change all the way through maintaining a successful change.

Resistance to change at the individual level translates to challenges implementing change at the organizational level. The general ADKAR model can help remind leaders where followers are in their change process. Change fatigue, overreliance on rationality, and failure to fully consider the risks are just some of the many barriers to effecting change.

Transformational leaders are contrasted with transactional leaders by their focus on advancing each follower to be their best self, versus simple compliance and organizational goal attainment. Adopting a transformational leadership approach, along with other interpersonal factors, comprises an initial step in executing change.

The I3 and Kotter models of change execution provide concrete steps for planning, executing, and maintaining organizational change efforts. Adding a design framework further highlights the transformational human aspect of the change process.

It takes a special person to lead change efforts. Suggesting change is rather easy, but implementing change is challenging. You will need to continue to develop your CORE™ to persevere through to successful change and design others' success.

Key Terms

CORE™ Attribute Builders: Build Now for Future Leadership Challenges

Attribute: Confidence

Builder: Align your strengths—take on a change challenge

Test your capacity to take on changing something of interest to you. First, align your change mindset, whether transformational, transactional, or a hybrid. Generate alternatives for solving either a person, interpersonal, or organizational issue confronting you today. Using the five-step design-thinking framework, along with the Kotter model that you learned in this chapter, select something that you would like to change on campus, at work, or in a community organization where a team of individuals is involved. Here is your guide:

1. Step #1—Justify the Challenge—(Level 1) (Level 2) (Level 3)—Give specifics

2. Step #2—Form a Coalition—Gather data from numerous sources

3. Step #3—Ideate Possible Solutions—Think laterally about alternatives

4. Step #4—Prototype for Credibility—Pretest alternatives for practicality

5. Step #5—Empower Others to Implement— Take a transformational or transactional role— Get your final alternative to work

Be prepared to discuss with others what worked and what did not work. As a result of this experience, how do you see yourself leading change?

Skill Builder Activity

Reflect upon a significant change you personally experienced while at work, at home, or at school. What was the change process? Was the leader transactional or transformational when acting as a change agent? How did you feel about the change process followed? What would you have done differently in bringing about that change if you were the leader at that time?

Skill Builder Activity

Learn from others how they addressed a change in their organization. Below are four organizations that have changed significantly in terms of moving from their original mission to a new product line. Select any one of the following and put together a profile of the process the leader used to change the behavior of those surrounding him or her. Was it a transformational change style or transactional—or perhaps a hybrid model? Put together a report no more than three pages long analyzing the process used and what you learned from this investigation.

Possible Alternatives to Select One for Study and Analysis

Netflix—starting as a DVD in the mail service to streaming of video/TV shows

Google—moving from a search engine to telephone access to cloud storage services

National Geographic—moving from a magazine to producing TV shows on Discovery and other channels

Nokia—transforming itself from a rubber producing company to cell phone distributor

Skill Builder Activity

Take a moment and study the leadership change style of specific individuals who have inspired others to stay on the cutting edge of their field. They challenged the status quo and generated solutions that others never thought of in their field. Select one of the following and determine how they were so different in their approach to be successful:

Anna Maria Chavez—CEO of Girl Scouts of America: How did she revamp an organization with a great history into the 21st century with a new direction?

Mark Cuban (Shark Tank TV)—CEO of Dallas Mavericks basketball team: Each basketball game is sold out. How did he change team marketing efforts to make millions of dollars?

Bill James—Sports Analyst: An analyst who discovered new approaches for helping sports teams, specifically in baseball, utilize data to produce winning seasons. How did he use design thinking to put together a strategy to convince others that he has the winning formula to be successful in baseball?

Marissa Mayer—Yahoo CEO: How did she change Yahoo from basically an e-mail service to a major advertiser of business services?

Design Culture
and Community

Over the past 10 chapters you have focused on designing yourself, your followers, and your relationship with them. Module 4 expands your leadership lens beyond the individuals involved to focus on the organization as a whole. Individuals make up an organization, but the organization also makes up the individuals. Here is a simple example: Holiday dinner with the family.

No matter who you are and how you act as an individual, when you return home for a holiday dinner with your family, there is a general feeling that influences everyone to act a certain way, to be a certain person. This applies regardless of where or what you call home, what your family looks like, and whatever holiday/special occasion you gather to celebrate. You feel the vibe, the relationships run deep, and the culture supersedes individual behavior. Simply put, culture is the way we do things. All groups have a culture—teams, organizations, communities . . . and families—a set of rules that defines the group. Culture happens, but a good leader *designs the culture* to influence others toward a common vision. The chapters in this section will guide your design of culture, with a special emphasis on leading effective teams and creating a culture that cares.

Recall Jim Collins's Level 5 leader from Chapter 2—the leader who brought great resolve coupled with humility in order to make the leap from good to great. Achieving that balance requires you to simultaneously appreciate the extraordinary complexity in the world and in most things, while disciplining yourself to have *piercing clarity*[1] about what you are passionate about and at what you are best. Now, consider a soccer team where

- Only 4 of the 11 players on the field would know which goal is theirs.

- Only 2 of the 11 would care.

- Only 2 of the 11 would know what position they play and know exactly what they are supposed to do.

- And all but 2 players would, in some way, be competing against their own team members rather than the opponent.[2]

Hardly a recipe for success. Yet Stephen Covey, in his book *The 8th Habit*, describes a poll of 23,000 employees drawn from a number of companies and industries. He reports the poll's findings:

- Only 37 percent said they have a *clear understanding* of what their organization is trying to achieve and why.

- Only one in five was *enthusiastic* about their team's and their organization's goals.

- Only one in five said they had a *clear line of sight* between their tasks and their team's and organization's goals.

- Only 15 percent felt that their organization *fully enables* them to execute key goals.

- Only 20 percent *fully trusted* the organization they work for.[3]

These numbers are the same as those of the dysfunctional soccer team and are clearly a problem for any leader.

Take a look at those elements again (in italics above), paraphrased here:

1. Clear understanding of purpose

2. Enthusiasm for goals

3. Clear connection between actions and goals

4. Fully enables to act

5. Trust one another

Strategic Planning

Strategic planning
the process by which an organization (a) clarifies (identify, develop, refine) values and vision; (b) translates those into goals; and then (c) creates action plans or strategy to achieve those goals

Effective leaders certainly can address each of these elements separately because they are each critical to individual and organizational success. But what if there were a larger process that conceptualized these elements as parts of a bigger whole? Fortunately, there is such a process—it is called strategic planning (among other names). **Strategic planning** is the process by which an organization (a) clarifies (identify, develop, refine) values and vision, (b) translates those into goals, and then (c) creates action plans or strategy to achieve those goals. Action plans generally include an analysis of the external and internal context and resources, activities tied to a specific goal or subgoal, a description of what success will look like, who is responsible, the timeline of activities, the resources needed, and how goal achievement will be assessed. Figure M4.1 (shown below) helps illustrate.

At first, strategic planning may appear to be a very logical, straightforward process. As explained, the process is quite simple. However, in practice strategic planning requires a good deal of time, focus, and thought. Consider how long it would take you to generate *your* core values and vision for your future and then to translate them into concrete action steps. Now multiply that by the number of individuals who comprise an organization—because together you are seeking a shared vision. The time and effort, though, is well worth it; strategic planning results in a clearer understanding of purpose and a clear connection between actions and goals (Items 1 and 3 above). The discussions, thinking,

---

FIGURE M4.1 ● Strategic Planning

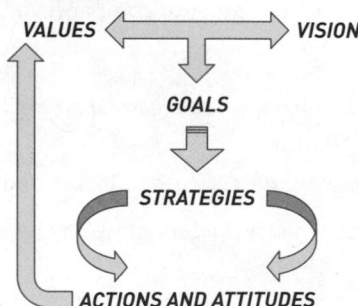

and decision-making done throughout the process bring individuals together in a shared understanding of both how they see the organization as well as how well they know and trust one another. In other words, strategic planning builds culture; and a well-designed and well-executed strategic planning process comprises a very powerful way leaders can design culture.

Strategic planning is like the creative problem-solving process introduced throughout this text. First, you must *understand* your organization, then you must *imagine* how to best achieve the goals and vision, and finally you craft a plan for *implementing* those activities. The process can be applied to designing culture and the path forward for organizations of any size, even groups of strangers seeking to build community and a shared vision. For example, a Collective Action Toolkit can be used to facilitate community leaders in a range of problem-solving and strategic planning activities.[4] As you can see from Figure M4.2, understanding, imagining, and implementing are all part of the process that centers around the shared goal.

As you continue developing your effective leader toolkit, strategic planning introduces a whole new set of tools that can be used to more effectively execute each phase of the process. Some of these tools have already been introduced, such as the creativity and idea-generating techniques to facilitate the Imagine phase that you learned about in Chapter 8. Before you move into this section's chapters that focus on the broader scope of culture, here are a few tools to help you better see how culture can be helpful. Strategic planning begins with understanding—first the organization and then the organization relative to the internal and external context. Organizational management legend Peter Drucker developed a self-assessment tool that poses five *most important*

FIGURE M4.2   ●   Collective Action Toolkit from Frog Design

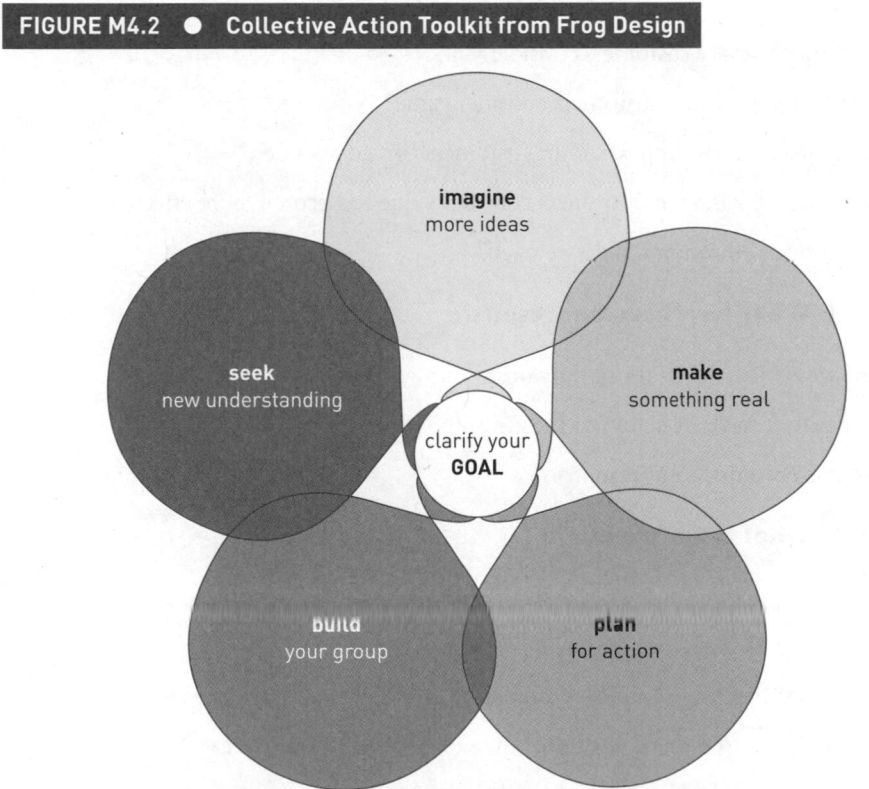

Source: Frog Design Inc. (2012). *Collective action toolkit: Groups make change* (p. 4).

questions (with many related prompts) from which organizational members can begin understanding themselves.[5] How many of these questions can you readily answer about an organization with which you work?

The Five Drucker Questions

Question 1: What is our mission?

What are we trying to achieve?

What specific results are we seeking?

What are our major strengths?

What are our major weaknesses?

Does our mission need to be revisited?

Question 2: Who is our customer?

Who are our primary customers?

Who are our supporting customers?

Have our customers changed?

Should we add or delete some customers?

Question 3: What does the customer consider value?

What do our primary customers consider value?

What do our supporting customers consider value?

How well are we providing what our customers consider value?

How can we use what our customers consider value to become more effective?

What additional information do we need?

Question 4: What have been our results?

How do we define results for our organization?

To what extent have we achieved these results?

How well are we using our resources?

Question 5: What is our plan?

What have we learned and what do we recommend?

Where should we focus our efforts?

What, if anything, should we do differently?

What is my plan to achieve results for my group/responsibility area?

What is our plan to achieve results for the organization?

REFLECTION QUESTIONS

Relook at the five important questions posed by Drucker. How would you answer each of those if you were examining your own leadership?

What is *your* mission? Who is *your* customer? What does the customer consider value? What have been *your* results? What is *your* plan?

Understanding your organization starts with introspective and aspirational questions like those posed by Drucker. The next step in understanding entails carefully examining the real and present internal and external attributes of the organization. A **SWOT analysis** is a strategic planning and decision-making tool used to evaluate the current Strengths, Weaknesses, Opportunities, and Threats relevant to an organization or specific situation that requires understanding. The typical SWOT matrix looks like Figure M4.3, illustrating the four categories for which you would analyze the organization. The SWOT analysis tool is simple to understand but very complex and powerful. A thorough SWOT analysis of your organization will yield both an assessment of current capacity as well as a glimpse of what might be possible.

SWOT analysis a strategic planning and decision-making tool used to evaluate the current Strengths, Weaknesses, Opportunities, and Threats relevant to an organization or specific situation that requires understanding

FIGURE M4.3 ● SWOT Analysis Matrix

	Positive/Helpful	Negative/Harmful
Internal: Attributes of the organization	Strengths	Weaknesses
External: Attributes of the environment outside the organization	Opportunities	Threats

REFLECTION QUESTIONS

Again, reinterpret an organizational tool like SWOT into a tool for better understanding yourself. You have likely already assessed your (internal) Strengths and Weaknesses. What are your external Opportunities? Your external Threats?

Identifying opportunities and mapping out how to pursue and attain those opportunities are the primary and most straightforward aim of strategic planning. Quite often leaders plan reactively based on immediate problems and challenges, rather than starting with values and vision to clarify what actions make the most sense. As Peter Drucker famously stated, "Doing the right thing is more important than doing the thing right."[6] The Drucker questions and the SWOT analysis are just two of many tools that can help identify the values, vision, mission, and specific goals your organization seeks. From this point the challenge is to craft a plan for meeting those goals. Typically, this step is called action planning, which involves working through the questions in Figure M4.4 for each goal.

FIGURE M4.4 ● Action Planning

Goal	Actions	Owner	Timeline	Resources Needed	Assessment Criteria
What is the specific goal?	What activities need to happen to reach the goal?	Who is responsible for leading, coordinating, and monitoring this activity?	What are the specific time goals for each activity and final goal?	What time, personnel, funds, or other resources are needed?	What does success look like, and how will progress be assessed?

Action plans can include many other categories to clarify the process. These might include a breakdown of long- and short-term goals, broad and subgoals, rationale for each goal, stakeholders involved or impacted by the activities, necessary partners or collaborations, and next steps or future actions after the goal is attained. Because strategic planning significantly catalyzes organizational progress, countless templates and technology-based tools have been developed to facilitate the process. However, there is no substitute for the actual time spent thinking and discussing among organization members.

One very useful tool that will help prompt action planning is the POWER Up method (see Figure M4.5). POWER is an acronym that stands for Positives, Objections, What else, Enhancements, and Remedies.[7] As you talk through possible actions to reach a goal, some of those ideas may be difficult to put into practice. The POWER Up method asks you to list out all of the Positive outcomes of that idea, then all the possible Objections that others might raise. Then, similar to effective creative problem-solving, the method asks you to set your idea aside for a moment and generate more ideas (What else?). Returning to the original idea (or another if you found a better one), you then revisit the list of Positives to discuss what Enhancements you could make to the idea. Finally, addressing the list of Objections, what Remedies would help address those objections?

FIGURE M4.5 ● POWER Up Method to Prompt Action Planning

The idea/solution: _____

Positives	Objections	What else?	Enhancements	Remedies
Positive outcomes of that idea:	Possible objections to that idea:	Additional ideas/solutions:	Ways to enhance those outcomes:	Ways to address those objections:

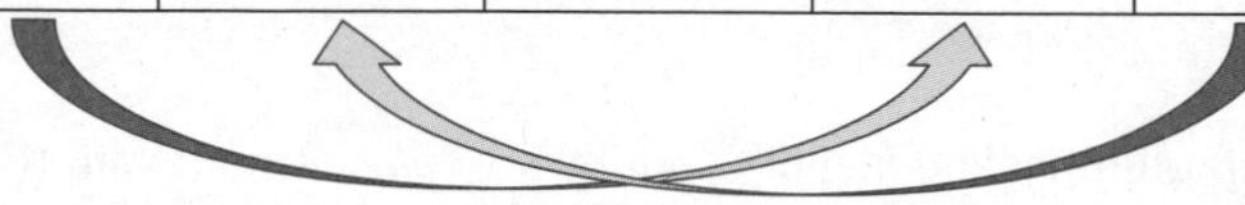

Strategic planning can be as fun as it is useful, and building in elements of culture (How do we all *want* to do things around here?) addresses the complete picture of what drives organizational success: the plans and the people. Highlighting what is amazing in your organization, what lofty and fantastic things you might achieve, and clarifying the ideal can add extraordinary energy to a strategic planning process. As a leader, it is about what you do and how you do it (recall Rule #1), all while making it about the organization's success and positive culture (Rule #2: It's not about you.). You will find that this balance continues to require your attention as you make your way through the chapters in this module: Chapter 11 on Culture, Chapter 12 on Leading a Team, and Chapter 13 on Designing a Culture That Cares.

Culture

In our early years, we didn't talk about culture much. We just built a business that we wanted to work in. And, that was great. But the real return on culture happened when we started getting more deliberate about it. By writing it down. By debating it. By taking it apart, polishing the pieces and putting it back together. Iterating. Again. And again.

—Dharmesh Shah

Culture eats strategy for breakfast.

—Peter Drucker

Learning Objectives

11.1 Compare culture from a personal, organizational, and societal perspective

11.2 Define an organization's culture and its subcultures

11.3 Examine societal cultures as they relate to organizational members' roles

11.4 Explain the leader's role in culture

11.5 Identify how values inform organizational culture

11.6 Describe the differences between organizational vision, mission, and values and how they relate to culture

11.7 Describe the various ways in which organizational culture can be designed

Detailed Chapter Outline

Leadership by Design Model

Design Self

How can I design myself as a leader?

Design Relationships

As a leader, how can I design my relationships with others?

Design Others' Success

As a leader, how can I design success for others?

DESIGN CULTURE

AS A LEADER, HOW CAN I DESIGN THE CULTURE OF MY ORGANIZATION?

Design Future

As a leader, how can I innovate?

Introduction

If you were asked to explore another culture, you would likely start thinking about where you were going to travel. The popular notion of culture brings forth images of foreign lands and native peoples with extremely different foods, clothing, language, housing, and other obvious visible characteristics. As you will learn in this chapter, the latter image is only a small example of culture, in terms of both where culture lies and what it entails. Here is another example that illustrates the depth and breadth of culture. Have you ever moved to a new neighborhood, joined a new group or club, switched schools, or started a new job with an established organization? If you have, you undoubtedly felt confused and a bit uncomfortable at first. You felt this way because you stepped into another culture.

Culture is a set of shared assumptions that guides the behavior of members of an organization of any size, from a small group of friends to a workplace to the larger society. Culture is the way things are done around here. Many of those things are invisible and unspoken. No one wrote them down; no one explained them to you. You are just expected to behave in accordance with the established culture. And until you do so, you are going to feel a bit out of place, uncertain, and uncomfortable.

Effective leaders design culture intentionally, establishing the values, norms, and beliefs that guide group members' daily behavior within the organization, as well as their interactions with those outside the organization. Culture within an organization can be deeply rooted as members of the organization share learning experiences that provide meaning to both themselves and the organization. As a leader, it will be important for you to ensure that there is a good fit between your values and the values and beliefs embraced by the members of the organization. This chapter assists you in understanding the origins and nature of culture for you personally, at the organizational and societal level, and how you as a leader can design and change culture.

Culture surrounds you every day, in every group to which you belong—your family, school, work, community, and the larger society. Maybe you only think about it when you see or meet someone from a *very* different culture from your own—someone who does not look or behave in the same way as you. In college, you may meet quite a few of those individuals, or you may experience cultural differences in the ways in which groups do things differently than you are used to. Maybe you selected a particular college because of its culture or the values that it articulates. Did you pick the party school, the religious institution, or maybe a field-specific university? However you selected your school, there was a cultural component that was in some way attractive to you.

In this chapter, you will learn how culture permeates every group, organization, and society; come to understand why it is important to you now and in the future; and learn how you can design and change culture. It is also important to learn how your personal and organizational values inform culture, how cultures originate, and most importantly, how you can design and change your group or organization's culture in the future.

LEADERSHIP THAT MAKES A DIFFERENCE

Imagine being a first grader walking an hour home from school to a remote village in the jungles of Bangladesh, crying the whole way because the teacher smacked your hands with a cane because you would not speak up when asked a question. But you could not speak up because you did not understand the teachers—your native language was Marma, and the teachers were speaking Bengali. It seems pointless for you to attend school since you do not understand the teacher, nor can you read the textbooks, so you beg your mother not to send you back to school. She finally agrees; however, you have to continue studying at home. You studied at your mother's side learning the Bengali language and went back to school four years later.

This is the story of Maung Nyeu, now a doctoral candidate working on his dissertation at Harvard University. Maung Nyeu was a first-grade dropout.

Decades-long internal strife in Bangladesh led to the resettlement of a significant number of the indigenous people of Chittagong Hill (where Maung grew up)—primarily to India. In fact, one night, when he was six years old, Maung and his family heard gunshots and were warned by the village headmaster to run, and into the jungle they escaped. The next day, they saw both their village and the Buddhist temple nearby burned to the ground. Tens of thousands of indigenous people fled to escape the civil war and social marginalization. When the children who had settled in refugee camps in India returned to their native Chittagong Hill, it was apparent that they had not been in school. Moreover, with Bengali now the official language, they lost most of what they knew of their native language. So too had Maung Nyeu.

Today, the schoolchildren continue to struggle with language issues. Less than 28% of individuals in Maung's village are literate, with 60% of students dropping out of primary school and even more dropping out in the higher grades. Maung was one of the lucky ones who won a scholarship to a residential school far from his home, and he was ultimately able to get into Harvard University and obtain his master's degree and work on his PhD. Still, he does not know how to write in his own language, like many of the children of his village.

So, he wanted to give back. In 2009, along with other community members, he opened a school and 12 students attended. Six years later, as a residential school on the grounds of a Buddhist Temple, the school serves 650 students, and Marma and other native languages are taught along with Bengali.

One issue that always bothered him was the absence of native stories from the Marma culture and for the children's lives to be validated (textbooks in Bengali barely referenced the indigenous people like him). He decided to do something about it. Tim Brookes, a faculty member at Champlain University and fiction writer, is passionate about saving vanishing languages through his project Endangered Alphabets.[8] He was excited to meet Maung and collaborate with him on a cultural preservation project. Endangered Alphabets is about preserving cultural identity: "In countries all over the world, members of indigenous cultures have their own spoken and written languages—languages they have developed to express their own beliefs, their own experiences, and their understanding of the world."[9]

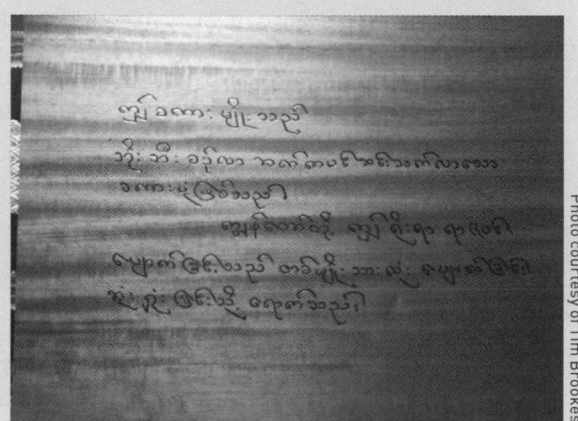

Photo courtesy of Tim Brookes

MARMA LANGUAGE IN MYANMAR SCRIPT

When the children attending Maung's school go home for vacation, they listen to the stories that their grandparents tell, practice the stories, and then tell them again when they return to school. Each story is captured on film and when Maung returns to Harvard with them, they are transcribed into Marma, illustrated, and a book is returned to the school. Because they have been so marginalized, it is important for the students to see that they have a voice and that their stories are as important as everyone else's. Now they are important, now they have a voice. Through his leadership, one man is changing lives, one culture, one story at a time.

Marma language in Myanmar script. Poem and carving by Tim Brookes. The poem reads, "All human beings are born free and equal in dignity and rights. They are endowed with reason and conscience and should act towards one another in a spirit of brotherhood."

The Way We Do Things Around Here: Understanding Culture

Learning Objectives

11.1 Compare culture from a personal, organizational, and societal perspective

11.2 Define an organization's culture and its subcultures

11.3 Examine societal cultures as they relate to organizational members' roles

Culture has been characterized as *the way we do things around here* and is considered a hot topic.[10] The word *culture* was the 2014 Word of the Year according to the number of hits on the Merriam-Webster online dictionary, and has only grown in relevance and importance. Moreover, it is taking center stage when college graduates are applying for jobs. Each year *Forbes* and *Fortune* report the top 100 companies to work for, taking into account organizational culture in their assessments, and *Glassdoor* reports the top 25 companies for culture and values. As individuals seek positions and enter the workforce, an engaging organizational culture with similar values is important to them. With the high cost of hiring, organizations that are transparent in their cultural values can ensure a good fit. Think about when you started applying to college or to your first job. Was a good *fit* important to you then? The same will be true when you graduate or consider future jobs.

MYTH OR REALITY?

THE BEST WAY TO UNDERSTAND AN ORGANIZATION'S CULTURE IS TO READ EXAMPLES OF EXIT INTERVIEWS WITH EMPLOYEES WHO LEAVE THE COMPANY.

Myth. People do not leave companies just because they do not like them; the reasons are many and varied. But often people are reluctant to give the *real* reason at an exit interview because they fear they will not get a good job reference when they need one next. To get the best pulse of your company, walk the floors of the organization and talk with people.

Culture is a very complex phenomenon.[11] Authors have tried to simplify the concept by defining it as how things are done around the organization[12] or how people behave when no one is looking.[13] But culture is much more complicated than those simple definitions would have you believe.[14] Consider the differences in what you might see and feel when visiting a friend's home for the weekend. What if they eat different types of food than you are used to, or what if they eat at a different time or in a manner that is more formal or more relaxed? There are differences you may also notice while traveling to different cities, such as the slow pace of life in some parts of the United States versus the frenetic activities in an urban center like New York City.

Traveling abroad often provides the most obvious cultural distinctions. For example, there may be an expectation to bargain for goods in a street market that is unlike the way that others accept prices as fixed when shopping at a market in the US. All these differences can be attributed to the various cultures within different types of groups or organizations, families, locals, and countries or societies. One notices different rules, different behaviors, and different values for the activities that take place. These experiences are differences in the observed behaviors that manifest from differences in cultural values. Despite how it may feel to you, those values and activities are not *weird*, they are just different . . . to you. For those who are part of that culture, it is simply the way things are done around here.

Leadership is a process of influencing others toward a common vision. This definition resonates well with understanding organizational culture. Organizational leaders influence members of their organization, and they guide them toward a common vision. An effective organizational vision will be deeply embedded in the culture of the organization through its values and norms, and manifest through what you see, hear, and feel when you interact with members of that organization.[15]

Every organization has a culture that has been crafted and created by founding members—whether family, partners, owners, or leaders.[16] Culture has been compared to an individual's personality—what you see on the outside (behavior) is the result of the personality (values) that you cannot see. Similarly, culture guides the behavior of individuals within the organization, which has a set of core values that you often do not see.

Culture Starts With People: Your Personal Culture Contribution

Take a moment to think back to what your home was like when you were young. Do you remember what the inside of the house looked like? What did you do after school? What was mealtime like? What kind of traditions did you have when you celebrated a holiday? Did you have any special routines, such as reading every night before bed?

Your first experiences with culture may have come from family or close friends. These people teach us about common values, beliefs, norms, and rules. They may share experiences in which they learned how to behave at home, in the groups in which they are a part (such as church, social groups, athletics), and in the greater society. The members of those groups reinforce the values and behaviors as well. Encountering people who did things differently may have felt a little strange. Culture is a powerful influence on how people see the world, and experiences with different groups and settings create expectations for the *way things are done around here*. That simple definition is enough to get you started exploring culture in this chapter.

Your foundational knowledge of culture, similar to that described above, is not unlike the culture in everyday organizations that you experience now or will in the future (e.g., like where you will work). As you grew up, you had the opportunity to experience different cultures in a variety of settings. For example, you may have attended a public school, where the focus was on making sure that the students successfully passed standardized tests; or you may have attended a college prep school where academics were rigorous and 100% of the student body got into good colleges. Now perhaps you attend a private liberal arts college that has as its foundation many long-standing traditions such as an outstanding football team where everyone goes to the game on Saturday, followed by a bonfire on the quad. Maybe you have experience at a community college where many of the students are working to put themselves through college, for whom extracurricular activities are not in the plan. These kinds of experiences help shape who you are, the values you have, your philosophies about life, and your understanding of organizational differences—differences in organizational culture.

Understanding Organizational Culture

Organizational Culture Defined

Culture has been researched and observed from a variety of different perspectives. With its roots in sociology and anthropology, researchers from management, leadership, organizational behavior, organizational development, and anthropology have studied culture, each from a slightly different perspective. Nearly all authors, no matter what their background, describe organizational culture as an abstraction, so *how* you experience culture is very different for each organization you encounter. That is, you experience culture specific to an organization through events and activities that you can see, such as symbols (the American flag), rituals (the fraternity/sorority initiation ceremony), group norms (the honors dorm—the quiet study area), and heroes (Nelson Mandela). These function as the outward signs (behaviors) of the inward culture (values) that result from integrating these various aspects of the organizational culture with your own values and background. Culture, originated by a group or organization's founding members, includes the values and beliefs that they thought were important to the organization—the shared basic assumptions of the group.

There are three levels of culture within organizations:

1. **Artifacts** and symbols—physical objects that represent organizational values (i.e., those things that you can see). These might include organizational logos, rituals (staff celebrations), language, and manner of dress;

2. Beliefs and Values—such as aspirations, goals, and ideals; and

Artifacts physical evidence (objects) that represent organizational values

3. Underlying Assumptions—unconscious beliefs and values that determine behavior but are unseen and often difficult to ascertain without significant time spent within the group.[17]

What does all this mean for you? You need to be aware that there are important underlying values and beliefs in groups, organizations, and societies that answer why and how its members behave in certain ways. You learn how to behave in different organizational cultures by interacting within various experiences where you learn the meaning of that particular world.[18] Much of this happens below the surface—out of your awareness, and thus, your understanding. "Every organization develops its own distinctive culture. . . . One can often tell within a few minutes of visiting a company, college, or even a restaurant whether employees enjoy their work, whether they take pride or some form of partial 'ownership' in their organization."[19] You will need to look more closely to understand the culture. Anyone not part of that culture is likely to make assumptions using their lean, mean, pattern-making machine brain, resulting in the usual partial and flawed mental model of that culture. The concept of the cultural iceberg may shed some light on understanding the various levels of culture.

Understanding the Iceberg

There is much about culture (whether organizational or societal) that you see and experience; however, there is a significant amount that remains unseen. The concept of the cultural iceberg has been attributed to Edward Hall, a cultural anthropologist. He explored the differences between and among the American cultural systems and the many other cultures in which he lived, studied, and visited—Navajo, Hopi, France, Germany, and Japan, among others. Hall inferred that there is only a small part of culture that is visible, and much of what drives you in your day-to-day life is below the surface, not visible to others, similar to an iceberg. In some respects, culture primarily operates at the unconscious level.[20]

One very important cultural dimension is context, which is what we pay attention to (or not) when we are experiencing events. Contexts provide individuals with *part* of the meaning of an event. Whether a context is high or low is determined by your culture and by what you have to pay attention to in order to gain meaning from the event. There are five categories of events that must be perceived to fully interpret an event: the activity, the present situation, your position/role within the social system, past experience, and culture.[21]

FIGURE 11.1 ● Iceberg

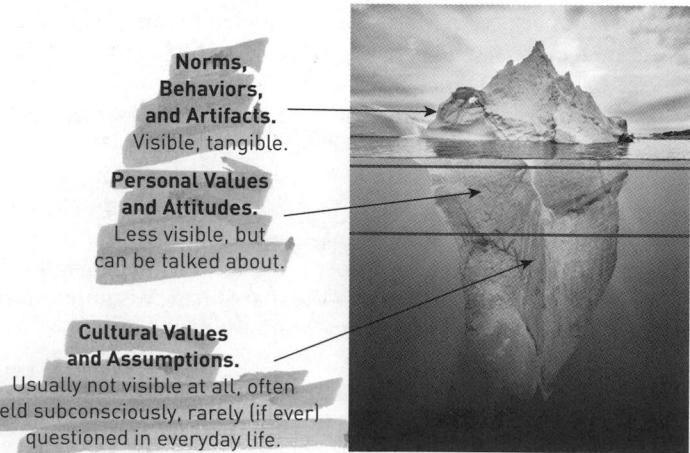

Norms, Behaviors, and Artifacts. Visible, tangible.

Personal Values and Attitudes. Less visible, but can be talked about.

Cultural Values and Assumptions. Usually not visible at all, often held subconsciously, rarely (if ever) questioned in everyday life.

Source: Photo ©iStock.com/posteriori.

To fully understand the meaning of a culture, you need to understand the context in which culture occurs and on *what* members focus their attention. An interesting example of cultural context is how you perceive personal space, which is based on how you grew up, where you live, and how you adapt to new contexts. You may have had a communication class in which you learned about norms for personal space—those are intimate space (typically one and a half feet), personal space (approximately four feet), social space (12 feet), and public space (25 feet). These distances can vary greatly from country to country, and you may find yourself quite annoyed and uneasy the first time you visit a country where the norm for space is significantly different from what you are used to experiencing. For example, in large cities in some Middle Eastern countries where there are large populations of individuals, personal space feels nonexistent due to overcrowding—individuals have gotten used to very little personal space and those individuals experience daily what Americans would consider intimate space.

Time is also a function of culture and is identified as either monochronic (M-time) or polychronic (P-time). Cultures that adhere to a monochronic time schedule, such as Americans and Northern Europeans, adhere to a strict time schedule where days are scheduled, and appointments are made and kept on time. In cultures that are polychronic, however, people juggle multiple tasks at one time and their focus is on people, not on the task. That is to say, it is more important for you to pay attention to the needs of the individual rather than adhere to a strict schedule.

REFLECTION QUESTIONS

Think about an organization to which you belong and reflect on the following questions:

- Are you aware of the founding members' values and beliefs for the organization? Can you articulate them?

- What are the underlying assumptions that guide the organization?

- What are the beliefs and values, the aspirations, goals, and ideas that organizational members espouse? Are they congruent with founding values?

- What kinds of artifacts represent those beliefs and values of the organization?

- What messages and values are taught to new members of the organization? How are those cultural values communicated?

Now that you have had a chance to learn about personal and organizational culture, a more micro view, take a step back and look at culture from the macro perspective—the societal level.

Culture at the Societal Level

Two primary views of societal culture have been put forth by those studying this concept. These groups of authors examine the differences in the behaviors, beliefs, and values of individuals based on their country of origin. One group defines culture as a social phenomenon that is "the collective programming of the mind that distinguishes the members of one group or category of people from others."[22] The other group believes the concept of culture should refer to societies (nations, ethnic or regional groups within or across nations). The first definition centers more on the individual and how they come to identify with the values of the group, while the second definition focuses more on specific societies

Societal cultures different cultures across nations, regions, or ethnicities

Stories the words, gestures, pictures, and objects that carry often complex meanings recognized as such only by those who share the culture

Heroes persons, alive or dead, real or imaginary, who possess characteristics that are highly prized in a culture and thus serve as models for behavior

Rituals collective activities that are technically unnecessary to the achievement of desired ends but that within a culture are considered socially essential, keeping the individual bound within the norms of the collectivity

as collectives. This text will use the second view, defining the term **societal cultures** as differences across nations, regions, or ethnicities.

Both organizational and societal cultures have visible elements, which include stories, heroes, and rituals.

- **Stories** are the words, gestures, pictures, and objects that carry often complex meanings recognized as such only by those who share the culture.

- **Heroes** are persons, alive or dead, real or imaginary, who possess characteristics that are highly prized in a culture and thus serve as models for behavior.

- **Rituals** are collective activities that are technically unnecessary to the achievement of desired ends but that within a culture are considered socially essential, keeping the individual bound within the norms of the collectivity.

These visible elements are known as *practices*. Although you (the outside observer) can see them, their meanings are not visible—those are only known to members of that culture. Many cultures around the world have different practices that are not immediately understood by others.

Several researchers over the years have collected data on cultural differences around the world. One of the largest studies collected data from more than 17,000 middle managers in 62 societies in what is called the GLOBE (Global Leadership and Organizational Behavior Effectiveness) study.[23] Similar to the definition provided earlier, this group defined culture as "shared motives, values, beliefs, identities, and interpretations or meanings of significant events that result from common experiences of members of collectives that are transmitted across generations." Looking at cultural practices and values in world cultures, their model incorporated numerous leadership-related theories resulting in 15 propositions that drove their research. For example, "Societal cultural norms of shared values and practices affect leaders' behavior" and "Societal cultural values and practices also affect organizational culture and practices."[24]

 If you were looking at leadership in another country, what would you focus on? The GLOBE research group used the following constructs to examine leadership practices and values:

1. Power Distance: The degree to which members of a collective expect power to be distributed equally.

2. Uncertainty Avoidance: The extent to which a society, organization, or group relies on social norms, rules, and procedures to alleviate unpredictability of future events.

3. Humane Orientation: The degree to which a collective encourages and rewards individuals for being fair, altruistic, generous, caring, and kind to others.

4. Collectivism I (Institutional Collectivism): The degree to which organizational and societal institutional practices encourage and reward collective distribution of resources and collective action.

5. Collectivism II (In-Group Collectivism): The degree to which individuals express pride, loyalty, and cohesiveness in their organizations or families.

6. Assertiveness: The degree to which individuals are assertive, confrontational, and aggressive in their relationships with others.

7. Gender Egalitarianism: The degree to which a collective minimizes gender inequality.

8. Future Orientation: The extent to which individuals engage in future-oriented behaviors such as delaying gratification, planning, and investing in the future.

9. Performance Orientation: The degree to which a collective encourages and rewards group members for performance improvement and excellence.

The GLOBE study resulted in some surprising outcomes. Despite all the differences across cultures, 22 of the leadership attributes were desirable across *all* societies. And eight attributes were universally undesirable. The study also found that, based on leader characteristics, there were three universally accepted theories of leadership that contributed to effective leadership across cultures: Charismatic/Value-Based leadership, Team Oriented leadership, and Participative leadership. Lastly, researchers were able to place societies into culture clusters based on how they scored on the nine cultural dimensions. How might this fascinating work connecting leadership to world cultures inform your leadership design work?

EXPERTS BEYOND THE TEXT

INSIGHTFUL LEADERS KNOW ABOUT . . . LEADERSHIP IN OTHER CULTURES

Features of Leadership in China

By Zhang Qianyu (with additions from Gaoxiang Chen)

Leaders in contemporary China usually have to possess good morality, pursue pragmatism, work within a well-connected personal network, and be aware of their political and cultural context. These values emanate from the dominant religions as well as the cultural values in China. In accordance with Kam-Cheung Wong, the Confucian tradition of China has always been focused on training "leaders on moral grounds" with a pragmatic base.[25] Pragmatism helps leaders in China to focus on cultivating abilities to implement plans. Guanxi (关系), "friendship with a continual exchange of favors," is a crucial tool for Chinese leaders for building business trust.[26]

Morality serves as a very important aspect in evaluating a leader in China. The Chinese have been focusing on developing ways of exercising morality through leadership instead of debating abstract concepts concerning morality. A student of the University of Hong Kong (HKU), Hou Liwei, thinks "moral" business leaders should be qualified to transition to political leaders, whose words indicate that higher responsibilities can be given only to ethical leaders. The current China in political and commercial worlds might be an irony to this belief, but what mediates morality here consists largely of pragmatism and having tangible benefits to the people.

Mastering Guanxi is another essential trait for Chinese leaders. Westerners build their trust based on the formal company system where everyone shares the same values. In China, it is necessary to earn personal trust. Chinese business leaders have to work in their Guanxi network to ensure trustworthy business deals. After repetitions of exchanging favors in the same Guanxi network, Chinese business leaders should be able to *minimize the risk of uncertainty* through trading with familiar people with whom they have established personal relations. This difference between East and West can lead to conflict. For instance, the Chinese would think Westerners are too rash to move forward, but Westerners would think it is hard to build the trust with Chinese.

There is a deeper exploration about the Guanxi called "Zhong Jian Ren" (中间人). It refers to a person who has an association with someone with whom you want to work. This person is usually someone with whom you have already built strong trust. Therefore, he/she can introduce you in a better way than you can. Moreover, it is strange to collaborate with a new business without a "Zhong Jian Ren" in China. So Zhong Jian Ren is a medium to create the good connection between you and your partner.

Finally, leaders in China should have strong sensitivity to the political environment. Takaaki Tanaka, the chairman and CEO of Toshiba China, articulates that "the Chinese business environment is changing so quickly that it is necessary to track changes in government policy at least every three months."[27] Keeping a close eye on

(Continued)

(Continued)

the changing political culture is important for company survival. Specifically, it is politically sensible for the leaders of state-owned companies to rank "keeping social stability" higher than "maximizing profits."

Many of these characteristics may apply to Western leadership. However, there is one unique and essential trait about Chinese leadership called "Zhong Yong" (中庸),

which is one of the Confucian principles.[28] The first word "Zhong" means in the middle or equilibrium; the second word "Yong" points to unchanging. This term refers to avoiding the extremes in the Chinese leadership, seeking moderation and harmony. It requires the leaders to be patient and wise. People in China would prefer their lives to be stable rather than in constant change.

REFLECTION QUESTIONS

Ask someone from another country or culture:

1. Describe a typical day [in your country or culture].

2. What are the types of foods that you eat? What is your favorite dish?

3. Tell me about the educational system.

4. How do individuals engage in business transactions? Do they quickly get to the point? Do they converse over a long, leisurely dinner?

The Leader's Role and Organizational Culture

Learning Objectives

11.4 Explain the leader's role in culture

11.5 Identify how values inform organizational culture

11.6 Describe the differences between organizational vision, mission, and values and how they relate to culture

Inculcating values throughout an organization starts with the leader, who sets standards of behavior for everyone in the organization. Someday that could be you. Leaders work hard every day to gain alignment with the company's values, reinforcing positive actions, and swiftly taking action with employees who do not emulate these values.[29] Leadership author and scholar Warren Bennis[30] wrote about the importance of understanding your own personal values, understanding the **organization's values**, and knowing any difference between the two. You will be happiest in your organization when there is congruence between your personal values and the values of your organization. Each person brings a personal set of values to the organization, and together those collective sets of values are what create the organization's culture.[31] For that reason, it is important for leaders to know and understand the values and beliefs of followers.

Organizational values
Generally emanating from founders, organizational values guide the behavior of organizational members.

Personal Values—Forming and Informing Organizational Culture

One of the most important elements of culture is values—both personal values and those reinforced at the organizational level. Based on the family in which you grew up, your social structures (e.g., religious, schools, groups), and your national and regional identity (e.g., American from the west coast), your values define who you are, what you believe, and how you interact with others. As you read in Chapter 4 on values, designing your leadership self requires a full understanding of the values by which you live, simply because when you join an organization you want to make sure that it is representative of those values.

One model for helping you see how your values align with those of an organization is the Competing Values Framework.[32] Two cultural dimensions comprise organizations in this model: an internal to external focus dimension and a flexibility to stability dimension. Within these emerge four generalized values-based cultures: Clan, Adhocracy, Hierarchy, and Market. The Clan is described as like a family, valuing nurturing, teamwork, loyalty, and concern for people. The Adhocracy is entrepreneurial, valuing risk, innovation, freedom, and challenges. These two cultures tend toward flexibility, while the next two—Hierarchy and Market—tend toward stability and control. The Hierarchy is described as controlled and structured, valuing organization, efficiency, security, and stability. The Market is competitive, valuing achievement in reaching goals and outdoing competition.

Each of the cultural types holds forth values important to the success of an organization, particularly in certain circumstances. For example, in times of disruption or uncertainty, organizations with more flexible cultures will more easily adapt. Each type also aligns with a set of leadership behaviors and follower expectations—the way things are done around here. How would you describe your current organizational culture? Would you call it a clan, where everyone is very involved similar to a big family, and the leader focuses on mentoring and nurturing followers? More important for you as a leader: Which of the four cultures described best aligns with your approach to leadership?

Do Your Values Align With the Organization's Values? Ensuring Fit

Just as important as the organizational culture is to the success of the organization, your success is driven by a match between personal and organizational values. The average cost to hire a new employee is roughly 20% to 50% of an individual's annual salary. That is a lot of money to any organization. So, losing employees because of poor values or cultural fit can be extraordinarily costly to the bottom line in both time and money (no matter what type of organization—public, private, governmental, or nonprofit). Organizational leaders hire individuals to get the best fit between new employees and the organizational culture—an important consideration regarding whether or not employees will stay the course. Moreover, prospective employees need to engage in self-reflection regarding their own values to determine whether the organizational values and culture are congruent with their own personal values.

The notion of aligned values for organizational success is a consistent theme for effective leadership. In the book *Leadership Matters*, the authors reported "that getting the culture right is a top priority" and "every organization has to create its own culture and encourage one that serves its particular mission."[33] While they acknowledged that there is no one *right* culture, there are certain characteristics that most organizations desire in their members. Use the following to do a quick assessment of a culture to which you belong. Do you

- take pride in the mission?

- have a sense of urgency about the work to be done?

- have a passion for their work?

- understand the way in which they are contributing to both their organization's success and society?

- recognize that although it is okay to make mistakes, they have to quickly learn from them?

- promote teamwork, collaboration, and trust?

- understand the importance of stopping to fix broken processes?

- understand the critical importance of honesty, integrity, and ethical considerations?

- have a skill set that matches the tasks at hand?

- understand customer needs, the competitive market, and the need to capitalize on comparative advantages?

- understand the importance of using good judgment in all situations?

- understand the importance of eliminating waste and inefficiencies?

- understand that high quality and continual innovation are everyone's responsibility?

- celebrate breakthroughs at all levels of the organization and encourage the joy and fun of solving problems, serving customers, and doing good?

- recognize the crucial importance of both personal renewal and organizational renewal strategies, all aimed at fostering agile, nimble, and adaptive flexibility?

- fight unnecessary bureaucracy and standard operating procedures that create bloat and kill spark?

Take a second look at the list you just read. Each of these items represents a design challenge for you as leader. Many represent multiple levels of leadership activity. For example, having a passion for your work can be designed in yourself, into your relationships with followers, and for others—all of which culminates in influencing culture. Identify the items that represent important challenges that you would like to see addressed. Note how you might utilize the past 10 chapters of this book to address these different culture design challenges you face as a leader.

LEADERSHIP BY DESIGN

Design Principle: Figure-Ground Relationship

Definition: Elements are perceived as either figures (objects of focus) or ground (the rest of the perceptual field).

In Other Words: Looking at anything, you will focus on some things while all the rest sits in the background.

For Example: Take a look at the picture to the right, entitled *Another Exciting Day of Class*. What is the first thing you notice? The sleeping student is the figure, all the rest is the ground. But what important things does the *ground* contain? Every picture, like every context, tells a story and raises questions. What class is this? What are they studying?

©iStock.com/PeopleImage

What put him to sleep? Is he sleeping or playing a game? The figure is key, but the ground can be important too.

For Leaders: Leaders must be aware of both figure and ground. When followers interact with you and the culture of your organization, what do you want them to notice and remember? If they cannot distinguish the figure from the ground, then they may not put their effort into the important things. Have you ever seen the optical illusion where a white vase sits on a black background, until suddenly that background appears to you as two profiles facing one another? This perceptual instability happens because it is unclear what is figure versus ground. For followers, this uncertainty diffuses their focus and results in frustration. Leaders should also consider what followers might be missing that may be getting lost in the background. What are the key elements that reinforce your culture?

Contemporary Approaches to Organizational Culture

The face of organizational cultural identity is changing. You need only look as far as Zappos or Google to see the contemporary approach to organizational culture. Numerous organizations have broken the mold, and gone are the days of the *white shirt and dark suit* that drove organizational culture in years past. Outlined in the *Zappos Family Culture* book are the 10 values on which their organization's culture is based:

1. Deliver WOW Through Service
2. Embrace and Drive Change
3. Create Fun and a Little Weirdness
4. Be Adventurous, Creative, and Open-Minded
5. Pursue Growth and Learning
6. Build Open and Honest Relationships With Communication
7. Build a Positive Team and Family Spirit
8. Do More With Less
9. Be Passionate and Determined
10. Be Humble[34]

In fact, to Zappos' CEO Tony Hsieh, culture is the most important priority because if the culture is right, everything else (great customer service, and a long-term enduring brand)[35] will fall into place.

Similar to Zappos, Starbucks, Apple, and many other contemporary organizations, Google's culture focuses on its people who "share common goals and visions for the company . . . . and reflect the global audience that we serve." Moreover, their corporate culture encourages interactions that focus on both work and play (similar to Zappos). Rather than a vision and/or mission, Google focuses on the "Ten things we know to be true":

1. Focus on the user and all else will follow.
2. It's best to do one thing really, really well.
3. Fast is better than slow.
4. Democracy on the web works.

5. You don't need to be at your desk to need an answer.

6. You can make money without doing evil.

7. There's always more information out there.

8. The need for information crosses all borders.

9. You can be serious without a suit.

10. Great just isn't good enough.[36]

Sounds like a great environment that focuses on both work and play. How does each set of values differ from the other? What would you need to value to succeed (or to lead) in each culture?

Vision, Mission, and Values in Organizational Culture

From lofty aspirations to day-to-day details, an organization's vision, mission, and values provide declarations to the world about who they are and for what they stand. A vision is a forward-thinking and aspirational image that sets the direction for the organization that others might follow. Unlike Alice in Wonderland, who did not know which way she ought to go, leaders must set a compelling vision that moves followers *somewhere* . . . and that somewhere is different for each organization. Excellent leaders listen to the wants and needs, the hopes and dreams of followers, and craft their vision of the organization around those, so that followers will feel a part of that vision. Crafting the vision is one of the first and most important tasks of the leader.[37]

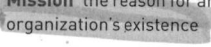

Mission the reason for an organization's existence

The organizational **mission** describes an organization's reason for existence—articulating the business that they are in. Mission statements guide organizational members in their day-to-day work and serve as a reminder of the reason the organization exists and that each and every activity in which they engage meets that end.

Finally, an organization's values inform the organizational culture. From the founders, there is reciprocity between organizational members and organizational leaders, and together they have a mutual understanding of what they stand for and in which direction they need to move the organization forward.

REFLECTION QUESTION

Think of a societal culture with which you are somewhat familiar (one such as Japan) and a story, hero, or ritual (such as bowing) that they have that you find odd or different. There is obviously some cultural meaning behind that practice that only insiders understand. Find a member of that culture, or someone who has lived in that culture for an extended time. Ask him or her about the practice, and try to understand the meaning behind the behavior.

Designing Organizational Culture

Learning Objective

11.7 Describe the various ways in which organizational culture can be designed

Changing Organizational Culture— It's Not as Easy as You Think

Often in response to changes such as fluctuations in the market, new leadership, fast-paced technological change, a changing workforce, a multigenerational and diverse workforce, increased scrutiny by stakeholders, more government oversight, and an ever-increasing global presence,[38] leaders are challenged to change organizational culture. Traditionally, organizational change occurs from the top down where executive leaders; in response to these internal and/or external pressures such as those noted above, respond each in his or her own way but often in a manner that imposes new requirements by others on the organization. In contrast, today organizational members want to be informed, involved, and engaged decision makers in the organizational processes that affect their work.

Organizational change has been defined as "planned alterations of organizational components to improve the effectiveness of the organization." These components include the "mission, vision, values, culture, strategy, goals, structure, processes or systems, technology, and people in an organization. When organizations enhance their effectiveness, they increase their ability to generate value for those they serve."[39]

Culture is the most difficult part of an organization to change. Culture is built from the ground up, by those who were there in the beginning, no matter the type of group or organization. It can take years to craft and years to change. Recall from the previous chapter the work of John Kotter and his eight-step change model. That model was introduced as a way to facilitate organizational change. Here are the steps again:

1. Establishing a sense of urgency

2. Creating the guiding coalition

3. Developing a vision and strategy

4. Communicating the change vision

5. Empowering broad-based action

6. Generating short-term wins

7. Consolidating gains and producing more change

8. Anchoring new approaches in the culture[40]

Note the last step—anchoring new approaches in the culture. Changing organizational culture can take quite some time, which can lead to frustration on the part of organizational members; enthusiasm can drop and changes that were made early on can be lost in the process. In fact, the point is that cultural changes need to be secured and built into the social norms and shared values if you hope to make organizational changes *stick*. Unfortunately, too many leaders fail to be attentive to the organization's culture during the process of implementing change. You cannot make changes to design success for others unless you also design the culture that will support and sustain that success.

Kotter's eight-step process for organizational change has stood the test of time. While the steps are numbered sequentially, Kotter noted that most organizations are engaged in various steps simultaneously, with some steps completed to various degrees, while others are being started. The majority of change efforts that fail are a result of leaders jumping ahead and trying to complete only Steps 5, 6, and 7. The *failure* to address the critical components of assisting members in understanding the importance of the change effort (urgency), getting key individuals on board (a guiding coalition), and creating and communicating a compelling vision can undermine all the subsequent steps to get the change implemented successfully. And as noted, the last step—the culture step—is critical to making the changes more permanent. Kotter reminds leaders that when they have been indoctrinated into and steeped in the culture of the organization's norms of behavior and shared values, change comes slowly; and although it can come, it must be anchored for change to be effective. Designing and facilitating organizational and cultural change is not easy, particularly at large corporations or organizations steeped in years of history, but it is nonetheless necessary for sustained organizational and individual success.

Tools to Facilitate Culture Change

Leadership guru Warren Bennis wrote about the importance of change to organizational leaders: "All of the leaders I talked with believe in change—in both people and organizations. They equate it with growth—tangible and intangible—and progress."[41] Growth and progress are extraordinarily relevant today given the rapid pace of change that continues to accelerate. In order to move *any* organization forward, leaders need to be cognizant of the types of pressures for change that affect their organizations—no matter what the organization type: for-profit, nonprofit, governmental, or educational. Environmental factors, most of which are beyond a leader's control (i.e., changing demographics, technology, globalization), affect all organizations. So, the question is not how do leaders react to external pressures, but rather how do leaders proactively engage their organization to be responsive to the changes they know are inevitable?

Organizational change, or any type of personal or professional change, can be difficult and stressful. As a leader, it will be important for you to recognize that and take measures to ensure a smooth transition for your team. Make sure that you have put into place and communicated an action plan that makes the change process transparent to everyone in the organization. The leader needs to be attentive to the following issues and decisions during the change:

- What are the strategies for dealing with the politics that will be involved in the change?

- What are the conditions for a successful change, and how will you know when you have achieved them?

- How will you communicate both the change plan and the results organization-wide?

- What strategies/resources will you use to generate new information to inform the plan?

- How will you support the staff through their emotional reactions to the change?

- How will you measure the success of the change effort (the new state) and the change process itself?

- What rewards will you implement to support the change process and the outcomes?

Again, while the change process will likely carry some stress for most individuals, being as transparent as possible will minimize that stress and keep the rumors to a minimum.

Appreciative Inquiry

Appreciative Inquiry This is the cooperative, coevolutionary search for the best in people, their organizations, and the world around them. It involves systematic discovery of what gives life to an organization or a community when it is most effective and most capable in economic, ecological terms.

Another method for facilitating organizational change is Appreciative Inquiry (AI).[42] **Appreciative Inquiry** is defined as the cooperative, coevolutionary search for the best in people, their organizations, and the world around them. This positive approach focuses on changing organizational cultures by examining what is *right* with the organization. It involves systematic discovery of what gives life to an organization or a community when it is most effective and most capable in economic, ecological terms. Conceived in the late 1980s, AI has gained momentum and is now considered one of the foremost methods for organizational change. Different from traditional change methods, AI focuses on organizational strengths and stories of success, rather than on problems and what has gone wrong—a glass half-full approach that is transformational for the organization.

AI's focus on what is right in the organization is uplifting and transforming for members who are used to always examining what is wrong. AI has been defined as "the study of what gives life to human systems when they function at their best."[43] AI uses process mapping to map the positive core of the organization. **Process mapping** is an activity where leaders and followers visually represent what an organization does, noting the flow of activities, decision points, roles, and any other variables involved in getting things done. AI engages the organization's entire community (or as many as possible), as well as all key stakeholders—board members, customers, suppliers, and so forth—in the process of inquiring into "extraordinary moments of high engagement, commitment, and passionate achievement."

Rather than focus on problem-solving, AI utilizes a structured *appreciative interview* process involving all stakeholders to glean out the best from the organization. Originally a four-step process called the 4-D Cycle, one author has added a fifth step. The five phases are as follows:

Process mapping
an activity where leaders and followers visually represent what an organization does, noting the flow of activities, decision points, roles, and any other variables involved in getting things done

- *Discovery*: Mobilizing the whole system by engaging all stakeholders in the articulation of strengths and best practices. Identifying "The best of what has been and what is."

- *Dream*: Creating a clear, results-oriented vision in relation to discovered potential and in relation to questions of higher purpose, such as, "What is the world calling us to become?"

- *Design*: Creating possibility propositions of the ideal organization, articulating an organization design that people feel is capable of drawing upon and magnifying the positive core to realize the newly expressed dream.

- *Destiny*: Strengthening the affirmative capability of the whole system, enabling it to build hope and sustain momentum for ongoing positive change and high performance.

- *Define*: Emphasizing the importance of a clear and compelling theme for the inquiry.

What follows are some sample AI interview questions for visioning for both individuals and groups. Notice the positive focus of the inquiry.

Individuals

1. Describe a time when you felt the team/group performed really well. What were the circumstances during that time?

2. Describe a time when you were proud to be a member of the team or group. Why were you proud?

3. What do you value most about being a member of this team/group? Why?

4. Tell about the time that you were most excited about your contributions to this group.

5. What are you most excited about with respect to future contributions?

Groups

1. Discuss examples of the best practices that people have seen within the organization.

2. Determine what circumstances made the best practices possible (describe in detail).

3. Take the stories and envision what might be. Write an affirmative statement (a provocative proposition) that describes the idealized future as if it were already happening.

When an AI effort is successful, an organization's culture change sticks. The power of focusing on the positive provides hope for organizational members. Moreover, the process is generative in that it focuses on coming to a collective understanding of what members want for the organization versus only solving problems.

Kotter's Eight-Step Change Model and Appreciative Inquiry are just two among a number of organizational change models that can be used as effective tools for designing culture. You might also look at models such as Lewin's Change Management Model, McKinsey's 7-S Model, ADKAR, and Kübler-Ross' Change Curve. When you realize that your organization is in need of cultural change, it will be important for you to examine the various models and determine which best serves your needs.

LEADERSHIP BY DESIGN

Design Principle: Immersion

Definition: A state of mental focus so intense that awareness of the *real* world is lost, generally resulting in a feeling of joy and satisfaction.

In Other Words: When you are so intensely engaged with something, time seems to fly by and you really enjoy the activity.

For Example: Have you ever been so engrossed in a great movie that when it ends you had to take a moment to remember where you were or what day it was? You may have had the same experience with a captivating book or a challenging role-playing video game, or even while engaged in a sport. Everything else disappears, and you are solely focused on the task at hand.

For Leaders: Immersion often occurs when you have found the zone between too much and too little cognitive and perceptual challenge. In other words, your context and task are neither overwhelming nor boring; they are just right—capturing your focus and energy to the exclusion of all else. Consider experiences you have had with immersion—in a job, at a party, at a museum, on an amusement park ride. What elements contributed to your immersion?

Leaders can apply the principle of immersion to increase satisfaction and enjoyment, enhance focus and engagement, deepen learning, and guide motivation. Creating a culture with clear and appropriate goals, limited distractions, and immediate feedback with tasks in that possible-but-not-easy challenge zone will help achieve that immersive experience. Leaders should monitor, assess, and adjust elements of context and culture to find and fully utilize immersion as they design culture. You may need to remind followers to eat and go home—immersion is a powerful state.

Chapter Summary

In this chapter, you have learned about the importance of culture from how individuals contribute to both organizational and societal culture. Organizational culture was defined and the elements that make up the visible and invisible parts of culture were outlined. Additionally, you learned about differences between individuals based on societal culture. Individual and organizational values as they define culture and the organization's vision and mission were described. Finally, changing organizational culture and new tools for facilitating cultural design were outlined.

Culture surrounds you every day in many ways. Personally and professionally, you navigate between worlds with values that may or may not be in concert with your own. No two cultures are the same. Groups have different values; organizations differ in their visions, missions, and values; and most importantly the people who belong to those groups and organizations differ in the backgrounds, skills, talents, and values that they bring. Culture is something individuals rarely think about, even though it is everywhere, and its roots run deep.[44] You are affected not only by the culture in the organizations to which you belong, but you acquire cultural roots from your family and groups, as well as society. Your own cultural roots run deep, are difficult to change, and are definitely influenced by where and how you spend your time.

Although organizational cultures are crafted by the beliefs and values of founding members, over time they are influenced by the beliefs and values of organizational members. Much of organizational culture is the visible norms, behaviors, and artifacts, which are significantly influenced by the less visible personal values and the usually not visible at all cultural values and assumptions. All culture is influenced by context,

which influences the differences between and among societal cultures. These differences are vitally important to understand when interacting in either a personal or business setting with individuals from around the world.

Last, individuals want to feel comfortable within their groups. The emotional aspects of culture fit or misfit result from ensuring that your own values align with the organization's values. When you become a leader in your own organization, it is important to take the time to listen to your followers. Make sure that you understand fully their values and beliefs and treat that culture with the same respect you would hope for your own.

Key Terms

Appreciative Inquiry 296
Artifacts 285
Heroes 288
Mission 294

Organizational Values 290
Process Mapping 297
Rituals 288
Societal Cultures 288

Stories 288
Strategic Planning 274
SWOT Analysis 277

CORE™ Attribute Builders: Build Now for Future Leadership Challenges

Attribute: Resilience and Engagement

Builder: Engage global events and persons

Many communities offer lots of opportunities for you to get involved with individuals from other countries, and through these opportunities, you can expand your cultural understanding. Many larger communities offer international cultural exchange programs for community members to visit other countries. Some communities have international festivals where local residents showcase their cultural background through food,

costumes, music and dance, and exhibits—take the time to visit and learn about your community members from other countries. Additionally, assimilating into a new country can be difficult for individuals—take the time to volunteer to help teach English as a second language to a new international member in your community or assist in helping him or her navigate through your city. However you engage with members from other countries, make sure to listen and absorb all you can about their culture—you never know when understanding differences might work in your favor.

CORE™ Attribute Builders: Build Now for Future Leadership Challenges

Attribute: Confidence (cultural)

Builder: Create a cultural guidebook

Developing your awareness of your own and other cultures will enhance your ability and comfort when encountering new cultures. With that increased confidence, you are more likely to explore and engage other cultures, which will broaden your sources for perspectives, approaches, solutions, and ideas for innovation.

Part I—Start building your cultural competence by exploring a group or organization

Individually or with a small group of peers, identify a group—the more different from you, the better. Interact with and explore all you can about that group. Visit places they visit, eat what they eat, listen to what they talk about and how, interview a few individuals in that culture—immerse yourself in any way possible. As you do this, take notes. What are the written rules of behavior and the unwritten and unspoken norms? Compare your observations and insights to your own culture. You are building what is called *cultural competence*, which

includes cultural knowledge, awareness, sensitivity, and ultimately the ability to effectively navigate and work with individuals in that culture.

Part II—Create a cultural guidebook

Organize your insights into a *guidebook* that you could hand to someone entering the culture you explored so that they would be able to read it and understand what to do and not do in order to be successful. Show your guidebook to some of the individuals in that culture to get their feedback on its accuracy. Consider what you got right . . . and what you missed.

Take a moment to reflect on what in *your* culture others need to know in order to succeed. How can you best communicate your culture to others?

Skill Builder Activity

My Cultural Perception

First, examine your world: Look around your classroom right now. What artifacts—those things that you can see—do you see that represent the culture in this specific room? How is the room set up? What does that tell you about the culture in the room? What beliefs and values are represented by the individuals around you? Ask the instructor too. And what underlying assumptions—unconscious beliefs and values—exist? Ask those around you.

Second, examine someone else's world: Find an organization or a local business where you can visit and observe. A local coffee shop or other place where you can linger without disruption is ideal. As you engage as a customer, observe the work culture of those employed (or members of an organization). Can you describe *the way things are done around here*? How do individuals interact and work with (or against) one another? How does the culture of the employees differ from the culture the customer or visitor experiences?

Leading a Team

Coming together is a beginning.

Keeping together is progress.

Working together is success.

—Henry Ford

You are not a team because you work together. You are a team because you trust, respect, and care for each other.

—Vala Afshar

Learning Objectives

12.1 Identify the skills necessary to be an effective team member

12.2 Describe the difference between teams and groups

12.3 Compare various types of organizational team models

12.4 Assess the essential elements of teams

12.5 Interpret Tuckman's stages of group development

12.6 Describe the key characteristics of team leadership

12.7 Summarize the factors that contribute to effective team members

12.8 Apply two assessments that assist team members with understanding themselves and others

12.9 Contrast the differences between organizational, team, and individual issues that can arise in teams

12.10 Assess three problems that can arise in teams

Detailed Chapter Outline

Leadership by Design Model
Design Self
How can I design myself as a leader?
Design Relationships
As a leader, how can I design my relationships with others?
Design Others' Success
As a leader, how can I design success for others?
DESIGN CULTURE
AS A LEADER, HOW CAN I DESIGN THE CULTURE OF MY ORGANIZATION?
Design Future
As a leader, how can I innovate?

Introduction: Designing Teams Within the Organizational Culture

It seems as if everywhere you look today, organizations are engaging in teamwork to accomplish organizational goals. At this point in your life, you have likely been a member of many different teams. Think back to a time when you were part of a team. Were you and the others focused on a common problem or goal? Did you have a choice as to who was part of the group? How did everyone relate and get along? What did the leader do that made the team more or less effective? As you recall, some teams seemed to work and some did not; some teams were fun and energizing, while others felt like a burden. What made the difference between those experiences? Would you have been better off working alone?

Even when there are no organized teams, groups will form in any organization, or anywhere, for that matter. However, it is up to leaders to purposefully design those groups to create the most effective and best performing group—in other words, design and lead a *team*. A team is defined as two or more individuals aligned in a common purpose. Today's complex, global work environment demands organizational teams that can respond quickly to internal and external environmental inputs, while maximizing the organizational outputs. Effective selection of team members for long- or short-term assignments provides the opportunity to bring the collective strengths of a group to organizational teams, while simultaneously creating motivated performance and continuous improvement toward achieving organizational objectives.

As far back as the late 1990s, leadership guru Warren Bennis commented that "the problems we face are too complex to be solved by any one person or any one discipline. Our only chance is to bring people together from a variety of backgrounds and disciplines who can refract a problem through the prism of complementary minds allied in common purpose."[1] The complexity of the world today has only magnified, needing solutions with broader viewpoints from multiple individuals. Bennis noted that "the more I look at the history of business, government, the arts, and the sciences the clearer it is that few great accomplishments are ever the work of a single individual."[2] Teams serve organizations much more effectively than a mere collection of individuals. This is a very important leadership lesson.

Teams have the distinct advantage of bringing synergy to a task, which would otherwise not occur. **Synergy** is defined as a group's energy, where the output of the entire group is greater than the combined output of each individual. That is to say, the output of a team far exceeds the sum of what each individual on the team can provide. When team members work collaboratively toward a shared vision and have developed into a team, each individual produces more in the team environment and the total outcome is greater still. Why does this happen? Team members provide mutual support for one another and contribute to continuous improvement and innovation.

The definition of leadership combined with the process of problem-solving comprise a process made more effective with a team. Leadership is the process of influencing others toward a common vision. Leaders intentionally design teams to effectively and efficiently meet the needs of the organization. An effective team often leads itself, with members influencing each other and reinforcing the common vision. Teams also solve problems more effectively. They mutually *understand* the vision of the organization, they utilize multiple brains and perspectives to *imagine* solutions to the problem at hand, and they complement one another to *implement* a solution to an issue or problem.

Just as organizations have a culture, so do teams. This chapter highlights the distinctions and advantages of designing and leading a team. The chapter begins by distinguishing between a group and a team, and then it describes various types of teams, the stages of team development, and the very important roles that members play in the effective functioning of a team. Finally, the notion of team leadership is introduced, examining several models of team leadership, your and others' role on the team, and how to take corrective actions when things go awry.

Synergy a group's energy where the sum of the energy of the group is greater than the combined output of each individual (the sum is greater than the total of the individual parts)

LEADERSHIP THAT MAKES A DIFFERENCE

Danny Iny and Mirasee

Successful entrepreneur Danny Iny, founder and CEO of Mirasee, successfully navigated an Internet marketing company from nothing to over $5 million in just 5 years.[3] Mirasee focuses on business training programs, calling their customers *students* and training programs *education* and *courses*. Mirasee is driven by six core values: empowerment through learning and growth; enthusiasm and positivity; innovation and adaptability; support, appreciation, and humility; openness and transparency;

(Continued)

(Continued)

and partnership and ownership. The company is committed to seeing that the companies it serves focus first on *their* audience, on making a difference second, and finally, on profits. Mirasee is a contemporary company, whose team conducts day-to-day business operations from around the globe—on four continents, in six countries, and in five different time zones. In those 5 years, Iny has mastered the art of successfully engaging and keeping connected with the members of his virtual team.

In an article on navigating successful remote teams, Iny answered the questions many of us would ask regarding how to keep connected in a virtual organization.[4] He offered 10 suggestions to keep the members of his team connected with one another—they communicate daily, weekly, and monthly, and actually convene in person on a periodic basis—noting these frequent connections as key to their team's success. Each week begins with Danny's Monday morning email, which highlights examples from team members who have exemplified one of the company's core values. Each day begins with team members checking in on their messaging app to see what was accomplished the previous day, see what is upcoming for the current day, and make requests for their work needs from team members. Additionally,

individuals instant message each other throughout the day to ask and answer questions, share information, or simply to share a joke.

Additionally, the Mirasee team has weekly all-team meetings via web conferencing. At the beginning of the meeting, each team member gets an opportunity to share, and each meeting concludes with an open session to ask questions of Danny. Periodically, extracurricular team meetings happen where members *get together* via web conferencing to chat over lunch or discuss topics of interest to members who choose to join in.

Each month, the chief financial officer provides a financial report to the team, which provides an incentive for all team members to work toward the company's success. Additionally, the team is committed to learning, so one day per month, they focus on the entire team learning a skill. Finally, once every eight months or so, they gather all team members from around the world to connect in person in order to "get away from distractions to brainstorm, deliberate ideas, and devise strategies."[5] As leader, Danny Iny has created a successful organization in the world of virtual teams. There is a lot to be learned from his ability to keep his staff members connected, engaged, and working together effectively as a team.

Just What *Is* a Team?

Learning Objectives

12.1 Identify the skills necessary to be an effective team member

12.2 Describe the difference between teams and groups

Growing up, your experience with teams might have included being on the basketball or football team, soccer or swim team, or maybe the debate team. In any case, you got an introduction to what the future might hold for you in working with teams, where individuals come together with specific knowledge, talents, or gifts, and work hard to win for the team. In college, you are likely to experience courses that include working in teams—from coming together for a short time, such as one class period, or a much longer time frame, such as a semester-long project. When groups are formed in classes, your professor is providing you with the opportunity to experience the benefits of and learn the skills necessary for teamwork that you will need when you start your job after graduation.

Today's work environment requires that graduates have a jump-start on the skills necessary for effective teamwork. Organizational leaders need to be on top of or ahead of the rapid pace of change, and they need individuals who have the flexibility to move in and out of teams as necessary to accomplish the work of the organization. In fact, employers purposefully look for individuals who have teamwork skills. Many of these skills you have learned about in this textbook, such as decision-making, problem-solving, and creativity. Many more skills are critical to working with an effective team, such as clear and direct communication; critical thinking; collaboration; and trust, support, and respect for one another.[6] Employers are imploring high school and college faculty members to prepare graduates for the challenges that they will face as new employees, and being an effective team member is top among them.

Teams Versus Groups

A group is defined as a collection of individuals who are coordinating their work for some reason or another. As contrasted with a team, groups of individuals have no mutual accountability, and they may likely work for personal gain over group gain and each have their own definition of *winning*. There are no shared consequences and no shared accountability.[7] While some groups may have a common end, group members work either individually or with each other; however, the ultimate focus is on "what's in it for me" without regard for the group as a whole. In fact, individual members often simply share information only so that each person's individual performance can be enhanced.

Team was defined earlier as a group of individuals with a common purpose, aligned with collective goals for the good of the entire team. Teams are "aligned toward a common purpose. They are guided by shared leadership and share a mutual understanding—and therefore accountability—of team roles, responsibilities, the scope of work to be accomplished and the purpose for which the team exists."[8] Think about the groups of individuals with whom you work in various settings—at work, in school, at home, or elsewhere. Are they a group or a team?

One difference between groups and teams is that groups designate a leader, while teams often have **shared leadership**[9] in which one individual may take a leadership role for a specific time and then another steps up to lead; or an individual may take a leadership role depending on the task at hand and on his or her areas of expertise, so that leadership is dependent on a specific task at any different moment.[10] Maybe you have experienced shared leadership in a team for a specific task in class—the team comes together and designates one individual to take the lead for a specific part of the project because of his or her expertise in that area, while at another time someone else takes the lead because of his or her knowledge. You have engaged in shared leadership in the team. Shared leadership is different from team roles. **Team roles** comprise the functions that each individual plays in the team (i.e., technical, interpersonal, etc.). Team roles are often discussed and agreed upon in advance, whereas shared leadership is more dynamic and emergent based on the current needs of the group.

Members of a group have individual accountability for completing group tasks, while team members have **shared accountability** for setting and meeting outcomes for the team.[11] In fact, for groups, the reasons for the specific work of the group reflect the purposes of the organization wherein they operate within the boundaries of the organization. However, members of teams often develop their own specific vision and/or purpose and are not constrained by organizational boundaries. Teams have a shared sense of mission and collective responsibility for carrying out that mission. After team members set the overall mission for the project and take shared responsibility for the outcome, members outline the specific tasks, assign *leads* for different parts of the project, and meet regularly to share progress. All team members are constantly cognizant of the big picture of the task at hand.

The appropriate size for a team seems to be a challenging question. What is the right number of members? Many authors suggest that between three to ten, but no more than 12, is a good and manageable size for a team. Larger than that, and it becomes difficult to find time to bring all members together. Moreover, members start to form subgroups, which can have a detrimental effect on the work of the team. Here is an amusing rule of thumb from Amazon's Jeff Bezos: "If I see more than two pizzas for lunch, the team is too big."[12]

It is very important that the team leader carefully select team members for the skills and talents they bring to the table. Designing your team means selecting team members intentionally and strategically so that all members understand their role on the team. Members need to trust one another and feel safe enough to open up to all members of the team. If

Shared leadership where one individual takes a temporary leadership role on the team based on his or her area of interest and/or expertise

Team roles the functions that each individual plays in the team (i.e., technical, interpersonal, etc.)

Shared accountability team members' focus on the work of and responsibility for the team, for the greater good of the organization

individuals have been included as a *favor* to the boss, people may not feel that they can open up and trust the entire team.

REFLECTION QUESTIONS

Besides taking this class, what are you doing to expand your team experience and develop your teamwork skills? Are you involved in clubs and organizations at school or in your community?

Essentials of Great Teams

Learning Objectives

12.3 Compare various types of organizational team models

12.4 Assess the essential elements of teams

Having experienced a team or two may lead you to believe that there exist only a couple of types of teams. However, in the workplace, there are a number of different types of teams that you may encounter. Primary among those are functional; cross-functional; self-directed or self-managed; permanent and temporary; and contemporary teams, such as virtual and high-performing. Each type of team has and serves a specific purpose. Moreover, different types may be more appropriate at different times or in different environments depending on the situation and tasks to be performed.

Types of Teams

Functional teams generally include department leaders and their subordinates. These types of teams typically operate within traditional organizational hierarchies and are structured along departmental lines. Leadership styles within these groups vary according to organizational and team needs.

Cross-functional teams are comprised of members from different departments who may be selected as a representative of that particular department or due to their areas of expertise. This type of team structure allows organizations to assemble teams that are quickly able to respond to problems or issues within the organization. Moreover, with such diverse organizational representation, members get a broader view of problems and their potential solutions.

Self-directed or *self-managed teams* are similar to cross-functional teams and are comprised of members from across department types within the organization. The primary difference is that self-directed team members take responsibility for the quality of the work process and the sharing of management and leadership functions, and they are involved in the training, hiring, and disciplining of group members. Self-management is related to high levels of performance and satisfaction.[13]

Permanent teams are those that work together continuously on various projects either simultaneously or consecutively. These teams can be composed of members with similar areas of expertise or with various complementary backgrounds for the projects to which they are assigned.

Temporary teams are comprised of members who come together for the specific purpose of completing a task or project and then disband when the work is complete, returning to their regular positions within the organization. They, too, can have similar or varied areas of skills and expertise, depending on the task at hand.

Virtual teams that are geographically dispersed have emerged as a result of today's mobile, global, and technological society. Virtual teams pose significant challenges for organizations. Many of the challenges that are present in traditional teams may be even more pronounced in virtual settings. Virtual organizations and virtual teams are the results of efforts to look for novel ways to manage rapid change and global reach, coupled with market forces that demand improved quality, service responsiveness, and tailored production. Specific to internationally dispersed teams, issues surrounding cultural differences (see Chapter 11) need to be top of mind for leaders, and attention must be paid to educating team members on both understanding and capitalizing on these cultural differences.[14]

High-performing teams are those teams that display extraordinary effort and productivity. As the name implies, the results-focused teams perform well beyond that of an average team. In one study, researchers[15] found seven characteristics of high-performing teams: (1) purpose and values; (2) empowerment; (3) relationships and communication; (4) flexibility; (5) optimal productivity; (6) recognition and appreciation; and (7) morale. Moreover, they discovered that "optimal productivity and morale are most important to be a high performing team. To be a successful team, the group must have a strong ability to produce results and a high degree of satisfaction in working with one another."[16] Additionally, "high performance teams don't just happen—they are developed and nurtured . . . [they] take the combined efforts of a visionary leader, willing and competent team members, and a facilitator with expertise in team building."[17]

REFLECTION QUESTIONS

Of the types of teams that have been outlined above, which are used most frequently in your college setting, for example, in your residence hall, sorority or fraternity, or athletic team? Are they working well? Would another team structure work better?

Essentials of Building a Great Team

Teams come together in a variety of ways. The organization may need to solve a specific problem, develop a new product, solve a complex task, or work with a specific client. Each of these needs requires that a leader craft a team based on skills needed or temperaments necessary for a specific project. Effective teams need to be comprised of members with complementary skills in the following three categories: technical or functional expertise; problem-solving and decision-making skills; and interpersonal skills—in short: Content, Process, and People.[18] While attempting to maintain an ideal team size of between three and 12, team members normally will be selected who are adept at *several* different skills (e.g., problem-solving and interpersonal; technical and decision-making).

How Do Teams Come Together, and What Makes Them Excellent?

Many individuals can describe their experience with an excellent team. The difficulty with that description is that it is from their perspective, which is likely to highlight those characteristics most meaningful and relevant to that team member. You will find many lists profiling the characteristics of an excellent team. Four well-established profiles are listed in Table 12.1. Several foundational elements are generally agreed upon by researchers and practitioners: a meaningful mission that is shared and understood by all members; a climate of respect and trust; clear, agreed-upon roles and processes; external organizational support; and attentive leadership that designs success.

TABLE 12.1 ● Profiling Characteristics	
Hackman (2010)	**Larson and LaFasto (1989)**
• Teams must be real. Everyone needs to know who is in and who is out. • Teams need a compelling direction. • Teams need enabling structures. • Teams need a supportive organization. • Teams need expert coaching. Too often organizations only focus on individual coaching.[19]	• a clear, elevating goal; • a results-driven structure; • competent members; • unified commitment; • a collaborative climate; • standards of excellence; • external support and recognition; and • principled leadership.[20]
Silva (2016)	**Crawford (2016)**
• Common purpose • Clear roles • Trust • Solid relationships • Competent leadership • Effective processes • Excellent communication[21]	• Embrace excellence • Accountable to each other • Excellent listening • Collaborative delegating • Flexible, adaptable • Ok with making mistakes • Sense of humor [22]

MYTH OR REALITY

A TALENTED LEADER AND TALENTED TEAM MEMBERS WILL RESULT IN A GREAT TEAM.

Myth and Myth. Effective teams are carefully, thoughtfully designed. Leaders create conditions for success, and research indicates that "condition-creating accounts for about 60% of the variation in how well a team eventually performs," along with another 30% for how the team is launched.[23] No amount of leader talent can make up for failing to design appropriate conditions for success.

There is indeed an *I* in team—it is called *individuals*. While the common sentiment of emphasizing the *we* aspect of shared vision, common purpose, and collaborative effort is important, you cannot overlook the individuals who comprise the team, both during the advance design of the team as well as during the team's work. Individuals have different perspectives, needs, strengths, ways of communicating, levels of investment, means of influence, and personal goals outside of work. Maximizing the engagement and enthusiasm of each individual enhances the team outcome.

The other *I* in team might be called *Irritating Innovation*. Although teams have a specific purpose or problem, typically a more innovative solution is preferred. Innovation, however, is not fostered by consensus, common perspectives, or compromising collaboration. Rather, as you should recall from Chapter 8 on creativity, innovative ideas emerge when individuals are forced to see differently. Teams comprised of purposefully differing perspectives are likely to conflict, and from that conflict springs innovation. Controlled conflict to catalyze innovation happens when leaders design the team, focusing on the roles, rules, and elevated common goals within which team members operate.

When creating a team, whether it is for a project for school, athletics, extracurricular, or beyond, it is important to make sure to clearly define each of the following elements for your team members. The more closely aligned members are to understanding and embracing them, the better performance your team will have on its tasks, purpose, or outcomes.

Key elements for teams include:

A meaningful mission that is shared and understood by all members. Teams need a common purpose, specifically one that is clear and compelling. Team members must have a clear understanding of the reasons why their task is being given to a team (rather than just an individual)—teams are the means to an end, not the end in and of itself. This must be clearly articulated to the team by organizational leaders or crafted by members of the team themselves. It is critical not to begin the work of the team before the purpose is clearly articulated and understood by all members.[24]

A climate of respect and trust. Trust forms one of the most important foundations of teams. As such, "being trustworthy means keeping confidences; carrying out assignments and following through on promises and commitments; supporting others when they need support; giving both honest, positive feedback and helpful constructive feedback; being present at team meetings; and being available to help other team members,"[25] in effect, being predictable and consistent. Trusting relationships in teams allows members to openly communicate and not feel threatened by other members. This openness of communication is what allows teams to become highly competent and successful. It is not necessary that team members be friends but simply that they have respectful, trusting relationships where they know that all members of the team have the best interest of the team at heart and that they can trust one another to do the right thing.

Clear, agreed-upon roles and processes. Critical to the effective functioning of the team is an understanding on the part of each member as to why he or she has been selected to be a member of the team (i.e., what unique skills and abilities he or she brings to the table). Each person needs an understanding of the role that every other team member plays and his or her skills and abilities. Leveraging the strengths of each team member together will increase the likelihood of a successful outcome for the project. Additionally, highly effective teams function because they have established effective processes. Consider any athletic team sport. The team works many hours in advance of the game to craft each of its plays with precise processes and then practices their moves over and over again. Organizational team processes include decision-making, problem-solving, innovation, project management, and many more.

Attentive leadership that designs success. Teams need attentive, effective leadership to design the team experience and launch. Attentive leadership then continuously ensures that the group is working within their agreed-upon roles and rules, has the resources they need, and is heading on the right path toward the mission.

Leaders must particularly attend to the team communication process. Excellent communication facilitates the work of the team. The more efficient the communication process, the more expeditiously the team can accomplish its work. Team members get straight to the point and say what they mean—members of the team do not waste time with beating around the bush or lack of straight talk, which can lead to miscommunication or misunderstandings. They work hard at making communication effective and efficient and *metacommunicate*. That is, they talk about the process of communication to ensure that all members are on the same page.

EXPERTS BEYOND THE TEXT

INSIGHTFUL LEADERS KNOW ABOUT . . . HUMAN CAPITAL MANAGEMENT (HCM)

Human Capital Management and Leadership: Investing in Your Human Resources

By Lauren Miltenberger, Villanova University
and Ralph A. Gigliotti, Rutgers University

Have you ever thought about the term "human resources"? Many organizations have an individual or an entire department called Human Resources (or HR), but consider the literal words: human beings—people—as a resource. HR functions typically administer all the organizational aspects of employees: Workforce planning and job analysis; employee recruitment and selection; compensation, benefits, and employee engagement; assessing and managing employee performance; and employee training and development. But what if HR retooled activities toward their literal aim—to maximize the value of the individuals in whom the organization invests? How would you treat followers if you were always reminded of their great value—not just as persons, but as a present and potential profit generator?

Human capital management (HCM) is an employee-centered approach for assessing individual performance, predicting organizational results, and guiding the investments made in the area of human resources.[26] In the HCM model, leaders strive to engage employees in meaningful work experiences, support their employees in achieving specific goals, and encourage their learning and development. Cultivating positive relationships with employees is rewarding for the leader and highly advantageous for the organization at large. Research suggests that companies with an HCM approach to employee relations produce higher financial returns and value to their shareholders.[27]

Great HCM leaders understand the needs of their employees, emphasize the importance of skill development, and seek to create a positive work environment that both engages the employee and contributes to their

ultimate success. Leaders can cultivate a human capital environment by doing the following:

- Focus on the strengths and strive to understand how to balance the skills and needs of the employee with the competencies and skills needed for the job.

- Recognize both extrinsic and intrinsic rewards: recognize and celebrate individual achievements, promote continual learning, draw connections to mission, encourage democratic decision-making, and build positive relationships grounded in trust and respect.

- Devote time and attention to the development of workplace plans, hiring strategies, and recruitment and selection techniques—all of which are aligned with the mission of the unit, department, and organization.

- Recognize the value of performance management. Instead of using evaluations as once-a-year opportunities to discuss employee performance, use them as real-time benchmarks to connect each employee to the larger purpose of the organization, as well as to co-create goals that clarify expectations and outcomes.

- Above all, demonstrate empathy and work with each employee to help develop strengths and achieve excellence.

As you learn more about building a great team and the mindful design of organizational culture, consider the extraordinary HCM impact of making the shift from seeing employees as something to manage versus resources that can exponentially grow and produce returns on investment.

Human capital management (HCM)
an employee-centered approach for assessing individual performance, predicting organizational results, and guiding the investments made in the area of human resources

Shared Vision, Values, and Culture—Key to Team Success

Teams need to establish their vision, values, and culture for the team. These provide both a shared purpose and reason for existence, as well as assist in keeping team members aligned with the same values and moving in the same direction toward the same goal. You have learned about the overall organizational vision, values, and culture elsewhere in this book. As you may recall, those terms were defined like this:

- Vision: An aspirational image that provides short- and long-term direction for an organization and its members

- Values: Beliefs or ideals that guide a person's behavior

- Culture: Shared values and assumptions by organizational (or group) members; the way we do things around here

Notice that all three have something very important in common—all of them are highly influential in motivating and guiding individual behavior. If team members do not embrace a common purpose and performance goals, they revert to subpar performance. Additionally, common values are especially important in virtual teams when individuals are not engaging in day-to-day activities with one another and can easily lose sight of the common goal.

LEADERSHIP BY DESIGN

Design Principle: Accessibility

Definition: Objects and environments should be designed to be usable without modification by as many people as possible.

In Other Words: Can everyone perceive, understand, and operate within the context, organization, and culture?

For Example: Online portals allow everyone to receive the same information efficiently and participate fully, no matter what their physical capabilities or geographic location.

For Leaders: Accessibility is generally associated with wheelchair ramps and other physical characteristics, but the principle really comprises a much broader range in what it means to have access. Accessibility is a very powerful design principle that also applies to designing the culture and community of your team. When those on your team are able to perceive the culture, understand and operate with it, and make a few mistakes without

©iStock.com/golero

getting too off-track, then you as leader have designed an accessible culture. As the team grows larger, how can you ensure you remain accessible to a diverse group of people? What must you consider when designing a community where information and social interaction flow unimpeded throughout the organization?

Teams also have a culture. If you have ever joined a well-established team, you felt that culture right away as you tried to figure out those invisible rules of behavior. While some team cultures mirror the culture of the larger organization, others create and live their own culture. In fact, Schumpeter observed that "teams work best if their members have a strong common culture."[28] Moreover, in virtual teams, where members represent cultures from around the world, expectations and understandings can differ, taking extra time and attention to make sure that all members understand and are clear on issues and goals facing the team. Refer back to Chapter 11 to refresh on the importance of culture in the organization.

From Group to Team: Stages of Development

Learning Objective

12.5 Interpret Tuckman's stages of group development

As individuals work together as a group, they inevitably move through various stages of development (much like you did when you were growing up). Leaders and team members who understand these developmental stages and what to expect can design ways to navigate those challenges more effectively and move the team to its next level more quickly. Sometimes the team can get stuck in one stage, sometimes it moves forward and then back again, and sometimes it works through the stages sequentially. The best team development is when everyone recognizes that there *are* developmental stages, *what* they are, and *how* to move through each one and on to the crucial stage of getting the work of the team completed. Finally, when the project is over, team members move on, either back to their regular positions or on to the next task.

Tuckman's Stages of Group Development

Tuckman's stages of group development stand as one of the most used and useful models describing how groups commonly move from strangers to team.[29] Originally conceived as four stages (forming, storming, norming, and performing), in a follow-up analysis, Tuckman and Jensen added a final stage (adjourning).[30]

In the first stage, **forming**, group members come together and behave in a very tentative way while trying to understand the task, the interpersonal dynamics, and each other. He referred to this as the stage of *testing and dependency*. The next stage, **storming**, is where individuals are in *conflict* as they attempt to find their place in the team and gain an understanding of the task, rules, and roles at hand. The third stage, **norming**, is where *cohesion and consensus* come together and teams establish their mission, goals, responsibilities, and culture. The fourth stage is the **performing** stage, which Tuckman indicated included *functional role relatedness* where members attend to their work and their interpersonal skills, and celebrate accomplishments.

Adjourning, the final stage, occurs when the work of the group is completed and the group as presently composed disperses. During this stage, members may mourn having to disband.[31]

As individuals and the group move through each stage of development, a number of needs must be addressed. Because individuals will behave in a manner that meets their own needs, a group will muddle through each stage. However, as stated at the outset, leaders can facilitate a group's progress (and thus their performance) by understanding those needs and taking action to address them. Table 12.2 lists the needs at each stage of development. What specific activities could you do to address any of the needs either before or during each stage?

Tuckman's stages of group development: Forming: the introductory stage of a group where members are getting to know one another and tend to act in very polite ways; **Storming:** the second stage of a group where members are vying for position in the group and attempt to establish their role in the group; **Norming:** the third stage of group development where members have settled into roles and begin to establish the mission, purpose, and culture of the group; **Performing:** the fourth stage of group development where team members have settled into their roles and focus on the work at hand; and finally, **Adjourning,** the last stage where the work of the group has concluded and the group members disband.

TABLE 12.2 ● Needs at Different Stages of Development			
		As Leader, How Could You Facilitate?	
Stage	**Individual Need**	**Before the Stage**	**During the Stage**
Forming	Understand the mission and vision		
	Channel excitement of new project		
	Allay fears of uncertainty		
	Get to know others		
	Understand culture and norms		
	Understand their role and how I fit		

| | | As Leader, How Could You Facilitate? | |
Stage	Individual Need	Before the Stage	During the Stage
Storming	Assurance that my contributions are noticed, appreciated, and important		
	Understand and address individual differences		
	Allay the uncertainty of others		
	Revisit mission and remember that progress takes time		
	Refocus goals		
	Acknowledge frustration and establish trust		
Norming	Elaborate on true feelings and ideas		
	Capitalize on differences		
	Deepen trust and engagement with others		
	Utilize critique for individual progress		
	Benchmark team progress		
Performing	Enhance team performance		
	Enhance engagement with others		
	Expand individual role and enrich others' work		
	Acknowledge and celebrate success		
	Reestablish goals and next steps		
	Assess and address internal and external changes		
Adjourning	Acknowledge relationships and connections with others		
	Celebrate and archive accomplishments		
	Allay impending fear of loss and feelings of sadness		
	Understand my next steps		

REFLECTION QUESTIONS

Think about the last time you were in a group . . . maybe it was in class, maybe it was the start of the new school year with new roommates, or maybe it was a new club or team; do you remember moving through Tuckman's various stages of group development? If your team ended—did you mourn the loss?

Leading and Being a Team

Learning Objectives

12.6 Describe the key characteristics of team leadership

12.7 Summarize the factors that contribute to effective team members

12.8 Apply two assessments that assist team members with understanding themselves and others

It is important to understand the difference between being a leader and leading a team. Where a leader generally oversees and directs the work of others, the team leader is an integral part of the team, participating in the work of the team—in many cases, this makes the team leader a leader among equals. Team leaders are principled leaders who show respect for team members and support an action-oriented, decision-making environment where team members are valued and encouraged.[32]

Models of Team Leadership

Leaders of great groups share four traits: They "provide direction and meaning; generate and sustain trust; display a bias toward action, risk taking, and curiosity; [and] are purveyors of hope."[33] Note how each of the four could facilitate a group working through the stages of development outlined in the previous section. For example, when leaders provide direction and meaning to followers in a variety of ways, and often, individuals maintain the direction of their work, the vision as shared is reinforced, minor relationships and communication issues are put in perspective, and followers feel that the leader is attentive and invested. A number of leadership theories, models, or styles work well for team leadership, including transformational (Chapter 10), servant (Chapter 13), and authentic (Chapter 16), which all focus on working closely with others.

One model specifically focused on leading a team is the Hill Model for Team Leadership (see Figure 12.2). This model frames the actions necessary for ensuring team effectiveness. Hill's model specifically delineates the decisions or actions necessary at the leadership level for the team to effectively problem solve at each decision level. As a team's agenda unfolds, the leader faces many issues and challenges. Hill's model directs the leader to ask three initial questions:

FIGURE 12.2 ● The Hill Model for Team Leadership

Source: Hill, S. E. K. (2016). Team leadership. In P. G. Northouse (Ed.), *Leadership: Theory and practice* (7th ed., p. 367). Thousand Oaks, CA: SAGE.

1. Should I simply monitor the situation or take action?

2. If taking action is necessary, does the most useful action address an internal or external aspect?

3. And, if the action should be internal, would the most useful action focus on tasks or relationships?

As you can see in the model, the answers to those three questions lead to a short menu of areas that might be the solution to the present issue. Hill's model is particularly useful in that it guides a leader to more accurately assess an issue before acting and highlights the idea that taking no action and simply monitoring can also sometimes be an effective answer.

Yet another model for effective team leadership (Katzenbach and Smith) suggests that team leaders do not need to be exceptional leaders, "they simply need to believe in their purpose and their people."[34] In that regard, they present six actions that make for good team leadership:

1. Keep the purpose, goals, and approach relevant and meaningful;

2. Build commitment and confidence [of the individuals and the team];

3. Strengthen the mix and level of skills;

4. Manage relationship with outsiders, including removing obstacles;

5. Create opportunities for others [allowing others to take on learning opportunities]; and

6. Do real work [in roughly equivalent amounts for all team members, including the leader].[35]

Your and Others' Role on the Team: What Makes a Good Team Member?

Over the course of this chapter, you have been asked numerous times to think back on your experience with teams. Similar to much of leadership, leading teams is about how effectively you can influence others, and that is most effectively accomplished (or thwarted) by how someone feels. If you felt lousy about a team experience, reflecting on why and what made it feel that way invariably advances your understanding and practice of leadership. Thinking again about your experience with teams, would you say you were a good team member? Why or why not? Who on those teams would you characterize as a good team member or who not? You might have said a good team member is someone who gets along with everyone, builds bridges, contributes great effort, or has some skill that makes a difference. Take a moment to reflect, discuss, and write a quick list of good and not so good team member characteristics.

The assets you think you bring to a team can often be different from what the team thinks you bring. As you consider your strengths and what you *could* bring to the team, you realize that individual attributes are more complicated than a short list of characteristics. The attributes of a good team member are dependent on what the team needs and who else is on the team and what they bring. In other words, what you might recall as your strength on a team may likely be your strength *in that particular role on that particular team*. That is why designing your team is such a critical activity for the leader.

One way of categorizing attributes is to separate the task from the people and process. LaFasto and Larson found that team members' abilities and behaviors matter in two areas:

1. Working knowledge factors

   • Experience (practical knowledge)

   • Problem-solving ability (clarifying, bringing them into focus, getting them understood, developing strategies for overcoming)

2. Teamwork factors

   • Openness: The basic ingredient for team success (willing to deal with problems, surface issues that need to be discussed, help create an environment where people are free to say what's on their minds, and promote open exchange of ideas—these folks are effective communicators)

   • Supportiveness

   • Action orientation

   • Personal style[36]

As noted earlier, team member selection can be based on a variety of factors, but it is critical that you have a good mix of content, process, and people members. In other words, individuals who know and are skilled at the task to be accomplished, those who understand and can facilitate the process, and those who are skilled in emotional and social intelligence—working well with, among, and between others. Many team members will likely have some of each, but leaders should strive to identify and design a complementary mix. A number of instruments provide insight into individual strengths, including the Myers-Briggs Type Indicator® (MBTI®), Multiple Intelligences, StrengthsFinder, DISC®, and the Big Five, to name a few.[37]

What Strengths Do I Bring to This Group?

This is a great time for you to do some self-analysis of the strengths you might bring to a team. If not required for this class or another, you may want to take one or more of the assessments listed above. Some of them can be taken online, some for free, and some for a small fee. Many of the online assessments offer interpretation of the results that can assist you in understanding your own preferences for interacting with others—very helpful for understanding the dynamics that occur in teams. For example, one assessment instrument that has been popular for quite some time, the MBTI®, assesses 16 different personality preferences along four dimensions: extraversion/introversion, sensing/intuition, thinking/feeling, and judging/perceiving. Knowledge of your own and your teammates' MBTI® profile can go a long way in assisting you in understanding the ways that others work in teams.

StrengthsFinder (SF) is another very insightful assessment that assists you with understanding the strengths that you bring to your team. The Gallup Strengths Center has numerous books, each of which has a code in order to take the StrengthsFinder assessment online.[38] Once you have taken the online assessment, you will learn your top five strengths and have access to a wealth of tools that can assist you in understanding how to leverage those strengths in the workplace. The 34 strengths as measured by SF will fall into one of four categories: executing, influencing, relationship building, and strategic thinking. The *ideal* team will have individuals who have strengths in each of those categories, either individually or in combination. The awareness of team members' strengths allows teams to leverage them for maximum team productivity. Numerous colleges and organizations have implemented SF in their programs and teams.

These are just several examples of assessments that can assist you in understanding yourself and your talents. Many organizations are using others to ensure the most productive of work and team environments.

When Teams Go Wrong

Learning Objectives

12.9 Contrast the differences between organizational, team, and individual issues that can arise in teams

12.10 Assess three problems that can arise in teams

At this point, you might be thinking, "Great, so if I just use all these tools, my team will run just fine." Not exactly. While the strategies you have learned so far will clearly help your team move along smoothly, teams are still made up of people with different personalities, different motives, and different agendas they bring to the team. Moreover, while some individuals may have great technical skills they bring to the team, they may lack effective communication or people skills to be successful team members or vice versa. This section examines how teams can fail and what you can do as a leader to avoid failure or minimize the consequences.

Top 10 Reasons Teams Fail

Things can go wrong on teams from an organizational perspective, within the group itself, or with individual team members. Here are 10 reasons researchers have found that teams fail:

1. Not taking time to clarify purpose and goals
2. Uncertainty about what requires team effort
3. Lack of mutual accountability

4. Lack of resources

5. Lack of effective leadership and/or shared leadership

6. Lack of focus on creativity and excellence

7. Lack of planning

8. Lack of support for a team culture

9. Inability to deal with conflict

10. Lack of training[39]

An awareness of these potential pitfalls allows teams to proactively take measures to ensure that they are addressed (i.e., design for success). Clearly, there are numerous issues or problems that can arise for teams—from within or outside the team and before or during team activity. Three additional, well-researched team pitfalls are explained in the next sections: Abilene Paradox, Groupthink, and the Five Dysfunctions of a team. As you read about how teams can go wrong, note which challenges are the responsibility of the team members, the leader, the organization, or a bit of each.

Abilene Paradox

Have you ever gone along with the group because you thought everyone wanted to do something, so you agreed to follow that particular plan? Well, the Abilene Paradox is just that—it is a story about a family that ends up on a car trip to Abilene, Texas, from their home in Coleman, because each individual thought all the others wanted to go, since that is what each person articulated to the group. It was not until their return home that everyone confessed to the group that they had not really wanted to go but would have preferred to stay in Coleman. There was plenty of blame to go around, as each blamed the other for not speaking up in opposition to going on the trip.

Professor Jerry Harvey, who conceived the Abilene Paradox, indicated that it is the *failure to manage agreement*, which means that in reality, even though individuals disagree with a particular decision, no one comes forward to indicate their disagreement.[40] As a result, the organization, team, or group ends up moving in a specific direction that no one wants to go. People do not speak up for fear of being ostracized by or left out of the group, no matter the negative consequences or outcome that might happen as a result of moving forward with the plan.

So what does the team do to overcome this dilemma? First, determine whether the organization is facing a *conflict-management* or an *agreement-management* problem. If it is the latter, all members of the team meet together, and one person expresses his or her real position on the decision or problem at hand. Results can be confronted on either a *technical* or *existential* level. The technical level addresses the ability or inability of the team to solve the problem or issue with the resources at hand. Conversely, the existential level exposes to the team true interpersonal conflict within the group. In either case, it opens the possibility for either satisfaction having come from confronting the problem or dissatisfaction with opening up to critical dialogue toward the problem-solving. Finally, the individual may simply have to face living with the consequences.

Groupthink

Groupthink is a theory of social conformity in groups that was developed by Irving Janis[41] after reviewing the group dynamics involved in several key historical blunders. He found that as group cohesion increases, so too does the incidence of groupthink. Groupthink occurs when members of a cohesive group fail to raise objections in group discussions for fear of being too harsh on colleagues, bow to group pressure to go along with the group, or desire not to create conflict and provide social support among group members. Janis summarizes eight symptoms of groupthink. As you read each, can you identify a time when you experienced this on a team?

1. An illusion of invulnerability, shared by most or all of the members, which creates excessive optimism and encourages taking extreme risks;

2. Collective efforts to rationalize in order to discount warnings which might lead the members to reconsider their assumptions before they recommit themselves to their past policy decisions;

3. An unquestioned belief in the group's inherent morality, inclining the members to ignore the ethical or moral consequences of their decisions;

4. Stereotyped views of rivals and enemies as too evil to warrant genuine attempts to negotiate, or as too weak and stupid to counter whatever risky attempts are made to defeat their purposes;

5. Direct pressure on any member who expresses strong arguments against any of the group's stereotypes, illusions, or commitments, making clear that this type of dissent is contrary to what is expected of all loyal members;

6. Self-censorship of deviations from the apparent group consensus, reflecting each member's inclination to minimize to himself the importance of his doubts and counterarguments;

7. A shared illusion of unanimity concerning judgments conforming to the majority view (partly resulting from self-censorship of deviations, augmented by the false assumption that silence means consent);

8. The emergence of self-appointed mindguards—members who protect the group from adverse information that might shatter their shared complacency about the effectiveness and morality of their decisions.[42]

Dysfunctional Teams

The Five Dysfunctions of a Team describes a fable about a new CEO who took over a previously successful company and taught them about the five dysfunctions that can derail a team.[43] Table 12.3 notes each of these dysfunctions, along with some possible ways to overcome each.

Finally, team problems can also arise from personal issues with individuals who are on the team. One primary concern is a lack of motivation to contribute to the goals of the team. Additionally, individuals may have ineffective communication skills that lead to problems between and among members. There may be difficulties getting an individual to adequately coordinate with team members, and individuals may have personal or professional conflicts with other team members. Some individuals may simply withdraw from participation in the team. *Harvard Business Review* offered these reasons why that may happen:

1. The presence of someone with expertise

2. The presentation of a compelling but inferior argument

3. Lack of confidence in their ability to contribute

4. The decision to be made seems unimportant or meaningless

5. Pressures from others to conform to the team's decision

6. There's a dysfunctional decision-making climate[45]

TABLE 12.3 ●   **Five Dysfunctions of a Team**

Dysfunction	Described as . . .	Could Be Overcome With	What Else Could You Do as Leader?
First: Absence of trust	team members are not open to one another about *mistakes and weaknesses* that are foundational to effective teamwork	personal histories, team effectiveness, and personality profiles	
Second: Fear of conflict	lack of open communication and debate of ideas	acknowledging that conflict can be constructive and giving themselves permission to raise issues and deal with them openly	
Third: Lack of commitment	lack of commitment to decisions	imposing a clear deadline or engaging in a worst-case scenario analysis	
Fourth: Avoidance of accountability	evidenced when team members "hesitate to call their peers on actions and behaviors that seem counterproductive to the good of the team"[44]	clarifying group goals and standards, regular progress reviews, and team (not individual) rewards	
Fifth: Inattention to results	where individual or other needs are put ahead of the needs of the team	publicly declaring the specifics of intended results and tying results to team-based rewards	

How Do I Fix It When Things Go Wrong?

Leadership is a process. Sometimes things go great, sometimes not. Leaders with strong CORE™ capacities are well-positioned to persistently and positively work through the challenges of teamwork. If you were steering a boat that drifted off course, you would guide it back, but it would not happen immediately. If you had a leak in the boat that slowed you down and threatened to sink your boat, you would fix the leak, but you would also need to bail out the water and recalculate your progress. Of course, if the boat falls apart, you abandon it and build a new boat. So, the notion of *fixing* a team is perhaps better stated as facilitating the process.

Too often the challenges of teamwork appear so daunting that organizations and individuals either avoid them or avoid teams altogether. However, many of those challenges are actually benefits in disguise, and (as per Hill's model) it only requires the patient monitoring of the leader to take effect. If you have ever thought to yourself, "If the leader would have just stayed out of this, it would be fine," then you know the power of purposeful nonaction. These challenge-benefit opportunities are nicely summed by Edmondson in the *Harvard Business Review*.[46] For example, the challenge of navigating individual differences yields the benefit of multiple perspectives finding innovation, expanding individual skill sets, and providing a broader, more cohesive view of the organization.

The teams of the future are moving toward a more dynamic, situational model, and thus, they are more challenging to lead. Edmondson distinguishes between traditional teamwork and the more agile, yet chaotic notion of teaming. **Teaming** represents a temporary group put together to solve a problem, often with a diverse group of experts. This is quite different from the more stable team that has worked their way through the developmental stages. In some ways, the classroom teams of which you have been a part were more teaming than traditional team. Leading teaming still requires advance planning of process and structure; however, the social and emotional aspects take on more importance and take greater skill to facilitate.

Teaming a temporary group put together to solve a problem, often with a diverse group of experts

LEADERSHIP BY DESIGN

Design Principle: Priming

Definition: The activation of specific concepts in memory for the purposes of influencing subsequent behaviors.

In Other Words: Exposure to certain things now will influence a later response.

For Example: Highlighting a preconceived stereotype before a task could influence performance. For example, there is a common misconception that females are poor at math. Indicating gender prior to taking the test primes the student to think a certain way and may influence performance.

For Leaders: Priming occurs outside of conscious awareness. Concepts in memory are automatically activated via the five senses, so as a leader you can capitalize on this natural phenomenon to reinforce culture and better lead your team. Set your team up for success by creating the desired environment within your followers' subconscious. What images, sounds, or interactions have been associated with organizational success? Priming that goes unnoticed is the most effective. What other behaviors might a leader require from followers that could be primed for later influence?

Just as leaders need to remember to reward individuals for their work accomplishments, teams also should be rewarded. When teams accomplish a major milestone, members should be rewarded *as a team*, not as individuals. While most companies claim they value teamwork, few really know what great teamwork looks like. If teaming were clear, then there would be more team-based rewards rather than corporate incentives that promote individualism.[47] Rewarding members as a team assists in keeping team cohesion and unity. Rewards can take the form of personal thank you notes, public praise, time off with pay, special celebrations, and special awards among many others. Bob Nelson has written a comprehensive book titled *1,001 Ways to Reward Employees* that outlines rewards that are just as appropriate for teams as they are for individual successes.[48]

REFLECTION QUESTIONS

While there is no foolproof way to avoid the problems outlined above, what do you need to look for when composing a team that might minimize the occurrence of issues? Take a look back through this entire chapter at the many aspects of effective teams and team leadership. What steps can you take to minimize teamwork issues?

Chapter Summary

More and more organizations are moving to the use of teams, recognizing the power and value in bringing different perspectives to a project. A group of individuals has the potential to bring more than the sum of individual contributions. This is known as synergy and can be accomplished by ensuring that the group has a shared purpose, vision, and accountability to one another. This is what makes a team different (and more than) a group.

Teams also have shared leadership. Although one person may have the leadership position, the strength of the team lies in the roles each person agrees to take. As different situations and needs arise, those roles may best serve the team by assuming the lead. Teams are carefully selected to include the right mix of content, process, and people skills and strengths.

There are many different kinds of teams, each suited for a different challenge or purpose. Effective teams are characterized by a meaningful mission that is shared and understood by all members; a climate of respect and trust; clear, agreed-upon roles and processes; external (to the team) support; and attentive leadership that designs success. A sense of humor helps, too.

Individuals remain an important element of the team as each person brings their unique motivations, attributes, and perspective. Bringing out the best in each individual team member requires considerable attention and ability by the leader, but inevitably, doing so provides great return in productivity and innovation.

Being a good team member depends on one's fit for the specific role. However, understanding your attributes and what you are capable of contributing to the team helps clarify.

In addition to their shared vision and values, teams share a culture. The culture of a given team goes through specific stages of development: Forming, Storming, Norming, Performing, and Adjourning. Understanding what each stage entails and feels like for team members informs a leader as they facilitate the group's formation into a team. Numerous models help further inform leader activity, including Hill's model that begins with asking whether action is even necessary (versus monitoring).

Teams can fail for many reasons. Preparation in designing the team and its launch is perhaps the most important preventative measure. Team leadership is a process comprised of people, and the attentive, mindful leader will choose from their many tools to facilitate the team to success.

Key Terms

Adjourning 312	Performing 312	Teaming 320
Forming 312	Shared Accountability 305	Team Roles 305
Human Capital Management	Shared Leadership 305	Tuckman's Stages of Group
(HCM) 310	Storming 312	Development 312
Norming 312	Synergy 303	

CORE™ Attribute Builders: Build Now for Future Leadership Challenges

Attribute: Optimism

Builder: Tuckman team development (on) stage

When you understand and can anticipate what is coming, it is much easier to be optimistic. Build your optimism for working with and leading a team by role-playing each stage of Tuckman's model. With a small group of peers, create a two- to three-minute skit based on one of the stages: Forming, Storming, Norming, Performing, or Adjourning. Strive to illustrate both

what happens and what it feels like at that stage. Following each performance, have a conversation about what you were trying to portray and what others would add to your performance.

Once you have gone through the performances, have your group change their focus, this time to create a new two- to three-minute skit illustrating how a leader could effectively facilitate a group through that specific stage.[49]

CORE™ Attribute Builders: Build Now for Future Leadership Challenges

Attribute: Resilience

Builder: Learn to do (something new to you)

Nothing requires resilience quite like learning to do something new, and doing so as a group can build your resilience as you see others acquiring the skill faster than you. Here is your group's task:

1. Your team must learn *to do* something new. All members must learn to do it proficiently. Only *one* member of the group may have tried it, and *no* member may be an expert in it.

2. What you choose to learn must be more interesting, creative, valuable, and challenging *than all the other groups*. This means no beer pong, t-shirt folding, simple recipe-making, flip cup, or other skills a small child could easily learn. *Be interesting, distinctive, and excellent.*

3. You must learn how to do it from a credible source.

4. Be prepared to *demonstrate* what you learned to do for the full group.

5. As a group, discuss:

   a. How did it feel to have to learn something new . . . at the start, as you learned, after you learned?

   b. What did you bring to the group?

   c. What did you need from the group?

   d. What traits and/or skills were most helpful for this task?

For an added challenge, have each group *assign* what another group needs to learn.

Skill Builder

Teamwork Is Like a Jigsaw Puzzle

List all the ways you can think of in which a jigsaw puzzle is similar to the composition and operation of a team.

Some possibilities:

1. There are boundaries (the straight-edged pieces).

2. Each piece plays a specific role in the solution.

3. Pieces are highly interconnected when teamwork occurs.

4. Each piece is unique in its nature (similar to the individual differences among people).

5. The solution is a fragile one (easily broken).

6. The whole is more (better) than the sum of its parts.

7. Some pieces are central, some are peripheral.

8. There are natural groupings (e.g., by color or design).

9. Pieces need someone to move them.

10. Rapid solution is aided by someone with an overall vision.

Discussion Questions

1. Are you surprised by the number of similarities?

2. What are the ways in which you can use this metaphor?

3. What action guidelines does this point toward?

13

Designing a Culture That Cares

A rich life (is fundamentally a life of serving others), trying to leave the world a little better than you found it . . . This is true at the personal level . . . (but there's also) a political version of this. It has to do with what you see when you get up in the morning and look in the mirror and ask yourself whether you are simply wasting time on the planet or spending time in an enriching manner.

—Cornel West

Learning Objectives

13.1 Reconceptualize designing others' success into designing a culture that cares

13.2 Describe the important characteristics of a caring culture

13.3 Explain the concept of service and the application of servant leadership

13.4 Translate a culture that cares into real-world leadership activities

13.5 Devise a plan for making a difference

Detailed Chapter Outline

Introducing a Culture
    That Cares
        Values and Intention
        Motivation and Maslow's
            Hierarchy of Needs

Leading With Service
        Servant Leadership and the
            Servant Leader
        Organizational Benefits of
            Servant Leadership

Leadership by Design Model

Design Self

How can I design myself as a leader?

Design Relationships

As a leader, how can I design my relationships with others?

Design Others' Success

As a leader, how can I design success for others?

DESIGN CULTURE

AS A LEADER, HOW CAN I DESIGN THE CULTURE OF MY ORGANIZATION?

Design Future

As a leader, how can I innovate?

Introducing a Culture That Cares

Learning Objectives

13.1 Reconceptualize designing others' success into designing a culture that cares

13.2 Describe the important characteristics of a caring culture

In what kind of place would you like to work—a place where colleagues do what they need to do for themselves to be successful or one where colleagues sincerely care for one another? At this point in the textbook, you have focused on the success of others—designing their success, designing your relationship with them, and designing the team and culture within which you and your followers will work. While you are always designing yourself as a leader, many of the last chapters move beyond that and focus on Rule #2 (It's not about you.). So, it is likely you have a pretty good vision for what kind of workplace or organization you are striving to build. However, set aside the notion of success and achievement for a moment and consider the idea of *care*. What might a culture of care look like? How do people communicate, make decisions, work through challenges and change?

The key question for designing culture asks, As a leader, how can I design the culture of my organization? The next important question is, What kind of culture do you want to promote? A culture that cares impacts employee morale, engagement, retention, and productivity; and consequently, it has a significant impact on achieving an organization's vision. As a leader, you can design a culture that cares, and thus, you can strengthen your organization, even its bottom line.[1] Caring in any organization begins with the top leaders and permeates throughout the entire organization. A *culture that cares* should be evident from a person's very first interaction with an organization.[2] Organizations that embrace caring in the workplace involve leaders and coworkers who provide support and empathy for one another; foster connections and conversations among employees; avoid blame, forgive mistakes, and use them as teachable moments; have a positive workplace; and focus on individual and team strengths.

Care acting in a manner that provides for and shows concern regarding another's needs and well-being

Individuals who **care** act in a manner that provides for and shows concern regarding another's needs and well-being. In Chapter 3, you learned about the style approach to leadership where, based on the current needs of the organization, leaders shift their emphasis and focus between task and relationship. Designing a culture of care goes well beyond what a leader emphasizes at a given moment in order for the group to be successful. A culture of care means that the unwritten rules emphasize concern for the health, wellness, and protection of the individuals—it is the way things are done around here.

LEADERSHIP THAT MAKES A DIFFERENCE

Tawanda Jones and the Camden Sophisticated Sisters

In a world filled with poverty, violence, and despair, there shines a bright, caring light in Camden, New Jersey. Camden, known for being one of the most violent cities in America, has often been referred to as a *war zone*. As a young teen, Tawanda Jones saw her friends having kids, dropping out of school, and struggling with poverty, a life that she did not want for herself. At age 13, Tawanda knew she needed to do something to change the course of her life and the lives of those around her.

Tawanda loved dance and drill team, so she went to the local community center to get involved with drill team—the director saw something in her and asked if she would help with the younger kids, and so she did. However, within a couple of years, the city program lost funding and it closed. At age 15, her grandfather challenged her to make a difference in her community; however, she was not sure she could. Her grandfather showed faith in her and told her he knew she would make it work. In 1986, he bought her 80 uniforms and one drum, and thus began the Camden Sophisticated Sisters (CSS). Tawanda set out to serve the youth in Camden and make a positive change in her community.

Students who enter the program come from very difficult circumstances where murder, drugs, single-parent homes, and families working multiple jobs to make a living wage are common. Students must have and maintain a *C* grade point average, audition, and complete an essay on *How Can I Improve Where I Live*. In addition, each student is required to participate in 200 hours of community service annually, instilling in them the importance of caring and giving back to their community. Tawanda exposes high school students to colleges, and out of over 5,000 students, 100% have graduated high school, and 80% of those have gone on to some form of post-secondary education—in a city where the high school graduation rate is only 48%.

Within the last few years, she has been recognized many times for the wonderful work and service she has provided to the children of Camden. Tawanda Jones is changing lives one kid at a time in Camden, New Jersey. "Under her unwavering leadership through many challenges, trials and tribulations, CSS has impacted lives, prepared young people for a successful life, and proved that, despite appearances, there is genuine goodness in Camden, New Jersey." Tawanda Jones exemplifies caring and service to others, and she credits her grandfather as the one who taught her to give back.[3]

Values and Intention

Individual values and intentions guide those actions that distinguish how a caring culture will feel and act. Culture, as you recall from Chapter 11, is ultimately a product of the individual actions that model the rules of behavior for others. While you and your followers may hold values and intentions that truly care about others, those values need to be both aligned with actions and reinforced by the culture. For a leader, the alignment of values and actions communicates credibility. More importantly, showing others that you care (in any situation) helps model the cultural expectations, helps followers feel good about themselves, and ultimately prompts them, in turn, to care for others. The cycle of caring can permeate throughout the organization, emphasizing values that many individuals hold deeply but did not believe were part of their work or organizational culture.

The notion of *care* for leaders represents a broad set of activities and intentions that incorporate elements from other leadership approaches. For example, in Chapter 10 you learned that transformational leadership was defined as a change process in which leaders and followers help each other advance to a higher level of morale and motivation.[4] Sounds very much like caring. Individual Consideration, one of the four Is used to describe trans-formational leader behavior, emphasizes the importance of communicating that you as a leader care about each and every individual within the organization. When you give others individualized consideration, you strongly communicate that you care—about who they are, what they are doing, what they need, and even why they are part of your team.[5]

Authentic Leadership is another approach that centers on an ethic and culture of care. (You will learn more about Authentic Leadership in Chapter 16.) Authentic leaders are working from a place where their central motivation is to help the movement, group, organization, or team.[6] They authentically care in a way that is both transparent and sincere. They do not take on a leadership role or engage in leadership activities for status, honor, or other personal rewards.

REFLECTION QUESTIONS

Revisit your values—the ones you explored in Chapter 4. Which of your values could contribute to a culture that cares? What important values do you hold that you hesitate to display because the culture does not support them? In what other ways does the culture of your group, organization, or society influence how much you behave in a way that cares?

Motivation and Maslow's Hierarchy of Needs

Have you ever been really hungry in the middle of class? All you can think about is ending the class and getting some food. Even if the class would normally be very interesting or engaging, your grumbling tummy has taken over your attention. Or imagine that you have an abusive classmate who glares at you in a threatening manner all through the class. You would likely put all your mental energy into wondering what you did, why they are targeting you, and what will happen to you after class rather than exploring and learning the course content. What if these situations (hungry or threatened) were a constant part of the classroom culture? This would definitely not be a culture that cares. But sometimes leaders rely on their values and intentions, and overlook some of the other forces that drive behavior and culture—forces that may distract from the vision.

The scenarios above describe one of the most well-known models for what drives individual behavior—Abraham Maslow's Hierarchy of Motivational Needs. **Maslow's Hierarchy of Needs** illustrates progressive categories of needs that drive human behavior.[7] There are four lower-order needs, which Maslow called *deficiency needs*, that must be satisfied (typically thought to be sequentially, but not always) before moving up to the higher-level needs. As individuals grow and fulfill needs, they are motivated by gratification of these lower-level needs. Then higher-level needs emerge and are pursued to satisfaction. This progression fosters continual growth in the person.[8] One way that you come to know and appreciate yourself is through an understanding of your own motivation and needs.

Maslow's Hierarchy of Needs This is a model of progressive categories of needs that drive human behavior. Four lower-order needs, which Maslow called *deficiency needs*, that must be satisfied (physiological— basics such as air, water, food; safety—from harm; belonging and love— relationships; esteem— esteem and respect from self and others) before moving up to the higher-level needs (cognitive, aesthetic, self-actualization, and transcendence).

The lower-level needs include:

- Physiological—basic air, water, food, and shelter; required for survival

- Safety—safety from harm, health, and economic security

- Belonging and love—family, friendships, social, community and religious groups, and intimate relationships

- Esteem—self-esteem and self-respect, respect and appreciation from others, and feelings of accomplishment[9]

Maslow's Hierarchy was originally developed with only one highest level need, called *self-actualization*. He later reexamined that top level and added three more, reordering the higher levels into the following: cognitive needs, aesthetic needs, then self-actualization, followed by transcendence, in which individuals move outside themselves to help others (see Figure 13.1).[10]

- Cognitive needs—gaining knowledge

- Aesthetic needs—understanding and appreciating beauty and the arts

- Self-actualization—realizing one's personal potential and being able to provide service to self

- Transcendence—helping others by being altruistic[11]

FIGURE 13.1 ● Maslow's Hierarchy of Needs

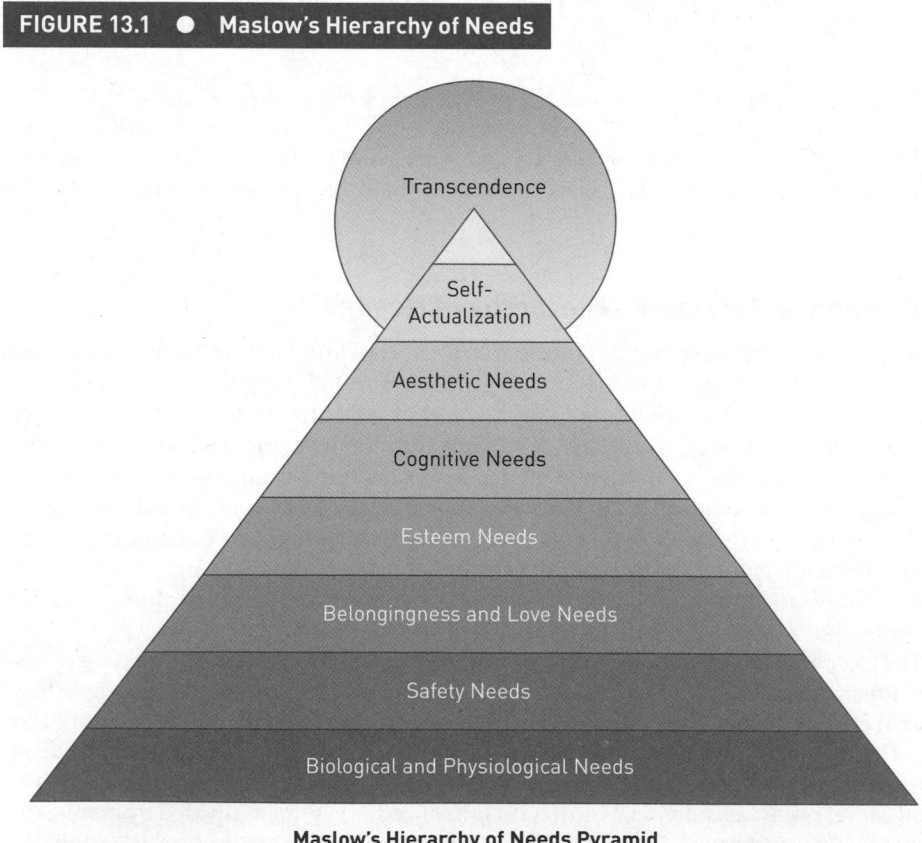

Maslow's Hierarchy of Needs Pyramid

Source: Maslow, A. H. (1969). The farther reaches of human nature. *Journal of Transpersonal Psychology, 1*(1), 1–9.

Maslow's Hierarchy illustrates an important point: Everyone has needs that drive them, and some of those basic needs must be satisfied before one can move on to other needs. Further, needs get satisfied in whichever order is important to life circumstances. Designing a culture that cares means you must also be aware of the individuals within that culture . . . and their needs.

As you design yourself as a leader, note what needs are driving *you*. Most of you have acquired your basic needs such as food and shelter from harm. But perhaps you are still working on a desire to feel a part of something bigger than oneself—friends, family, and community. At some point, everyone wants to be self-actualized and live a life that is happy and fulfilled. The ultimate outcome in the leadership quest is to attain Transcendence—to give of yourself. Through transcendence you are able to focus on caring for and serving others. Maslow reminds you that you must design your leadership self before you can (or are willing to) focus on designing a culture that cares.

REFLECTION QUESTIONS

Where are you in the hierarchy? Are all your lower-order needs met? Are you currently pursuing your cognitive needs by taking a college class or program? What do you think it means to become self-actualized? What more information do you need or what intrapersonal issues do you need to resolve to achieve self-actualization? Are you ready to help others?

Leading With Service

Learning Objective

13.3 Explain the concept of service and the application of servant leadership

Designing a culture that cares includes your values and intentions, aligning your actions with those values, and meeting the individual needs of your followers. When you shift your focus from your needs and well-being to those of others, you are leading with service. **Service** can be defined as action that is done for others—putting others' needs ahead of your own. The concept of service to others as an aspect of leadership goes back at least 2000 years. Every Christian and non-Christian religion in both ancient and contemporary history describes (and promotes) some form of service to others as a part of its foundational principles. Recent leadership authors also note the importance of service. For example, Peter Northouse identifies *serving others* as one of five key components of what ethical leaders do.[12] And in Kouzes and Posner's *The Leadership Challenge* (see intro to Module 2), the first practice, "Model the Way," speaks to the importance of understanding and following your own guiding principles and values.[13] All around the world, many organizations exist specifically to serve others. Many schools, businesses, and organizations have embraced the idea of providing service to others to benefit the organization and its members, local communities, and society in general.

Leading with service means changing the way you fundamentally see your goal—elevating achieving a culture of care to an equal place as part of the vision of the organization. Former AT&T executive Robert Greenleaf is credited with the modern leadership notion of placing oneself in the service of others as a core component of leading. Organizations with cultures that espouse a leadership model of service not only have employees with high loyalty but also high engagement, high performance, and high productivity. This section examines the nature of service to others and of leadership *with* others for positive good.

The idea of service with others is critical to the definition of leadership: the process of influencing others toward a common vision. Organizations today are moving toward

Service action that is done for others—putting others' needs ahead of your own

designing organizations that give back to the community and to the world as well. But even more than giving back, organizations want to be positive contributing citizens. The idea of sustainability as an organizational goal includes the common notion of environmental sustainability, yet it also includes financial sustainability (so you do not go out of business) and the idea of social sustainability—creating a culture within your organization such that individuals thrive and want to stay. This description of sustainability is referred to as the triple bottom line (environment, finance, social), and it will be explored more extensively as you design your future in the final chapter of this book.

In a growing number of organizations, individuals are given time off from work to volunteer in the community. Teams of individuals travel the world to effect change in countries less fortunate than ours. The challenge as you move into a leadership role is to determine how and when your organization can give back and how the culture encourages sustainable behavior. The vision of making the world a better place is important to engaging today's employees in the workplace because it provides a sense of purpose and a feeling that you are working toward something bigger than yourself. Look to very involved contemporary organizations for the new model of how this is working. In the most recent list of the Best Places to Work, there is also a list of Best Workplaces for Giving Back, where you will find such places as Nationwide Insurance, Cisco, PricewaterhouseCoopers, Etsy, and American Express.[14]

Servant Leadership and the Servant Leader

Servant leadership
a leadership approach that focuses first on others' needs, aspirations, and success

The concept of **servant leadership** has been around since 1970, when Robert Greenleaf wrote an essay titled *Servant as Leader* and subsequently expanded the concept.[15] His concept of servant as leader came after reading Hermann Hesse's novel entitled *Journey to the East*. In the story, a character named Leo acts as a servant to a group of travelers. He does chores, but he also keeps up the spirits of a group of travelers, which keeps them together. One day he disappears, and then the travelers fall apart—they cannot make it without him. Years later, Leo is found, and it is discovered that he is a "great and noble leader" (who first served).

Greenleaf asked the question, "Who is the Servant-Leader?" In the most often quoted passage he noted,

> The servant-leader *is* servant first—as Leo was portrayed. It begins with the natural feeling that one wants to serve, to serve *first*. Then conscious choice brings one to aspire to lead. That person is sharply different from one who is *leader* first. . . . The difference manifests itself in the care taken by the servant-first to make sure that other people's highest priority needs are being served. The best test, and difficult to administer, is: Do those served grow as persons? Do they, *while being served*, become healthier, wiser, freer, more autonomous, more likely themselves to become servants? *And*, what is the effect on the least privileged in society; will they benefit, or, at least, not be further deprived?[16]

Thus, servant leadership is defined as a leadership approach that focuses first on others' needs, aspirations, and success. Over the years since Greenleaf's first writing about servant leadership, numerous authors have tried to capture and articulate the concept of servant leadership and define it in a way that is easily communicated. Authors have examined traits, behaviors, and characteristics of servant leaders; various concepts related to servant leadership; and personal values of servant leaders. Larry Spears, who led the Greenleaf Center for Servant Leadership for 17 years, had the opportunity to dive deeply into Greenleaf's writings and found that "servant leadership seeks to involve others in decision-making, is strongly based in ethical and caring behavior, and enhances the growth of workers while improving the caring and quality of organizational life."[17] He identified the following 10 characteristics, which he views as being critical to the development of servant leaders:

1. *Listening*—listening intently to others for both what is said and what is unsaid, clarifying the will of the group after a period of reflection

2. *Empathy*—striving to both understand and empathize with others; accepting and recognizing others for who they are

3. *Healing*—taking the opportunity to heal oneself and others and "help make whole those with whom they come in contact"[18]

4. *Awareness*—self-awareness, especially regarding ethics, power, and values

5. *Persuasion*—the ability to convince others, especially through effective consensus building within the group

6. *Conceptualization*—the ability to dream and conceptualize beyond the day-to-day with a delicate balance between conceptual and operational thinking

7. *Foresight*—the ability to learn from the past and apply lessons to future decisions

8. *Stewardship*—the ability to hold the organization and its people (staff and trustees alike) for the greater good of society with the commitment to serving others

9. *Commitment to the growth of people*—individual members of the organization have intrinsic value and the servant leader commits to providing resources that will add to the personal and professional growth of each one

10. *Building community*—moving toward a focus on building community for those individuals within an organization

Leadership is a process; the leader is the person. Beyond these 10 characteristics of servant leadership, there are several scholars who looked for the most important characteristics of servant leadership. From the over 100 they found in the literature, they found the following 12 characteristics most important for servant leaders: valuing people, humility, listening, trust, caring, integrity, service, empowering, serving others' needs before their own, collaboration, unconditional love, and learning.[19]

Organizational Benefits of Servant Leadership

An article in the *Harvard Business Review* suggests that a new style of leadership is needed for individuals in today's workforce, who often work in a team environment (see Chapter 12) and want organizational leaders to be honest, open, transparent, and trustworthy. They want to feel respected, and they want to contribute in a meaningful way to the organization's work.[20] Servant leadership fits the bill for today's workers. In order to gain the influence that most leaders desire, the servant leader removes the attention from him- or herself and focuses on the achievements of the organization, the success of team members, and their contribution to the organization. The leader becomes the facilitator between the employee and the success of the organization.

The servant leader will "ask more questions, listen more carefully, and actively value others' needs and contributions. The result is more thoughtful, balanced decisions." Moreover, "an employee who believes her boss understands her strengths, values her input, and encourages her growth is likely to stick around for the long-term."[21] The benefits of servant leadership include increased worker morale and greater organizational commitment by employees, thus leading to lower employee attrition.

Why is it important for a leader to understand and apply servant leadership? Organizations that are led by servant leaders are extraordinarily successful from both a financial and personnel point of view. For example, one study compared the 10-year average performance of the S&P 500 with Jim Collins' Good to Great Companies[22] and servant-led companies. The S&P 500 averaged a 10.8 percent gain, Collins' companies averaged a 17.3 percent gain, and the servant-led companies averaged a 24.2 percent gain.[23] That is a massive financial and productivity difference.

Servant leaders lead a significant number of top-performing organizations. They are "people-centric, value service to others and believe they have a duty of stewardship."[24]

Spiritual capital individual dispositions that manifest as a sense of meaningfulness through (a) belief in something larger than self; (b) a sense of interconnectedness; (c) ethical and moral salience; (d) a call or drive to serve; and (e) the capability to transfer the latter conceptualizations into individual and organizational behaviors, and ultimately added value

High-performing organizations have included (among others) Chick-fil-A, Home Depot, the U.S. Marine Corps, Ritz-Carlton, Whole Foods, Starbucks, and Southwest Airlines.[25] Ritz-Carlton, which has consistently been among the top servant-led organizations on numerous lists, stands out not only for being an exemplar in service, but for having a corporate training arm that focuses specifically on teaching servant leadership principles both in house and to others who want to emulate their extraordinary service philosophy.

Servant leadership blogger Ben Lichtenwalner found an absence of a comprehensive list of organizations that embraced servant leadership principles and set about to create his own list. To date his list contains 112 companies that value servant leadership.[26] Additionally, each year more and more companies that espouse servant leadership principles are popping up on lists of best companies to work for. He noted that five of the top 10 *Fortune* magazine's Best Companies to Work For had servant leaders who run the organizations.

EXPERTS BEYOND THE TEXT

INSIGHTFUL LEADERS KNOW ABOUT . . . LEADERSHIP AND SPIRITUAL CAPITAL

Leadership Success as Redefined Through Spiritual Capital

By Alain Noghiu

Being a leader is a popular aspiration and a coveted organizational and societal status. Yet there is something both inspiring and troubling about the notion of leadership, both leading back to the same source: human nature. Leadership authors, of course, distinguish between less ("authoritarian") and more desirable ("transformative" or "servant") forms of leadership, but the field of study as a whole tends to abstain from judgments, instead focusing on presenting nearly all forms of leadership as valid in particular contexts. Hence, individuals must grapple with questions of right and wrong—the why and to what end—to pursue leadership and ponder how they need to address prevailing leader-follower dynamics.

Judging by the course of history, it may seem pointless to challenge power-based leader-follower paradigms, since it appears that most societies have structured themselves along these lines. One might conclude that such a dynamic represents a "natural societal order." The 21st century, however, is not "business as usual." Our globe and societies are transforming at an incredible pace, characterizing this time as one of complexity and interconnectedness. These come with evident social benefits, such as technological progress and global communication, as well as considerable costs, like environmental degradation. Might this new reality require a rethink of how leadership acts and what it wants?

The concept of **spiritual capital** addresses complexity and interconnectedness, and takes a stance about society and the future. Spiritual capital is a form of value,

but unlike other forms (like money, time, social connections, etc.). Samuel Rima, perhaps the most thoughtful author on the topic, defines the notion as

a metaphysical impulse that animates and leverages other forms of capital to build capacity for advancing the common good. As such, spiritual capital exists to bring life, vitality and empowerment to people and the societies in which they live, rather than for the material or economic satisfaction and advancement of one individual, social group or corporate entity.[27]

Spiritual capital speaks to the fact that if leaders seek positive impact, they need to connect with something deeper, something transcendent. Within themselves, aspiring leaders need to seek sources of motivation more noble, principled, and moral. Toward others, leaders must "disappear" so that their peers may also gather "life, vitality and empowerment." Spiritual capital as a form of leadership value looks like

individual dispositions that manifest as a sense of meaningfulness through: (a) belief in something larger than self, (b) a sense of interconnectedness, (c) ethical and moral salience, (d) a call or drive to serve, and (e) the capability to transfer the latter conceptualizations into individual and organizational behaviors, and ultimately added value.[28]

Spiritual capital challenges leadership to rise above itself, transcending organizational structures to inspire human progress. As such it fully represents the exciting paradoxical reality of our times.

LEADERSHIP BY DESIGN

Design Principle: Veblen Effect

Definition: A willingness and at times tendency to find a product desirable and pay a higher price simply because the product has a high price.[29]

In Other Words: It must be good because it costs more . . . so I want it.

For Example: Brand-name clothing, brand-name shoes, brand-name foods, pretty much brand-name everything.

For Leaders: The perception of high value influences others. Valuable things are sought after, elicit great effort, and are cherished and kept nice. In reality, price does not always equate to quality or efficacy. But price does often compel individuals to perceive and desire one thing over another. As a leader designs a culture of service, the Veblen Effect (and research on engagement and motivation) suggests that followers will more likely want to be a part of an organization that has explicitly high value. Individuals want to be a part of something valuable—they desire the feeling of status, which in turn provides a feeling of belonging. While excellent service can translate into profits, it more often arises from efforts to better the human condition. How can you as a leader recast the common good as uniquely great? Where and when might you need to unveil the misperception of overvalued, unproductive goals?

REFLECTION QUESTIONS

Have you ever worked for an organization that cares? How did you see that play out? What can you do in the future to ensure that your organization engages in caring?

Make a Difference: Designing a Culture That Cares

Learning Objectives

13.4 Translate a culture that cares into real-world leadership activities

13.5 Devise a plan for making a difference

In what kind of a place would you like to work? That was the question posed at the start of this chapter. Some say that if you want a workplace that employees love, you need to create a high-energy workplace where work is fun, employees have space to dream, and everyone shares the success so that employees feel like owners and have a real incentive to contribute to the organization's success.[30] Sounds like a great culture. But what if within that high-energy culture no one *authentically* cares about each other? Although everyone has their own set of values and goals, everyone—every single person—wants to feel like they matter. Adopting a servant leadership approach and incorporating those specific behaviors into your culture will make a great difference.

Designing a culture where each individual matters means fully engaging *The Leadership Challenge* exemplary practice entitled Encourage the Heart.[31] In their workbook by the same title, Kouzes and Posner outline seven essential activities. Take a moment to look over each of these seven practices listed in Table 13.1 and try to complete the table: What are you doing now that helps meet that essential for encouraging the heart? What could you be doing?

TABLE 13.1 ● Seven Essentials for Encouraging the Heart[32]	What Are You Doing Now?	What *Could* You Be Doing?
Tell the story		
Set clear standards		
Expect the best		
Pay attention		
Personalize recognition		
Celebrate together		
Set the example		

Source: Kouzes, J. M., & Posner, B. Z. (2011). *Encouraging the heart workbook.* San Francisco, CA: Jossey-Bass.

Tell the story of your organization. What makes you excellent? Who are the main characters and what role do they play? What challenges do you overcome, and how do you do it? When you tell the story of your organization, you are setting the example and clear standards. Your story is about expecting the best, working together with everyone's strengths, and celebrating your accomplishments. Telling this story again and again, in word and deed, models and reinforces a culture that cares. The story, through the culture, becomes a self-fulfilling prophecy—if much is expected from an individual, he or she will rise to the occasion and achieve higher goals. You may want to revisit the Leadership by Design featuring "Storytelling" in both Chapter 4 and ahead in Chapter 16.

When you feel like you matter, people notice when you do a good job and then provide recognition for that job well done. Recognition that is personal. Personalized recognition singles out a person and specifically notes what they did, why it mattered, and how that person contributes to the greater mission and overall good. Appreciation for a great job goes a long way to make a person feel that he or she is an important part of the organization. Sometimes, a simple *thank you* can go a long way to making an individual feel valued as well. If you currently work on a team, with a group, or in an organization, who could use a personal thank you or note of accomplishment? In what ways could you make individual recognition a regular activity such that it becomes the way things are done around here (as culture is simply defined)?

LEADERSHIP BY DESIGN

Design Principle: Personas

Definition: A technique to build data-based archetypes of fictitious users/clients/customers to profile their needs, wants, and expectations in order to guide decision-making regarding features, interactions, and aesthetics.

In Other Words: Who are the *typical* users, and what do they tend to be like?

For Example: Visitors can log into a university website from a number of different perspectives—a student, an alumnus, a parent, a faculty/staff member, and so forth. The subsequent information each person sees is tailored specifically to that subpopulation.

For Leaders: A leader's role is often ambiguous. There are no guidelines for every specific situation, context, time, and individual follower that demonstrate how to lead. Crafting personas comprising different roles in the organization and different stakeholders helps a leader anticipate and better design culture and community. In the same way that a persona helps make the intended user more real to a designer, a leader can use personas to more effectively find the *common* vision across many individuals. Personas provide a framework around which a leader can test decisions, understand situations, and further develop. Personas ensure that different needs are being met, while also creating empathy and expanding perspectives.

Social Change Model of Leadership Development

One model that many universities have adopted to help students develop their capacity to design a culture that cares and make a difference is the Social Change Model of Leadership Development (SCM) (shown in Table 13.2 below).[33] Often used as a foundation for co-curricular programs, the SCM asserts that the hub of leadership development is the pursuit of positive social change (the first of seven Cs in the model). The model emphasizes the interplay between three sets of values: individual values (Consciousness of self, Congruence defined as alignment of values and actions, and Commitment), group values (Collaboration, Common purpose, and Controversy with civility), and community values (Citizenship). Each of the seven *C* values within the model provides a prescriptive goal around which many college programs have built leadership programs to develop social responsibility and drive positive social change. How might you translate each of the values into a practicable action?

TABLE 13.2 ● The Seven Cs of the Social Change Model of Leadership Development	
	Start Making a Difference by Doing the Following:
Consciousness of self	Find what motivates you to take action.
Congruence	Find what values your actions communicate, then find the right actions that align.
Commitment	Find the social issue or challenge that inspires your investment of time and energy.
Collaboration	Find others who share your commitment, and find ways to work with them.
Common purpose	Find the shared values, visions, and aspirations of those sharing your commitment.
Controversy with civility	Find where others disagree, and then find resolution (even if it is agree to disagree).
Citizenship	Find how your values and your issues connect with others and the community, and find your responsibility to those others.
Change	Find out more about change management, and how your service can effect positive social change.

Making a Difference Now and Later: Opportunities and Actions

Reflect back on several of the "Leadership That Makes a Difference" stories that you have read throughout this book. What you were reading were actual stories of caring and service to others. Remember in Chapter 4, Ryan Hreljac at age 6 was determined to solve the issue of access to clean drinking water? He was serving others, doing something greater than just for himself. And in Chapter 11, Maung Nyeu sought to save his native language for future generations of his hometown. And in this chapter, you learned about Tawanda Jones, who cared about and served her community by saving 5,000 children from the devastating effects of murder and drugs in the streets of Camden, New Jersey. These three examples of caring and service to others reflect ordinary people doing extraordinary things and touching the lives of many individuals. These leaders made a difference by serving others, and they acted from the heart to serve as leaders for their communities and their causes.

MYTH OR REALITY?

PARTICIPATING IN A SERVICE PROJECT IS A GREAT WAY TO GET EXPERIENCE FOR A JOB UPON GRADUATION.

Reality. Not only does gaining service experience look great on a resume, it provides you with an opportunity to gain skills that are important and useful in today's work environment, especially if you have worked in a team environment.

Nonprofit organization
This is an organization that focuses on achieving a type of value different from financial. As an organization, they strive to achieve a cause or mission, funneling any financial profit back into serving the organization's efforts (versus paying investors or stockholders).

Perhaps the best training for designing a culture that cares is through practicing service yourself. The more mindful, reflective service engagement you experience, the more you will notice what is and is not effective. Service to others is embedded in many families, communities, organizations, and national cultures. Service plays out in many different ways, through many different organizations. **Nonprofit organizations** focus on achieving a type of value different from financial. As an organization, they strive to achieve a cause or mission, funneling any financial profit back into serving the organization's efforts (versus paying investors or stockholders). Many nonprofit organizations are service-oriented, with missions to tackle difficult social challenges. Working with or for a nonprofit organization can be extraordinarily rewarding because serving others and a culture that cares are often built into the mission. For-profit companies can also serve or make a difference. But their underlying responsibility is to maximize profit and/or shareholder value.

It is quite likely you have already participated in service. Every major religion engages in service to others in numerous ways—this call to service, to serve others, is reflected in each of the holy books. Maybe when you were growing up, your church, synagogue, temple, or other religious institution engaged in feeding the poor or building or cleaning up homes for those less fortunate. Possibly you were involved with a nonprofit organization such as the local animal shelter and helped walk dogs or clean cages. Perhaps you had a bake sale to donate the proceeds to a specific charity or visited with senior citizens at a community center. Each of these provided you an opportunity to feel good about making a difference in your community. Moreover, it provided an opportunity to improve your community, meet new people, and gain work and leadership experiences. But most important, these activities shape and reinforce the culture people seek to encourage. Consider the many ways you can continue and extend your involvement—this time as a leadership learning opportunity.

Service to Others in College

Although some students come to college already having engaged in service learning or volunteerism in high school, often students have their first experience with service learning in college.[34] **Service learning** refers to campus-based volunteer opportunities that combine academic learning with principles of service to community. **Volunteerism** comprises individual or group engagement with others and/or an organization for no compensation. In fact, many colleges and universities have created service learning opportunities both inside and outside the classroom. Most sororities and fraternities have had some type of socially responsible service opportunities since early in their inception; and now, more college clubs and organizations outside of fraternities have taken on service projects. Colleges and universities are most interested in assisting the local community, being good community partners, and stewards of the neighborhoods in which they reside. Many universities offer lots of opportunities for students to become involved.

Besides the simple benefit of feeling like you are doing something to help the greater good of the community, the organization Idealist lists three reasons why it is important for students to become engaged in service as a part of their college experience: (1) "staying involved in college strengthens the foundation for lifelong volunteerism"; (2) students can learn "new skills and expand their personal and professional networks"; and (3) "volunteerism offers college and university students the opportunity to marry theory and practice beyond academia's gates."[35]

Service learning campus-based volunteer opportunities that combine academic learning with principles of service to community

Volunteerism individual or group engagement with others and/or an organization for no compensation

Types of College Service

The types of student engagement in service or volunteerism that are offered are quite varied and are foundational for a lifetime of volunteering:

- *Service learning*—typically engages students in combining learning goals with service in the community, usually making a difference for some local nonprofit organization. This type of activity enhances student growth and the common good.

- ***Community engagement***—focuses on community action goals, combined with learning. Beneficial outcomes occur for learning, personal, and social outcomes, and career development.

- *Volunteerism*—often not as structured as service learning or community engagement but can provide just as valuable a service to external (or internal) organizations.

Community engagement where like-minded individuals come together to engage with and effect change in the local community

In addition to on-campus resources for service learning (e.g., your professor, the service learning office), there are numerous off-campus groups that coordinate service experiences. Among some are the Corporation for National and Community Service; Campus Compact; College Students Helping America; BreakAway (alternative breaks); and Idealist. Several colleges stand out as exemplars in service learning—or creating service for others. Brandeis University has consistently provided a service-learning program as well as being actively engaged in research on service learning. You only need to do a web search for "best colleges for community service" to come up with a list of the top 10 colleges most involved with community service. For colleges that are interested in participating in education for civic and social responsibility, Campus Compact has been a leader in coordinating activities for college since the 1980s. It offers "research, online tools, and other initiatives to help campuses create effective service-learning programs that meet academic and service goals."[36]

Service Outside College

If you are fortunate, college represents a time and context where the full responsibilities of adult life have been put off. This time-out from full adult expectations ideally helps students focus on developing themselves (like your CORE™), so that you can be even more impactful when you graduate. Service activities in college are excellent practice for leading the design of a culture that cares across many contexts. These opportunities to practice and make a difference continue after college. And in fact, your participation is critical to the success of others and community—it is the citizenship value in the Social Change Model. You will find some of these opportunities within your career field or organization, and there are also many venues to make a difference outside your organization.

One context that will always appreciate your attention is your community. Every individual exists in a community of one type or another. Some people are very involved, while others prefer to simply act as good citizens. Either way, communities usually have individual and societal needs—needs that can be addressed through community service. In her blog, *PrepScholar*, Christine Sarikas defines community service as "work done by a person or group that benefits others." She poses four questions that can guide your thinking about your involvement in community service:

1. Who would you like to help?

2. Do you want a community service activity that is reoccurring or a one-time event?

3. What kind of impact do you want to have?

4. What skills would you like to gain?[37]

The list of opportunity ideas in this article seems endless, and indeed there are many, many creative and interesting ways that you can contribute. Once you have thought about and discussed those questions with others, consider what *you* are interested in, have specific strengths and skills in, and would find fun and fulfilling. Then, realistically consider how much time you can devote to community service. As with leadership, the more you know about yourself, the more likely you will identify your preferred avenue for serving . . . and creating a culture that cares.

REFLECTION QUESTIONS

What worlds, hobbies, activities, or ideas do you find important or interesting? Then, research groups or organizations in your community that align with those interests? Who could you contact to find out how you could get involved? Remember, service is not about fixing, it is about engaging.

Service Within the Organization

In today's turbulent times, many organizations are encouraging employees to spend time in service to others in both the local community and beyond, sometimes even internationally. Often called names such as volunteerism, community service, or corporate volunteering, many allow these opportunities during the work hours.

Volunteering is alive and well in America. The most recent statistics on volunteering from the Corporation for National and Community Service found that "1 in 4 Americans volunteered through an organization," and that adults volunteered 7.8 billion hours; time that is valued at $184 billion. Additionally, they found that volunteers are "twice as likely to donate to charity as non-volunteers." In their study, Gen X had the highest volunteer rate (28.9%), followed by Baby Boomers (25.7%), and 21.9% of Millennials volunteered. Individuals attending college volunteered at twice the rate of non-college peers (25.7% vs. 13.6%), and working mothers have the highest rate of volunteerism (36%).[38] The latest research by the Higher Education Research Institute (2017) on Gen Z indicated that 79% of college seniors volunteered or provided community service either occasionally or frequently.[39]

Volunteerism provides numerous benefits to the organization. It can assist with attracting engaged employees who are motivated to work in an organization that gives back to the community, it can improve a corporate image, it can enhance employees' skills, and it can build stronger local communities in which the organization resides. The best kind of volunteer program is one that is employee driven, which leads to more organizational engagement by employees.

Service Outside the Organization

In the United States, the federal government offers numerous opportunities for service. Public service and volunteer opportunities are available at https://www.usa.gov/volunteer, which includes a repository for information on Peace Corps, Citizen Corps, and Volunteer.gov, and a link to the Corporation for National & Community Service, where one can find information on AmeriCorps and Senior Corps. Information is also available on disaster services, education, vets and military families, and environmental stewardship. Gaining experience in one of these meaningful types of service organizations can position college students or recent graduates for significant leadership experiences upon return and be looked upon favorably by employers when seeking a permanent position.

The United States also has numerous **service clubs** made up of people whose purpose in belonging to those organizations—in addition to fellowship—is to serve others. Three highly regarded international organizations that were founded in the United States are Rotary International,[40] Kiwanis International,[41] and Lions Clubs International.[42] The mottos for each of these organizations are "Service Above Self" (Rotary), "Serving the Children of the World" (Kiwanis), and "We Serve" (Lions). In turn, each of the service organizations has social issues that its members undertake to solve and give back—whether those are for local, state, or international communities (sometimes for all three). For example, Rotary strives to foster intercultural peace; fight diseases such as polio and malaria; provide clean water, sanitation, and hygiene; save mothers and children; support education; and grow local economies, and they engage in these activities both here and abroad. No matter the type of service organization, all have similar desires for the outcomes of their service—to make the world a better place than they found it, to solve a need that affects large numbers of individuals.

The concept of organizational caring may seem like the latest *buzzword* in the lexicon of leadership and management. But an organizational culture that provides a culture of care is a setting that employees (and others) would love to spend their time in every day. The website FastCompany.com wrote an article titled "How to Create a Workplace People Love Coming To" in which they found the five traits in organizations that made them "Employers of Choice" in the annual list of Best Places to Work.[43] Those traits are people matter; employees feel heard; people are empowered to grow; leaders are strong; and employees are appreciated. In other words, these organizations and their leaders *care* about their employees.

So, now it is up to you. What steps will you take to design a culture that cares? How will you make a difference? Take the Service Learning Preference Inventory (SLPI) at the end of this chapter to learn which type of service learning activity fits best with your personality type. Are you a *Direct* type, where you like to be involved in direct contact with people in need of service? Maybe you are *Indirect*, where you prefer to work on resources to solve problems that affect individuals in need. Alternatively, you might be into *Advocacy*, where

Service clubs organizations that usually were originally formed for social purposes that have evolved into making changes in the world

your skills fit the opportunity to solve specific problems. Finally, you might be more interested in participating in a *Research-based*, task-oriented service-learning project by researching the underlying causes for specific community problems. Whatever fits your specific style of involvement, there is always a place for you in serving others.

REFLECTION QUESTIONS

If you were to engage in service learning in your class today, what type of organization would you engage with and why? Based on your skills and expertise, what type of contribution can you make to a service project?

Chapter Summary

In what kind of a place would you like to work? Designing a culture of care significantly impacts both individual and organizational performance. Organizations that embrace caring in the workplace involve leaders and coworkers who provide support and empathy for one another; foster connections and conversations among employees; avoid blame, forgive mistakes, and use them as teachable moments; have a positive workplace; and focus on individual and team strengths. The concept of care is rooted in the values, intentions, and motivations of leaders and followers. Many of the practices in Transformational and Authentic leadership further contribute to a culture that cares.

Leading with service, and the approach of servant leadership, comprises one of the most impactful approaches to designing a culture that cares. While people have been serving others for millennia, leading with service is more complex than helping or fixing. Robert Greenleaf, who created the idea of servant leadership, found servant leaders in business who were making a difference

in their organizations. Numerous attributes characterize the servant leader, including listening, empathy, healing, awareness, foresight, stewardship, building community, and a commitment to the growth of others. Valuing people and caring are at the heart of the servant leader.

Designing a culture that cares is really about making a positive social difference, whether in your organization, your community, or the larger world. Many strategies, approaches, and venues exist for maximizing your impact, such as those related to *Encouraging the Heart* of others or the seven *C* values that comprise the Social Change Model of Leadership Development.

Many of today's organizations are engaged with local, national, and international community projects where giving back and assisting others is a primary end goal. This chapter includes suggestions for numerous types of opportunities for service to community as well as a number of organizations that provide those opportunities.

Key Terms

Care 326
Community Engagement 337
Maslow's Hierarchy of Needs 327
Nonprofit Organization 336

Servant Leadership 330
Service 329
Service Clubs 339

Service Learning 337
Spiritual Capital 332
Volunteerism 337

CORE™ Attribute Builders: Build Now for Future Leadership Challenges

Attribute: Confidence and Engagement

Builder: Engaging servant leadership

Complete each of the following activities by yourself or with a small group of others. Explain how you accomplished each item, and consider which characteristics of servant leadership are most applicable for each activity:

Help someone.

Do something exceptionally courteous.

Interact with positive people.

Praise someone.

Make someone else feel good.

Work on something with a positive person.

Tell someone that you care about her or him.

Meet someone new (more than just *hello*).

Recognize someone for something.

Listen to someone talk through their goals and ambitions.

Make an unhappy person laugh.

Recognize someone for doing something excellent.

Send someone a thank you note.

(Adapted from http://gx.gallup.com/dipper.gx)

CORE™ Attribute Builders: Build Now for Future Leadership Challenges

Attribute: Resilience and Engagement

Builder: First-year student servant leader care package

First, review the 10 characteristics of a servant leader:

1. Listening
2. Empathy
3. Healing
4. Awareness
5. Persuasion for empowerment
6. Conceptualizing a positive vision
7. Foreseeing possibilities
8. Stewardship and sustainable behavior
9. Commitment to the growth of people
10. Building community

Second, remember when you were a first-year student in college? What aspects of servant leadership would have facilitated your success?

Third, design and put together a care package for a first-year student at your school incorporating as many of the servant leadership characteristics as possible. Explain which characteristics you used, why you chose them, and how you incorporated them into your care package.

Finally, deliver your care package to a deserving first-year student.

Skill Builder Activity

Service Learning Preference Inventory (SLPI)

STEP 1: Conduct Inventory

Each row contains descriptions of two service activity options. Circle the number closest to the service activity you would *most likely* prefer of the two options given in each numbered row. Look at the sample, then begin when you are ready.

Wash cars to raise money	1 2 ③ 4	Research social issues and create a report

Begin Inventory Here

1. Visit elderly in long-term care facility	1 2 3 4	Organize a letter-writing campaign
2. Deliver food to needy families	1 2 3 4	Collect/analyze data to solve organizational problem
3. Assist a group with cleaning a local park	1 2 3 4	Conduct a nonpartisan voter registration effort
4. Create marketing materials (flyers, brochures)	1 2 3 4	Analyze survey data for a school district
5. Help people register for recreation classes	1 2 3 4	Assist a political office with a social issue
6. Mentor teens on basic living skills or career preparation	1 2 3 4	Evaluate effectiveness of a new program
7. Design a web site or use social media to market an agency	1 2 3 4	Design and deliver presentations on a social issue (e.g., poverty, obesity)
8. Assist with raising funds to build a local playground	1 2 3 4	Conduct energy audits in public buildings

Horizontal score = _____

Add your circled responses and place the sum on the line above

This is your *Horizontal* score

Continue With Inventory . . .		
9. Pack boxes to send shoes to third world countries	1 2 3 4	Create community awareness for Alzheimer's
10. Conduct an analysis to determine impact of agency on its community	1 2 3 4	Give series of presentations regarding resources for diabetics
11. Serve *behind the scenes*	1 2 3 4	Work directly with people
12. Analyze data—look for trends	1 2 3 4	Work one-on-one with people
13. Arrange baskets of food for local pantry	1 2 3 4	Give small group presentations in the community
14. Conduct a needs analysis on an organization	1 2 3 4	Create community awareness for a social issue
15. Serve while working among a group, following their lead	1 2 3 4	Serve by working independently, taking your own initiative
16. Service focused on a *project* (tasks)	1 2 3 4	Service focused on *people* (relationships)

Vertical score = _____

Add your circled responses and place the sum on the line above

This is your *Vertical* score

Estimate (plot) your horizontal and vertical scores on the graph's horizontal and vertical lines. Draw a line to connect your two scores to create an intersecting mark in one of the quadrants as shown in the sample. For example, scores of 30 (horizontal) and 14 (vertical) would display like this to show *Research-Based* as the preferred type of service:

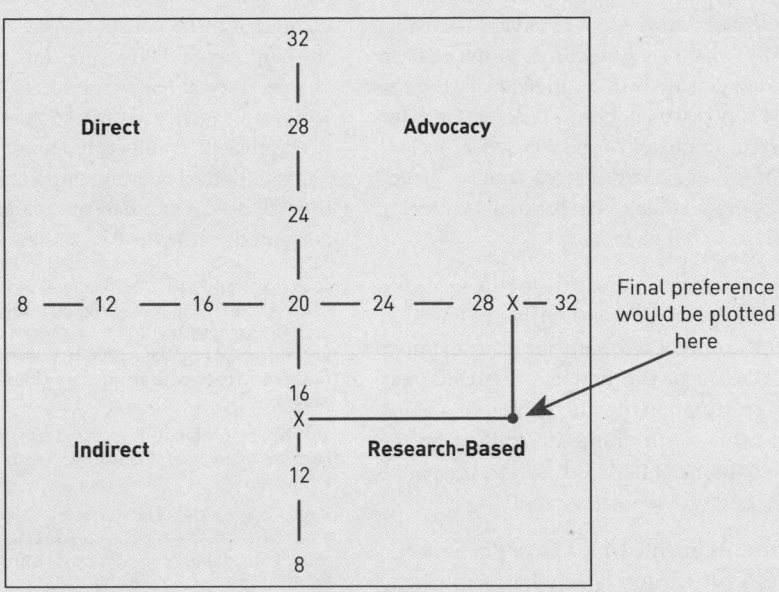

STEP 2: Chart Your Scores

On the graph below, plot your Horizontal and Vertical scores; then connect the two to view your preferred type of service.

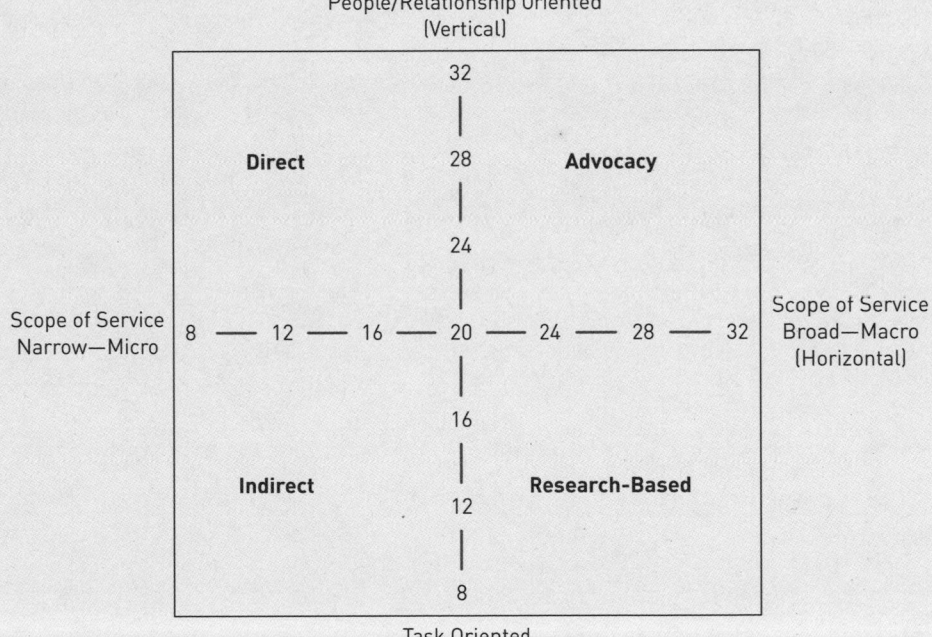

Service Learning Preferences

Direct (people oriented; narrow scope of service)—Activities that require personal contact with people in need. This type of service is generally the most rewarding since you often receive immediate positive feedback during the process of helping others. Examples of direct service activities include working with senior citizens, providing direct services to the homeless, or being the front receptionist at a women's center.

Indirect (task oriented; narrow scope of service)—Activities that are centered in channeling resources to the problem rather than working directly with an individual who may need the service. Often you do not come in contact with the people being served. Examples of indirect service include collecting food or toys for disadvantaged families, participating in landscaping a community park, or transferring hard-copy policies to an online format.

Advocacy (people oriented; broad scope of service)—Requires you to lend your skills and talents to the effort of eliminating the causes of a specific problem and/or to make the public aware of the problem. Activities may include making presentations to the community about particular social issues, distributing literature about the issues throughout the neighborhood, or making phone calls to help raise funds for a notable cause.

Research-Based (task oriented; broad scope of service)—can be defined as a partnership of students, faculty, and community who collaboratively engage in research with the purpose of solving a pressing problem or initiative for change. Typical research projects include creating survey tools for an agency in order to assess a specific community need/problem, conducting a needs analysis to implement a new initiative, or evaluating a current process or organizational need. Once data are analyzed, recommendations are typically developed to address the needed change.

Source: © Dan Noel, 2015. Direct, Indirect and Advocacy types of service learning were originally suggested by Dunlap, Drew, and Gibson (1994). All four types of service are mentioned and supported by Kaye (2004) as well as used by other institutions of higher education (i.e., Colorado State University-tilt program).

Dunlap, N. C., Drew, S. F., & Gibson, K. (1994). *Serving to learn: High school manual.* Columbia: South Carolina Department of Education.

Kaye, C. B. (2004). *The complete guide to service learning: Proven, practical ways to engage students in civic responsibility, academic curriculum, & social action.* Minneapolis, MN: Free Spirit Publishing.

Design the Future

Would you like to swing on a star

Carry moonbeams home in a jar

And be better off than you are[1]

—Bing Crosby

There has been a lot of talk over the decades about the future in space. After successful use of satellites, trips to the moon, shuttles, and space stations, the next big thing seems to be getting people to Mars. A personal trip to Mars requires a lot of planning and inventing a few things that do not yet exist. The more scientists, engineers, policymakers, and all of those involved learn about what such a trip might entail, the more clearly the challenges can be anticipated and prepared for. Designing a successful trip to Mars means knowing what you will need to have, know, be able to do, and be like—all so that you can expect the unexpected and survive if the worst possibilities happen. Everyone, using all that they know, strives to build accurate scenarios that can then be analyzed for best and worst cases. The best-case/worst-case scenario analysis is a tool used in many fields to predict risk and guide decisions.

You have a much more difficult challenge on your hands than designing a trip to Mars. You have to design *you* . . . to make a successful trip into the future. No one has been to the future, nor have any probes been sent to gather information. Despite the best efforts of many very smart people through time, none have consistently predicted what the future will bring—what challenges, new ideas, or even accurate best-/worst-case scenarios. Many have imagined the future, and in some cases, those imaginations helped guide those designing the future. The hard reality is that no one knows what to expect, how it will feel, what needs to be known, and so forth. That reality is one of the essential tenets of this textbook: How do you prepare for that unknown future?

Designing in the 5th Dimension

Throughout this text you have been challenged to translate the design process, which typically applies to the concrete world (like designing a chair), into the abstract notion of designing leaders, leadership, and culture. Design as a process is an action—a verb. As a noun, design has multiple dimensions (2-D, 3-D, 4-D, 5-D) that illustrate the breadth of design applications.[2] Two-dimensional (2-D) objects have only length and width, so 2-D design objects are things similar to posters, brochures, logos, and the home page of a website. When a 2-D movie is turned into 3-D, it looks like things are coming at you off the screen. Adding that third dimension, depth, brings 3-D design into things like product design—remember, pretty much every product you see around you right now was designed.

The next dimensions of design—4th and 5th—start to get quite interesting. A product is what it is . . . until someone interacts with that product in some way. This is the fourth dimension. A 4-D design focuses on the human interaction element, which can include systems, services, and how people experience something. Finally, the 5-D design focuses on time and the future. Designers considering the fifth dimension are thinking about how an organization within a specific market is going to operate and maneuver over time or how the use of a product will change as the user acquires expertise or experience.

Here is an easy example of how these four dimensions all come together. Imagine you have started a healthy and tasty fast food restaurant. To maximize your success, you have designed a great product (the food) and space that is comfortable and attractive (3-D). You have also designed intriguing and appealing ads online and in publications that feature your super cool logo (2-D). The best part about your restaurant, however, is the customer experience (4-D). There is no *drive thru* but rather a drive up, where you order on your smart phone, and your order is delivered to your window—fast, fresh, hot, and with a smile—or they staple a $20 bill to the bag. Your restaurant may be a success . . . today . . . but what about into the future? Times and tastes change, and the fifth dimension of design addresses that element of time. So, you incorporate a customer idea board and send teams around the world to discover new food ideas. These 5-D design additions generate strategy for how a designer wants the other dimensions to unfold over time.

Now you have designed a great restaurant experience. But focusing on your product is only part of your design challenge. You cannot achieve success in a consistent, sustained manner without designing the leadership, too. All the dimensions work together to make a great organization. Purposefully considering each dimension relative to different facets of the organization, including the leadership design, increases your awareness of where design efforts might lead to innovation. Use Table M5.1 (below) to prompt some ideas for what you could do to design effective leadership within the restaurant example:

TABLE M5.1 ● Designing Leadership Across Different Dimensions

	2-D What written materials will facilitate:	3-D What products will facilitate:	4-D What experiences will facilitate:	5-D What will facilitate success over time:
Design leadership self	You as leader put a photo collage of all employees right in front of your desk to remind you of what matters most.			
Design leadership relationships				Each week, a leader and two employees have a *no work talk allowed* lunch.
Design others' success		Every employee receives a smart watch that is synced to their schedules, sends reminders, and can reference instructions.		
Design culture and community	Motivational posters? You post these only if they actually motivate. How about a compliment wall?			
Design the future			Quarterly "Share What You Like" meetings where employees share examples of competitors' products they like as feedback for improvement.	

What do you need to do to design the future—and your future leadership? Many experts postulate about what future leaders will need for success. The authors of this text assert that you need to develop your Confidence, Optimism, Resilience, and Engagement (CORE™). Many of your professors will insist you develop an expertise in a discipline, while practitioners will want expertise in a field. "The leaders and experts of tomorrow have to be either polymaths (deep multi-domain experts), curators (those who collect or collate different domains), polyglots (the overlay and meaning makers), or all three," notes designer Denise Gershbein in *Extinction of the Expert*.[3] Everyone's journey and requisite applicable characteristics will certainly differ, but perhaps your most valuable tool moving into the future is understanding how to facilitate the process of designing.

LEADERSHIP BY DESIGN

Design Principle: Hierarchy of design needs[4]

Definition: Design success requires meeting basic and deficiency needs before attempting to satisfy higher-level needs.

In Other Words: Basics then additions.

For Example: A cake must be edible before you concern yourself with the color of frosting. No one buys a phone that does not work just because it fits sleekly in their pocket.

For Leaders: The notion of a hierarchy of needs was made famous by the psychologist Abraham Maslow's hierarchy of motivational needs.[5] As you may recall from the previous chapter, the hierarchy illustrates that people are motivated to fulfill basic needs (such as food) before more complex needs, such as connecting with friends or finding themselves and their calling. The hierarchy of design needs outlines the needs of a design from the most fundamental to the most desirable (see Figure M5.1).

Throughout this textbook you have been designing various facets of your leadership. The hierarchy of design needs provides important guidance as you design your future leadership. Have you met each level before moving to the next? Have your followers? Examine the questions that follow to help prompt and inform your plans.

FIGURE M5.1 ● Hierarchy of Design Needs/Criteria

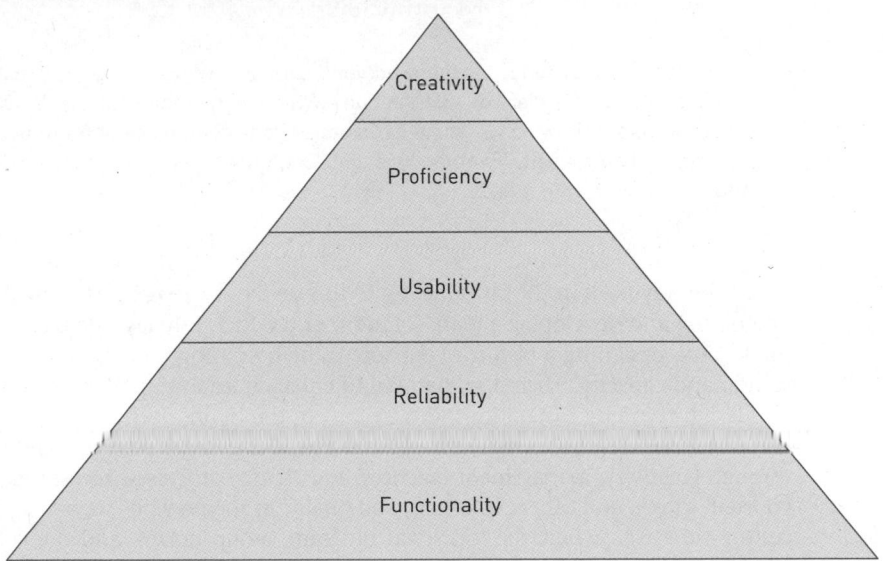

- Creativity
- Proficiency
- Usability
- Reliability
- Functionality

(Continued)

(Continued)

Functionality

- What, at a minimum, must you know, do, and be like as a leader?
- What do you need to learn?

Reliability

- Can you maintain consistent performance, and do you do what you say you will do (a.k.a. credibility)?
- What do you need to practice?

Usability

- How adaptable are you to different contexts and situations?

- How accessible are you to your followers and other stakeholders?
- What do you need to experience?

Proficiency

- What do you do as a leader that makes your organization and your followers better than they would be elsewhere?
- Do you continue to assess and improve your leadership?

Creativity

- In what new and innovative ways can you lead your followers and the organization?

No one can predict the future, but there is much information to guide your preparations. Effectively designing your leadership at all levels means learning and innovating, the confidence to continuously pursue the latter, and the humility to always remember that "It isn't what we don't know that gives us trouble, it's what we know that ain't so."[6]

REFLECTION QUESTIONS

When was the last time you followed your curiosity? Who was Bing Crosby, the author of the quote at the start of this section? Who was Stephen Covey? What do we know about Mars, and how do we know it? Exercise your confidence and humility by indulging your curiosity. After all, "Everybody is ignorant, only on different subjects."—Will Rogers (and, by the way, who is he?).

All the way back in the introduction to this textbook, design was defined as the process of originating and developing a plan, solution, or product. Initially, the plan was all about you, the leader—designing a plan for your success by becoming more aware of your conceptions, values, and capacity. Then it was a plan to enhance leadership relationships by understanding design-thinking dispositions, dimensions of the brain, decision-making, and motivation and influence. The focus shifted to the follower, designing a plan to facilitate others' success through creativity, management practices, and change processes. You shifted your focus from yourself, to you and others, to others, and finally, in the previous set of chapters, to the larger culture—the we—where the focus was on team, group norms, and the collective action of a culture of service. This final module moves into the future—"Design the Future"—first by building a culture of innovation (Chapter 14), then by learning more about how to forge your own way as an entrepreneurial leader (Chapter 15), and finally understanding the broad notion of sustainability and how to develop systems that will perpetuate your success (Chapter 16).

14

Creating a Culture of Innovation

by Jules Bruck, PhD

When you come into an organization, you bring with you
an arcane potency, which stems, in part, from your uniqueness.
That, in turn, is rooted in a complex mosaic of personal history
that is original, unfathomable, inimitable. There has never been
anyone quite like you, and there never will be. Consequently,
you can contribute something to an endeavor that nobody else can.
There is a power in your uniqueness—an inexplicable,
unmeasurable power. . . . a magic.

—Gordon Mackenzie[7]

Learning Objectives

14.1   Summarize innovation's role in the advancing marketplace of the future

14.2   Interpret innovation as a process and how it differs from creativity

14.3   Demonstrate convergent thinking techniques for innovation

14.4   Compare design thinking dispositions to innovation culture

14.5   Apply the dimensions of the brain to innovation for individuals and teams

14.6   Design your future innovative workplace

Detailed Chapter Outline

Leadership by Design Model
Design Self
How can I design myself as a leader?
Design Relationships
As a leader, how can I design my relationships with others?
Design Others' Success
As a leader, how can I design success for others?
Design Culture
As a leader, how can I design the culture of my organization?
DESIGN FUTURE
AS A LEADER, HOW CAN I INNOVATE?

Why Innovate? Designing the Future

Learning Objective

14.1 Summarize innovation's role in the advancing marketplace of the future

Innovation is perhaps one of the most overused and misunderstood terms in leadership. Take a minute to search online for a *process of innovation*. You may be surprised to find about 447,000,000 results in less than one second (thank you, Google). It would take a lifetime to sort through all the results. Even if you review the first three screens of results, you find many resources with vastly different advice, definitions, tips, and ideas. Some of the information online is misleading. Innovation is not merely invention, nor is it always *new*. Innovators may work to bring a product to the marketplace, but they also deliver new processes, services, and experiences to consumers. And for the most part, innovation is built upon prior advances in a field of study.

What do *you* think of when you hear the word innovation? Often technology comes to mind because major technological advances and discoveries are significant drivers of large periods of innovation. **Technology** is the practical, material, and human application of scientific knowledge. This means technology includes everything from the most complicated machines to the most simple, everyday devices—such as a pencil. As you learn more about innovation in this chapter, know that the ideas, objects, and processes familiar to you were once the cutting-edge technology. Those now-common ideas sprung from prior ideas, and in turn, they will prompt the next set of ideas, in a chain of inspiration that will continue on into the future.

Technology the practical, material, and human application of scientific knowledge

This chapter focuses on you as the designer of the future, specifically how you can effectively foster a culture of innovation. Throughout this textbook you have been challenged to design leadership. Designing for innovation means addressing all levels of leadership—building your own innovative capacity, developing creativity and innovation in other individuals and teams, and designing a culture that encourages and sustains innovative thinking. In this chapter, you will discover processes, perspectives, and possibilities that will enhance idea generation and the translation of those ideas into value.

LEADERSHIP THAT MAKES A DIFFERENCE

All successful innovative organizations involve collaboration, but it is often the case that certain charismatic individuals become the face of the organization's success. Individuals possessing creative confidence (see Chapter 8) trust in themselves as creative individuals, and they are courageous enough to pursue their unique ideas. When you hear the word innovation, you likely think about those highly creative tech geniuses. Their genius, however, lies not in the idea attributed to them, but more to their leadership and ability to foster a culture of innovation relative to the problem they address. These leaders have the creative confidence to innovate: Marissa Mayer, Julie Zhuo, and Jane Marie Chen. How were they able to come up with new ideas, and what gave them the courage to try them out?

New ideas define the career of Marissa Mayer, the former president and CEO of Yahoo! In her prior role at Google, and subsequently for Yahoo!, she embraces ideas that come from all levels of the organization. Mayer says, "Ideas come from everywhere." In a video filmed for Stanford's eCorner, she explains there are "myriad of different places that ideas come from," and the goal is to set up a system where people feel they can contribute those ideas. "The best ideas will rise to the top in sort of a Darwinistic way by proof of concept of

the powerful prototype, by demonstrating that it's going to fill a really important user need."[8] She continuously built platforms for people throughout the organization to share their ideas leading to a culture of innovation. She also believes creativity comes from constraint. At Google, she evaluated the vision, which was to have Google run on 90 percent of computers, and concretely set down the constraints created by the vision. For Google to run on so many machines, it had to have a small memory footprint, and it could only consume a certain amount of disk space. Ruling out features based on size constraints led to very exciting levels of product innovation. According to Mayer, "That's when you see a lot of really interesting innovation happen, is when you actually pen in the constraints."[9] You can read more about constraint as a design principle later in this chapter.

Facebook's vice president of product design, Julie Zhuo, refers to the generation of new ideas in concrete terms of problem-solving and asks is the problem worth solving? She asks, "Is this one the one we should pick out of thousands or millions of problems that are out there?"[10] Confidence comes from knowing that the problem is not being solved because of organizational self-interest, rather it is decidedly a problem faced by their audience. To determine the right problem at Facebook, Zhuo relies

(Continued)

(Continued)

on talking to a lot of people and looking at a lot of data. Courage to try out new ideas comes from knowing the implementation of the idea will solve a real problem.

Embrace Innovations CEO and cofounder, Jane Marie Chen, gets her courage from optimism. Embrace Innovations aims to help over 20 million premature and low-birth-weight babies born into vulnerable populations by providing low-cost infant warmers. After years of working within *corrupt and broken systems* and witnessing a lot of pain and suffering, she began to feel negative and pessimistic. Her conscious choice to see the beauty around her motivated her to continue generating ideas to bring the vision to reality. She meets amazing, selfless doctors, nurses, parents, and community workers who provide her hope.[11]

Innovation is bigger than individual personality traits and more intricate than the end product. The individuals described above are the face of their organization's success because they generate creative ideas and lead their organization guided by a strong vision of the future.

Innovation and Technology

Technological innovation generally brings to mind things like the Internet and perhaps some of the big Internet companies such as Google. Everyone is familiar with Google the company and search engine, and individuals even use the word Google as a verb meaning to search for answers or information online. What was Google's innovation? Larry Page and Sergey Brin, who founded Google, actually designed a PageRank algorithm to rank web pages, making the search engine faster and more accurate for users. They did not invent the idea of search engines—they creatively improved the process. From there, creativity in advertising-based financial innovations drove their business, allowing them to expand and innovate in new directions.

You live in an amazing time where search engines give you answers to most of the questions you can dream up—in fact, it is more challenging to think up the questions than acquire the answers. Access to knowledge is easier than it has ever been. So, what might differentiate you, your team, or your organization from others who have the same access to information? You possess an un-Googleable talent—creativity. Innovation is powered by creativity, so to distinguish yourself from others, it is imperative that you maximize and capitalize on your creativity and learn to lead an organization that collects and fosters individual and team creativity.

Innovation is defined as the collaborative process of translating creative ideas into something of value. Through time, individuals have contributed personal creativity to the development of exciting new technologies that transformed access to new markets and ideas. Yet, the practical reality is that innovation remains collaborative. As a collaborative process, innovation benefits from today's connectivity, which allows for efficient sharing of information. Not surprisingly, innovation occurs more rapidly now than in any other point in history. If two parties are working on ideas to solve the same problem on opposite sides of the globe, they can connect and collaborate to expedite new discoveries. This was not always the case.

One of the most important innovations of all time, the magnetic compass, became readily available for European explorers in the 15th century, but it was originally invented in China over 1000 years earlier. In today's world, we navigate easily with the help of satellites within the Global Positioning System (GPS). Without innovation, there would be no GPS, nor all the jobs along the way as humans moved from star navigation to magnetic compasses to the present technology.

Likewise, organizations that failed to innovate, and chose instead to propagate the then-current technology, inevitably became as obsolete as the technology they embraced. Effective leaders (and designers) accurately read the current marketplace. Innovative leaders read the *future* marketplace, continually questioning the market and the process, and iterating existing ideas or selecting new creative ideas to translate into value.

Drivers of Innovation

The development of navigation story highlights several facets of the innovation definition. Again, innovation is the collaborative process of translating creative ideas into something of value. In the upcoming sections you will learn more about two key concepts within this definition: collaboration and translating ideas into value. For now, notice how creativity is embedded in the definition of innovation. Creativity was defined in Chapter 8 as the personal capacities and process of generating a unique product that has value. Innovation and creativity processes are indeed similar. However, there are additional features that differentiate innovation from creativity, including a number of unique tools to help in the thoughtful selection of bringing an idea to reality.

From the beginning of time, humans have innovated to survive and thrive in their environment. The creation of basic tools over thousands of years represents many examples of how humans innovate to create items of value. Through time, innovation in tools used to hunt, carry and store food, build secure shelters, and move easily from place to place have meant everything from basic survival to increased quality of life and additional leisure time. Several factors continually drive innovation throughout time including *necessity*, *desire*, and *advances*.

Innovation From Needs

Necessity is perhaps the most fundamental reason for innovation. Look around the room and notice all the things you see around you. What do you categorize as items you need? Certainly, you need the shelter of the room, food, and drink. What about electricity? The need for electricity is debatable—but it is unfathomable to exist without it in most parts of the world today. As you explore the drivers of innovation, you could focus on the evolution of absolutely anything you see, but a quick study of something all humans need allows for an easy exploration. Stop for a moment to think about how building techniques for shelters, vessels to hold and conveniently carry water, or even the clothes on your back have evolved over time.

Innovation driven by necessity extends beyond basic needs to higher-order needs. You looked at a hierarchy of design needs in the introduction to Module 5, but recall Maslow's Hierarchy of Needs from the previous chapter, Maslow's model of what motivates human behavior. Each of those levels (physical, safety, belonging, esteem, cognitive, aesthetic, self-actualization, and up to transcendence) contributes a set of needs and thus provides potential for future innovation. What innovations are possible in each of these various need categories?

Innovation From Desires

When considering what items were in the room that you *need*—you likely differentiated between two types of items. The ones you need and the ones you want. There are many items that are not necessary to own but are desirable. *Desire* is a second driver of innovation. The desire for entertainment and fun has driven creativity and innovation in many industries. Most notably, Disney has capitalized on the desire for both a safe escape from everyday life as well as high-quality entertainment. Fitness is another industry capitalizing on desire. The promise of improved physical health based on new programs or equipment is desirable over the alternative, not to mention the many desirable conveniences of modern health clubs.

Innovation From Advances

The third driver of innovation is advances. *Advances* in materials, machines, manufacturing, and processing (i.e., technology—applications of scientific knowledge) change the look, durability, use, and cost of our everyday products and services. Drive through an old neighborhood and you will find houses made of stone and brick. Advances in composite materials and plastics have transformed many industries resulting in many new product introductions. You can tell the age of a newer housing development by the use of composites for siding, railings, fences, shutters, decks, and patios. Creative people and organizations continually dream up new uses for new materials and machines, and innovators translate those uses into value.

The three drivers of innovation—needs, desires, and advances—provide you with an accessible framework to begin imagining a new and different future. This useful framework provides prompts for innovative thinking and demonstrates that creativity and innovation do not necessarily come from a place of creative genius, but rather from an ability to reframe existing information.

Need will always be a primary driver of innovation, so as you consider how to design the future of an organization, think about the problems you want to solve. What will people need in the future? What material advance might provide a strong barrier against increasing UV exposure? How might nanotechnology be used to improve health at the molecular scale? Could microbes be used to create self-healing fabrics or structures? What materials and equipment would be required to monitor the health of or provide safe shelters for refugees?

REFLECTION QUESTIONS

Innovation will change the marketplace of the future.

How do you imagine the needs and desires of the future?

What current trends can you find in technology and material innovations?

Can you connect knowledge about recent breakthroughs with human needs and desires? How might sustainability factor into the future marketplace? Will society continue to have a tolerance for products that consume natural resources and are quickly obsolete, or will consumers demand innovation shifts that consider a healthier environment?

In your daily life, you have seen how innovation is driven by needs and desires as well as advances in materials, machines, manufacturing, and technology. Right now, inventors, scientists, and entrepreneurs are working on ideas for new products and processes to introduce to the marketplace of the future. The future holds promise of many wondrous innovations that you will interact with over time. The ability to combine advances with a need or desire in a way that creatively solves a problem will lead you to innovation and provide countless opportunities to generate creative ideas. The ideas and activities of innovation are just as applicable to your work as an effective leader as you design the future.

Understanding Innovation

Learning Objective

14.2 Interpret innovation as a process and how it differs from creativity

"Innovating requires identifying the problems that matter and moving through them systematically to deliver elegant solutions."

—Larry Keeley[12]

This section highlights key components of the definition of innovation: the collaborative process of translating creative ideas into something of value. Each of these elements prompts you to start thinking about ways to clearly identify and articulate problems as a means to communicate a clear organizational goal. Importantly, innovation requires both individual and collective creativity, and it takes place within an environment that supports creativity. Those additional aspects of innovation related to creativity, culture, and climate are discussed in the sections that follow.

Collaborative Process

In *Ten Types of Innovation*, Keeley states, "Innovation is a team sport. In fact, an organization that depends on individual innovators alone is destined to fail."[13] **Collaboration** is two or more people working together to create or achieve greater success than can be achieved individually. Naturally, collaboration involves both teamwork and partnerships, and therefore, it has importance as an *internal* organizational tool (recall Chapter 12 on Leading a Team) and as a means to communicate with experts and stakeholders outside the organization (*external* partnerships). The most valuable collaborators are those who are open to new ways of looking at existing information and who engage in multidisciplinary exploration. Leaders who wish to foster a collaborative organization should expertly define problems so all members of the organization have a strong sense of purpose and clarity of vision.

Collaboration two or more people working together to create or achieve greater success than can be achieved individually

Defining a Problem

Albert Einstein is reported to have said that if he only had an hour to solve a problem, he would spend 55 minutes thinking about the problem and 5 minutes solving it. Whether proper attribution belongs to Einstein or someone else, the point is an emphasis on problem definition over solution. A poorly defined problem results in an ineffective solution, or worse, it results in a solution that does not even address the problem. Effective collaboration requires leaders who are able to clearly define the problems they are seeking to solve. Leaders want to solve real problems that will make a big difference over time, so it is important to get into the habit of actively defining problems as long-range challenges that you can tackle within your organization.

If you are going to design the future, you must think proactively—anticipating and preparing for a possible outcome. Proactively exploring problems is the key to innovative leadership. As discussed in Chapter 8, looking for problems may seem a bit odd, but practicing this mental habit now allows you to think more critically in the future. Once you see problems, you will automatically want to generate ideas to solve them. At that point, stop your innovation process and take the time to fully define the problem. Only by clearly defining a problem are you able to identify areas for further exploration, select measures for how to successfully solve the problem, and articulate a clear vision of the problem to share with others.

Have you ever used Mad-Libs™? Filling in blanks to complete a sentence is a fun game that is likely to lead to hilarious answers. The Buck Institute for Education (BIE)[14] created a helpful problem-defining tool called a TUBRIC™. The tool functions similar to Mad-Libs™ and provides an easy structure to fill in blanks to generate a clear problem statement. There are four blanks you must fill in to complete the problem statement: Frame, Person/Entity, Action/Challenge, and Audience/Purpose.

In the first blank, called the Frame, select a word or phrase to frame the statement as a question, such as how might, could, what if, and so forth. The partially completed chart in Table 14.1 provides examples for each of the blanks. For the second blank, Person/Entity, write down the group who is taking action. This could be you (I), your organization (We), a school or community, or a group such as all high school seniors or moms. The third blank is for the Action/Challenge. It requires a strong and concise verb such as create, design,

TABLE 14.1 ● TUBRIC Tool for Problem-Finding and Defining			
Frame	Person/Entity	Action/Challenge	Audience/Purpose
How might	universities	design a campus facility	to engage students in creativity?
How can	supermarket managers	create networks	to provide food to hungry individuals?
How might	health providers in low-income communities	engage parents to ensure	children thrive in their first five years?
Could	we	improve delivery strategies	to cut back on fuel costs?

plan, solve, propose, or decide, followed by a challenge. For example, *design a network* or *organize a better process*. The last blank identifies the Audience/Purpose. The more specific your answers, the better your problem definition. Try filling in each blank for a problem relevant to you. Here is an example: "Could (frame) universities (entity) consolidate the application process (action/challenge) to save applicants time and money (audience/purpose)?"

 A strongly defined problem often reads as a challenge. Formulating the challenge takes time and may be one of the hardest parts of the creative process. But a well-defined problem is well on its way to being solved. The problem gives you clues as to where to seek ideas, who to engage, and where to start to look for a better understanding of the problem including what has been done before to solve the problem.

As highlighted in this chapter's "Leadership That Makes a Difference" feature, the future requires you to define challenges that solve real problems. Practice defining problems using the method above. Keep track of problems you have defined so you can see how your ideas evolve over time. Once you have identified a clear problem—practice communicating your idea to someone to see if it is clear and concise before embarking on the next steps of the design process, which are highlighted subsequently.

REFLECTION QUESTIONS

What are some ways you could mindfully build your collaboration network? How does clearly defining a problem lead you to seek out additional collaborators?

Translating Ideas

Creativity comprises the personal capacities and process of generating a unique product that has value. Innovation is the collaborative process of *translating* creative ideas into something of value. At first glance, these two definitions seem pretty similar. As you analyze both terms you will begin to see the differences.

Creativity requires divergent thinking. As you learned in Chapter 8, there are many techniques you can use to think divergently and generate many, many ideas. Individuals and teams able and willing to generate many ideas will develop more creative solutions to a defined problem. Innovation also requires generating ideas that solve a well-defined problem but includes selecting one idea and moving it toward the marketplace or other measure of value.

Imagine you were hired to work at the Idea Factory. Your job description states your compensation is based on quantity of ideas generated for a given problem. This would require creativity fluency, the ability to generate many ideas. If you were successful at your job you would generate many ideas each day and become well-compensated. What if your pay was reduced each time your colleague thought of the same idea as you? You would have to ramp up your originality to keep up your earnings. Originality in idea-generating refers to a unique idea. Think of each unique idea as an individual marble, and then imagine all the marbles together in a canvas bag. It took a lot of creativity to generate all those ideas, and you are holding a large bag of marbles. You are a divergent-thinking success.

Now it is time to choose an idea. Which one do you select? How do you pick one idea from a big bag of unique ideas? It requires a different skill set called convergent thinking. **Convergent thinking** is the mental process of finding a single best solution to a problem.

Imagine *innovation* is represented by arrows pointing in all directions (Figure 14.1). The arrows suggest movement toward the implementation of a given idea—movement toward greater value. Select an idea and put it in the center of the arrows as a way of visualizing innovation. Is it possible to have creativity without innovation? Absolutely. Creativity gets you a bag of marbles. Can you have innovation without creativity? No, because you have nothing unique to *move* to the next phases of the process, which is implementation. You need to select a creative idea (or combination of ideas) to move forward for innovation. If the selected idea is prototyped and tested, it may be put into the marketplace. Some of those arrows lead to very valuable implementations, and some do not. The next part of the innovation definition highlights how the idea is translated into *something of value*, and later in the chapter, you will learn about several convergence methods for how to select one idea from many.

Convergent thinking
the mental process of finding a single best solution to a problem

Translating Ideas Into Something of Value

There are many ways to return value to the organization. Economic viability requires that an innovation generate enough revenue to sustain the organization. The innovation may be in the form of a product, system, process, or service. Innovation within an organization frequently includes other forms of value such as social or environmental strategies, which may also be good for an organization's bottom line. Note that there are many forms of value beyond economic.

Identifying the full range of possible innovation-value connections can be driven by the value you seek or by the idea and its possibilities. As you design for the future, what are the values that you and your organization seek to enhance? Likewise, consider the many ways innovation in different areas of your organization can return value to you and others. A number of models have been developed that explicate many of the different types of innovation, each offering a different form of value. One concise model based on the work of Keeley organizes the innovation into 10 types across four major categories. Table 14.2 illustrates these innovation types along with a key descriptor and prompting question.

FIGURE 14.1 ● Creativity versus Innovation

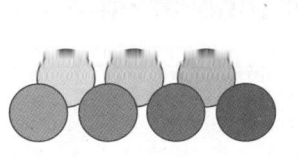

Creativity = generating a lot of ideas

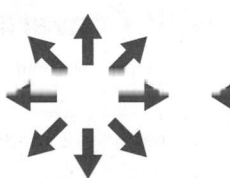

Innovation = translating an idea to action, requires selection of an idea!

TABLE 14.2 ● Ten Types of Innovation

Innovation Type[15]	Description	Ask Yourself	Example—Not-for-Profit Summer Camps
Finance—business model	How you make money	How might I generate extra capital?	Create new for-profit division to support your not-for-profit work
Finance—networks and alliances	How you join forces with other companies for mutual benefit	How might I partner to eliminate local or regional duplication of services?	Offer advanced lessons (tennis, golf, swimming) through local partners
Process—enabling	How you support the company's core processes and workers	How might I enhance compensation or benefits for my employees?	Provide an educational development pipeline for staff wanting to become school teachers
Process—core	How you create and add value to your offerings	How might I create a new system that will optimize resources?	Design a new bus scheduling system reducing bus rental costs
Offerings—product performance	How you design your core offerings to improve performance	In what ways might I improve my product's performance?	Offer campers high-tech training on useful design programs
Offerings—product system	How you link and/or provide a platform for multiple products	How might I link programs, products, and processes to enhance offerings?	Turn school-year activities into clubs, and transition clubs to camp themes
Offerings—service	How you provide value to customers and consumers beyond and around your products	How might I enhance services or special offerings to my customers?	Add before and after camp care, parents' nights, and advanced booking
Delivery—channel	How you get your offerings to market	What are the key channels through which my audience finds products, services, and so forth?	Partner with students' home school for location
Delivery—brand	How you communicate your offerings	What unique message will capture the attention of my audience?	Focus marketing campaign on student achievement
Delivery—customer experience	How your customers feel when they interact with your company and its offerings		Provide team t-shirts and hold a youth expo to highlight projects

Diverge for Creativity, Converge for Innovation

Learning Objective

14.3 Demonstrate convergent thinking techniques for innovation

Generating many ideas is a hallmark of creativity. Remember, the more ideas you generate, the more likely you are to find that unique and valuable idea. Divergent thinking—a mindset of generating many, many ideas for a single problem—and divergent techniques are critical to creativity. But the opposite—convergence—is key to the process of innovation and the selection of one idea to move into action.

Convergent thinking was defined as the mental process of finding a single best solution to a problem. Sometimes it is described as the ability to give the *correct* answer, but this is misleading. Unlike a standardized exam question, there is hardly ever one right answer, especially in design or leadership. It is best to think of convergence as a process. Convergence as a process gives room for a level of creativity in choosing an idea—whether combining two or more ideas or allowing for iteration on an original idea. You use convergence every day when you work to support an argument in writing or conversation. For example, you may know many facts and figures about gun safety, but when you are responding during a discussion, you have to evaluate the particular facts that best support the idea you are sharing.

In contrast to divergent thinking, a process focused on wildly outward directions, convergence is centered. Both are critical for innovation, and both are generally associated with the imagination phase. Before you can implement, you must evaluate each of the best ideas to select one to put into action.

Convergent thinking is a disposition (habit of thinking) that you have been well trained in over a lifetime of schooling. Unfortunately, your convergent habit is usually put to use in cutting off the idea-generating process and choosing an answer. Effective innovators (and those that lead them) learn to manage both divergent and convergent thinking within the process. Convergent thinking is also a skill set with many techniques that are used to select and prepare an idea for action. Deciding which technique to use is often based on the situation. Using convergent techniques is a good way to choose an idea without biasing the process, which is very useful when groups are involved in decision-making. For example, you may find your team has a bias toward solving problems with ideas that are easy to implement or seem familiar (see Constructive Dimension: Seeking and Seeing Differently). If that is the case, they may be seriously limiting innovation. Convergence strategies allow you to evaluate ideas free from bias and make decisions free of judgment.

Benchmarking

One method to converge on an idea is a process called benchmarking. **Benchmarking** is evaluating ideas by comparison with a standard. Consider a team of engineers asked to design something new such as an innovative floating wetland. A floating wetland is a manufactured floating island designed to provide filtration and treatment services to waterways to improve water quality. The engineers will compare their idea, as well as several others including solutions already on the market (standard), against criteria developed during the definition of the problem. Perhaps they were asked to design a floating wetland treatment that reliably floats, supports plants, eliminates nesting waterfowl, and is safe for the environment. After creating the matrix, each person on the project team independently scores each product, ranking each idea using a numerical system (for example, 1 to 4) against the criteria. The addition of each product's score will yield a number that represents a quantitative result. Benchmarking allows ideas to be numerically ranked to determine the best idea of several.

As seen in Table 14.3, the high score based on the four criteria seem to indicate a clear best choice. However, using the tool to see where other products/ideas scored higher than the overall winner in different categories is useful too. In this example, it may lead the team to consider changes to *Our Innovative Idea* based on *Market Product B*'s score on Criterion 4, and *Another Idea We Had*'s score on Criterion 3. Use the scoring to guide team discussion. Work to understand differences in individual values.

Benchmarking evaluating ideas by comparison with a standard

TABLE 14.3 ● Benchmarking

Product	Criterion 1—Reliably Floats, No Sinking	Criterion 2—Supports Plants	Criterion 3—Does Not Allow for Nesting	Criterion 4—Safe for the Environment	Score
Our Innovative Idea	4	3	2	3	12
Market Product A	4	2	1	1	8
Market Product B	3	1	2	4	10
Another Idea We Had!	1	1	4	3	9

How? Now, Wow![16]

Another useful tool to select ideas while making sure no potentially viable ideas are lost is a technique called *How? Now, Wow!* This convergence tool is also a matrix that has two selection criteria—*originality* and *ease of implementation*. To use the tool, draw four boxes—two stacked on top of two (see Figure 14.2).

The top two boxes represent ideas *impossible* to implement, and the bottom two are for *easy* ideas to implement. Looking at the four boxes—the two on the left are for *normal ideas* and the two on the right are for *original ideas*. This tool allows a team to quickly sort through the many ideas they generated during the imagination phase to converge on the most suitable idea to develop. The value of this matrix is that it also enables the group to look at all ideas simultaneously. A team using this tool then has an opportunity to look beyond practical project selection criteria (How much weight does it hold? How stable is it? How durable is it?) that solve the problem to actively deciding to pursue a more innovative idea. As a team, ideas are reviewed and each one placed into a box. *HOW* ideas are original but impossible to implement. These are ideas for the future—dreams and challenges that inspire awe and wonder—think human colony on Mars. *NOW* ideas are the ones that are easy to implement and low risk. They are pre-accepted—maybe because they are slightly different versions of an older idea. The *WOW* ideas are easy and original breakthrough ideas that are exciting because they are feasible and ready for action.

As a leader, you help determine which type of idea is most feasible for the organization. Do you have the time, resources, and talent to go for a HOW idea? Is this the direction you want to move into as an organization? What may be needed to help you achieve those original, impossible ideas? Perhaps it requires you to focus on a product or process in the NOW category that becomes the ongoing revenue generator for the development of a HOW idea. WOW ideas are those that will be easy but position the organization as unique or innovative.

FIGURE 14.2 ● How? Now, Wow!

Impossible to implement/ Normal ideas	Impossible to implement/ Original ideas HOW?
Easy to implement/ Normal ideas NOW!	Easy to implement/ Original ideas WOW!

Force Field Analysis

Another useful convergence technique is Force Field Analysis. You can use Force Field Analysis when you want to explore the forces for and against several ideas once you have narrowed down your possibilities. To use this technique, at the top of a blank page write down the idea under consideration. Draw a line down the middle of the page. On one side of the line begin to list all the forces *for* the idea. In other words, list out all the things that might promote the idea or change. This could be specific individuals, connections, assets, trends, policies, partnerships, funds—absolutely anything. On the other side of the line, list the forces *against* the idea. Similar to making a pro/con list, use logic to determine different

FIGURE 14.3 ● Force Field Analysis

Force Field and Change Analysis Template

Describe the current situation or problem (what is happening now, or what the status quo is).		
Outing Club is exclusively for registered university students. Only registered students can attend outings.		

Describe the contemplated change (desired goal) that needs analysis.		
Proposed change to allow alumni of the outing club to attend trips.		

List the driving forces that are promoting change.	Weight (1–5)	List the restraining forces or obstacles that are opposing change.	Weight (1–5)
Alums have experience they can share with the club members	4	University liability will not cover alums	4
Alums have friends in the club post-graduation and want to participate	2	May limit younger students from emerging as leaders	5
Alums may provide additional financial support for larger trips	3	Alums may take the place of undergraduates on trips with limited space	3
Are there some common themes?		Why are these forces occurring?	
		Are there some common themes?	
Totals	9		12

forces that have the potential to act on a solution if those are understood. For example, if a team generated an idea to create a *shared food pantry* for a community to combat food waste while feeding people in need, there would be forces for the pantry and forces against. The forces for a shared food pantry may be a new policy that limits food waste in household garbage, centrally available space near a homeless shelter, and an existing transportation network of deliveries from a single distribution to neighborhood grocery stores. Forces against the idea may be health concerns, high transportation costs, and high rent.

Once you have the forces defined and written into the diagram, you can lead a team in determining how to neutralize or otherwise address the forces against the idea, as well as capitalize on and/or increase the forces in the for category. Figure 14.3 illustrates the Force Field Analysis using another example. After looking it over, choose an example of your own and briefly outline the forces for and against your desired goal. The act of purposefully thinking about these two seemingly obvious sides of a change leads to insights that ultimately facilitate addressing the issue.

The $100 Test

Benchmarking is a method used to determine the quantifiable ranking of an idea. Economists see the world differently. Through the lens of an economist, the way to gauge the acceptability of a product or policy is to equate it to something valuable that everyone can relate to—dollars. Would you put your money on an idea?

People make very different decisions about how to allocate dollars versus points on a chart. Another convergence technique is *The $100 Test*. Assume each team member has $100 to spend on developing several ideas. After presenting a range of suitable ideas, each team member distributes their money across the ideas under consideration. This works best if team members have money (real or play) to allocate. Direct the team to think of each allocation as a real investment and allow members to divide their $100 to different ideas. After everyone invests, add up the total dollar amounts for each of the ideas to determine how the team values each idea. This can lead to a deeper conversation about how distributions were made among team members.

Convergence is part of the ideation phase of the innovation process. It leads to the selection of an idea to move forward into implementation phases of the process. As a leader, you now have selected an idea—so what is your next move? You should consider ways of testing the idea. During the implement phase you must practice an iterative mindset—constantly assessing and improving on ideas. Circle back to revisit old ideas and be open to new ideas along the way. As you can see, there is a balance between multiple variables, ideas, and design constraints. The innovation process is about creatively resolving the tensions between multiple factors. As a leader, you should continuously ask, "What if . . .?" regardless of how satisfied you are with your solution and be willing to make design decisions conditionally with the awareness that they may or may not work out as you continue toward a final solution.

Design Thinking for Innovation Culture

Learning Objective

14.4 Compare design-thinking dispositions to innovation culture

What would an organizational culture look like if it were designed to support creativity and innovation? One way of approaching this question is to think about ways creative individuals are *taught* from their earliest encounter with a culture outside their family—in school. Educators, similar to all professionals, must strike a balance between competing constraints. The culture of a school is likely to prioritize many values above creativity in part because of time constraints. If achievement is high on the list of priorities, resources dedicated to the development of individual skills related to creativity may be lacking.

Have you ever wondered why leaders, especially political and business leaders, always seem so concerned about education? They are interested in education because what students are taught now will influence who they become and how they think about business and politics as adults. If you want to design the future, you start where the future lies—within the developing minds of children. The same is true of developing minds of adults and those you lead. As you think about creating a culture of innovation, consider what you might do now that will affect your organization 10 or 20 years from now. Read about what creativity expert Ronald Beghetto highlights about creativity in the classroom and note those things you can do now in the teaching aspects of your leadership.

EXPERTS BEYOND THE TEXT

INSIGHTFUL LEADERS KNOW ABOUT . . . CREATIVITY IN THE CLASSROOM

Creativity in the Classroom: Quick Insights for Leaders

By Ronald A. Beghetto, University of Connecticut

What do leaders need to know about creativity in the classroom? In what follows, I provide a brief overview of what creativity is and what it means in the context of the classroom. I then highlight a few important things to know about creativity. Specifically, I highlight a few problematic beliefs that can undermine classroom creativity and offer alternative perspectives from the creativity studies literature. I close by briefly discussing why it is important for leaders to know about this topic.

What Is Creativity?

Creativity researchers generally agree that creativity is some combination of originality and meeting task constraints as defined within a particular context.[17]

One way to think about creativity in the classroom is striking a balance between helping students share their own ideas, interests, perspectives, and ways of doing things (originality) while at the same time helping them learn how to meet academic criteria, standards, and expectations (task constraints) during particular learning activities and assignments (context).

Here's an example that may help. Imagine a student who is asked to provide an illustration of the life cycle of a plant on a science test. The student draws a picture of a plant turning into a zombie. Although such a drawing is an *original* response, it would not be considered creative in the *context* of the science test (because it did not meet the *task constraints* of representing the features of the plant life cycle). Similarly, a student who copies a picture found on Google Images would not be considered creative because it lacks originality, even though it meets the task constraints (i.e., has all the required features of the life cycle). A creative response, in the context of the science test, would require students to come up with their own, unique way of illustrating the required features of the plant life cycle.

Important Things to Know About Classroom Creativity

Here are a few problematic beliefs about creativity in classrooms and some new ways of thinking about them based on the creativity studies literature:

- **Problematic belief:** Only certain people can be creative

- **Response from the literature:** There are different levels of creative experiences and actions. Learning something new and meaningful (even if it is only new and meaningful to you) can still be considered a creative act. This is called mini-c creativity and is a sign of creative potential.[18] Mini-c creativity can grow into larger C creativity through (among other things) honest and supportive feedback, hard work, deliberate practice, sensible risk-taking, persistence, the development of expertise, and time.[19] There are no short cuts or magical strategies for developing creative potential into creative achievements.

- **Problematic belief:** Creativity is only about the arts

- **Response from the literature:** Creative thought and action are possible in any subject area.[20] Just because someone is creative in one subject area (science), however, doesn't mean they will be creative in another (language arts). Creative accomplishment requires developing domain-specific knowledge and skills.

- **Problematic belief:** Creativity is about thinking outside the box

- **Response from the literature:** In the context of classrooms, it's often more about thinking and acting creatively inside the box rather than outside of it. Of course, there are times when it is necessary to imagine and build a new box. In most cases, however, it's about being creative within curricular constraints.[21]

- **Problematic belief:** Creativity is always good

- **Response from the literature:** There is a time and a place for creativity. Creative thought and action always involve risk, which sometimes involves negative, unintended consequences. Taking creative risks makes sense when old ways of thinking and acting don't work or when we are trying to make improvements.

- **Problematic belief:** Schools kill creativity

- **Response from the literature:** The possibility for creative thought and action is always and already present in schools and classrooms. Schools can't give creativity to students, take it away, or kill it, but schools can establish situations that suppress or support it.[22]

Why Is It Important for Leaders to Know About This Topic?

A common goal of education is to prepare young people for the future. This is a challenge because the future is uncertain. Creativity is a capacity that enables people to successfully navigate the uncertainty they face, solve complex and ill-defined problems, and make necessary changes in thought and action. Moreover, if we want students to engage in possibility thinking and take the risks necessary for creative thought and action, then we need to lead the way by doing so ourselves.

Another way of approaching the question of how to foster creativity is to think about ways creative individuals *habitually think* as they approach each stage of the creative process—in other words, design thinking. As you learned in Chapter 1, design thinking is a set of dispositions defined as habits of mind that are often seen as a tendency or characteristics. Leaders who provide the cultural conditions to support the characteristic dispositions of creative individuals as they progress through each stage of their process will set the organization on a path to innovation.

In Chapter 10, culture refers to "a set of shared assumptions that guide the behavior of members of an organization of any size from a small group of friends to a workplace to the larger society." Effective leaders design culture *intentionally*, which means actively designing the shared set of beliefs and values that drive behaviors as well as all aspects of organizational conduct. You want meaningful organizational values to be the driver of culture, rather than empty words. In other words, stating "At this organization we value excellence, service, and innovation" does not mean a whole lot because the words have little clarity. Instead consider, "At this organization, we value innovation and believe in adopting a user-centered approach to problem solving." The second statement clearly shares how the value is related to the belief and is influential in shaping the organization's behavior.

Design-thinking dispositions can guide your efforts as a leader to create a culture of innovation. Look at the design-thinking dispositions in Table 14.4. The specific dispositions include User-centered, Explorative, Divergent, Multidisciplinary, Iterative, Collaborative, and Integrative. As you review the column titled "We make it so by . . ." consider ways a statement in each category could be expressed as part of the organizational values and beliefs. On the left are the dispositions by phase of the design process, and on the right are the ways leaders can *make it so* by engaging in the specific tasks.

TABLE 14.4 ● Creating a Culture of Innovation With Design Thinking

Design-Thinking Disposition	Creating a Culture of Innovation—Our Vision
Design thinking is a cognitive approach to engaging problems that embodies a specific mindset that is:	We make it so by . . . We encourage/foster the notion of . . .
Understand the Problem, Person, Process, Context	
User-centered—mindset that focuses on the user and how they experience and feel	Adopting a user-centered approach Engaging in user research to acquire a deeper understanding of the user Looking toward users to define problems rather than those who successfully solved the problem before
Explorative—mindset that assumes purposeful ambiguity and curiosity	Allowing time and space for preflection and reflection on the problem, person, process, and context Proactively seeing opportunities to improve by unearthing new problems Embarking on the unknown with optimism
Imagine the Possibilities and Impossibilities	
Divergent—mindset of generating many, many ideas for a single problem	Modeling and pushing beyond preconceived limits of generating ideas Incentivizing the generation of new ideas Encouraging people to speak up with new ideas
Multidisciplinary—mindset that engages many minds and pursues multiple areas of expertise	Imagining and/or engaging using multiple disciplines and perspectives Purposefully displacing people out of routine thinking Engaging a diverse group of colleagues

Iterative—mindset of always seeing solutions in process—assessing and improving	Incorporating revisions and multiple iterations
	Testing new ideas
	Prototyping
	Providing constant feedback
Implement, Assess, Iterate	
Collaborative—mindset that working with others is always far more effective	Inviting collaboration and co-design
	Engaging across functional boundaries
Integrative—mindset of attending to and balancing multiple criteria, particularly viability, feasibility, and desirability	Assessing competing goals of the solution and revising

Culture is complex and multifaceted. Organizational leaders strive to influence members of their organization and guide them toward a common vision. The most effective visions are deeply embedded in the culture through the expression of values and norms. Most importantly, the expression of values and norms influences how people within the organization act (i.e., "the way we do things around here"). The *ways we make it so* in Table 14.4 demonstrate several possibilities to guide the development of clear organizational values that are supportive of creativity and innovation.

REFLECTION QUESTIONS

Evaluate which statements in Table 14.4 you believe are most important, necessary, and true to support a culture of creativity and innovation. Imagine an organization you are familiar with while evaluating the design-thinking dispositions and the innovation culture statements. Does the organization you are thinking about support one or more aspects of creativity? Which ones do they value and where could they become more supportive?

Creating a Climate of Innovation With the Dimensions of the Brain

Learning Objectives

14.5 Apply the dimensions of the brain to innovation for individuals and teams

14.6 Design your future innovative workplace

The design of an organization's culture based upon the design-thinking mindsets ensures the values of an organization will support creativity. The culture sets the overall tone for a group, but it does not address individual needs within the context of the workplace. Therefore, it is important to consider how people within an organization function at a fundamental and perceptual level and how they relate to one another to further design a workplace climate conducive to creativity.

The organizational climate differs from the culture. An organization's culture is a stable articulation of beliefs, values, and norms. The **organizational climate** is the recurring, often dynamic, patterns of behaviors, attitudes, and feelings that characterize what it is like to work within an organization. The difference can be thought of as what the team *values* versus what the team members experience. It is well-documented that a supportive, creative climate increases levels of innovation, well-being, and even profitability.

In Chapter 5—"Design Thinking and Brain Leading"—you explored how understanding six dimensions of the brain could inform your leadership. These six dimensions were Physiological, Emotional, Social, Constructive, Dispositional, and Reflective. In this section, three of the dimensions are revisited to provide a valuable framework for leaders interested in designing an innovative organizational climate supportive of and enhancing individual and team creativity. While all six dimensions have implications for addressing individual needs as both an innovator and as a contributing factor to a creative climate, the Social, Constructive, and Reflective Dimensions are particularly useful when designing the future.

Organizations of the future will compete for talented individuals. When designing for either climate or culture, it is important to start with an understanding of the many different people who share the work environment. Because each individual has a unique set of motivators, attitudes, and personal preferences, there is no one-size-fits-all approach to creating a perfect climate for all. The most impactful leaders maintain open and honest communication with teams about the positive and negative aspects of the working environment. Leaders familiar with applying the dimensions of the brain have a great head start in conceiving of a workplace environment in tune with a variety of individual needs and styles.

Social Dimension: Collaboration and Community

At this organization, we foster interaction and the notion that there is a collaborative spirit where individuals are able to take risks while advancing a shared vision.

Collaboration is key to innovation. As discussed earlier in this chapter, innovation does not happen individually in a vacuum. Rather, it requires the dedication and creativity of many people with unique skill sets coming together to focus on the collective vision of the solution to a problem. How does collaboration fit within the overall context of a society that values individual achievement and success? What do high schools do to foster collaboration among students in the classroom? On the playing field? In the band? And as students prepare college applications? It may be hard to imagine since some level of competitive structures are in play in almost every one of those examples, and individuals are not taught *how* to collaborate.

In a collaborative environment, people must enjoy working on teams, accepting critical feedback, and putting into place systems for selecting valuable ideas, and they must be willing to leave good ideas behind. For these reasons, it is perhaps asking a lot of an organization to expect individuals to have the ability to collaborate effectively and efficiently. Instead, assume people are not accustomed to collaboration and foster team and external interaction deliberately. It is also critical to articulate the goals of the group clearly. Investing in a shared vision is the best way to overcome any obstacles to collaboration.

TABLE 14.5 ● **Creative Climate Using the Social Dimension**	
Actively Support the Social Dimension of Creativity and Innovation by Providing:	**In My Organization, I Could . . .**
Opportunities for collaboration with and within diverse individuals and groups from inside and outside the organization	Join a team and become a co-collaborator Provide collaboration training Hire/populate teams with diversity in mind

Actively Support the Social Dimension of Creativity and Innovation by Providing:	In My Organization, I Could . . .
Freedom to make mistakes and room to fail	
Clear problems to solve, criteria for success, and a project plan to recognize successful solutions	Use a methodology to clearly define problems and help teams craft a vision for successful solutions
A strong sense of community	
Rewards to teams that take appropriate risks	Nominate groups for awards based on their process rather than their end result

Constructive Dimension: Seeking and Seeing Different

At this organization, we believe in other ways of seeing the problem and we seek to challenge the existing constructions of knowledge.

Your brain is a lean, mean, pattern-making machine (remember that phrase?). To challenge a construction of knowledge requires one to determine how individual mental models influence your way of seeing a problem. Mental models were defined way back in Chapter 2 as your mental representation of things in the world, including how you understand things and how you process information. On the positive side, the constructive dimension helps you and your team establish a clear and shared vision of what you are trying to achieve. On the troubling side, differences in mental models can affect how two people arrive at different conclusions when provided the same information. Generally speaking, it is common for people to pay attention to some but not all data presented to them, while others may pay attention to different aspects of the data. The way both individuals impose their interpretation of the data and draw conclusions has a profound effect on the conclusion. It is easy to lose sight of your personal thinking process and obtain conclusions that seem obvious. When conclusions seem obvious, but are different from others, it can lead to disagreements. It is often difficult to resolve a conflict that arises from your constructed reality for a given situation.

Mental models frame how one sees a problem, which consequently limits how one sees a problem and the possibilities for solution.[23] By definition, it inhibits new ways of seeing and limits innovation. In a culture of innovation, there needs to be a conscious effort to recognize the constructions that are dictating how you are seeing problems and solutions and look beyond mental models to frame a problem in a unique way. Are you open to different ways of seeing the world?

What are some ways to challenge your mental model? First, understand the nature of your mental model and how it works to frame information. *Reflect* on your mental model—how are you defining things, describing situations, assuming—what are the ways you see the world that may influence how you make decisions and process information? *Inquire* about others' mental models; specifically, learn to ask questions that shed light on what data people are paying attention to and how they interpret the data. *Advocate* for your way of thinking and the conclusions you draw by clearly expressing your thought and reasoning process.

According to Confucius, "True wisdom is knowing what you don't know." Being aware of mental models and actively expanding your knowledge base are useful ways of thinking about your own constructions of the world. If you were asked to make a list of what you do not know, it should be very, very long. If it is not, you are not even aware of what you do not know, which means raising that awareness is your first step. Find out more about the world, explore different perspectives. It is helpful to explore cultures different from your own, to travel, and to be open to new ways of seeing the world.

Mental models structure what individuals see, how they respond, and the conclusions they draw. Mental models describe how information is organized in your mind and what you draw on when faced with complex yet seemingly familiar situations. They also describe how an individual may adapt to a new situation or see a new problem or frame the future. As you design a culture of innovation, what ways of seeing the world do you bring to the table? How similar are the constructed mental models of those in your organization? What perspectives are you missing that could spark innovation?

TABLE 14.6 ● Creative Climate Using the Constructive Dimension

Actively Support the Constructive Dimension of Creativity and Innovation by Providing:	In My Organization, I Could...
Opportunity to travel	Send groups to new places to gather information
	Hold a meeting in a new location—somewhere unexpected
Time to explore and understand before being asked to draw conclusions	Give my team excused time off of e-mail to allow time for focused problem solving
	Work with my team to create a labyrinth—encourage people to use it and lead the way
Opportunity to get involved with a culture different from your own	Host cultural events that allow individuals to share foods and customs
Explore societal mental models when implementing ideas	Provide the team prompts to ensure societal mental models are considered

LEADERSHIP BY DESIGN

Design Principle: Constraint

Definition: A method of limiting the actions that can be performed on a system.

In Other Words: Challenge your creativity with limits—advance your innovation

For Example: A spending limit on your credit card constrains how much shopping, and acquisition of debt, you can do.

For Leaders: Constraints may seem like the last thing a leader should be imposing on a creative project, but constraints can prove beneficial when implemented correctly. When the sky is the limit, many people become paralyzed by the infinite opportunities. As a leader, helping to take away some of the choices can provide a more focused path to begin exploring. Constraints are put in place as a means to simplify systems and minimize errors. Constraints also help with the convergence process, helping to identify the best ideas from the long list of divergently generated ideas.

When would a leader want to limit the actions of their followers? How might counterintuitive approaches make a culture more creative? It is important to use constraint wisely, and only when appropriate. Wouldn't innovation come to a halt without the occasional dissent?

Reflective Dimension: Time, Space, and Structure

At this organization, we believe in supplying time, space, and structure for other ways of seeing the problem.

Every Sunday night Julie looks at her calendar to see what she has on the schedule for the week ahead. Recently, she had a week that was jam-packed with meetings. Back-to-back meetings. Each meeting required some preparation on the front end, and of course, each required follow-up afterward. But with each meeting stacked one on top of the next, there was no time to *reflect* on the purpose or conclusion of any meeting. What was decided? Was it a good decision? Does it require additional follow-up? Where is the best source of follow-up information? What does the outcome of the meeting mean for the project?

In a work climate that requires a lot of meetings, who is allowing for and protecting the important non-meeting time where individuals have a chance to think and be thoughtful? This thoughtful thinking time is called reflection. It may come naturally directly following the meeting if you are fortunate enough to have a decent walk (15–20 minutes) outside of a building between meetings or if you schedule time between meetings for reflection, exercise, meditation, or naps. These mental breaks after intense collaborative or individual work often lead to the greatest ideas, and they can foster creativity as well as reduce stress.

When working in groups, reflective time may seem more like the alternative definition of reflective—as in images or sounds *bouncing back* at you. Your brain needs individual reflection time, and teams need their people engaging in both individual and group reflection to fully foster their creativity (recall the idea-generating technique called incubation from Chapter 8). What opportunities are provided for your organization to reflect on current decisions, process, ideas, or products? How have you and your team structured time and space to actually think about decisions already made?

Reflection is an essential dimension of the brain, and it is a key component of all work; but it is an inseparable part of creative work. When during the work day are you provided time to reflect? Is time to reflect valued in the organization? Promoted? Understood? Do you understand it? Think about it. Now read this section again, and then put the book down. Go for a 20-minute walk. You may prefer to reflect quietly—or to the sound of nature or music—but try both. When you walk, you think about things differently. In fact, the authors of this textbook did just that—took a break and walked a bit to think about how to organize and write up the idea of reflection for this section.

TABLE 14.7 ● Creative Climate Using the Reflective Dimension

Actively Support the Reflective Dimension of Creativity and Innovation by Providing:	In My Organization, I Could . . .
Time for people to reflect	Structure my meeting blocks to keep the most productive part of the day open for creative work and reflection
Space for people to reflect	Seek out places and encourage team members to exercise after long meetings
	Seek out places for team members to work on hobby projects or engage in mindful meditation; encourage people to take a break and work on alternative hobby projects
Opportunities for people to relax during the work	Encourage people to enjoy time in a café
	Take a walk together
Education about the value of reflection	End the meeting 15 minutes early; prompt your team to stop and write down their thoughts before they leave
	Take time to share success stories

LEADERSHIP BY DESIGN

Design Principle: Von Restorff Effect

Definition: A phenomenon of memory in which noticeably different things are more likely to be recalled than common things.

In Other Words: Leverage the element of surprise to increase memory

For Example: The Macy's Thanksgiving Day Parade uses the von Restorff Effect every year to deliver a memorable experience to its millions of viewers. Nowhere else would you see Smurfs and a giant ice cream cone floating through the streets of New York City. Macy's capitalizes on these unique sights and experiences to engrain themselves in people's memory.

For Leaders: Leaders can create a culture of innovation by applying the von Restorff Effect in order to raise awareness of the mental models that may be restraining the team, to emphasize important points, and to generally spark individuals thinking in new ways. What do I really need followers, clients, or stakeholders to notice or remember? How can I introduce that message in a manner that is very, very different than they might expect? Note that this technique in leadership should be used sparingly—if everything is highlighted, then nothing will stand out.

©iStock.com/RightFramePhotoVideo

While the dimensions of the brain applied to innovation for individuals and teams provides a broad framework to design a creativity-supporting climate, there are several other dispositions a leader should consider when designing a future innovative workplace. Recall the concept of *press* introduced in Chapter 8. Press refers to those things in the environment that press on your creativity, either inhibiting or encouraging. Beyond what was discussed with the dimensions of the brain, what other ways could you strategically engage elements of the creative press to influence creative behavior?

Finally, recall that the CORE™ capacities discussed throughout this textbook are fundamental to your overall leadership success. They are also key to you and your team's innovation capacity. When designing the workplace of your future, note what might inhibit those CORE™ capacities and what you might do to design a culture that is encouraging of each one. Think critically about what would inhibit or undermine *confidence* in a workplace environment. Perhaps it would be inhibited by fear stemming from lack of information or an impending change that was not well explained. Undermining *optimism* may be an overall pessimism that pervades the culture. What is the source of pessimistic viewpoints? Are there misunderstandings around deadlines or availability of resources? How might *resilience* be undermined? Perhaps there are significant challenges that are not addressed in a timely manner. This may lead to discouragement and the overall feeling that there are insurmountable deterrents to organizational success. In what ways might *engagement* be inhibited? When individuals or teams are not recognized for their efforts or if the people in the organization do not understand how their work fits into the overall goals of the organization, lack of engagement ensues.

Many of these prompting questions about confidence, optimism, resilience, and engagement point to the value of clear and meaningful communication as a standard for organizational success. While it is often not explicit in the values and beliefs that comprise an organizational culture, there is no reason to discount the importance of communication in making sure the culture is not undercut by pessimism, misunderstandings, discouragement, or lack of engagement. Your job as the leader of an innovative culture is to understand all the cultural and climate variables that lead to greater innovation and to communicate to ensure the press encourages an individual's CORE™ capacities.

MYTH OR REALITY?

TRANSFORMATIONAL LEADERSHIP IS THE BEST APPROACH FOR ENCOURAGING FOLLOWERS' CREATIVITY AND ORGANIZATIONAL INNOVATION.

Myth . . . and Reality. Transformational leadership—characterized by the four Is of individual consideration, intellectual stimulation, inspirational motivation, and idealized influence—generally feels like the leadership approach that would most likely establish the conditions for individuals and organizations to innovate. And, the reality is that there are numerous studies suggesting transformational leadership has significant effects on creativity at both the individual and organizational levels.[24] At the individual level, transformational leadership influences employees' creativity through psychological empowerment. At the organizational level it is positively associated with organizational innovation. But . . . in some cases, the effect is mediated by promotion focus and creative process engagement,[25]

by emphasizing a learning orientation,[26] or by applying leadership to a specific part of the creativity process.[27] But . . . other studies indicate limited effects of transformational leadership, and even negative effects such as increasing follower dependency that decreased creativity.[28]

This is a great example of why leadership needs to be a mindful process that you design. There are no simple recipes that say do this leadership style and it will result in that performance outcome. Leadership, and innovation, are simply too complicated, individual-based, context-based, and situational. Nonetheless, research on what factors promote and inhibit creativity, and the variables that mediate those effects, are worth exploring, understanding, and applying as appropriate.

Chapter Summary

When you think of the future of innovation, it is likely that you think about technology. Technology and innovation are closely related because major advances in technology tend to drive the largest periods of progress throughout time. Innovation would not be possible without creativity. Innovative leaders accurately read the future marketplace, continually questioning the market to iterate upon existing ideas or select new creative ideas to translate into value.

Innovation is enhanced if you understand the drivers of innovation, which include necessity, desire, and advances

(in methods, materials, etc.). Innovative leaders have an understanding of how to use these drivers of innovation as a starting point to imagining future possibilities.

Innovation is a collaborative process of translating creative ideas into something of value.

The best leaders and collaborators have a clear understanding of the problem they are trying to solve. You benefit from learning how and practicing defining problems clearly. A clearly defined problem is well on its way to being solved.

Innovation is a creative process that relies on iteration and the translation of creative ideas into something of value for an organization. Many types of innovation result in value for an organization, and you can select one or more once you choose the type of value that you and your organization seek to enhance. As you look at the many creative ideas that you generate, you also use a process to find a single best solution to a problem. Selecting the one idea, out of many, to translate to value occurs through convergence. There are many convergence techniques used to help you understand a variety of ways to go about selecting an idea to pursue.

Innovative organizations are designed to support creativity. Supporting creativity requires an understanding of how creative individuals habitually think as they approach the creative process. Using design-thinking dispositions as a guide to create a culture of innovation allows you to design a culture that is sympathetic to creative individuals' characteristics and mindsets. Culture is the values and beliefs of an organization, but climate is the patterns of behavior and attitude that characterize what it is like to work within an organization. It is equally important to design culture and climate. With no one-size-fits-all approach, using the six dimensions of the brain as a way to design the climate of an innovative workplace environment is a good place to start.

Key Terms

Benchmarking 359
Collaboration 355

Convergent Thinking 357
Organizational Climate 366

Technology 351

CORE™ Attribute Builders: Build Now for Future Leadership Challenges

Attribute: Engagement

Builder: Read, post, or comment to OpenIDEO.com or Innocentive.com

How might mobile technology help improve access to health care? How might we better prepare all learners for the needs of tomorrow by reimagining higher education? These are two of the current open challenges offered on the online open source innovation platform called OpenIDEO. According to their website, "A challenge is usually a three to five-month collaborative process that focuses our attention on a specific issue and creates a space for community members to contribute, refine and prototype solutions."[29] Innocentive.com offers a similar platform for you to engage your creative, problem-solving leadership.

Get involved. Read, comment, or post on the current challenge. The most valuable part of their platform is the engagement of *innovators* from all over the world connected and actively involved in solving pressing global issues.

CORE™ Attribute Builders: Build Now for Future Leadership Challenges

Attribute: Confidence and Resilience

Builder: Space and feeling awareness

What kind of space brings out the best or most creative in you? Raising your awareness of how different spaces elicit different emotions in you empowers you to both seek out the spaces that best fit you as well as know what spaces might require an extra effort to deal with unwanted feelings. Try this activity to build your confidence and resilience through awareness of space and feeling:

1. Go to three separate locations:

   a. One space that feels really good to you—a place you really enjoy spending time and where you feel focused and energized.

   b. Another space that seems very unique

   c. And another space that seems very popular or that many individuals walk through or occupy

2. What feelings does each space communicate and incite in you as you occupy the space?

3. What about the space, specifically, do you think brings on those feelings?

Here are a number of feeling words to help you describe your experience:

Feelings When Needs *Are Not* Being Met		
Angry: enraged, furious, incensed	Annoyed Aggravated, Dismayed	Hostile Animosity, Appalled, Aversion
Afraid: apprehensive, dread, foreboding	Confused: ambivalent, baffled	Embarrassed: ashamed, chagrined, flustered
Sad: depressed, dejected, despair	Vulnerable: fragile, guarded helpless	Disconnected: alienated, aloof, apathetic, bored, cold, detached, distant
Upset: agitated, alarmed, discombobulated, disconcerted	Tense: anxious, bitter, cranky, distressed, distraught, edgy	Pain: agony, anguished, bereaved, devastated, grief, heartbroken
Yearning: envious, jealous, longing	Fatigue: beat, burned out, depleted	Surprised: disbelief, shocked, startled

Feelings When Needs *Are* Being Met		
Joyful: amused, delighted, glad	Excited: amazed, animated, astonished	Affectionate: compassionate, friendly
Hopeful: expectant, encouraged	Inspired: amazed, awed, radiant	Exhilarated: blissful, ecstatic, elated
Grateful: appreciative, moved, thankful	Confident: empowered, open, proud, safe	Intrigued: interested, fascinated
Peaceful: calm, clear-headed, relaxed	Engaged: absorbed, alert, curious	Refreshed: enlivened, rejuvenated

http://www.celebrateempathy.com/Needs-&-Feelings.pdf

Skill Builder Activity

Creative Climate Interview and Memo

Choose an organization (not your own). Observe and talk to folks about the creative context and culture. Analyze the data you collect. Write a one- to two-page memo to the organization highlighting what they should start doing, stop doing, and keep doing to facilitate creativity.

Interview someone in that career about the role, process, and context of creativity. Choose five to seven questions from the following list:

- Do you believe in divergent thinking? What methods do you use?

- What do you do to inspire creativity?

- What do you do when you encounter someone who is not creative?

- How do you recover from failing?

- What is the most effective way to start your day in your organization?

- Why do you do what you do?

- What is the key factor to make you successful?

- What is the future of your industry?

- How do you generate ideas?

- What do you fear?

- What brings you joy?

- Where do you come up with your ideas?

- What is involved in your daily routine?

- Does your family influence your creativity?

- Do you intentionally surround yourself with creative people?

- How do you overcome adversity to your creative idea?

- How do you remain entrepreneurial?

- Do you feel pressured to maintain a level of creativity?

- When did you know being different was a good thing?

- How do you find new ways to stay creative?

Skill Builder Activity

Build a Better Block

As a leader, individuals look to you for guidance, assurance, answers, decisions, and success. Individuals also look to you to foster a culture of innovation. This *Skill Builder Activity* challenges you to create a space that encourages creativity and innovation, specifically redesigning a city block in your neighborhood or town.

The Build a Better Block program is a relatively new social design endeavor that has grown exponentially. Why? Because it is critically needed, is flexible to accommodate a variety of locations, and engages individuals in a real-world effort to make a difference. You can (should) read more about it here: http://betterblock .org/

From the website http://betterblock.org/how-to-build-a-better-block/, it is best to address the following four areas when developing a Better Block, which we will break down in greater depth:

1. **Safety (Real and Perceived)**—First and foremost, if an area feels unsafe then everything breaks down. Whether it be businesses, schools, or neighborhood revitalization, the key to changing a place is addressing its perceived safety. When approaching blocks, we ask the questions: Does it feel safe to cross the street? Does it feel safe to stand on the sidewalk? Does it feel safe to linger in the area?

2. **Shared Access**—The next goal we focus on is looking at ways to bring more people into the area by various modes of transportation. We ask the questions: Do pedestrians have easy and clear access to the area? Do bicycles feel welcome in the area? Is the area easily accessible from neighborhoods? Are there way-finding signs that direct people into and out of the area? Are there amenities that allow people to linger in the space (seating, tables, etc.)?

3. **Stay Power**—How can we encourage people to visit the area, have them linger, and invite their friends?

4. **8—80, Dog-Owners**—Lastly, we look at amenities that create invitations for children, seniors, and dog owners on a block. These groups tend to be indicators of a healthy environment that feels welcoming and attracts other people.

You can attempt this challenge individually, but it is far more fun as a group or as a class project.

You will need to *understand* the problem, its history, context, efforts to solve, and so forth.

You will need to *imagine* great ideas . . . thinking divergently far beyond *the box*.

And you will need to *iterate* your ideas until you have something feasible, viable, desirable, and innovative.

15

Entrepreneurial Leadership

by Tony Middlebrooks, PhD, and Dan Freeman, PhD

*When you grow up, you tend to get told that the world is the way
it is and your life is just to live your life inside the world, try not
to bash into the walls too much, try to have a nice family, have fun,
save a little money. That's a very limited life. Life can be much
broader, once you discover one simple fact, and that is that
everything around you that you call life was made up by people
that were no smarter than you. And you can change it, you can
influence it, you can build your own things that other people can
use. Once you learn that, you'll never be the same again.*

—Steve Jobs[1]

Learning Objectives

15.1   Describe the broad domain of entrepreneurship

15.2   Transform your mindset to see leadership as entrepreneurial

15.3   Interpret the entrepreneurial mindset

15.4   Distinguish the entrepreneurial process

15.5   Design your future as an entrepreneurial leader

Detailed Chapter Outline

Leadership by Design Model

Design Self

How can I design myself as a leader?

Design Relationships

As a leader, how can I design my relationships with others?

Design Others' Success

As a leader, how can I design success for others?

Design Culture

As a leader, how can I design the culture of my organization?

DESIGN FUTURE

AS A LEADER, HOW CAN I INNOVATE?

Introduction

Did you ever play musical chairs as a kid? Musical chairs is that game where you and a group of others walk around a bunch of chairs while music is playing. Then, when the music stops, everyone has to find a chair and sit in it. The challenge, however, is that there is always one less chair than people playing, which of course means someone is left standing and that person is out of the game. The marketing guru Seth Godin shared this analogy in regard to how individuals approach their career—constantly competing and looking over your shoulder, making sure you have a chair when the music stops.[2] This is playing the game within rules that only exist in your head. The reality of today's rapidly changing technology means career path instability and organizational disruption. In other words, disappearing chairs. But what if you brought your own chair or even built your own chair and made your own music? That is the essence of entrepreneurship.

Being a leader often requires designing and making your own path. The previous chapter introduced creating a culture of innovation, fostering yourself and others to generate unique ideas and translate them into value. This chapter introduces the broad domain of entrepreneurship, and more importantly, the elements from entrepreneurship that can make you a more effective, innovative leader—the *entrepreneurial leader*. At a fundamental level, entrepreneurship can be viewed as an exercise in leadership that involves bringing people together around a shared vision to launch something new into the marketplace and make a positive impact on others. **Entrepreneurial leadership** comprises a unique set of concepts, mindsets, and activities used by leaders to identify opportunities, deepen understanding, and initiate and develop innovation—in other words, leaders who spot value, translate that value, develop it, and then put the ideas into action to realize greater value for their organization and beyond.

> **Entrepreneurial leadership** a unique set of concepts, mindsets, and activities used by leaders to identify opportunities, deepen understanding, and initiate and develop innovation

Entrepreneurial leadership is more important and needed than ever. Although every era has enjoyed the benefits of new ideas and the individuals who translated these ideas into real-world value, the trending patterns indicate an acceleration of invention and innovation, faster adoption of new technologies, and increasing disruption to products and services resulting in shorter life spans for companies that cannot adapt.[3] These trends impact individuals and their career choices and options. Within the next decade, nearly half of all current jobs will be replaced with automation and artificial intelligence, and upwards of one third of the work force will be independent contract workers.[4] All of this adds up to a critical need for entrepreneurs and strong career advice to acquire and develop the mindsets and skills of entrepreneurial leadership. Design the future before it designs you.

LEADERSHIP THAT MAKES A DIFFERENCE

"Chase the vision, not the money." —Tony Hsieh, co-founder of Zappos.com

Tony Hsieh joined the online shoe store Zappos as CEO in 2000, shortly after the company's founding. Less than a decade later, his leadership had helped to grow the company from less than $2 million in annual revenue to more than $1 billion. How did Hsieh's leadership make such a big impact? According to many interviews and media reports, Hsieh's emphasis on creating an appealing company culture and ensuring that all employees felt like they were part of something bigger than themselves made a huge difference. Among the many things Hsieh did to establish the Zappos culture and gain buy-in for its larger purpose were

- communicating openly and honestly with employees and making sure that all employees feel comfortable openly voicing their opinions.

- focusing on fun as a priority through company events, allowing time to pursue passion projects and creating other opportunities to share enjoyable experiences with coworkers.

- working at a desk placed among the cubicles of other employees instead of isolating himself in a corner office, thus demonstrating a sense of humility and esprit de corps.

- admitting and taking responsibility for mistakes, including a pricing error that cost Zappos more than $1.5 million in less than 6 hours.

Who would not want to work for a leader like Tony Hsieh?

Entrepreneurship: Re-envisioning Leadership

Learning Objectives

15.1 Describe the broad domain of entrepreneurship

15.2 Transform your mindset to see leadership as entrepreneurial

What comes to mind when you hear someone mention *entrepreneurship*? Do you think about starting and operating small businesses, taking risks, and seeking to make a profit? Do you think about famous entrepreneurs like Mark Zuckerberg (Facebook), Bill Gates (Microsoft), and Jeff Bezos (Amazon)? If so, you are certainly not alone. Many definitions of entrepreneurship focus on starting businesses, and popular culture has made celebrities out of a handful of entrepreneurs who have founded companies and become exceptionally wealthy by creating innovative goods and services used by millions of consumers. These are some of the many misconceptions individuals hold regarding entrepreneurship.[5]

Defining Entrepreneurship

Entrepreneurship originates from the French verb *entreprendre*, which means to undertake or do something, and that *something* has been to start a business venture for hundreds of years. As entrepreneurship has evolved to the present day, it has come to comprise four very important distinguishing features that were added to entrepreneurship over centuries: creating value, managing that value, assuming risk, and innovating.[6] Indeed, the notion of reaching for something new and taking action is fundamental to entrepreneurship, as the origins of the word go even deeper into history, combining the Latin words *entre* (to swim out) and *prendes* (to grasp, understand, or capture). This chapter presents a richer perspective on entrepreneurship that extends beyond startup businesses to include innovation within existing companies, social venturing, and other entrepreneurial endeavors. This broader perspective is anchored by an updated definition of **entrepreneurship** stated as the process of pursuing opportunity through the conception, validation, and launch of new ideas into the marketplace. Each element of this definition tells a story about who entrepreneurs are, how they think, and what they do as leaders to make an impact on the world.

Entrepreneurship
the process of pursuing opportunity through the conception, validation, and launch of new ideas into the marketplace

Entrepreneurship Is a Process

Entrepreneurship involves engaging in a series of actions in an attempt to achieve a desired outcome. In *Disciplined Entrepreneurship*,[7] Bill Aulet describes the first 24 steps needed to launch a successful startup, beginning with "Step 1—market segmentation" and ending with "Step 24—develop a product plan." Although few entrepreneurial endeavors progress in the type of orderly, linear sequence implied by numbered steps (on the contrary, most are characterized by repeated false starts, pivots, iterations, and feedback loops), descriptions like Aulet's help to elucidate the many actions involved in executing the entrepreneurial process.

Entrepreneurship Involves Pursuing Opportunity

Opportunity recognition
occurs when entrepreneurs become aware of a problem, dissatisfaction, or gap in current offerings that they find interesting and believe themselves capable of solving

Like all processes, entrepreneurship has a defined beginning. It starts with the recognition and pursuit of opportunity. **Opportunity recognition** occurs when entrepreneurs become aware of a problem, dissatisfaction, or gap in current offerings that they find interesting and believe themselves capable of solving. Opportunity pursuit occurs when an entrepreneur decides to take action. For example, Seth Goldman, co-founder of Honest Tea, noticed a gap in the market for iced tea that was not heavily sweetened and decided to develop a new lightly sweetened formulation to pursue this opportunity. Similarly, Muhammad Yunus recognized a common problem for many would-be entrepreneurs in developing countries—they were poor and lacked access to even small amounts of startup capital. Yunus pursued this opportunity through the founding of Grameen Bank, a microcredit and microfinancing organization that has helped countless people to break out of poverty, and was awarded the 2006 Nobel Peace Prize for his efforts.

REFLECTION QUESTION

"What do you believe that no one else does?" That's a question Peter Thiel, co-founder of PayPal, asks the people he interviews. Seeing a truth that others are missing may represent an opportunity to change the world.

Conception, Validation, and Launch of New Ideas

The pursuit of opportunity involves three major buckets of activities corresponding to the conception, validation, and launch of new ideas. Conception-related activities include problem exploration, creativity, idea generation, and visioning (using many of the techniques you have learned in prior chapters). Validation-related activities include identifying risky assumptions, conducting tests, and iterating based on evidence. And launch-related activities include influencing others, building a team, and establishing a sustainable business or social impact model.

As Figure 15.1 shows, the conception, validation, and launch of new ideas require a broad and diverse skill set that goes far beyond small business management. It also requires a strong leadership CORE™, as entrepreneurship tends to be similar to riding a roller coaster—there are a lot of uncontrollable ups and downs that will test your confidence, optimism, resilience, and engagement.

Into the Marketplace

The final component of this updated definition of entrepreneurship—into the marketplace—implies that someone or some entity (a business, governmental organization,

FIGURE 15.1 ● Knowledge and Skills Relevant to the Broad Domain of Entrepreneurship				
Recognizing Opportunity	**Idea Conception**	**Validation**	**Launch**	**Growth and Management**
• Adaptability • Effectual thinking • Entrepreneurial mindset • Resourcefulness	• Creativity • Design thinking • Problem-solving • Visioning	• Evidence-based decision-making • Experimentation • Mindfulness • Prototyping and iteration	• Boundary spanning • Networking • Pitching and selling • Teamwork	• Business fundamentals • Continuous learning • Efficient execution • Goal setting
Confidence	Optimism		Resilience	Engagement

Invention the creation of a new method, device or process

or nonprofit) must benefit from the entrepreneur's new idea. In other words, mere **invention**—the creation of a new method, device, or process—is not sufficient for entrepreneurship. Rather, the new creation must provide value to a customer or a beneficiary by helping them to solve a problem or address an unmet need. If so, then the new creation can be referred to as an innovation—a new method, device, or process that is useful to people—that is developed and delivered into the marketplace through the process of entrepreneurship.

The Broad Domain of Entrepreneurship

Social entrepreneurship the process of utilizing the marketplace to solve social problems (generally wicked social problems) in a novel manner

Intrapreneurship entrepreneurial behaviors within an existing organization, such as risk-taking and generating ideas

Defining entrepreneurship as involving the pursuit of opportunity through new ideas broadens its domain to include entrepreneurial activity across many contexts. These contexts might look like new ideas for policies, projects, and programs that solve important problems and create benefits for people within the entrepreneurial domain. For example, **social entrepreneurship** is the process of utilizing the marketplace to solve social problems (generally wicked social problems) in a novel manner. It encompasses new ideas for social ventures to address chronic societal problems such as environmental degradation, poverty and access to health care, education, and clean water. **Intrapreneurship** comprises entrepreneurial behaviors within an existing organization, such as risk-taking and generating ideas for new products and services to be developed as companies seek to remain competitive or grow revenues and profitability. The entrepreneurial leader brings a mindset and understanding of how to execute the entrepreneurial process and a skill set that is relevant and useful across the broad domain of contexts where opportunity can be turned into value.

Entrepreneurship and Leadership

Founder's syndrome an organizational disorder characterized by over-reliance on the charisma, involvement, and decisions of one or more founding members in place of mindful, collaborative, and strategic management and leadership

Entrepreneurs need the leadership skills and dispositions that build relationships and engage others to realize the potential of their venture. Yet, interestingly, entrepreneurial success stories are filled with tales of vexing problems solved by someone with a brilliant insight and then a series of heroic journeys—challenging situations; tough decisions; and a path to growth, enlightenment, and often unexpected outcomes. As you hear these stories you may get the mistaken impression that leading an entrepreneurial venture is the act of a single great leader who initiates and drives everything—the *great man* theory that represented one of the early notions of leadership. Entrepreneurs may mistake their willingness and initial effort to *do something* with an image that they do everything. This shortsighted conception often results in considerable organizational difficulties, and it is referred to as founder's syndrome. **Founder's syndrome** is an organizational disorder characterized by overreliance on the charisma, involvement, and decisions of one or more founding members in place of mindful, collaborative, and strategic management and leadership.

The moment any endeavor begins to develop beyond an idea, other individuals become involved. At that point, you are trying to facilitate a process of influencing others toward a common vision (i.e., leadership). Researchers have found significant overlap between the characteristics of leaders and entrepreneurs.[8] The dynamic nature of a growing venture requires different knowledge, skills, attitudes, and others at every stage of the entrepreneurial journey—and consequently different types and facets of leadership.

Leading an entrepreneurial venture differs from entrepreneurial leadership.[9] Entrepreneurial leadership begs the question, What would you know, do, or be like as a leader if you were more entrepreneurial? The most basic notion of entrepreneurship by Jean-Baptiste Say in 1804 states, "The entrepreneur shifts economic resources out of an area of lower and into an area of higher productivity and greater yield."[10] In other words, the entrepreneur finds ways to make the most out of things—to bring out the greatest value—not just in economic terms but in other currency aligned with the context such as greater employee engagement, a more accessible bike trail, less diabetes in a community, more indictments of corrupt officials, or more citizens voting. Successfully achieving these kinds of outcomes requires that leaders see and think differently—like an entrepreneur. Thus, a recent definition states, "Entrepreneurial leaders are individuals who, through an understanding of themselves and the contexts in which they work, act on and shape opportunities that create value for their organizations, their stakeholders, and the wider society."[11]

The Entrepreneurial Mindset

Learning Objective

15.3 Interpret the entrepreneurial mindset

Entrepreneurs think differently. They notice problems and dissatisfactions that others fail to recognize. They utilize effectual thinking to develop a vision of what is possible given the means at hand. And they draw from a deep reservoir of passion and persistence to overcome the many impediments to developing novel solutions that make people's lives better. Some people seem to be wired this way, and they naturally see themselves as surrounded by abundant opportunity and feel compelled to take action. However, most do not possess this hardwiring, and instead, they need to develop the ability to see the world through an entrepreneurial lens. Doing so can provide incredible rewards—empowerment and the capacity to capitalize on unlimited possibilities for having a good and fulfilling life.

Take a moment to revisit the quote at the start of this chapter by Steve Jobs, founder of Apple and creator of iMacs, iPods, and iPhones: "Everything around you that you call life was made up by people that were no smarter than you. And you can change it, you can influence it, you can build your own things that other people can use." This quote captures the distinction between two general approaches for how you see the world: a fixed mindset versus a growth mindset.[12] With a **fixed mindset** you see your abilities and capacity as a change agent as set traits—they are what they are. The **growth mindset**, by contrast, is your belief that you can acquire and develop new abilities and that your capacity is only limited by your effort. Note how the growth mindset underpins the more specific entrepreneurial mindsets discussed in this section.

Fixed mindset a state of mind wherein you see your abilities and capacity as a change agent as set traits—they are what they are

Growth mindset a state of mind wherein you believe that you can acquire and develop new abilities, and that your capacity is only limited by your effort

REFLECTION QUESTIONS

If you had the power to change anything in the world, what would you change? What in your life right now is getting in the way of your success? What could you add to your life, real or magical, that would enhance your success?

Now, really believe the advice of Steve Jobs: You have the power to make things change. Do it.

The next sections discuss the entrepreneurial mindset—a series of dispositions or mental habits that drive the process of pursuing opportunity through the conception, validation, and launch of new ideas into the marketplace (Table 15.1).

TABLE 15.1 ● Entrepreneurial Mindset
See More Opportunity: Mindful, Observant, and Open to New Ideas
See Different: Reframing Problems as Opportunities
See More Answers: Ideation, Effectuation, and Resourcefulness
See It Started: Predilection for Action . . . and Reflection
See It Through: Remembering Your Purpose

See More Opportunity: Mindful, Observant, and Open to New Ideas

Have you ever wondered why school starts early in the morning and ends in the afternoon? Have you ever thought about why we frequently eat food such as eggs and cereal for breakfast but choose them less often for other meals? Have you ever sat at a red light in the middle of the night with no other cars around and wondered why you are required by law to just sit there? As Steve Jobs rightly pointed out, everything in the world—from the schools we attend to our food consumption patterns to the traffic laws we are required to follow were made up by people and can be changed.

Training yourself to be open and observant is a lot like trying to see your surroundings through the eyes of a foreign traveler. It involves continuously questioning your understanding of the *what* and the *why* of the people, products, processes, and other things that we encounter on a daily basis. Most of the time we take the what and the why for granted and just accept the world at face value. Seeing the world through an entrepreneurial lens involves actively looking deeper to discover the hidden cracks of opportunity that surround us. For example, you likely have heard of TOMS Shoes, the company that gives a pair of shoes to someone in need for every pair it sells. What you may not know is that the founder, Blake Mycoskie, was already a serial entrepreneur. He thought up the idea for TOMS while traveling in Argentina. There he noticed how many individuals were lacking shoes and the effect it had on their health and success. While many would simply see an interesting culture and people, Blake Mycoskie saw a problem . . . and then he saw an opportunity.

Seeing opportunities is not as easy as the stories of entrepreneurship make it seem. Yes, you may find an opportunity simply jumps out at you, particularly if you have developed the habit of looking for them. Throughout this text, you have read about many other developing leaders and their moments of awareness. As an entrepreneurial leader, *you need to seek out* and maximize those moments, raising your awareness of opportunities. Try this exercise:

Take a trip to a public place such as a park or a mall and watch the people around you. Try to understand what they are doing and why. Are there unspoken social norms guiding their behaviors? If so, what are they? Start a few conversations and really listen to what others are saying—are they complaining about things that could be addressed by an entrepreneurial venture? Next time you use a product, consider why you are really using it and whether it truly meets your needs. Next time you are at work, map out the steps involved in doing your job and ask yourself whether there might be a better way.

Take notes during and after each of these experiences. Then consider how you might meet a need, enhance an experience, add to a current use, make something more user-friendly, or create the next evolution in a product, service, or experience. The great news is that there are many techniques that you can utilize to both direct your focus as well as develop the mindset of mindfully observing. Try the specific opportunity-finding methods in this section to raise your awareness. Table 15.2 outlines six general approaches to explore opportunities along with a few of the many user-centered data collection techniques that can guide your explorations. Purposely find some time individually or with a partner to engage in some of these activities. See what opportunities you can discover.

See Differently: Reframing Problems as Opportunities

Think about the last time you encountered a problem. How did you react? Did you try to avoid it, or did you embrace the problem and immediately begin to consider solutions? Back in Chapter 8 on creativity, you learned about being reactive and proactive—dealing with problems as they occur or trying to anticipate problems and address them before they became problematic. Entrepreneurs completely reframe problems and see them as opportunities—a hint that there is something of value missing that can be filled by a venture. Entrepreneurs love to encounter people who have problems because they know that their complaints, frustrations, and pains represent opportunities to make a positive impact. Consider the examples of persistent problems listed below. Try to reframe them to represent opportunities to make a positive impact on the world through the conception, validation, and launch of a new idea into the marketplace.

TABLE 15.2 ● Opportunity-Finding Methods*	
Explore Data and Analyze It	**En/Vision the Ideal**
Historical Analysis—Compare features of an industry, organization, group, market segment, or practice through various stages of development. **Competitive Product Survey**—Collect, compare, and conduct evaluations of the product's competition.	**Predict Next Year's Headlines**—Invite clients to project their company into the future, identifying how they want to develop and sustain customer relationships.
Observe, Map, Analyze	**En/Vision the Worst Cases**
Fly on the Wall—Observe and record behavior within its context, without interfering with people's activities to see what people actually do within real contexts and time frames. **A Day in the Life**—Catalog the activities and contexts that users experience throughout the entire day.	**Error Analysis**—List all the things that can go wrong when using a product and determine the various possible causes.
Recognize and Map (Your/User) Culture & Concepts	**Investigate Personal Preferences**
Extreme User Interviews—Identify individuals who are extremely familiar or completely unfamiliar with the product and ask them to evaluate their experience using it.	**Personal Inventory**—Document the things that people identify as important to them as a way of cataloging evidence of their lifestyles.

*Methods directly quoted from IDEO Method Cards[13]

- People are unhappy about their weight

- People are busy and feel time-poor

- People want to find fulfilling employment

- People lack access to affordable medical care

Can you see the connection between people being unhappy about their weight and the thousands of diet and exercise solutions that have been introduced into the marketplace? How about time poverty and the invention of countless time-saving devices (many of which do not actually save time and end up failing to gain traction in the marketplace)? The point is that the world is full of problems. As a result, when you learn to view the world through an entrepreneurial lens you will see that these problems represent opportunities, and opportunities are everywhere.

LEADERSHIP BY DESIGN

Design Principle: Simplicity (a.k.a. Ockham's Razor, the law of parsimony)

Definition: "Simplicity is about subtracting the obvious and adding the meaningful."[14]

In Other Words: Keep it simple. Unnecessary elements decrease efficiency, increase the likelihood of unanticipated consequences, and discourage use.

For Example: A single-speed bicycle rarely needs a tune-up.

For Leaders: When asked to improve something, people generally add a new feature. What is better than a car that performs well? A car with cup holders . . . and seat warmers . . . and keyless entry . . . and, and, and. While these features may be desirable, they also add layers of necessary instruction and possible repair. Complexity is simple addition, but simplicity requires seeing the bigger system and designing a more fundamental solution. For example, when followers are not performing, leaders often add more instruction or more rules. The principle of simplicity, however, would suggest starting with asking why.[15]

- Why are followers doing this?

- Why are we concerned about this performance?

- Why are we adding this?

- Why are we taking this away?

- Why would users care?

- Why can they do this?

- Why will they still do this?

What can be reduced, reorganized, relocated, or relearned, rather than added? This may take time. Added time is also added complexity, and some things cannot be made simple. But simplicity frees up room for new activities and innovative directions.

See More Answers: Ideation, Effectuation, and Resourcefulness

Ideation the mental process of forming ideas

Entrepreneurs see more opportunities, and they see more ways to take advantage of those opportunities using two mental habits: ideation and effectuation. **Ideation** is the mental process of forming ideas. Entrepreneurs envision what *could be* as they encounter opportunity. In other words, what would the ideal outcome look like? Applying divergent thinking to generate many possibilities enhances this approach. However, another kind of thinking helps entrepreneurs flexibly alter their venture as new opportunities emerge.

When researcher Saras Sarasvathy conducted a study involving 27 expert entrepreneurs, she discovered that they think differently.[16] Rather than using **causal reasoning** to set a goal and then consider the means through which the goal can be accomplished, entrepreneurs use effectuation. **Effectuation** is defined as a type of reasoning that starts with one's given resources that subsequently forge goals as the resources are applied.[17] Effectual thinkers start by considering their means: Who am I, what do I know, whom do I know? Entrepreneurs also consider the other resources at their disposal—facilities, funding, equipment, and more—to determine what they can accomplish.

The distinction between causal reasoning and effectuation is perhaps best illustrated with a cooking metaphor. If you were going to prepare dinner for yourself, which approach would you take: Do you decide what you want to eat and use a recipe to cook it? Or do you look around to see what you have on hand, and then figure out how to use the ingredients to make something you want to eat. Typical businesspersons tend to plan their actions based on the goal (i.e., the recipe). Entrepreneurs, however, often begin with their means. Activities from that starting point result in emergent goals, which in turn produce new means, in a cycle that drives their venture in unexpected but fruitful new directions.[18] To begin to think like an entrepreneur, start by considering your means and resources. What opportunities can you pursue with your ingredients?

Causal reasoning a type of reasoning characterized by first setting a goal and then considering the means through which the goal can be accomplished

Effectuation a type of reasoning that starts with one's given resources that subsequently forge goals as the resources are applied

See It Started: Predilection for Action . . . and Reflection

Entrepreneurs are doers. They do not just sit around dreaming of new ideas. Rather, they think about what they can do to pursue an opportunity, and they take action. This approach has been described as *ready-fire-aim*[19], but it might be better to think of it as *ready-fire-reflect* because the most successful entrepreneurs thoughtfully consider the outcomes resulting from their actions. They ask themselves, "why did the action succeed or fail?" and "what might work better next time?" as they search to find solutions that will win in the marketplace. The single most valuable resource entrepreneurs possess is their time. Having a mental bias toward action and reflection enables entrepreneurs to efficiently allocate their time while executing a continuous series of dream, do, learn, and repeat loops.

MOMENT OF AWARENESS

There's no such thing as being fearless. If that's something you aspire to, you've been duped! But fear not, I was duped too. Being a Misfit Entrepreneur requires that you be fear-facing. For me, fear manifested as debilitating, getting-in-my-own-way self-doubt. It literally stopped me from doing necessary things, and for no good reason.

It's one thing to feel doubt; it's another to let it limit your potential and hold you back. My self-doubt would stop me from following up with a potential client. I would meet someone at a networking event who seemed interested in my elevator pitch. I'd get their card and think to myself, I should follow up with them and schedule a coffee meeting. But then I'd tell myself, I need to get a flyer together—it's more professional to have packages I can

show. Days would go by, and I hadn't made a flyer. A week later, I still hadn't followed up. Then I would tell myself that I'd missed the magic 48-hour window to follow up, which just showed how much I was failing at business, so why should I even bother.

You must learn to listen from within and distinguish between the voice of your inner critic and the wisdom of your inner genius. Understanding yourself isn't about making excuses. It's not saying, "It's just the way I am—there's nothing I can do about it." Understanding yourself is a constant process of self-discovery.

—Ariana Friedlander, from
*A Misfit Entrepreneur's Guide to
Building a Business Your Way*[20]

Adaptive cycles cycles that are natural to the evolution of living systems that occur at all levels of scale

Panarchy These are the deep patterns that occur in the transformation cycles all human and natural systems go through. This specific cycle looks like an infinity loop, and it includes the following phases: exploitation, conservation, release, and reorganization.

See It Through: Remembering Your Purpose

Conceiving, validating, and launching a new idea into the marketplace is a *huge* challenge. To succeed, you will need to overcome obstacles, push through points of resistance, avoid pitfalls, and quickly recover from rejection and failure. During dark times it is important to remember your purpose—the *why* behind your actions. With a strong and clear purpose— for example, providing world-class educational opportunities, creating jobs and economic well-being for others, making a strong positive impact on people's lives—you can keep yourself on track. Having such a purpose will also help you to bring people together around a shared vision and keep your team on track while you execute the entrepreneurial process.

EXPERTS BEYOND THE TEXT

INSIGHTFUL LEADERS KNOW ABOUT . . . PANARCHY AND ADAPTIVE CYCLES

Thinking in Adaptive Cycles

By Dr. Kathleen E. Allen

When we see a living system, like nature or an individual person, there are cycles that are natural to the evolution of these systems that occur at all levels of scale. One of these **adaptive cycles** is called panarchy.[21] **Panarchy** names the deep patterns that occur in the transformation cycles all human and natural systems go through. This specific cycle looks like an infinity loop, and includes the following phases: exploitation, conservation, release, and reorganization (see Figure 15.2).

The front side of this loop includes exploitation and conservation. Exploitation occurs when there is a buildup of resources that can be used to launch a new phase of business or life cycle, and this front loop continues into conservation when things become systematized and the successful forms that have achieved the function become set. The front loop is slow. At some point

the focus on conservation builds rigidity and an adherence to form. This rigidity makes the system vulnerable to a collapse, which starts the back loop of this adaptive cycle. The collapse creates a release of resources that are needed to build the next stage of evolution for an ecological system, business model, or individual transformation. This release occurs when the system is not adapting to changing conditions and creates a reset in the system. The other part of the "back loop" is reorganization, which is in the upper left side of the loop. After the collapse of the system, an exploration phase occurs that allows for the system to adapt or reset.

When disruptive technologies occur in business, this panarchy cycle is seen. A business develops a business plan that launches a successful enterprise. They move to launch their product and solidify their market niche. One example of this was the shift from desktop computers to mobile devices, or from internal data storage to the cloud. Swiss watchmakers and their successful

FIGURE 15.2 ● Panarchy

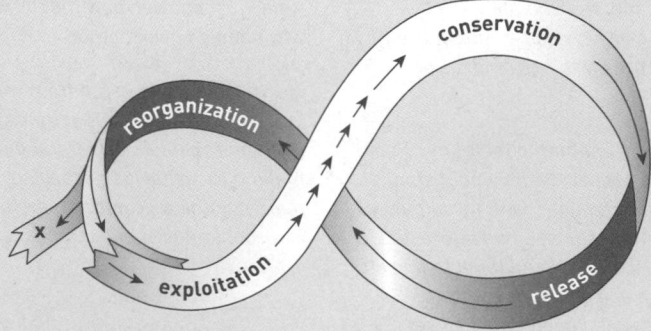

dominance of the analogue watch design had their business model collapse when digital watchmaking emerged as a disruptive technology. This triggered a release of the traditional paradigm of watchmaking and created a lot of creative energy to explore and reorganize the assumptions behind how to tell time. New businesses and market share were created that split the analog market niche into analog and digital time pieces.

In human organizations and communities there is a constant evolution occurring. In business, disruptive technologies are occurring all the time, even if we can't see them coming.[22] Leaders of the future will need to learn how to think in adaptive cycles. Organizations are built on structures. Systems aren't just structures, they are also movements.[23] These movements have a pattern, one of which is panarchy. The concepts of panarchy have been adapted into using an **ecocycle framework** for understanding movements and cycles in organizational systems and applying it to planning and leading.[24] The ecocycle in Figure 15.3 shows four main phases cycling in an infinite loop.

Traditionally, businesses think of strategic planning as a linear process moving the organization forward. However, in typical strategic plans there is no space for release or creative destruction of what an organization is doing. An ecocycle invites an intentional letting go of all preconceived assumptions or structures to release energy and resources. These resources are then used to explore and launch new products or thinking. The questions that leaders need to focus on are related to the ecocycle.

- What needs to be explored?
- What needs to be launched?
- What needs to be sustained and systematized?
- What needs to be let go of or released to make room for the next innovation?

This allows for intentional releasing of energy, capital, attention, and form that no longer serves the organization's main function.

FIGURE 15.3 ● Ecocycle

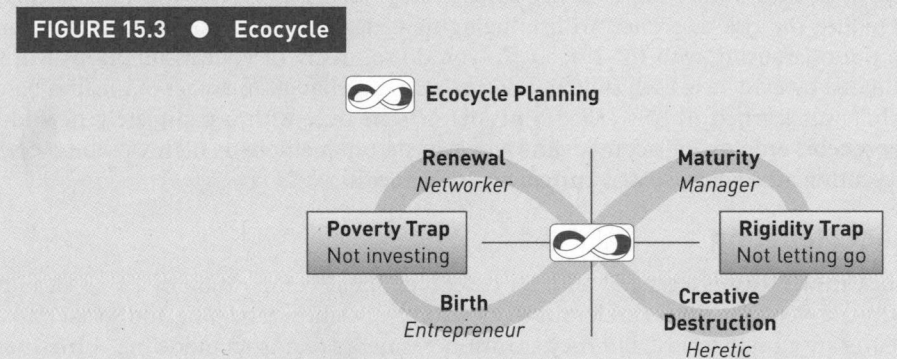

Leading the Entrepreneurial Process

Learning Objective

15.4 Distinguish the entrepreneurial process

Entrepreneurs, and their unique way of seeing and thinking, design the future by seeing opportunities and translating them into value. Leaders adopting these entrepreneurial mindsets can apply them to any context to maximize innovation. Entrepreneurs also engage in unique processes that can further enhance leadership. The entrepreneurial process is best described as a sequence of activities that includes opportunity recognition, idea conception, validation, launch, and growth. However, in practice, it is decidedly nonlinear, often involving false starts and pivots before launch into the marketplace and continuous

Ecocycle framework explains the movements and cycles in organizational systems, often used in planning and leading and comprising four main phases (birth, maturity, creative destruction, and renewal) cycling in an infinite loop iteration thereafter. Until recently, best practices for executing the entrepreneurial process once an idea was conceived involved emulating the strategic planning process of large companies. Specifically, entrepreneurs would allocate their time to developing a comprehensive business plan that describes the company, its organization and management, products, marketing plan, and financial projections for the next three to five years. They would then seek to execute their plans, often resulting in failure because the plans relied on critical untested assumptions, which are inherent to bringing any truly new idea into the marketplace.

A new set of best practices has begun to emerge for executing an *evidence-based* entrepreneurial process based on a key book: *Four Steps to the Epiphany*.[25] **Evidence-based decision-making** means that decisions are researched and made based on collected data, rather than relying on your experience and expertise, personal observations, advice, hopes, or hunches. These practices build from the observation that all new ideas are associated with a variety of untested assumptions. When left untested prior to launch, each of these assumptions represents a potential cause of failure. For example, if you conceived of a new program to reduce homelessness, then the success of your idea would likely depend on untested assumptions about why the people you want to help are homeless, how the specifics of your program would benefit them, how you would reach beneficiaries to let them know about the program, the extent to which participating in the program would appeal to prospective beneficiaries, and how the program would be funded for sustainability. If any one of your assumptions ultimately proved to be invalid, then the program would be likely to fail.

The basic idea underlying evidence-based entrepreneurship is that you can systematically reduce the risk associated with bringing new ideas into the marketplace by testing assumptions, starting with the riskiest. As you do so, many of your assumptions will be invalidated by evidence. Each time this occurs, you can change an aspect of the idea based on what was learned (this is called a **pivot**) or start over with a completely new idea. Entrepreneurs employ impact modeling and lean startup methods as highly useful toolsets for executing an evidence-based entrepreneurial process.

Impact Modeling

Impact modeling is a general term for describing the decomposition of a new idea into constituent elements that are relevant to its viability. Business modeling and social impact modeling are closely related, but they are distinct varieties of impact modeling. A **business model** represents a company's rationale for how it creates value for customers, delivers its products to them, and captures value to make a profit. A category of tools called **business model canvas** are useful for illustrating the components of a business model. The first such tool to gain widespread use, which was developed by Alexander Osterwalder and Yves Pigneur,[26] is aptly named the business model canvas. The business model canvas decomposes businesses into nine components: (1) key partners, (2) key activities, (3) key resources, (4) value proposition, (5) customer relationships, (6) channels, (7) customer segments, (8) cost structure, and (9) revenue. Figure 15.4 displays the common business model canvas; however, it is important to know that other versions of this tool have been developed for different contexts, types of organizations (such as nonprofits), and different facets of entrepreneurship, such as social entrepreneurship.

In combination, these components describe how the company creates value (through its key partners, activities, and resources), the value it offers and to whom it is offered (its value proposition and customer segments), how value is delivered (through its customer relationships and channels), and the economics of capturing value from customers (its cost structure and revenue streams).

Another form of business model canvas is the lean canvas developed by Ash Maurya[27] for startup businesses. The lean canvas decomposes new business ideas into nine components: (1) problem, (2) solution, (3) key metrics, (4) unique value proposition, (5) unfair advantage, (6) channels, (7) customer segments, (8) cost structure, and (9) revenue streams.

Evidence-based decision-making decisions are researched and made based on collected data, rather than relying on your experience and expertise, personal observations, advice, hopes, or hunches

Pivot changing an aspect of your idea, solution, or approach (or starting over) to reduce risk based on evidence and testing assumptions

Impact modeling a general term for describing the decomposition of a new idea into constituent elements that are relevant to its viability

Business model represents a company's rationale for how it creates value for customers, delivers its products to them, and captures value to make a profit

Business model canvas This is a tool that illustrates the nine key business components: (1) key partners, (2) key activities, (3) key resources, (4) value proposition, (5) customer relationships, (6) channels, (7) customer segments, (8) cost structure, and (9) revenue.

FIGURE 15.4 ● Business Model Canvas

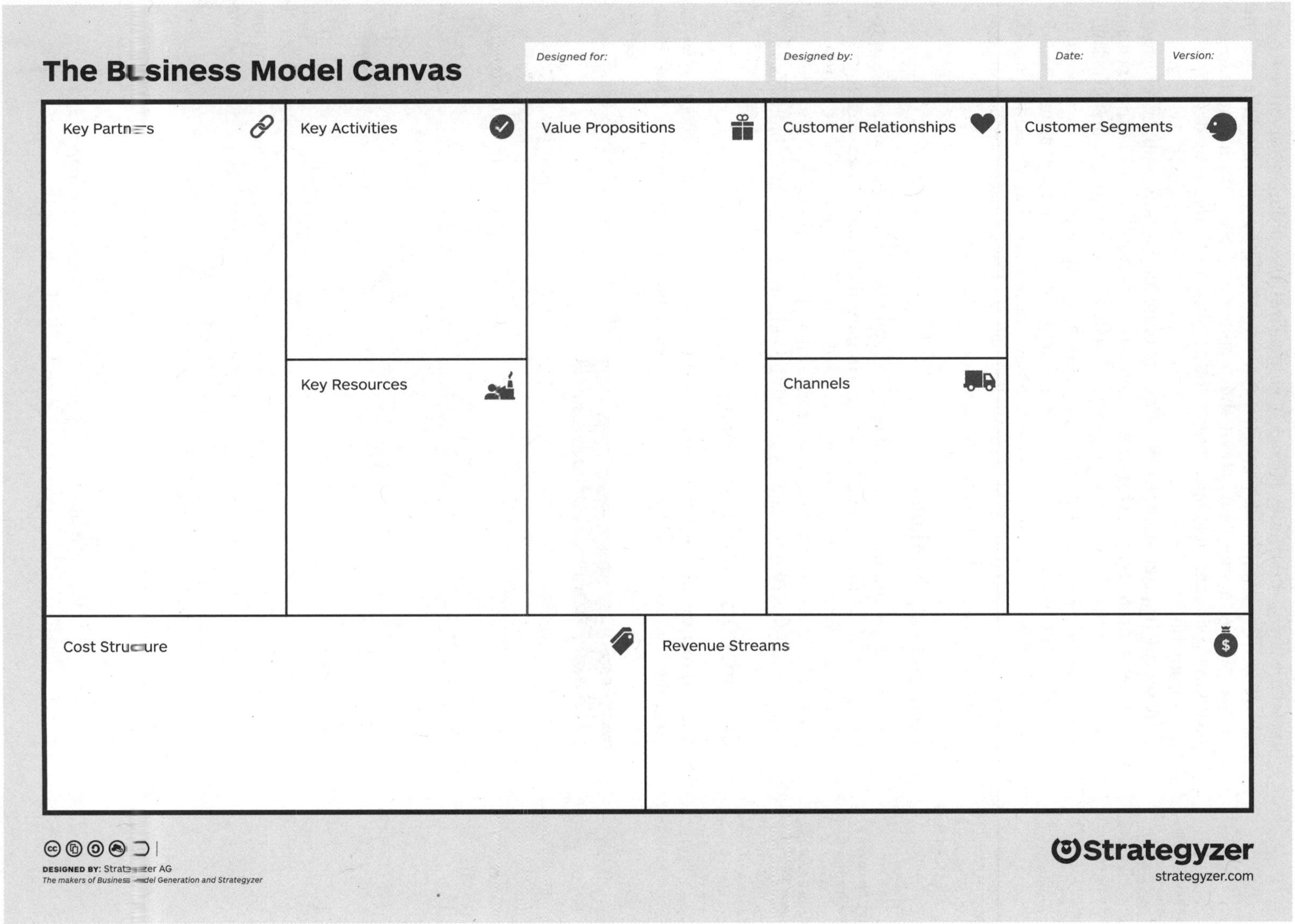

The B siness Model Canvas
Designed for:
Designed by:
Date:
Version:
Key Partn s
Key Activities
Key Resources
Value Propositions
Customer Relationships
Channels
Customer Segments
Cost Stru ure
Revenue Streams
DESIGNED BY: Strat zer AG
The makers of Busines del Generation and Strategyzer
Strategyzer
strategyzer.com

Source: Strategyz *Business Model Canvas*, https://strategyzer.com/canvas/business-model-canvas via CC BY-SA 3.0 (https://creativecommons.org/licenses/by-sa/3.0).

Social impact model
a representation for the rationale for how a policy, program, project, or social venture creates value for beneficiaries, delivers the value to beneficiaries, and sustains its impact over time

Lean an approach to organizational development that engages flexible, rapid methods to test and revise products and services before heavily investing

Customer discovery interviewing using a structured interview script to qualify an interviewee as a member of your assumed target segment and elicit beliefs and experiences relevant to the problem you are trying to solve and the solution you are working to develop

One benefit of using the lean canvas as part of the evidence-based entrepreneurial process for startup businesses is that it emphasizes the problem (or unmet need) being addressed. The biggest risk most startups face is building a solution that no one wants. By identifying assumptions about the problem and who has it, the lean canvas can save entrepreneurs from spending a lot of time and money to develop solutions to non-problems.

A **social impact model** represents the rationale for how a policy, program, project, or social venture creates value for beneficiaries, delivers the value to beneficiaries, and sustains its impact over time. A variety of social impact canvases are available, most of which include key partners, value proposition, channels, customer segments, and other elements. The best one for decomposing your idea into constituent assumptions for testing will depend on the nature of your idea. Some components that are unique to social impact canvases include type of intervention, key points of resistance, intended societal impact, and potential unintended consequences (see Figure 15.5).

Lean Startup Methods

Once you have modeled your idea using an appropriate canvas, you can begin to identify and test your riskiest assumptions using lean startup methods.[28] **Lean** refers to an approach to organizational development that engages flexible, rapid methods to test and revise products and services before heavily investing. Two of these powerful methods include customer discovery interviewing and prototyping minimum viable products.

Customer Discovery Interviewing

The **customer discovery interview** involves using a structured interview script to qualify an interviewee as a member of your assumed target segment and elicit beliefs

FIGURE 15.5 ● Social Impact Canvas

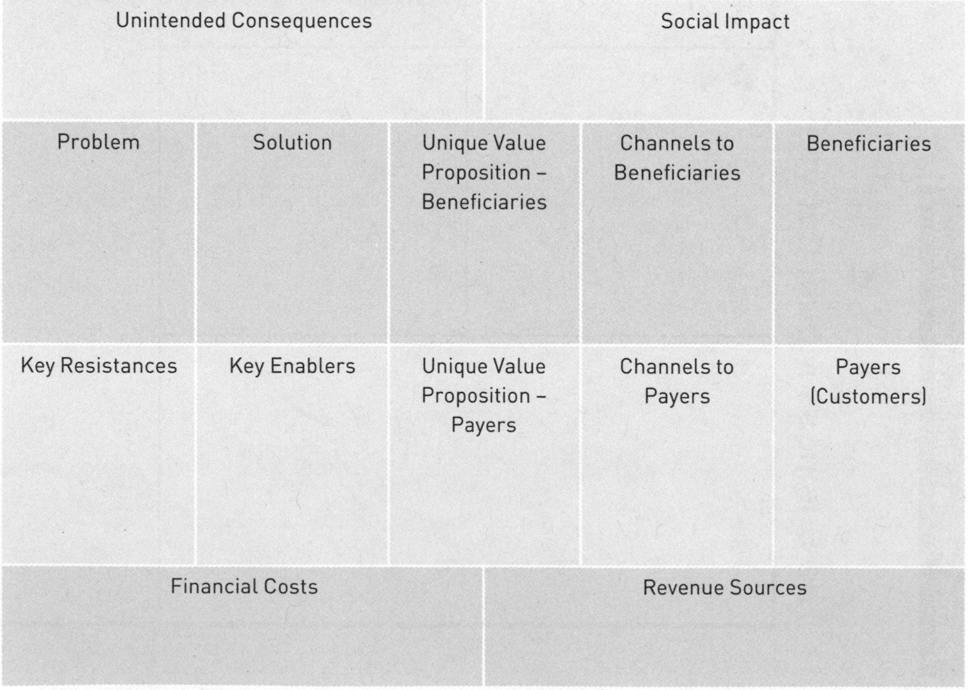

Source: Dan Freeman.

and experiences relevant to the problem you are trying to solve and the solution you are working to develop. One of many user-centered data collection techniques discussed previously, customer discovery interviewing tests and/or enriches understanding of the problem members of the customer segment experience and identifies core *must-have* features and benefits that your solution will need to offer to deliver compelling value. The most important guideline for customer discovery interviewing is simply to do it early and often during the entrepreneurial process.

The second most important guideline is to remember that a pitch is *not* included. Customer discovery interviews should focus on the interviewee's experiences, pains, and desires. Listen, do not talk. As Seth Godin notes, "The other person is always right. You'll need to travel to this place of 'right' before you have any chance at all of actual communication or understanding" and influence.[29] Table 15.3 provides a few sample interview questions.[30]

Prototyping Minimum Viable Products

Once you have validated your ideas for core product features and benefits, you can prototype a minimum viable product to test its appeal. A **minimum viable product** (MVP) is the smallest, simplest thing you can build that conveys the product's value proposition to customers. Your MVP does not need to be a physical prototype, but it could be a promotional flyer or a landing page that describes the product and what it offers. Different variations of MVPs provide information from customers that allow you to iterate based on evidence before spending the time and money needed to actually develop a marketable version of your product or service.

Minimum viable product (MVP) the smallest, simplest thing you can build that conveys the product's value proposition to customers (and potentially captures value back)

The lean practices associated with evidence-based entrepreneurship can be successfully applied to the process of bringing any type of new idea—including ideas for programs, policies, social ventures, products, and startup businesses—into the marketplace.

The Evolving Role of the Entrepreneurial Leader

Learning Objective

15.5 Design your future as an entrepreneurial leader

Up to this point, entrepreneurial leadership has been described largely as mental habits and process activities such as idea generation and validation. However, there are at least four

TABLE 15.3 ● Sample Customer Discovery Interview Questions	
To Qualify an Interviewee	• Who in your [household, business] makes decisions about [the type of product or service you are envisioning]?
Problem Discovery	• What is the most challenging part of your day? • What tasks do you spend the most time on?
Problem Validation	• Tell me about the last time you [experienced the problem] • If you had a solution to [the problem], what would it mean to you?
Product Feature and Benefit Discovery	• How would you describe your ideal solution to [the problem]? • What are you currently doing to solve [the problem]?

Source: Adapted from Fishbein, M. (2013). *The ultimate list of customer development questions.* Retrieved from http://mfishbein.com/the-ultimate-list-of-customer-development-questions (accessed January 2, 2017).

distinct roles that entrepreneurial leaders can play as they execute the entrepreneurial process by conceiving, validating, and launching new ideas into the marketplace: the founder, the innovator, the team builder, and the chief executive. This section describes these roles as well as the tremendous challenges associated with any one person attempting to fill all of these roles by going from founder to CEO.

The Founder

The entrepreneurial process begins with the recognition and pursuit of opportunity by a founder (or inventor/creator). The founder's role as an entrepreneurial leader involves seeing opportunity and utilizing creativity to conceive of a new idea that has the potential to disrupt the status quo. New ideas are inherently associated with greater uncertainty and risk vis-à-vis established ideas. As uncertainty and risk are aversive, an important part of the founder's role involves developing and communicating a compelling vision for the unique value that will be provided by the new idea. This vision needs to articulate who will benefit, how they will benefit, why it matters, and why the benefits should be expected to greatly outweigh any potential risks. For founders, creativity, compulsion to disrupt the status quo, and vision are essential personal characteristics.

MYTH OR REALITY?

YOU CANNOT BE AN ENTREPRENEUR UNLESS YOU HAVE A DISRUPTIVE IDEA.

Myth! There are many entrepreneurial roles— founder, innovator, team builder, and chief executive. Only one requires that you be involved in idea generation. In other words, you can still be an entrepreneur if you are involved in the validation and launch of a new idea into the marketplace or guide the growth of an entrepreneurial venture as its chief executive. Ideas emerge from engaging other ideas and perspectives. The more you are involved in entrepreneurial activities, and the more you are mindful, observant, and open to new ideas, the more likely you will one day see that opportunity and find that disruptive idea. But that activity is just one small part of entrepreneurship.

The Innovator

Once a vision has been developed, the entrepreneurial leader's role transitions to that of the innovator. Recall that innovation is defined as the collaborative process of translating creative ideas into something of value. Thus, the innovator's role is to translate the vision into a series of testable impact model assumptions, prioritize and conduct tests, and iterate as needed until a viable model is identified or the project is terminated. This process, which often involves active collaboration with members of the founding team and many turns of the do–learn–repeat loop, requires the innovator to maintain flexibility and persistence in response to a roller coaster of excitement, rejection, and uncertainty. Riding the roller coaster is not for everyone. Possession of the passion and optimism needed to persist through difficult times and the capacity to continuously reprioritize and rapidly adapt based on learning are essential characteristics for innovators.

LEADERSHIP BY DESIGN

Design Principle: Fun

Definition: A feeling of enjoyment or pleasure (as a noun), a way to describe something as such (as an adjective—that was a fun game—or even a verb if you think "funning" is a word).[31]

In Other Words: A purely and often instantaneously pleasurable experience. For example, you fill in the blank: "I have fun doing _____." Fun is subjective.

For Leaders: Fun can play a key role in every facet of your leadership design. Designing fun into yourself and your time has positive effects on health and creativity. Fun in your leadership relationships increases engagement, job satisfaction, and performance, while reducing anxiety and emotional exhaustion.[32]

Fun increases organizational citizenship behavior and creates a culture of connectedness and innovation (see Chapter 14). Fun, and funny, often emanates from connecting ideas that generally do not belong together—such as when a comedian makes an unexpected or inappropriate face relative to their joke. Or why do witches fly around on broomsticks? Because vacuum cleaners do not have long enough cords. Fun can catalyze innovation and designing the future.

Because everyone defines fun in their own way, leaders must buy in, facilitate, and find ways to bring everyone in on the fun—to make it a shared experience.[33] Likewise, too often, activities and interactions imposed by managers are perceived as juvenile, condescending, and inauthentic, resulting in employee cynicism. That is no fun.

What can you do to design fun into your leadership?

The Team Builder

After the innovator succeeds in validating a novel impact model, the entrepreneurial leader's role shifts to growing the team. Leadership is the process of influencing others toward a common vision. At this point the entrepreneurial leader's role of team builder focuses most heavily on effective leadership activities, such as recruiting new personnel and communicating a purpose that will align everyone's activities and make all team members feel as if they are part of something important and larger than themselves (i.e., a shared vision). Recent research on motivation shows that purpose is often more powerful than money in promoting high performance among the types of employees who are most likely to drive the growth of an entrepreneurial venture—those who are creative problem solvers and knowledge workers.[34] Therefore, being growth oriented, willing to make personal sacrifices to advance a shared purpose, and capable of influencing others are essential characteristics for team builders.

The Chief Executive

Once the core team is assembled and scope and scale of the venture have expanded, often with considerable velocity, the entrepreneurial leader's role transitions to chief executive. In this capacity, the leader becomes responsible for setting strategic direction and accountable for the overall performance/impact of the business, social enterprise, project, or program. Providing strategic direction requires cognitive ambidexterity.[35] Similar to being able to use both hands equally well, cognitive ambidexterity describes the ability of someone to think creatively as well as logically. The chief executive must guide the development of rigid policies and processes to extract efficiencies from existing products. On the other hand, the chief executive must also encourage ongoing experimentation to explore and pursue new opportunities. Accountability for performance requires managerial discipline, while energizing innovation requires leadership autonomy and inspiration. Thus, characteristics pertaining to mental agility, efficiency, and management are essential for chief executives.

REFLECTION QUESTIONS

What entrepreneurial leadership role are you best suited for—founder, innovator, team builder, or chief executive? Do you think you have the characteristics and skills needed to go from founder to chief executive?

The Leadership Challenge: From Founder to Chief Executive

The skills approach to leadership explained in Chapter 2 outlined the shifting skills required of leaders as they rose in the organization—transitioning from the technical skills of doing the job to the human skills of managing to the conceptual skills of heading the organization. These shifts also apply to the value of personal characteristics in the transition from founder to chief executive, with each level demanding new skills from entrepreneurial leaders. Two skill set-based challenges associated with making this transition are going from technician to strategist and going from star player to coach of the year.[36]

During idea generation, validation, and launch, entrepreneurial leadership is about pace setting and being actively involved in all aspects of value creation, delivery, and capture. Throughout these stages of the entrepreneurial process, leaders need to be close to customers to ascertain whether they are on the right track. Technical expertise and operational skills are valuable in this context, as they enable the leader to meet the challenge of execution, which is about doing things right.

However, as the business grows, entrepreneurial leadership transitions to being about doing the right things. Chief executives simply do not have enough time to be actively involved in the day-to-day operational aspects of a business or social venture. Rather, they need to focus on setting the strategic direction of the company and determining how to put their limited time to its highest and best use. Transitioning from working in the business to working on the business can be difficult for many entrepreneurial leaders (thus, founder's syndrome). Whereas working in the business emphasizes attending to details and constantly making decisions in real time, working on the business emphasizes big picture and making a relatively small number of strategic decisions. This requires a different skill set. Table 15.4 summarizes the shifting focus of entrepreneurial leadership.

Transitioning from a nascent startup to a growing company also involves a shift in the nature of leaders' relationships with team members. The shift from founder to chief executive is akin to going from the star player to coach of the year. During startup, entrepreneurial leaders are the stars of their teams; others look to them for direction and making the big plays that result in the company beginning to win in the marketplace. Growth forces entrepreneurial leaders to rely more on the operational capabilities of others and less on their own abilities to execute the company's business model. This means another shift in skills—away from execution and toward talent development. Just as in sports, the star player does not necessarily translate to excellent coach, or scout, or trainer. The entrepreneurial leader must focus on and develop new skills to become an effective coach who prepares top executives and devises a strategic game plan that puts them in the best position to succeed.

TABLE 15.4 ● Entrepreneurial Leadership Roles and Shifting Focus		
Role	Venture Focus	Leadership Focus
Founder	Find opportunity Generate idea Craft vision Initiate venture	Clarify and communicate vision Inspire and recruit partners Model CORE™ amidst risk
Innovator	Translate value Develop viable model	Manage collaborative iteration work Maintain optimism and resilience
Team builder	Maximize value Engage and manage others	Identify, screen, onboard Communicate vision and purpose Clarify direction and strategy Engage, motivate, and manage
Chief executive	Maximize, sustain, and reinvent value Set strategic direction	Foster innovation Create management systems Inspire and model the ideal

REFLECTION QUESTIONS

With which entrepreneurial leadership role are you least comfortable? What are your personal shortcomings and weaknesses that might affect your success as an entrepreneurial leader? The capacity to conduct an honest self-assessment and strive for personal improvement will make you a better entrepreneurial leader.

Chapter Summary

This chapter added another perspective and set of tools to your leadership toolbox—that of the entrepreneurial leader. Entrepreneurs benefit greatly from understanding leadership, but leaders who seek to thrive in times of change must learn to innovate and take on an entrepreneurial leadership mindset. As you continue to learn more about leadership, it should become more and more apparent that leadership is about you and not about you simultaneously. Navigating that balance will allow you to harness innovation and maximize your success.

The classic children's book *Harold and the Purple Crayon* tells the story of young Harold, who decides to create his own world and adventure by drawing what he wants with his purple crayon and then watching it come to life. At heart, it is a story about creating your own opportunities and solving problems with your imagination and effort. Harold draws a mountain from which to see, "But as he looked down over the other side he slipped—And there wasn't any other side of the mountain. He was falling, in thin air. But, luckily, he kept his wits and his purple crayon. He made a balloon and he grabbed on to it."[37] Effective leaders must design and make their own path, seeing and pursuing opportunities for innovation. The field of entrepreneurship provides a unique set of concepts, mindsets, and activities that can help leaders spot, translate, and develop value.

Entrepreneurship is the process of pursuing opportunity through the conception, validation, and launch of new ideas into the marketplace. This activity goes beyond the field of business and can include every field including social, political, and within existing organizations. Each action within the definition requires specific knowledge and skills, as well as a number of mindsets that enable entrepreneurs to see differently. This includes a growth mindset, being mindful and observant, reframing problems as opportunities, ideating and effectuating, taking reflective action, and staying focused on purpose.

Leading the entrepreneurial process using tools such as the business model canvas and lean start-up methods enable entrepreneurial leaders to minimize risk and iterate to find the most successful path forward.

As a venture grows, entrepreneurial leaders must shift their role and focus from founder to innovator to team builder to chief executive. Each role requires a differing skill set aligned to the needs of the developing venture.

Key Terms

Adaptive Cycles 386
Business Model 388
Business Model Canvas 388
Causal Reasoning 385
Customer Discovery
    Interviewing 390
Ecocycle Framework 387
Effectuation 385
Entrepreneurial Leadership 377

Entrepreneurship 378
Evidence-Based
    Decision-Making 388
Fixed Mindset 381
Founder's Syndrome 380
Growth Mindset 381
Ideation 384
Impact Modeling 388
Intrapreneurship 380

Invention 380
Lean 390
Minimum Viable Product
    (MVP) 391
Opportunity Recognition 378
Panarchy 386
Pivot 388
Social Entrepreneurship 380
Social Impact Model 390

CORE™ Attribute Builders: Build Now for Future Leadership Challenges

Attribute: Engagement

Builder: "Eye of the Tiger," by Steve Boerner

Can you recall a movie where the hero is facing terrible obstacles, and then the hit soundtrack kicks in, and the hero has that moment of conviction—a moment that marks the beginning of a determined journey toward conquering the impossible? In the Academy Award-winning movie *Rocky*, that song is "Eye of the Tiger" (by the band Survivor). In the movie, Rocky is faced with the impossibility of rising from the streets of South Philadelphia to become a world-champion

boxer. Only when he truly commits (and fully engages) does he take on the eye of the tiger—the tenacious will to reach his goals.

Your challenge: Choose an implausible outcome you desire. Then pursue it with a new lens, a creative approach, and with heightened ambition.

Apply your eye of the tiger to accomplish a micro-success, and then another, and another. Perhaps you want to meet someone? Learn a skill?[38]

What do you really want, but right now think is impossible? Get the eye of the tiger and take the first step!

CORE™ Attribute Builders: Build Now for Future Leadership Challenges

Attribute: Confidence and Resilience

Builder: 25 things to celebrate

Entrepreneurs are on the lookout for opportunities, take risks, spearhead initiatives, and constantly try things for the purpose of assessing and improving. They are always looking for the next thing on their to-do list. And effective leaders are often no different. What both fail to do often enough is note and celebrate their success.

1. Take a moment right now to write out 25 things of which you are proud. These can be accomplishments big or small, interactions or reactions, a risk taken, a moment of emotional intelligence, or anything that *you* are proud to have done, been like, and so forth.

2. When you are done with the list, read it out loud to yourself without comment or judgment. You will be surprised how you feel.

3. Date your list and file it somewhere. Repeat this activity every so often, and soon you will have quite a record of your big and small accomplishments. Taking the time to remind yourself of these accomplishments boosts your confidence, knowing that your work is more than the list that remains undone. The list also builds resilience, reminding yourself of the many things that you have managed to achieve.

As an added dimension, do this activity with friends and/or colleagues. Remind them that during the reading there is no judgment or comment. Of course, there will be lots of smiles and congrats afterward.

Skill Builder Activity

Practice Your Pitching

Develop a 30-second description of your business (an elevator pitch) and field test it at a community networking event. Do people seem to get it? What can you learn from their reactions?

Skill Builder Activity

Plan a Venture

Planning an entrepreneurial venture takes a good deal of time, information, collaboration, and leadership. Use the list of activities below to guide you and/or a team through the venture planning process.

	Prompt/Activity	Business Model Canvas	Innovation Process Phase
1	Consider and list issues of interest to you—what do you want to know more about and make a difference regarding?	Pre-canvas	Understand
2	Write a brief history of your issue—both a professional history and your personal history with the issue.	Pre-canvas	Understand
3	Create a visual model of your issue—a mental map or a systems diagram.	Pre-canvas	Understand
4	Write the story of solutions as it regards your issue, and highlight best practices (using the storytelling framework). If customers have a problem, right now they are doing something to solve it. What has been done? What is being done?	Pre-canvas	Understand

	Prompt/Activity	Business Model Canvas	Innovation Process Phase
5	Engage user-centered methods to collect information about your issue, identifying the stakeholders and potential customer segments. Consider what kind of relationship you want with each customer segment.	Customer segments Customer relationships	Understand
6	Envision the ideal solutions and/or outcomes of your issue—what would/could it look like and how?		Understand Imagine
7	Generate many, many, many ideas for *solving* your issue.		Imagine
8	Examine multiple views and perspectives on both your issue and some of your proposed solutions.		Imagine
9	Research and establish criteria by which you will judge the success of your solution; create metrics as applicable.	Key metrics	Implement
10	Engage in customer discovery interviewing and other techniques to determine solution viability and desirability.		Iteration
11	Assess unique value proposition and how to frame it.	Unique value proposition	Implement
12	Assess your unfair advantage: Why are *you* the one to take on this problem? What do *you* have that no one else has or can buy? What gives you an advantage that others can only dream of?	Unfair advantage	Implement
13	Craft a strategic implementation plan for your solution using the business model canvas or other applicable tool.	Overall canvas Sales channels Key resources Key activities	Iterate Implement
14	Add a plan to maximize value and revenue.	Revenue streams (or value types)	
15	Consider and plan possible cross-sector collaborations and further innovations in the solution and/or implementation of your solution. Who could help you advance your venture?	Key partners	Iterate Implement
16	Consider unintended consequences, worst cases, and ethical issues arising from your solution.	Overall canvas	Iterate
17	Create and test a minimum viable product.		Iterate
18	Envision the next iteration and innovation.	Revisit problem and solution, then overall canvas	Iterate

Systems and Sustainability

Experiences aren't truly yours until you think about them, analyze them, examine them, question them, reflect on them, and finally understand them. The point, once again, is to use your experiences rather than being used by them, to be the designer, not the design, so that experiences empower rather than imprison.

—Warren Bennis[1]

We shall not cease from exploration, and the end of all our exploring will be to arrive where we started and know the place for the first time.

—T. S. Eliot[2]

Learning Objectives

16.1 Explore how systems thinking is critical to the success of leaders

16.2 Identify systems thinking as a key part of a learning organization.

16.3 Summarize the concept of sustainability

16.4 Describe several dimensions of sustainability

16.5 Personalize the concept of authentic leadership

Detailed Chapter Outline

Leadership by Design Model

Design Self

How can I design myself as a leader?

Design Relationships

As a leader, how can I design my relationships with others?

Design Others' Success

As a leader, how can I design success for others?

Design Culture

As a leader, how can I design the culture of my organization?

DESIGN FUTURE

AS A LEADER, HOW CAN I INNOVATE?

Introduction

Great leaders design a future of success long past their time as leader. This chapter focuses on systems thinking and sustainability in the broadest sense. How can the leader ensure long-term financial viability, environmental stewardship, socially just practices, and development of the next generation of leaders for the organization? The chapter concludes with a discussion of authentic leadership as a foundation for sustainable leadership.

Designing the future as a leader means understanding two facts: Everything is more complicated and interconnected than it appears, and actions in the present will impact the future in some way. In other words, individuals, groups, organizations, and cultures are all part of complex systems and may or may not be sustainable over time. Sustainable, effective leadership is less about having the answers and much more about a leader's ability to see wider, deeper, and into the future. Most senior leaders would agree that leadership is about identifying the right questions to help achieve mission— questions that help unmask hidden variables and influences that drive activity and attitudes. It is a complex endeavor to determine what an organization needs to hold on to and what it needs to let go of to live into a better future (see IBM and Kodak for two interesting case studies). Consider the poem below entitled "The Blind Men and the Elephant" by American poet John Godfrey Saxe (1816–1887) based on an Indian folktale. The individuals in the poem are big on firmly held answers but lack the questions that could have changed their results.

The Blind Men and the Elephant*

It was six men of Indostan,
To learning much inclined,
Who went to see the elephant,
(Though all of them were blind),
That each by observation
Might satisfy his mind.

The first approached the elephant,
And happening to fall
Against his broad and sturdy side,
At once began to bawl:
"God bless me! But the elephant
Is very like a wall!"

The second, feeling of the tusk,
Cried: "Ho! What have we here,
So very round and smooth and sharp?
To me 'tis very clear,
This wonder of an elephant
Is very like a spear!"

The third approached the animal,
And happening to take
The squirming trunk within his hands,
Thus boldly up and spake:
"I see," quoth he, "the elephant
Is very like a snake!"

*Source: Saxe, J. G. (1873). The blind men and the elephant. Retrieved from https://www.commonlit.org/texts/the-blind-men-and-the-elephant

The fourth reached out an eager hand,
And felt about the knee.
"What most this wondrous beast is like
Is might plain," quoth he;
"Tis clear enough the elephant
Is very like a tree."

The fifth, who chanced to touch the ear,
Said: "E'en the blindest man
Can tell what this resembles most:
Deny the fact who can,
This marvel of an elephant
Is very like a fan."

The sixth no sooner had begun
About the beast to grope,
Than seizing on the swinging tail
That fell within his scope,
"I see," quoth he, "the elephant
Is very like a rope."

And so these men of Indostan
Disputed loud and long,
Each in his own opinion
Exceeding stiff and strong.
Though each was partly right,
All were in the wrong.

Moral:
So oft in theologic wars,
The disputants, I ween,
Rail on in utter ignorance
Of what each other mean,
And prate about an Elephant
Not one of them has seen!

"The Blind Men and the Elephant" encapsulates the focus of this final chapter. The elephant could be said to represent an organization; however, the world is full of complex, interconnected systems in which there are elephants everywhere. Even this textbook is an elephant—without reading and understanding the overall structure, and how each idea fits with the others, each idea could be interpreted a variety of ways, many of which would not be accurate without the big picture.

Looking at individual parts of a larger system can be an exercise in futility. As you read in earlier chapters, developing an ideal culture means understanding and addressing the many hidden variables at work in the more extensive system. You need to understand the system to facilitate long-term, lasting change. It is more likely that a system of interventions will lead to a sustainable organization versus a single solution. And to better understand the system and create sustainability (defined broadly), there are some characteristics and tools that you will need—things like remaining humble, surrounding yourself with an incredible team, and identifying central questions for the group to explore.

LEADERSHIP THAT MAKES A DIFFERENCE

Many of you reading this text may not think of Walmart and sustainability as compatible terms. Similar to many corporations, Walmart has its challenges and is not perfect. But leadership is a process. Walmart is a leader among large corporations and has made significant effort to embrace the notion of sustainability. In fact, Walmart has made sustainability core to its business operations and strategy. A look at its 2016 Sustainability Report makes a convincing case that the company values sustainability (broadly defined) and has set a clear course for improving its hiring of a diverse workforce and veterans, increasing wages among employees, supporting female business owners, reducing packaging, and using renewable energy for its facilities. In fact, the company uses terms like *whole systems change* and is focusing on improving the industry with initiatives such as its responsible packaging initiative—"Working with others, we aspire to reshape whole systems to achieve significant and lasting improvement in social, environmental and economic outcomes."[3] Below are a few facts on Walmart's efforts.

- **Renewable energy:** Walmart has an explicit goal to be 100% supplied by sustainable energy. As of 2015, it received about 25% of its power from green sources (e.g., wind, solar).[4]

- **Targeting zero waste:** A goal of Walmart is to achieve zero waste for each of its stores. This means that 100% of waste from each store is diverted from landfills. As of 2016, 81% of the material is diverted in the United States, and stores in Japan and the U.K. divert more than 90%.[5]

- **Supporting women-owned businesses (WOB):** According to its 2016 Sustainability Report, "In 2011, we promised to spend $20 billion to purchase products for our U.S. stores from WOBs over a five-year period. Since 2012, Walmart has sourced $16.46 billion in products and services from WOBs in the U.S., including $4.76 billion in the past year."[6]

- **Plastic bag waste:** Through many programs at the local level, Walmart reduced plastic bag use by 38% between 2007 and 2013.[7]

- **Responsible packaging:** Walmart is working with suppliers to reduce packaging. In fact, the organization met its goal of reducing packaging by suppliers by 5% between 2007 and 2013.[8] Likewise, the organization introduced a packaging scorecard as a "measurement tool that allows suppliers to evaluate themselves relative to other suppliers, based on specific metrics."[9]

- **Local sourcing:** Walmart doubled sales of local produce between 2009 and 2015.[10]

While only a fraction of Walmart's initiatives are highlighted in this brief section, it is apparent that the organization is working to improve on multiple fronts. Current CEO Doug McMillon sums up Walmart's efforts well when he suggests the following: "We don't pretend for a moment that we have this all figured out. The issues are complex, and the work is difficult. But our role is to get up every day, roll up our sleeves and lead. As we do, we're thankful to be joined by so many great suppliers, NGOs, community groups and other stakeholders."[11]

Systems and Systems Thinking

Learning Objectives

16.1 Explore how systems thinking is critical to the success of leaders

16.2 Identify systems thinking as a key part of a learning organization.

"Every system is perfectly designed to get the results it gets."—Dr. Paul Batalden

A **system** comprises a group of interconnected, interdependent parts that make up a complex whole. A bag of marbles is not a system because each marble functions independently. However, the ball in a pinball machine is part of a system—without the other parts of the game, there is no game (and no fun). The concept can sound complicated and confusing. However, you interact and work with systems every day. A primary example is the Earth. There is a system—multiple variables interacting with one another—all in place to facilitate life on planet Earth. A similar system does not exist on Pluto, Venus, or Mercury. Another

System a group of interconnected, interdependent parts that make up a complex whole

example is your weight. Based on your metabolism, eating habits, workout regimen, environment, culture, microbiome, and any number of other variables, there is a system in place that yields your weight. One final example is your family—a system as well. For example, if your primary caregivers modeled a healthy relationship with strong communication, valued education, modeled moral integrity, and promoted a growth mindset, you likely come from a family system that set you up for a well-adjusted life.

Organizations have systems in place as well. Chapter 7 highlighted the importance of engagement in organizational life. Some organizational systems facilitate a culture of engagement, while others do not. As a leader, establishing a culture of engagement is no small task. You have to focus on many variables such as how you set the vision, hire, conduct performance management, reward and recognize, assign work, develop your employees, model norms of behavior, and so on.

REFLECTION QUESTIONS

Think back to your last job or internship. Did the system facilitate engagement of employees? Why or why not?

Leaders influence others toward a common goal; they affect the relationships, context, and culture of a group or organization. Influencing such a complex system requires the ability to see and think about the systems making up the whole. **Systems thinking** is a habit of mind (disposition) used to examine and understand the connections and interactions between individual parts making up a complex whole.

Systems thinking a habit of mind (disposition) used to examine and understand the connections and interactions between individual parts making up a complex whole

Systems thinking was first introduced in organizational life as a tool for decision-making. Systems thinking is a way to *see the whole* of a problem or opportunity versus the individual parts (as highlighted in the poem at the beginning of the chapter). Only seeing or addressing the *parts* of a problem can lead to unintended consequences or failed efforts. For instance, a community experiencing low unemployment and an increase in crime could push full steam ahead on business development—attracting several new businesses to town. However, unless the community has the educated workforce, resource infrastructure (e.g., roads, water, airport), and other components (e.g., resources for families, high-quality education, strong police force) to accommodate the new demand, their efforts will fail. The issue of unemployment and high crime links to education, skills training, community resources, and so on.

As you become more and more familiar with systems, certain archetypes emerge. An archetype is a *typical example* of something. For instance, one archetype of system thinking is Fixes That Fail. These solutions often tackle a symptom of the problem versus the root cause. For instance, many popular diet plans provide tools or *fixes* that often do not address the actual root cause of overeating and/or low activity levels (e.g., depression, addiction, environment). As a result, they often fail to work long term—thus, resulting in the multibillion-dollar diet industry. If these diets worked, the obesity epidemic would have been eradicated by now.

Another systems-thinking archetype is known as Limits to Growth, which occurs when resource constraints eventually limit growth, quality, and service. Imagine a college campus that is growing its international population rapidly. If the school does not have the support resources (e.g., housing over breaks, year-round meal plans, onboarding programs) to accommodate large numbers, the quality of their experience will diminish. Only so much growth will occur under the current system. For the organization to move to another level, it will need to address other dimensions of the system.[12]

Seeing Interconnections

As discussed, systems thinking means that you can see the many interconnections and relationships among the variables. Leaders can often default to looking for a single cause for low motivation among employees (e.g., "we are hiring the wrong people") or a lack of results; however, in reality, the system is yielding results for many reasons. At least, that is a real possibility. As a result, think about your organizations with a level of complexity so you can push past simplistic thinking as you work to create a better future. Peter Senge, a leader in this realm, suggests the following:

> Systems Thinking helps us challenge counterproductive assumptions about authority in a productive way. Rather than pointing fingers, it fosters compassion. We realize that systems work the way they do, not because of any one person's individual agency, but because of our collective agency.[13]

Similar to the leader/follower relationship, everyone owns a piece of what works and what does not work. Everything that *functions* and the dysfunction as well. At times, you are a bystander to dysfunctional behavior, which allows or creates a culture that will not yield desired results. In reality, everyone is shaping culture. A common misconception is that you need to have a position of authority to influence or change the system. By now, you know this is not necessarily the case. Great acts of leadership have occurred throughout history by men and women who did not have a formal position of authority (e.g., Gandhi, Martin Luther King, Jr., Harvey Milk, Susan B. Anthony, Malala Yousafzai).

If we were mapping a human being, the major systems to be mapped would include circulatory, respiratory, digestive, nervous, immune, skeletal, and so forth. A heart cannot function without other parts of the system, and it will be difficult to understand the system by merely exploring the heart. Thus, to understand a human being, you need to look at the whole to better understand the system. Interestingly, the universe, a rain forest, and a corporate community are systems as well. For example, when an organization embraces a community, the two become more and more interdependent.

REFLECTION QUESTIONS

Think about your campus as a system. What are some of the major components of the system? Which components are successful and filled with energy? Which struggle and why?

EXPERTS BEYOND THE TEXT

INSIGHTFUL LEADERS KNOW ABOUT . . . CYNEFIN FRAMEWORK AND EMERGENT PRACTICE

Cynefin Framework: Decision-Making for Complex Times

By Dr. Kathleen E. Allen

The global economy, social media, the internet of things, political unrest, and the environment are connected to each other. Change in one area impacts changes in other domains. Nothing seems to "stay put" anymore. As the world becomes more interconnected and interdependent, leaders no longer lead a closed system organization. This new reality has implications for how we think about leadership and decision-making.

Traditional decision-making frameworks held a deep background assumption that organizations and businesses were closed systems. If a problem came up, leaders sought to identify and analyze all the variables to the problem. Once the parts were understood, the solution would show up as good or best practice. In closed systems, solutions are found in the parts, not the whole.

(Continued)

(Continued)

When leading in open complex organizations, many problems have multiple systems that impact one another. The turbulent external environment shows up inside the organization, and traditional decision-making of good or best practice doesn't fit these situations. As systems become more open, interconnected, and sophisticated, decision-making practices also need to shift.

In open complex systems, solutions are found by going up to the balcony and observing the dance floor to see the patterns of the dance. In other words, leaders need to seek out and see the bigger picture. Once the patterns are found, a strategy can be designed through emergent practice. Sometimes open systems are very dynamic and become chaotic. Chaotic challenges require novel practice instead of best practice because nothing is static or known.

The Cynefin Framework helps leaders see how open systems develop an emergent practice approach to decision-making.[14] These open systems have many different variables that impact the system. The weather system is an example of a non-linear dynamic system where the interdependent nature of weather variables can create disturbances at a distance. The popular idea from chaos theory that the flap of a butterfly's wings in China can create a snowstorm in New York City is an example of how open and interdependent systems have unexpected events as a natural part of the system.[15] The non-linear nature of the dynamics of an open complex system fits with emergent practice rather than best or good practice.

Figure 16.1 is a visual of four different kinds of problems and the decision-making practice that best fits the problem. A *Simple* or *Complicated* problem occurs in a closed system. The variables are either known or can be known, and no new variables show up. The leader seeks to analyze all the variables and then decide based on good or best practice.

Complex or *Chaotic* problems can't use "best practice" because there are always new variables that emerge as the problem is being solved. The situation is dynamic and changing, so the leader must shift their decision-making process to emergent or novel practice. Emergent practice has an element of adaptation and experimentation, which is necessary for leaders seeking a culture of adaptation and innovation.

FIGURE 16.1 ● The Cynefin Framework

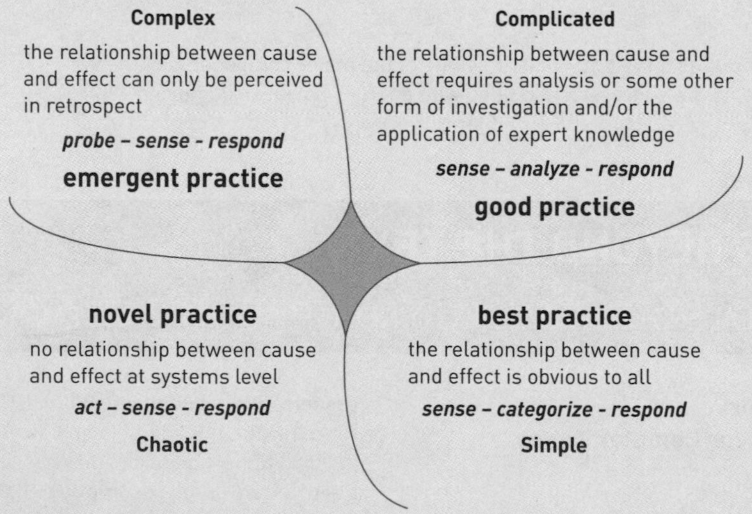

Complex
the relationship between cause and effect can only be perceived in retrospect
probe – sense – respond
emergent practice

Complicated
the relationship between cause and effect requires analysis or some other form of investigation and/or the application of expert knowledge
sense – analyze – respond
good practice

novel practice
no relationship between cause and effect at systems level
act – sense – respond
Chaotic

best practice
the relationship between cause and effect is obvious to all
sense – categorize – respond
Simple

Source: Snowden, D. J., & Boone, M. E. (2007, November). A leader's framework for decision making: Wise executives tailor their approach to fit the complexity of the circumstances they face. *Harvard Business Review, 85*(11). Retrieved from https://hbr.org/2007/11/a-leaders-framework-for-decision-making.

Where's the Energy in the System?

Energy is an important concept to consider when discussing systems. All systems use energy. As discussed in Chapter 7, an organizational system is unleashing positive energy and engagement, or in many cases, it is quite the opposite, according to Gallup's research. Leaders need to have a keen eye for energy, and in their article "Energy Optimization and the Role of the Leader," Kathy Allen and William Mease highlight this point elegantly.

> Energy exists in all systems. When energy is used positively, it is optimized, and like the riptide, is generative instead of continually consuming resources. Positive energy naturally flows in a direction that brings the system into greater alignment with itself. We've all had the expansive experience of being "on the same wave length" with others. It is a freeing, energizing experience.[16]

Leaders have an opportunity to unleash energy in a system. This phenomenon has occurred throughout history—for good and evil. For instance, Gandhi unleashing the power of the Indian people or Mandela focusing the energy of the South African people. In a similar vein, Adolf Hitler tapped into the fear and unrest of the German people, which led to evil and destruction. You likely experience this on a daily basis in the classroom, at your job, on your team, or in your student organizations. In some contexts, the professor, coach, or supervisor does an excellent job of unleashing and focusing energy. At other times, this is not the case—and you can feel it—almost instantly.

REFLECTION QUESTIONS

Can you think of a teacher, coach, clergy member, supervisor, or relative who was skilled at unleashing the untapped energy in a group? What attributes made him or her have such an impact on others?

Once energy is released, what does success look like? Some would say that in a capitalistic society, profits will determine success. Others define success more broadly—in more of a systemic manner. For instance, proponents of the triple bottom line assert that long-term, sustainable success is about three fundamental factors: people, planet, and profit.[17] Does the culture engage and develop people? Does the organization sustainably use natural resources? Does the firm minimize its footprint? And does the company maximize profits for shareholders? By defining *success* more broadly, some would assert that there is a better likelihood of long-term, sustainable results.

The Learning Organization

The notion of systems, interconnections, systems thinking, and energy can be nebulous and confusing. It is likely that no one individual has a clear understanding and awareness of the whole. As a result, it is crucial that leaders establish an environment where individuals and groups can learn together. To further develop this notion, Peter Senge coined the term *learning organization*. According to Senge, learning organizations are "organizations

TABLE 16.1 ● Component Technologies for Fostering a Learning Organization	
Systems Thinking	Seeking to better understand the *whole* and seeking to better understand the relationships and interconnections of the *parts*
Personal Mastery	Living in a state of continuous learning, exploration, and sensemaking
Mental Models	Exploring (and at times challenging) the assumptions, biases, generalizations, and mental pictures that shape and inform our world
Building Shared Vision	Unleashing energy in others to work above and beyond toward a desired future
Team Learning	A habit of dialogue that fosters an environment where individuals are engaged in shared learning and collective meaning making

where people continually expand their capacity to create the results they truly desire, where new and expansive patterns of thinking are nurtured, where collective aspiration is set free, and where people are continually learning to see the whole together."[18] Senge identified what he termed five disciplines or *component technologies* (in Table 16.1) for developing and fostering a learning organization.

In essence, a learning organization maximizes the use of systems thinking to make sense of complexity. Systems thinking is rarely the work of one individual—it is a collective effort that requires a culture where individuals are invited to own and engage in the design of a better future. The creation of a learning organization is perhaps the ultimate goal of a leader. By doing so, the leader will ensure a focus on dialogue, collective energy, and continuous growth, and a better understanding of the larger whole.

Design for Sustainability

Learning Objectives

16.3 Summarize the concept of sustainability

16.4 Describe several dimensions of sustainability

Sustainability the ability to endure, specifically the process of using the resources of the present to ensure success in the future

Sustainability is defined as the ability to endure, specifically the process of using the resources of the present to ensure success in the future. Another definition developed by the Brundtland Commission is that "Sustainable development is development that meets the needs of the present without compromising the ability of future generations to meet their own needs."[19] Although the term sustainability is often associated with the environment, there are many more facets to the concept and its applicability (see Figure 16.2). As a leader, you have a responsibility to *design* systems that facilitate long-term success. To this point, the concept of systems and the energy within a system have been explored. It is essential that as a leader you have both in mind—the system and energy within the system. Healthy systems will yield desired results. This text is all about designing your leadership, and the ultimate end of your design work is a team and organization that will be a successful and thriving organization for years to come.

This section explores several aspects of sustainability. The ultimate goal is to build a *sustainable system* that addresses the areas explored (and others). Given what you have learned about systems and complexity, a lack of balance in one area will impact other areas. For instance, if an organization is placing too much priority on giving back to the community and pleasing employees, it could lose sight of its economic sustainability. Likewise, if it is too focused on only benefiting shareholders, it may lose good employees and have a poor reputation in the community. The key is clarity of values and a long-term, balanced approach.

FIGURE 16.2 ● Many Facets of Sustainability

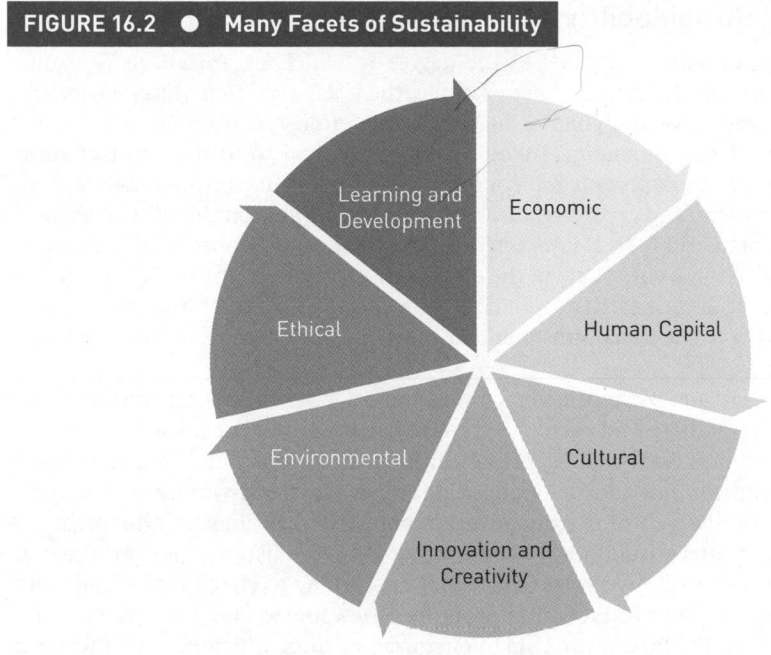

The Sustainable Culture

Culture was defined as the shared values and assumptions by organizational (or group) members (from Chapter 11). Creating a sustainable culture means maintaining what is good and healthy about organizational culture. Likewise, there will always be areas for improvement as contextual shifts occur (e.g., changing employee demographics, economic forces). The thing to remember is that culture is like a plant—metaphorically speaking, it needs sunlight and water to thrive. While some plants are sturdy and can withstand many environmental shifts, others are much more delicate and susceptible to the elements. The key is that as a leader, you have a consistent eye on culture. Is the system yielding the results you would like? Are your team members engaged, energized, and excited?

After the death of Apple's long-time chief executive officer, Steve Jobs, the role was turned over to former chief operations officer Tim Cook. A primary concern among investors, long-time Apple enthusiasts, and employees was how the organization would shift under new leadership. And while this story is still being told, it is interesting to explore how Jobs attempted to solidify norms for the culture of Apple—even before his death. Cook has reported that the single most significant piece of advice from Jobs was to "never ask what he would do" and to just "be himself."[20] In fact, in their article, "Why Apple Doesn't Need Steve Jobs," the authors suggested that "Jobs has managed to perform the ultimate feat of leadership—he's embedded himself so deeply within the cultural fabric of Apple that the company no longer needs him."[21]

REFLECTION QUESTIONS

Think of an organization to which you belong. What aspects of the culture have endured, and which components are based on the personalities of key individuals involved? What could be done to solidify the features that are dependent on one or two key personalities?

Environmental Sustainability

Environmental sustainability is defined as the degree to which organizations can minimize their impact on the environment. For example, the *Leadership That Makes a Difference* segment at the beginning of the chapter highlights the efforts of Walmart to minimize its footprint, utilize renewable energy, invest in its people, and so forth. While environmental sustainability is an important topic, organizations take three distinct approaches—compliance, commitment, and core. Organizations that are simply compliant with external regulations such as state and federal laws often see the topic of environmental sustainability as a *necessary evil* versus a core value of the organization. At times, the term *greenwashing* is used to describe organizations that publicize their efforts as more of a promotional or marketing tactic than a sincere commitment to renewing resources that have been harvested or depleted.

Organizations that are authentically committed to environmental sustainability have found ways to prioritize and perhaps monetize their efforts. For instance, Walmart makes millions of dollars each year recycling cardboard. Walmart has identified a way to help the environment *and* add revenue for doing so. This win-win approach facilitates commitment on the part of the organization and its stakeholders. Other organizations have environmental sustainability at the core of their existence. For instance, in 2016, Patagonia donated 100% of its profits from Black Friday to charity.[22] Perhaps their business strategy rests upon products that promote renewable energy such as wind and solar power. Or maybe the business exists to encourage a more efficient use of water in faucets, showerheads, or toilets. Or maybe Patagonia has a deep commitment to more than just the bottom line, as exemplified in its mission statement: "Build the best product, cause no unnecessary harm, use business to inspire and implement solutions to the environmental crisis."[23]

MYTH OR REALITY?

SUSTAINABILITY INITIATIVES ARE JUST ANOTHER COST TO THE ORGANIZATION.

Myth and Reality. It is potentially true if the sustainability initiatives lack alignment with the organization's core strategy or mission. For instance, an organization that allows employees to give time to the community but has no substantial purpose or reason for doing so may be missing an opportunity to achieve the mission and do good for the community. The statement becomes a myth if the organization can achieve the win-win. For example, Walmart has identified a way to profit from their goal of targeting zero waste. In fact, not only does it divert waste from landfills, across the many stores, the organization adds hundreds of millions of dollars in revenue each year selling its recycled goods to companies that use the materials in any number of ways (e.g., cardboard, plastic, fryer grease).[24]

Sustaining Creativity and Innovation

In Chapter 14, you learned how to foster a culture of innovation, much of which you can use as a leader to ensure that innovative behavior continues into the future. By definition, innovation is an experimental activity—generating lots and lots of ideas, choosing the best, testing and assessing, iterating, and then putting those solutions to work as quickly as possible. Various tools for divergent thinking (Chapter 8) and convergent thinking (Chapter 14) contribute to establishing and perpetuating this culture. Innovative teams "know that integrative decision-making often involves more than simply and mechanically combining ideas. Rather, it requires a willingness to play with ideas and experiments until they *click*."[25]

In the article "The Capabilities Your Organization Needs to Sustain Innovation," the authors suggest three capabilities: creative abrasion, creative agility, and creative resolution.[26] Creative abrasion means creating a culture where people with different values, viewpoints, knowledge, and life experiences can search for solutions, discuss ideas, and passionately explore new directions. As discussed, this requires a culture with strong norms that encourage multiple perspectives and a willingness to openly share, dialogue, and search for the best idea. These groups can maintain their focus on the problem at hand and drop their egos in search of the best outcome.

Ethical Sustainability

The foundation of a sustainable career is a solid grounding in who you are and what you stand for. Given the topic of this chapter (sustainability), it is essential to think about ethical sustainability at a few different levels. The first is the individual level, which was the focus of Chapter 4: Your Values and Ethical Actions. Two others are the group and organization levels.

Ethical sustainability at the group level means that you have developed shared norms that the team is committed to living. As a leader, you must engage your team in this conversation to ensure the team members have a clear understanding of what is and is not acceptable. If you think about organizations on campus or in your community, you can understand why this is critical. For instance, it is likely you can identify incidents on your campus where the actions of a few individuals have reflected poorly on the entire organization or campus community. Not only do leaders need to have their *own shop in order*, they need to ensure the group level norms are established and followed as well.

At the organizational level, cultural norms are even more critical. While the point seems obvious, a leader must have a keen eye for many organizational dimensions that could lead to (or even encourage) unethical behavior. An example is the incident at Wells Fargo that began in 2016 and resonated in the news for years. More than 5,300 employees created false accounts. According to one news source, "The phony accounts earned the bank unwarranted fees and allowed Wells Fargo employees to boost their sales figures and make more money."[27] The organizational culture of *meeting numbers* was creating an environment where thousands of employees acted unethically. By some estimates, employees opened more than 1.5 million unauthorized accounts. This is just one example of many that could be considered. Thus, unethical behavior at the individual, team, and organizational level is not sustainable. As a leader, you must have an eye on how the system influences behavior. A culture with strong behavioral norms and accountability for not meeting said norms is vital. One final point—it is easy to feel like this topic is foreign and far away. In reality, it exists all over campus. Just look at an organization that you belong to. Does the culture promote ethical behavior, look the other way, or worse, actively enable unethical behavior?

Economic Sustainability

In a general sense, sustainability is about a sensible use of resources. From an economic standpoint, the primary resources are money, capital resources, intellectual property, and so forth. One can tell a great deal about the values and priorities of an organization based on its allocation of resources. For instance, an organization that balances shareholder returns with employee benefits and salary is different from an organization solely focused on maximizing shareholder returns. Likewise, an organization that invests in (and even looks for ways to profit from) recycling, green energy, and minimizing environmental impact displays its priorities and values in a different manner.

The key is planning and balance. While it is important to be generous in some circumstances, long-term financial viability is another priority and objective. Ensuring financial health and sustainability is essential and a solid starting point. Also, it is necessary to have clarity on the organizational mission and vision to ensure that the economic model is helping the organization achieve objectives.

Sustainable Learning and Development

At first glance, it may seem odd to place *learning* in a section on sustainability, but it is a central element of ensuring that your organization is on the cutting edge of your industry and how it will interface with artificial intelligence, automation, sensor technology, virtual reality, and any number of other disruptive technologies. As you read this text, humans are on the cusp of a significant shift in machine learning and artificial intelligence (AI). Technology continues to permeate all aspects of organizational life. A few interesting facts to pique your interest:

- Artificial intelligence has composed a pop song[28]
- Artificial intelligence has created its own movie trailer[29]
- Artificial intelligence has solved a 100-year-old biology problem[30]
- At Hitachi, artificial intelligence has been placed in charge of the warehouse management system to assign tasks to employees[31]
- Robots are performing surgery on animals with a high level of success[32]
- Harvard is working to develop an AI that is as fast as the human brain[33]

What does all of this mean? Technology and capitalism have shifted many jobs to developing countries, but that was just the beginning. As technology continues to replace humans, your role as a manager or leader may become more and more in danger of being replaced. For instance, Foxconn, the company that makes the iPhone, recently cut 60,000 jobs and replaced them with robots.[34] This is only going to continue. As machines replace surgeons, attorneys,[35] and managers, how will you and your organization compete?

Bottom line, you, your team, and your organization need to be on the cutting edge of your industry and how it will interface with machine learning, autonomous vehicles, virtual reality, and robotics. Entire industries are being disrupted, and this reality will impact you in ways that can only be imagined. Futurists foresee an existence that sounds more like science fiction than fact.[36] What systems will you put in place that foster continuous learning of you and your team?

LEADERSHIP BY DESIGN

Design Principle: Weakest Link

Definition: The use of a weak or highly sensitive element that will fail in order to protect from or warn of further damage within a system.

In Other Words: Small failures can protect big systems.

For Example: A sprinkler system in a building or dormitory is designed to release water after something within the system breaks due to excessive heat but before a raging fire destroys everything.

For Leaders: Everyone is familiar with the cliché: A chain is only as strong as its weakest link. Knowing that organizations, teams, and industries are all part of a system—a chain, if you will—the weakest link represents the point of vulnerability, the place where the system could be broken or changed. There is always a weak link because elements are not uniform or equal. Identifying that weak link can be of great value, but what if you intentionally inserted a weak link as a warning (like when a fuse blows out and warns of a greater electrical malfunction)?

One way to use the weakest link in leadership is to reframe weakness as an acute sensitivity. Hire someone with high emotional intelligence and ask them to report on team dynamics. A concern from that person would serve as a warning that relationships need tending. Or identify the weakest point in the system and accommodate it as a learning tool. For example, interns or temporary workers may be the least competent and/or committed employees, but that perspective is advantageous as an early warning of miscommunication, lack of clarity, lack of transparency, or complacency. Those individuals will be the first to run to a competitor because they have the least to lose.

Think through "applying the weakest link principle:

1. identify how something might fail;

2. identify or define the weakest link in the system for that failure;

3. further weaken the weakest link and strengthen the other links as necessary to address the failure condition; and

4. ensure that the weakest link will only fail under the appropriate, predefined failure conditions."[37]

The weakest link is intended to deliberately fail to minimize damage. Use this concept to protect systems, facilitate change, and design the future.

Sustainable Results

Sustaining results is the ultimate goal that employees at Apple, Google, or any other successful organization seek. Many corporations come and go, but only a few have the longevity to succeed for decades amid multiple shifts (see IBM for an interesting case study). So, what are the ingredients of a winning culture? Exploring this topic at the individual and organizational levels is essential.

At the individual level, scholars have found that two components, thriving and learning (see the previous section), relate to employees with better performance, less burnout, and increased job satisfaction. Employees who thrive have a sense of vitality (e.g., enthusiasm, excitement, passion). They are intrinsically motivated, and as discussed in Chapter 7: Influence, Power, and Motivation, there is a sense that their work makes a difference. The second component, learning, means that thriving employees have the drive to learn and develop their knowledge, skills, and abilities.[38]

At an organizational level, what factors foster a culture that wins over time? According to *Harvard Business Review*, there are two distinctions: (1) "unique personality and soul based on shared values and heritage" and (2) "cultural norms and behaviors that translate the organization's unique personality and soul into 'customer-focused actions and bottom-line results.'"[39]

The authors also explore five key steps to instilling a winning culture, shown in Table 16.2.[40] While the steps in the table seem like common sense depending on the complexity of the organization, they can be challenging to implement. The good news is that for many of you reading this text, student organizations provide a practice field to work and achieve much of the content in the table.

Sustainable Personal Growth and Development

Finding your authentic voice and approach to leadership is an important first step. Many, however, believe that their personal work ends after those initial efforts to grow and develop. How do you make personal development a systematic, sustainable, life-long process? In many ways, you are on your own when it comes to your continued learning and development, particularly once you exit formal education. Nevertheless, you have a great responsibility to ensure that you are in a constant state of growth and sensemaking or "a 'process' that includes the use of prior knowledge to assign meaning to new information."[41]

TABLE 16.2 ● Sustainable Results—Steps to a Winning Culture	
Perform a culture audit and set new expectations	What aspects of the culture are healthy, core to the business, and critical drivers? What is missing?
Align the team	Is the senior team aligned with the vision and ready to adjust systems and old habits, and build enthusiasm?
Focus on results and build accountability	Are key metrics clear and aligned, and is everyone driving toward the same vision?
Manage the drivers of culture	Are systems such as hiring, training, performance management, and incentives/rewards aligned with objectives?
Communicate and celebrate	Are organizational leaders communicating progress and celebrating wins (large and small)?

Source: Based on Meehan, P., Rigby, D., & Rogers, P. (2008). Creating and sustaining a winning culture. *Harvard Management Update.* Retrieved from https://hbr.org/2008/02/creating-and-sustaining-a-winn-1.

LEADERSHIP BY DESIGN

Design Principle: Exposure Effect[42]

Definition: Individuals tend to like and have a preference for stimuli that are familiar.[43]

In Other Words: The more you see/hear/interact with something, the more you like it.

For Example: When that new song comes out, and you think, "Eh . . . it's ok." Then you hear it over and over and over and over . . . and soon, to your surprise, you like it. And then, even stranger, you hear it years later and fondly remember it as a favorite. Marketers know the exposure effect and replay songs frequently to increase exposure and thus listeners' sentiments.

For Leaders: Familiarity plays a role in appeal and acceptance—the more a leader is around and present, the more they will be liked. Of course, this is not automatic or assured. The exposure effect is most prevalent when the stimulus (leader in this case) is neutral, and the exposure is subtle. Leaders can leverage the exposure effect to help reinforce and build commitment to the mission or vision. Do certain facets of your vision need greater buy-in and/or positive responses? In what ways can you increase exposure to that message? Be cautious—there is such a thing as overexposure, and that can lead to negative feelings or boredom.

As you design the future, what message do you as a leader need to really have followers know and love?

Self-monitoring the act of observing your own actions—the good, the bad, and the ugly

Reflection the mental act of considering and modifying information and understanding, often replaying interactions in an effort to understand your behavior and the behavior of others

A few concepts are essential to understand as you think about your growth and continuous development. A primary objective of your work is to remain in a continual state of mindfulness and reflection. Mindfulness means the mental state of being in the present and in tune with all that is happening in your immediate environment. You are noticing the nonverbal communication of others, paying attention to what is not being said, and so on. Mindfulness keeps you locked into the present and truly *in the game.*

Another concept is **self-monitoring**, which means the act of observing your actions—the good, the bad, and the ugly. You can monitor your emotions, energy level, motivations, self-talk, interventions, and the people, places, and things that *trigger* you.

The final concept is **reflection**, which is the mental act of considering and modifying information and understanding, often replaying interactions to understand your behavior and the behavior of others. If you are practicing mindfulness, self-monitoring, and engaging in reflection, you will develop a habit of mind that is in a continuous state of development.

Leaders seeking sustainable personal growth create external systems to help prompt, reinforce, and guide their development. For instance, you could secure a mentor or development coach who can help you identify areas for growth, potential steps forward, and the accountability needed to help you stay on track. You could also join a group or club that is designed to help you grow and develop (e.g., faith-based, leadership-oriented).

Sustainable Leadership—Authentic Leadership

Learning Objective

16.5 Personalize the concept of authentic leadership

This chapter on systems and sustainability, and the entire textbook, ends where it began—with the design of you. As discussed, leadership is the process of influencing others toward a common vision. An interesting nuance to the conversation about effective leadership is highlighted by George, Sims, McLean, and Mayer when they suggest that

> during the past 50 years, leadership scholars have conducted more than 1,000 studies in an attempt to determine the definitive styles, characteristics, or personality traits of great leaders. None of these studies has produced a clear profile of the ideal leader. Thank goodness. If scholars had produced a cookie-cutter leadership style, individuals would be forever trying to imitate it. They would make themselves into personae, not people, and others would see through them immediately.[44]

The reality is that you have to discover your personal, authentic, and unique approach to leadership. A sustainable approach to leadership likely has at least four primary ingredients—many of which are highlighted throughout this text. First, you are focused on the ultimate objective of *intervening skillfully*. The leader understands that as the players (followers, team members) and the context shift, so will the calculus for success. As a result, a skillful intervention in one setting or situation may not work in another. The sustainable leader is aware of this fundamental reality and adjusts and adapts.

A second attribute of the sustainable leader is an *awareness of default mindsets* (i.e., mental models and dispositions). Everyone reading (and working on) this book has defaults. In some contexts, defaults serve you beautifully; in many cases, they are the reason you have experienced success. A strong work ethic is a valuable default to have—but it can be taken to an extreme, become unhealthy, and create long-term problems with relationships, health, and identity. By intentionally choosing when to go with your defaults, you are more present and conscious of how you work, live, and play.

REFLECTION QUESTION

Take a moment (or much more) to craft a leadership summary for yourself by reflecting on and responding to the prompts below.

1. Here is what I know about leadership that is most important . . .

2. Here is how it all fits together . . .

3. This is what works best for me as a leader (now) . . .

4. These are the most important leadership lessons—the ones I will take with me into the future . . .

5. I will apply all of the above to make this difference as a leader . . .

A third attribute of a sustainable leader is a *thriving and robust support network*. Sustainable leaders have a network of mentors, peers, and friends who will provide unfiltered feedback, guidance, and perspective. Leadership is difficult, and a sustainable leader has a strong supporting cast to help him or her stay on track, continuously grow, and adjust as needed.

Finally, a sustainable leader is an *authentic leader*. **Authentic leadership** is your unique, ethical, and honest way to help the work of the group move forward. While this text has been at the crossroads of leadership and design, it is a book about you, specifically how you design the many dimensions of you. Former Medtronic CEO and Harvard business professor Bill George suggests that "No one can be authentic by trying to imitate someone else."[45] Shamir and Eliam suggest four attributes of authentic leaders:

> **Authentic leadership** your unique, ethical, and honest way to help the work of the group move forward

1. Authentic leaders do not fake their leadership. Authentic leaders are not playing a part outside of their true self. In other words, there is a high *person/role merger*, which means "they think of themselves in terms of that role and enact that role at all times, not only when they are officially in role."[46]

2. Authentic leaders do not take on a leadership role or engage in leadership activities for status, honor, or other personal rewards. Authentic leaders are working from a place where their central motivation is to help the movement, group, organization, or team.

3. Authentic leaders are originals, not copies. Authentic leaders are not working to copy or replicate another leader or their style and approach. They are comfortable *in their own skin* and understand their values, motivations, strengths, and areas for development.

4. Authentic leaders are leaders whose actions are based on their values and convictions. Authentic leaders are connected to a strong sense of mission and belief in the objective at hand. The objective aligns with their *actual* passions.[47]

The roots of authentic leadership stem from Greek philosophy (e.g., "To thine own self be true") and humanistic psychology.[48] And in many ways, this sums up the notion of authentic leadership (and this text). As an authentic leader, you must discover your unique way to help the work of the group move forward. Of course, this takes a great deal of self-exploration, and perhaps this text has provided you with some exciting ways to begin thinking about and exploring leadership. The reality is that each one of you must find your voice, and that process is a lifelong journey.

LEADERSHIP BY DESIGN

Design Principle: Storytelling (again)

Definition: A method of creating imagery, emotions, and understanding of events through an interaction between a storyteller and an audience. The elements of story typically consist of setting, characters, plot, theme, and mood.

In Other Words: Once upon a time . . . I worked with this team . . . with this organization . . . something really interesting happened . . . and we were awesome. Let's do it again.

©iStock.com/PeopleImages

For Example: What is your story as a follower and as part of a great team?

For Leaders: The story of sustainable organizations is one of intertwined logic and emotion. Create a strong foundation for your story using both. Winning hearts can pique interest, increase commitment, or help resolve a conflict. Using emotion shows how your idea will affect them personally. Appeal to logic while storytelling to overturn a past decision, address a complex problem, or gain the support of analytic, data-driven people. Design both the story and how you share the story.

Legendary leaders and organizations make people feel wonderful, whether through their products or practices. Good stories become part of the listener and are remembered for a long, long time. What story will you design?

Chapter Summary

This chapter focused on systems thinking, sustainability, and authentic leadership. Systems thinking is a core activity of leadership because, from a problem-solving perspective, leaders need to see the *whole* system to make decisions that are more integrated and fully account for the complexity involved.

Systems thinking is central to the success of leaders. Systems thinking, along with other components, can foster a learning organization. Likewise, the hope is that systems thinking will lead to sustainability.

Sustainability is defined as a sensible use of resources on many different dimensions. In fact, it is essential to think of sustainability as a system as well. It is likely that sustainable results are predicated on many different dimensions such as ethical decision-making, environmental impact, creativity and innovation, fiscal responsibility, and more. Viewing these dimensions as a system is vital for long-term organizational health and wellness.

The chapter concludes with a discussion on the topic of authentic leadership, which means that you have discovered a style and approach to leadership that naturally aligns with your gifts, talents, passions, and values. Authentic leadership is not developed overnight—it is a long-term, lifelong endeavor that requires you to *know thyself* and ultimately prepare the next generation of leaders who follow.

Key Terms

Authentic Leadership 416
Reflection 414

Self-Monitoring 414
Sustainability 408

System 403
Systems Thinking 404

CORE™ Attribute Builders: Build Now for Future Leadership Challenges

Attribute: Optimism

Builder: Read up on the GOOD news

There is a great deal of good being done to help foster sustainability across the globe. It is easy to focus on what is going wrong (and there are significant issues). However, there is good news as well. For instance, in the last 100 years, the number of people living in extreme poverty has decreased dramatically, literacy has increased, child mortality has decreased, and youth are more educated than ever before.[49] Another piece of good news is that the UN Global Compact proposes that business can be a "force for good" and its mission suggests that business "can take shared responsibility for achieving a better world."[50] The UN Global Compact has identified 17 Sustainable Development Goals to be achieved by 2030. In fact, more than 9000 companies and 3000 non-business organizations throughout the globe have committed. Each year, participants submit a communication on progress (COP) report. Organizations around the globe submit these reports and highlight the good occurring. They present an optimistic view of the efforts of millions of men and women. Look up some of your favorite organizations and see how they are contributing to the greater good. You can use your favorite search engine (search: UN Global Compact COP Reports), and you will likely land on "The Communication on Progress (COP) in Brief" page. From there, you can view organizations (e.g., KPMG, Symantec, Royal Bank of Scotland, Intel, Dow Chemical, Accenture) participating at various levels.

Skill Builder Activity

Observing Leadership Theory in Action

Choose an organization to which you belong but are not in a formal leadership position. You might also engage in this activity with a small group.

Identify a meeting and/or event of the group where you are likely to observe the group's leader/s in action.

Attend the event and observe the leader and his or her interactions with followers. Specifically, observe each of the following listed below—prompting questions are provided to guide your thinking.

Take notes. From this experience, craft a one-page memo to the leader of the group you observed providing feedback as to what they did well and suggestions for making them more effective. (It is your decision as to whether you give the leader a copy of the memo.)

1. **Traits and Skills**

   Observe the leader.

   - What traits and skills tend to be used?
   - Which traits or skills seem to be effective, and how so?

2. **Style, Situational**

   - Is the leader more task or relationship focused?
   - Does the leader adapt to the commitment and competence of the followers and move between support, coach, delegate, and direct?

3. **Path-Goal**

   Observe the relationship between the leader and each individual in the group.

   - What does the leader use to influence?
   - How do the followers respond?

   - What motivates the followers?
   - Does the leader remove barriers to their motivation?

4. **Leader-Member Exchange**

   Observe the relationship between the leader and each individual in the group.

   - Does the leader give individualized consideration to each person?
   - Does the leader appear to treat everyone equally?

5. **Transformational Leadership**

   Again, observe the leader.

   - Does the leader serve as a role model who inspires you?
   - Does the leader stimulate your intellect?
   - Does the leader attend to each person individually?

6. **The Vision—Servant Leadership**

   - Does he or she act as servant, facilitating the success of others and the group?
   - Do they build community?
   - Do you observe empathy?

7. **Group Dynamics**

   Observe the dynamics of the group.

   - How do they communicate?
   - Are they open and honest with one another?
   - Are they constructive? Critical? Overly polite?
   - How does the group make decisions?
   - How do they deal with conflict?

• Glossary •

Achievement oriented: *See* Leadership style

Adaptive cycles: cycles that are natural to the evolution of living systems that occur at all levels of scale

Adjourning: *See* Tuckman's stages of group development

ADKAR model of change: This is a model of change starting with Awareness of a needed change, Desire to make the change, Knowledge about how to make the change, Ability to do so, and Reinforcement of the change once in place.

Algorithmic problem: a problem with a well-defined set of rules or instructions for solving

Appreciative Inquiry: This is the cooperative, coevolutionary search for the best in people, their organizations, and the world around them. It involves systematic discovery of what gives life to an organization or a community when it is most effective and most capable in economic, ecological terms.

Artifacts: physical evidence (objects) that represent organizational values

Authentic leadership: your unique, ethical, and honest way to help the work of the group move forward

Authority figure: an individual whose role provides them with formal power to determine the fate of individuals or groups

Autonomy: *See* Sources of motivation

Benchmarking: evaluating ideas by comparison with a standard

Biomimicry: a problem-solving technique that looks to see how nature has solved a similar problem and then tries to mimic that solution

Blocks: the many things that stifle your creative thinking

Business model: represents a company's rationale for how it creates value for customers, delivers its products to them, and captures value to make a profit

Business model canvas: This is a tool that illustrates the nine key business components: (1) key partners, (2) key activities, (3) key resources, (4) value proposition, (5) customer relationships, (6) channels, (7) customer segments, (8) cost structure, and (9) revenue.

Calculated risk-taking: making a decision that involves careful consideration of the possible outcomes

Care: acting in a manner that provides for and shows concern regarding another's needs and well-being

Career pathing: *See* Sources of motivation

Causal reasoning: a type of reasoning characterized by first setting a goal and then considering the means through which the goal can be accomplished

Change: the process of becoming different yourself or fostering difference in other persons or things

Change fatigue: a general state of disengagement from the change process due to natural cognitive, emotional, and social demands

Character: the moral qualities of an individual

Charisma: the personal quality that commands attention, respect, and attraction

Closure: Design principle—we tend to see complete figures even when part of the information is missing, which means what you do not show people, they will fill in the blanks on their own.

Code of ethics: often a document that seeks to clarify right or wrong behavior in a profession or organization

Collaboration: two or more people working together to create or achieve greater success than can be achieved individually

Community engagement: where like-minded individuals come together to engage with and effect change in the local community

Community solidarity: unity (as in a group) which produces collegial interests, objectives, and points of view; refers to the ties in a society that bind people together

Comparison: Design principle—to accurately understand and assess something, you must look at it next to things that relate.

Confidence: Latin root *con+fidere*, which means with intense trust—trust in yourself; the state of knowing you are capable and effective; as part of leadership CORE™ it is your ability to learn, adapt, and succeed.

Constructive dimension: *See* Dimensions of the brain

Convergent thinking: the mental process of finding a single best solution to a problem

Creative confidence: trust in yourself as a creative individual or a "natural ability to come up with new ideas and the courage to try them out"

Creativity: the personal capacities and process of generating a unique product that has value

Credibility: the quality of being believed, and in practice, doing what you say you are going to do

Crucible (of leadership): a difficult challenge that has the potential to transform your values, assumptions, and future capabilities as a leader

Culture: shared values and assumptions by organizational (or group) members; the way we do things around here

Customer discovery interviewing: using a structured interview script to qualify an interviewee as a member of your assumed target segment and elicit beliefs and experiences relevant to the problem you are trying to solve and the solution you are working to develop

Decide: the process of making a choice or determining a course of action

Decision-action gap: That space between deciding what you *should* do and actually *doing it*, which exists when an individual or group knows what the correct course of action should be, but struggles to make the *right* or *best* decision.

Decision criteria: factors deemed important to consider in the process of choosing a course of action

Decision-making: a specific process of choosing the best option

Design: (noun) a proposed plan, solution, or product; (verb) the process of originating and developing a plan, which comprises three phases: understand, imagine, and implement

Design principle: rules that designers apply to help guide their process and enhance their product

Design process: a general problem-solving process consisting of three major phases: understand, imagine, and implement; with iteration occurring throughout

Design thinking: This is a cognitive approach to engaging problems that embodies a specific mindset that is **Explorative:** mindset that assumes purposeful ambiguity and curiosity; **User-centered:** mindset that focuses on the user and how they experience and feel; **Divergent:** mindset of generating many, many ideas for a single problem;

Multidisciplinary: mindset that engages many minds and pursues multiple areas of expertise; **Integrative:** mindset of attending to and balancing multiple criteria, particularly viability, feasibility, and desirability; and **Iterative:** mindset of always seeing solutions in process—assessing and improving. Also, habits of mind (dispositions) that designers use to help enhance and guide their process.

Digital competence: having a set of skills, attitudes, and abilities that enables an individual to use a variety of technical tools (the Internet, platforms, mobile tools, and computers, etc.) when seeking, gathering, and analyzing data, and communicating findings to others

Dimensions of the brain: This is an organizational scheme for understanding and applying information about the brain to leadership activity. The six dimensions are the **physiological dimension**, which recognizes that there is a fundamental connection between your brain and your body; the **emotional dimension**, which influences how individuals see and react to situations and others based on feelings; the **social dimension**, which focuses on the critical and inextricable role that others play in how you see and react to the world; the **reflective dimension**, which is the capacity to consider and modify information and understanding; the **constructive dimension**, which emphasizes your process of conceptualizing the world based on what you interact with in the world; and the **dispositional dimension**, which highlights habitual ways of processing information, also seen as mental habits that influence what individuals perceive and how they conceive information.

Directive: *See* Leadership style

Disposition: habits of mind often seen as tendencies or characteristics

Dispositional dimension: *See* Dimensions of the brain

Divergent: *See* Design thinking

Double-bind: the phenomenon wherein even when women use the same leadership behaviors as men, they are judged more harshly than their male counterparts

Ecocycle framework: explains the movements and cycles in organizational systems, often used in planning and leading and comprising four main phases (birth, maturity, creative destruction, and renewal) cycling in an infinite loop

Effectuation: a type of reasoning that starts with one's given resources that subsequently forge goals as the resources are applied

Elaboration: the degree of detail in a given idea as a measure of creativity

Emotional dimension: *See* Dimensions of the brain

Emotional intelligence: a person's ability to know and regulate their own feelings, perceive and understand the feelings of others, and effectively work between their own and others' feelings

Empathy: the ability to sense the feelings of others with the capacity to detect another's mindset

Empowerment: *See* Sources of motivation

Engagement: the degree of individual involvement, investment, and enthusiasm within and for a specific context or situation

Entrepreneurial leadership: a unique set of concepts, mindsets, and activities used by leaders to identify opportunities, deepen understanding, and initiate and develop innovation

Entrepreneurship: the process of pursuing opportunity through the conception, validation, and launch of new ideas into the marketplace

Essence: the process, the thought, the intent, and the motivation of the individual; that being, the actions of people who congregate for a common purpose

Ethical perspectives: This describes five lenses through which to view ethical decisions including **Utilitarianism**, which means that one should do the highest good for the most significant number of people; **Kant's Categorical Imperative**, which posits that an individual must do what is right at all costs; **Justice as fairness**, which asserts that individuals in a free and democratic society should have equal access and opportunity to benefit from specific rights; **Altruism**, which means that you should *love thy neighbor* and make decisions from a place of benefitting others; and **Pragmatism**, which engages any of the ethical perspectives to address ethical issues, understanding that no one perspective can be correct all of the time.

Ethics: an area of study that is concerned with codifying and defending right or wrong behavior in multiple contexts

Evidence-based decision-making: decisions are researched and made based on collected data, rather than relying on prior experience and expertise, personal observations, advice, hopes, or hunches

Explorative: *See* Design thinking

Extrinsic motivation: engaging in an activity because of external rewards for doing so

Five Es: This describes the skill set for future leaders: Exhibit empathy, Engage digitally, Enhance a collaborative work culture, Enact social intelligence, and identify your Essence.

Fixed mindset: a state of mind wherein you see your abilities and capacity as a change agent as set traits—they are what they are

Flexibility: the number of different answer categories comprising ideas as a measure of creativity

Fluency: the total number of ideas generated as a measure of creativity

Formal power: legitimate power bestowed upon an individual who holds a position or role (e.g., judge, police officer)

Forming: *See* Tuckman's stages of group development

Founder's syndrome: an organizational disorder characterized by overreliance on the charisma, involvement, and decisions of one or more founding members in place of mindful, collaborative, and strategic management and leadership

4Ps: This defines creativity: product, person, press, and process. **Product:** the qualities and criteria that distinguish a solution as creative; **Person:** the knowledge, skills, and dispositions that support individual creative activity; **Press:** the contextual variables that foster or inhibit creative thinking and behavior; **Process:** the steps of thinking and doing that maximize creative possibilities

Freelance workers: an individual who desires to work for more than one employer on a part-time basis rather than full-time for only one organization

Group: a collection of individuals who are coordinating their work for some reason or another

Groups: two or more individuals who come together but have no mutual accountability, and a propensity for personal gain rather than a team focus

Group/Team level decision-making: decisions made by a group/team

Growth mindset: a state of mind wherein you believe that you can acquire and develop new abilities, and that your capacity is only limited by your effort

Heroes: persons, alive or dead, real or imaginary, who possess characteristics that are highly prized in a culture and thus serve as models for behavior

Heuristic problem: an open-ended problem with no specific formula for solution and thus needs a general set of guidelines to address

Human capital management (HCM): an employee-centered approach for assessing individual performance, predicting organizational results, and guiding the investments made in the area of human resources

Ideation: the mental process of forming ideas

Impact modeling: a general term for describing the decomposition of a new idea into constituent elements that are relevant to its viability

Incremental change: that extra effort needed in order to build effective working relationships for gaining the confidence of those with whom your future success depends

Incubation: a purposeful stepping away from consciously focusing on the problem to allow unconscious processing and connections

Individual-level decision-making: decisions made by an individual

Influence: the process of moving individuals or groups to a desired mindset, position, behavior, or place

Influence tactics: These are actions designed to move others to a desired mindset. Examples include (a) **Rational persuasion:** Sharing facts and using logic to persuade others; (b) **Lead a coalition:** Convening a group of like-minded people to convince decision makers; (c) **Win-win:** Helping others see how they will benefit from your idea or solution; (d) **Inspirational appeal:** Aligning your proposed direction with the values, mission, and vision of the group or organization; and (e) **Ingratiation:** Increasing the level of positive feelings among the key decision makers.

Informal power: power derived from an individual characteristic such as charisma, expertise, experience, wisdom, and so forth

Ingratiation: *See* Influence tactics

Innovation: new things or methods that deliver value; the collaborative process of translating creative ideas into something of value

Inquisitiveness: an inclination to ask questions, seek information, or otherwise inquire

Inspirational appeal: *See* Influence tactics

Integrative: *See* Design thinking

Integrity: having strong moral character; assumes alignment of word to deed

Intrapreneurship: entrepreneurial behaviors within an existing organization, such as risk-taking and generating ideas

Intrinsic motivation: engaging in an activity for the inherent joy of the task

Intuitive decision-making: relies heavily on an individual or group's gut feeling, hunch, or intuition

Invention: the creation of a new method, device, or process

Iterate: the act of trying things out and improving the design based on feedback

Iterative: *See* Design thinking

Large-scale change: a more complex change process that requires integrating a strategic vision into change initiatives that redirect attention to entirely new processes, systems, or structures

Lateral organizational model: a structure that enables individuals to come together in varying arrangements based on personal preferences for getting things done

Lateral thinking: attempting to look at a situation from a unique or unexpected point of view; having individuals step beyond the obvious solutions

Laws: rules developed by a social institution (e.g., state or nation) that govern correct behavior

Lead a coalition: *See* Influence tactics

Leadership: the process of influencing others toward a common vision

Leadership brand: identifying your assets—strengths, skills and other desirable characteristics—and packaging them in a manner that enhances leadership efficacy and credibility

Leadership capacity: your fundamental attributes that can be applied to any leadership challenge in the future

Leadership (extended): Leadership comprises your perceptions, strengths, style, skills, and the way you make decisions and solve problems, including how you persuade, guide, teach, and build relationships with others. But leadership goes beyond you—it is also how you help others succeed and create a culture of success so that you, your followers, your organization, and your society can make a positive difference in the world.

Leadership style: This is how a leader goes about addressing the four elements of defining the goal, clarifying the path, removing obstacles, and providing support. Styles include **Directive:** The leader provides guidance and psychological structure; **Supportive:** The leader provides nurturance; **Participative:** The leader provides involvement; and **Achievement oriented:** The leader challenges others to work to the next level.

Lean: an approach to organizational development that engages flexible, rapid methods to test and revise products and services before heavily investing

Legitimate power: *See* Sources of power

Level 5 leadership: leadership consisting of high-level resolve coupled with compelling personal humility

Management: the process of organizing, controlling, and coordinating resources to achieve organizational value

Manipulation: similar to influence but often with more of a hidden or inauthentic intent

Maslow's Hierarchy of Needs: This is a model of progressive categories of needs that drive human behavior. Four lower-order needs, which Maslow called *deficiency needs*, that must be satisfied (physiological—basics such as air, water, food; safety—from harm; belonging and love—relationships; esteem—esteem and respect from self and others) before moving up to the higher-level needs (cognitive, aesthetic, self-actualization, and transcendence).

Mental model: your mental representation of things in the world—not just the picture in your head but how you understand things and even how you process information

Metacognition: thinking about your own thinking

Mindfulness: the mental state of being in the present and in tune with all that is happening in your immediate environment; being aware of the full, present moment; individuals; context; and/or situation

Minimum viable product (MVP): the smallest, simplest thing you can build that conveys the product's value proposition to customers (and potentially captures value back)

Mission: the reason for an organization's existence

Moral principles: principles deemed *correct* or *incorrect* by individuals, groups, and societies

Motivation: the internal desire for a person to act

Multidisciplinary: *See* Design thinking

Nondecisions: controversial issues or topics that have been consciously or unconsciously *taken off the table* by an individual or group

Nonprofit organization: This is an organization that focuses on achieving a type of value different from financial. As an organization, they strive to achieve a cause or mission, funneling any financial profit back into serving the organization's efforts (versus paying investors or stockholders).

Norming: *See* Tuckman's stages of group development

Open-minded: the mindset of being receptive to new ideas and perspectives

Opportunity recognition: occurs when entrepreneurs become aware of a problem, dissatisfaction, or gap in current offerings that they find interesting and believe themselves capable of solving

Optimism: the ability and tendency to see the positive, both now and into the future

Organizational climate: the recurring, often dynamic, patterns of behaviors, attitudes, and feelings that characterize what it is like to work within an organization

Organizational culture: a way of life for a group of individuals that has been learned and developed over a period of time

Organizational values: Generally emanating from founders, organizational values guide the behavior of organizational members.

Originality: the total number of unique ideas as a measure of creativity

Outmatched effort: *See* Sources of power

Panarchy: These are the deep patterns that occur in the transformation cycles all human and natural systems go through. This specific cycle looks like an infinity loop, and it includes the following phases: exploitation, conservation, release, and reorganization.

Participative: *See* Leadership style

Performing: *See* Tuckman's stages of group development

Perseverance: a steady persistence in a course of action in spite of unexpected delays

Person (creative): *See* 4Ps

Personal values: beliefs or ideals that guide a person's behavior; what you find *personally* important or of some *worth*

Physiological dimension: *See* Dimensions of the brain

Pivot: changing an aspect of your idea, solution, or approach (or starting over) to reduce risk based on evidence and testing assumptions

Positive engagement: your initiation and participation in ways that add value in a reflective and mindful manner, critically and carefully integrating new information into your understanding

Practice: an activity used typically to maintain or improve one's performance

Press (creative): *See* 4Ps

Proactive: anticipating and preparing for a possible outcome

Problem: a challenge or difficult matter of uncertain outcome

Process: *See* 4Ps

Process mapping: an activity where leaders and followers visually represent what an organization does, noting the flow of activities, decision points, roles, and any other variables involved in getting things done

Product (creative): *See* 4Ps

Project management: the application of knowledge, skills, tools, and techniques to a broad range of activities in order to meet the requirements of a particular project

PsyCap: an individual's positive psychological state of development characterized by confidence, optimism, hope, and resilience

Psychological safety: *See* Sources of motivation

Rational decision-making: relies heavily on a logical process for the individual or group to make a decision

Rational persuasion: *See* Influence tactics

Referent power: *See* Sources of power

Refining personal change capacity: modest changes in your own behavior that people notice and at the same time convince them to follow your lead during the change process

Reflection: the mental act of considering and modifying information and understanding, often replaying interactions in an effort to understand your behavior and the behavior of others

Reflective dimension: *See* Dimensions of the brain

Resilience: Latin root *resilire*, which means to spring back—your ability to withstand and recover from difficulties

Rituals: collective activities that are technically unnecessary to the achievement of desired ends but that within a culture are considered socially essential, keeping the individual bound within the norms of the collectivity

Satisficing: a process of *satisfying* minimal criteria with a solution that will *suffice*

Self-monitoring: the act of observing your own actions—the good, the bad, and the ugly

Servant leadership: a leadership approach that focuses first on others' needs, aspirations, and success

Service: action that is done for others—putting others' needs ahead of your own

Service clubs: organizations that usually were originally formed for social purposes that have evolved into making changes in the world

Service learning: campus-based volunteer opportunities that combine academic learning with principles of service to community

Shared accountability: team members' focus on the work of and responsibility for the team, for the greater good of the organization

Shared leadership: where one individual takes a temporary leadership role on the team based on his or her area of interest and/or expertise

Situational leadership: behaviors utilized by leaders of an organization adjusting to fit the development level of the followers they are trying to influence

Skills: what leaders can do—their competencies

Social dimension: *See* Dimensions of the brain

Social entrepreneurship: the process of utilizing the marketplace to solve social problems (generally wicked social problems) in a novel manner

Social impact model: a representation for the rationale for how a policy, program, project, or social venture creates value for beneficiaries, delivers the value to beneficiaries, and sustains its impact over time

Social intelligence: the ability to get along well with others by getting them to collaborate and eventually partner with you for achieving a specific result

Societal cultures: different cultures across nations, regions, or ethnicities

Sources of motivation: These are the conditions that you design to alter someone's internal desire to act. Examples include (a) **Empowerment:** You feel a sense of ownership/control and competence in your work; (b) **Autonomy:** You feel ownership in how tasks are accomplished; (c) **Career pathing:** You have a clear sense for how you can progress and move forward in the organization; and (d) **Psychological safety:** You have trust in the organization, your supervisor, and your peers.

Sources of power: This is the specific origin of your capacity to influence others. Examples include (a) **Referent power:** You attract others through your enthusiasm, energy, humor, and optimism; (b) **Outmatched effort:** You consistently display superior effort; (c) **Legitimate power:** You have actual authority over an individual or group.

Spiritual capital: individual dispositions that manifest as a sense of meaningfulness through (a) belief in something larger than self; (b) a sense of interconnectedness; (c) ethical and moral salience; (d) a call or drive to serve; and (e) the capability to transfer the latter conceptualizations into individual and organizational behaviors, and ultimately added value

Stories: the words, gestures, pictures, and objects that carry often complex meanings recognized as such only by those who share the culture

Storming: *See* Tuckman's stages of group development

Strategic planning: the process by which an organization (a) clarifies (identify, develop, refine) values and vision; (b) translates those into goals; and then (c) creates action plans or strategy to achieve those goals

Strengths-based leadership: workers excelling in four specific domains: executing, influencing, relationship building, and strategic thinking

Supportive: *See* Leadership style

Sustainability: the ability to endure, specifically the process of using the resources of the present to ensure success in the future

SWOT Analysis: a strategic planning and decision-making tool used to evaluate the current Strengths, Weaknesses, Opportunities, and Threats relevant to an organization or specific situation that requires understanding

Synergy: a group's energy where the sum of the energy of the group is greater than the combined output of each individual (the sum is greater than the total of the individual parts)

System: a group of interconnected, interdependent parts that make up a complex whole

Systems thinking: a habit of mind (disposition) used to examine and understand the connections and interactions between individual parts making up a complex whole

Team: a collection of individuals with a collective goal

Teaming: a temporary group put together to solve a problem, often with a diverse group of experts

Team roles: the functions that each individual plays in the team (i.e., technical, interpersonal, etc.)

Technology: the practical, material, and human application of scientific knowledge

Third industrial revolution: the integration of science, technology, and personal choice for creating collaborative work strategies for getting people focused on the future

Traits: well-habituated, stable, and consistent personal characteristics

Transactional leadership: a process whereby those in leadership roles directly supervise change by setting clear objectives and goals for followers as well as by using either punishments or rewards in order to encourage compliance with these goals

Transformational leadership: a change process in which leaders and followers help each other advance to a higher level of morale and motivation

T-shaped person: This is a metaphor for expertise within and across disciplines. The stem of the T represents an individual's depth of knowledge in their own field, while the cross of the T models an individual's capacity to collaborate and work with other disciplines.

Tuckman's stages of group development: Forming: the introductory stage of a group where members are getting to know one another and tend to act in very polite ways; **Storming:** the second stage of a group where members are vying for position in the group and attempt to establish their role in the group; **Norming:** the third stage of group development where members have settled into roles and begin to establish the mission, purpose, and culture of the group; **Performing:** the fourth stage of group development where team members have settled into their roles and focus on the work at hand; and finally, **Adjourning,** the last stage where the work of the group has concluded and the group members disband.

User-centered: *See* Design thinking

Vertical operational model: a rigid structure that relies upon the leadership practices of senior executives to direct others for getting tasks done efficiently

Virtues: a continuum of traits, behaviors, and/or habits

Vision: an aspirational image that provides short- and long-term direction for an organization and its members

Volunteerism: individual or group engagement with others and/or an organization for no compensation

Wicked problem: a problem that is difficult or impossible to solve because of incomplete information, multiple perspectives, dynamic variables, and interconnections with other problems

Win-win: *See* Influence tactics

• Notes •

Introduction

1. This concise definition can be found in Northouse, P. (2016). *Leadership theory and practice* (7th ed.). Thousand Oaks, CA: SAGE. Northouse provides a clear, brief overview of the evolution of leadership definitions in Chapter 1. This definition may have origins with Seeman, M. (1960). *Social status and leadership.* Columbus, OH: Ohio State University, Bureau of Business Leadership; and later with Rauch, C., & Behling, O. (1984). Functionalism: Basis for an alternate approach to the study of leadership. In J. G. Hunt, D.-M. Hoskins, C. A. Schriesheim, & R. Stewart (Eds.), *Leaders and managers.* Elmsford, NY: Pergamon.

2. Among the many resources listing definitions of leadership: http://www2.warwick.ac.uk/fac/sci/wmg/ftmsc/modules/modulelist/le/content_store_2012/leadership_definitions.doc

3. This is a real term describing problems that are difficult and likely impossible to solve because they are interconnected with other problems, have many competing and dynamic variables, and have many possible causes, and because of all this we have incomplete or contradictory knowledge. Wicked problems include things like poverty, homelessness, racism, wellness, and so forth. You should learn a bit more about wicked problems here: https://www.wickedproblems.com/1_wicked_problems.php

4. There is no single source that says leadership matters; rather, there are hundreds of specific studies across many fields of practice that describe successful organizations and the leadership activities that were critical to that success.

5. Lidwell, W., Holden, K., & Butler, J. (2010). *The universal principles of design.* Beverly, MA: Rockport Publishers. Available at http://universalprinciplesofdesign.com/books/

6. Senge, P. M. (1994). *The fifth discipline fieldbook: Strategies and tools for building a learning organization.* New York, NY: Currency, Doubleday.

7. Cards developed by Middlebrooks, T. (2011). Self-published.

Chapter 1

1. Burns, J. M. (1978). *Leadership.* New York, NY: Harper & Row.

2. Burns (1978), p. 18.
3. Burns (1978), p. 4.
4. Burns (1978), p. 20.
5. Burns (1978), p. 43.
6. Burns (1978), p. 461.
7. Burns (1978), p. 460.
8. Safian, R. (2013). *10 lessons for design-driven success.* Retrieved from http://www.fastcodesign.com/3016247/10-lessons-for-design-driven-success

9. Dundon, E. (2002). *The seeds of innovation: Cultivating the synergy that fosters new ideas.* New York, NY: AMACOM.

10. IDEO. (2015). *Our approach.* Retrieved from https://www.ideo.org/approach

11. Bruck, J., & Middlebrooks, A. (2010). Design-based learning for leadership. *Academic Exchange Quarterly, 14*(2), 17–22.

12. Lovett, J. (2018). *Original design overview.* Retrieved from http://www.johnlovett.com/test.htm

13. Luthans, F., Youssef, C. M., & Avolio, B. J. (2007). *Psychological capital: Developing the human competitive edge.* Oxford, UK: Oxford University Press.

14. Luthans, F. (2012). Psychological capital: Implications for HRD, retrospective analysis, and future directions. *Human Resource Development Quarterly, 23*(1), 1–8. Retrieved from https://onlinelibrary.wiley.com/doi/abs/10.1002/hrdq.21119

15. This outcome of leader confidence has been found in numerous studies, including Mowday, R. (1979). Leader characteristics, self-confidence, and methods of upward influence in organizational decision situations. *Academy of Management Journal, 22*(4), 709–725; and DeCremer, D., & van Knippenberg, D. (2004). Leader self-sacrifice and leadership effectiveness: The moderating role of leader self-confidence. *Organizational Behavior and Human Decision Processes, 95*(2), 140–155.

16. Karlsberg, R., & Adler, J. (n.d.). Building confidence: The number 1 challenge for new leaders. *Expert Performance.* Retrieved from http://docplayer.net/20922971-E-xpert-performanc-e-building-confidence-charting-your-course-to-higher-performance-the-number-1-challenge-for-new-leaders.html

17. Kanter, R. (2011, April). Cultivate a culture of confidence. *Harvard Business Review.* Retrieved from https://hbr.org/2011/04/column-cultivate-a-culture-of-confidence

18. Bandura, A. (1997). *Self-efficacy: The exercise of control.* New York, NY: Freeman.

19. http://www.ted.com/talks/amy_cuddy_your_body_language_shapes_who_you_are

20. For example—https://www.mindtools.com/pages/article/newTCS_84.htm

21. Van Zant, A. B., & Moore, D. A. (2013). Avoiding the pitfalls of overconfidence while benefiting from the advantages of confidence. *California Management Review, 55*(2), 5–23.

22. Shipman, A. S., & Mumford, M. D. (2011). When confidence is detrimental: Influence of overconfidence on leadership effectiveness. *The Leadership Quarterly, 22*(4), 649–665.

23. Kouzes, J., & Posner, B. (2003). *Encouraging the heart: A leader's guide to rewarding and recognizing others.* San Francisco, CA: Jossey-Bass.

24. Lounsbury, J. W., Sundstrom, E. D., Gibson, L. W., Loveland, J. M., & Drost, A. W. (2016, March). Core personality traits of managers. *Journal of Managerial Psychology, 31*(2), 434–450.

25. Chemers, M. M., Watson, C. B., & May, S. T. (2000, January). Dispositional affect and leadership effectiveness: A comparison of self-esteem, optimism, and efficacy. *Personality and Social Psychology Bulletin, 26*(3), 267–277; Scheier, M. F., Weintraub, J. K., & Carver, C. S. (1986, January). Coping with stress: Divergent strategies of optimists and pessimists. *Journal of Personality and Social Psychology, 51*(6), 1257–64.

26. Kirschenbaum, D. (1984). Self-regulation and sports psychology: Nurturing and emerging symbiosis. *Journal of Sport Psychology, 6*(2), 159–183. Retrieved from http://www.worldcat.org/title/self-regulation-and-sport-psychology-nurturing-an-emerging-symbiosis/oclc/6826359882&referer=brief_results

27. Losada, M., & Heaphy, E. (2004, February). The role of positivity and connectivity in the performance of business teams: A nonlinear dynamics model. *American Behavioral Scientist, 47*(6), 740–765.

28. Kovic, D. (2010, February 23). *Leading with optimism—10 ways to be optimistic.* Retrieved from http://www.selfgrowth.com/print/843605

29. Edmondson, A. C. (2011, April 1). Strategies for learning from failure. *Harvard Business Review, 89*(4); Seligman, M. E. P. (1991). *Learned optimism.* New York, NY: A. A. Knopf; Seligman, M. E. P. (2011, January 1). Building resilience. *Harvard Business Review, 89*(4), 100–106.

30. Bartone, P. T. (2006, January). Resilience under military operational stress: Can leaders influence hardiness? *Military Psychology, 18*(3), 131.

31. Birkinshaw, J., & Haas, M. (2016, January 1). Increase your return on failure. *Harvard Business Review, 94*(5).

32. Sommer, S. A., Howell, J. M., & Hadley, C. N. (2016). Keeping positive and building strength: The role of affect and team leadership in developing resilience during an organizational crisis. *Group & Organization Management, 41*(2), 172–202.

33. Reid, J. (2008, May/June). The resilient leader: Why EQ matters. *Ivey Business Journal.* Retrieved from http://iveybusinessjournal.com/publication/the-resilient-leader-why-eq-matters/

34. Motto, A. L., Seneca, & Campbell, R. (1970, January 1). Seneca, letters from a stoic: Epistulae morales ad lucilium. *The Classical World, 63*(5), 172.

35. Many resources are available providing suggestions for building resilience, including: http://www.apa.org/helpcenter/road-resilience.aspx and https://www.mindtools.com/pages/article/resilience.htm.

36. Martel, P., & Perkins, J. (2016, March). Building career resiliency: Hone your ability to grow from adversity. *Public Management, 98*(2), 6–9.

37. Salovey, P., & Mayer, J. D. (1990). Emotional intelligence. *Imagination, Cognition, and Personality, 9*(3), 185–211.

38. Bar-On, R. (2007). The Bar-On model of emotional intelligence: A valid, robust and applicable EI model. *Organisations & People, 14*, 27–34; Petrides, K. V., & Furnham, A. (2000). On the dimensional structure of emotional intelligence. *Personality and Individual Differences, 29*(2), 313–320.

39. Goleman, D., Boyatzis, R., & McKee, A. (2002). *Primal leadership: Realizing the power of emotional intelligence.* Boston, MA: Harvard Business School Press.

40. Goleman, D. (2000). Emotional intelligence: Issues in paradigm building. In D. Goleman & C. Cherniss (Eds.), *The emotionally intelligent workplace: How to select for, measure, and improve emotional intelligence in individuals, groups, and organizations.* San Francisco, CA: Jossey-Bass.

41. Mayer, J. D., Salovey, P., & Caruso, D. R. (2004). Emotional intelligence: Theory, findings, and implications. *Psychological Inquiry, 15*(3), 197–215.

42. Ramo, L. G., Saris, W. E., & Boyatzis, R. E. (2009). The impact of social and emotional competencies on effectiveness of Spanish executives. *Journal of Management Development, 28*(9), 771–793.

43. Boyatzis, R. E. (1999). From a presentation to the Linkage Conference on Emotional Intelligence Chicago, IL, September 27, 1999. Cited in Cherniss, C. (1999). The business case for emotional intelligence. *Consortium for Research on Emotional Intelligence in Organizations, 4*, p. 1.

44. Hay/McBer Research and Innovation Group (1997). This research was provided to Daniel Goleman and is reported in his book (Goleman, 1998). Cited in

Cherniss, C. (1999). The business case for emotional intelligence. *Consortium for Research on Emotional Intelligence in Organizations, 4*, p. 2.

45. Nohe, C., Michaelis, B., Menges, J. I., Zhang, Z., & Sonntag, K. (2013, April). Charisma and organizational change: A multilevel study of perceived charisma, commitment to change, and team performance. *The Leadership Quarterly, 24*(2), 378–389.

46. https://www.salzburgglobal.org/news/latest-news/article/are-we-becoming-disconnected-by-our-love-of-devices//.html/https://theworldunplugged.wordpress.com/about/#anchor1

47. Safian, R. (2013). *10 lessons for design-driven success*. Retrieved from http://www.fastcodesign.com/3016247/10-lessons-for-design-driven-success

Chapter 2

1. Bennis, W., & Thomas, R. (2002). *Geeks and geezers*. Boston, MA: HBS Press.

2. Bennis, W., & Thomas, R. (2002), p. 3.

3. Galbraith, J. K. (1971). A contemporary guide to economics, peace, and laughter. In A. D. Williams (Ed.), *Essays, Chapter 3: How Keynes came to America*. Boston, MA: Houghton Mifflin Company. (p. 50)

4. Bregman, P. (2015). Quash your bad habits by knowing what triggers them. *Forbes*. Retrieved from http://www.forbes.com/sites/peterbregman/2015/10/09/quash-your-bad-habits-by-knowing-what-triggers-them/#25f0429194f6

5. The Emotional Intelligence Network. (2016). Retrieved from http://www.6seconds.org/

6. Credit to Dr. Michael Dickmann, Emeritus Professor of Leadership for the Advancement of Learning and Service at Cardinal Stritch University.

7. Bransford, J., National Research Council (U.S.). (2000). *How people learn: Brain, mind, experience, and school*. Washington, DC: National Academy Press.

8. Soygüt, G., & Savasir, I. (2001). The relationship between interpersonal schemas and depressive symptomatology. *Journal of Counseling Psychology, 48*(3), 359–364.

9. Collins, J. C. (2001). *Good to great: Why some companies make the leap—and others don't*. New York, NY: HarperBusiness.

10. There are many definitions of vision, but this classic concise definition, along with an extensive explanation and toolkit relative to building shared visions, can be found in Senge, P. M. (1990). *The fifth discipline: The art and practice of the learning organization*. New York, NY: Doubleday/Currency.

11. Lidwell, W., Holden, K., & Butler, J. (2010). *The universal principles of design*. Beverly, MA: Rockport Publishers.

12. Although leadership is exemplified and discussed all the way back to antiquity, possibly the two earliest published scholarly works directly focused on leadership are Terman, L. (1904). A preliminary study of the psychology and pedagogy of leadership. *Journal of Genetic Psychology, 11*, 413–451 and Mumford, E. (1909). *The origins of leadership* (Dissertation). University of Chicago.

13. Stogdill, R. M. (1974). *Handbook of leadership: A survey of the literature*. New York, NY: Free Press.

14. Northouse, P. G. (2015). *Leadership: Theory and practice*. (7th ed.). Thousand Oaks, CA: Sage.

15. Stadler, C., & Dyer, D. (2013, March 1). Why good leaders don't need charisma. *MIT Sloan Management Review, 54*(3); Tasler, N. (2015, October 27). You don't need charisma to be an inspiring leader. *Harvard Business Review*.

16. Tarakci, M., Greer, L. L., & Groenen, P. J. F. (2015, January 1). When does power disparity help or hurt group performance? *Journal of Applied Psychology, 101*(3), 415–429.

17. Collins, J. (1997, October). *The death of the charismatic leader (And the birth of an architect)*. Retrieved from www.Jimcollins.com

18. Katz, R. L. (1955, January/February). Skills of an effective administrator. *Harvard Business Review*, 33–42.

19. Bolden, R., Gosling, J., Marturano, A., & Dennison, P. (2003). *A review of leadership theory and competency frameworks*. Edited version of a report for Chase Consulting and the Management Standards Centre. Centre for Leadership Studies, University of Exeter. Retrieved from https://ore.exeter.ac.uk/repository/handle/10036/17494

20. Fayol, H. (1949). *General and industrial management*. London, UK: Pitman.

21. Zaleznik, A. (2004, January). Managers and leaders: Are they different? *Harvard Business Review*. Retrieved from https://hbr.org/2004/01/managers-and-leaders-are-they-different

22. Bennis, W. G. (1989). *On becoming a leader*. Reading, MA: Addison-Wesley.

23. Yukl, G., & Lepsinger, R. (2005). Why integrating the leading and managing roles is essential for organizational effectiveness. *Organizational Dynamics, 34*(4), 361–375.

24. Bransford, J., National Research Council (U.S.). (2000). *How people learn: Brain, mind, experience, and school*. Washington, DC: National Academy Press.

25. Klein, G. A. (1999). *Sources of power: How people make decisions*. Cambridge, MA: MIT Press.

26. Allen, S. J., & Middlebrooks, A. (2013, December 1). The challenge of educating leadership expertise. *Journal of Leadership Studies, 6*(4), 84–89.

27. Kouzes, J. M., & Posner, B. Z. (2012). *The leadership challenge: How to make extraordinary things happen in organizations*. (5th ed.). Hoboken, NJ: Wiley.

28. Kouzes, J. M., & Posner, B. Z. (2012), p. 38.

29. Goffee, R., & Jones, G. (2005, January 1). Why should anyone be led by you? *Harvard Business Review, 1*.

30. Lawrence-Lightfoot, S. (1999). *Respect: An exploration*. Reading, MA: Perseus Books.

31. Bichard, M. (2000). The modernization and improvement of government and public services: Creativity, leadership and change. *Public Money and Management, 20*(2), 41–46.

32. http://etad.usask.ca/skaalid/theory/gestalt/closure.htm

33. Emmons, R. A., & McCullough, M. E. (2004). *The psychology of gratitude*. Oxford, UK: Oxford University Press.

Chapter 3

1. Goleman, D. (1998, November/December). What makes a leader? *Harvard Business Review*, pp. 82–91.

2. Burns, J. (1978). *Leadership*. New York, NY: Harper & Row.

3. Mack, T. (2015). Leadership in the future. In M. Sowcik, A. C. Andenoro, M. McNutt, & S. E. Murphy (Eds.), *Leadership 2050: Critical challenges, key contexts, and emerging trends* (pp. 9–22). Bingley, England: Emerald.

4. Hempel, J. (2014, July 21). Instagram is ready to take its shot. *Fortune, 170*(1), 34–40.

5. Kearns, K. (2015). 9 great examples of crowdsourcing in the age of empowered consumers. Retrieved from http://tweakyourbiz.com/marketing/2015/07/10/9-great-examples-crowdsourcing-age-empowered-consumers/

6. Kanawattanachai, P., & Yoo, Y. (2012). Dynamic nature of trust in virtual teams. *Journal of Strategic Information Systems, 11*(3–4), 187–213.

7. Brandt, V., England, W., & Ward, S. (2011). Virtual teams. *Research Technology Management, 54*(6), 62–63.

8. Colvin, G. (2015, July 23). Humans are underrated. *Fortune*. Retrieved from http://fortune.com/2015/07/23/humans-are-underrated/

9. Redman, P. (2013, October 7). Five essentials of strategic planning. *Stanford Social Innovation Review*. Retrieved from https://ssir.org/articles/entry/five_essentials_of_strategic_planning

10. Conservation International. (2016). *Climate change: 11 things you need to know*. Retrieved from https://www.conservation.org/stories/Pages/11-things-you-need-to-know-about-climate-change.aspx?gclid=EAIaIQobChMI_Ompp6m12wIVGMZkCh0JbAU7EAAYASAAEgIwufD_BwE; NASA. (2018, January 18). Long-term warming trend continued in 2017: NASA, NOAA. Release 18-003. Retrieved from https://www.nasa.gov/press-release/long-term-warming-trend-continued-in-2017-nasa-noaa

11. National Pay Equity Committee. (2016). *The wage gap continues over time: Women see a continuing gap*. Retrieved from https://www.pay-equity.org/info-time.html

12. Muñoz, P., & Cohen, B. (2018, March 1). Sustainable entrepreneurship research: Taking stock and looking ahead. *Business Strategy and the Environment, 27*(3), 300–322.

13. Kanawattanachai, P., & Yoo, Y. (2012). Dynamic nature of trust in virtual teams. *Journal of Strategic Information Systems, 11*(3–4), 187–213.

14. Giambusso, D. (2012, May 13). Power plant is approved and Newark residents are outraged. *NJ.com—True Jersey*. Retrieved from http://www.nj.com/news/index.ssf/2012/05/power_plant_is_approved_and_ne.html

15. Gropius, W. (1925). *Internationale architektur*. München, Germany: Albert Langen Verlag.

16. Colvin, G. (2015, January 1). Humans are underrated. *Fortune, 172*(2), 34–43.

17. Bear, M. (2015). *Why empathy is the critical 21st century skill*. Retrieved from https://www.linkedin.com/pulse/20140424221331-1407199-why-empathy-is-the-critical-21st-century-skill/

18. Patnaik, D., & Mortensen, P. (2009). *Wired to care: How companies prosper when they create widespread empathy*. Upper Saddle River, NJ: FT Press.

19. Pavlovich, K., & Krahnke, K. (2014). *Organizing through empathy*. New York, NY: Routledge.

20. Randall, P. (2001). *Bullying in adulthood: Assessing the bullies and their victims*. New York, NY: Taylor & Francis.

21. Stephan, W., & Finlay, K. (2001). Role of empathy in improving intergroup relations. *Journal of Social Issues, 55*(4), 729–743.

22. Capgemini Consulting. (2012). The digital advantage: How digital leaders outperform their peers in every industry. *MIT-CDB and Capgemini Consulting*. Retrieved from https://www.capgemini.com/wp-content/uploads/2017/07/The_Digital_Advantage__How_Digital_Leaders_Outperform_their_Peers_in_Every_Industry.pdf

23. Hackman, M., & Johnson, C. (2013). *Leadership: A communication perspective* (6th ed.). Long Grove, IL: Waveland Press.

24. Dukes, E. (2014). 4 ways technology has changed the modern workplace. *The iOFFICE*. Retrieved from https://www.iofficecorp.com/blog/4-ways-technology-has-changed-the-modern-workplace

25. Blanchard, K. (2010, January 25). *Leading at a higher level. Peter Drucker Institute keynote speaker* [Video File].

Retrieved from https://www.youtube.com/watch?v=_hNYu4cdU2k

26. Colvin, G. (2007, September 20). How top companies breed stars. *Fortune.* Retrieved from http://archive.fortune.com/magazines/fortune/fortune_archive/2007/10/01/100351829/index.htm?postversion=2007092010

27. Kim, W. C., & Mauborgne, R. (2015). *Blue ocean strategy: How to create uncontested market space and make the competition irrelevant.* Boston, MA: Harvard Business School Publishing Corporation.

28. Kellerman, B. (2008). *Followership: How followers are creating change and changing leaders.* Boston, MA: Harvard Business School Press.

29. Hurwitz, M., & Hurwitz, S. (2015). *Leadership is half the story: A fresh look at followership, leadership, and collaboration.* Toronto, Canada: University of Toronto Press.

30. Kelley, R. E. (1985). *The gold collar worker: Harnessing the brainpower of the new workforce.* Reading, MA: Addison-Wesley.

31. Hollander, E. P. (2012). *Inclusive leadership: The essential leader-follower relationship.* New York, NY: Routledge. (p. 130)

32. Chaleff, I. (2009). *The courageous follower: Standing up to & for our leaders* (3rd ed.). San Francisco, CA: Berrett-Koehler.

33. Koonce, R. (2014). Introductory remarks. Proceedings of the 2014 International Followership Symposium, 16th Annual ILA Global Conference. *Journal of Leadership Education* (pp. 5–8). doi:10.12806/V13/I4/C2

34. Follett, M. P. (2013a). XII. Leader and expert. In H. C. Metcalf & L. Urwick (Eds.), *Dynamic administration: The collected papers of Mary Parker Follett* (pp. 247–269). Mansfield Centre, CT: Martino Publishing. (p. 262)

35. Carsten, M. K., Harms, P., & Uhl-Bien, M. (2014). Exploring historical perspectives of followership: The need for an expanded view of followers and the follower role. In L. M. Lapierre & M. K. Carsten (Eds.), *Followership: What is it and why do people follow?* (pp. 3–25). Bingley, England: Emerald. (p. 4)

36. Clerkin, C. (2015). Creative leadership and social intelligence: The keys to leading in the digital age. In M. Sowcik, A. C. Andenoro, M. McNutt, & S. E. Murphy (Eds.), *Leadership 2050: Critical challenges, key contexts, and emerging trends* (pp. 175–187), Bingley, England: Emerald.

37. See Wiest, B. (2018, March 13). 13 things socially intelligent leaders do differently. *Forbes.* Retrieved from https://www.forbes.com/sites/briannawiest/2018/03/13/13-things-socially-intelligent-leaders-do-differently/#40b32cdf4dbd for one of many examples of practical advice for social intelligence and leadership.

38. Goleman, D., & Boyatzis, R. (2008, January 1). Social intelligence and the biology of leadership. *Harvard Business Review, 86,* 9.

39. Blanchard, K. (2010, January 25). *Leading at a higher level. Peter Drucker Institute keynote speaker* [Video file]. Retrieved from https://www.youtube.com/watch?v=_hNYu4cdU2k

40. Buckingham, M., & Clifton, D. O. (2001). *Now, discover your strengths.* New York, NY: Free Press.

41. Strengths and their definitions loosely quoted from the Clifton StrengthsFinder measure, which can be found here: http://www.gallup.com/poll/166991/clifton-strengthsfinder-theme-descriptions-pdf.aspx; Students can take the measure (for a fee) here: https://www.gallupstrengthscenter.com/Purchase/en-US/Index/?utm_source=En_US&utm_medium=Ad&utm_campaign=SF2SiteAd

42. Rath, T., & Conchie, B. (2009). *Strengths based leadership: Great leaders, teams and why people follow.* New York, NY: Gallup Press.

43. Judge, T. A., & Hurst, C. (2008, January 1). How the rich (and happy) get richer (and happier): Relationship of core self-evaluations to trajectories in attaining work success. *Journal of Applied Psychology, 93*(4), 849–63.

44. Gallup, Inc. (2013). *State of the American workplace.* Retrieved from file:///C:/Users/tmidd/Downloads/State%20of%20the%20American%20Workplace%20Report%202013.pdf

45. Ulrich, D., & Smallwood, N. (2007). *Leadership brand: Developing customer-focused leaders to drive performance and build lasting value.* Boston, MA: Harvard Business School Press.

46. Bass, B., & Riggio, R. (2006). *Transformational leadership.* Mahwah, NJ: Lawrence Erlbaum.

47. Heifetz, R., Grashow, A., & Linsky, M. (2009). *The practice of adaptive leadership: Tools and tactics for changing your organization and your world.* Boston, MA: Harvard Business School Press.

48. Norman, D. (1988). *The design of everyday things.* New York, NY: Doubleday.

49. Ulrich, D., & Smallwood, N. (2007). *Leadership brand: Developing customer-focused leaders to drive performance and build lasting value.* Boston, MA: Harvard Business School Press.

50. Blanchard, K. (2010, January 25). *Leading at a higher level. Peter Drucker Institute keynote speaker* [Video file]. Retrieved from https://www.youtube.com/watch?v=_hNYu4cdU2k

51. Collins, J. (2001). *Good to great.* New York, NY: HarperCollins.

52. Reuters. (2016, January 26). *Comedian Carol Burnett 'gobsmacked' at SAG lifetime award.* Retrieved from http://www.reuters.com/article/us-awards-sag-carolburnett-idUSKCN0V4223

53. Safian, R. (2012, October 29). Terry Kelly: The "UN-CEO" of W. L. Gore, on how to deal with chaos: Grow up. *Fast Company.* Retrieved from http://www

.fastcompany.com/3002493/terri-kelly-un-ceo-wl-gore-how-deal-chaos-grow

Chapter 4

1. Burns, J. M. (1978). *Leadership*. New York, NY: Harper Torchbooks. (p. 455)
2. George, B. (2007). *True north*. Hoboken, NJ: Wiley. (p. 47)
3. Smith, P. (2015). The UpBeat: Ryan's Well Foundation reaches milestone in clean water drive. *The Ottawa Citizen*. Retrieved from http://ottawacitizen.com/news/local-news/the-upbeat-ryans-well-foundation-reaches-milestone-in-clean-water-drive
4. Ibid.
5. Giles, S. (2016, March 15). The most important leadership competencies, according to leaders around the world. *Harvard Business Review*. Retrieved from https://hbr.org/2016/03/the-most-important-leadership-competencies-according-to-leaders-around-the-world
6. United Nations. (1948). *The universal declaration of human rights*. Retrieved from http://www.un.org/en/universal-declaration-human-rights/
7. American Medical Association. (2016). *AMA code of medical ethics: AMA principles of medical ethics*. Retrieved from https://www.ama-assn.org/sites/default/files/media-browser/principles-of-medical-ethics.pdf
8. Hoban.org. (n.d.). *4 universal moral principles: Lessons of the ages*. Retrieved from https://www.hoban.org/s/1098/images/editor_documents/2009-10%20School%20Year/Bulgrin/4%20Basic%20Moral%20Principles.pdf?sessionid=f9e8cb31-22cc-4159-9676-b18595ccbc90&cc=1
9. Kinnier, R. T., Kernes, J. L., & Dautheribes, T. M. (2000). A short list of universal moral values. *Counseling & Values*, 45, 4–16.
10. King, M. L., Jr. (1963, August 28). *I have a dream*. Lincoln Memorial, Washington, DC.
11. Peterson, C., & Seligman, M. E. (2004). *Character strengths and virtues: A handbook and classification*. Oxford, UK: Oxford University Press.
12. Ibid.
13. Joachim, H. H., & Rees, D. A. (1953). *Aristotle: The Nicomachean ethics*. Oxford, UK: Clarendon Press.
14. Retrieved from http://www.thirteenvirtues.com
15. Ibid.
16. Lickona, T. (1993). *The return of character education*. Retrieved from http://www.ascd.org/publications/educational-leadership/nov93/vol51/num03/The-Return-of-Character-Education.aspx
17. Berkowitz, M. W. (2002). The science of character education. In W. Damon (Ed.), *Bringing in a new era in character education* (pp. 43–63). Stanford CA: Hoover Institution Press. (pp. 55–56)
18. Ibid.
19. Ibid.
20. Kuh, G. D., & Umbach, P. D. (2004). College and character: Insights from the National Survey of Student Engagement. *New Directions for Institutional Research*, 2004(122), 37–54.
21. Astin, H. S., & Antonio, A. L. (2004). The impact of college on character development. *New Directions for Institutional Research*, 2004(122), 55–64.
22. Berkowitz, M. W. (2002). The science of character education. In W. Damon (Ed.), *Bringing in a new era in character education* (pp. 43–63). Stanford, CA: Hoover Institution Press.
23. Ibid.
24. Stefaner, M. (2010, June 14). Proportional density in visualization. *Well-Formed Data*. Retrieved from http://well-formed-data.net/archives/495/propositional-density-in-visualization
25. Center for Character and Leadership Development. (2011). *Developing leaders of character at the United States Air Force Academy—A conceptual framework*. USAF Academy, CO: Author.
26. Ibid.
27. Schwartz, A. (2015, Summer). Inspiring and equipping students to be ethical leaders. *New Directions for Student Leadership*, 2015(146), 5–16.
28. Jones, T. (1991). Ethical decision-making by individuals in organizations: An issue contingent model. *Academy of Management Review*, 16(2), 366–395.
29. Bandura, A. (1999). Moral disengagement in the perpetration of inhumanities. *Personality and Social Psychology Review*, 3(3), 193–209.
30. Detert, J. R., Trevino, L. K., & Sweitzer, V. L. (2008). Moral disengagement in ethical decision making: A study of antecedents and outcomes. *Journal of Applied Psychology*, 93(2), 374–391. (p. 374)
31. Hannah, S., Avolio, B., & May, D. (2011). Moral maturation and moral conation: A capacity approach to explaining moral thought and action. *Academy of Management Review*, 36(4), 663–685.
32. Schwartz, A. (2015, Summer). Inspiring and equipping students to be ethical leaders. *New Directions for Student Leadership*, 2015(146), 5–16.
33. Lipman-Blumen, J. (2005). The allure of toxic leaders: Why followers rarely escape their clutches. *Ivey Business Journal*. Retrieved from http://iveybusinessjournal.com/publication/the-allure-of-toxic-leaders-why-followers-rarely-escape-their-clutches/ (para. 9)
34. Ibid.
35. I. Challeff, personal communication, January 19, 2016.
36. Carsten, M. K., Uhl-Bien, M., West, B. J., Patera, J. L., & McGregor, R. (2010). Exploring social constructions of followership: A qualitative study. *The Leadership Quarterly*, 21(3), 543–562. (p 551)

37. Carsten, M. K., & Uhl-Bien, M. (2013). Ethical followership: An examination of followership beliefs and crimes of obedience. *Journal of Leadership & Organizational Studies, 20*(1), 49–61.

38. Kelley, R. E. (1988). In praise of followers. *Harvard Business Review, 66,* 142–148.

39. Chaleff, I. (2009). *The courageous follower: Standing up to & for our leaders.* Oakland, CA: Berrett-Koehler.

40. Graber, S. (2015, December 4). The two sides of employee engagement. *Harvard Business Review.* Retrieved from https://hbr.org/2015/12/the-two-sides-of-employee-engagement

41. Center for Character and Leadership Development. (2011). *Developing leaders of character at the United States Air Force Academy—A conceptual framework.* USAF Academy, CO: Author.

42. Schwartz, A. (2015, Summer). Editor's notes. *New Directions for Student Leadership, 2015*(146), 5–16.

43. Gentile, M. C. (2010). Giving voice to values: A brief introduction. Retrieved from http://store.darden.virginia.edu/Syllabus%20Copy/GVV-Brief-Introduction_S.pdf

44. Gentile, M. C. (2010). *Giving voice to values: Speaking your mind when you know what's right.* New Haven, CT: Yale University Press.

45. Hannah, S., Avolio, B. J., & May, D. R. (2011). Moral maturation and moral conation: A capacity approach to explaining moral thought and action. *Academy of Management Review, 36*(4), 663–685.

46. Lau, C. (2010). A step forward: Ethics education matters! *Journal of Business Ethics, 92*(4), 565–584.

47. Johnson, C. E. (2013). *Meeting the ethical challenges of leadership: Casting light or shadow.* Thousand Oaks, CA: Sage.

48. Nash, L. (1981). Ethics without the sermon. *Harvard Business Review, 59,* 79–90.

49. Greenleaf, R. (2002). The servant as leader. In D. Kim (Ed.), *Foresight as the central ethic of leadership* (p. 1). Atlanta, GA: The Greenleaf Center for Servant Leadership.

50. Hannah, S., Avolio, B. J., & May, D. R. (2011). Moral maturation and moral conation: A capacity approach to explaining moral thought and action. *Academy of Management Review, 36*(4), 663–685.

Chapter 5

1. Kouzes, J. M., & Posner, B. Z. (1987). *The leadership challenge: How to get extraordinary things done in organizations.* San Francisco, CA: Jossey-Bass.

2. Graen, G. B., & Uhl-Bien, M. (1995). Relationship-based approach to leadership: Development of leader-member exchange (LMX) theory of leadership over 25 years: Applying a multi-level multi-domain perspective. *The Leadership Quarterly, 6*(2), 219–247; Uhl-Bien, M., & Maslyn, J. M. (2003, January 1). Reciprocity in manager-subordinate relationships: Components, configurations, and outcomes. *Journal of Management, 29*(4), 511–532.

3. Torka, N., Schyns, B., & Looise, J. K. (2010). Direct participation quality and organisational commitment: The role of leader-member exchange. *Employee Relations, 32*(4), 418–434.

4. Othman, R., Ee, F. F., & Shi, N. L. (2010). Understanding dysfunctional leader-member exchange: Antecedents and outcomes. *Leadership & Organization Development Journal, 31*(4), 337–350.

5. IDEO. (2018). *About IDEO.* Retrieved from https://www.ideo.com/about/

6. IDEO. (2018). *Tools.* Retrieved from https://www.ideo.com/by-ideo/#articles

7. Tischler, L. (2009). IDEO's David Kelley on design thinking. *Fast Company.* Retrieved from http://www.fastcodesign.com/1139331/ideos-david-kelley-design-thinking

8. IDEO. (2018). *About IDEO.* Retrieved from https://www.ideo.com/about/

9. Framework based on Dickmann, M., & Stanford-Blair, N. (2003). *Mindful leadership: A brain-based framework.* Thousand Oaks, CA: Corwin.

10. This activity was brilliantly conceived and executed by Dr. Michael Dickmann, Professor Emeritus at Cardinal Stritch University. Many others in this chapter were inspired by the latter.

11. Specifically, there are 43 quintillion variations of the Rubik's cube—that is 43,252,003,274,489,856,000.

12. Robinson, K. (2006). Do schools kill creativity? Retrieved from http://www.ted.com/talks/ken_robinson_says_schools_kill_creativity/transcript?language=en

13. National Institute of Mental Health. (n.d.). *5 things you should know about stress.* Retrieved from http://www.nimh.nih.gov/health/publications/stress/index.shtml; Sanders, L. (2014). New evidence that chronic stress predisposes brain to mental illness. *Berkeley News.* Retrieved from http://news.berkeley.edu/2014/02/11/chronic-stress-predisposes-brain-to-mental-illness/

14. Consortium for Research on Emotional Intelligence in Organizations. (n.d.). *Welcome to the Emotional Intelligence Consortium website.* Retrieved from http://eiconsortium.org/; Six Seconds. (n.d.). The case for emotional intelligence. *Six Seconds.* Retrieved from http://www.6seconds.org/case/

15. Galbraith, J. K. (1971). *A contemporary guide to economics, peace, and laughter.* Boston, MA: Houghton Mifflin.

16. Lidwell, W., Holden, K., & Butler, J. (2010). *The universal principles of design.* Beverly, MA: Rockport Publishers.

17. Tishman, S., Perkins, D. N., & Jay, E. (1995). *The thinking classroom: Learning and teaching in a culture of thinking.* Boston, MA: Allyn & Bacon.

18. Schraw, G. (1998). Promoting general metacognitive awareness. *Instructional Science, 26*(1–2), 113–125.

19. The application ideas are only the beginning—see *Connecting Leadership to the Brain* by M. Dickmann and N. Stanford-Blair (pp. 196–211) for many more specific ideas.

20. Durant, W. (2005). *The story of philosophy: The lives and opinions of the great philosophers of the Western world.* Bremen, Germany: Outlook Verlag. (p. 87)

21. Cross, N. (1982). Designerly ways of knowing. *Design Studies, 3*(4), 221–227; Cross, N. (2010, October 19–20). *Design thinking as a form of intelligence.* Proceedings of the 8th Design Thinking Research Symposium (DTRS8), Sydney, Australia. (pp. 99–105).

22. Kimball, L. (2011). Rethinking design thinking. *Design and Culture, 3*(3), 285–306. doi: 10.2752/175470811X13071166525216 (pp. 290–291)

23. Ibid.

24. Brzozowski, L. (2015, August 4). Innovating a mature product—The Sealy Case. *LinkedIn.* Retrieved from https://www.linkedin.com/pulse/innovating-mature-product-sealy-case-len-brzozowski; Ketter, P. (2016, May). Design thinking: A company's DNA. *TD Magazine.* Retrieved from https://www.td.org/Publications/Magazines/TD/TD-Archive/2016/05/Design-Thinking-a-Companys-DNA

25. Wicked Problems. (n.d.). An introduction to wicked problems. Retrieved from https://www.wickedproblems.com/1_wicked_problems.php

26. Also referred to as the Conscious Competence Matrix or Learning Matrix; most attributed to Noel Burch at Gordon Training International, http://www.gordontraining.com/free-workplace-articles/learning-a-new-skill-is-easier-said-than-done/; and nicely explained here: Mind Tools Content Team. (n.d.). *The conscious competence ladder: Keeping going when learning gets tough.* Retrieved from: https://www.mindtools.com/pages/article/newISS_96.htm

27. http://www.ted.com/talks/tim_harford/transcript?language=en

28. Schwartz, M. A. (2008, January 1). The importance of stupidity in scientific research. *Journal of Cell Science, 101*(11), 1771.

29. Middlebrooks, A. (2016). Global leadership competencies: Inquisitiveness. In M. Mendenhall (Ed.), *International leadership: A reference guide.* Santa Barbara, CA: Mission Bell Media.

30. Gregersen, H. (2016, April 1). When was the last time you asked, "Why are we doing it this way?" *Harvard Business Review.* Retrieved from https://hbr.org/2016/04/when-was-the-last-time-you-asked-why-are-we-doing-it-this-way

31. Smith, K. (2008). *How to be an explorer of the world: Portable life museum.* New York, NY: Penguin. (p. 5)

32. http://www.luckyironfish.com/about-us

33. IDEO. (n.d.). *Design kit: The human-centered design toolkit.* Retrieved from https://www.ideo.com/work/human-centered-design-toolkit/; IDEO. (n.d.). *Method cards.* Retrieved from https://www.ideo.com/work/method-cards

34. IDEO. (n.d.). *Method cards.* Retrieved from https://www.ideo.com/work/method-cards

35. Fidelity. (2016, April 7). *Better quality of work life is worth a $7,600 pay cut for millennials.* Retrieved from https://www.fidelity.com/about-fidelity/individual-investing/better-quality-of-work-life-is-worth-pay-cut-for-millennials

36. Kolko, J. (2014). *Well-designed: How to use empathy to create products people love.* Boston, MA: Harvard Business Review Press.

37. Turnali, K. (2016, January 17). Empathy, design thinking, and an obsession with customer-centric innovation. *Forbes.* Retrieved from http://www.forbes.com/sites/sap/2016/01/17/empathy-design-thinking-and-an-obsession-with-customer-centric-innovation/#5620a4c64285

38. Kellett, J. B., Humphrey, R. H., & Sleeth, R. G. (2002, January 1). Empathy and complex task performance: Two routes to leadership. *The Leadership Quarterly, 13*(5), 523–544.

39. http://www.margaretwheatley.com/articles/listening healing.html

40. Johnson-Laird, P. N. (1983). *Mental models: Towards a cognitive science of language, inference, and consciousness.* Cambridge, UK: Cambridge University Press.

41. Linton, W. J. (1878). *Poetry of America.* London, UK: George Bell & Sons.

42. Gershbein, D. (2014) *Extinction of the expert: How the knowledge economy is changing the innovation game.* Retrieved from http://daoofstrategy.blogspot.com/2014/08/succeeding-in-information-economy-as.html

43. Guest, D. (1991, September 17). The hunt is on for the Renaissance Man of computing. *The Independent.*

44. Martin, R. (2007). How successful leaders think. *Harvard Business Review, 85*(6), 60–7

Chapter 6

1. Stone, B. (2011). Steve Jobs: The return, 1997–2011. *Bloomberg Businessweek.* Retrieved from https://www.bloomberg.com/news/articles/2011-10-06/steve-jobs-the-return-1997-2011

2. Ohnesorge, L. (2016). Report: IBM to sell significant stake in Lenovo. *Triangle Business Journal*. Retrieved from http://www.bizjournals.com/triangle/blog/techflash/2016/03/report-ibm-to-sell-significant-stake-in-lenovo.html

3. Addady, M. (2016). Patagonia's donating all $10 million of its Black Friday sales to charity. *Fortune*. Retrieved from http://fortune.com/2016/11/29/black-friday-2016-patagonia/

4. Mumford, M. D., Zaccaro, S. J., Harding, F. D., Jacobs, T. O., & Fleishman, E. A. (2000). Leadership skills for a changing world: Solving complex social problems. *Leadership Quarterly, 11*(1), 11–35.

5. Blesch, C. (n.d.). Biomedical engineering student leads team to build a prosthesis for little girl's hand. *Rutgers School of Engineering*. Retrieved from http://soe.rutgers.edu/story/biomedical-engineering-student-leads-team-build-prosthesis-little-girl%E2%80%99s-hand (para. 2)

6. Hawkins, A. J. (2016). MIT wins SpaceX's Hyperloop competition, and Elon Musk made a cameo. *The Verge*. Retrieved from http://www.theverge.com/2016/1/30/10877442/elon-musk-spacex-hyperloop-competition-awards

7. iGem. (n.d.). Welcome to iGem. *Internationally Genetically Engineered Machine Competition*. Retrieved from http://igem.org/Main_Page, para. 1.

8. Bender, J. (2015). How college students are advancing the fight against cancer. *From The Grapevine*. Retrieved from http://www.fromthegrapevine.com/innovation/how-college-students-are-advancing-fight-against-cancer#!

9. Bender, J. (2015), para. 3.

10. Pink, D. (n.d.). Pinkcast 1.1: One question to help you make better decisions. Retrieved from https://www.danpink.com/pinkcast/episode-1/

11. Heifetz, R. A., & Linsky, M. (2002). *Leadership on the line: Staying alive through the dangers of leading*. Boston, MA: Harvard Business School Press.

12. Trefis Team. (2014). How the fast casual segment is gaining market share in the restaurant industry. *Forbes*. Retrieved from http://www.forbes.com/sites/greatspeculations/2014/06/23/how-the-fast-casual-segment-is-gaining-market-share-in-the-restaurant-industry/#23f527a1d48f

13. Nutt, P. C. (2002). Selecting decision rules for crucial choices: An investigation of the Thompson framework. *The Journal of Applied Behavioral Science, 38*(1), 99–131.

14. Wansink, B., & Sobal, J. (2007). Mindless eating: The 200 daily food decisions we overlook. *Environment and Behavior, 39*(1), 106–123.

15. Singh, K. (2010). *Organizational behaviour: Text and cases*. New Delhi, India: Dorling Kindersley. Adapted from Maier, N. R. (1967). Assets and liabilities in group problem solving: The need for an integrative function. *Psychological Review, 74*(4), 239–49.

16. Center for Character and Leadership Development. (2011). *Developing leaders of character at the United States Air Force Academy—A conceptual framework*. USAF Academy, CO: Author; Simon, H. A. (1987). Making management decisions: The role of intuition and emotion. *The Academy of Management Executive* (1987–1989), 57–64.

17. Miller, S. J., Hickson, D. J., & Wilson, D. C. (1999). Decision-making in organizations. In S. R. Clegg, C. Hardy, & W. R. Nord (Eds.), *Managing organizations: Current issue* (pp. 43–62). London: SAGE.

18. Simon, H. A. (1987). Making management decisions: The role of intuition and emotion. *The Academy of Management Executive* (1987–1989), 57–64.

19. Hammond, J., Keeney, R., & Raiffa, H. (2002). *Smart choices: A practical guide to making better decisions*. New York, NY: Broadway Press.

20. Doyle, J. (1999). Rational decision-making. In R. A. Wilson & F. C. Kiel (Eds.), *The MIT encyclopedia of the cognitive sciences* (pp. 701–703). Cambridge, MA: The MIT Press; Simon, H. A. (1979). Rational decision-making in business organizations. *The American Economic Review, 69*(4), 493–513.

21. Parker, A. M., De Bruin, W. B., & Fischhoff, B. (2007). Maximizers versus satisficers: Decision-making styles, competence, and outcomes. *Judgment and Decision-Making, 2*(6), 342; Simon, H. A. (1959). Theories of decision-making in economics and behavioral science. *The American Economic Review, 49*(3), 253–283.

22. Dane, E., & Pratt, M. G. (2007). Exploring intuition and its role in managerial decision-making. *Academy of Management Review, 32*(1), 33–54. (p. 40)

23. Mui, C. (2011). Five dangerous lessons to learn from Steve Jobs. *Forbes*. Retrieved from http://www.forbes.com/sites/chunkamui/2011/10/17/five-dangerous-lessons-to-learn-from-steve-jobs/#1821263860da

24. Mintzberg, H., & Westley, F. (2001). Decision-making: It's not what you think. *MIT Sloan Management Review, 42*(3), 89.

25. Hick's Law (Hick-Hyman Law). (n.d.). Retrieved from https://www.usability.gov/what-and-why/glossary/hicks-law-hick-hyman-law.html

26. Vroom, V. H. (2000). Leadership and the decision-making process. *Organizational Dynamics, 28*(4), 82–94.

27. Eisenhardt, K., & Zbaracki, M. (1992). Strategic decision-making. *Strategic Management Journal, 13*, 17–37; Mintzberg, H., Raisinghani, D., & Theoret, A. (1976). The structure of unstructured decisions. *Administrative Science Quarterly, 21*, 246–75; Simon, H. A. (1965). *The shape of automation*. New York, NY: Harper and Row.

28. Hammond, J., Keeney, R., & Raiffa, H. (2002). *Smart choices: A practical guide to making better decisions*. New York, NY: Broadway Press.

29. Beyth-Marom, R., Fischhoff, B., Quadrel, M. J., & Furby, L. (1991). Teaching adolescents decision making. In J. Baron & R. Brown (Eds.), *Teaching decision making to adolescents* (pp. 19–60). Hillsdale, NJ: Erlbaum.

30. Guo, K. L. (2008). DECIDE: A decision-making model for more effective decision-making by health care managers. *The Health Care Manager, 27*(2), 118–127.

31. Kalbar, P. P., Karmakar, S., & Asolekar, S. R. (2012). Selection of an appropriate wastewater treatment technology: A scenario-based multiple-attribute decision-making approach. *Journal of Environmental Management, 113*, 158–169.

32. Saaty, T. L. (2008). Relative measurement and its generalization in decision-making: Why pairwise comparisons are central in mathematics for the measurement of intangible factors—The analytic hierarchy/network process. *RACSAM-Revista de la Real Academia de Ciencias Exactas, Fisicas y Naturales. Serie A: Matematicas, 102*(2), 251–318.

33. Henderson, D. R. (2008). *The concise encyclopedia of economics*. Indianapolis, IN: Liberty Fund.

34. Nickerson, R. S. (1998). Confirmation bias: A ubiquitous phenomenon in many guises. *Review of General Psychology, 2*(2), 175.

35. Snowden, D. J., & Boone, M. E. (2007). A leader's framework for decision-making. *Harvard Business Review, 85*(11), 68.

36. Esser, J. K. (1998). Alive and well after 25 years: A review of groupthink research. *Organizational Behavior and Human Decision Processes, 73*(2), 116–141. (p. 123)

37. McCauley, C. (1989). The nature of social influence in groupthink: Compliance and internalization. *Journal of Personality and Social Psychology, 57*(2), 250.

38. LeBoeuf, R. A., & Shafir, E. (2003). Deep thoughts and shallow frames: On the susceptibility to framing effects. *Journal of Behavioral Decision-Making, 16*(2), 77–92.

39. Dunning, D., Griffin, D. W., Milojkovic, J. D., & Ross, L. (1990). The overconfidence effect in social prediction. *Journal of Personality and Social Psychology, 58*(4), 568.

40. Parkinson, C. N. (1955). *Parkinson's Law*. Retrieved from http://www.berglas.org/Articles/parkinsons_law.pdf

41. Newman, M. (2005). Congress opens hearings on steroid use in baseball. *The New York Times*. Retrieved from http://www.nytimes.com/learning/teachers/featured_articles/20050318friday.html

42. Alloy, L. B., & Abramson, L. Y. (1982). Learned helplessness, depression, and the illusion of control. *Journal of Personality and Social Psychology, 42*(6), 1114.

43. Langer, E. J. (1975). The illusion of control. *Journal of Personality and Social Psychology, 32*(2), 311.

44. Kuhberger, A. (1998). A meta-analysis. *Organizational Behavior and Human Decision Processes, 75*(1), 23–55.

45. Loewenstein, G., & Lerner, J. S. (2003). The role of affect in decision-making. In R. Davidson, H. Goldsmith, & K. Scherer (Eds.), *Handbook of affective science*, (pp. 619–642). Oxford, UK: Oxford University Press; Simon, H. A. (1987). Making management decisions: The role of intuition and emotion. *The Academy of Management Executive (1987–1989)*, 57–64.

46. Heifetz, R. A., & Linsky, M. (2002). *Leadership on the line*. Cambridge, MA: Harvard Business Review. (p. 27)

47. Goleman, D. (2001). Emotional intelligence: Issues in paradigm building. In C. Cherniss & D. Goleman (Eds.), *The emotionally intelligent workplace: How to select for, measure, and improve emotional intelligence in individuals, groups, and organizations* (pp. 13–26). San Francisco, CA: Jossey-Bass.

48. Van Boven, L., Loewenstein, G., Dunning, D., & Nordgren, L. F. (2013). Changing places: A dual judgment model of empathy gaps in emotional perspective taking. *Advances in Experimental Social Psychology, 47*, 117–171. (p. 118)

49. Eisenhardt, K., & Zbaracki, M. (1992, Winter). Strategic decision-making. *Strategic Management Journal, 13*, 17–37.

Chapter 7

1. Harter, N. (2018, August 26). Personal correspondence.

2. Sanders, E., & Stappers, P. J. (2008). Co-creation and the new landscapes of design. *CoDesign, 4*(1), 5–18; Schuler, D., & Namioka, A. (1993). *Participatory design: Principles and practices*. Hillsdale, NJ: Erlbaum.

3. Dugan, J. P. (2017). *Leadership theory: Cultivating critical perspectives*. San Francisco, CA: Jossey-Bass.

4. House, R. J. (1996). Path-goal theory of leadership: Lessons, legacy, and a reformulated theory. *The Leadership Quarterly, 7*(3), 323–352.

5. Northouse, P. G. (2013). *Leadership: Theory and practice* (6th ed.). Thousand Oaks, CA: SAGE.

6. Blanchard, K., Zigarmi, P., & Zigmari, D. (1985). *Leadership and the one minute manager*. New York, NY: Morrow.

7. Chaney, M. (2015). Hazing on school campuses: What parents and students need to know. *The Clay Center for Young Healthy Minds*. Retrieved from http://www.mghclaycenter.org/parenting-concerns/young-adults/hazing-school-campuses-parents-students-need-know/

8. Chaney, M. (2015), para. 1.

9. Higgins, C. A., Judge, T. A., & Ferris, G. R. (2003). Influence tactics and work outcomes. A meta-analysis. *Journal of Organizational Behavior, 24*(1), 89–106.

10. Heifetz, R. A. (2010). Adaptive work. *The Journal of Kansas Civic Leadership Development, 2*(1), 72–77. (p. 72)

11. Ford, J. (2013). Are you being influenced or manipulated? *Psychology Today*. Retrieved from https://www.psychologytoday.com/blog/focus-forgiveness/201309/are-you-being-influenced-or-manipulated

12. Tost, L. P., Gino, F., & Larrick, R. P. (2013). When power makes others speechless: The negative impact of leader power on team performance. *Academy of Management Journal, 56*(5), 1465–1486.

13. Harford, T. (2011). Tim Harford: Trial, error and the God complex [video file]. *Ted.* Retrieved from http://www.ted.com/talks/tim_harford

14. Kotter, J. P., & Schlesinger, L. A. (1979, January 1). Choosing strategies for change. *Harvard Business Review, 57,* 106–114.

15. Allen, K. E., & Mease, W. P. (2001). Optimizing energy: The theory of action energy. Retrieved from https://kathleenallen.net/wp-content/uploads/2017/12/ILA-Energy-Handout.pdf

16. Soegaard, M. (2016). Horror vacui: The fear of emptiness. *The Interaction Design Foundation.* Retrieved from https://www.interaction-design.org/literature/article/horror-vacui-the-fear-of-emptiness

17. https://www.youtube.com/watch?v=e-ORhEE9VVg

18. Lerner, J. S., Li, Y., Valdesolo, P., & Kassam, K. S. (2015). Emotion and decision making. *Annual Review of Psychology, 66,* 799–823.

19. Cable, D. M., & Judge, T. A. (2003). Managers' upward influence tactic strategies: The role of manager personality and supervisor leadership style. *Journal of Organizational Behavior, 24*(2), 197–214.

20. Redelmeier, D. A., & Cialdini, R. B. (2002). Problems for clinical judgement: 5. Principles of influence in medical practice. *Canadian Medical Association Journal, 166*(13), 1680–1684.

21. Yukl, G., & Tracey, J. B. (1992). Consequences of influence tactics used with subordinates, peers, and the boss. *Journal of Applied Psychology, 77*(4), 525.

22. Yukl, G., Kennedy, J., Srinivas, E. S., Cheosakul, A., Peng, T. K., & Tata, J. (2001, August). Cross-cultural comparison of influence behaviour: A preliminary report. *Academy of Management Proceedings, 2001*(1), D1–D6.

23. Pratkanis, A. R. (2007). Social influence analysis: An index of tactics. In A. R. Pratkanis (Ed.), *Frontiers of social psychology. The science of social influence: Advances and future progress* (pp. 17–82). New York, NY: Psychology Press.

24. Falbe, C. M., & Yukl, G. (1992). Consequences for managers of using single influence tactics and combinations of tactics. *Academy of Management Journal, 35*(3), 638–652.

25. Redelmeier, D. A., & Cialdini, R. B. (2002). Problems for clinical judgement: 5. Principles of influence in medical practice. *Canadian Medical Association Journal, 166*(13), 1680–1684.

26. Falbe, C. M., & Yukl, G. (1992). Consequences for managers of using single influence tactics and combinations of tactics. *Academy of Management Journal, 35*(3), 638–652.

27. Plouffe, C. R., Bolander, W., & Cote, J. A. (2014). Which influence tactics lead to sales performance? It is a matter of style. *Journal of Personal Selling & Sales Management, 34*(2), 141–159.

28. Yukl, G., & Tracey, J. B. (1992). Consequences of influence tactics used with subordinates, peers, and the boss. *Journal of Applied Psychology, 77*(4), 525.

29. Riggio, R. (2009). Bosses from hell: A typology of bad leaders. *Psychology Today.* Retrieved from https://www.psychologytoday.com/blog/cutting-edge-leadership/200904/bosses-hell-typology-bad-leaders

30. Riggio, R. (2009). How power corrupts leaders. *Psychology Today.* Retrieved from https://www.psychologytoday.com/blog/cutting-edge-leadership/200908/how-power-corrupts-leaders

31. Rabaut, M. (2016, February 17). Closing in on victory. *Eliminate.* Retrieved from http://www.kiwanis.org/kiwanis/programs/eliminating-maternal-neonatal-tetanus

32. French, J. R. P., Jr., & Raven, B. (1959). The bases of social power. In D. Cartwright (Ed.), *Studies in social power* (pp. 150–167). Ann Arbor, MI: Institute for Social Research.

33. Yukl, G., & Falbe, C. M. (1991). Importance of different power sources in downward and lateral relations. *Journal of Applied Psychology, 76*(3), 416.

34. Mechanic, D. (1962). Sources of power of lower participants in complex organizations. *Administrative Science Quarterly, 7*(3), 349–364.

35. French, J. R., Raven, B., & Cartwright, D. (1959). The bases of social power. *Classics of Organization Theory,* 311–320.

36. Bal, V., Campbell, M., Steed, J., & Meddings, K. (2008). The role of power in effective leadership. *Center for Creative Leadership.* Retrieved from http://insights.ccl.org/wp-content/uploads/2015/04/roleOfPower.pdf

37. Ibid.

38. Ibarra, H., & Hunter, M. L. (2007). How leaders create and use networks. Retrieved from https://hbr.org/2007/01/how-leaders-create-and-use-networks

39. Whetten, D. A., & Cameron, K. S. (2011). *Developing management skills.* Upper Saddle River, NJ: Prentice Hall/Pearson.

40. French, J. R. P., Jr., & Raven, B. (1959). The bases of social power. In D. Cartwright (Ed.), *Studies in social power* (pp. 150–167). Ann Arbor, MI: Institute for Social Research.

41. Ryan, R. M., & Deci, E. L. (2000). Intrinsic and extrinsic motivations: Classic definitions and new directions. *Contemporary Educational Psychology, 25*(1), 54–67. (p. 54)

42. Deci, E. L. (1971). Effects of externally mediated rewards on intrinsic motivation. *Journal of Personality and Social Psychology, 18*(1), 105.

43. Deci, E. L., Koestner, R., & Ryan, R. M. (1999). A meta-analytic review of experiments examining the effects of extrinsic rewards on intrinsic motivation. *Psychological Bulletin, 125*(6), 627.

44. Cerasoli, C. P., Nicklin, J. M., & Ford, M. T. (2014). Intrinsic motivation and extrinsic incentives jointly predict performance: A 40-year meta-analysis. *Psychological Bulletin, 140*(4), 1–20.

45. Chamorro-Premuzic, T. (2013, April 10). Does money really affect motivation? A review of the research. *Harvard Business Review Blog Network.* Retrieved from https://hbr.org/2013/04/does-money-really-affect-motiv; Judge, T. A., Piccolo, R. F., Podsakoff, N. P., Shaw, J. C., & Rich, B. L. (2010). The relationship between pay and job satisfaction: A meta-analysis of the literature. *Journal of Vocational Behavior, 77*(2), 157–167; Katzenbach, J. R., & Khan, Z. (2010). Money is not the best motivator. *Forbes.* Retrieved from http://www.forbes.com/2010/04/06/money-motivation-pay-leadership-managing-employees.html

46. Coffee & Company. (2016, July 18). Starbucks expands health benefits for all eligible U.S. full- and part-time partners. *Starbucks Newsroom.* Retrieved from https://news.starbucks.com/press-releases/starbucks-expands-health-benefits

47. Branson, C. M. (2008). Achieving organisational change through values alignment. *Journal of Educational Administration, 46*(3), 376–395.

48. Michaelson, C. (2010). The importance of meaningful work. *MIT Sloan Management Review.* Retrieved from http://sloanreview.mit.edu/article/the-importance-of-meaningful-work/

49. Isaac, R. G., Zerbe, W. J., & Pitt, D. C. (2001). Leadership and motivation: The effective application of expectancy theory. *Journal of Managerial Issues, 13*(2), 212–226.

50. Cacioppe, R. (1999). Using team-individual reward and recognition strategies to drive organizational success. *Leadership & Organization Development Journal, 20*(6), 322–331.

51. Sohail, M., & Malik, S. A. (2016). Impact of leader-follower interactions and employee satisfaction: Mediating effect of employee empowerment. *International Journal of Complexity in Leadership and Management, 3*(1–2), 85–100.

52. Conger, J. A., & Kanungo, R. N. (1988). The empowerment process: Integrating theory and practice. *Academy of Management Review, 13*, 471–482.

53. Adkins, A. (2016). Employee engagement in U.S. stagnant in 2015. *Gallup.* Retrieved from http://www.gallup.com/poll/188144/employee-engagement-stagnant-2015.aspx (para. 3)

54. Clifton, J. (2016). Unhappy state, local government workers cost U.S. billions. *Gallup.* Retrieved from http://www.gallup.com/opinion/gallup/193490/unhappy-state-local-government-workers-cost-billions.aspx?g_source=EMPLOYEE_ENGAGEMENT&g_medium=topic&g_campaign=tiles

55. Nohria, N., Groysberg, B., & Lee, L. E. (2008). Employee motivation. *Harvard Business Review, 86*(7/8), 78–84.

56. McClelland, D. C. (1961). *The achieving society.* New York, NY: Free Press.

57. Seifert, M., Brockner, J., Bianchi, E. C., & Moon, H. (2016). How workplace fairness affects employee commitment. *MIT Sloan Management Review, 57*(2), 15–17.

58. Hogg, M. A. (2001). A social identity theory of leadership. *Personality and Social Psychology Review, 5*(3), 184–200.

59. Hackman, J. R., & Oldham, G. R. (1976). Motivation through the design of work: Test of a theory. *Organizational Behavior and Human Performance, 16*(2), 250–279.

60. Ibid.

61. Barney, C. E., & Elias, S. M. (2010). Flex-time as a moderator of the job stress-work motivation relationship: A three nation investigation. *Personnel Review, 39*(4), 487–502.

62. Watts, G. A. (1992). Work values, attitudes and motivations of women employed in administrative support occupations. *Journal of Career Development, 19*(1), 49–64.

63. Nembhard, I. M., & Edmondson, A. C. (2006). Making it safe: The effects of leader inclusiveness and professional status on psychological safety and improvement efforts in health care teams. *Journal of Organizational Behavior, 27*(7), 941–966.

Chapter 8

1. Carasco-Saul, M., Kim, W., & Kim, T. (2015). Leadership and employee engagement: Proposing research agendas through a review of literature. *Human Resource Development Review, 14*(1), 38–63.

2. Jin, M., McDonald, B., & Park, J. (2016). Followership and job satisfaction in the public sector: The moderating role of perceived supervisor support and performance-oriented culture. *International Journal of Public Sector Management, 29*(3), 218–237.

3. Gallup. (n.d.). *Gallup employee engagement center.* Retrieved from https://q12.gallup.com/

4. Gallup. (n.d.). *State of the American manager.* Retrieved from http://www.gallup.com/services/182138/state-american-manager.aspx

5. Aon Hewitt. (2015, June). *Say, stay, or strive? Unleash the engagement outcome you need.* Retrieved from http://www.aon.com/attachments/human-capital-consulting/2015-Drivers-of-Say-Stay-Strive.pdf

6. Seppala, E., & Cameron, K. (2015, December 1). Proof that positive work cultures are more productive. *Harvard Business Review.* Retrieved from https://hbr.org/2015/12/proof-that-positive-work-cultures-are-more-productive

7. Eiseley, L. C. (1969). *The unexpected universe.* New York, NY: Harcourt, Brace & World.

8. World Economic Forum. (2016, January 18). *The future of jobs.* Retrieved from https://www.weforum.org/reports/the-future-of-jobs/

9. https://www.wurman.com/

10. https://www.design.upenn.edu/alumni/events/2015-lisa-roberts-david-seltzer-integrated-product-design-lecture-richard-saul-wurman

11. TED Conferences, LLC. (n.d.). *History of TED.* Retrieved from https://www.ted.com/about/our-organization/history-of-ted

12. https://www.ted.com/about/our-organization/history-of-ted

13. Wurman, R. S. (2009). *33: Understanding change & the change in understanding.* Norcross, GA: Greenway Communications.

14. Madjar, N., Greenberg, E., & Chen, Z. (2011). Factors for radical creativity, incremental creativity, and routine, noncreative performance. *Journal of Applied Psychology, 96*(4), 730–743.

15. Mueller, J. S., Melwani, S., & Goncalo, J. A. (2012). The bias against creativity: Why people desire but reject creative ideas. *Psychological Science, 23*(1), 13–17.

16. May, M. (2016, April 14). Ideacide: The perils of self-censoring (and how you can stop it). *99u.* Retrieved from http://99u.com/articles/53751/ideacide-the-perils-of-self-censoring-and-how-you-can-stop-it

17. Olien, J. (2013, December 6). Inside the box: People don't actually like creativity. *Slate.* Retrieved from http://www.slate.com/articles/health_and_science/science/2013/12/creativity_is_rejected_teachers_and_bosses_don_t_value_out_of_the_box_thinking.html

18. Michalko, M. (2011). *Creative thinkering: Putting your imagination to work.* Novato, CA: New World Library; Michalko, M. (2011, December 11). *The twelve things you are not taught in school about creative thinking.* Retrieved from http://creativethinking.net/the-twelve-things-you-are-not-taught-in-school-about-creative-thinking/#sthash.UJt7sQFv.dpbs

19. Gonzalez, C., Dana, J., Koshino, H., & Just, M. (2005, January 1). The framing effect and risky decisions: Examining cognitive functions with fMRI. *Journal of Economic Psychology, 26*(1), 1–20.

20. Ackoff, R. L., Magidson, J., & Addison, H. J. (2006). *Idealized design: Creating an organization's future.* Upper Saddle River, NJ: Wharton School.

21. Brown, M. W., & Weisgard, L. (1949). *The important book.* New York, NY: Harper.

22. Drucker, P. F. (1963). *Managing for business effectiveness.* Boston, MA: Harvard University.

23. For an overview of research connecting personality characteristics and traits to creativity, read among others: Runco, M. A. (2014). *Creativity: Theories and themes: Research, development, and practice* (2nd ed.). Amsterdam, Netherlands: Elsevier Academic Press.

24. Guilford, J. P. (1960). *Alternate uses, Form A.* Beverly Hills, CA: Sheridan Supply; Barron, F. (1963). *Creativity and psychological health.* Oxford, UK: Van Nostrand.

25. Loyd, S. (1976). *Sam Loyd's cyclopedia of 5000 puzzles, tricks and conundrums: With answers.* New York, NY: Pinnacle.

26. Vance, M., & Deacon, D. (1995). *Think out of the box.* Franklin Lakes, NJ: Career Press.

27. Kelley, T., & Kelley, D. (2013). *Creative confidence: Unleashing the creative potential within us all.* New York, NY: Crown Business.

28. Kelley, T., & Kelley, D. (2012, December). Reclaim your creative confidence. *Harvard Business Review.* Retrieved from https://hbr.org/2012/12/reclaim-your-creative-confidence

29. Wallas, G. (1926). *The art of thought.* New York, NY: Harcourt, Brace and Company.

30. Young, J. W. (1986). *A technique for producing ideas.* Lincolnwood, IL: NTC Business Books.

31. Creating Innovative Thinkers. (n.d.). Retrieved from http://www.creativeeducationfoundation.org/

32. Osborn, A. F. (1952). *Wake up your mind: 101 ways to develop creativeness.* New York, NY: Scribner.

33. von Oech, R. (1983). *A whack on the side of the head: How to unlock your mind for innovation.* New York, NY: Warner Books; von Oech, R. (1986). *A kick in the seat of the pants: Using your explorer, artist, judge, & warrior to be more creative.* New York, NY: Perennial Library.

34. von Oech, R. (1986), p. 16.

35. Johnson, S. (2010, July). Where good ideas come from. *TED Global 2010.* Retrieved from http://www.ted.com/talks/steven_johnson_where_good_ideas_come_from/transcript?language=en; Johnson, S. (2010). *Where good ideas come from: The natural history of innovation.* New York, NY: Riverhead Books.

36. Osborn, A. F. (1963). *Applied imagination: Principles and procedures of creative problem-solving.* New York, NY: Scribner.

37. Eberle, B. (1996). *Scamper: Games for imagination development.* Waco, TX: Prufrock Press.

38. Thanks to Nat Measely and the Fun Dept for this example, which they use to create fun *deliveries.*

39. Brown, T. (2008). Tales of creativity and play. *TED.* Retrieved from http://www.ted.com/talks/tim_brown_on_creativity_and_play

40. The Biomimicry Institute—Inspiring Sustainable Innovation. (n.d.). Retrieved from https://biomimicry.org/

41. The Biomimicry Institute (n.d.). *Biomimicry 101, biomimicry examples.* Retrieved from https://biomimicry.org/biomimicry-examples/#.WAqWx4WcHIU

42. von Oech, R. (1986). *A kick in the seat of the pants*. New York, NY: Perennial Library.
43. Culatta, R. (n.d.). Iterative design. *Instructionaldesign.org*. Retrieved from http://www.instructionaldesign.org/models/iterative_design.html
44. Baas, M., De Dru, C. K. W., & Nijstad, B. A. (2008, January 1). A meta-analysis of 25 years of mood-creativity research: Hedonic tone, activation, or regulatory focus? *Psychological Bulletin, 134*(6), 779–806.
45. von Oech, R. (1986). *A kick in the seat of the pants: Using your explorer, artist, judge, & warrior to be more creative*. New York, NY: Perennial Library. (p. 143)

Chapter 9

1. Fishman, M. (2015, November 25). Horizon Services co-owner grounded in gratitude. *Wilmington News Journal*. Retrieved from http://www.delawareonline.com/story/news/local/2015/11/25/grounded-gratitude/76316706/
2. Cooperrider, D. L., & Whitney, D. K. (2005). *Appreciative inquiry: A positive revolution in change*. San Francisco, CA: Berrett-Koehler.
3. Smith, J. (2013). 20 people skills you need to succeed at work. *Forbes*. Retrieved from http://www.forbes.com/sites/jacquelynsmith/2013/11/15/the-20-people-skills-you-need-to-succeed-at-work/2/#6da3723
4. Hinchcliffe, D. (2013). Today's enterprise collaboration landscape: Cloudy, social, mobile. *ZDNet*. Retrieved from http://www.zdnet.com/article/todays-enterprise-collaboration-landscape-cloudy-social-mobile/
5. Catalyst. (2016, October). *Women earn more degrees than men*. New York, NY: Catalyst; Snyder, T. D., & Dillow, S. A. (2012). *Digest of education statistics 2011 (NCES 2012–001)*. Washington, DC: National Center for Education Statistics, Institute of Education Sciences, U.S. Department of Education.
6. Ely, R. J., Ibarra, H., & Kolb, D. M. (2011). Taking gender into account: Theory and design for women's leadership development programs [Special Issue]. *Academy of Management Learning & Education, 10*(3) 474–493.
7. DeFrank-Cole, L., & Tan, S. J. (2017). Reimagining leadership for millennial women: Perspectives across generations. *Journal of Leadership Studies, 10*(4), 43–46.
8. Ibid.
9. Eagly, A. J., Johannesen-Schmidt, M. C., & van Engen, M. L. (2003). Transformational, transactional, and laissez-faire leadership styles: A meta-analysis comparing women and men. *Psychological Bulletin, 129*(4), 569–591.
10. Eagly, A. H., Karau, S. J., & Makhijani, M. G. (1995). Gender and the effectiveness of leaders: A meta-analysis. *Psychological Bulletin, 117*(1), 125–145.
11. Eagly, A. H., & Karau, S. J. (2002). Role congruity theory of prejudice toward female leaders. *Psychological Review, 109*(3), 573–598.
12. Bohnet, I. (2016). *What works: Gender equality by design*. Cambridge, MA: Belknap Press; Eagly, A. H., & Heilman, M. E. (Eds.). (2016). Gender and leadership: An introduction to the special issue [Special Issue]. *The Leadership Quarterly, 27*(3), 349–353; Eagly, A. H., & Karau, S. J. (2002). Role congruity theory of prejudice toward female leaders. *Psychological Review, 109*(3), 573–598; Heilman, M. E. (2001). Description and prescription: How gender stereotypes prevent women's ascent up the organizational ladder. *Journal of Social Issues, 57*(4), 657–674.
13. Eagly, A. H., & Karau, S. J. (2002). Role congruity theory of prejudice toward female leaders. *Psychological Review, 109*(3), 573–598; Heilman, M. E. (2001). Description and prescription: How gender stereotypes prevent women's ascent up the organizational ladder. *Journal of Social Issues, 57*(4), 657–674.
14. Eagly, A. H., & Karau, S. J. (2002). Role congruity theory of prejudice toward female leaders. *Psychological Review, 109*(3), 573–598; Hoyt, C. L. (2010). Women, men, and leadership: Exploring the gender gap at the top. *Social and Personality Psychology Compass, 4*(7), 484–498.
15. Kan, M. Y., Sullivan, O., & Gershuny, J. (2011). Gender convergence in domestic work: Discerning the effects of interactional and institutional barriers from large-scale data. *Sociology, 45*(2), 234–51.
16. Hoyt, C. L. (2010). Women, men, and leadership: Exploring the gender gap at the top. *Social and Personality Psychology Compass, 4*(7), 484–498.
17. Hoffman, L. R., & Maier, N. (1961). Quality and acceptance of problem solutions by members of homogeneous and heterogeneous groups. *Journal of Abnormal and Social Psychology, 62*(2), 401–407.
18. Kanter, R. (2013). Three things that actually motivate employees. *Harvard Business Review*. Retrieved from https://hbr.org/2013/10/three-things-that-actually-motivate-employees
19. Kanter, R. (2004). *Confidence: How winning streaks and losing streaks begin and end*. New York, NY: Crown Publishing Group.
20. Burns-Callander, R. (2015, January). Unilever boss Paul Polman slams capitalist obsession with profit. *The Telegraph*. Retrieved from https://www.telegraph.co.uk/finance/newsbysector/epic/ulvr/11372550/Unilever-boss-Paul-Polman-slams-capitalist-obsession-with-profit.html
21. Gotkin, Z. (2012, December 17). America's innovative companies are going flat. *Huffpost Business*. Retrieved from https://www.huffingtonpost.com/zev-gotkin/corporate-hierarchy-work_b_1962345.html

22. Riftkin, J. (2011). *The third industrial revolution: How lateral power is transforming energy, the economy, and the world.* New York, NY: St. Martin's Press. (p. 291)

23. Riftkin, J. (2011), p. 215.

24. Graen, G., & Uhl-Bien, M. (1995). Relationship-based approach to leadership: Development of leader-member exchange (LMX) theory of leadership over 25 years: Applying a multi-level multi-domain perspective. *Leadership Quarterly, 6*(2), 219–241.

25. Kouzes, J., & Posner, B. (2012). *The leadership challenge* (5th ed.). San Francisco, CA: Jossey-Bass.

26. Quotes by Jack Welch can be retrieved from https://www.goodreads.com/author/quotes/3770.Jack_Welch

27. Graen, G., & Uhl-Bien, M. (1995). Relationship-based approach to leadership: Development of leader-member exchange (LMX) theory of leadership over 25 years: Applying a multi-level multi-domain perspective. *Leadership Quarterly, 6*(2), 219–241.

28. Quotes by Jack Welch can be retrieved from https://www.goodreads.com/author/quotes/3770.Jack_Welch

29. Collins, J. (2011). *Great by choice.* New York: NY: HarperCollins.

30. Conger, J., & Benjamin, B. (1999). *Building leaders: How successful companies develop the next generation.* San Francisco, CA: Jossey-Bass.

31. Levering, R. (2016, March 3). This year's best employers have focused on fairness. *Fortune, 173*(4).

32. Conger, J., & Benjamin, B. (1999). *Building leaders: How successful companies develop the next generation.* San Francisco, CA: Jossey-Bass.

33. Senik, S. (2009). How great leaders inspire action. *TED.* Retrieved from https://www.ted.com/talks/simon_sinek_how_great_leaders_inspire_action?language=en

34. Annual Report. (2014). *What is a benefit corporation?* Retrieved from https://bcorporation.net/about-b-corps

35. Krueger, K. (2016, April 12). Freelance workers are the new HR disruptors, Deloitte Human Capital Trends 2016. *LinkedIn.* Retrieved from https://www.linkedin.com/pulse/freelance-workers-new-hr-disruptors-deloitte-human-capital-krueger-6123247708862959616

36. Senge, P. (2006). *The fifth discipline: The art and practices of a learning organization.* New York, NY: Crown Business Publishers.

37. Buckley, P., Viechnicki, P., & Barua, A. (2016). A new understanding of Millennials: Generational differences reexamined. *Deloitte Insights.* Retrieved from https://www2.deloitte.com/insights/us/en/economy/issues-by-the-numbers/understanding-millennials-generational-differences.html

38. Blanchard, K., Hersey, P., & Johnson, D. (2012). *Management of organizational behavior.* Upper Saddle River, NJ: Pearson-Prentice Hall.

39. Ibid.

40. Anderson, M. (2015, October 29). Technology device ownership: 2015. *Pew Research Center.* Retrieved from http://www.pewinternet.org/2015/10/29/technology-device-ownership-2015/

41. Porter, L., & McLaughlin, G. (2006). Leadership and the organizational context: Like the weather? *The Leadership Quarterly, 17*(6), 559–576.

42. McLaughlin, D. (2016). Developing an attractive work cultures is key to performance. *Smart Business Online.* Retrieved from http://www.sbnonline.com/article/126024/

Chapter 10

1. Donaldson, K. (2011). 40 under 40: Krista Donaldson. *Silicon Valley Business Journal.* Retrieved from http://www.bizjournals.com/sanjose/news/2011/11/28/40-under-40-krista-donaldson.html

2. Dinwoodie, D., Pasmore, W., Quinn, L., & Rabin, R. (2015). Navigating change: A leader's role. *Center for Creative Leadership* (White Paper). Retrieved from https://www.ccl.org/wp-content/uploads/2015/02/NavigatingChange.pdf

3. Kübler-Ross, E. (1969). *On death and dying.* New York, NY: Touchstone.

4. Danes, S. (1993). Change: Loss, opportunity, and resilience. *University of Minnesota Extension.* Retrieved from https://conservancy.umn.edu/bitstream/handle/11299/118663/1/Danes.pdf

5. Prochaska, J. O., Redding, C. A., & Evers, K. (2002). The transtheoretical model and stages of change. In K. Glanz, B. K. Rimer, & F. M. Lewis (Eds.), *Health behavior and health education: Theory, research, and practice* (3rd ed.). San Francisco, CA: Jossey-Bass.

6. Goodstein, L., & Burke, W. (1991). Creating successful organization change. *Organizational Dynamics, 19*(4), 5–17.

7. ProSci. (2005). *Change management toolkit: Using Prosci's ADKAR model for managing the people side of change.* Fort Collins, CO: Author. Also see https://www.prosci.com/adkar

8. Lieberman, M. (2013). *Social: Why our brains are wired to connect.* New York, NY: Crown Publishers.

9. Aiken, C., & Keller, S. (2009, April). The irrational side of change management. *McKinsey Quarterly.* Retrieved from https://www.mckinsey.com/business-functions/organization/our-insights/the-irrational-side-of-change-management

10. http://www.get2test.net/index.html#academic; Courtney, H., Lovallo, D., & Clarke, C. (2013, November). Deciding how to decide. *Harvard Business Review.* Retrieved from https://hbr.org/2013/11/deciding-how-to-decide

11. Beaudan, E. (2006, January/February). Making change last: How to get beyond change fatigue. *IVEY Business Journal.* Retrieved from https://iveybusinessjournal.com/publication/making-change-last-how-to-get-beyond-change-fatigue/

12. Higgs, M., & Rowland, D. (2011). What does it take to implement change successfully? A study of the behaviors of successful change leaders. *Journal of Applied Behavioral Science, 47*(3), 309–335.

13. Odumeru, J. A., & Ogbonna, I. G. (2013). Transformational vs. transactional leadership theories: Evidence in the literature. *International Review of Management and Business Research, 2*(2), 355–361.

14. Burns, J. M. (1978). *Leadership.* New York, NY: Harper & Row.

15. Maslow, A. H. (1943). A theory of human motivation. *Psychological Review, 50,* 370–396.

16. Bass, B. M., & Avolio, B. J. (1994). *Improving organizational effectiveness through transformational leadership.* Thousand Oaks, CA: Sage.

17. Ibid.

18. Ibid.

19. Kotter, J. (2007, July). Leading change: Why transformational efforts fail. *Harvard Business Review,* 59–67.

20. Fullan, M. (1982). *The meaning of educational change.* New York, NY: Teachers College Press; Fullan, M., & Stiegelbauer, S. (1991). *The new meaning of educational change* (2nd ed.). New York, NY: Teachers College Press; Miles, M. B., & American Educational Research Association. (1986). *Implementing change, toward a data-based theory.* Chicago, IL: Teach'em.

21. Ewenstein, B., Smith, W., & Sologar, A. (2015, July). Changing change management. *McKinsey & Company.* Retrieved from http://www.mckinsey.com/global-themes/leadership/changing-change-management

22. Gladwell, M. (2000). *The tipping point: How little things can make a big difference.* Boston, MA: Little, Brown and Company.

23. Heath, C., & Heath, D. (2007). *Made to stick: Why some ideas survive and others die.* New York, NY: Random House.

24. Kotter, J. P. (1996). *Leading change.* Boston, MA: Harvard Business School Press.

25. Sloane, P. (2006). *The leader's guide to lateral thinking skills: Unlocking the creativity and innovation in you and your team.* London, UK: Kogan Page.

26. Ewenstein, B., Smith, W., & Sologar, A. (2015). Changing change management. *McKinsey & Company.* Retrieved from http://www.mckinsey.com/global-themes/leadership/changing-change-management

27. Kerzner, H. (2009). *Project management: A systems approach to planning, scheduling and controlling.* New York, NY: John Wiley.

28. Ibid.

29. Carroll, J. M. (1983). Presentation and form in user interface architecture. *Byte, 8*(12), 113–122; Carroll, J. M., & Carrithers, C. (1984). Blocking learner error states in a training-wheels system. *Human Factors, 26*(4), 377–389.

30. Tierney, P. (1988). Work relations as a precursor to a psychological climate for change: The role of work group supervisors and peers. *Journal of Organizational Change Management, 12*(2), 120–133.

31. Lynch, P. (2010). 7 ways to achieve lasting behavioral change. *Business Alignment Strategies, Inc.* Retrieved from http://www.businessalignmentstrategies.com/articles/behavioral-change.php

Chapter 11

1. Collins, J. C. (2001). *Good to great: Why some companies make the leap… and others don't.* New York, NY: Harper Business.

2. Heath, C., & Heath, D. (2007). *Made to stick: Why some ideas survive and others die.* New York, NY: Random House. (p. 145)

3. Heath, C., & Heath, D. (2007), p. 144.

4. Frog Design. (n.d.). *We are a global design, innovation and strategy firm.* Retrieved from http://www.frogdesign.com/work/frog-collective-action-toolkit.html

5. Drucker, P. F., & Drucker, P. F. (2010). *The five most important questions self-assessment tool: Participant workbook.* San Francisco, CA: Jossey-Bass.

6. Drucker, P. F. (2016). *The Peter F. Drucker reader: Selected articles from the father of modern management thinking.* Boston, MA: Harvard Business School Press.

7. Hurson, T. (2008). *Think better (your company's future depends on it—and so does yours): An innovator's guide to productive thinking.* New York, NY: McGraw-Hill.

8. http://www.endangeredalphabets.com/

9. Endangered Alphabets. (n.d.). *Why we care.* Retrieved from http://www.endangeredalphabets.com/about-us/why-we-care/

10. Bersin, J. (2015, July/August). *The new culture wars.* Retrieved from http://www.hrpatoday.ca/article/the-new-culture-wars.html

11. Hall, E. T. (1981). *Beyond culture.* New York, NY: Anchor Books.

12. Cameron, K. S., & Quinn, R. E. (2011). *Diagnosing and changing organizational culture: Based on the competing values framework* (3rd ed.). San Francisco, CA: Jossey-Bass.

13. Bersin, J. (2015, July/August). The new culture wars: Becoming irresistible through year-round engagement. *HR Professional, 32*(5), 33–34.

14. Bremer, M. (2015, August 28). Edgar Schein on culture. *Leadership & Change.* Retrieved from

https://www.leadershipandchangemagazine.com/
edgar-schein-on-culture/

15. Schein, E. H. (2004). Organizational climate and culture. In G. R. Goethals, G. J. Sorenson, & J. M. Burns (Eds.), *Encyclopedia of leadership* (pp. 1113–1117). Thousand Oaks, CA: Sage.

16. Deal, T. E., & Kennedy, A. A. (2000). *Corporate cultures: The rites and rituals of corporate life.* New York, NY: Perseus Books.

17. Schein, E. H. (2010). *Organizational culture and leadership.* San Francisco, CA: John Wiley.

18. Janicijevic, N. (2011). Methodological approaches in the research of organizational culture. *Economic Annals, 56*(189), 69–99.

19. Cronin, T. E., & Genovese, M. A. (2012). *Leadership matters: Unleashing the power of paradox.* Boulder, CO: Paradigm Publishers.

20. Hall, E. T. (1989). *Beyond culture.* New York, NY: Random House.

21. Ibid.

22. Hofstede, G., Hofstede, G. J., & Minkov, M. (2010). *Cultures and organizations: Software of the mind: Intercultural cooperation and its importance for survival.* New York, NY: McGraw-Hill. (p. 6)

23. House, R. J., Hanges, P. J., Javidan, M., Dorfman, P. W., & Gupta, V. (2004). *Culture, leadership and organizations: The GLOBE study of 62 societies.* Thousand Oaks, CA: Sage.

24. Ibid., pp. 17–18.

25. Wong, K.–C. (2001). Chinese culture and leadership. *International Journal of Leadership in Education, 4*(4), 309–19.

26. Wong, Y. H. (1998). The dynamics of Guanxi in China. *Singapore Management Review, 20*(2), 25–42.

27. Huang, D. H. (2010). Leadership in China: Challenges and practice. In D. Dotlich, P. Cairo, R. Meeks, & Oliver Wyman Leadership Development (Eds.), *The 2010 Pfeiffer annual: Leadership development for the new economy* (pp. 59–71). San Francisco, CA: Wiley.

28. Gallo, F. T. (2011). *Business leadership in China: How to blend best Western practice with Chinese wisdom.* Singapore: Wiley.

29. George, B. (2003). *Authentic leadership: Rediscovering the secrets to creating lasting value.* San Francisco, CA: Jossey-Bass.

30. Bennis, W., & Goldsmith, J. (2010). *Learning to lead: A workbook on becoming a leader* (4th ed.). New York, NY: Basic Books.

31. Fairholm, M. R. (2013). *Putting your values to work: Becoming the leader others want to follow.* Santa Barbara, CA: Praeger.

32. Cameron, K. S., & Quinn, R. E. (2011). *Diagnosing and changing organizational culture: Based on the competing values framework.* San Francisco, CA: Jossey-Bass.

33. Cronin, T. E., & Genovese, M. A. (2012). *Leadership matters: Unleashing the power of paradox.* Boulder, CO: Paradigm Publishers.

34. Zappos Insights. (2014). *Zappos culture book, 2014.* Retrieved from http://www.zapposinsights.com/culture-book/digital-version/download-cb

35. Zappos. (2014), p. 18.

36. Google. (n.d.). *Ten things we know to be true.* Retrieved from https://www.google.com/about/philosophy.html

37. Bennis, W. (2009). *On becoming a leader.* Philadelphia, PA: Perseus Book Group.

38. McGuire, J. G., Palus, D. J., Pasmore, W., & Rhodes, G. B. (n.d.). *Transforming your organization* (White Paper). Greensboro, NC: Center for Creative Leadership. Retrieved from: https://www.ccl.org/articles/white-papers/transforming-your-organization/

39. Cawsey, T. F., Desza, G., & Ingols, C. (2016). *Organizational change: An action-oriented toolkit.* Thousand Oaks, CA: Sage.

40. Kotter, J. P. (2012). *Leading change.* Boston, MA: Harvard Business Review Press.

41. Bennis, W. (2009). *On becoming a leader.* Philadelphia, PA: Perseus Book Group.

42. Stavros, J. M., Godwin, L. N., & Cooperrider, D. L. (2015, January 1). Appreciative inquiry: Organization development and the strengths revolution. In W. Rothwell, J. Stavros, & R. Sullivan (Eds.), *Practicing organization development: Leading transformation and change* (4th ed., pp. 96–116). Hoboken, NJ: Wiley; More information on AI can be found at https://www.centerforappreciativeinquiry.net/ and https://appreciativeinquiry.champlain.edu/

43. Whitney, D., & Trosten-Bloom, A. (2010). *The power of appreciative inquiry: A practical guide to positive change.* San Francisco, CA: Berrett-Koehler.

44. Kotter, J. P. (2012). *Leading change.* Boston, MA: Harvard Business Review Press.

Chapter 12

1. Bennis, W. (1997, December 1). The secrets of great groups. *Leader to Leader, 3*, 29–33. (p. 29)

2. Bennis, W. (1997), p. 29.

3. Iny, D. (2016, March). 10 habits of successfully remote teams. *Inc.com.* Retrieved from http://www.inc.com/danny-iny/10-habits-of-highly-successful-remote-teams.html

4. Ibid.

5. Iny, D. (2016, March), para. 9.

6. Day, D. V., Gronn, P., & Salas, E. (2004). Leadership capacity in teams. *The Leadership Quarterly, 15*(6), 857–880; Katzenback, J. R., & Smith, D. K. (2003). *The wisdom of teams.* New York, NY: HarperCollins;

Larson, C. E., & LaFasto, F. M. J. (1989). *Teamwork: What must go right, what can go wrong.* Newbury Park, CA: Sage.

7. Boss, J. (2016, July). Accelerate your understanding of teams with these 3 facts. *Forbes.com.* Retrieved from http://www.forbes.com/sites/jeffboss/2016/07/25/accelerate-your-understanding-of-teams-with-these-3-facts/#4c533f6a44ed

8. Ibid.

9. Day, D. V., Gronn, P., & Salas, E. (2004). Leadership capacity in teams. *The Leadership Quarterly, 15*(6), 857–880.

10. Dyer, W. G., Dyer, J. H., & Dyer, W. G. (2013). *Team building: Proven strategies for improving team performance.* San Francisco, CA: Jossey-Bass; Wheelan, S. A. (2010). *Creating effective teams: A guide for members and leaders.* Thousand Oaks, CA: Sage.

11. Ibid.

12. Shumpter, J. (2016, March). Team spirit. *The Economist.* Retrieved from http://www.economist.com/news/business-and-finance/21694962-managing-them-hard-businesses-are-embracing-idea-working-teams

13. Amos, B., & Klimoski, R. J. (2014). Courage: Making teamwork work well. *Group & Organizational Management, 39*(1), 110–128. doi: 10.1177/1059601113520407

14. Berry, G. R. (2011). Enhancing effectiveness on virtual teams: Understanding why traditional team skills are insufficient. *Journal of Business Communication, 48*(2), 186–206.

15. Blanchard, K., Carew, D., & Parisi-Carew, E. (1996). How to get your group to perform like a team. *Training & Development, 50*(9), 34–37.

16. Blanchard, K., Carew, D., & Parisi-Carew, E. (1996), p. 36.

17. Blinn, C. (1996). Developing high performance teams. *Online, 20*(6), 56.

18. Katzenback, J. R., & Smith, D. K. (2003). *The wisdom of teams.* New York, NY: HarperCollins.

19. Hackman, J. R. (2010). Leading teams: Imperatives for leaders. In G. R. Hickman (Ed.), *Leading organizations: Perspectives for a new era* (2nd ed.). Thousand Oaks, CA: Sage.

20. Larson, C. E., & LaFasto, F. M. J. (1989). *Teamwork: What must go right, what can go wrong.* Newbury Park, CA: Sage.

21. Silva, R. (2016, June 24). Management and good leadership a process to build high-performance teams. *LinkedIn.* Retrieved from https://www.linkedin.com/pulse/management-good-leadership-process-build-teams-ricardo-antonio-silva

22. Crawford, B. (2016, January). Developing an all-star leadership team. *AboutLeaders.* Retrieved from http://aboutleaders.com/developing-star-leadership-team

23. Hackman, J. R. (2011). *Collaborative intelligence: Using teams to solve hard problems.* San Francisco, CA: Berrett-Koehler.

24. Katzenback, J. R., & Smith, D. K. (2003). *The wisdom of teams.* New York, NY: HarperCollins.

25. Dyer, W. G., Dyer, J. H., & Dyer, W. G. (2013). *Team building: Proven strategies for improving team performance.* San Francisco, CA: Jossey-Bass. (p. 69)

26. Bassi, L., & McMurrer, D. (2007, January 1). Maximizing your return on people. *Harvard Business Review, 85*(3), 115–123.

27. Willis Towers. (n.d.). *U.S. workers say performance management doesn't make the grade.* Retrieved from https://www.towerswatson.com/en/Insights/Newsletters/Americas/Insider/2004/us-workers-say-performance-management-doesnt-make-the-grade

28. Shumpter, J. (2016, March). Team spirit. *The Economist.* Retrieved from http://www.economist.com/news/business-and-finance/21694962-managing-them-hard-businesses-are-embracing-idea-working-teams

29. Tuckman, B. W. (1965). Developmental sequence in small groups. *Psychological Bulletin, 63*(6), 384–399.

30. Tuckman, B. W., & Jensen, M. A. C. (1977). Stages of small-group development revisited. *Group & Organization Studies, 2*(4), 419–427.

31. Ibid.

32. Larson, C. E., & LaFasto, F. M. J. (1989). *Teamwork: What must go right, what can go wrong.* Newbury Park, CA: Sage.

33. Bennis, W. (1997). The secrets of great groups. *Leader to Leader, 3,* 29–33.

34. Katzenback, J. R., & Smith, D. K. (2003). *The wisdom of teams.* New York, NY: HarperCollins. (p. 138)

35. Katzenback, J. R., & Smith, D. K. (2003), pp. 139–144.

36. Larson, C. E., & LaFasto, F. M. J. (1989). *Teamwork: What must go right, what can go wrong.* Newbury Park, CA: Sage.

37. Shapiro, M. (2015). *HBR guide to leading teams.* Boston, MA: Harvard Business School Publishing Corp.

38. Gallup Strengths Center. (2016). Retrieved from https://www.gallupstrengthscenter.com/

39. Carew, D., Parisi-Carew, E., Good, L., & Blanchard, K. (2010). Situational team leadership. In K. Blanchard (Ed.), *Leading at a higher level: Blanchard on leadership and creating high performing organizations.* Upper Saddle River, NJ: FT Press. (p. 167)

40. Harvey, J. (1974). The Abilene paradox: The management of agreement. *Organizational Dynamics, 3*(1), 63–80.

41. Janis, I. L. (1971). Groupthink. *Psychology Today, 5*(6), 84–90.

42. Janis, I. L. (1973, September 1). Groupthink and group dynamics: A social psychological analysis of defective policy decisions. *Policy Studies Journal, 2*(1), 19–25. (pp. 21–22)

43. Lencioni, P. (2002). *The five dysfunctions of a team: A leadership fable*. San Francisco, CA: Jossey-Bass.

44. Lencioni, P. (2002), p. 189.

45. Harvard Business Review Press. (2004). *Teams that click*. Boston, MA: Author.

46. Edmondson, A. C. (2012). Teamwork on the fly. *Harvard Business Review, 9*(4), 72–80.

47. Boss, J. (2016, July). Accelerate your understanding of teams with these 3 facts. *Forbes.com*. Retrieved from http://www.forbes.com/sites/jeffboss/2016/07/25/accelerate-your-understanding-of-teams-with-these-3-facts/#4c533f6a44ed

48. Nelson, B. (1994). *1001 ways to reward employees*. New York, NY: Workman Publication.

49. This idea was contributed by David Rosch during the 2014 Great Ideas Share and Teach Forum at the International Leadership Association Conference in San Diego, CA.

Chapter 13

1. Scudamore, B. (2015, December 5). 3 tips to create a workplace culture that employees love. *Forbes.com*. Retrieved from https://www.forbes.com/sites/brianscudamore/2015/12/05/creating-culture-its-all-about-people/#1eb65c667ad5

2. Cole, M. B. (2015, April 21). A culture of care, without compromise. *Stanford Social Innovation Review*. Retrieved from https://ssir.org/articles/entry/a_culture_of_care_without_compromise

3. Brown, C. (2014, September 30). *Toyota awards $25,000 to Camden Sophisticated Sisters Drill Team*. Retrieved from http://www.blackenterprise.com/lifestyle/toyota-awards-25000-to-sophisticated-sisters-drill-team/; Bush, D. (2013, February 19). *Tawanda Jones: Mother, friend and mentor to youth of Camden, N.J.* Retrieved from https://whyy.org/articles/tawanda-jones-mother-friend-and-mentor-to-youth-of-camden-nj/; Burling, S. (2013, April 13). Trying out for Camden's Sophisticated Sisters. *The Philadelphia Inquirer*. Retrieved from http://www.lexisnexis.com; Griffith, J. (2013, June 29). Changing lives for Camden kids: Drill team provides stability through dance, discipline. *NJ.com*. Retrieved from http://www.nj.com/news/index.ssf/2013/06/camden_drill_team_sophisticated_sisters.html; WYSK. (2013, May 2). Tawanda Jones is turning the city of Camden around one kid at a time. *Women You Should Know*. Retrieved from http://www.womenyoushouldknow.net/tawanda-jones-is-turning-the-city-of-camden-around-one-kid-at-a-time/

4. Burns, J. M. (1978). *Leadership*. New York, NY: Harper & Row.

5. Willoughby, A. (2014, March 31). How to create a workplace people love coming to. *FastCompany*

.com. Retrieved from https://www.fastcompany.com/3028368/how-to-create-a-workplace-people-love-coming-to

6. Shamir, B., & Eilam, G. (2005). "What's your story?" A life-stories approach to authentic leadership development. *The Leadership Quarterly, 16*(3), 395–417.

7. Maslow, A. H. (1943). A theory of human motivation. *Psychology Review, 50*(4), 370–396.

8. Maslow, A. H. (1968). *Toward a psychology of being*. New York, NY: Van Nostrand Reinhold.

9. Maslow, A. H. (1943). A theory of human motivation. *Psychology Review, 50*(4), 370–396.

10. Maslow, A. H. (1969). The farther reaches of human nature. *Journal of Transpersonal Psychology, 1*(1), 1–9.

11. Ibid.

12. Northouse, P. G. (2016). *Leadership: Theory and practice*. Thousand Oaks, CA: Sage.

13. Kouzes, J. M., & Posner, B. Z. (1987). *The leadership challenge: How to get extraordinary things done in organizations*. San Francisco, CA: Jossey-Bass.

14. https://www.greatplacetowork.com/best-workplaces/giving-back/2017

15. Greenleaf, R. K. (1977). *Servant leadership: A journey into the nature of legitimate power and greatness*. Mahwah, NJ: Paulist Press.

16. Greenleaf, R. K. (1977), pp. 13–14.

17. Spears, L. C. (2010). Character and servant leadership: Ten characteristics of effective caring leaders. *The Journal of Virtues & Leadership, 1*(1), 25–30. Retrieved from https://www.regent.edu/acad/global/publications/jvl/vol1_iss1/Spears_Final.pdf

18. Spears, L. C. (2010), p. 27.

19. Focht, A., & Ponton, M. (2015). Identifying primary characteristics of servant leadership: Delphi study. *International Journal of Leadership Studies, 9*(1), 44–61.

20. Marabella, S. D. (2014). Serving our employees and volunteers: Teaching, mentoring, and spirit-building in the workplace. *Leader to Leader, 74*, 7–12. (p. 8)

21. Walker, C. A. (2015). New managers need a philosophy about how they'll lead. *Harvard Business Review*. Retrieved from https://hbr.org/2015/09/new-managers-need-a-philosophy-about-how-theyll-lead (para. 3)

22. Collins, J. (2001). *Good to great: Why some companies make the leap and others don't*. New York, NY: HarperCollins.

23. Sipe, J. W., & Frick, D. M. (2015). *Seven pillars of servant leadership: Practicing the wisdom of leading by serving*. Mahwah, NJ: Paulist Press.

24. Hess, E. (2013, April 28). Servant leadership: A path to high performance. *The Washington Post*. Retrieved from https://www.washingtonpost.com/business/capitalbusiness/servant-leadership-a-path-to-high-performance/2013/04/26/435e58b2-a7b8-11e2-8302-3c7e0ea97057_story.html?noredirect=on&utm_term=.5f3bac5d1bb7 (para. 6)

25. Hess, E. (2013, April 28), para. 4.

26. Lichtenwalner, B. (2017, April 20). Servant leadership companies [Web post]. Retrieved from http://modernservantleader.com/featured/servant-leadership-companies-list/

27. Rima, S. D. (2013). *Spiritual capital: A moral core for social and economic justice.* Aldershot, UK: Gower.

28. Middlebrooks, A., & Noghiu, A. (2010). Leadership and spiritual capital: Exploring the link between individual service disposition and organizational value. *International Journal of Leadership Studies, 6*(1), 67–85.

29. Bagwell, L. S., & Bernheim, B. D. (1996). Veblen effects in a theory of conspicuous consumption. *The American Economic Review, 86*(3), 349–373.

30. Scudamore, B. (2015, December 5). 3 tips to create a workplace culture that employees love. *Forbes.com.* Retrieved from https://www.forbes.com/sites/brianscudamore/2015/12/05/creating-culture-its-all-about-people/#1eb65c667ad5

31. Kouzes, J. M., & Posner, B. Z. (2012). *The leadership challenge: How to make extraordinary things happen in organizations* (5th ed.). Hoboken, NJ: Wiley.

32. Kouzes, J. M., & Posner, B. Z. (2011). *Encouraging the heart workbook.* Hoboken, NJ: Wiley.

33. Komives, S. R., & Wagner, W. (2017). *Leadership for a better world: Understanding the social change model of leadership development.* Hoboken, NJ: John Wiley.

34. Soria, K. M., & Mitchell, T. D. (2016). *Civic engagement and community service at research universities: Engaging undergraduates for social justice, social change and responsible citizenship.* London, UK: Palgrave Macmillan.

35. http://www.idealist.org/info/volunteerMgmt/Student

36. http://compact.org/initiatives/service-learning/

37. Sarikas, C. (2015, October 10). 129 great examples of community service projects [Web log post]. *PrepScholar.* Retrieved from http://blog.prepscholar.com/129-examples-of-community-service-projects

38. Corporation for National and Community Service. (2016, November 15). New report: Service unites Americans; Volunteers give service worth $184 billion. Retrieved from https://www.nationalservice.gov/newsroom/press-releases/2016/new-report-service-unites-americans-volunteers-give-service-worth-184

39. Higher Education Research Institute. (2017). College senior survey [HERI]. Retrieved from https://heri.ucla.edu/college-senior-survey/

40. https://www.rotary.org/

41. http://www.kiwanis.org/

42. http://www.lionsclubs.org/

43. Willoughby, A. (2014, March 31). How to create a workplace people love coming to. *Fast Company.* Retrieved from https://www.fastcompany.com/3028368/how-to-create-a-workplace-people-love-coming-to

Chapter 14

1. Burke, J., & Van, Heusen, J. (1944). Swinging on a star [Recorded by Bing Crosby]. [Record]. Los Angeles, CA: Decca Records.

2. Nerenberg, S. (2011, March 31). Dimensions of design. *Core77.* Retrieved from http://www.core77.com/posts/18914/dimensions-of-design-by-sami-nerenberg-18914

3. Gershbein, D. (2009, October 26). Extinction of the expert: How the knowledge economy is changing the innovation game. *The Collaborative View.* Retrieved from http://collaboration360.blogspot.com/

4. Lidwell, W., Holden, K., Butler, J., & Elam, K. (2010). *Universal principles of design: 125 ways to enhance usability, influence perception, increase appeal, make better design decisions, and teach through design.* Beverly, MA: Rockport Publishers.

5. Maslow, A. H., & Frager, R. (1987). *Motivation and personality.* New York, NY: Harper & Row.

6. Quote attributed to Will Rogers, Mark Twain, and others.

7. Mackenzie, G. (1998). *Orbiting the giant hairball: A corporate fool's guide to surviving with grace.* New York, NY: Viking.

8. Mayer, M. (2006). Ideas come from everywhere. *Stanford University eCorner.* Retrieved from http://ecorner.stanford.edu/videos/1524/Ideas-Come-From-Everywhere

9. Ibid.

10. Zhuo, J. (2016). Solve only real problems. *Stanford University eCorner.* Retrieved from http://ecorner.stanford.edu/videos/4697/Solve-Only-Real-Problems

11. Chen, J. (2016). Choose to see beauty. *Stanford University eCorner.* Retrieved from http://ecorner.stanford.edu/videos/4674/Choose-to-See-Beauty

12. Keeley, L. (2013). *Ten types of innovation: The discipline of building breakthroughs.* Hoboken, NJ: Wiley.

13. Ibid., p. 13.

14. A downloadable TUBRIC template can be found at the Buck Institute for Education at http://www.bie.org

15. From the model introduced in Keeley, L. (2013). *Ten types of innovation: The discipline of building breakthroughs.* Hoboken, NJ: Wiley.

16. Gray, D., Brown, S., & Macanufo, J. (2010). *Gamestorming: A playbook for innovators, rulebreakers, and changemakers.* Sebastopol, CA: O'Reilly Media. Retrieved from http://gamestorming.com/games-for-decision-making/how-now-wow-matrix/

17. Beghetto, R. A. (2016a). *Big wins, small steps: How to lead for and with creativity.* Thousand Oaks, CA: Corwin.

18. Beghetto, R. A. (2007). Ideational code-switching: Walking the talk about supporting student creativity in the classroom. *Roeper Review, 29,* 265–270; Beghetto, R. A., & Kaufman, J. C. (2007). Toward a broader

conception of creativity: A case for mini-c creativity. *Psychology of Aesthetics, Creativity, and the Arts, 1,* 73–79.

19. Kaufman, J. C., & Beghetto, R. A. (2009). Beyond big and little: The Four C Model of creativity. *Review of General Psychology, 13,* 1–12.

20. Beghetto, R. A. (2013). *Killing ideas softly? The promise and perils of creativity in the classroom.* Charlotte, NC: Information Age Publishing.

21. Beghetto, R. A. (2016b). Leveraging micro-opportunities to address macroproblems: Toward an unshakeable sense of possibility thinking. In D. Ambrose & R. J. Sternberg (Eds.), *Creative intelligence in the 21st century: Grappling with enormous problems and huge opportunities.* Rotterdam, Netherlands: Sense.

22. Ibid.

23. For more information on mental models, see https://mentalmodels.princeton.edu/about/what-are-mental-models/

24. Gumusluoglu, L., & Ilsev, A. (2009, January 1). Transformational leadership, creativity, and organizational innovation. *Journal of Business Research, 62*(4), 461–473; Khalili, A. (2016, January 1). Linking transformational leadership, creativity, innovation, and innovation-supportive climate. *Management Decision, 54*(9), 2277–2293.

25. Henker, N., Sonnentag, S., & Unger, D. (2015, June 1). Transformational leadership and employee creativity: The mediating role of promotion focus and creative process engagement. *Journal of Business and Psychology, 30*(2), 235–247.

26. Jyoti, J., & Dev, M. (2015, January 5). The impact of transformational leadership on employee creativity: The role of learning orientation. *Journal of Asia Business Studies, 9*(1), 78–98.

27. Hyypia, M., & Parjanen, S. (2013, May 6). Boosting creativity with transformational leadership in fuzzy front-end innovation processes. *Interdisciplinary Journal of Information, Knowledge, and Management, 8,* 21–41.

28. Eisenbeiss, S. A., & Boerner, S. (2013, March 1). A double-edged sword: Transformational leadership and individual creativity. *British Journal of Management, 24*(1), 54–68.

29. Retrieved from https://openideo.com/

Chapter 15

1. Jobs, S., & Silicon Valley Historical Association. (2013). *Steve Jobs: Visionary entrepreneur.* Menlo Park, CA: Silicon Valley Historical Association.

2. Godin, S. (2014, March 25). The debilitating myth of musical chairs. *Seth's Blog.* Retrieved from http://sethgodin.typepad.com/seths_blog/2014/03/the-debilitating-myth-of-musical-chairs.html

3. Mochari, I. (2016, March 23). Why half of the S&P 500 companies will be replaced in the next decade. *Inc. Magazine.* Retrieved from http://www.inc.com/ilan-mochari/innosight-sp-500-new-companies.html; Also see http://www.wipo.int/portal/en/; http://www.singularity.com/charts/page17.html

4. Heikkila, A. (2016, March 16). Jobs that don't exist yet: How to prepare for the future of work. *Business 2 Community.* Retrieved from http://www.business2community.com/human-resources/jobs-dont-exist-yet-prepare-future-work-01484828#2XAJ46EhZTY07RJB.97; http://www.oxfordmartin.ox.ac.uk/downloads/academic/The_Future_of_Employment.pdf

5. Neck, H., Neck, C., & Murray, E. (2017). *Entrepreneurship: The practice and mindset.* Thousand Oaks, CA: Sage.

6. Sobel, R. S. (2008). Entrepreneurship. *The Library of Economics and Liberty.* http://www.econlib.org/library/Enc/Entrepreneurship.html; for the earliest mentions of entrepreneur, see Cantillon, R. (1756). *Essai sur la nature du commerce engénéral: Traduit de l'anglois.* London, UK: F. Gyles.

7. Aulet, B. (2013). *Disciplined entrepreneurship: 24 steps to a successful startup.* Hoboken, NJ: John Wiley.

8. Zimmerman, J. (2014, September 29). Toward a hypothesis connecting leadership and entrepreneurship. *International Journal of Management & Information Systems, 18*(4), 291.

9. Greenberg, D., McKone-Sweet, K., & Wilson, H. J. (2011). *The new entrepreneurial leader: Developing leaders who shape social and economic opportunity.* Oakland, CA: Berrett-Koehler.

10. There have been many editions and translations of Say's original work first published in 1800 in Paris. The latest, in English, is Say, J. B., Quddus, M., & Rashid, S. (2017). *A treatise on political economy.* New York, NY: Cosimo Classics.

11. Greenberg, D., McKone-Sweet, K., & Wilson, H. J. (2011). *The new entrepreneurial leader: Developing leaders who shape social and economic opportunity.* Oakland, CA: Berrett-Koehler.

12. Dweck, C. S. (2008). *Mindset: The new psychology of success.* New York, NY: Ballantine Books.

13. IDEO. (2003, November). *Method cards.* Retrieved from https://www.ideo.com/work/method-cards

14. Maeda, J. (2006). *The laws of simplicity.* Cambridge, MA: MIT Press.

15. Selway, J. (2013, March 5). The complexity of simplicity. *UXMag.com.* Retrieved from http://uxmag.com/articles/the-complexity-of-simplicity

16. Sarasvathy, S. D. (2009). *Effectuation: Elements of entrepreneurial expertise.* Cheltenham, UK: Edward Elgar.

17. Society for Effectual Action. (n.d.). *Effectuation 101.* Retrieved from http://www.effectuation.org/?page_id=207

18. Sarasvathy, S. D. (2001). *Effectual reasoning in expert entrepreneurial decisions: Existence and bounds* [ENT D1–D6]. Paper presented at the meeting of the Academy of Management 2001 Meeting Best Paper Proceedings.

19. Masterson, M. (2007). *Ready, fire, aim: Zero to $100 million in no time flat.* Hoboken, NJ: John Wiley.

20. Friedlander, A. (2016). *A misfit entrepreneur's guide to building a business your way.* Fort Collins, CO: Rosabella Consulting.

21. Gunderson, L. H., & Holling, C. S. (2002). *Panarchy: Understanding transformations in human and natural systems.* Washington, DC: Island Press.

22. Bower, J. L., & Christensen, C. M. (1995). Disruptive technologies: Catching the wave. *Harvard Business Review, 73*(1), 43–53; Kiuchi, T., & Shireman, B. (2002). *What we learned in the rainforest: Business lessons from nature.* San Francisco, CA: Berrett-Koehler.

23. Hurst, D. K. (2012). *The new ecology of leadership: Business mastery in a chaotic world.* New York, NY: Columbia University Press.

24. Lipmanowicz, H., & McCandless, K. (2013). *The surprising power of liberating structures: Simple rules to unleash a culture of innovation.* Seattle, WA: Liberating Structures Press.

25. Blank, S. (2013). *Four steps to the epiphany.* Pescadero, CA: K&S Ranch.

26. Osterwalder, A., & Pigneur, Y. (2010). *Business model generation: A handbook for visionaries, game changers, and challengers.* Hoboken, NJ: John Wiley.

27. Maurya, A. (2012). *Running lean: Iterate from Plan A to a plan that works.* Sebastopol, CA: O'Reilly Media.

28. Ries, E. (2011). *The lean startup: How today's entrepreneurs use continuous innovation to create radically successful businesses.* New York, NY: Crown Business.

29. Godin, S. (2016, December 6). The other person is always right. *Seth's Blog.* Retrieved from http://sethgodin.typepad.com/seths_blog/2016/12/the-other-person-is-always-right.html

30. Adapted from Fishbein, M. (2013). *The ultimate list of customer development questions.* Retrieved January 2, 2017, from http://mfishbein.com/the-ultimate-list-of-customer-development-questions/

31. Middlebrooks, A. (2016). The paradox of serious fun. In R. A. Beghetto & B. Sriraman (Eds.), *Creative contradictions in education: Cross disciplinary paradoxes and perspectives* (pp. 265–280). New York, NY: Springer-Verlag.

32. Fluegge-Woolf, E. R. (2014). Play hard, work hard. *Management Research Review, 37*(8), 682.

33. Measley, N., & Gianoulis, N. (2015). *Playing it forward: The definitive "how to" model for creating a winning workplace culture.* Wilmington, DE: The Fun Dept.

34. Pink, D. (2009). *Drive: The surprising truth about what motivates us.* New York, NY: Riverhead Books.

35. Tushman, M. L., Smith, W. K., & Binns, A. (2011). The ambidextrous CEO. *Harvard Business Review, 89*(6), 74–81.

36. Freeman, D., & Siegfried, R. L. (2015). Entrepreneurial leadership in the context of company startup and growth. *Journal of Leadership Studies, 8*(4), 35–39.

37. Johnson, C. (1955). *Harold and the purple crayon.* New York, NY: HarperCollins.

38. For a great example of this, check out: The social graph: The journey from Francis to Bono, in Baehr, E., & Loomis, E. (2015). *Get backed: Craft your story, build the perfect pitch deck, and launch the venture of your dreams.* Boston, MA: Harvard Business Review Press.

Chapter 16

1. Bennis, W. G. (1989). *On becoming a leader.* Reading, MA: Addison-Wesley.

2. Eliot, T. S., Eliot, T. S., Hodgson, A., & Mairet, P. (1942). *Little gidding.* London, UK: Faber and Faber.

3. Walmart. (2016). *Walmart 2016 global sustainability report.* Retrieved from http://cdn.corporate.walmart.com/9c/73/3f9abcef444397f2c771e081e095/2016-global-responsibility-report.pdf

4. Clancy, H. (2014). Apple, IKEA, Walmart: 12 leaders in on-site renewables. *Greenbiz.* Retrieved from https://www.greenbiz.com/article/Apple-Google-Walmart-corporate-renewables-leaders; Helman, C. (2015). How Walmart became a green energy giant, using other people's money. *Forbes.* Retrieved from http://www.forbes.com/sites/christopherhelman/2015/11/04/walmarts-everyday-renewable-energy/#107ec12c4894; Lozanova, S. (2015). Walmart leaps toward 100% renewable energy with wind deal. *TriplePundit.* Retrieved from http://www.triplepundit.com/2015/10/walmart-leaps-towards-100-renewable-energy-wind-deal/; Wahba, P. (2016). Walmart aims to generate half its energy from renewable sources by 2025. *Fortune.* Retrieved from http://fortune.com/2016/11/04/walmart-sustainability-2025/

5. Walmart. (n.d.). Sustainability. Retrieved from http://corporate.walmart.com/global-responsibility/sustainability/ (para. 4)

6. Miu, Y. (2011). Wal-Mart pledges billions to aid women businesses. *The Washington Post.* Retrieved from https://www.washingtonpost.com/business/economy/wal-mart-pledges-billions-to-aid-women-businesses/2011/09/13/gIQAap53QK_story.html; Walmart. (2016). *Walmart 2016 global sustainability report.* Retrieved from http://cdn.corporate.walmart.com/9c/73/3f9abcef444397f2c771e081e095/2016-global-responsibility-report.pdf

7. Walmart. (n.d.). *Sustainability.* Retrieved from http://corporate.walmart.com/global-responsibility/sustainability/ (para. 2)

8. Sasine, R. (2013). Walmart: Lessons learned from a commitment to packaging reduction. *Packaging Digest.*

Retrieved from http://www.packagingdigest.com/sustainable-packaging/walmart-lessons-learned-commitment-packaging-reduction

9. Walmart. (2006, November 1). Wal-Mart unveils "packaging scorecard" to suppliers. Retrieved from http://corporate.walmart.com/_news_/news-archive/2006/11/01/wal-mart-unveils-packaging-scorecard-to-suppliers

10. Walmart. (2016). Walmart 2016 global sustainability report. Retrieved from http://cdn.corporate.walmart.com/9c/73/3f9abcef444397f2c771e081e095/2016-global-responsibility-report.pdf

11. Walmart. (2016), p. 1.

12. Bellinger, G. (2004). Archetypes. *Systems Thinking.* Retrieved from http://www.systems-thinking.org/arch/arch.htm

13. Sullivan, T. (2011). Embracing complexity. *Harvard Business Review.* Retrieved from https://hbr.org/2011/09/embracing-complexity

14. Snowden, D. J., & Boone, M. E. (2007, November). A leader's framework for decision making: Wise executives tailor their approach to fit the complexity of the circumstances they face. *Harvard Business Review, 85*(11). Retrieved from https://hbr.org/2007/11/a-leaders-framework-for-decision-making

15. Gleick, J. (1987). *Chaos: Making a new science.* New York, NY: Penguin Books; Taleb, N. N. (2007). *The Black Swan: The impact of highly improbable fragility.* New York, NY: Random House.

16. Allen, K. E., & Mease, W. P. (2001). Energy optimization and the role of the leader. Retrieved from http://www.kathleenallen.net/index.php/writings/leadership-change/24-ila-energy-opt-2/file (p. 2)

17. Savitz, A. W., & Weber, K. (2006). *The triple bottom line: How today's best-run companies are achieving economic, social, and environmental success—and how you can too.* San Francisco, CA: Jossey-Bass.

18. Senge, P. (1990). *The fifth discipline: The art and science of the learning organization.* New York, NY: Currency Doubleday. (p. 3)

19. United Nations. (n.d.). *Our common future, Chapter 2: Towards sustainable development.* Retrieved from http://www.un-documents.net/ocf-02.htm#III

20. McGregor, J. (2016). The biggest "gift" Steve Jobs gave Apple CEO Tim Cook before he died. *Washington Post.* Retrieved from https://www.washingtonpost.com/news/on-leadership/wp/2016/08/16/the-biggest-gift-steve-jobs-gave-apple-ceo-tim-cook-before-he-died/

21. Allworth, J., Wessel, M., & Wheeler, R. (2011). Why Apple doesn't need Steve Jobs. *Harvard Business Review.* Retrieved from https://hbr.org/2011/08/why-apple-doesnt-need-steve-jo

22. Farber, M. (2016). Patagonia is donating all its Black Friday sales to charity. *Fortune.* Retrieved from http://fortune.com/2016/11/22/black-friday-2016-patagonia-sales/

23. Patagonia. (2016). *Patagonia's mission statement.* Retrieved from http://www.patagonia.com/company-info.html

24. Biddle, D. (1993). Recycling for profit: The new green business frontier. *Harvard Business Review.* Retrieved from https://hbr.org/1993/11/recycling-for-profit-the-new-green-business-frontier

25. Hill, L., Brandeau, G., Truelove, E., & Lineback, K. (2015). The capabilities your organization needs to sustain innovation. *Harvard Business Review.* Retrieved from https://hbr.org/2015/01/the-capabilities-your-organization-needs-to-sustain-innovation (para. 18)

26. Hill, L., Brandeau, G., Truelove, E., & Lineback, K. (2015). The capabilities your organization needs to sustain innovation. *Harvard Business Review.* Retrieved from https://hbr.org/2015/01/the-capabilities-your-organization-needs-to-sustain-innovation

27. Egan, M. (2016). 5,300 Wells Fargo employees fired over 2 million phony accounts. *CNN Money.* Retrieved from http://money.cnn.com/2016/09/08/investing/wells-fargo-created-phony-accounts-bank-fees/ (para. 3)

28. Lobenfeld, C. (2016). Hear the first ever pop song composed by artificial intelligence. *Fact.* Retrieved from http://www.factmag.com/2016/09/22/hear-first-complete-pop-song-composed-artificial-intelligence/

29. 20th Century Fox. (2016, August 31). Morgan: IBM creates first movie trailer by AI [HD]. *YouTube.* Retrieved from https://www.youtube.com/watch?v=gJEzuYynaiw

30. Herkewitz, W. (2015). A computer just solved this 100-year-old biology problem. *Popular Mechanics.* Retrieved from http://www.popularmechanics.com/science/a15886/computer-scientific-theory

31. Yahoo Tech. (2015, September 9). Meet the new boss: The world's first artificial-intelligence manager? *Yahoo! Finance.* Retrieved from https://www.yahoo.com/tech/meet-the-new-boss-the-worlds-first-128660465704.html

32. Strickland, E. (2016, May 4). Autonomous robot surgeon bests humans in world first. *Spectrum.* Retrieved from http://spectrum.ieee.org/the-human-os/robotics/medical-robots/autonomous-robot-surgeon-bests-human-surgeons-in-world-first

33. Pascual, K. (2016, January 27). Harvard to develop AI that works as fast as human brain. *Tech Times.* Retrieved from http://www.techtimes.com/articles/127773/20160127/harvard-to-develop-ai-that-works-as-fast-as-human-brain.htm

34. Statt, N. (2016, May 25). Foxconn cuts 60,000 factory jobs and replaces them with robots. *The Verge.* Retrieved from http://www.theverge.com/2016/5/25/11772222/foxconn-automation-robots-apple-samsung-smartphones

35. Chowdhry, A. (2016, May 17). Law firm Baker Hostetler hires a "digital attorney" named ROSS. *Forbes*. Retrieved from http://www.forbes.com/sites/amitchowdhry/2016/05/17/law-firm-bakerhostetler-hires-a-digital-attorney-named-ross/#717cbe221caa

36. Diamandis, P. (2015, January 26). Ray Kurzweil's mind-boggling predictions for the next 25 years. *Singularity Hub*. Retrieved from http://singularityhub.com/2015/01/26/ray-kurzweils-mind-bogglingpredictions-for-the-next-25-years/; Galeon, D. (2016). AI will colonize the galaxy by the 2050s, according to the "father of deep learning." *Futurism*. Retrieved from https://futurism.com/ai-will-colonize-the-galaxy-by-the-2050s-according-to-the-father-of-deep-learning/

37. Lidwell, W., Holden, K., Butler, J., & Elam, K. (2010). *Universal principles of design: 125 ways to enhance usability, influence perception, increase appeal, make better design decisions, and teach through design*. Beverly, MA: Rockport Publishers.

38. Spreitzer, G., & Porath, C. (2012). Creating sustainable performance. *Harvard Business Review, 90*(1), 92–99.

39. Meehan, P., Rigby, D., & Rogers, P. (2008, February 27). Creating and sustaining a winning culture. *Harvard Business Review*. Retrieved from https://hbr.org/2008/02/creating-and-sustaining-a-winn-1

40. Ibid.

41. Schwandt, D. R. (2005). When managers become philosophers: Integrating learning with sensemaking. *Academy of Management Journal, 4*(2), 176–92.

42. Zajonc, R. B. (1968, January 1). Attitudinal effects of mere exposure. *Journal of Personality and Social Psychology, 9*(2), 1–27.

43. Fournier, G. (2016). Mere exposure effect. *Psych Central*. Retrieved from http://psychcentral.com/encyclopedia/mere-exposure-effect/

44. George, B., Sims, P., McLean, A. N., & Mayer, D. (2007). Discovering your authentic leadership. *Harvard Business Review, 85*(2), 129.

45. George, B., Sims, P., McLean, A. N., & Mayer, D. (2007), p. 129.

46. Shamir, B., & Eilam, G. (2005). What's your story? A life-stories approach to authentic leadership development. *The Leadership Quarterly, 16*(3), 395–417. (p. 398)

47. Shamir, B., & Eilam, G. (2005). What's your story? A life-stories approach to authentic leadership development. *The Leadership Quarterly, 16*(3), 395–417.

48. Avolio, B. J., & Gardner, W. L. (2005). Authentic leadership development: Getting to the root of positive forms of leadership. *The Leadership Quarterly, 16*(3), 315–338.

49. Roser, M. (2016). The short history of global living conditions and why it matters that we know it. *Our World in Data*. Retrieved from https://ourworldindata.org/a-history-of-global-living-conditions-in-5-charts/

50. United Nations Global Compact. (n.d.). *Who we are*. Retrieved from https://www.unglobalcompact.org/what-is-gc/mission

• Index •

Employees:
    bring your own work strategy and, 236
    collaborative organizational culture and, 79–80, 236
    empowerment of, 236
    engagement of, 188, 195–196
    exit interviews of, 284
    freelance workers and, 241
    information technology and, 236
    open architecture workspace and, 80
    person/job fit and, 190
    productivity, technology and, 78
    wage gap and, 74–75
    workspaces and, 73–74, 80
    workplace inequalities and, 77
    See also Followers' success; Human capital management
        (HCM); Management activities; Success of others
Empowerment, 79, 187, 189 (table), 236, 238, 267–268
    See also Motivation
Encourage the Heart practice, 333–334, 334 (table)
Engagement attribute, xviii, xix, 9, 13, 20, 21 (figure),
        29–30, 30 (figure), 32
    attribute builder activity and, 90, 146–147, 169,
        190–191, 299, 341, 372, 396
    creativity, engagement in, 201–202
    mindful engagement, 12–13
    positive engagement, 29
    social media/mobile devices and, 31
    strengths-based leadership and, 84
    success of others and, 195–196
    See also CORE™ (confidence/optimism/resilience/
        engagement) Model
Entrepreneurial leadership, 376–377, 380
    answers, recognition of, 384–385
    business model/business model canvas and,
        388–390, 389 (figure)
    causal reasoning and, 385
    chief executive role and, 393–394, 395 (table)
    contemporary challenges/trends and, 377
    customer discovery interviewing and, 390–391, 391 (table)
    definition of, 381
    ecocycle framework and, 387, 387 (figure)
    effectuation and, 385
    entrepreneurial mindset and, 381–386, 382 (table)
    entrepreneurial process, leading of, 387–391
    entrepreneurship and, 380–381
    evidence-based decision-making and, 388, 391
    fixed mindset and, 381
    founder role, 392, 395 (table)
    founder-to-chief executive transition and, 394
    founder's syndrome and, 380
    framing problems as opportunities and, 383–384
    growing venture, dynamic nature of, 380
    growth mindset and, 381
    ideation process and, 384

impact modeling and, 388–390, 389–390 (figures)
    innovator role and, 392, 395 (table)
    leader role, evolution of, 195 (table), 391–394
    lean startup methods and, 390–391
    minimum viable product, prototyping of, 391
    misconceptions about, 378
    opportunity recognition and, 382–383,
        383 (table)
    panarchy/adaptive cycles and, 386–387, 386 (figure)
    pivoting and, 388
    planning a venture and, 397–398
    seeing differently, capacity for, 383–384
    social impact model/social impact canvas and,
        390, 390 (figure)
    team builder role and, 393, 395 (table)
    translating ideas into real world value and, 377
    See also Designing the future; Entrepreneurship;
        Innovation; Sustainability
Entrepreneurship, 378
    action, predilection for, 385
    broad domain of, 380
    causal reasoning and, 385
    CORE™ attributes and, 379, 379 (figure)
    definition of, 378–380
    effectuation and, 385
    fear/doubt and, 385
    founder's syndrome and, 380
    intrapreneurship and, 380
    invention and, 380
    leadership process and, 380–381, 387–391
    marketplace, new idea launch and, 379–380, 386
    new idea conception/validation/launch process and,
        379, 379 (figure)
    opportunity recognition and, 378–379
    process of, 378
    ready-fire-reflect approach and, 385
    reflection and, 385
    social entrepreneurship and, 380
    See also Entrepreneurial leadership
Environmental sustainability, 330, 408, 410
Equal Pay Act of 1963, 74
Essence, 82
Estes, B., 55
Ethical leadership, 93
    academic domain and, 103
    choice of followers and, 106
    community domain and, 103
    courageous followers, dissent and, 106–108
    credibility and, 112
    decision-action gap and, 104, 105 (table), 108
    ethical decision-making and, 93, 108–109,
        113–114
    ethical domains, issues in, 103
    extracurricular domain and, 103

growth mindset and, 381

metacognition and, 129, 134

open-mindedness and, 207, 208

See also Brain dimensions; Creative thinking; Creativity; Design thinking; Influence tactics; Problem-solving process; Reflection

Redman, P., 74

Referent power, 182, 185 (table)

Reflected Best Self (RBS) exercise, 67–68

Reflection, 414

insight and, 43

self-awareness and, 72–73, 175, 187, 208

self-monitoring and, 23, 111, 414

Reflective dimension of the brain, 123, 127–128, 130, 131 (table), 369, 369 (table)

Relationships. *See* Brain dimensions; Design thinking; Friendships; Leadership relationships design; Systems thinking

Reputation, 64

Resilience attribute, xviii, xix, 13, 20, 21 (figure), 25–27, 30 (figure), 32, 82, 146–147, 269, 299, 323, 341, 372–373, 396–397

See also CORE™ (confidence/optimism/resilience/ engagement) Model

Reward power, 182, 185 (table)

Riggio, R., 181

Rima, S., 332

Risk-taking:

calculated risk-taking and, 260–261

collaborative organizational culture and, 79–80

imagination and, 73

leadership capacity and, 73

open organizational culture and, 80

passion and, 73

perseverance and, 73

pivoting and, 80, 105, 378, 387, 388

Rituals, 288

Robbins, A., 115

Robinson, K., 124

Roosevelt, T., 149

Rotary International, 339

Ryan's Well Foundation, 94

Sagmeister, S, 200

Saltiel, T., 43

Sarikas, C., 338

Satisficing process, 138, 154

Saxe, J. G., 139, 401

Say, J. -B., 380

SCAMPER (substitute/combine/adapt/modify/put to another use/eliminate/reverse attributes) technique, 214

Schwartz, A., 104, 105

Schwartz, M., 134

Seeley, A., 52

Self-awareness, 72–73, 175, 187, 208

Self-efficacy, 22

Self-monitoring, 23, 111, 414

Seneca, L. A., 26–27

Senge, P., 407, 408

Servant leadership, 314, 330–332, 333

Service, 329, 336

Service clubs, 339

Service learning, 336, 337, 339–340

Service Learning Preference Inventory (SLPI), 339–340, 341–344

Shah, D., 280

Shamir, B., 416

Shared accountability, 305

Shared leadership, 305

Shared vision, 74, 177, 178

Signal-to-noise ratio principle, 176

Silva, R., 308

Simplicity principle, 384

Sims, P., 415

Situational Leadership approach, 244

buy-in, securing of, 248

definition of, 245

entrusting/delegating behaviors and, 245 (figure), 246

flexible leadership-management practices and, 247

implementation process for, 246

individual needs categories and, 246

information/communications technology and, 248

innovative processes and, 247

model components and, 245–246, 245 (figure)

organizational culture, respect for, 247–248

relationships, development of, 247

selling/coaching behaviors and, 245 (figure), 246

supporting/participating behaviors and, 245 (figure), 246

team efforts, preparation for, 247

telling/directing behaviors and, 245 (figure), 246

worker developmental level, leader instructions/ guidance and, 246–247

See also Followers' success; Leadership by design framework; Leadership styles; Management activities

Skills approach to leadership, 10, 59 (table), 61

closure principle and, 66

competency framework and, 62

conceptual skills and, 61, 62

credible leaders and, 64–66, 65 (table)

cutting-edge skills, dynamic world stage and, 76–82

expert leaders and, 63–64, 63 (table)

flexible leadership model and, 63

human skills and, 61, 62

Katz's three-level model of skills and, 61–62

leadership vs. management approaches and, 63